CRITICAL SURVEY
OF
LONG FICTION

CRITICAL SURVEY
OF
LONG FICTION

Foreign Language Series

Authors
A-Dod

1

Edited by
FRANK N. MAGILL

Academic Director
WALTON BEACHAM

SALEM PRESS
Englewood Cliffs, N. J.

LIBRARY OF CONGRESS CATALOG CARD NUMBER: 84-51791
Complete Set: ISBN 0-89356-369-2
Volume 1:   ISBN 0-89356-370-6

PRINTED IN THE UNITED STATES OF AMERICA

PREFACE

THE FOREIGN LANGUAGE SERIES of *Critical Survey of Long Fiction* is a continuation of the eight-volume English Language Series on long fiction published in 1983. This work becomes the fifth set in the *Critical Survey* Series, joining the other multivolume references covering short fiction, poetry, and English-language long fiction. The forthcoming *Critical Survey of Drama*, originally scheduled for 1984, has been delayed until 1985.

The format of this Series conforms to that of the earlier works in the project. The first four volumes provide critical studies of 182 writers whose works have made important contributions to the development of the bodies of long fiction literature in their native languages. Individual articles include seven sections: Principal long fiction; Other literary forms; Achievements; Biography; Analysis (the most extensive section); Major publications other than long fiction; and Bibliography. Volume 5 comprises a collection of sixteen essays, most of them devoted to a history of the novel's development in various geographical areas of the world where English is not the indigenous language. Volume 5 also includes the index for the set.

Although *Critical Survey of Long Fiction* is designed to offer introductory articles on the canon of 182 important individual novelists, the essays add an extra dimension by providing background reference material concerning the time, place, and circumstances under which many of the creative artists produced their works.

For example, the essay "Chinese Long Fiction" explains that, until the twentieth century, fiction was largely ignored in China as trivial and unimportant; "literature" was considered to include only classics, history, philosophy, and belles lettres (poetry and literary criticism). Whereas critics ignored everything else, the average Chinese was not so selective and earlier enjoyed such novels as Lo Kuan-chung's *The Romance of the Three Kingdoms* (fourteenth century), Wu Ch'eng-en's *The Journey to the West* (1592), and Ts'ao Hsüeh-ch'in's *Dream of the Red Chamber* (1792), along with much more long fiction as it became available. The essay also points out that Chinese literature in the twentieth century has shown changes and promise, good omens for broadening the base of popular literature.

The literature of the Far East has not always been readily available to the West but fortunately this condition has changed. In addition to Chinese works, many Japanese novels now appear in the West, so that Lady Murasaki Shikibu's early eleventh century *The Tale of Genji* need no longer be our only recognized Japanese long fiction. We may now relish Nobel Prize winner Yasunari Kawabata's *Snow Country* and *Thousand Cranes* as well as *The Master of Go*; enjoy Kōbō Abe's *The Woman in the Dunes*; and appreciate Kenzaburo Ōe, one of Japan's major contemporary novelists. Also in translation are many of the works of Yukio Mishima, praised by many critics as a genius of modern Japanese letters before his ritual suicide in 1970. Among his major works are *The Sound of Waves*, *The Temple of the Golden Pavilion*, and *The Sea of Fertility* (a tetralogy, completed in 1970).

"African Long Fiction" is another essay of considerable interest to today's serious reader. As a form, the African novel is less than half a century old, reaching back at best to the late 1940's. From the first, however, African novelists have resisted Western (mainly European) impositions of its own established mores; and, considering the short training period, African novelists have learned fast and done well in depicting their social complexities— personalizing their unique problems without benefit of centuries of human experimentation.

"Latin American Long Fiction" is yet another essay which deals with a geographical area that was greatly influenced by the European cultural tradition, most of the indigenous findings having been suppressed, as is the custom with repressive conquerors.

The first Latin American novel is reputed to be *The Itching Parrot* (1816), by Mexico's José Joaquín Fernández de Lizardi. This work has sold many millions of copies over the years, ensnaring generations of readers through its picaresque episodes. Most Latin American long fiction of the nineteenth century, however, consists of novels of protest, José Mármol's *Amalia: A Romance of the Argentine* being such a work against Argentina's dictator Juan Manuel de Rosas. Almost a century later, however, the excellent Argentine novelist Eduardo Mallea could turn his attention to more artistic matters with his *Fiesta in November* and *The Bay of Silence*. At about the same time, Brazil's Jorge Amado produced *The Violent Land*, a historical romance evoking the turbulence attendant upon cacao production on the plantations of Bahia. In 1941, Ciro Alegría published *Broad and Alien Is the World*, a beautifully written novel presenting a powerful plea for justice for the Peruvian Indians. Colombia's Nobel Prize winner Gabriel García Márquez in 1967 published the central work of his Macondo cycle, *One Hundred Years of Solitude*, which was received with much enthusiasm by critics and readers alike.

Mexican authors have been very productive and influential in the area of Latin American literature. Ignacio Manuel Altamirano, himself of pure Indian blood, wrote *El Zarco* (1894), the story of a bandit, in an attempt to substitute realism for Romanticism in Latin American literature. Greatly admired in his later years, his ashes were placed in Mexico City's Hall of Fame when he died. Mexican writers continued the flow of excellent fiction into the mid-twentieth century and beyond with works such as Mariano Azuela's Mexican Revolution novel, *The Underdogs*; with *The Edge of the Storm*, by Agustín Yáñez; with Juan Rulfo's compelling *Pedro Páramo*, in which the violent story is told by the voices of characters already dead; and with three fine novels by Carlos Fuentes: *Where the Air Is Clear*, *The Death of Artemio Cruz*, and *Terra Nostra*, the latter perhaps his most important work.

Virtually all of Latin America has contributed admirably to the continual literary output. One is reminded of Guatemala's Nobel Prize winner Miguel Ángel Asturias (the first Latin American to win that prize); Venezuela's Rómulo Gallegos and his popular *Doña Bárbara*; Nicaragua's Rubén Darío; Chile's José Donoso; Jorge Icaza, from Ecuador; and two fine novels, *The Kingdom of This World* and *The Lost Steps*, by Cuba's Alejo Carpentier.

The Continental mother tongue that supplied Latin America with its means of expression also handed down some matchless examples of the novel form, such as Miguel de Cervantes' *Don Quixote de la Mancha*, called "the first modern novel"; Fernando de Rojas' *La Celestina*; Mateo Alemán's *The Life and Adventures of Guzman de Alfarache*; and the anonymous *Lazarillo de Tormes*, often considered the first picaresque novel. Surely the Latin American tradition can claim kinship with the brilliance of Spain's Golden Age, a most noble ancestor.

All of Europe was fertile ground for the spread of long fiction from the eighteenth century onward. Italy, divided politically, was slower to take up long fiction—and even short fiction—and also there was no universal language prevalent in the "Italy" of the time. Before the middle of the nineteenth century, however, Alessandro Manzoni's *The Betrothed* had appeared and sparked a trend. Manzoni's "heir presumptive," Antonio Fogazzaro, published *The Patriot* before the end of the century and *The Saint* shortly thereafter. More up to date are Nobel Prize winner Grazia Deledda's *The Mother* and Ignazio Silone's *Bread and Wine*. Once established, the Italian novel flourished and, among other things, served to portray for the world the poverty and backwardness of Southern Italy.

A long, slow process of development also characterized the French novel. Following Madame de La Fayette's *The Princess of Clèves*, Stendhal, George Sand, and Madame de Staël provided some leadership toward maturity of the French novel, which culminated in Gustave Flaubert's *Madame Bovary*, a trendsetting work whose artistic excellence is still much admired today. Émile Zola with his Naturalism soon followed Flaubert and greatly influenced the work of the Goncourts, Alphonse Daudet, Guy de Maupassant, and others until post-Naturalists Joris-Karl Huysmans, André Gide, and Marcel Proust— with his *Remembrance of Things Past*—appeared on the scene. The twentieth century has seen the French continue to hold their own among the world's influential novelists, with writers such as Nobel Prize winners Romain Rolland, whose massive novel depicting a sensitive musician was highly regarded in the early twentieth century; Roger Martin du Gard, whose multivolume family chronicle was especially well received in the 1930's; and Albert Camus, whose accidental death in 1960 cut short a brilliant career that seemed destined for even greater achievements.

Like France, Germany has a long and noble literary history, out of which the novel developed from the early poetic tradition represented by the works of Wolfram von Eschenbach and Hartmann von Aue. The period of the Enlightenment showed Germany entering the mainstream of the European novel development, and the sentimental fiction its authors had created undoubtedly influenced Henry Fielding, Samuel Richardson, and Laurence Sterne. This period was followed by *Sturm und Drang*, "Exhibit A" of which may be considered to be Johann Wolfgang von Goethe's *The Sorrows of Young Werther*.

With Germany's defeat in World War I, its artistic thrust was devastated, and for a time its major writers were mostly silent, although Erich Maria Remarque spoke eloquently in *All Quiet on the Western Front*, and in 1927 another shaken writer, Hermann Hesse, sought to erase the lost-generation years with the hallucinatory *Steppenwolf*. The postwar period following World War II seems to have had a similar dampening effect in West Germany, although Heinrich Böll and Günter Grass have been active since the late 1950's. In East Germany, workers' literature has been strong under the Eastern Bloc influence.

Central and Southeastern Europe, also wartorn, have longer histories of military conquest and total social disruption than Germany and seem to have learned to adjust with resignation to their intermittent social traumas. Great novels have come out of this area in the past century. Poland's Henryk Sienkiewicz, Stefan Żeromski, and Władysław Reymont—a Nobel Prize winner—are among the most esteemed Polish novelists. Czech writers of note include Jaroslav Hašek, Karel Čapek, and Milan Kundera. Prominent Slovak novelists who should be cited are Martin Kukucín and Jozef Cíger-Hronský, whose *Jozef Mak* is part of a trilogy of superior novels. Influential Hungarian novelists are Mór Jókai and Kálmán Mikszáth, while one of Yugoslavia's most significant novelists was Ivo Andrić, whose *The Bridge on the Drina* (1945) was his masterpiece. Thus the creative urge, while impeded and dominated by external events, refused to be wholly denied.

Russia's first novelist was Fyodor Emin, who published his first novel, an adventure story, in 1763. The defeat of Napoleon in 1812 spurred great interest in Russian literature, especially the infant novel. National pride was now a favorite subject, and scenes from everyday life the favorite fare. For a few years the historical novel was very popular, but that interest soon faded in favor of novels of contemporary life. Russia's greatest novelists of the nineteenth century were Nikolai Gogol, Ivan Turgenev, Leo Tolstoy, and the incomparable Fyodor Dostoevski.

The momentum of the late nineteenth century did not carry far into the twentieth century. Ivan Bunin was the first Russian to win the Nobel Prize. His *The Village*, first published in 1910, and Andrey Bely's *Petersburg*, published in 1916, were the two most noteworthy Russian novels of the early twentieth century. After the advent of Stalinism in the 1920's, Russian literature shriveled to an echo of the revolutionary dogma of the new masters. A great novel of the revolutionary period, however, was Mikhail Sholokhov's *The Silent Don*, a series of four books about the Don Cossacks from World War I to the end of the Civil War. With the advent of Stalin's Five-Year Plans (1928 onward), however, the independence of authors entirely evaporated, and writers seemed to become subject to orders by the State to produce literature on call.

Scandinavian literature has not been subjected to such pressures, and Iceland's Snorri Sturluson (1179-1241), with his *Heimskringla*, a history of Norse kings to 1177, provided an early example of the Scandinavian fondness for literature. Despite its small size and relative remoteness, Iceland has produced considerable fiction of worth, including that of twentieth century novelists Gunnar Gunnarsson and Nobel Prize winner Halldór Laxness. Mainland Norway has generated an admirable body of literature, including novels by Jonas Lie, Olav Duun, Sigrid Undset, Bjørnstjerne Bjørnson, and Knut Hamsun, whose impressionistic novel *Hunger* was widely acclaimed upon its publication in 1890. The latter three writers each won the Nobel Prize.

Sweden, home of the Nobel Prize, has produced several twentieth century novelists who have been awarded that honor. Among these writers are Verner von Heidenstam, Pär Lagerkvist, and Selma Lagerlöf, whose *Gösta Berling's Saga* is a true masterpiece.

Denmark's contribution to Scandinavian literature has also been continuous and outstanding. Major novelists include Jens Peter Jacobsen, Martin Anderson Nexö, Henrik Pontoppidan, and Johannes V. Jensen, whose six-volume novel *The Long Journey* is a stunning racial history of the Nordic forefathers who surged all across Europe. Jensen and Pontoppidan each were awarded a Nobel Prize, Pontoppidan's 1917 award being shared with Karl Gjellerup.

This five-volume set completes another section of the Salem Genre Series. The volumes dealing with drama are scheduled for completion in 1985. I wish to acknowledge with thanks the dedication of all those who have contributed to the development of the Foreign Language Series of our long fiction survey.

FRANK N. MAGILL

CONTRIBUTORS

Writing Staff for Essays

Lowell A. Bangerter
Thomas Banks
Stanisław Barańczak
Richard P. Benton
András Boros-Kazai
Todd C. Hanlin
Feroza Jussawalla
Vasa D. Mihailovich
George Mihaychuk
Peter Petro

Sven H. Rossel
Murray Sachs
Jack Shreve
William L. Siemens
Thomas J. Sienkewicz
Gilbert G. Smith
Christopher J. Thaiss
James A. Winders
Harry Zohn
Leon Zolbrod

Writing Staff for Author Articles

Linda C. Badley
Thomas P. Baldwin
Lowell A. Bangerter
Thomas Banks
Stanisław Barańczak
Jean-Pierre Barricelli
Fiora A. Bassanese
Joseph F. Battaglia
Richard P. Benton
Harold Branam
Joseph Bruchac
Mitzi M. Brunsdale
Susan K. Burks
Jean-Pierre Cap
John Carpenter
Luisetta Elia Chomel
Richard N. Coe
Steven E. Colburn
John J. Conlon

Julian W. Connolly
Mark Conroy
Natalia Costa
J. Madison Davis
Mary E. Davis
Thomas Di Napoli
Lillian Doherty
Robert S. Dombroski
Paul F. Dvorak
William L. Felker
Margot K. Frank
Howard Fraser
L. H. Goldman
Roberto González Echevarría
Stephen I. Gurney
Franz P. Haberl
Klaus Hanson
John P. Harrington
Robert Henkels

David K. Herzberger

Marie-France Hilgar

Helen Mundy Hudson

Barbara L. Hussey

Joe W. Jackson, Jr.

Angela M. Jeannet

Alfred W. Jensen

Djelal Kadir

Lothar Kahn

Irma M. Kashuba

Steven G. Kellman

Charles L. King

Jeanne Larsen

Robert W. Leutner

Avril S. Lewis

Leon Lewis

Ward B. Lewis

Naomi Lindstrom

John D. Lyons

Fred B. McEwen

Iole F. Magri

Carol S. Maier

Richard A. Mazzara

Laurence W. Mazzeno

Jeremy T. Medina

Siegfried Mews

N. J. Meyerhofer

Jennifer Michaels

Vasa D. Mihailovich

Mark Minor

Harold K. Moon

Gene M. Moore

Christer L. Mossberg

Carol J. Murphy

F. William Nelson

James O'Brien

John C. O'Neal

Robert M. Otten

Ana María F. Parent

David B. Parsell

Carole Deering Paul

Genaro J. Pérez

Janet Pérez

Peter Petro

Linda Schelbitzki Pickle

Philippe Radley

Paul Reichardt

Helene M. Kastinger Riley

J. Thomas Rimer

Michael Ritterson

Sven H. Rossel

Victor Anthony Rudowski

Murray Sachs

F. C. St. Aubyn

Jan St. Martin

John K. Saunders

Joachim Scholz

Lucy M. Schwartz

Jack Shreve

Anne M. Sienkewicz

Armand E. Singer

Jan Sjåvik

Carol J. Sklenicka

Philip H. Solomon

Brian Stableford

Sonja G. Stary

Wojtek Stelmaszynski

Irwin Stern

Stan Sulkes

Victor Terras

Janet G. Tucker

Kim Vivian

Hans Wagener

John Michael Walsh

CONTRIBUTORS

Joan M. West

David Allen White

Raymond L. Williams

Timothy C. Wong

Sanroku Yoshida

Harry Zohn

Leon Zolbrod

LIST OF AUTHORS IN VOLUME 1

CRITICAL SURVEY
OF
LONG FICTION

KŌBŌ ABE

Born: Tokyo, Japan; March 7, 1924

Principal long fiction

Daiyon kampyōki, 1959 (*Inter Ice Age 4*, 1970); *Suna no onna*, 1962 (*The Woman in the Dunes*, 1964); *Tanin no kao*, 1964 (*The Face of Another*, 1966); *Moetsukita chizu*, 1967 (*The Ruined Map*, 1969); *Hakootoko*, 1973 (*The Box Man*, 1974); *Mikkai*, 1977 (*Secret Rendezvous*, 1980).

Other literary forms

Kōbō Abe has gained international renown not only for his novels but also for his short stories, plays, essays, radio dramas, and film scenarios. As the title of his collection of essays, *Mōken-no kokoro-ni keisanki-no te-o* (1957; with the hand of an adding machine in the heart of a vicious dog), suggests, virtually all of his writings reflect—in however oblique a way—moral indignation at the state of mankind. Abe has tried to expose the alienation and despair that so easily possess lonely or isolated people, particularly in modern urban society. He has demonstrated a willingness to experiment, and his stage pyrotechnics, as well as his halting and fragmented mode of narration, have been deliberately calculated to expose the irony and paradox of human existence.

Achievements

By means of his short stories, which were first published in journals and then collected in books during the early 1950's, Abe carved a special niche in the postwar Japanese literary scene. His story "Akai mayu" ("Red Cocoon"), first published in December, 1950, was awarded the Post-war Literature Prize. His first collection of short stories, *Chin'nyūsha* (1952; intruders), took its title from one of his best-received tales, a satiric allegory on counterfeit democracy in postwar Japan. Later, the title story, "Intruders," became transformed into the play *Tomodachi* (1967; *Friends*, 1969). Two of Abe's early stories, "Kabe" ("The Wall") and "S. Karuma-shi-no hanzai" ("S. Karuma's Crime"), were awarded the coveted Akutagawa Prize for portraying a Kafkaesque world that stresses the qualities of irrationality, surrealism, and frustration in contemporary life. His radio drama, *Bō ni natta otoko* (1957, 1969; *The Man Who Turned into a Stick*, 1975—a later version for theater), received a Cultural Festival Prize. Another of his radio dramas in 1958 earned second place in the Public Broadcasting Cultural Festival. His masterpiece, *The Woman in the Dunes*, won the Yomiuri Literature Prize in 1960 on the basis of an earlier, serialized version. As the doyen of living Japanese writers who enjoy an international reputation, Abe transcends the cultural code of his native country. His work deals with issues that relate to individuals and societies everywhere. The basic theme that underlies his best-known novels deals with the matter of alienation and identity, two poles that regulate human existence in social groups.

Biography

The circumstances of Kōbō Abe's early life and education suggest why he was especially predisposed to treat the question of alienation and identity with clinical detachment as well as with verve and imagination. The son of a physician on the staff of the Manchurian School of Medicine in Mukden (now Shenyang, China), Abe was born in Tokyo while his father was there on a research assignment. When Abe was barely a year old, the family returned to Mukden, where Abe lived until the age of sixteen. His early life and schooling, partly in Mukden and partly in Tokyo, took place during a turbulent period of social and political unrest in North China. Japanese military occupation included the area where he lived. In due course, World War II broke out, and eventually Tokyo and the other main cities of Japan were devastated by bombs and fire. All of this was part of Abe's direct experience. It is no wonder that his novels are dotted with references to warfare and human conflict.

Exempted from military service because of a respiratory illness, Abe stood apart from other young men of his age. Being forcibly separated by virtue of the Japanese defeat from the place where he grew up, he became almost a displaced person in his own country. His birthplace was Tokyo, yet his youth had been spent mostly in Mukden. His official family residence was on the northern island of Hokkaido. Abe himself has said that he is a man without a homeland. After going back to Tokyo in 1941 for schooling and military training and traveling under wartime conditions several times between Japan and Manchuria, Abe eventually finished medical school in 1948.

Deciding against medical practice, however, in favor of a writing career, Abe allied himself with a literary group led by Kiyoteru Hamada, which was committed to the goal of fusing surrealistic techniques with Marxist ideology. An avant-garde, experimental style quickly won for Abe praise from the younger generation of readers, who admired his short stories, novels, and plays that exposed the emptiness of life in modern society. His wife, Machi, whom he married while still a student, is an accomplished artist and stage designer. She has also illustrated many of Abe's works. In recent years, Abe has devoted much time to directing his own theater group, which he took to the United States in 1979.

Analysis

Human loss, disappearance, allocation of responsibility, anguish, and futility stand out as the main issues that figure in Kōbō Abe's writings. At first,

Abe treated such matters mostly in a serious way. Gradually, from the under-lying absurdity and irrationality of the imaginary situations about which he wrote, a kind of gallows humor emerged, giving a sense of situation comedy, albeit black comedy. Abe recognizes, on the one hand, that without cohesive units of interdependent people, human life, at least as it is now known, could scarcely exist. He also observes, on the other hand, that people everywhere suffer under the pressure to model their behavior on conventionally accepted manners and mores. Abe's characters' resistance to such pressures (or perhaps their unconscious wish to suffer) results in a desire to assert their individuality. Ironically, such assertion leads to alienation, creating a Catch-22 situation and a sense of absurdity.

Thus, in Abe's novels, human relationships are shown to be in disorder, partly reflecting the particular quality of his artistic imagination and partly reflecting his own youthful experiences. Except for the case of *The Woman in the Dunes*, which is set in a remote seaside hamlet, the main action in his narratives typically takes place against the urban landscape and amid the impersonalized locations and institutions with which modern city dwellers are most familiar—hospitals, offices, laboratories, department stores, movie the-aters, waiting rooms, and apartments. Conversation and human intercourse are fragmented and interrupted, contributing to a sense of incompleteness. Success, fruition, and fulfillment constantly evade his protagonists, who are usually depicted as well-educated people, deserving to reap the rewards of their prudence and perseverance. The underlying irony of Abe's narratives suggests that human beings have learned to govern many of the forces of their external environment, but that they know so little about themselves that they flounder helplessly at the mercy of satanic workings that lurk in the irrational depths of the mind. Sexuality in many of Abe's novels perversely turns out to exert a divisive impact on men and women, reducing them to a bestial level.

Sometimes, it would seem, gratuitous detail clogs Abe's narratives, slowing down the forward thrust of the action and creating what amounts to a form of static. The sequence of time is often juggled, creating a confusion of past and present. Lists of objects, minute descriptions of surface appearances, and clinical analyses of emotional responses try the reader's patience, giving an impression of awkwardness. Actually, however, what appear as technical deficiencies contribute to the overall effectiveness of the author's style. Besides imparting a sense of verisimilitude to the situations described—however absurd and irrational they would seem to be—the interruptions, false starts, and narrative shifts convey the state of suffering from which the characters in the end find it impossible to be freed; periodic breaks in the flow of a story are essential to the ultimate completion of the event.

Another intrusive characteristic in Abe's novels that deserves mention relates to the didactic impulse. As critics have recognized, his novels are imbued with an implicit desire for men and women, parents and children, and family or community to work for social good. A strong social conscience drives through all the novels like a compelling organic force. It is easy to understand why at the beginning of his career Abe immersed himself in philosophical writings. Not only did he feel empathy for Marxism, but also he studied Friedrich Nietzsche, Martin Heidegger, and Karl Jaspers. As a founding member of two postwar Japanese groups of left-wing authors, as well as someone involved in a cross section of European literary movements, Abe, like Jean-Paul Sartre and Albert Camus, stands out as an intellectual writer of cosmopolitan bent who deals not in themes of localized scope but with universal problems. As such, he deserves to be counted as the leading Japanese exponent of the novel of ideas.

Yet, in pinpointing the sources for Abe's moral sensibility, one must go beyond twentieth century ideologies and consider the same Chinese and South-Asian Buddhist and Confucian sources that led earlier Japanese authors such as Bakin to treat themes touching on good and evil behavior and on the individual's place in the larger framework of human society. For example, in terms of theme, Abe's idea that the search for the other—typically a missing or estranged person—becomes a search for the self relates to fundamental insights of Zen. Similarly, the concept of a realm of nothingness owes as much to Buddhist philosophy as to modern nihilism. Social criticism based on the techniques of irony and satire harkens back to popular Japanese literature of the late eighteenth and early nineteenth century, with its pronounced Confucian orientation and its express purpose of encouraging good and castigating evil.

Even in terms of technique, the idea of a postscript in the author's voice, which suggests removal of the narrator's mask, resembles Bakin's practice. The ending of *Inter Ice Age 4*, for example, insists on the open-ended nature of literature and fiction, in which each person must form his or her own conclusion about the meaning of the tale, yet Abe in his own voice observes in the last words of the postscript, "The most frightening thing in the world is discovering the abnormal in that which is closest to us." Few modern authors would dare to make such an observation about their own fiction, at least in the text itself, but Bakin frequently did so in his day. Nevertheless, unlike Bakin, Abe refrains from simplistic characterization of certain kinds of behavior as being praiseworthy or reprehensible.

Paradox and irony in Abe's writings give rise to positive and negative polarities. On the negative side, one finds situations such as running away, disappearing, losing one's identity, and desiring to escape, all of which lead to destruction, loss, and denial of self. On the positive side, a sense of rebirth, regeneration, and reshaped identity emerges from the narratives. *The Woman in the Dunes*, in particular, suggests a case in point. Toward the end of the story, the omniscient narrator states pointedly about the protagonist, "Perhaps, along with the water in the sand, he had found a new self." Returning to a communal structure, as Niki Jumpei does, on the one hand binds and imprisons; on the other hand, it also shelters and supports.

To sum up the constituent elements of Abe's long fiction, his main theme involves exposition of the condition of the outsider in modern society. His technique is based on allegory, irony, and satire. His narratives are often constructed by means of a series of reverses. Whenever some hopeful sign appears that communication between people is about to take place, some obtrusion appears, rendering further development impossible, as if the lights were suddenly turned on in a lovers' bedroom or someone knocked on the door. His style is often stiff and formal, like a student in a celluloid collar always preparing for examinations. Order is what one arbitrarily imposes on experience. Logic represents an abstraction incapable of fathoming reality, which constantly changes in shape and inexorably exerts the power to move people, however reluctant they may be.

In cumulative effect, Abe creates parable and myth. By inverting, destroying, or denying meaning to the rational foundations of society and its values, Abe invents a new reality, which takes the shape of an ironic affirmation of a future without form. A brief discussion of six texts of long fiction that have appeared in English translation will serve to demonstrate the salient characteristics of Abe's art and philosophy.

Essentially about artificial intelligence, computers, and the moral issues that surround abortion, *Inter Ice Age 4* involves a scientist and laboratory administrator, Dr. Katsumi (whose name literally means "Win-see"). He supervises the reduction of a slain man's intelligence to a computer program. Toward the end of the novel, Dr. Katsumi is ordered killed by the computer that he himself programmed. Mostly in the form of a first-person narrative, the novel combines elements of murder mystery and science-fiction fantasy. In a subplot, aborted fetuses are kept alive, and by means of sordid biological experimentation that involves "planned evolution," a new form of human life is created—namely, "aquans." Aquans become heirs to the earth, owing to climatic change that brings a dramatic warming of temperatures and a precipitous rise in the level of the sea.

Ironically, the investigators turn out to be the perpetrators of the crime. Besides murder, racketeering in human fetuses, computer programming, and aquan research, the bizarre plot includes strange telephone calls and the intense rivalry that can lead scientists into reckless or irresponsible behavior. As a computer designed to predict the future comes to speak with its own intelligence, Gothic horror merges with science fiction. Dr. Katsumi's own wife unknowingly contributes her aborted fetus to aquan research. "Was I . . . trying to protect her or was I . . . trying to use her. . . ?" muses the husband. "Compared with this fate, infanticide was a refined and humane act."

In the climactic episode, Dr. Katsumi's subordinate colleagues place him on trial in a kangaroo court. Such a development suggests victimization, lynching, and scapegoating, which abound in Abe's work and which Rene Girard has treated in his book, *"To Double Business Bound": Essays on Literature, Mimesis, and Anthropology* (1978). Characteristically, the narrative mode of *Inter Ice Age 4* toward the end changes to a representational mode. Televised pictures of an aquan breeding farm are described with commentary by the scientist in charge, Professor Yamamoto, who serves partly as a foil and partly as a double for Dr. Katsumi. *Inter Ice Age 4* originally appeared in serial form between July, 1958, and March, 1959, in the wake of the launching of the first Soviet sputnik and a heightened degree of awareness of futuristic science and technology.

The Woman in the Dunes is Abe's most widely read novel. It has been translated not only into English but also into more than twenty other languages. A film production by Hiroshi Teshigahara in 1963 became a huge commercial success. As William Currie has said in *Approaches to the Modern Japanese Novel* (1976), *The Woman in the Dunes* is a narrative of "almost mythic simplicity," in which Abe probes the "roots of existence" and the "difficulty people have in communicating with one another," touching on the "discrepancy between the mind and the external world, or between inner and outer reality."

Central to the novel is the metaphor of sand. It suggests the shifting reality with which the protagonist, Niki Jumpei, must come to terms; often used in Buddhist scriptures, the image of sand represents that which is universal and which can grind or pulverize other material. Niki Jumpei's name has a significance that goes beyond his identity as a schoolteacher who likes to travel to remote places to collect insects. Written with Chinese characters that may be translated as "Humanity-tree Conform-to-average," the name suggests allegorically a kind of victimized Everyman.

From the narrative, the idea emerges that people living under conditions of permanent crisis on the one hand are forced by public circumstances to pull together. On the other hand, private desire and primitive instinct compel them to withdraw into isolation. The specific conditions that led Abe to grapple with people's contradictory impulses in literary and imaginative terms may well derive from the experience of coming of age during wartime and witnessing the social disorder and transformation that came in the wake of defeat. To say so, however, should not imply that Abe's work is limited to any special time or place. The beauty of *The Woman in the Dunes* lies in the transcendence of any locality or period. It reminds one that life everywhere, now as always, lurches from crisis to crisis. The future remains as uncertain as the shifting sands on the shore. A person's well-being depends on a precarious balance between identity with others and alienation from a social group.

Alienation and identity, the paired concepts crucial to an appreciative reading of Abe's novels, also figure prominently in *The Face of Another*. The idea of deceitfully masking one's true identity and thereby alienating oneself from the possibility of love is developed in a first-person narrative that involves a brilliant scientist who has lost his face in a laboratory explosion. By creating a new face mask, he acquires a new self, "which ironically leads to his own psychological death as a person," as Philip Williams has stated in *Studies On Japanese Culture* (1973).

The Ruined Map is a first-person narrative about a detective whom a missing man's wife has hired to search for her husband. In a metamorphosis resembling that of *Inter Ice Age 4*, the detective is transformed into the ghostly man whom he is relentlessly pursuing. As his personality progressively disintegrates, he is carried to the edge of madness. By the end of the novel, he has given up "looking for a way to the past." As the woman—his wife or the person who hired him to find her husband—apparently gives up searching for him, he leaves his "crevice in the darkness." He begins "walking in the opposite direction," relying on a map he does not comprehend, "perhaps in order to reach her." Such is the nature of the paradox and irony that distinguish Abe's mode of narration.

Similarly, *The Box Man* also describes a person's futile effort to escape from himself. Here the protagonist tries to achieve this end by taking a large, empty cardboard box, cutting a peephole in it, and placing it over his head. Thus he expects to walk away from his anxieties. The main danger lies in the possibility of meeting another "box man." Part of the narrative involves intercourse between a true box man and a fake box man, suggesting the literary device of doubling and splitting, about which R. Rogers has written in *Psychoanalytical Study of the Double in Literature* (1970). As Abe himself has said of the novel, "Being no one means at the same time that one can be anyone." Aversion to ordinary existence and the question of what is genuine and what is counterfeit are expressed by means of the box as a shield from the world, a symbol that represents disposability and concealment.

One unusual feature of the novel consists of nine leaves of photographs, all but one having enigmatic or aphoristic captions. For example, the text for the fifth of these, that in the middle position, reads:

In seeing there is love, in being seen there is abhorrence. One grins, trying to bear the pain of being seen. But not just anyone can be someone who only looks. If the one who is looked at looks back, then the person who was looking becomes the one who is looked at.

The appropriateness of such a graphic and textual appendage to *The Box Man* stems from the former identity of the fictional narrator, who has become a box man. He was a photographer, albeit not of portraits or landscapes but rather of such prosaic subjects as women's underwear and incidents in public parks, and took surreptitious snapshots—seeing without being seen.

Secret Rendezvous is a surrealistic detective story about an unidentified thirty-two-year-old man, a director of sales promotion for "jump shoes," special athletic footwear with "air-bubble springs" built into the soles. Early one morning, his wife, who was perfectly healthy, suddenly disappears, a typical occurrence in Abe's fictional world. An ambulance comes to pick her up and take her to a hospital. When the husband attempts to check on the situation, he encounters a tangle of red tape and is unable to obtain any solid information.

One of the underlying social issues involves the quality and dependability of health care. Titillating and yet frightening incidents such as "a deliberate prearranged rendezvous" with a physician are introduced. In a narrative that mixes both first- and third-person modes, one of the suspected doctors turns out to be involved in collecting his own sperm for sale to an artificial insemination agency. Besides the matter of inexplicable loss and the struggle to come to terms with a reality that lies beyond the power of human comprehension (which are common to all of Abe's principal works of long fiction), there is also the puzzling business of human sexuality, of institutional continuity, and of providing effective health care in a world marred by petty jealousy, internecine rivalry, and haphazard medical diagnosis. "Secret rendezvous among patients" are handled as a common occurrence, and hospital surveillance techniques necessitate "automatic recording of love scenes." Abe's topsy-turvy world, which inexorably requires scapegoats and hapless victims, unfolds in such a way that it becomes impossible for the protagonist to distinguish the aggressor from the victim.

Outwardly stiff and awkward, Abe's novels reveal his preoccupation with ideas rather than style. Using concepts and language drawn from science and philosophy, Abe trains a critical focus on human society and institutions. Allegory, irony, and satire lend artistic force and credibility to his concern for the dangers of alienation from society and the difficulty of achieving a constructive identity of the self within the confines of the social groups among whose members people must live.

Major publications other than long fiction
SHORT FICTION: *Chin'nyūsha*, 1952; *Four Stories by Kōbō Abe*, 1973.
PLAYS: *Bō ni natta otoko*, 1957, 1969 (radio drama; *The Man Who Turned into a Stick: Three Related Plays*, 1975); *Tomodachi*, 1967 (*Friends: A Play by Abe Kōbō*, 1969); *Omae nimo tsumi ga aru*, 1978 (*You, Too, Are Guilty*, 1979).
NONFICTION: *Mōken-no kokoro-ni keisanki-no te-o*, 1957.

Bibliography
Currie, William. "Abe Kōbō: *The Woman in the Dunes*," in *Approaches to the Modern Japanese Novel*, 1976. Edited by K. Tsuruta and T. E. Swann.

Kimball, Arthur G. *Crisis in Identity and Contemporary Japanese Novels*, 1973.
Richter, Frederick. "A Comparative Approach to Abe Kōbō's 'S. Karumashi no Hanzai,'" in *Journal of the Association of Teachers of Japanese*, 1974.
Rimer, J. Thomas. *Modern Japanese Fiction and Its Traditions*, 1978.
Williams, Philip. "Abe Kōbō and Symbols of Absurdity," in *Studies on Japanese Culture*, 1973 (volume 1). Edited by S. Ota and R. Fukuda.
Yamanouchi, Hisaaki. "Abe Kōbō and Ōe Kenzaburō: The Search for Identity in Contemporary Japanese Literature," in *Modern Japan: Aspects of History, Literature and Society*, 1975. Edited by W. G. Beasley.

Leon Zolbrod

SHMUEL YOSEF AGNON
Shmuel Yosef Czaczkes

Born: Buczacz, Austria-Hungary (now Poland); July 17, 1888
Died: Jerusalem, Israel; February 17, 1970

Principal long fiction

Hachnasat Kala, 1931 (*The Bridal Canopy*, 1937); *Bilvav Yamim: Sippur Agadah Shel S. Y. Agnon*, 1934 (*In the Heart of the Seas: An Allegorical Tale of S. Y. Agnon*, 1947); *Sippur Pashut*, 1935; *Oreach Nata Lalun*, 1939, 1950 (*A Guest for the Night*, 1968); *T'mol Shilshom*, 1945; *Shira*, 1971; *Bachanuto Shel Mar Lublin*, 1974.

Other literary forms

Many of Shmuel Yosef Agnon's writings are available in two comprehensive collections, both called *Kol Sippurav Shel Shmuel Yosef Agnon*. The first collection appeared in 1931 in Berlin. It included two novels, *The Bridal Canopy*, parts 1 and 2, and *Sippur Pashut* (a simple story), and three collections of short stories, *Me'az Ume'ata* (1931; from then and from now), *Sippurei Ahavim* (1931; stories of lovers), and *b'Shuva v'Nachat* (1935; with repentance and joy). This edition was expanded to eleven volumes: Volumes 7 and 8, including the novel *A Guest for the Night* and a collection of stories, *Elu v'Elu* (1941; of this and that), were printed in Jerusalem. Volumes 9 through 11, published both in Jerusalem and Tel Aviv, included the novel *T'mol Shilshom* (a day before yesterday) and two more volumes of short stories, *Samuch Venir'e* (1951; near and apparent) and *Ad Hena* (1952; thus far). The second comprehensive edition was published in Tel Aviv in eight volumes, seven of them in 1953 and another in 1962. In addition to his fiction, Agnon published a number of nonfiction works. They include *Yamim Nora'im* (1938; *Days of Awe*, 1948), an anthology of High Holiday traditions; *Sefer, Sofer, v'Sippur* (1938, 1978; book, writer, and story), excerpts on booklore from various sources; *Atem R'item* (1959; you have witnessed), a compilation of rabbinic responsa; and *Sifreihem Shel Zaddikim* (1961; tales of the Zaddikim), stories of the Baal Shem Tov and his disciples. Posthumous publications of Agnon's works include: the two novels, *Shira* and *Bachanuto Shel Mar Lublin* (in Mr. Lublin's store); three collections of stories, one concerning Agnon's hometown in Galicia, entitled *Ir Umeloah* (1973; a city and the fullness thereof), and two others, *Lifnim Min Hachomah* (1975; inside the wall) and *Pitchei Devarim* (1977; introductions); a book of Agnon's letters and speeches, *Meatzmi El Atzmi* (1976; from myself to myself); and a work tracing Agnon's family tree, *Korot Bateynu* (1979; pillars of our house). Some of his works have been translated into French, Spanish, and German.

Achievements

Affectionately known in Israel by the acronym "Shai," Agnon was, during his lifetime, as one critic notes, "uncontestably the dean" of Hebrew letters. He is widely read and almost a household word in his own country but is not as well-known to English-speaking audiences. His works, deceptively simple, are so complex that they do not lend themselves well to translation. He was a prolific writer, the author of more than a hundred tales, yet only two of his major novels have been translated into English (and those translations are considered of poor quality), *The Bridal Canopy* and *A Guest for the Night*, in addition to one shorter novel, *In the Heart of the Seas*, the anthology *Days of Awe*, and two long stories, *Shevu'ath Emunim* (1943; *Betrothed*) and *Edo ve Enam* (1950; *Edo and Enam*) that are translated together in the volume *Two Tales*, 1966.

Agnon is unique in many respects: He was a religious Jew who wrote fiction rather than biblical commentaries, an intellectual writer who appeals to the simple as well as to the highly sophisticated. Most of his writings appeared in local periodicals, either in Europe or in Israel, prior to their incorporation in the volumes of collected works. In his extraordinary Hebrew prose style, which assimilates biblical phrases and Talmudic parables, Agnon insists upon a return to Jewish sources. He is an allusive writer who writes with the erudition of his rabbinic background, using the language of the Jewish scholar. His Hebrew is classical rather than modern. Agnon's works have a timeless, dreamlike, magical quality that takes them beyond the reality he presents. The issues with which he deals are not explicit; they are veiled in layers of symbolism, making his works so elusive that scholars are reluctant to attempt translations. The surface of his fiction, however, is realistic, offering a detailed picture of Eastern European Jewry of the nineteenth and twentieth centuries.

Agnon was the recipient of numerous honors and prizes. In 1966, with Nelly Sachs, he received the Nobel Prize for Literature—the first time this award was granted to a Hebrew-language writer.

Biography

The oldest of five children, Shmuel Yosef Agnon was born Shmuel Yosef Czaczkes in the small village of Buczacz in Eastern Galicia (a small East European province that has belonged alternately to Poland and Austria). His father, Shalom Mordecai, an ordained rabbi, earned his livelihood as a fur merchant. Religiously, the family was traditionally observant; economically, it was strongly bourgeois; culturally, it was erudite in Jewish literature. Agnon received a traditional and liberal education, studying the Talmud, Midrash, Jewish medieval philosophers, and Hasidic and rabbinic lore, as well as the early Galician enlightened writers, modern Hebrew and Yiddish literature, and German literature. His broad education developed in him two loves, which became his *modus vivendi*: his love for literature and for Zion.

In his Nobel Prize speech, Agnon claimed that he wrote his first poem at the age of five as a tribute to his father, who was away on a business trip, because he missed him. His early interest in writing was no doubt generated by a desire to emulate both his father, who wrote poetry and scholarly articles, and his cousin, Hayim Czaczkes, a writer whose works were often published in the Galician press. He was fortunate that his family was well off and did not need his help in its support, and he was encouraged to pursue his own interests. At fifteen, he published his first poem in the Krakow Hebrew weekly. By the time he was eighteen, he was considered a promising young writer.

Agnon, a strong Zionist, left for Palestine in 1907, and although he returned to Buczacz twice, in 1913 and once in 1930, he could stay only for short periods. His journey to Eretz Yisrael, the Land of Israel, was a difficult one, requiring a train trip to Trieste and then a sea voyage to Jaffa. Agnon's short novel, *In the Heart of the Seas*, records this hazardous trip. Upon entering Palestine, he settled in Jaffa, the scene of a number of his stories, including his first published tale in 1908, entitled "Agunot" ("Deserted Wives"). Following a trend adopted by earlier Hebrew writers, such as Mendele Mokher Seforim (pseudonym for Sholom Yaakov Abramowitz) and Sholom Aleichem (pseudonym for Sholom Rabinowitz), young Shmuel Yoseph Czaczkes signed this tale with the name of "Agnon," adopting it officially as his family name in 1924. It is significant that he chose this particular name, for it would seem to indicate his own relationship to the world.

In Jewish law, the *agunah*, or deserted woman, is not free to remarry, because she has not been divorced. She is anchored in a relationship which can last forever. This image of being in limbo was pursued a decade after Agnon's story by S. Ansky in his classical drama, *Dybbuk* (1916; English translation, 1917), and some thirty-five years later by Saul Bellow in his depiction of the *Dangling Man* (1944). In all three cases, the characters are not free. They are constricted by an invisible thread which they do not control and cannot sever. This condition is not a form of alienation, an estrangement from a person or society; rather, it suggests an eternal rootedness that cannot be easily extirpated. At the age of twenty, Agnon felt like the *agunot* of his tales: uprooted, yet eternally bound to his native village of Buczacz and the world of his youth. In 1911, he moved to Jerusalem and settled permanently in that city, even though he left it for one extended period and other brief periods. He was proclaimed an honorary citizen of Jerusalem in 1962.

Agnon went to Berlin in 1913. The time spent in Germany proved to be very significant to him. (He made a brief trip to his hometown to visit his ailing father, who died November 20, 1913. His mother had died earlier, in 1908.) There he met Zalman Schocken, a merchant and Zionist and patron of the Jewish arts who became Agnon's admirer, his Maecenas, and his sole publisher. Agnon was one of those fortunate artists who never had to struggle for a livelihood and who was free to concentrate on his writing.

Germany was then a hub of cultural activity, and Agnon moved in a dynamic circle of philosophers, writers, Zionist leaders, and industrialists. In 1920, he married Esther Marx, a member of one of Germany's most respected Jewish families. The couple moved to Homburg, where two children were born, a daughter, Emunai, in 1921, and a son, Hemdat, in 1922. Agnon's years in Germany were productive ones, but in 1924, his home was destroyed by a fire which consumed much of his unpublished material. He never entirely recovered from the trauma of this conflagration. In his Nobel speech, he claimed to have lost, at that time, not only everything he had written once he left Israel, but also a rare library of four thousand Hebrew books. He left Berlin alone, after sending his wife and children to her parents' home, and returned to Jerusalem in 1924. In 1925, his family joined him. They made their home in Talpiot, a suburb of Jerusalem. Agnon was busy at this time working on his epic novel, *The Bridal Canopy*.

In 1929, Agnon lost his home again, this time to marauding Arabs, who attacked numerous Jewish settlements in that year. The family escaped unhurt, but his house and library were in shambles. In a letter to his friend Schocken, he described the scene and wrote that he was able to save his manuscripts, but most of his archives and the history of Eretz Yisrael were destroyed. His new library of three thousand books, many of which he had inherited from his father-in-law, also suffered: Books were "overturned and scattered and torn."

The loss of his home a second time was a crushing blow to Agnon. The family spent four months at his wife's sister's home in Bat Galim, near Haifa. In January, 1930, he traveled to Germany to see Schocken, who had decided to publish Agnon's collected works. During this time, Agnon also made a trip to Buczacz. He stayed only a week, but this trip provided the material for his novel *A Guest for the Night*.

The Berlin edition of his collected works was enthusiastically received, and from that time on, Agnon's life was a series of artistic and critical triumphs. Since his death in Israel on February 17, 1970, a number of his works have been edited by his daughter and published posthumously by Schocken Books.

Analysis

Two dominant forces ruled Shmuel Yosef Agnon's life: the Torah as the essence of a meaningful life, and Eretz Yisrael, the Land of Israel, as the ancestral homeland for the Jew. On a personal basis, Agnon integrated these passions into his existence at an early age. He was brought up in a religious home. For a brief time, he abandoned his piety, but he shortly realized that his life was empty without it. He returned to his orthodox ways and lived as a Jew committed to the Torah, albeit in secular surroundings. He made Eretz Yisrael his home when most religious Jews still looked upon the Holy Land as a suitable burial place but not a place to live. They felt that settlement in Israel could take place only with the advent of the Messiah.

On an artistic level, Agnon's early works, those that are best known and have been widely translated, present a nostalgic evocation of the milieu of the Eastern European shtetl, specifically his native village of Buczacz. The works that are set in the nineteenth century depict a hermetically sealed community, governed by piety and love and watched over by the omnipresent and benevolent Almighty. Agnon, however, was a man of his times, fully aware of contemporary events and their effect upon the Jewish community. Eretz Yisrael is a motif in all of his works, which reflect the ongoing dissolution of the shtetl as it became increasingly vulnerable to the intrusions of the age. Although Agnon made brief visits to Buczacz as an adult, all of his works are drawn from his childhood memories of his hometown. At times, the image is ebullient and joyful, as in *The Bridal Canopy*; at times fanciful, as in *In the Heart of the Seas*; at other times, somber and depressing, as in *A Guest for the Night*.

The Bridal Canopy is the first of a trilogy of novels dealing with the experience of Eastern European Jewry. Written in 1931 (although based on a short story completed in 1920), a time of upheaval between two major wars, the novel focuses on the Jewish community in Galicia of the 1820's. In a mood of fantasy and nostalgia, Agnon presents a work that is both realistic and unrealistic: realistic in its depiction of the Jewish milieu, the piety of the Jew, and his devotion to the Torah; unrealistic in its childlike attitude toward life, where the concerns of men are limited to the amassing of a bridal dowry and to the telling of tales of past saints and wonder-workers.

The theme of this major work, as suggested in the title, is the brotherhood of the Jewish people, which is achieved through the upholding of God's commandments, especially those of charity and hospitality. The title, *Hachnasat Kala*, a Hebrew idiom meaning bridal dowry, has been loosely translated as *The Bridal Canopy* (see I. M. Lask's translation of the novel). This is a mistranslation. The focus of the work is on the collection of the dowry; the wedding itself, which takes place under the "bridal canopy," is of relatively minor significance. Agnon deals with the marriage process, which involves not only the protagonist, Reb Yudel, but also the entire Jewish community. All participate in the preservation of the social institution of marriage and in the fulfillment of God's commandment of procreation. The bridal dowry, an ancient concept, well-known in the time of Abraham, who sent his servant, Eliezer, loaded with gifts, to seek a wife for his son, Isaac, is an integral element of the traditional Jewish marriage. With this initial novel, Agnon falls into the category of Jewish writers who depict Jewish social institutions humorously. Many of them, such as Yosef Perl and Mendele Mokher Seforim, writing during the period of the Haskalai—the Enlightenment—parodied and satirized traditional Jewish customs. Agnon's novel more closely resembles the work of Israel Zangwill, who at the turn of the century wrote the marvelously funny work *King of the Schnorrers* (1894), depicting, with a combination of humor and love, the Jewish mendicant, who is considered a vital aspect of the community. It is through him that the community is able to fulfill God's commandment of charity. The protagonist, the schnorrer, never allows the community to forget that he is the instrument of their salvation. Similarly, in Agnon's work, Reb Yudel, by raising a bridal dowry for his daughter, allows the community to participate both in hospitality to a stranger and in charity to the poor. Through the peregrinations of Reb Yudel, one sees a cohesive Jewish community, its members flawed but united, a community wherein each is his brother's keeper.

The plot is simple, if somewhat improbable. Provoked by his wife's complaints, the protagonist leaves the relative comforts of his home and the house of study in his native village of Brod and travels to various neighboring communities to raise enough money for the bridal dowry of his eldest daughter. He is accompanied by his faithful friend, the wagon-driver Nota, and Nota's trusty and intelligent horses, Mashkeni and Narutza. (These names whimsically play on a passage in Song of Songs, where the beloved says to her betrothed, "draw me after thee"—*mashkeni*—"and we will run together"—*narutza*.) After spending months on the road, he yearns for a return to the simple life and decides to make up for lost time by settling in an inn, studying the Torah and using the collected dowry money to pay for his stay. While at the inn, he is mistaken for a wealthy man who coincidentally happens to bear his same name and lives in the same town as he does. This mistaken identity is the vehicle for the ensuing events: an alliance in the form of an engagement with a wealthy family, the return to his home, the inadvertent intercession of the aristocratic Yudel Nathanson, who unwittingly becomes the patron of Yudel the Hasid, the discovery of the treasure in a cave, the wedding itself, Yudel's blessed and prosperous life, and his eventual settling in the Land of Israel.

Agnon's language in *The Bridal Canopy* is a combination of the Yiddish vernacular and biblical and post-biblical Hebrew. It was the medium of popular Hebrew texts of the seventeenth, eighteenth, and nineteenth centuries and also the language of the pious Jew of the period depicted. Eclectic in style, the novel is essentially a series of tales or anecdotes held together by the tale of Reb Yudel. Most of the tales in *The Bridal Canopy* were published as individual stories; some are well integrated in the novel, while others seem superimposed. These tales are, at times, didactic, at other times fanciful. Some are folktales; others are Agnon's own creations. The narrative of Reb Yudel's odyssey and the tales within the narrative illuminate the character of the protagonist and the inhabitants of the community of Brod, his hometown, and those whom he meets in the neighboring villages. The tale within the tale is also symbolic of the Jew within his community: Each has his own personality; together they make up a larger entity.

The novel itself is a depiction not so much of Reb Yudel as it is of the entire environment he traverses. It establishes Agnon's posture in his fictive world as well, an attitude of respect for religious tradition in spite of instances of hypocrisy and ignorance. The work is divided into two parts. Book 1 deals with the departure of Reb Yudel, the raising of the bridal dowry, and the quest for a successful match for his daughter; book 2 deals with his return home and the wedding.

The opening chapter describes Reb Yudel's high spiritual aspirations and his lowly materialistic circumstances. He lives in an unfurnished cellar. His only possession is a cock, known as Reb Zerach, that functions at the beginning of the work simply as an alarm clock, awakening Reb Yudel at dawn for the morning worship. At the end of the work, it becomes clear that the cock's function is a more subtle one. Reb Yudel's character, as the work progresses and he becomes a wanderer, combines three Jewish stock figures: the *batlon* (the idler), the *meshulach* (the messenger or schnorrer), and the *maggid* (the itinerant preacher and storyteller).

Reb Yudel, a *batlon*, known affectionately, if somewhat ironically, as "the Chasid," the student, is one of that society's pious men who is incapable of earning a living and spends all day in the house of study. The author indicates his attitude toward the protagonist (and the work itself) by referring to him by the descriptive diminutive "Reb Yudel" or "little Jew." It is the name given to a child or to one of lowly stature, *dos kleine Mensch*, and lacks the reverence that would be found in the scholar's appellation. At no time is he referred to as "Rav Yehuda ha Chasid"—Rabbi Judah, the pious. Agnon wants his audience to recognize the humble nature, the childlike quality of his protagonist, and the inherent comedy of the work. This is reflected not only in Yudel's naïveté but also in his attitude to life and the world at large, an attitude indicated in the subtitle of the work, "The Wonders of Reb Yudel, the Chasid from Brod . . .," which supports the mood of fantasy and nostalgia in which this novel was written. Reb Yudel is not a saint and does not perform miracles, but he depends upon and believes in miracles. Like a child, Reb Yudel interprets experiences and expressions in their most literal context. Like the unscholarly, nonsaintly individual, he misquotes the sages, misapplies biblical and Talmudic sayings, and misassesses situations.

Agnon's depiction of Reb Yudel is not harshly critical. Reb Yudel represents a world that no longer exists, a world that was reassuring in its simplicity, in its belief in the goodness of God and man, a world where one could spend one's life recounting the marvels of the sages while enjoying the hospitality of one's host and brethren. Some critics find a troubling ambiguity in the novel, an uncertain combination of acceptance and rejection of the world so painstakingly delineated. This ambiguity is felt only if the reader mistakes Agnon's comedy for criticism. In fact, Agnon wrote as a devoted traditionalist;

he makes this obvious in his depiction of Heshel, the *maskil*, the man of the Enlightenment whom Reb Yudel meets during his odyssey. Heshel, ready to discard tradition without replacing it with anything substantial ("grammar is the foundation of the world," he claims), receives the harshest treatment of any character in the work. He begins as a wealthy man, and Yudel goes to him for a contribution to his bridal fund, but he ends in a state of abject penury, ill-clothed, pockets empty, starving. He comes as a beggar to the wedding of Yudel's daughter. The point Agnon makes is obvious: Life is impoverished when it is devoid of tradition. In contrast to Heshel, Reb Yudel, the believer, is amply rewarded for his faith with material fortune, a prosperous life with its spiritual culmination in the Land of Israel, where he settles in his old age.

It has been suggested that *The Bridal Canopy* is modeled after Miguel de Cervantes' *Don Quixote de la Mancha* (1605, 1615) and that Agnon treats his protagonist ambivalently, both as saint and fool. Actually, Agnon's style, like Sholom Aleichem's, more closely resembles that of the American humorist Mark Twain, in its use of the vernacular, folk humor, tall tale, literal interpretation of metaphor, and comic treatment of cloistered religion. The protagonist, Reb Yudel, is not a romantic; he does not fight windmills, nor does he reach for the impossible dream, as does Don Quixote. He is a firm believer in the beneficence and magnanimity of God and has utmost faith that all of his needs will be met. Ultimately, they are. It is not a romantic concept but a religious one.

The Bridal Canopy is an eclectic work. In his Nobel speech, Agnon voiced his indebtedness to the Jewish sources: to the Bible, and its major commentator, Rashi; to the Talmud and *Shulhan ᶜarukh*; to Jewish sages and authorities on Jewish law; to medieval poets and thinkers, especially Maimonides; and to contemporary Hasidim and pious men with whom he had spent time.

In the Heart of the Seas, the second of the trilogy begun with *The Bridal Canopy*, is a shorter novel which has much in common with its predecessor. The time period of the second novel is the same as that of the earlier work, about 1820; the milieu, the city of Buczacz (instead of Brod) in Galicia. While *The Bridal Canopy* ends with Reb Yudel's ascent to the Holy Land, *In the Heart of the Seas* begins with the last-minute preparations for the departure of a group of pious Hasidim who have decided to emigrate to Eretz Yisrael. The work deals with the journey itself, the perils, the trials, the anguish involved in this trip, and the determination of these pilgrims, in spite of all hardships.

It is a tale which commingles reality and fantasy. In 1934, the year the novel was published, Agnon was witness to the Fifth Aliya (ascent to the Land of Israel), which brought two hundred and fifty thousand Jews to the country. Most of them were refugees from Nazi Germany who managed to leave before all exits were closed. They were not necessarily religious people.

They were those who had the means and the foresight to leave. In *In the Heart of the Seas*, Agnon reflects upon what it would be like to emigrate to the Holy Land out of love and religious commitment, rather than the political necessity of the times. It is a fantastic concept. The single individual may move whenever he desires, but communities of people are not so mobile and will reestablish themselves, or move from the security of their environment, only when forced to do so. This was the case with the Jewish community of Eastern Europe. *In the Heart of the Seas* is a wistful tale with a realistic veneer.

The work assumes even greater significance if considered in the context of the secular writings of the Hebraists and the cultural climate of the time. Zionism was viewed mainly as a secular and political movement within the Jewish world and was frowned upon by the religous Jews, who, like the rabbi of Buczacz in *In the Heart of the Seas*, believed that it was sacrilege to go to Israel prior to the coming of the Messiah. Agnon takes the traditional image of Zion, which the ancient poets and pietists glorified in psalms and poetry, and transforms it into a realistic destination of the pious Hasidim of this Eastern Galician village.

Although the action takes place in the early part of the nineteenth century, the author includes himself as one of the travelers. He is the last to join the group. He is mentioned by name, Rabbi Shmuel Yosef, the son of Rabbi Shalom Mordechai ha-Levi, who is married to a woman named Esther and who has a penchant for storytelling. The tale is related by an omniscient narrator who is replaced at times by the author's own persona. He purports to be chronicling the adventures of a man named Chananiah exactly as he heard them.

On a literal level, Chananiah is the character who frames the story. The story starts with him and ends with him. Chananiah—meaning "God has graced"—is a saintly mysterious stranger, an evanescent figure. He joins the group of Hasidic pilgrims to the Holy Land. Before starting out on their journey, he tells them his own story, a tale of robbers, immoral men, and their hideouts in a country that knows no Sabbath; the chief of the villains wears phylacteries, even though he is not Jewish. Chananiah is a jack-of-all-trades; he emerges in time of need to help the travelers with their preparations, making boxes for their belongings, while his own he keeps in a kerchief. He disappears for the voyage itself but is seen riding the waves on this same kerchief, reaching the destination much before his fellow travelers. He also appears on the last page of the work, where the narrator states that the book is a tribute to the memory of Chananiah. This would seem to suggest a realism that is contradicted by the subtitle of the story, *Sippur Agadah Shel S. Y. Agnon* (*An Allegorical Tale of S. Y. Agnon*). In its allegorical context, the work suggests that all life is a pilgrimage, fraught with dangers and hardships, cloaked in mystery. The good, those "graced by God," will ride the rough seas under His aegis, protected by His garment. The work, then, becomes a tribute not to the evanescent Chananiah of this particular tale, but to all of those Chananiahs who embark on the journey into time or who journey from night to day, from ignorance to illumination, donning the protective mantle of God's covering, the Torah.

Chananiah is also the author himself, who narrates allegorical tales for the reader to interpret. The kerchief is the imagination of the author, which can take him over the seas, or back in time, or any place he desires to go.

The style of this work is, like that of *The Bridal Canopy*, eclectic. Agnon draws from biblical sources, the Book of Jonah, Psalms, Song of Songs, the Midrash, among others, and also from travel literature describing voyages to the Holy Land, especially a work published in 1790 entitled *Ahavat Zion*, an autobiographical account of Rabbi Simcha of Zalozitz's voyage to Eretz Yisrael. Less fanciful than *The Bridal Canopy* despite its allegorical quality, *In the Heart of the Seas* acts as a bridge to the realism and sobriety of the last novel of the trilogy, *A Guest for the Night*, Agnon's greatest work.

In *A Guest for the Night*, Agnon changes his mode of storytelling from the comic and fanciful to the tragic. Originally published in daily installments in *Ha'aretz*, a Tel Aviv newspaper, from October 18, 1938, to April 7, 1939, the novel reflects the unrelenting gloom that pervaded both Europe and Palestine during this period.

Agnon, distraught upon losing his home for the second time, made a sentimental journey to his native village of Buczacz in 1930, attempting to recapture some of the serenity and security of his childhood. The trip was unsuccessful. Within five days, Agnon realized that he could not reenter the protective womb of his childhood. The key to his security was not to return to or re-create a chimerical past but to build a strong foundation in the present, to ensure a firm and stable future. The novel is an extended re-creation of this visit. It deals with the return of the narrator to his native town of Shibush (the Hebrew word for "error") after his home in Jerusalem has been destroyed by Arab marauders. It is a bleak work evincing none of the gaiety and merriment of Agnon's previous novels. Realistically drawn, it reveals Agnon at the height of his powers.

In a complex interweaving of historical and psychological themes, Agnon develops the idea that one's childhood is best left to the imagination. Reality belongs to the present, and the real present can never be as beautiful as the imagined past. The theme of the *ēgun*, the "dangling man," is used to convey the character of the protagonist. He is a man in limbo, ejected from his home, estranged from his family. Just as the *agunah*, the deserted woman, is still tied down to her evanescent husband, and just as the dangling man dangles from the end of an imperceptible cord, so the protagonist of *A Guest for the Night* is securely linked to the home and land from which he flees, to the family from which he separates and the traditions which bind him for all time.

Early in the novel, the narrator is given the key to the Bet Midrash (the House of Study) by the townspeople of his native village. On a literal level, the key opens the door to the House of Study. The narrator, however, misplaces it immediately and must have a new one made. The old key turns up once again at the end of the story, when he has returned to Jerusalem, found by his wife in a corner of his suitcase. The villagers have no need for the key. Most of the oldtimers have left town, and those who remain await an opportune moment to leave. The new key suggests that the Bet Midrash needs new life to restore its grandeur. The narrator's presence is temporary, and his effect on the town is limited. Symbolically, the old key represents the old tradition, which has served the townspeople heretofore but which seems to be in disharmony with the present time and inadequate to meet contemporary needs. Daniel Bach's tale of his wartime comrade who was shot while still wearing his phylacteries illustrates this point. That the old key reappears at the end of the story, when the protagonist has returned to his home in Jerusalem, suggests Agnon's concept of tradition: It recedes into the background when it is unceremoniously dropped; it will, however, resurface eventually to take its necessary place within one's life. On a psychological level, the key opens the door for the narrator to a secure world where he can close himself off from harm, and although he allows everyone to enter, he knows that whoever comes is a *landsman* and friend. The four walls of the Bet Midrash represent a return to the secure embrace of his childhood.

Eretz Yisrael is another primary theme in this work. Agnon settled in Israel during the time of the Second Aliya, the second wave of Zionist immigration to Israel, which spanned the decade from 1904 to 1914. Those who participated in this *aliya* (literally, "ascent") were mainly from Eastern Europe. Many of them became workers and settled in the port city of Jaffa, where Agnon himself settled before moving to Jerusalem. Others settled in existing *moshavim* (agricultural settlements) or established kibbutzim. Agnon depicts this period of Zionism in *A Guest for the Night* in his portrayal of the Jewish pioneer group preparing themselves for life in Israel by working as a group on a farm in Poland and also in vignettes of the various members of the Bach family, including the patriarch, Reb Shlomo Bach, who settles in Israel in his old age. The narrator has left Israel after the attack on his home, but he considers his leaving a form of therapy and not a permanent emigration. He expresses his love for Eretz Yisrael by the tales he tells and by his positive attitude to the Holy Land in conversations with various members of the community. In fact, at one point he says that one of the reasons he does not like to visit with the local rabbi is that he is disturbed by the rabbi's antagonism toward Israel. In *The Bridal Canopy*, Reb Yudel's journey to Israel is the culmination of his life, and he settles there in his old age. In *In the Heart of the Seas*, an entire Hasidic group, a quorum of ten, moves to the Holy Land. In *A Guest for the Night*, young and old strive to achieve the same goal. Not all are fortunate in their endeavors. Some cannot make it for familial, economic, or political reasons. Zvi, the young man who prepares himself for life in the Land of Israel by working on a farm in Poland, cannot afford the cost of proper papers and attempts to enter the country illegally; he is turned back by the British. Some who do make it are disillusioned and do not stay, as is the case with Yerucham Freeman. In fact, Yerucham Freeman's harsh criticism of the protagonist's relationship to Israel and his influence upon others illuminates another theme of this work: illusions and realities.

For most of the Jews of Eastern Galicia (and, for that matter, worldwide), the Land of Israel at this period was indeed a dream, the subject of poetry, literature, prayers, and communal deliberations. It gave direction to one's life, but it remained generally an unattainable quest, an illusion, as it were. The narrator of this work, having settled in the Land of Israel while still a youth, transforms this illusion into a reality for his community. He becomes an exemplar for others and, in time, personifies the Land itself. Yerucham Freeman also falls in love with the Land of Israel, but he does not realize that he is exchanging one illusion for another. For this reason, he cannot find fulfillment when he does immigrate to the Holy Land. Entering the new country, he finds that the narrator has left for a sojourn abroad. This information shatters Yerucham's dream, which was thoroughly interwoven with its personification, and (expelled from the Land of Israel for Communist activities) he returns to his native village to gain a foothold in reality.

The narrator makes a similar movement, but for opposite reasons. Reality for him is the home he has established for himself in the Land of Israel, encompassing both its beauty and its harshness. The narrator would like to erase its harshness by returning to a state of illusion—a return to his childhood and his juvenile vision of the Holy Land. His prolonged stay in Shibush attests the fact that one cannot go "home" again, one cannot recapture the past. The narrator arrives in Shibush on the eve of Yom Kippur, the most solemn day in the Jewish calendar, a day of judgment for all. By bringing the narrator in at the onset of this holy day, the author is suggesting that the protagonist needs to take stock of himself and repent for his sins, the most obvious of which is his decision to leave his family and home in the Land of Israel. Just as Shibush is no longer the place that he knew, so must Israel take a more realistic place in his life. Reality may at times be beautiful, but it is also brutal.

All the themes of the novel coalesce within a historical perspective spanning two time periods. The work was written during a six-month period from October, 1938, to April, 1939, a period that witnessed the upheaval of the Jewish communities in Europe prior to the outbreak of World War II and the ultimate destruction of the shtetl way of life. Indeed, the work has been referred to as "an elaborate elegy on the lost shtetl culture." The story itself takes place in 1930, a time between wars, a time when the entire European world had not had a chance to recover from the devastating effects of the maelstrom of World War I before it was thrown into another cycle of death and destruction. The Jewish community was caught in this vertigo. Agnon's work captures all the bleakness of this "no exit" situation: Europe, the shtetl, could no longer be the home of the Jew, and Eretz Yisrael, the Land of Israel, was not considered a viable alternative. As a British mandate, Palestine was inhospitable and unsympathetic to Jewish immigration, while the Yishuv, the Jewish settlement in Israel, was not developed sufficiently to be a replacement for the Jewish community of the shtetl.

Agnon re-creates this dilemma in the narrative of *A Guest for the Night*. Allegorically, the title (taken from Jeremiah 14:8) suggests the historical situation of the Jew, who comes as a guest to a foreign country, intending to stay for a short while; remains for as long as he can maintain his status as a guest; and then, when the realities of life force him to do so, leaves.

Agnon is above all a storyteller, and although the mood of *A Guest for the Night* differs from that of *The Bridal Canopy*, the style is characteristically Agnon's. In both works, the inn or the house of study represents the centrifugal force of the novel: The protagonist employs his vantage point as a hotel guest to narrate his own tales and the tales of the people with whom he comes in contact, or allows them to tell their own tales. The protagonists of both novels are passive characters and sedentary people; they are not adventure-seekers. Agnon's heroes are humble, gentle, and compassionate people who are imbued with a love and fear of God and a love for their fellowman. Their tales comprise the chronicles of the Jewish people.

Agnon's later works continue to reflect upon the situation of the Jew in modern society. Although the Holocaust is not a major theme of his works, it is an underlying current in many of his novels. In *A Guest for the Night*, the gloom and sterility of the village seem to foreshadow the destruction of the culture about to take place. Agnon's next novel, *T'mol Shilshom*, set in Palestine in the early part of the twentieth century, symbolically suggests, with its protagonist being eaten by a mad dog, the fate of the Jewish people.

Perhaps what has endeared Agnon so much to his people is the love that he expresses for them throughout his writings and the understanding and compassion for their situation, one of uprootedness, which he echoed in the name he adopted for himself. In a fluctuating, chaotic world, his steadfast traditionalism, coupled with his artistic complexity, is appreciated by a general audience as well.

Major publications other than long fiction
    SHORT FICTION: *Me'az Ume'ata*, 1931; *Sippurei Ahavim*, 1931; *b'Shuva v'Nachat*, 1935; *Elu v'Elu*, 1941; *Shevu'ath Emunim*, 1943 (*Betrothed*); *Edo ve Enam*, 1950 (*Edo and Enam*); *Samuch Venir'e*, 1951; *Ad Hena*, 1952; *Al Kapot Hamanul*, 1953; *Haesh Vehaetzim*, 1953; *Two Tales*, 1966 (includes *Betrothed* and *Edo and Enam*); *Twenty-one Stories*, 1970; *Ir Umeloah*, 1973;

Lifnim Min Hachomah, 1975; *Pitchei Devarim*, 1977.

NONFICTION: *Sefer, Sofer, v'Sippur*, 1938, 1978; *Yamin Nora'im*, 1938 (*Days of Awe*, 1948); *Atem R'item*, 1959; *Sifreihem Shel Zaddikim*, 1961; *Meatzmi El Atzmi*, 1976; *Korot Bateynu*, 1979.

MISCELLANEOUS: *Kol Sippurav Shel Shmuel Yosef Agnon*, 1931-1952 (11 volumes); *Kol Sippurav Shel Shmuel Yosef Agnon*, 1953-1962 (8 volumes).

Bibliography

Band, Arnold J. *Nostalgia and Nightmare: A Study in the Fiction of S. Y. Agnon*, 1968.

Fisch, Harold. *S. Y. Agnon*, 1975.

Halkin, Simon. *Modern Hebrew Literature*, 1950.

Hochman, Baruch. *The Fiction of S. Y. Agnon*, 1970.

Sadan, D., and E. Urbach, eds. *Le Agnon, Shai (About "Shai" Agnon)*, 1959.

L. H. Goldman

ALAIN-FOURNIER
Henri-Alban Fournier

Born: La Chapelle-d'Angillon, France; October 3, 1886
Died: Éparges, France; September 22, 1914

Principal long fiction

Le Grand Meaulnes, 1913 (*The Wanderer*, 1928; also as *The Lost Domain*, 1959); *Colombe Blanchet*, 1922, 1924 (fragment).

Other literary forms

In addition to *The Wanderer*, upon which his fame principally rests, Alain-Fournier published stories, poems, and essays. His correspondence with Jacques Rivière (collected by Alain-Fournier's sister, Isabelle, in a post-humous edition) is especially noteworthy; indeed, it is generally regarded as among the most valuable cultural documents to come out of France at the beginning of the twentieth century. As painstaking records of the growth of a novel and the evolution of an aesthetic, these letters are comparable to the journals of André Gide; as a scrupulous exercise in psychological introspection and as meditations on and records of the contemporary arts in the Paris of *la belle époque*, they are of inestimable value. Similarly, Alain-Fournier's letters to his family and to his friend René Bichet are distinguished by the same arresting qualities which inform *The Wanderer*: an ability to describe impressions suggestively and economically; a keen and nostalgic sense of that which is irretrievable in human experience; a lucid and discriminating appreciation of human character.

In addition to the letters, there are the stories, poems, and reviews edited by Jacques Rivière under the title *Miracles* (1924). Most of these works bear the earmarks of Alain-Fournier's early infatuation with the French Symbolists, and they betray the hand of an apprentice. There are, however, an equal number of pieces here—especially "Le Miracle des trois dames"—which prefigure the tempered artistry of *The Wanderer*. Finally, there are the unfinished sketches for a play, "La Maison dans la forêt," and a novel left incomplete at the time of Alain-Fournier's death.

Achievements

Alain-Fournier's novel *The Wanderer* is universally regarded as one of the signal achievements of French fiction in the first half of the twentieth century. In a review that appeared on April 19, 1953, in *The Observer*, the eminent English critic Sir Harold Nicolson claimed, "Were I asked what was the most impressive novel published in France during my own lifetime, I should answer 'Alain-Fournier's *Le Grand Meaulnes*.'" He concluded his evaluation of Alain-Fournier's novel with the following critical judgment: "Certainly I should place this novel among those which every literate person should have read."

Scholars of French literature have demonstrated an indefatigable interest in this writer. In volume 6 of *A Critical Bibliography of French Literature* (1980), Alain-Fournier—along with Marcel Proust, Gide, and a handful of other writers—is accorded a separate chapter of eighteen double-columned pages. The quarterly journal of the Association des Amis de Jacques Rivière et Alain-Fournier contains essays, notes, and reviews on the life and works of these two authors. In Paris, there is a famous bookstore called Au Grand Meaulnes, and the local high school, or *lycée*, in Bourges is named after Alain-Fournier. In 1967, Jean Gabriel Albicocco directed a film version of *The Wanderer* (with screenplay by Alain-Fournier's sister, Isabelle); the film has gone on to become a veritable *objet de culte* among discriminating French moviegoers. In short, on the level of both critical appreciation and popular response, *The Wanderer* has achieved the status of a classic in modern French fiction.

Biography

Henri-Alban Fournier (Alain-Fournier is a partial pseudonym) was born October 3, 1886, at La Chapelle-d'Angillon. After a childhood passed in Sologne and the Bas-Berry, where his parents were schoolteachers, he began his secondary education in Paris and then prepared in Brest for entry into the École Novale. Unable to suppress a passionate attachment to the countryside of his childhood, he returned closer to home and enrolled in a course of philosophical studies at Bourges. He subsequently attended the Lycée Lakanal at Sceaux, where he met and developed a profound friendship with the future editor of the *Nouvelle Revue française*, Jacques Rivière, who married Alain-Fournier's younger sister, Isabelle, in 1909.

Together, Alain-Fournier and Rivière dedicated themselves to the study, evaluation, and analysis of the contemporary arts: painting, music (especially the music of Claude Debussy), and, above all, literature. They were among the first to discover and celebrate those writers destined to become the acknowledged masters of twentieth century French literature, including Paul Claudel, Charles Péguy, and Gide.

On Ascension Day of June, 1905, while leaving an exhibition of contemporary art in Paris, Alain-Fournier encountered the woman whom he subsequently transformed into the heroine of *The Wanderer*, Yvonne de Galais. Yvonne de Quièvrecourt (her real name) was the daughter of a French naval officer and, in consequence, moved in a higher social milieu than the young Alain-Fournier. A brief conversation they once had as they strolled by the quais of the Seine was abruptly terminated when the young lady responded to Alain-Fournier's importunities with the following remark: "À quoi bon?" ("What's the use?"). These are the precise words that Yvonne de Galais addresses to Augustin Meaulnes in Alain-Fournier's novel. Despite the brevity of this colloquy, Alain-Fournier regarded his encounter with Yvonne as the most decisive event in his life. Eight years later, after ineffectual attempts to renew relations, he met her for a second time: She was then married and the mother of two children.

Alain-Fournier's studies were interrupted in 1907 by two years of military service. In the meantime, he had begun to publish diverse poems, essays, and studies (later collected by Rivière in the volume *Miracles*). Work on *The Wanderer*, however, was painstaking and slow.

It was several months after the second encounter with Yvonne that *The Wanderer*, the novel in which Alain-Fournier's years of ineffectual devotion are enshrined, finally appeared. A year later, the author was dead.

Alain-Fournier was one of the first casualties of World War I. The young French lieutenant was struck down during an ambush of his troop on September 22, 1914, at Éparges. According to the accounts of survivors, Alain-Fournier raised his hand in a gesture of command when a bullet passed through it. He fell to one knee but was lost sight of in the ensuing confusion and presumed dead. His body was never recovered.

After the death of Rivière in 1925, Isabelle published her husband's and brother's correspondence as *Correspondance avec Jacques Rivière (1905-1914)* (1926-1928); this volume was followed by *Lettres au Petit B.* (1930; letters to René Bichet, a young comrade of Alain-Fournier at Lakanal) and *Lettres d'Alain Fournier à sa famille (1905-1914)* (1930).

Analysis

In *The Wanderer*, Alain-Fournier has written one of those few novels whose riches are not exhausted by analysis, however prolonged. Its multivalent textures, organic use of imagery, psychological depth, and contrapuntal themes reveal a structural integrity that is peculiarly modern. At the same time, it summarizes and brings to consummate expression a variety of concerns, preoccupations, and attitudes germane to the French Symbolists. It may be construed simply and straightforwardly as a novel of adventure or, on a complementary level, as a quest for the Absolute that makes abundant, though discreet, reference to medieval legend, ancient myth, folk and fairy tale, and the symbols and procedures of religious initiation. It may be relished for the haunting, restrained lyricism of its prose, its delicate evocations of a landscape flickering with Impressionist light and Symbolist overtones, its unprecedented fusion of fantasy and factuality, its insights into adolescent psychology, and, finally, as a mythopoeic search for salvation.

Its opening pages immediately enunciate the themes and dramatic situations subsequently borne out by the novel's hapless protagonists: François Seurel, the diffident yet deeply compassionate narrator; Augustin Meaulnes, the figure of youthful valor who betrays his best impulses and precipitates those around him into tragedy and regret; and Frantz de Galais, the wayward, erratic embodiment of those demoniac forces that explode toward the novel's conclusion. These characters, although sharply differentiated and thoroughly believable as dramatic figures, are, to a certain extent, psychological counterparts of one another. (Triadic figures are, of course, a common ingredient of fairy tales, as in "The Three Bears" or "The Three Little Pigs.") Here, however, the three protagonists of Alain-Fournier's novel represent, on a psychological level, individual aspects of a single, fragmented ego. The resemblance between the names "Frantz" and "François" is not merely fortuitous; nor is it merely accidental that Meaulnes, at one point in the novel, sustains wounds to the head and knee—the respective locations of Frantz's scar and François' affliction.

The very first words of the novel evoke that sense of an irretrievable happiness which, through François' delicate and subtly cadenced prose, envelops the characters, scenes, and situations of *The Wanderer* with a profound and poignant sense of nostalgia. After mentioning a nameless "He" who will turn out to be the principal subject of the book, François remarks of the house, the neighborhood, and the countryside of his early adventures that "we shall not be going back to it." Here, then, is one of those themes, casually broached and tentatively suggested, which colors the lives and attitudes of the chief characters: namely, the search for a lost paradise variously identified with an idealized childhood, an uncorrupted heart, or a state of pure and disinterested love. "My credo in art and literature," wrote Alain-Fournier, "is childhood: to render this state without puerility, but with a profound sense of its mystery."

Childhood is, of course, the period of human life most frequently extolled by the Romantic school of the nineteenth century. The child enjoys a continued imaginative transformation of reality; the boundaries between ego and world are nebulous. Hence, the child becomes the type and emblem of the poet himself. Moreover, the sense of oneness with the whole of Being is more readily available in childhood (before the process of ego-building has begun) than at any other period. In consequence, the child's unconscious participation in the whole of reality is analogous to the conscious awareness of that wholeness which is deliberately cultivated by the mystic. It is one thing to be an adult, however, and to cherish childhood as emblematic of the spiritually awakened conscience; it is another thing altogether to be an adult and wish to return to a condition from which, by virtue of one's temporality, one is debarred.

Alain-Fournier's novel is informed by a growing awareness that the celebration of childhood, when protracted beyond its limits, becomes demoniac and obsessive; concomitantly with this awareness emerges a collateral theme: "the dialectic of desire." This dialectic, as outlined by C. S. Lewis in his preface to *The Pilgrim's Regress* (1933), may be described as follows. Human beings are so constituted that they perpetually feel the paucity of present satisfactions. In order to hide this emptiness and discontent, one is perennially engaged in the search for some object that can fill the vacuum of existence. Each object pursued or desired is inevitably disappointing insofar as it fails to secure everlasting happiness. In consequence, one scuttles from object to object, goal to goal, in the hope of securing that without which one is miserable. The fallacy inherent in the pursuit becomes evident, however, when the attainment of some cherished and sought-for treasure does not produce the lasting effect desired. Sometimes, when present objects do not satisfy expectations, one wrongly believes that if it were in one's power to return to some luminous moment in the past, one could again be happy. Such a return, however, would reveal only that the "luminous" moment similarly involved the pursuit of a distant goal or the longing for a vanished past. Hence, one is obliged to resign oneself to a moody cynicism or, through an act of secondary reflection, to arrive at a greater understanding of the dilemma—namely, a recognition that one is created to enjoy a felicity not available in the world of spatiotemporal objects. The things sought—the wonder of childhood, the purity of first love, the ecstasy of sexual union—have an analogous relationship to the true object of the quest but should not be confused with it.

The divine discontent of Romanticism points, then, to a reality of ultimate and transcendent worth, and it is the recognition of this reality (or the failure to recognize it) that is thematically central to *The Wanderer*. Indeed, one of Alain-Fournier's signal achievements in this novel lies in his ability to make the reader conscious of that reality as it impinges on human existence, and it is through an especially cunning stylistic device—the consistent use of marine imagery—that this effect is achieved. Through repeated and strategic references to the sea, Alain-Fournier is able to achieve that sense of what the French call *dépaysment*, the feeling of being transported from one's present surroundings into a more mysterious dimension of existence. Hence, Alain-Fournier, in a letter to Rivière, claimed that his intention in the novel was not simply to reproduce the sights, sounds, and impressions associated with his childhood home in the landlocked region of the Sologne, but to capture "that other mysterious landscape" at which the real landscape hints or which it suggests, to "insert the marvellous into reality" without straining credulity or surpassing the world of concrete objects and living forms. To achieve his effects, Alain-Fournier fused the idealized conventions of romance narrative with the low mimetic style of realistic fiction.

Thus, after a matter-of-fact inventory of the household and schoolroom associated with Meaulnes' adventure, Seurel suddenly introduces an image that has the effect of transposing the reader above the immediate scene into an atmosphere of haunting suggestivity and alien coldness: "This was the setting in which the most troubled and most precious days of my life were lived; an abode from which our adventurings flowed out, to flow back again like waves breaking on a lonely headland." The haunting image of the "lonely headland" coupled with the fairy-tale superlatives "most troubled" and "most precious" has the effect of jolting the reader out of the present and into that vast Symbolist "beyond" which Alain-Fournier inherited from the poets and artists of his generation. Throughout the novel, sea imagery is used to expand the sense of horizon, to make one conscious of a quest that is essentially religious. Significantly, as the novel progresses and the characters fail to live up to their early impulses, the imagery darkens, as connotations of shipwreck and loss supplant the first hopeful sense of adventure.

Before engaging the novel further, a summary of the essential features of the plot are in order. François Seurel, the narrator of the story, recounts the events associated with his family's move, fifteen years earlier, to the village of Sainte-Agathe. A shy and reclusive adolescent suffering from a slight limp, Seurel is gradually cured after the arrival of a dynamic and imperious youth named Augustin Meaulnes. Dominant and intense, the seventeen-year-old Meaulnes becomes the accepted leader of the other schoolboys. When Monsieur Seurel (François' father) chooses another student to join François in meeting his grandparents at the local train station, Meaulnes rebels by stealing a horse and cart and taking off on his own.

Meaulnes soon becomes lost and, after a night in the woods, arrives at an isolated château where, as he later discovers, festivities are in preparation for a marriage between the spoiled son of the house, the sixteen-year-old Frantz de Galais, and his fiancée, an impoverished seamstress named Valentine Blondeau.

After entering the château through a window, Meaulnes is mistaken for a guest and subsequently joins in a masked ball arranged by the children of the domain. Diverted, along with the other revelers, by the antics of a costumed Pierrot, Meaulnes soon retires to a secluded portion of the house, where his attention is arrested by the sound of a distant piano. Entering a small chamber occupied by children turning the pages of storybooks, Meaulnes beholds, seated at a piano, a young girl who later proves to be Frantz's sister, Yvonne de Galais.

The next day, during a boating party, Meaulnes meets and talks briefly with Yvonne. He returns to the château to find the revelers in a state of consternation and disarray. Frantz has failed to return with his bride, and the guests, tired of waiting, grow restless, moody, and cynical, entertaining one another with bawdy songs and off-color jokes.

As he is about to leave, Meaulnes is accosted by a youth in naval costume; this youth turns out to be Frantz de Galais. His fiancée, mistrusting the effects of his lofty ideals, has abandoned him. Frantz orders Meaulnes to suspend the proceedings. As Meaulnes is hurried from the château in a rolling carriage, a flash of light accompanied by the report of a gun explodes from the depths of the forest. This is followed by the apparition of the costumed Pierrot carrying the inert body of Frantz de Galais.

The rest of the novel is devoted to Meaulnes' unsuccessful attempt to return to the lost domain. After a brief interval following Meaulnes' return to Sainte-Agathe, a mysterious stranger, his head wrapped in bandages, arrives at the village in the company of a dissolute strolling player named Ganache. (They turn out to be Frantz and the erstwhile Pierrot.) Before disclosing any information concerning the whereabouts of his sister, Frantz departs, having chosen to lead the itinerant life of a gypsy.

Meaulnes travels to Paris in the hope of seeing Yvonne at the Galais' city residence, but the house is abandoned. Waiting outside the house, like Meaulnes, is another figure: a girl, dressed in black with a white collar like a "pretty Pierrot." Like Meaulnes, she is companionless. Despairing of ever seeing Yvonne again, Meaulnes accepts Valentine (for this chance-met girl is indeed Frantz's former fiancée) as his mistress.

In the meantime, Seurel has discovered the whereabouts of Yvonne. She is a regular customer at his uncle's country store. Having lived vicariously for so long in Meaulnes' adventure (and knowing nothing of Meaulnes' relations with Valentine), Seurel now hopes to bring Meaulnes and Yvonne together. He arranges to meet Meaulnes at his parental home but is astonished at Meaulnes' apparent reluctance to give up an intended journey. (As is later disclosed, Meaulnes had abandoned Valentine after discovering that she was Frantz's fiancée. Hence, Seurel's arrival with news of Yvonne synchronizes unmercifully with Meaulnes' intention to find and retrieve the self-destructive Valentine.)

In any event, Seurel convinces Meaulnes to meet Yvonne at a country outing organized by Seurel and Monsieur de Galais. The meeting proves to be a disaster. To Yvonne's mortification (for her father has lost his fortune in paying off the accumulated debts of his son), Meaulnes dwells obsessively on the vanished splendor of the lost domain. Finally, Meaulnes starts an argument with Yvonne's father over his imprudence in saddling the broken-down cart horse, Belisaire. That evening, in a fit of remorse, Meaulnes asks Yvonne to be his wife.

On the evening of the wedding, Frantz returns. He persuades Meaulnes to accompany him on a search for his lost fiancée. To Seurel's incredulity and dismay, Meaulnes departs with Frantz. Seurel becomes, in consequence, both surrogate husband to Yvonne and substitute father to the child conceived on the night before Meaulnes' departure. Following the birth of her child, Yvonne dies and Seurel is appointed guardian. After an indeterminate interval, Meaulnes returns, having successfully reunited Frantz with Valentine. Presently Meaulnes departs with his daughter to a nameless destination. Seurel is left with nothing save a host of indelible memories and the book in which they are enshrined.

Notwithstanding the intricacies of the narrative, the reader is aware from the very beginning that the plot—like a bass line in music—sustains an imposing edifice of suggestive details, symbolic episodes, and allegorical events. Virtually every paragraph hints of or highlights the book's implicit themes or comments, through oblique but dexterously chosen effects, on the significance of the characters and dramatic situations. When, for example, Seurel as a small boy first arrives at Sainte-Agathe under the protection of his parents, the first problem that concerns his mother is the distressing abundance of doors and windows that need to be "blocked before the place is habitable." From this point on, images of doors and windows ramify in an exceedingly suggestive manner. They belong to that network of images in the novel which opposes interiors to exteriors, warmth to cold, and darkness to light. For Seurel, the warmth and security of the maternal home is both a starting point and orientation. Throughout the novel, he persists in identifying happiness or fulfillment with the domestic hearth. Meaulnes, on the other hand, is associated with roads and cold. In fact, his arrival occurs on "a cold Sunday in November," and it is he who, as Seurel later reflects, "extinguishes the lamp around which we had been a happy family group at night-time when my father had closed all the wooden shutters." Unlike Seurel, however, Meaulnes is continually tempted by the allure of a ceaseless journey toward an indeterminate goal.

Meaulnes is the demoniac force that makes Seurel and the other schoolboys conscious of their limitations. He initiates the transition to adulthood by compelling his schoolfellows to recognize impulses that no longer pertain to the period of childhood. In the final analysis, however, Meaulnes is less a hero than an antihero. He is able to carry the urge to self-actualization only so far; he arrives at the threshold of adult reality but remains, to the last, unable to pass through the door. It is not surprising that Seurel first glimpses Meaulnes as he stands in the shadowed contours of a doorframe—a literal threshold which is the first of several that make the reader conscious of the opposition between interiors and exteriors and which highlight Meaulnes' tendency to vacillate between antagonistic impulses.

Meaulnes' first action at Sainte-Agathe epitomizes his power to evoke mystery and magic in the realm of the humdrum and mundane. When he sets off a skyrocket in the school courtyard, the crepuscular glow that illumines the humble village of Sainte-Agathe is a tangible emblem of his ability to transfigure reality. The burst of black and red light at this moment is replicated in subsequent situations: the sparks in the shadowed smithy where Meaulnes conceives of stealing the horse and cart, the blast of Frantz's pistol, the wavering candlelight by which Meaulnes discovers Frantz, the red light of Ganache's Gypsy caravan, the red and black drapes in the room that Meaulnes shares with Valentine, and finally, the black-frocked priest and the boy "wearing the red cap of an acolyte," both of whom Seurel confronts as a portent of Yvonne's death. The imagery, with its increasingly sinister connotations, mirrors Meaulnes' failure to develop; it further parallels the manner in which a creative potential, distorted or frustrated by the hero's immaturity, turns into its destructive opposite. Significantly, Meaulnes' appearance at Sainte-Agathe occurs on a day when Seurel comments, apropos of the village bells: "Then, abruptly, the pealing of the baptismal bells left off—as though someone issuing a joyous summons to a fête had become aware of a mistake in the date, or the parish." The canceled baptism prefigures Meaulnes' aborted rite of passage, while the reference to a "fête" anticipates the broken-off wedding party at Les Sablonnières, where Meaulnes will remain, in an emotional sense, permanently arrested.

The "fête étrange" itself is at once the starting point and the goal of the novel's various adventures. In consequence, it carries enormous symbolic weight, notwithstanding the matter-of-fact account to which it is reduced in the increasingly disenchanted context of the novel's third and last part. Yet it is especially here that the reader recognizes Alain-Fournier's dexterity in weaving commonplace incidents into a highly wrought fabric which blends the marvelous with reality. Meaulnes' adventure, it should be noted, begins as an inglorious schoolboy prank; it is only gradually, as he becomes lost, that the suggestive details which heighten the sense of mystery begin to build imperceptibly. (Hence Meaulnes falls asleep immediately before his arrival and after his departure from the domain. This adds to its dreamlike quality but also underlines its significance as a symbolic projection of unconscious processes unfolding in the adolescent Meaulnes.)

Moreover, the whole journey to the "fête étrange" not only bears the earmarks of the Grail legend but also duplicates the customary rites and events associated with primitive initiation rituals. Like an archetypal hero of medieval or ancient mythology, Meaulnes strays from the limited and myopic confines of Sainte-Agathe, engages in the quest for a nameless goal which transfigures his existence, and then returns to his former state with the presumed intent of lifting his associates to an awareness of their potentialities. It is at this point, however, that the analogy between Meaulnes and the legendary hero of romance breaks down. Although Meaulnes' journey reflects the tripartite movement of separation, initiation, and return (which Joseph Campbell, in his 1949 book, *The Hero of a Thousand Faces*, sees as paradigmatic in Western myth), Meaulnes fails to complete successfully the return journey. Instead of pointing the way to his fellow students, Meaulnes remains stuck in one phase of his development. Instead of accepting a workaday existence and transforming it from the perspective of his adventure, he clings to the thrills and trappings of the mysterious fête, refusing to accept anything of lesser intensity or to prize any goal of slighter significance. In a word, Meaulnes' journey to the domain bears the earmarks of a rite that misses completion.

After coming to a crossroads (which is perhaps more significant when understood psychologically than topographically), Meaulnes, in descending from the cart, stumbles, hurting both his head and his knee. Not only do these wounds connect him symbolically with Frantz and Seurel; they are also equivalent to the symbolic wounds sustained, in primitive cultures, by young novices in preparation for adulthood. These wounds represent the death of the old unawakened self and signal the candidate's rebirth into a higher, more complex plane of existence. Moreover, Meaulnes' first glimpse of the domain is provided by children (who, the reader simultaneously learns, are totally in charge of the proceedings), and, on the evening prior to his "initiation," Meaulnes sleeps in an abandoned sheepfold where, in an effort to keep warm, he wraps himself in his smock, drawing up his knees in an embryonic pose. As Mircea Eliade has demonstrated in his book *The Sacred and the Profane* (1959), the primitive initiation rite customarily begins with a ceremony in which the novice is cared for and led by the hand like a child; his rebirth requires a preliminary reversion to the state of primal virtuality associated with infancy. Hence, Meaulnes' symbolic pose and his return to childhood are preparatory to his rebirth as an adult.

On the two evenings prior to his first glimpse of Yvonne, moreover, Meaulnes has a series of dreams—one of his mother seated at the piano, the other of a girl sewing in a long green room—which forecast his encounter with Yvonne. (As Eliade has noted, the rite of passage involves the recognition of three dimensions of existence: sexuality, death, and the sacred. Meaulnes' meeting with Yvonne reflects the first of these dimensions.) Interestingly, pianos and sewing machines function as symbolic counterparts throughout the novel and connect each of the female figures with Meaulnes' subconscious image of the "eternal feminine." Seurel's mother is a seamstress who makes her own hats; Yvonne is first seen, like Meaulnes' mother in his dream, seated at the piano; and Valentine earns her living as a seamstress. Each of these women is a variant of that buried feminine component which each man carries in his unconscious—what the Swiss psychologist, Carl Gustav Jung, calls the "anima," or feminine portion, of the male ego. At the moment of "falling in love," according to Jung, this unconscious image—partly derived from ancestral memories, partly colored by the child's first contact with women—attaches itself to a particular woman; hence the coalescent images of femininity that cluster about Yvonne. (Significantly, both Meaulnes' mother and Yvonne are associated with mother hens whose fledglings are missing from their brood.)

Meaulnes' courtship of Yvonne at the lost domain involves both of them in a primitive reversion to childhood—a reversion which is not that unusual when placed in the context of modern psychology. Scientists have observed that the mating calls of birds resemble the sounds of fledglings in their nests, and everyone is familiar with the endearing diminutives and the so-called billing and cooing which characterize the private talk of lovers. Unfortunately for Meaulnes, however, this stage of psychological projection and childhood reverie, which diversifies the initial stages of courtship before the lovers are "reborn" into the world of adult responsibility, is never transcended; in consequence, he fails to discriminate between the projected image of Yvonne and the real flesh-and-blood woman with distinct needs and perceptions of her own. Moreover, it is his failure to integrate his concept of woman into a composite whole which divides him between Yvonne and Valentine. Each of the women is associated with a fragmentary portion of Meaulnes' anima. In consequence, Meaulnes remains divided between the chaste and disincarnate image of Yvonne and the seductive, potentially explosive image of Valentine. It would be a mistake, however, to assume that the episode of the "fête étrange" is entirely reducible to clinical psychology. Meaulnes' predicament has both an ethical and a religious dimension, which Alain-Fournier has been at pains to suggest.

The sleep with which Meaulnes' adventure is rounded out not only connects the events at the lost domain with Meaulnes' subconscious but also hints of the atemporal nature of Meaulnes' experience. Commenting on that moment in the rite of passage when the novice reverts to a childlike state, Eliade observes that "this state is not meant only in terms of human physiology but also in terms of a regression to virtual, pre-cosmic life: the womb of uncreated Being." In short, the "fête étrange" involves a recognition of that second component in the rite of passage: the reality of the sacred. Like the Gardens of Adonis in Edmund Spenser's *The Faerie Queene* (1590, 1596), the lost domain represents the original ground of being or "pre-cosmic womb" out of which all life proceeds. Thus, the revelers dress in period costumes, embracing and, hence, transcending the manifold changes of history. The party itself is a Saturnalia and takes place during Christmas. Although it is mid-winter, a springlike warmth in the air adds to the sense of atemporality. "Midwinter spring is its own season/ Sempiternal though sodden towards sundown" writes T. S. Eliot on the moment of Pentecost in *Four Quartets* (1943). Here, too, a "mid-winter spring" suggests the moment of the intersection of eternity with time, the sense of an infinite present, an eternal now which both Alain-Fournier and Eliot associated with the immediacy of childhood. (Significantly, Alain-Fournier was Eliot's French tutor, so the connection is less fortuitous than it might seem.)

Why, then, given all of these positive ingredients and connotations, is Meaulnes irretrievably ruined by the experience of the fête? To answer this question, one must turn to Yvonne's brother, Frantz de Galais. If Seurel comes close to embodying Meaulnes' ethical sense, then Frantz is representative of Meaulnes' id: the urge, namely, to self-gratification regardless of consequences. Frantz's love for Valentine caricatures Meaulnes' love for Yvonne in the same way that Frantz's gypsylike wanderings are a distorted and counterfeit version of Meaulnes' quest for the ideal. Meaulnes progressively succumbs to the lure of Frantz's emotional restlessness. While childhood and adolescence are celebrated in this novel as stages that, in the development of the ego, must be assimilated rather than left behind, Alain-Fournier demonstrates, in the character of Frantz, the fatal consequences that befall those who fail to integrate the freshness of childhood and the self-dedication of adolescence into the mature perspectives of adulthood. Frantz is the "spoiled child" unable to apply an inner check to his expansive impulses.

Despite his efforts to return to the lost domain, Meaulnes finally prefers to live on the memory of Yvonne and in the spell of his former adventure. When he meets Yvonne a second time at the outing arranged by Seurel, he evokes two items (significantly compared to bits of "wreckage") from his first night's stay at Les Sablonnières: the lute with the broken strings and the large oval mirror. The broken lute recalls the figure of Orpheus; the mirror, Narcissus. Like the mythic poet Orpheus, Meaulnes fails to retrieve his lost Eurydice from the underworld (which, in Meaulnes' instance, must be construed as a failure to dissociate and, hence, liberate Yvonne from her status as an idealized projection of Meaulnes' ego); like Narcissus, Meaulnes never outgrows the self-infatuation of adolescence. (The episode at the fête in which Meaulnes admires his reflection in a standing pool is especially pertinent.)

The items that clutter Meaulnes' bed at Les Sablonnières (the candelabra and broken lute) point to the sexual element in Meaulnes' rite of passage. They are symbolic descendants of the lance and cup sought by the Knights of the Holy Grail; like the lance and cup, they may be construed, on one level, as emblems of sexual fertility. Meaulnes' polarized conception of femininity—Yvonne and Valentine, virgin and whore—is never fully resolved; in consequence, he vacillates between opposing images of womanhood and fails to establish an authentic relationship with either his mistress or his wife. In addition, Meaulnes remains hopelessly divided between opposing impulses: celibacy contra marriage, the contemplative life contra the domestic life. At one point, he writes to Seurel apropos of his experience at the domain: "Our adventure is ended. The winter of this year is as dead as the grave. Perhaps when we come to die, death will be the meaning and the sequel and the ending of this unsuccessful adventure." Meaulnes, here, demonstrates a clear-sighted Christian stoicism. Rejecting the "dialectic of desire," he recognizes that, for him, the lost domain must not be construed narrowly as a final resting place or identified simplistically with the figure of Yvonne. A return to the scene of his former afflatus would not produce the desired effect; as his words denote, it is only in another dimension that he will find the elusive essence that he seeks. Unfortunately, this insight is not sustained for long. Immediately following his letter to Seurel, Meaulnes engages in an affair with Valentine Blondeau—entirely unconscious of her former relations with Frantz.

At this point, the novel deepens in moral complexity. Is the reader to believe, as Meaulnes would have it, that if Valentine had remained faithful to Frantz (instead of retreating in the face of her fiancé's lofty ideals), an unbroken felicity would have been guaranteed for all? When Meaulnes discovers Valentine's identity, he throws this accusation in her face and abandons her to what, in the context of the novel's Victorian mores, is her only alternative: a life of prostitution. Yet Meaulnes' accusation is more accurately applicable to himself: If *he* had remained faithful to his former impulses, if he had clearly discriminated between the love of woman and the search for the absolutes of perfection, if he had been able to recognize the difference between emotional restlessness and divine discontent, then neither Valentine, Yvonne, Seurel, nor himself would be subject to the disequilibrium of Meaulnes' undisciplined will. In a preliminary version of the novel, Alain-Fournier intended to have Meaulnes pursue a religious vocation (an ending which the author wisely revised on recognizing its incompatibility with the novel's elusive textures). Still, traces of Meaulnes' religious orientation are preserved in the following words, which he addresses to Seurel: "But how can a man who has once strayed into heaven ever hope to make terms with the earth! What passes for happiness with most people seemed contemptible to me. And when I tried deliberately and sincerely to live like the rest of them I stored up enough remorse to last me a very long time." (Significantly, even Seurel is not devoid of culpability; he entirely misses the point of Meaulnes' words and pushes his friend in the direction of Yvonne without reflecting on Meaulnes' unfitness for domestic life.)

Meaulnes' remorse is associated with his treatment of Valentine, but it is not Valentine alone who is victimized by his vacillation. On the evening of his marriage to Yvonne, Meaulnes abandons his bride, presumably to assist Frantz in recovering his fiancée. Although Meaulnes is able to reunite Frantz and Valentine, his exertions on Frantz's behalf are self-deceiving. The short-lived nature of Frantz's liaison with Valentine becomes apparent when, on their return to Les Sablonnières, they enter the playhouse formerly constructed by Monsieur de Galais for his errant son. They are no more than two children playing "house" before the onset of a mutual, estranging tantrum. On the pretext of aiding his friend, Meaulnes has been able to circumvent his greatest fear: a candid and responsible relationship with a mature woman.

A final word remains to be said about the novel's enigmatic heroine, Yvonne de Galais. It is difficult to assess the precise nature of her role in the novel. On the one hand, she is tender, domestic, maternal, and down-to-earth. Seurel finds her, after all, in the least exotic of settings: the country store of his Uncle Florentin. Moreover, she enunciates a position that is in every way antagonistic to the romantic excesses of her brother and would-be lover. As she says to François on learning that he intends to teach school like his father: "But most of all, I would teach those boys to be sensible. I'd impress upon them a kind of wisdom I do know something about. I wouldn't fill their heads with a desire to go roaming about the world, as you will probably do, Monsieur Seurel, once you're an instructor. I'd teach them how to find the happiness which, if they only knew it, is within easy reach. . . ." At the same time, Yvonne is regarded, at least by Meaulnes and Seurel, as a sort of Dantesque mediator between the divine and the human: a breathing incarnation of the absolutes of purity and grace.

To the end, however, these estimates of Yvonne are ambiguous. Like Simone Weil's God, a "beggar waiting for our love," she waits patiently and without censure for the love that neither Frantz nor Meaulnes is mature enough to give, yet this uncritical acceptance of her brother's petulance and her husband's shortcomings contributes to her demise. Whether she is considered a pathetically exploited victim or a Christ figure, she is, at any rate, destroyed by a male mentality that distorts the interpersonal situation of love by regarding the woman almost exclusively from an aesthetic point of view. Only Seurel can see her from a point of view other than his own.

It is especially in her death that Yvonne repudiates the emotional restlessness of the male protagonists and reaffirms her conviction that authentic existence is to be grasped not in some remote and alluring never-never land but in the quotidian world of relationships and commitments. When her coffin proves too bulky to fit up the stairs, one of the bearers suggests that it may be hoisted up through the window and lowered in the same way. At this point, Seurel intervenes and carries the inert body of Yvonne down the steps in a sequence that lends a cruel irony to the traditional image of the groom carrying the bride over the threshold. (This episode, with its macabre sexual overtones, reveals that Seurel, as Meaulnes' follower, is equally afflicted with a fear of woman: It is only in death that Yvonne may be safely embraced.) Yvonne cannot be lowered through the window, for from the inception of the novel, window imagery repeatedly signals a flight from reality or a transposition to another dimension of experience. Meaulnes' arrival at Sainte-Agathe is heralded by his mother tapping on Seurel's window; both Meaulnes and Frantz enter the lost domain through a window, and Meaulnes is awakened in the carriage bearing him away from his adventure by a tap on the window. Frantz's disruption of Meaulnes' happiness is foreshadowed by the sound of a dead rose branch tapping the window of the newlyweds' cottage; it is at the shuttered windows of the Galais' Parisian residence that Meaulnes stands vigil prior to his meeting with Valentine. Before her death, Yvonne watches steadfastly at the window for Meaulnes' return; yet inasmuch as, at the end of the novel, the window imagery loses its initial connotations of mystery, transcendence, and wonder and declines into a motif associated with irresponsible escapism, it is impossible, given her scale of values, for Yvonne to pass through a window, even in death.

By the same token, one of Yvonne's last gestures summarizes and brings to final significance the pattern of images associated with birds and nests. In an evening walk prior to her confinement, Yvonne and Seurel are caught in a sudden shower which obliges them to seek shelter in the abandoned playhouse of Frantz. On the threshold, they discover a brood of newly hatched chickens, most of which have died. Yvonne separates the living ones in a gesture of maternal solicitude. This moment consummates the series of images which, from the novel's inception, foreshadow disaster and defeat. Meaulnes' mother, upon her first appearance at Sainte-Agathe, is described as having "the look of a hen whose wild changeling is missing from the brood." When Meaulnes meets Seurel's mother, she clutches her hat (which is compared to a nest) close to her breast in a gesture with strong psychological overtones: The domestic nest needs to be protected against an intruder like Meaulnes. The dead squirrel, in a basket brought by a student on the day of Meaulnes' departure, is a permutation of the same image. Ganache supports himself and Frantz by stealing chicken eggs, and on the day when Seurel receives a hint of Meaulnes' lost trail, the other schoolboys are "playing hooky" to hunt for nest eggs. The violated or overturned nest becomes, in consequence, another image that obliquely comments on the novel's themes: the molestation of childhood, the loss of innocence, the failure to develop emotionally and spiritually.

By the end of the novel, this failure, beginning with Meaulnes, radiates outward and affects everyone with whom he comes in contact. Hence, Meaulnes' head wound on the way to the lost domain is reiterated in the bruised head of his baby, the wound that Yvonne sustains as she rushes outside to intercept her brother and bring back her husband, and the scar that disfigures the forehead of Frantz de Galais.

The Wanderer, ultimately, is a cautionary tale; it embodies a sense of reality that is distinctly antiromantic and implicitly warns against the extravagances to which an untempered romanticism is prone. Its hero, Meaulnes, is a conspicuous example of bad faith. He leaves Yvonne for the putative purpose of reuniting Valentine with Frantz—but the reader realizes, and so must he, that such a union is ill-advised and without substance. He seeks for a purity that is not of this world, but he marries a woman who exists for him exclusively as a symbol of that purity. He both solicits and recoils from the demands of marriage and the responsibilities of parenthood, confusing Heaven with earth, the supernatural with the natural, the divine with the human. Desiring all or nothing, he wrecks the happiness that comes with an acceptance of human limit yet lacks the dedication, the disdain for comfort, and the single-minded tenacity of the hero or the saint. Yet a final estimate of Meaulnes is leavened with compassion. Seurel's grave and musical prose, his sense of the sadness and inscrutability of human existence, and his fidelity to the memories of Meaulnes and Yvonne are a palliative to the novel's grim conclusion and temper the tragedy with grace notes.

Major publications other than long fiction
NONFICTION: *Correspondance avec Jacques Rivière (1905-1914)*, 1926-1928;

Lettres au petit B., 1930; *Lettres d'Alain-Fournier à sa famille (1905-1914)*, 1930.

MISCELLANEOUS: *Miracles*, 1924.

Bibliography

Gibson, Robert. *The Land Without a Name: Alain-Fournier and His World*, 1975.

Gurney, Stephen. "The 'Dialectic of Desire' in *Madame Bovary* and *Le Grand Meaulnes*," in *Romanticism Past and Present*. VII, no. 1 (Winter, 1983), pp. 37-62.

Houston, John Porter. *Fictional Technique in France: 1802-1927*, 1972.

March, Harold. "The 'Other Landscape' of Alain-Fournier," in *PMLA*. LVI (1941), pp. 266-279.

Stubbs, Marcia. "The Pilgrim Spirit," in *Accent*. XVIII (Spring, 1958), pp. 121-133.

Turnell, Martin. *The Rise of the French Novel*, 1978.

Ullmann, Stephen. *The Image in the Modern French Novel*, 1963.

Stephen I. Gurney

CIRO ALEGRÍA

Born: Sartimbamba, Peru; November 4, 1909
Died: Lima, Peru; February 17, 1967

Principal long fiction

La serpiente de oro, 1935 (*The Golden Serpent*, 1943); *Los perros hambrientos*, 1938; *El mundo es ancho y ajeno*, 1941 (*Broad and Alien Is the World*, 1941); *Lázaro*, 1973.

Other literary forms

In addition to the works above, Ciro Alegría wrote a collection of short stories, *Duelo de los caballeros* (1963), two nonfictional works, *La revolución cubana* (1973) and *Sueño y verdad de América* (1972), and one poetic work, *Cantos de la revolución* (1934).

Achievements

Imprisoned in his native Peru for his liberal, antidictatorial convictions and political activism, then exiled to neighboring Chile, Ciro Alegría, at around the age of thirty, wrote the three prizewinning novels that echoed around the world as a powerful voice for the rights of the oppressed and exploited Indians of his native country. These *novelas indigenistas* (indigenist novels, so called because they deal with the problems of the indigenous Indian peoples of Latin America) are lyric, direct, and honest, portraying the hard life of the Indians and half-breeds of the Andes with deep sympathy and condemning the actions of their persecutors. Despite this tremendous beginning, however, Alegría did not continue to write novels, and, apart from the posthumously published *Lázaro*, which was written in Cuba in 1953 and never quite finished, these three first novels remain his entire opus in the genre. Though written with freshness and vigor, they were in a style reminiscent of the best nineteenth century fiction, and so to a later, post-World War II generation, which witnessed the rise of a new, technically more sophisticated school of Latin American fiction, Alegría's indigenist realism seemed too one-dimensional and too undisciplined structurally. Unfortunately, this postwar reappraisal kept the author from writing any further novels, and so from 1941 until 1963 Alegría went into a period of total literary silence. Indeed, his novels do have a loose, rather jumbled structure; yet they have a great emotional and aesthetic impact because they portray their sector of human life with great credibility and humanitarianism and because they are vibrant with the author's commitment to human rights.

Biography

Ciro Alegría was born on November 4, 1909, in Sartimbamba, Huamachuco province, in Peru. During his childhood on the ranch, he learned a great deal about the life and problems of the Peruvian Indians, and his grandfather taught him to sympathize with their hard life. In high school, one of his teachers, the famous poet César Vallejo, influenced his political thinking and encouraged him to write. Alegría's career as a journalist began in 1925; two years later, at the age of eighteen, he was already editor in chief of *El norte*, an opposition newspaper, and a member of Alianza Popular Revolucionaria Americana, a group advocating democratic socialism. He registered at the University of Trujillo in 1930 but dropped out after half a year and returned to journalism. Soon he was arrested and given a ten-year jail sentence for his editorials against the government. After serving two years of his sentence, he emigrated to Chile, where he wrote his three famous novels in order to win prize money to supplement his scanty earnings as a reporter. During his Chilean exile, two attempts on his life as well as a kidnaping attempt were made by the Peruvian secret service. His first novel, *The Golden Serpent*, won a coveted literary prize. As a result of hunger and hardships suffered in prison, Alegría contracted tuberculosis and spent some time in a sanatorium in Chile, where he wrote his second novel, *Los perros hambrientos* (the hungry dogs). The English translation of his third novel, *Broad and Alien Is the World*, was published in the United States even before the Spanish edition appeared. The book was quickly translated into sixteen other languages, making Alegría world-famous. During his twenty-six-year exile, Alegría taught literature at Columbia University, at the University of Puerto Rico, and later at Oriente University in Cuba. He finally returned to Peru in 1960 and was elected Senator, as a member of the social democratic Acción Popular Party. He died in Lima, Peru, in 1967, at the age of fifty-seven.

Analysis

Ciro Alegría's novels are distinguished from prior works in the Latin American tradition of indigenist literature because they depict the Andes Indians realistically, and they avoid the extremes of either an exotic picturesque idealization of the "noble savage" or a warped negative portrayal of criminalistic and pathological primitivism amid the crudest living conditions. Like other novelists of the school of indigenist realism, which thrived in the 1920's and 1930's throughout Latin America, Alegría wrote novels of protest against the hard lot and oppressed condition of the Indians and was not concerned primarily with literary quality for its own sake. His works, perhaps for that very reason, give an impression of great spontaneity and directly perceived reality.

Alegría's first novel, *The Golden Serpent*, focuses not on the tribal Indians, who appear occasionally in the background, but on the *cholos* (half-breeds), rivermen in a jungle valley along the treacherous Marañon River, where they earn their living as ferrymen transporting men, goods, and cattle on their balsa rafts at the risk of their lives. The great struggle of the book is between the rushing river, its dangerous currents and rapids, its cliffs, jungles, and sandy, gold-dust rich beaches, and the men who match their wits and brawn with the river's primeval power. The title *The Golden Serpent* refers to the river; this metaphor was applied to it by a young engineer from Lima, Don Osvaldo, because from a cliff top this "world of yellow mud" looks like a "great yellow serpent"; its secondary reference is to a company by the same name which the engineer planned to establish to obtain financing and machinery to mine the river's rich gold deposits; finally, it refers to the little yellow viper that bit the engineer fatally in the neck, preventing him from ever returning to civilization. All three meanings intermingle in the chthonic symbolism of the river and its jungles, teeming with both life and death. In Alegría's rich, poetic prose, the river becomes a symbol of man's life itself, powerful and multivalent: ". . . life always triumphs. Man is like the river, deep, having his ups and downs, but always stout-hearted." "Not everything went smoothly, for life is like the river, full of turns and rough crossings." Such comparisons, both explicit and implicit, are woven into the texture of many vivid descriptions of the tropical environment.

In *The Golden Serpent*, the central focus is on man's struggle with nature; the exploitation or oppression of man by man plays only a small role here. The river, whose ominous roar can always be heard in the background, is the main challenge as well as the life-giving force. Among its more tangible dangers are landslides, treacherous rapids, seasonal floods that sweep away whole settlements, and tremendous logjams that fling the flimsy balsa rafts against jutting cliffs or cause them to be swallowed up by whirlpools. The deadly disease *uta*, which rots the flesh off one's living bones, affects mainly outsiders who venture into the tropical valleys. Snakes, mosquitoes, and other vermin are ubiquitous, and larger denizens of the jungle also make their presence felt; in one chapter, a *cholo* woman outwits and kills a puma which has been slaying the farm animals and spreading panic in the village. Early in the novel, the plight of two brothers stranded in the middle of the shallows in the low-water season, separated from shore on both sides by deep water and steep cliffs and slowly starving, is described graphically. Only one of the brothers survives; the other is caught in the swift current and drowns in a desperate but unwise attempt to swim to shore.

The *cholos* are uneducated men, heavy drinkers, hard workers, impetuous, proud of their hazardous life and grateful to the river for their livelihood, aware of its beauty and its unexpected dangers, which could kill them suddenly when they least expect it. They face its challenges boldly, matching their courage to its strength.

The narrative perspective is quite complex. The overall narrative vantage point is the first-person plural, denoting "we *cholos*"—as opposed, on the one hand, to the pure-blooded tribal Indians who are further from civilization, and, on the other hand, to the occasional representatives of white, civilized authority, both of whom appear only rarely and peripherally to the lives of the *cholo* river-valley dwellers in their remote habitat. Gradually, a first-person-singular narrator emerges out of the plural "we" and becomes a particular *cholo* close to the main protagonists, though his name, Lucas Vilca, is not mentioned until near the end of the book in a chapter in which, by falling hopelessly in love with the widow of one of his dead friends, he momentarily becomes no longer only a sympathetic observer but the main protagonist. Framed within the comprehensive unity of the *cholo* riverman Vilca's "we" and "I" narrative are numerous stories-within-a-story told by other narrators, so that the result is a colorful patchwork quilt of narrative perspective.

Los perros hambrientos begins with an idyllic scene that sets the tone for the entire first part of the book: A shepherd girl, La Antuca, is herding a large flock of sheep high in the mountains with the help of four faithful dogs. Between sorties to bring back various stray sheep, her companion dog, Zambo, snuggles close to her so that they "mutually share the warmth of their bodies" against the cold wind and mist. The dogs have been raised to be sheepdogs from birth, and they enjoy their work and perform it intelligently. The girl, too, is happy at this lonely work, sometimes singing, or calling to the elements, or remaining still "as if united with the vast and profound silence of the *cordillera*, which consists of rock and immeasurable, lonely distances."

The shepherd girl's father, Simón Robles, is famous throughout the region for this breed of dogs, as well as for his other talents, such as playing the flute and the drum, telling stories, and exercising sound, humane judgment. The dogs are not purebred, but of a stock "as mixed as that of Peruvian man." They are "*mestizos* like their master." The dogs share the simple but good life of their masters "fraternally," and they feel attached to their owners. Yet even in the idyllic first part, some mishaps occur. One dog is accidentally blown to bits by exploding dynamite; another is killed with a single jugular-severing bite by a vicious dog that belongs to the local feudal landlord. The exploits of Robles' dogs are described with pride. They never mistreat the sheep but get them to obey by yapping at their ears. One dog is skilled at partridge-hunting; another keeps a frightened herd of cattle from turning back disastrously at midstream in a swift river. They all are courageous and feel a comradeship with man. Their birth and their naming is an occasion of joy. Sometimes they receive traditional names: For example, two dogs are called *Pellejo* (skin) and *Güeso* (bones), and Simón Robles, the great story-teller, jovially explains how once an old widow, guessing that a thief was hiding in her house, kept saying more and more loudly as if to herself, "All I am is *skin and bones*, that's all, just *skin and bones*," until her two dogs by those names finally heard and came to her rescue. Sometimes, a dog gets its name from a special occasion. One pup is the perpetual companion of Robles' little grandson Damián. "He seems just like his brother," the boy's mother remarks. The little boy overhears and keeps repeating his baby version of the word "brother" (*mañu, mañu*), and so the dog is named Mañu. It is a good life, in which each being, man or animal, feels sheltered within the communal pattern of existence.

Two major parallel events signaling the approaching end of the idyllic phase are the coerced conscription of Damián's father into military service (he is never to return), and the stealing of La Antuca's lead sheepdog by two cattle rustlers. By chapter 7, the dismal anti-idyllic phase begins with the words "It was a bad year," which in agrarian language means "a year without good crops." Men and animals are put on half-rations. Eventually all the chickens have been eaten, and even wheat is in short supply. After a hard year, Simón Robles is still able to make his family laugh by telling a funny story, which—practical man that he is—he follows up by giving the order for a sheep to be killed the next day. The plight of the dogs "at half-ration" is somewhat worse. They "cannot tell or listen to stories," and they have "sheep to guard but not to slaughter." So they howl continuously at night and roam the fields in search of food. Some raid a fenced field of standing green corn and blunt their hunger with the unripe grain, until the owner ambushes them and shoots three of them. The next calamity involves the political machinations which lead to the siege of the two cattle rustlers, Julián and Blás Celedón, and their death by poisoning, while Güeso, who has meanwhile become their faithful companion, dies attacking their killers.

The next year's crop also fails, and now truly dire times are upon the land. Simón Robles forgets his stories. The dogs are no longer fed at all. People are haggard and sad-faced. The social contact between men and men and between men and animals begins to fall apart, for "the animal loves the one who feeds him. No doubt, the same is true of that higher animal which is man, though he receives his ration in less ostensible equivalencies." Even toward the higher forces, Christian or pagan, this contract seems broken. Ironically, during a procession along a mountain road, as the crowd is singing a hymn, "This and much more/ Our Lady deserves," the statue of Mary falls off its stand and is smashed to pieces at the bottom of a cliff. By the end of chapter 14, La Antuca, in a sad scene that counters the opening idyll, is seen again herding her considerably diminished flock on the mountain slopes. She still calls to the elements, "Cloud, cloud, cloooud . . ." and "Wind, wind, wiiind . . . ," but it is not as before, for "with the pantheistic sentiment of her Indian ancestor she understood that the dark and powerful forces of nature had turned against animal and man." As man feels abandoned by nature, so the hungry dogs feel abandoned by man; the dog Wanka kills a sheep and the other dogs join her in devouring it, atavistically, like prehistoric dogs in the Stone Age.

When the dogs finally return to Simón's farm, they are chased away with sticks and stones, because once a dog has begun to kill the herd, he will not stop unless he is killed or driven away. Thus the dogs begin the sad life of homeless marauders. Meanwhile, Damián, abandoned by his mother, who has gone to seek her husband, dies of starvation on the road to his grandfather's village, and his faithful dog, Mañu, tries to protect the little corpse against scavenging condors. For a time, Mañu then helps to guard La Antuca's sheep, but eventually, unfed and uncaressed, he, too, joins the "nomadic" dogs, for "the suffering of the outcasts was his own, and moreover he no longer had any ties to man."

Eventually, two parallel attacks on the big landowner's house result in tragedy for the respective invaders. First, the desperate dogs invade the big house itself, slaying domestic animals, and the landowner kills most of them by laying out poisoned meat. In the second incursion, some fifty half-breeds and Indians appear at the big house, and Simón Robles, their spokesman, questions the landowner's claim that there is no food to be distributed to the starving: "Master, how can there be nothing? Your mules and horses are eating barley. Isn't a person worth more than an animal? . . . But now the time has come to kill your animals so that your people can eat. We are worse than dogs. . . . Yes, we are just like hungry dogs." Simón then asserts that all the landowner's harvests, and whatever he and his animals eat, has been accumulated through the peasants' work. Instead of showing commiseration, the landlord harps snidely on his feudal right: "Isn't the land mine? Do you think I give you the land for your pretty faces?" The outraged peasants then attempt to capture the big house but are routed by a barrage of rifle fire and suffer three deaths.

Finally the drought ends, and the only surviving dog, Wanka, mother of the rest, returns to Simón Robles' farm. Simón bursts into tears and, feeling the dog's sufferings to be his own, he caresses her and says, "You know what it is when the poor man and the animal have no land and water. . . . You know, and so you have come back. Wanka, Wankita, . . . you have returned like the good rain."

The great all-encompassing theme of *Los perros hambrientos* is life itself. Although the negative drought-ridden second part of the book is longer than the idyllic first five chapters, the picture of a happier life in more normal times is portrayed convincingly as the more usual lot of men and animals, so that even under crushing adversity, the memory of a happy life lingers hauntingly. The times of extreme hardship serve as a touchstone for social inequity, tearing asunder the social arrangements that had been considered quite adequate by the frugal peasants during times of less stress. These lower classes, the *cholo* tenant-farmers and the landless Indian farmhands, ranked little above the dogs in the economy of things when the landlord had to choose between them and his livestock. Yet they are not revolutionary firebrands; all they seek is "a tiny place" within the broad horizon of the world. Alegría got the idea for *Broad and Alien Is the World* while writing *Los perros ham-brientos*. Like the dog Wanka that returns from her outcast state to the warmth and social functionality of human companionship as soon as living conditions will permit, so Simón Robles and his peers, after the famine is over, gladly return to the feudal order which allows them to till the land and draw a modest livelihood from it. *Los perros hambrientos* is a masterpiece in its depiction of the brave, robust, and generous character of the simple, unedu-cated men and women of the Andes highlands; in its use of the dog perspective to represent the nobility and basic claims of life itself on an elemental level and as an allegory of the socially low status of the unpropertied classes; and finally, in its breathtaking beauty and grandeur in some scenes set in the great Andean *cordillera*.

Alegría's third novel, *Broad and Alien Is the World*, deals with an organized tribal community of full-blooded Indians. A proud and simple people, the Indians of the Andean village of Yumi lived free and independent lives, working hard on their communal property and sharing the produce equitably. Theirs was an almost idyllic existence. Under the wise leadership of their elected mayor, old Rosendo Maqui, the village thrived and the people lived happily within their communal system—a relic of the pre-Columbian Inca order which they retained because "work ought not to be to prevent someone from dying or falling sick but to provide well-being and happiness." Then, in the person of a powerful and ruthless neighbor and rancher, Don Alvaro Amenábar, disaster struck: Rosendo was imprisoned, and troops attacked the village, leaving it a ghost town, an empty, uninhabited shell of the once-happy place it had been. Some of the Yumi dwellers were scattered in all directions and were reduced to a subhuman state of semiserfdom in the mines or on coconut and rubber plantations in the coastal jungles, where they eked out an exploited and unfree existence and eventually died of hunger and exhaustion. Another part of the Yumians stayed together and retreated even higher into the mountains to steeper, less fertile land, where they established a harsher, scantier semblance of their former, comparatively opulent com-munity. Even this did not satisfy the rancher: What he wanted, in destroying the village, was, mainly, not the land but the people themselves to use as cheap labor on his land and in his house. Troops were sent, the Indians were defeated in battle, many of them were killed, and even the second Yumi was left desolate and vacant.

The title *Broad and Alien Is the World* expresses the Indians' hopeless final state when they realized how defenseless and exposed they were—unable to defend their most basic rights or even their very lives. Neither legal means nor armed self-defense had proved adequate. Their power within the "broad" society is nil, and so they feel "alienated" from it. The broad society does not provide the foundation for them to maintain their integrity and dignity or even their physical existence within its framework; the broad society does not provide the proper sociopolitical context for their village, which, with its rich interpersonal links and close relation to the soil and to their mountainous habitat, represents home to them as opposed to the "alien" outside world; the broad society fails to recognize even their most vital interests and leaves them prey to human predators who covet not only their property but also their very persons, subjecting them to inhuman drudgery, exploitation, and death. The destruction of the village of Yumi marks the destruction of the humanity of the individuals who composed it. It is a crime bordering on genocide, because it destroys their dignified life of self-sustaining cooperative labor in their own community and replaces it with loneliness, pain, servitude, and death in a cruel and impersonal society.

By traditional standards, *Broad and Alien Is the World* suffers from a serious structural disunity. The first half of the book has a close perspectival unity centering mostly on the observations of the wise old mayor Rosendo Maqui, but when the villagers are scattered, and especially after Rosendo has been killed, the perspective necessarily shifts away from this internal, character-linked viewpoint to that of a more anonymous omniscient narrator orchestrating the whole, which leaves the reader with an impression of a breach of style. This shift, however, permits Alegría to follow the various fates of individual villagers scattered to all parts of the country after their community has been destroyed. Alegría's overriding concern was not stylistic unity but thematic comprehensiveness: He was not writing the story of only one man but of an entire village, and it was essential to this purpose to follow the outcome of its destruction for at least a cross section of the villagers. Also, consonant with the epic treatment typical of the indigenist genre, Yumi represents all similarly oppressed Indian villages of Peru; it gives a collective picture of the status of the Indians in Peruvian society at the time (1910 to 1928). This panoramic perspective, which gradually replaces the more intimate personal vantage point of the first part of the book, corresponds to the work's intention to be a realistic exposé and sociological documentary; the persecutions (jail, exile, murder, and kidnaping attempts) which the author suffered from the Peruvian authorities, as well as the great acclaim given him and the political office to which he was elected at the end of his twenty-five-year exile, prove amply that the political and humanitarian message of his works was understood by his countrymen—however unreceptive to this message they were for many years.

Major publications other than long fiction
SHORT FICTION: *Duelo de los caballeros*, 1963.
POETRY: *Cantos de la revolución*, 1934.
NONFICTION: *Sueño y verdad de América*, 1972; *La revolución cubana*, 1973.

Bibliography

Aldrich, Earl M., Jr. *The Modern Short Story in Peru*, 1966.

D'Onofrio, Mario Leonardo. *La construcción de la narrativa indigenista Andina: Ciro Alegría*, 1979.

Early, Catherine Eileen. *The Narrative Art of Ciro Alegría*, 1973.

Onis, Harriet de. "Afterword," in Ciro Alegría's *The Golden Serpent*, 1963.

Rodríguez-Florido, Jorge Julio. *Ciro Alegría, el hombre: Temas y aspectos de su prosa narrativa*, 1975.

Vázquez Amaral, José. *The Contemporary Latin American Narrative*, 1970.

Ana María F. Parent

JORGE AMADO

Born: Near Ilhéus, Brazil; August 10, 1912

Principal long fiction

O país do carnaval, 1931; *Cacáu*, 1933; *Suor*, 1934; *Jubiabá*, 1935; *Mar morto*, 1936; *Capitães da areia*, 1937; *Terras do sem fim*, 1943 (*The Violent Land*, 1945); *São Jorge dos Ilhéus*, 1944; *Seara vermelha*, 1946; *Os subterrâneos da liberdade*, 1954 (includes *Agonia da noite*, 1961; *A luz no túnel*, 1963; *Os ásperos tempos*, 1963); *Gabriela, cravo e canela*, 1958 (*Gabriela, Clove and Cinnamon*, 1962); *Os velhos marinheiros*, 1961 (2 parts; part 1 as *A morte e a morte de Quincas Berro D'Agua* [*The Two Deaths of Quincas Wateryell*, 1965]; part 2 as *A completa verdade sôbre as discutidas aventuras do Comandante Vasco Moscoso de Aragão, capitão de longo curso* [*Home Is the Sailor*, 1964]); *Os pastores da noite*, 1964 (*Shepherds of the Night*, 1967); *Dona Flor e seus dois maridos*, 1966 (*Dona Flor and Her Two Husbands*, 1969); *Tenda dos milagres*, 1969 (*Tent of Miracles*, 1971); *Tereza Batista cansada de guerra*, 1972 (*Tereza Batista: Home from the Wars*, 1975); *O gato malhado e a andorinha sinhá: Uma historia de amor*, 1976 (*The Swallow and the Tom Cat: A Love Story*, 1982); *Tieta do Agreste*, 1977 (*Tieta, the Goat Girl*, 1979); *Farda fardão, camisola de dormir*, 1979; *O menino grapiuna*, 1982.

Other literary forms

Although known primarily for his long fiction, the prolific Jorge Amado has also written much nonfiction, including journalism and several books. His nonfiction indicates his interests even more obviously than does his fiction, as translation of the following titles shows: *Bahia de todos os santos: Guia das ruas e dos misterios da cidade do Salvador* (1945; Bahia: a guide to the streets and mysteries of Salvador), *Homens e coisas do Partido Comunista* (1946; men and facts of the Communist Party), *O mundo da paz: União Sovietica e democracias populares* (1952; the world of peace: Soviet Union and popular democracies), and *Bahia boa terra Bahia* (1967; Bahia, sweet land Bahia). Also pertinent here are two biographies of Brazilians, *ABC de Castro Alves* (1941), about a Romantic nineteenth century abolitionist poet known as "the poet of the slaves," and *Vida de Luíz Carlos Prestes* (1942, 1945), featuring a twentieth century revolutionary and Marxist hero.

Efforts in other genres include a collection of prose poems, *A estrada do mar* (1938); a play, *O amor de Castro Alves* (1947; also published in 1958 as *O amor do soldado*); and various film scenarios.

Achievements

During the first stage of his career, in the 1930's, Amado was frequently criticized for writing propagandistic novels, for allowing his left-wing politics to take precedence over his novelistic art. Though Amado proudly admitted such a priority, part of the explanation for his early awkwardness is that he was only beginning to learn his art. Of his novels of the 1930's, the best is *Jubiabá*. Amado's early novels are now his least read, still untranslated into English, but they do establish his credentials as a writer of the people and help account for his 1951 Stalin International Peace Prize.

With *The Violent Land*, Amado's first acknowledged masterpiece, his politics became less overt. Samuel Putnam, Amado's early translator into English, maintained that Amado succumbed to the repressive censorship of the Getúlio Vargas dictatorship in Brazil, but, if so, argues Fred P. Ellison, the ironic result was more effective art. Part of the explanation again seems to be that Amado's art simply matured in *The Violent Land*, that he developed from thesis novels to a fuller version of reality.

Gabriela, Clove and Cinnamon, Amado's next masterpiece, marked another shift in his career—adoption of a humorous stance. The entertaining novels of this period represent the height of Amado's art. Other comic masterpieces include *Dona Flor and Her Two Husbands* and the volume *Os velhos marinheiros*, which contains two novels translated as *The Two Deaths of Quincas Wateryell* and *Home Is the Sailor*.

With *Tereza Batista* and *Tieta, the Goat Girl*, Amado's art has become flaccid, as he indulges in shallow (and wordy) repetition of previously successful formulas, such as centering his novel on a sexy woman. The effect of flabbiness is magnified in translation, wherein Amado's famed lyricism is mostly lost, but even in the original Portuguese, Amado has been prone to repeat himself from novel to novel and within the same novel.

Despite his faults, Amado is an immensely popular writer—the best-known Brazilian novelist in his own country and in the world. His work has been translated into more than forty languages, and it has also gained mass circulation via radio and film. Amado has always had a good eye for popularity, even in the early days when proletarian novels were in vogue. Perhaps his popularity explains why he has been a perennial candidate for the Nobel Prize for Literature.

Biography

A *Nordestino* (a person from the Brazilian northeast), Jorge Amado writes about the people and places he has experienced at first hand, the cacao plantations and seacoast towns of his native state of Bahia. Son of João Amado de Faria and Eulália Leal Amado, he was born August 10, 1912, on his father's cacao plantation near Ilhéus. It was a turbulent and violent period, as documented in *The Violent Land*, where Amado depicts himself as a fascinated child observing a much publicized murder trial. He attended primary school in Ilhéus; his headmistress, Dona Guilhermina, appears briefly in *Gabriela,*

Clove and Cinnamon, where her reputation for severity is "legendary." Amado went on to secondary school in Salvador, first at the strict Jesuit Colégio Antônio Vieira (from which he ran away) and then at the progressive Ginásio Ipiranga. He attended law school at the Federal University of Rio de Janeiro, receiving his degree in 1935.

While a student at the Ginásio Ipiranga, Amado began writing for newspapers and magazines and joined the Academia dos Rebeldes (academy of rebels), a Bohemian group of writers and artists. Similar activities continued in Rio de Janeiro, where Amado published his first novel when he was nineteen. By that time, he was already attracted to leftist politics, and his second novel, *Cacáu*, branded subversive, landed him briefly in jail. Thus began a whole series of clashes with censors, detentions and imprisonments (1935-1936, 1938), and exiles (1936-1937, 1941-1943, 1948-1952).

In 1945, Amado married Zélia Gettai of São Paulo; they have two children, João Jorge and Paloma. Also in 1945, after the military overthrew the Vargas dictatorship, Amado, running on the Communist Party ticket, was elected Federal Deputy of the Brazilian Parliament and helped draft a new constitution. His political career ended in 1948 after the Communist Party was outlawed and Amado was forced into exile.

During his exiles, Amado traveled through the rest of South America, Mexico, the United States, Western and Eastern Europe, and Asia, living perhaps for the longest periods in Mexico, Argentina, Uruguay, Paris, Czechoslovakia, and Poland. Since 1952, as Amado's worldwide popularity has increased, conditions have improved for him in Brazil. From 1956 to 1959, he edited *Para todos*, a prominent cultural periodical in Rio de Janeiro. In 1961, he was appointed to the Literary Committee of the Conselho Nacional de Cultura and elected to the Academia Brazileira de Letras. His home is now in Salvador, capital of Bahia, but he sometimes retires to a remote farm to write his novels.

Analysis

Some critics are made uneasy by the coexistence in Jorge Amado of Marxist commitment and the Bahian version of *far nièntè* or "Let the good times roll." Amado's duality is evidenced by his popularity on both sides of the Iron Curtain, by the unlikely conjunction of his early propagandistic novels and his recent spate of sexy best-sellers. Yet there is more consistency in Amado's career than first appears. As Amado himself maintains, his sympathies throughout his writing have been with the working class and the poor. In part, Amado's metamorphoses indicate his strategy: He has had to present his case in the face of disinterest, opposition, and censorship. After all, if sex and humor can be used to sell toothpaste and automobiles, then they can be used to sell Marxist views. Amado also answers the question of what to do while one waits for the revolution: One has a good time and invites the rich to a party. Indeed, in Amado's easygoing Marxism, revolution might not even be necessary, since modern society seems to be evolving on its own toward a humane civilization free of want, repression, and prejudices.

The duality in Amado's outlook is reflected in his depiction of the working-class poor. On the one hand, they are ground down by hunger and serfdom, yet, paradoxically, they are also heroic. As a class they are heroic because it is mainly with their blood, sweat, and tears that civilization has been built. The working-class poor also furnish most of Amado's individual heroes and heroines. In the early novels, heroic proletarians abound, the most notable being the black António Balduíno, who becomes a labor leader in *Jubiabá*. Later examples are the mulatto beauties Gabriela and Tieta, who subvert the bourgeois social order with their sexual freedom; the Syrian immigrant Nacib Saad, who has to choose between Gabriela and bourgeois *macho* respectability, might also be included here. In general, the Bahian poor, with their urge to enjoy life, best exemplify Amado's ideal of humane civilization, whereas the repressed bourgeoisie are driven by greed, puritanism, snobbery, and other demons. The bourgeoisie rule, but when they want a good time they have to go to the Bahian poor. Through the interaction of these two classes, Amado shows the evolution of society taking place.

The most primitive stage of social organization is represented in *The Violent Land*, set in early twentieth century Bahia. Although Bahia has been at least sparsely settled for centuries, frontier conditions reminiscent of the Wild West still prevail in the novel. The main enemy is the dark rain forest, the Sequeiro Grande, full of fearsome animals and imagined goblins presided over by an old witch doctor who delivers his voodoo curse. The jungle constantly threatens to reclaim the cacao plantations carved out of it, a threat symbolized by the cries of frogs being swallowed by snakes in a pond next to a plantation house. The darkness lurking in the hearts of men and women—ignorance, lawlessness, amorality, and greed—also threatens. To bring order out of this impending chaos and drive the wedge of conquest deeper into the jungle requires a few strongman types; therefore, the resulting social order is a feudal plantation system presided over by the strongmen-owners, such as Sinhô and Juca Badaró and Colonel Horacio da Silveira.

The defects of this feudal strongman system, however, are immediately apparent. Only the strongmen (the "colonels") and their close henchmen benefit substantially; the workers live on a subsistence level, laboring long hours daily and completely subject to the will of the strongmen. The social order achieved at such high cost is minimal: The only law is the whim of the strongmen. Corrupted by their power, the strongmen corrupt their followers; this moral morass is symbolized by the sticky cacao ooze which clings to the hands and feet of the workers, who can rise in the order only by becoming assassins for their bosses (a description which also gives some notion of how the social order is enforced). The only ideal is a *macho* code of personal courage (which, however, is flexible enough to allow bullying and bush-whacking; beating women is also considered acceptable). Most of the women serve as cooks or whores, though Ana Badaró impresses everyone with her ability to shoot as straight as any man.

Paradoxically, the strongman social order is very weak. Dependent on the head man, it waits for his orders before anything gets done, and then it is limited by his vision. The system's fragility is demonstrated most clearly when the strongmen clash, as happens in *The Violent Land*. The principle of survival of the fittest returns: In the cacao war between Colonel Horacio and the Badarós, the Badarós are decimated and their plantation burned to the ground.

Amado thus shows the feudal strongman system to be only one step beyond the jungle, a primitive stage which belongs to a civilized country's past. As long as it stays in the past, it can be celebrated, and *The Violent Land* thus possesses epic qualities: a grand design, sweeping action, a lyric prose style that breaks out into ballads. The colorful characters tend toward the mock-heroic—gamblers, whores, assassins, adulterers, colonels. Above all, Amado has an epic theme, the struggle and sacrifice required to achieve progress: He never tires of saying that the land was fertilized by human blood, mainly the blood of workers. To lose what has been achieved at such great cost would be a betrayal.

Gabriela, Clove and Cinnamon shows the next step up for society, the transition from a feudal order to a crude form of democracy. The novel is set in Ilhéus in 1925-1926, during a boom period for the cacao industry. Significantly, material change, especially the growth of cities, has preceded political change. Representing the old feudal order is the octogenarian Colonel Ramiro Bastos, in addition to a clutch of other colonels, some sporting scars of the cacao wars. Representing the new order is the cacao exporter Mundinho Falcão, who gathers a following of town dignitaries and a few enlightened colonels. Ruling by decree, Colonel Ramiro Bastos stands in the way of further progress—schools, roads, sewers, and especially a port which will accommodate large ships. Throughout the novel, the political campaign between Colonel Ramiro Bastos and Mundinho Falcão heats up. Colonel Ramiro's followers propose to bring back the old-style violence, but their plans fizzle when the old man dies. Ultimately the issues are settled peacefully, by an honest election, itself an innovation for the region.

Significantly, Mundinho Falcão, the agent of change, is not a native of the region but the youngest son of a rich and politically prominent Rio de Janeiro family. Another, humbler agent of change is also an outsider: the Syrian Nacib Saad, owner of the Vesuvius Bar. The novel's other main line of action concerns Nacib's love for the beautiful backlander Gabriela, a mulatto whom he hires as cook at a migrant labor pool called the Slave Market. When Gabriela proves to be as good in bed as she is in the kitchen ("color of cinnamon, smell of clove"), Nacib marries her. A flower of the people, generous and loving, Gabriela seems an ideal woman, but the marriage is a mistake, like the caged bird Nacib gives her as a present. Free and easy as a bird, Gabriela cannot stomach the middle-class restrictions of marriage in Ilhéus.

When Nacib finds Gabriela in bed with the town Romeo, he is faced with a dilemma: The old *macho* code decrees that he must kill her and her lover, but the easygoing Nacib, however heartbroken, is no killer. The solution is another triumph for civilization in the region: Nacib and Gabriela's marriage is declared legally void, and, after a period of separation, they go back to living and loving together. The triumph is underlined when a cacao colonel who had killed his wife and her lover is sent to prison—the first such conviction in Ilhéan history.

These cases and others are discussed nonstop in the homes, businesses, and taverns of Ilhéus, especially in the Vesuvius Bar. Amado's characters do like to talk, and they tell it all. As Amado notes here and elsewhere, the main entertainment in small-town Bahia is gossip. Obviously the Ilhéans are well entertained, as are Amado's readers: In *Gabriela, Clove and Cinnamon*, a masterpiece of plotting, character, and theme, gossip is raised to a fine art.

A smaller masterpiece is *The Two Deaths of Quincas Wateryell*. Here, in a funny, fantastic little story that verges on allegory, Amado attacks middle-class pretensions and restrictions head-on. His hero is Joaquim Soares da Cunha, an exemplary family man and bureaucrat who, at the age of fifty, retires from the State Rent Board and inexplicably leaves his home and family to become a bum, roaming the slummy Salvador waterfront in the company of drunks and whores. In his new identity, Joaquim Soares da Cunha becomes Quincas Wateryell, named after the outraged scream he lets out when he drinks a glass of water thinking it is white rum. After ten years, Quincas' convivial life of drinking, whoring, and gambling catches up with him: When the novella opens, he lies dead on a rancid flophouse bed, his big toe sticking out of a hole in his dirty sock. Still, there is a smile on the corpse's face.

As his relatives gather to give Quincas a "decent" burial, his reason for running away from home becomes clear. His straitlaced family, scandalized and mortified all of those years, is finally relieved by his death. In particular, his smug daughter Vanda determines to put the domestic screws to Quincas in death, just as her "saintly" mother did in life. That is, she symbolically dresses him up and has the undertaker make him up as Joaquim Soares da Cunha. Nothing, however, can be done about his immoral smile, which Vanda thinks is mocking her. Indeed, she thinks she hears the corpse whistle and call her "Viper!" Her efforts to reclaim Quincas for respectability are defeated when four of his buddies appear at the wake. Left alone with the corpse, they revive it with rum and take it for a last night on the town, including a fight in a bar and a visit to Quincas' mistress. The drunken party ends up out at sea in a fishing boat, from which the corpse "leaps" to its death in the cleansing waters—a proper end for an old salt like Quincas.

A similar attack on bourgeois values informs *Tieta, the Goat Girl*, an example of Amado's later work. *Tieta, the Goat Girl*, however, is neither little nor a masterpiece. The wordy, rambling story runs on interminably (672 pages in the English translation), as silly as it is raunchy. The first half or so details the 1966 return of a "prodigal daughter," Tieta "the goat girl," to her poor hometown of Agreste on the Bahian seacoast. Twenty-six years before, her father beat her and drove her from home for giving away sexual favors. Now, supposedly the widow of a rich São Paulo industrialist, the beautiful and generous Tieta is enfolded in the bosom of her family, and the dazzled town declares her a saint. The joke is that Saint Tieta became rich by learning to sell her sexual favors, eventually becoming madam of the fanciest whorehouse in Brazil. When this joke wears thin, Amado tries, in the book's last half, to whip up reader enthusiasm for an ecological battle: A polluting titanium-dioxide factory wants to move into town and spoil the beaches and fishing.

Despite the novel's sophomoric plot and characters, *Tieta, the Goat Girl* is still entertaining. Amado's unrestrained style is not merely wordy; it has a veritably Rabelaisian range and exuberance. Consistent with his uninhibited style is Amado's satiric attack on bourgeois hypocrisy and greed, including recent extremes manifested in the consumer society and destructive industries. Amado's attack reaches its literal and symbolic climax in Tieta's seduction of her nephew Ricardo, a seventeen-year-old seminarian. Saint Tieta, the expert, teaches Ricardo a new life-affirming religion, as Ricardo is assured by the liberation theologian Frei Thimóteo, a Franciscan friar. Other characters representing this religion in the novel are a group of hippies who visit the fabulous beach of Mangue Seco and a group of fishing families who have always lived there.

Frei Thimóteo, the liberation theologian, makes an appropriate figure on whom to end this analysis of Amado's fiction. Coming from another direction, but deriving its inspiration from Marx as well as Jesus, liberation theology is not too far away from Amado's own easygoing Marxism. The appearance of liberation theology in recent decades supports Amado's view that modern society—at least in Brazil—is evolving toward a humane civilization free of want, repression, and prejudice. Both liberation theology and Amado represent the frustration and optimism of Brazil—and the new combinations of thought emanating from that vital land.

Major publications other than long fiction

PLAY: *O amor de Castro Alves*, 1947 (also as *O amor do soldado*, 1958).

POETRY: *A estrada do mar*, 1938.

NONFICTION: *ABC de Castro Alves*, 1941; *Vida de Luíz Carlos Prestes*, 1942, 1945; *Bahia de todos os santos: Guia das ruas e dos misterios da cidade do Salvador*, 1945; *Homens e coisas do Partido Comunista*, 1946; *O mundo da paz: União Sovietica e democracias populares*, 1952; *Bahia boa terra Bahia*, 1967; *Bahia*, 1971 (English translation, 1971).

Bibliography
Almeida, Alfredo Wagner Berno de. *Jorge Amado: Politica e literatura*, 1979.
Ellison, Fred P. *Brazil's New Novel: Four Northeastern Masters*, 1954.
Hamilton, Russell. "Afro-Brazilian Cults in the Novels of Jorge Amado," in *Hispania*. C (May, 1967), pp. 242-252.
Lins, Álvaro. *Sagas literárias e teatro moderno do Brazil*, 1967.
Lowe, Elizabeth Schlomann. "The 'New' Jorge Amado," in *Luzo-Brazilian Review*. VI (December, 1969), pp. 73-82.
Tavares, Paulo. *O Baiano Jorge Amado e sua obra*, 1980.

Harold Branam

IVO ANDRIĆ

Born: Dolac, Bosnia; October 10, 1892
Died: Belgrade, Yugoslavia; March 13, 1975

Principal long fiction
Travnička hronika, 1945 (*Bosnian Story*, 1958; better known as *Bosnian Chronicle*, 1963); *Na Drini ćuprija*, 1945 (*The Bridge on the Drina*, 1959); *Gospodica*, 1945 (*The Woman from Sarajevo*, 1966); *Pričo o vezirovom slonu*, 1948 (*The Vizier's Elephant: Three Novellas*, 1962; includes *Pričo o vezirovom slonu* [*The Vizier's Elephant*]; *Anikina vremena* [*Anika's Times*]; *Zeko* [English translation]); *Prokleta avlija*, 1954 (novella; *Devil's Yard*, 1962).

Other literary forms
Ivo Andrić began his writing career with two volumes of poems in 1918 and 1920 and continued to publish poetry in magazines throughout his life. During the 1920's and 1930's, he published several volumes of short stories and brought out a fourth volume in 1948. His essay "Conversations with Goya" (1934) sets out his creed as a writer and a humanist. Between 1945 and his death in 1975, he also published essays on various philosophical, aesthetic, and literary subjects. A selection of his short stories from all periods of his career, *The Pasha's Concubine and Other Tales*, was published in English in 1968.

Achievements
Ivo Andrić is undoubtedly best known in the English-speaking world as the author of what has been called one of the great novels of the twentieth century, *The Bridge on the Drina*. Primarily for this novel, and for two others about life in his native Bosnia published at the same time, he won the Nobel Prize for Literature in 1961. Until this "Bosnian Trilogy" brought him considerable fame, he had not been widely known outside his own country. His reputation has gone through three distinct phases. From 1918 to 1941, Andrić came to be recognized, primarily in Yugoslavia, as that nation's leading writer of short stories and as one of its better poets and essayists. The second phase, from 1941 to 1961, established his fame as a writer of novels and novellas, culminating in the Nobel Prize. In this period, especially in the 1950's, he gained his first wide readership throughout the Western Hemisphere. Finally, in the period from the Nobel Prize onward, he gained worldwide recognition, with his novels and short stories translated into more than thirty languages and many paperback reprints.

Andrić is one of a very few Nobel Prize winners whose work continues to be admired equally by professional critics and the general public. As a novelist, he has been praised especially for his vivid and lifelike characterizations, for his ability to relate individual dilemmas to larger social forces, and for "the epic force with which he has depicted themes and human destinies drawn from the history of his country," in the words of the Nobel Prize Committee. It was Andrić's fame which first drew the attention of the rest of the world to the high quality of Yugoslav literature in general.

Biography

Ivo Andrić's family origins embody that ethnic, religious, and cultural diversity of modern Yugoslavia which has always been one of the underlying subjects of his fiction. He was born in the tiny hamlet of Dolac, in Bosnia (then a province of the Austro-Hungarian Empire and now in Yugoslavia) on October 10, 1892. His father, a Serb of the Orthodox faith, was a poor coppersmith; his mother was a Croat and a Roman Catholic. When Ivo was an infant, his father died, and his mother took him to live with her parents in Visegrad, where he played on the bridge erected by the Turks which was later to be the location and subject of his greatest novel. A brilliant student, he had translated some of Walt Whitman's poetry into Serbo-Croatian by the time he was nineteen. His education, however, was interrupted by his political activities. As a youth he had joined Young Bosnia, an organization dedicated to creating an independent nation for the South Slavs. When another member of the organization assassinated the Archduke Franz Ferdinand in 1914 (the event that precipitated World War I), Andrić was arrested and imprisoned for three years.

Andrić always said that his imprisonment forced him to mature rapidly, both as a writer and as a human being. He read extensively, especially the Danish philosopher Søren Kierkegaard, whose work gave substance to Andrić's already developing pessimism. Released in 1917, he began to publish poetry written in prison, joined the editorial staff of a literary journal, and resumed his academic career. During the next six years, Andrić studied languages, philosophy, and history at universities in Poland, Austria, and Yugoslavia, earning a Ph.D. in history from the University of Graz, Austria, in 1923. His thesis, a study of Bosnian spiritual and intellectual life during four centuries of Turkish rule, provided a solid underpinning of historical knowledge for his later novels and stories of Bosnian life. That same year, Andrić, then thirty-one, joined the diplomatic corps of the new kingdom of Serbs, Croats, and Slovenes, a country roughly equivalent to contemporary Yugoslavia, created out of the ruins of the Austro-Hungarian and Ottoman empires after World War I. He was to serve in a variety of posts in Rome, Madrid, Budapest, Geneva, Trieste, Graz, and Bucharest over the next eighteen years, rising to be the Yugoslav ambassador to Germany from 1939 to 1941.

Andrić had published his first piece of fiction, the long story "Voyage of Ali Djerzelez," in 1920 while still in the university, but his diplomatic career allowed little time for sustained writing. He did manage to write and publish three volumes of short stories—in 1924, 1931, and 1936—but had to postpone writing several novels for which he had developed sketches and done considerable research. His diplomatic career ended, and his years as a novelist began, with the Nazi invasion of Yugoslavia in April of 1941. Arriving in Belgrade just ahead of the first German bombers, Andrić placed himself under voluntary house arrest in his apartment. There he spent the remainder of the war, enduring the destruction and writing novels and short stories. He refused to flee the city in the periodic bombardment and panic because, he said later, "I had nothing to save but my life and it was beneath human dignity to run for that." The three novels he wrote at that time all deal with the suffering and endurance of his native Bosnia at various times in its history.

With the end of the war in 1945, Andrić quickly published *Bosnian Chronicle*, *The Bridge on the Drina*, and *The Woman from Sarajevo*, as well as a volume of translations from Italian. Yugoslavia had become a Communist Federated Republic under Marshal Tito. Andrić joined the Communist Party, served as president of the Yugoslav Writers' Union, and in subsequent years sat as a representative for Bosnia in the Yugoslav Parliament. Throughout the 1940's and 1950's, he continued to write prolifically, publishing four novellas, a number of short stories, philosophical and travel essays, and critical studies of key figures in Western art, including Petrarch and Francisco Goya. He won many awards in Yugoslavia for his writing, and, in 1961, he was awarded the Nobel Prize for Literature. Advancing age and the burdens of fame slowed Andrić's output after that time. A bachelor for most of his life, he married Milica Babic, a well-known painter and theatrical designer, in 1959. He died in Belgrade at the age of eighty-two on March 13, 1975.

Analysis

Ivo Andrić's native Bosnia, the setting for almost all of his fiction, functions as a microcosm of human life. It is for his characters a land of fear, hatred, and unrelenting harshness. To all who enter it, mere survival becomes a victory. Its effect on outsiders especially is one of confusion, panic, and sometimes even insanity. Bosnia's strategic location in southern Europe has given it a peculiar character which Andrić exploits fully in his novels. In ancient times, it formed a border between Eastern and Western empires, and later between Roman Catholic and Eastern Orthodox forms of Christianity and culture. In the sixteenth century, it became an outpost of the Ottoman Empire, which was Turkish and Muslim. All of these religions, in addition to Judaism, existed in uneasy juxtaposition in Bosnia, with periodic outbursts of religious, ethnic, and political violence between various religious and ethnic groups. Subject to constant nationalistic upheaval, foreign conquest, and the crude violence of Turkish rule, Bosnian history is for Andrić the epitome of the dangers, sufferings, and uncertainties of human life. All people live in a kind of prison as they struggle against one another and against their own fears and insecurities. Undoubtedly, certain facts of Andrić's life help to explain his views. He spent both world wars in confinement, able to write yet unable to act in other ways. His efforts to keep Yugoslavia out of World War II failed, showing him his powerlessness as a diplomat to change the course of history. Finally, the literary heritage of Bosnia that Andrić knew so thoroughly offers several important writers and cultural figures with similar views of human life.

Andrić's fiction is concerned not only with the unpredictability of human life but also with his characters' attempts to understand their place in history, to escape their fears, and to find some measure of constancy and hope. He presents his characters against a background of the inexorable flow of time and its cumulative effect on future generations. His concept of history is not one of discrete periods of time, but rather of the constant change that is to him the basic fact of human existence. His characters fail whenever they attempt to relive time rather than to understand its flow, when they concentrate on mere memory of the past rather than on its meaning for the future. In an essay, he stated: "Only ignorant and unreasonable men can maintain that the past is dead and by an impenetrable wall forever separated from the present. The truth is rather that all that man once thought and did is invisibly woven into that which we today think, feel, and do."

Andrić has been praised most often for the masterful character portrayals in his novels. His main characters are usually figures of lesser importance: priests, consuls, wealthy local farmers, petty bureaucrats, and small merchants; yet they are chosen by Andrić for detailed treatment because on them the whole weight of the injustices, cruelties, and irrationalities of life tend to fall most heavily. As he says of his protagonist in *Bosnian Chronicle*: "He is one of those men who are predestined victims of great historic changes, because they neither know how to stand with these changes, as forceful and exceptional individuals do, nor how to come to terms with them, as the great mass of people manage to do." His other characters are drawn with equal skill. It has been said that there is no such thing as a flat character in an Andrić novel. This pattern results from the fact that he explores carefully the background of every person whom he introduces, however briefly each appears. As a result, the reader knows all the characters intimately, yet the narrative flow is never unnecessarily interrupted in order to impart this information. It is a technique which serves Andrić's thematic purposes as well, for it embeds his characters more deeply in the stream of time. The plots of his novels develop out of this careful delineation of his characters' past. The meaning of their lives is the product of that confluence of personal and national history of which all humans are made yet which relatively few novelists have portrayed as successfully as does Andrić.

Although Andrić's first three novels were published simultaneously in 1945, *Bosnian Chronicle* was the first to be written after he returned to Belgrade in 1941. He began writing, he says, because

> it was a way of surviving. I remembered the moments in history when certain peoples
> seemed to lose out. I thought of Serbia and Bosnia blacked out in the Turkish tide of the
> sixteenth century. The odds against one were so monstrous . . . even hope was an aspect
> of despair. . . . I pulled the past around me like an oxygen tent.

The act of writing under these conditions, he goes on, was "like drawing up a testament." *Bosnian Chronicle* is set in the town of Travnik during the height of Napoleon's power, from 1806 to 1814. Its main characters are the consuls and viziers who represent the various governments having an interest in Bosnia. The Turkish vizier is there because his Empire "owns" Bosnia; the French consul because the French are trying to extend their power inland from the coast; the Austrian consul because the Austrians fear French power as a threat to their own. The protagonist of the novel is the French consul, Jean Daville, and the plot grows out of his efforts as a European to comprehend the strange mixture of Oriental and Occidental cultures that is Bosnia. He is alternately bewildered, frustrated, and horrified at the barbarity of Turkish rule, the ignorance of the peasantry, and the endless intrigues of the contending powers represented in Travnik. Daville's ideals, formed during the French Revolution, are slowly being eroded and betrayed in this outpost of the Empire; he comes to see that he is merely a pawn in a game of international politics played without principle or mercy.

Daville has trouble working with his friends as well as with his enemies. He and his assistant, Desfosses, a generation apart in age, epitomize the opposite approaches that Westerners take toward the Orient. Daville follows the "classical" strategy: He emphasizes order and form, tradition, pessimism about sudden change, and a refusal to take local culture seriously. Desfosses, on the other hand, follows the "Romantic" attitude: He approaches problems with optimism, energy, impatience with tradition, and a great respect for local culture. The several Turkish viziers with whom the French consul must deal present him with complex moral and political dilemmas. The first one, Husref Mehmed Pasha, poisons an emissary from the Sultan who has come to order the Husref Pasha's removal. Daville is shocked but can see no ready way to deal with the situation or even to reveal it to anyone. The second vizier, Ibrahim Halimi Pasha, is, like Daville, incurably pessimistic but even more violent than Husref Pasha. Just when Daville believes he has found someone with whom he can solve diplomatic problems rationally, Ibrahim Pasha gives Daville a present of a sack full of ears and noses purportedly severed from the heads of rebellious Serbs but actually taken from Bosnian peasants massacred at a religious festival. Ibrahim Pasha also shoots one of his own army captains merely because the Austrians ask him to do so. Daville must acknowledge that "morbid circumstances, blind chance, caprice and base instincts" are simply taken for granted in Bosnia. A mindless anarchy seems to pervade everything when the bazaar riots against some captured Serbs, brutally torturing and executing some of them in the town square. The third vizier to appear in Travnik, Silikhtar Ali Pasha, makes no pretense of using anything but unbridled terror as his main instrument of policy.

One of Andrić's most common themes is the various ways human beings attempt either to live with or to escape from the dismal conditions of human life. Desfosses and the Austrian consul's wife try to escape through sexual desire, but their efforts are frustrated by chance, and, in the wife's case, by extreme instability. Cologna, physician at the Austrian consulate, converts to Islam to save his wife during the bazaar riots but is found dead the next morning at the base of a cliff. Daville himself attempts to bring order to his life through an epic he is writing about Alexander the Great; he never finishes it because, the narrator implies, he has no roots in this culture and therefore no way to nourish his creativity. Only Daville's happy family life keeps him from losing his reason as the years pass. As he nears the end of his tenure in Travnik (Napoleon has been defeated in Russia and will soon abdicate), he concludes that there is really no such thing as progress in human affairs:

> In reality all roads led one around in a circle. . . . The only things that changed were the men and the generation who travelled the path, forever deluded. . . . One simply went on. The long trek had no point or value, save those we might learn to discover within ourselves along the way. There were no roads, no destinations. One just travelled on . . . spent oneself, and grew weary.

Even though the reader undoubtedly must take Daville as a "chorus" character reflecting Andrić's own views, Daville does not have the last word in the novel. The work begins and ends not with Europeans but with native Bosnians in the small coffeehouses as they assess the import of the events in their region. The narrator shows that, ultimately, the Bosnian people will survive these various foreign occupations, their character having been tested in these trials of the body and spirit. As one of them says to Daville while the latter prepares to leave Bosnia forever: "But we remain, we remember, we keep a tally of all we've been through, of how we have defended and preserved ourselves, and we pass on these dearly bought experiences from father to son." The stream of history carries away much good along with the bad, but their cumulative knowledge has formed the bedrock of the Bosnian character, and they will survive.

The fact that Andrić did not write his first novel until he had had more than twenty years' experience with successful short stories meant that *Bosnian Chronicle* emerged as an unusually mature work. One of its weaknesses, however, is the characterization of its protagonist, Jean Daville. Even though the story is narrated from his point of view, he is never as fully developed or as believable as most of the other characters in the novel. The plot also suffers from being too episodic, lacking the sense of direction which a journey, for example, can give an episodic plot. Nevertheless, *Bosnian Chronicle* remains an impressive work, showing Andrić's extraordinary descriptive powers and his great gift for developing a memorable group of characters.

Nowhere in Andrić's fiction is the handling of the great flow of history more impressive than in his second novel, *The Bridge on the Drina*. It is a marvelous condensation of four centuries of Bosnian culture, as acted out in the town of Visegrad and on its bridge across the Drina, linking Bosnia and Serbia, East and West. In its structure, this novel, too, is episodic, a fact that Andrić emphasizes by labeling it a "chronicle." Yet its plot is more successful than that of *Bosnian Chronicle* because the episodes, though they cover many years, are unified by the novel's two great symbols, the bridge and the river. In addition, the author wisely devotes about half of the novel to the fifty-odd years before the destruction of the bridge at the beginning of World War I, the years in which all that the bridge represents is most severely tested.

The bridge originated in the early sixteenth century in the dreams of the Grand Vizier of the Ottoman Empire, Mehmed Pasha. As a young peasant growing up in the nearby Bosnian village of Sokolovici, he had witnessed the horror of children being ferried across the Drina as blood sacrifices for the Empire. Later, though he was tc serve three sultans for more than sixty years and win battles on three continents, he would still remember his boyhood home by ordering a bridge across the Drina at Visegrad as a way of exorcising his memory of the ferry of death. Ironically, in the first of many arbitrary deaths in the novel, Mehmed Pasha himself is assassinated shortly after the bridge is completed.

The Bridge on the Drina, like all of Andrić's fiction, is filled with memorable characters. Early in the novel there is Abidaga, the ruthless supervisor of construction of the bridge. He catches a young Bosnian attempting to sabotage the project and has him impaled alive on a huge stake, in what is undoubtedly one of the most horrifying scenes in Western literature. There is Fata Avda-gina, the ravishingly beautiful merchant's daughter on her way to a wedding with a man she does not want to marry. There is Alihodja Mutevelic, the Moslem merchant and cleric whose fate in the last half of the novel personifies that of the bridge and of the Ottoman Empire: He dies gasping on the hill above the town, old and worn out, as the bridge just below him is destroyed by the opening salvos of the war. He cannot believe that a work made centuries ago for the love of God can be destroyed by man. There is Salko Corkan, the one-eyed vagabond who, drunk one night, dares to attempt what no one has done before: to walk the ice-covered parapet of the bridge. He succeeds and becomes in later generations part of the folklore of the town. There is Milan Glasicanin, a wealthy young man who cannot stop gambling. One night on the bridge, he meets a mysterious stranger who, in a game of chance, takes him for everything he has. Andrić had a great interest in and respect for the folklore of Bosnia. His merging of history and folklore in *The Bridge on the Drina* is one of the novel's most impressive characteristics.

The symbolic function of the bridge and the river is obvious enough, verging on cliché, yet in Andrić's hands, these obvious symbols become profoundly suggestive of what is ephemeral and what is permanent in human life. The river represents, above all, the ceaseless flow of time and history which continually threatens to obliterate all evidence of human effort. The bridge is many things. It is permanence and therefore the opposite of the river: "Its life, though mortal in itself, resembled eternity, for its end could not be perceived." It is the perfect blend of beauty and utility, encouraging and symbolizing the possibilities of endurance: Life is wasted, and life endures. It is a symbol of man's great and lasting works, of his finest impulses as expressed in the words of its builder: "the love of God." Like all great works of art, though it is not completely safe from the ravages of time, it remains for generations and centuries to inspire humankind, to provide comfort and constancy in an uncertain universe. The bridge says to human beings that they need not become paralyzed by fear and by change. In this novel, as in Andrić's other fiction, no one can escape the fear and uncertainty that is the human lot, but the bridge enables the reader to perceive those aspects of life in their true proportions. In the end, the people will endure, because the bridge sustains their vision as well as their commerce.

Ivo Andrić's achievement in the novels written during World War II is all the more remarkable in that the three works he produced are so different in purpose, plot, and setting. In *The Woman from Sarajevo*, instead of the vast canvas of four centuries of history or the political intrigues of diplomats, he concentrates on one ordinary person: a moneylender, Raika Radakovich. "Miss," as she is universally known, lives an outwardly uneventful life, dying old and alone in a Belgrade apartment in 1935. Yet Miss Raika becomes for Andrić an example of how human beings often attempt, unsuccessfully, to fend off the dangers and uncertainties of life. His exploration of the development of her personality from childhood to old age is one of the masterpieces of characterization in world literature.

Miss Raika can deal with life only through an extreme miserliness. For her, thrift is something almost spiritual in character. Her miserliness originates in her youth, when the father whom she idolizes loses everything and dies a pauper. On his deathbed, he tells her she must suppress all love of luxury, "for the habit of thrift should be ruthless, like life itself." Thereafter, as a young woman in Sarajevo, she becomes an extremely shrewd manager of her money, relishing the power that having money to lend gives her over the lives of other people. Money enables her, she believes, to avoid the desperation and unhappiness which she perceives in the eyes of those who come to her to borrow. If through thrift and careful lending she can become a millionaire, only then will she be able to atone for her father's death. She vows never to make his mistakes, such as feeling compassion for or generosity toward another human being. If one has no emotional ties to anyone, then one is not obligated to be compassionate.

The outbreak of World War I seriously threatens her financial situation. Surrounded by people who feel intensely the great social and political changes then taking place in Bosnia and in Eastern Europe, she searches desperately for someone with whom she can have a strictly "business" relationship, but there is no one except the memory of her dead father. Shunned by the town as a "parasite," abandoned by her advisers (who are ruined by the war), unable to lend money at interest, she leaves Sarajevo in 1919 and moves to Belgrade. There, among relatives whom she detests, she resumes her career. In one of the most revealing episodes in the novel, she repeatedly loans money to a charming young man despite clear evidence of his irresponsibility. The narrator makes the point that because her miserliness never allowed her to develop either knowledge of others or self-knowledge, she cannot prevent herself from making the same mistake again and again. Her last years are increasingly lonely, as money turns out not to be the proof against unhappiness that she had imagined. More and more fearful of robbery, she bars doors and windows to guard her gold. In the powerful last scene of the novel, Miss Raika dies of a heart attack brought on by her irrational fear that every sound she hears is that of a thief breaking in to steal her money.

In this novel, like his others with a much vaster canvas, Andrić's strength is to be able to relate the life of Miss Raika to the historical currents of her time and place. The acid test for Andrić's characters is always how well they can adapt to the constant change and uncertainty that is human life and human history. Miss Raika fails not simply because hoarding money is somehow "wrong" but because, in being a miser, she fails to understand either her own life or the lives of others. There is perhaps also a hint that Miss Raika fails because she represents the decay of the capitalist ethic, which can think of no other response when its values are challenged but to hoard what it has left. More tightly plotted than *Bosnian Chronicle* or *The Bridge on the Drina*, *The Woman from Sarajevo* is, in its structure and in the characterization of its protagonist, Andrić's most successful novel.

In answer to an interviewer's question, Andrić stated that he thought the novella form more congenial to the Yugoslav temperament than the full-length novel. *The Vizier's Elephant*, one of three novellas which Andrić wrote in the first few years after the war, is based on a kind of folktale which circulated unrecorded in Bosnia during the nineteenth century. The story takes place in Travnik in 1820 (in the same location as, and only a few years later than, *Bosnian Chronicle*). A new vizier, Sayid Ali Jelaludin Pasha, proves to be unusually cruel even for a Turkish imperial official. The Ottoman Empire is decaying in its outlying regions, so the Sultan has sent a man known for his viciousness to conquer the anarchic Bosnian nobility. The new Vizier has a two-year-old pet elephant which in its rambunctiousness destroys the town market, frightens people away, and in general causes havoc in the town. The Vizier's retinue makes things worse by punishing anyone who dares to object to the elephant's behavior. Finally, the merchants decide they must act. One of their number, Alyo, volunteers to go see the dreaded Vizier about the problem. He is too frightened to go into the palace, so instead, he fabricates a story about his "visit," claiming that he has told the Vizier that the people of the town love the elephant so much, they wish to have more elephants. Finally, the merchants make repeated attempts to poison the beast—attempts which never succeed—until the Vizier himself commits suicide when he learns he is to be replaced because his cruelties have only created more, not less, anarchy.

As always, Andrić tells an interesting story. However, *The Vizier's Elephant* is perhaps his least successful novella, especially in its halting attempts to attach a larger significance to the eccentricities of its characters. The narrator does encourage the reader to view the elephant as a symbol of the Empire: Causing constant fear and apprehension, behaving in a mindless, destructive way, the elephant is ungainly and out of place in a changing world. Andrić, however, never commits himself completely to this or any other narrative approach. The Vizier and Alyo never emerge as more than stereotypes, and Alyo's motives especially are too often left unexplained. The reader tends not to be as affected by the anguish of human existence as he usually is in an Andrić story; the comic effects of the elephant's behavior are not developed enough to make the humor dominant, yet these same comic effects dilute the force of the tragedy that lies behind the Vizier's cruelties.

Anika's Times, a novella also published in 1948, is more complex and satisfying than *The Vizier's Elephant*. It is set in the village of Dobrun in two different time periods. The first part concerns Father Vuyadin Porubovich, the Orthodox parish priest, and takes place in the 1870's. After the death of his wife, who died in childbirth, Father Vuyadin gradually loses his grip on reality. He comes to feel enormous disgust for the people whose spiritual needs it is his job to satisfy. His behavior becomes erratic, and he refuses to speak to anyone. Finally, no longer able to stand the strain of his own hypocrisy, he seizes his rifle and fires at some peasants visible from his window. He then flees into the night but is later captured and confined to an insane asylum. How, the narrator asks, is one to explain the priest's behavior?

The narrator's "answer" to this question takes the reader back to the times of Vuyadin's grandparents. The story at this point concerns a beautiful young woman named Anika, her feebleminded brother, Lale, and the various men who cannot resist Anika's charms. She first has an affair with a young man named Mihailo. They break up, and Mihailo takes up with a married woman whose husband he unintentionally helps the wife to murder. Though returning to Anika in the hope of forgetting his guilt, Mihailo cannot hold her, and she develops into the classic "evil woman," inflaming men and causing them to act like fools. She takes up with Yaksha Porubovich, who will become the grandfather of Father Vuyadin. This is too much for Yaksha's father, who calls the police to have Anika arrested. Hedo Salko, the chief of police in Visegrad, is reluctant to carry out the order. He believes that no problem is ever solved: "evil, misfortune and unrest are constant and eternal and . . . nothing concerning them can be changed." On the other hand, he says, "every single problem will somehow be resolved and settled, for nothing in this world is lasting or eternal: The neighbours will make peace, the murderer will either surrender himself or else flee into another district. . . ." Since Salko will not act, the Mayor intervenes, but Anika seduces the Mayor.

Anika's tangled *amours* now begin to trap her. When she visits a religious festival in Dobrun, huge mobs surround her, and Yaksha's father attempts to shoot her from the same window from which his great-grandson Vuyadin will try to kill the peasants seventy years later. The family steps in, however, and Yaksha's father can only curse Anika from his darkened room. Yaksha himself attempts to kill the Mayor in a fit of jealousy, but he fails and flees into the hills. It is here that Andrić shows his supreme skill at managing the climax of a narrative involving many characters. Mihailo reappears, still haunted by the murder of the husband eight years before and convinced that the husband's death foretold his own. No longer able to distinguish Anika from the married woman he had also loved, he goes to her house intending to kill her, but he finds that someone else has already done it and fled. No one is arrested, though it appears that Lale may have been the killer. Yaksha is reconciled with his father, but his father predicts that Anika will poison the town for a century.

Andrić's handling of theme and atmosphere in *Anika's Times* is similar to that in many stories of the American writer Nathaniel Hawthorne. Like Hawthorne, Andrić in this novella is concerned with the ways in which "the sins of the fathers are visited on the sons." He is able to suggest in subtle and complex ways how behavior patterns in the village are constantly changing yet remain fundamentally the same. A number of his characters, even those, such as Salko, who appear only briefly, come vividly alive. Andrić knows how mysterious human behavior can be, how ambiguous and tentative explanations of it must often remain.

The longest of the three novellas published in 1948, *Zeko* is Andrić's only piece of long fiction concerned with the World War II period in Yugoslav history. It is the story of a meek little man, Isidore Katanich, nicknamed "Zeko" (meaning "Bunny"), who in the course of his various tribulations comes to understand the meaning of his own and his country's life during the years of depression and war. The other main character besides Zeko is his domineering wife, Margarita—nicknamed "Cobra." She is full of aggressive energy, constantly twitching, with "greedy, mistrustful, deadly eyes." Her occupation is managing the apartment building which she and Zeko own. They have a son, Mihailo, a handsome, egocentric, and entirely shiftless young man without moral values, who has been nicknamed "Tiger." Since he and his mother take sides constantly against Zeko, it is an uneven match: Cobra and Tiger versus Bunny.

There are signs in the book that Andrić intends Zeko's life to parallel and therefore to comment upon the development of the Yugoslav people during the twentieth century. Though not strictly speaking an allegory, *Zeko* shows through its protagonist the developing national consciousness and desire for freedom of the South Slavs. Zeko had been a gifted artist, but he lost confidence in himself and went to law school at the time of the Austrian annexation of Bosnia in 1908. When the 1912 Balkan War begins, Zeko joins the army but suffers continually from typhus and is finally forced to return home. He marries Margarita, but World War I intervenes. He returns home in 1919 to find his wife a horrible shrew. He hears rumors that Mihailo was fathered by someone else while he was away at war, but he cannot establish the truth or falsehood of the rumor. "Everything around him was changed, turbulent, shattered . . . this was a time of fatigue and of the acceptance of half-truths." As the years go on, Zeko is increasingly desperate to find a way out of his marriage (his years with Margarita corresponding to the years of the "marriage" of the Serbs, Croats, and Slovenes in the Kingdom of Yugoslavia— that is, 1919 to 1941).

Zeko finds several forms of escape. He associates more and more with his sister-in-law and her family, and he discovers the subculture of those who live on and by the Sava River. Their lives are uncertain and dangerous—what the narrator calls "the true life of most people." Zeko does manage to find true peace and acceptance among these "strenuous, unsettled lives, full of uncertainty, where efforts invested in work were out of proportion to the rewards." The members of his sister-in-law's family become Communists, and symbolically, as it were, Zeko gravitates increasingly toward their values, away from the greed and selfishness of his capitalistic wife and son. Zeko becomes, then, a true man of the people and, in embracing their fate and their future, finds meaning for his own life.

With the coming of Hitler's invasion, Cobra and Tiger, because of their fear and lack of self-knowledge, do not have the inner resources necessary to withstand the despair of war. Zeko, however, does: Becoming more aware of the need for meaningful action, he is less tempted to hide from conflict, as he had done on the river: "The most important thing was to do away, once and for all, with a barren and undignified life, and to walk and live like a man." Like Yugoslavia itself, Zeko learns the value of independence. He finally joins the Partisans (Tito's anti-Nazi guerrilla organization), while his wife and son, finding it difficult to orient themselves amid the suffering of war, flee Belgrade and disappear. On Zeko's first mission against the Germans, he is caught in an ambush and, attempting to flee, drowns in the Sava River. Yet Zeko's death is not a defeat, for, like his country, he was finally learning how to live with dignity; like his country, he had finally decided what creed he would follow.

One of the chief virtues of *Zeko* is that Andrić allows the parallels between Zeko and Yugoslavia to resonate within the story without ever forcing them on the reader. The other main characters have a vividness which prevents them from fading into stereotypes. The gradual awakening of Zeko's consciousness is portrayed with much of the same skill that Andrić had shown in the characterization of Miss Raika in *The Woman from Sarajevo*.

If each of Andrić's novels and novellas has important images representing the dangers and uncertainties characteristic of human life, in his last novella, *Devil's Yard*, such an image for the human condition comes to dominate everything in the story: "Devil's Yard," the notorious prison in Istanbul under the Ottoman Empire. One can be thrown into this prison on suspicion of almost anything, on the principle that it is easier to release a man who has been proved innocent than to track down one who has been proved guilty. The inmates are mostly the weak, the poor, the desperate of society. In Devil's Yard (and in roughly the first half of the novella), the dominant character is the warden, Karadjos. His name means "shadow show," and he will appear anywhere in the prison without warning, trying to trick or frighten a confession out of a prisoner. He is overweight, horribly ugly, with a powerful, piercing eye. His governing principle is that, because everyone is guilty of something, everyone who ends up in Devil's Yard belongs there, whether guilty or not of the particular crime with which he is charged.

In *Devil's Yard*, the prison is a metaphor for human life, with Karadjos as its "god," or fate. He is inscrutable, unpredictable, and tyrannical. In addition to the constant fear felt by the inmates, there is the constant mingling of truth, half-truth, and falsehood which, according to Andrić, is a basic characteristic of human existence. Karadjos fosters this climate of rumor and suspicion with an endless series of threats, cajolery, incredible jokes, and surprise remarks. The prisoners "complained about him the way one complains about one's life and curses one's destiny. Their own damnation had involved them with him. Therefore, despite their fear and hate, they had grown to be one with him and it would have been hard for them to imagine life without him."

Andrić's *Devil's Yard* is his only piece of long fiction told as a story within a story (in fact, it includes several stories within stories). This technique, which he handles with great ease, seems meant to reinforce the notion that in life itself there are layers of truths, half-truths, and falsehoods among which one must try to distinguish. The outermost frame-story concerns a young monk: He is helping sort through the effects of another monk named Brother

Petar, who has recently died. As the young monk does so, he recalls Brother Petar's story of having once been held for several months in Devil's Yard while on a visit to Istanbul. The next frame is that of Brother Petar narrating his stay in the prison. While there, he meets a young, educated Turk, Djamil Effendi. The story of Djamil's life is actually narrated by a depressed, apprehensive, and talkative Jew from Smyrna, named Haim. This Haim has "a passion for narrating and explaining everything, for exposing all the errors and follies of mankind." The story he tells of Djamil's life, though at times incredible, has a ring of truth about it simply because its teller has such a passion for the truth, or at least for detail.

It seems that Djamil has studied the history of the Turkish Empire to the point where he has begun to imagine himself one of its ill-fated sultans— Djem Sultan, who in the late fifteenth century was bested in a struggle for the throne by his brother. When Djamil himself returns to the prison yard after several days' interrogation, he tells Petar the story of Djem Sultan. Djamil's story of Djem Sultan is the innermost tale in this intricately narrated novella. He has been confined in Devil's Yard because his complete identification with Djem Sultan bears an uncomfortably close resemblance to the life of the current sultan, whose own throne is threatened by his own brother. Thus Djamil seems to illustrate the danger of people accepting too completely the accounts of their own history and therefore the meaning of their lives as embodied in that history. Djamil finally disappears, and the very mystery of his fate—is he free? was he murdered? confined in a hospital for the insane?— only underlines the confusion that passes for human knowledge.

As his imprisonment drags on, apparently for no reason except the arbitrary will of some higher authority, Brother Petar realizes that he is becoming irrational. He cannot find anyone whose talk seems sane. The brutal Karadjos has dominated the first half of the novella, and Djamil Effendi, equally irrational, has dominated the second half. Under their influence, Brother Petar could not have retained his own sanity had he remained in prison much longer. Like most of Andrić's protagonists, Brother Petar has had to spend all of his energy simply to escape madness and despair. When the first narrator, the young monk, resumes his own frame-tale at the end of *Devil's Yard*, he is forced out of his reverie by the "dull clang of metal objects thrown on the pile" of Petar's earthly possessions. This is a "reality" which the reader views in a far different light from that of his earlier impression.

There is no use pretending that Andrić is an optimist about the human condition. His impressive accomplishments in the novel and the novella hinge on other things: an impeccable style; a depth of insight into human motivation almost unmatched in Western literature; a profound sympathy for the sufferings of his characters; vivid dramatization of the ethnic character of his province, built up over the centuries against oppression and civil war; and perhaps most important, an ability to turn local history into universal symbols, so that readers knowing nothing of Bosnia can see in his fiction the common lot of mankind.

Major publications other than long fiction

SHORT FICTION: *Pripovetke*, 1924, 1931, 1936; *Nove pripovetke*, 1948; *The Pasha's Concubine and Other Tales*, 1968.

POETRY: *Ex Ponto*, 1918; *Nemiri*, 1920.

Bibliography

Dzadzic, Petar. *Ivo Andric*, 1960.

Goy, E. D. "The Work of Ivo Andric," in *Slavonic and East European Review*. XLI (1963), pp. 301-326.

Kadic, Ante. *From Croatian Renaissance to Yugoslav Socialism*, 1969.

Lord, Albert B. "Ivo Andric in English Translation," in *Slavic Review*. XXIII (1964), pp. 563-573.

Mihailovich, Vasa D., and Mateja Matejic, eds. *Yugoslav Literature in English*, 1976.

Moravcevich, Nicholas. "Ivo Andric and the Quintessence of Time," in *Slavic and East European Journal*. XVI (1972), pp. 313-318.

Simon, John. "Afterword," in *The Bridge on the Drina*, 1967.

Mark Minor

SHOLEM ASCH

Born: Kutno, Poland; November 1, 1880
Died: London, England; July 10, 1957

Principal long fiction

Dos Shtetl, 1905 (*The Little Town,* 1907); *Motke Ganev,* 1917 (*Mottke the Thief,* 1917); *Onkl Mozes,* 1918 (*Uncle Moses,* 1920); *Kiddush Hashem,* 1920 (English translation, 1926); *Toyt Urteyl,* 1926 (*Judge Not*); *Khayim Lederers Tsurikkumen,* 1927 (*Chaim Lederer's Return*); *Farn Mabul,* 1927-1932 (*Three Cities,* 1933); *Der Tilim Yid,* 1934 (*Salvation,* 1934); *Three Novels,* 1938 (includes *Uncle Moses, Judge Not,* and *Chaim Lederer's Return*); *Der Man fun Notseres,* 1943 (*The Nazarene,* 1939); *The Apostle,* 1943; *Ist River,* 1946 (*East River,* 1946); *Mary,* 1949; *Moses,* 1951; *Der Novi,* 1955 (*The Prophet,* 1955).

Other literary forms

Although Sholem Asch is remembered chiefly as a novelist, much of his early work consists of dramas. When *Der Got fun Nekome* (1907; *The God of Vengeance,* 1918) was performed on Yiddish stages in Russia and Poland, Max Reinhardt, who understood Yiddish, decided to produce it at the Deutsche Theater. This was the first time that a work of Yiddish literature had appeared in the international literature. This play, in which a brothel owner purchases a Torah to place in his daughter's room, hoping it will protect her from the impurities in the apartment below, was widely condemned as sacrilegious. Many other dramas followed, including adaptations of such novels as *Mottke the Thief,* which enjoyed considerable success on Yiddish stages.

Asch also published *The Collected Stories of Sholem Asch* (1958) and other collections of short fiction, as well as an autobiographical essay, *What I Believe* (1941), in which he reacted to criticism levied against him by the Jewish community.

Achievements

Until 1950, Asch was indisputably the best-known, most translated, most successful of Yiddish writers. More than anyone before him, he managed to inject the Yiddish word into world culture, making the world aware of a major literature that had been unjustly ignored. This broader world sometimes seemed more kindly disposed to him than the segment of his Jewish readers who objected to his delineation of the seamier aspects of Jewish life in some works and to his sympathetic treatment of Christianity in others. The bulk of his Jewish readers remained faithful and recognized in him a lover of the poor and weak, a God-seeker, a gentle soul keenly aware that man did not live by bread alone. In spite of his high regard for Christianity, Asch remained faithful to Jewish life and tradition, acutely aware of the anti-Semitism all about him. While his characters accept this intolerance as a fact of life, Asch himself could not always assume the same stance. He returned a medal awarded to him by the Polish government when he realized that the policies of that government permitted a heightened anti-Jewish feeling.

A student of the revered I. L. Peretz, whose influence he acknowledged as late as 1951, Asch went beyond the teachings of this master and dealt with topics that Yiddish literature had theretofore avoided. His work marks an abandonment of the rational ways that the Jewish enlightenment had made obligatory for Jewish writers. Like Isaac Bashevis Singer, who replaced him as *the* Yiddish writer on the world stage, Asch was attracted to folkloristic and irrational elements. Because of the diversity of his oeuvre, critics have found it difficult to classify Asch. There is the Romantic who idealized the life of simple Jews and insisted on the primacy of tradition and faith in faith; there is the Naturalist who brilliantly depicted the milieus of thieves, jugglers, and prostitutes; there is the didactic moralist who strove to teach the meaning of the good life. There is even a hint of the publicist who fought Hitlerite anti-Semitism by underscoring the basic nobility of Jewish existence and demonstrating the common bonds uniting Judaism and Christianity. This very multiplicity suggests Asch's enduring appeal.

Biography

The tenth child of a pious and prosperous Hasid, Sholem Asch underwent an early formal education in Hebrew language and literature, especially the Bible. His progress indicated sufficient promise for his father to entertain hopes for him in a rabbinic career. In his mid-teens, Asch came upon his first secular book and became "enlightened." He found employment as a "scribe," writing letters for the illiterate, which likely gave him unique insights into the human psyche. At the same time, he was teaching himself German, Russian, and Polish and reading whatever books by major writers became available to him.

At the age of sixteen, Asch visited Peretz, whose stories he had admired, and requested that the master comment on his own efforts, which he was then writing in Hebrew. Peretz liked what he read but urged the youngster to change to Yiddish. Asch's first story, "Moshele," appeared in *Der Jud* in late 1900. A collection of Hebrew stories published in 1902 was followed in 1903 by another in Yiddish. (His writing then, as later, was colored by the dark and dingy places in which he had lived, the hunger he had suffered and which he was never to forget.) Asch married Mathilda Shapiro, the daughter of a teacher and minor poet. In 1904, he serialized his "poem in prose" *The Little Town* in *Der Freint*; in 1905, it was published as a book that quickly established him at the forefront of Yiddish writers.

Asch visited Palestine in 1907 and the United States in 1909. He was awed by biblical sites in Palestine and the evidence of Jewish and Christian events. In America, the landscapes impressed him, but he was repelled by the sweatshops, the tenements, and the quality of the life he observed.

In the ten years preceding World War I, Asch completed ten plays. He lived mostly in France but was forced to leave upon the outbreak of the conflict. Besides *Mottke the Thief*, his wartime writing, emanating mostly from New York, included *Uncle Moses*, a novel of immigrants in their initial years in New York.

After the war, Asch revisited Eastern Europe as the representative of a Jewish relief agency. He was horrified by the slaughter of Jews at the hands of Cossacks and White Russians. What he saw reminded him of a seventeenth century Ukrainian slaughterer of Jews whose soldier-peasants terrorized the countryside. The result was the first of his historical novels, *Kiddush Hashem* (sanctification of the name).

In the words of Sol Liptzin, Asch in the postwar years continued "glorifying Jewish deeds of brotherly love and quiet heroism." Before Adolf Hitler rose to power, Asch believed that contrasting such quiet deeds of Jews with the crude Hitlerite reliance on force would be his way of fighting the Nazi menace. *Salvation*, written in 1932, was the most spiritual novel he wrote, and he was embittered by its poor reception.

Asch's spiritual orientation, accompanied by the desire to strengthen the Jewish position, led to novels on Jesus (*The Nazarene*), Paul (*The Apostle*), and Mary (*Mary*). These works alienated his Jewish readers, who feared a case of apostasy at a time when Hitler was decimating European Jewry. *The Nazarene* was published in English before a Yiddish publisher would touch it. The controversy continued for nearly a decade. The resilience of European Jews and the establishment of a Jewish state tore Asch out of his isolation and prompted him to turn to *Moses*, which he had begun long before and had laid aside in favor of his Christian novels.

In 1954, having lived in the United States and France, Asch settled permanently in Israel, where, in 1955, he wrote *The Prophet*. As the chronicler of a world that had disappeared, Asch became again an object of admiration—a condition that his insatiable ego demanded. In 1957, he suffered a mild stroke. While in London for an operation, he died before surgery could be performed.

Analysis

Nearly all of Sholem Asch's works are related, in a broad sense, to some religious concern. His many themes are clearly intertwined: the simple, traditional life of the Jew; saintliness in the quest for God and service to man; the ugliness of poverty but the distinct possibility of meaningful beauty even in poverty; the emptiness of a purely material existence; the Jewish roots of Christianity and the need to close the gap between the two faiths. In fact, faith in both its meanings—trust in God and different institutionalized ways of reaching Him—is a thread running through all of Asch's works, but especially his later works.

Even in his first major work, *The Little Town*, Asch had romanticized the inwardness of Jewish life in the shtetl, a different approach from the ridicule usually heaped upon the backward enclaves in literature. Asch perceived nobility and charm in the poverty-ridden, filth-infested shtetl.

Similarly, he had dealt with spiritual and sacrificial heroism before dealing with it directly in *Kiddush Hashem*. Living far out in the Padolian steppe, a Jewish innkeeper, Mendel, dreams of the day when other Jews will join him in the town and enable him to build a synagogue and lead a Jewish existence. Mendel eventually overcomes the threats of the local priest, and a small but flourishing Jewish community comes into being. Mendel and the congregation are dangerously sandwiched between the machinations of the Catholic priest and the Greek Orthodox priest. The former is intent upon humbling the latter. What better means of debasing his rival than to force him to go to the Jew Mendel to obtain the key to his own church? In his frustration, the Orthodox priest threatens Mendel: Sooner or later "the little brothers" will come to liberate the peasants from the Polish lords and the filthy Jews.

The "little brothers" eventually come, under the leadership of Bogdan Chmelnitzky, and lay waste not only to Mendel's but also to every Jewish community far and wide. Mendel's attachment to his synagogue is such that he refuses to leave, but the rabbi reminds him that the synagogue is only stone, while a human life is a human life. Mendel's Jews flee, joining the stream of refugees; they put up a heroic fight with virtually no weapons. They are finally conquered through the betrayal of the Polish lords, who are only too willing to sacrifice their Jewish allies in the mistaken belief that they can thereby save themselves.

Through Mendel and his family, which includes a learned son and his beautiful wife, Asch depicts the simplicity and piety of Jewish life and the Jews' willingness to live and die for "the sanctification of the name." Jews are offered a chance to save their lives by bowing before the Cross, but they will bow only before their one and only God. All resist the easy way out, sacrificially preferring to suffer cruelty, death, and martyrdom. Although the body may be destroyed, the will and spirit are indestructible. Asch only inferentially says that the Jews' imperishable faith in God has ensured their survival in the past and will ensure it in the future.

Charles Madison has stated that "Asch's compassionate brooding gives the tragic tale the poignant quality of imaginative truth." This critic has also distinguished between two forms of martyrdom—Mendel's, which is not a pure martyrdom in that it is wholly passive, and his daughter-in-law's, which is active: She persuades the Cossack captor who loves her that he should shoot her, on the pretense that no bullet can hurt her.

Kiddush Hashem is perhaps Asch's only novel in which religious motifs and Jewish historical destiny, especially the Jews' suffering for their survival as a group, fuse successfully. The structure of the novel, on the other hand, is awkward, which prevents it from becoming the masterpiece it might have been.

If *The Little Town* and *Kiddush Hashem* are, to use Sol Liptzin's words, in a Sabbath mood, *Mottke the Thief* is decidedly workaday. Asch abandons the idealized Jews of earlier works to offer such sad human specimens as Blind Layb and Red Slatke, Mottke's parents. Layb is a vicious, irresponsible father whose only guidance to his child is the lash, which he uses freely and cruelly. Not only is Jewish life imperfect in *Mottke the Thief*, in spite of some obedience to forms and tradition, but also it exists on the lowest levels of humanity. Asch shows an exceptional virtuosity in this novel. The first half combines picaresque with gargantuan, larger-than-life features; the second half is Zolaesque in its depressing Naturalism. The abused Mottke, first open enough to seek affection even from a curious dog, is transformed into a callous pimp and murderer, a development that calls for considerable skill, which Asch demonstrates in good measure.

His earlier work might have given rise to the impression that there was something do-goodish in Asch, that his feet were not firmly planted on the ground. With the creation of Mottke, this impression was swept aside. From the moment Mottke joins a group of vaudevillians, uses and abuses them, seduces or is seduced by Mary, the rope dancer, and competes with the treacherous Kanarik, he becomes a character apart from any that Asch had previously created. The erstwhile thief's descent into total depravity continues. With Mary's help, he kills Kanarik, assumes Kanarik's identity, and acquires his own small staff of prostitutes. Yet the Mottke who had once enjoyed something of a Jewish upbringing, however atypical, is not wholly dead. He is fatally attracted to a decent girl, and his love generates decent impulses that have long been submerged. The desire for chastity, piety, and living in the love of and reverence for God, however, has been resurrected too late. Perhaps Mottke's conversion, which comes to naught, is not the most persuasive part of the book; in any case, Mottke is betrayed by the sweet girl he loves. Yet even in the novel's variety of depressing settings, Asch still emerges as a man with a profound faith in faith.

Salvation, a story of the saintly Jekhiel and his quest for God and ways of serving man, is more in the mainstream of Asch's fiction than is *Mottke the Thief*. It is probably the most purely "spiritual" of Asch's novels—a term he himself used to describe it—and he attributed its relative failure with the reading public to the refusal of the modern world to address spiritual questions.

Jekhiel's father was a Hasid who left his wife and younger son to join his rabbi in study. Jekhiel was a deep disappointment to him, for, unlike Jekhiel's older brother, Jekhiel has failed to grasp the subtleties of the Talmud. Jekhiel, oppressed by a sense of failure, helps his mother eke out a bare living in the marketplace. She dies, and the youngster serves as tutor to an innkeeper's children, to whom he teaches the elements of the Hebrew language. Jekhiel is heartened one day by a wise stranger, who tells him that knowing the Psalms, with their simple yet warm teachings, is every bit as important in the sight of God as the subtle shadings of Talmudic disputation. Soon Jekhiel is known as the Psalm-Jew (which was, indeed, the original Yiddish title of the novel).

In this first half of *Salvation*, Asch poses several questions, to which his answers are clear. He is not enamored of the father, who puts study—however strong an ethic in Jewish tradition—ahead of his familial obligations; Asch does not place learning the Talmud above simpler aspects of the Jewish obligation to ponder the ways of God. A cold, rational approach to religion attracts him less than a warmer, human, perhaps less rational mode.

Jekhiel, without wishing it, develops a following of his own, becoming the rabbi of the Psalms, simple and humble. He is also known for miracles, for which, however, he claims no credit. On one occasion, Jekhiel, under great pressure, commits God to giving a child to a hitherto barren woman. A girl is born. When Jekhiel's wife dies shortly thereafter, the pious rabbi sees it as a sign from Heaven. He leaves home and, in the manner of ascetic saints of all faiths, roams the countryside in rags. He is finally recognized and forced to return.

The years pass, and the girl whose birth he had promised has grown to maturity and fallen in love with a strapping young Polish soldier. They plan to marry. In preparation for her conversion to Catholicism, she enters a convent. There is consternation in the girl's family. Torn by conflicting pressures, the girl jumps to her death. Jekhiel, who had fought the conversion, is troubled for the second time: Has he overstepped proper bounds again? Was not human life and the search for God more precious than the particular way of reaching Him: the Jewish or the Christian?

Asch's implied tolerance of intermarriage again brought him into conflict with his Jewish readers. *Salvation* paved the way for a work that would nearly lead to a rupture with these readers: the story of Jesus of Nazareth, whose emphases within Judaism were not that different from those of Jekhiel the Psalm-Jew.

The problem of Christian anti-Semitism is omnipresent in the oeuvre of Sholem Asch. Considering the author's vision of Jesus, an extension of his characterization of Jekhiel, it is not surprising that Asch often felt bitter about the crimes against Jews committed in the name of the saintly Nazarene. Throughout *The Nazarene*, Asch has his Rabbi Jeshua repeat that he has not come to destroy the Law but to fulfill it. Jeshua observes all but one or two of the ritual commandments, but it is his failure to observe those that his wealthy detractors use against him. Asch's Jesus is learned in the Torah; the character appears to be depicted in the tradition of the great teacher Hillel; he is a man of infinite wisdom and compassion. If, in spite of its strengths, *The Nazarene* fails to satisfy completely, that failure must be attributed to the nature of the subject. Jeshua as man, as self-revealed Messiah, and as Son of Man (interpreted to mean the Son of God) is a difficult fusion to achieve. Asch is as successful as any novelist who has ever attempted it or, for that matter, biographers and interpreters. There are times, however, when Jeshua, ever mysterious—now very human, now very enigmatic, even furtive—suggests ever so slightly the religious charlatan. Yet this was far from Asch's intent and has not been the impression of all readers.

Jeshua's teachings are within the frame of Jewish tradition, but as he himself says, the fulfillment of that tradition requires new interpretations and emphases. The occasional impressions of hucksterism are held only by the more cynical modern reader, reacting to Jesus' refusal to answer questions directly, to speak in parables only, to select carefully his moments of healing and revealing, to satisfy the doubts of the most searching and spiritually avid of his disciples and admirers. Rabbi Jeshua has a talent for the grand gesture and for the attention-getting phrase or figure of speech, but this image is not one created by Asch; it is, rather, inherent in the subject matter, which he derives entirely from New Testament sources. There are few famous sayings of Jesus that are not quoted, and the endless quotations, although necessary, at times slow the pace of the narrative. Asch underscores the innovations of the teachings of Jesus: compassion for the poor, the sick, the neglected; the emphasis on the spirit, not the forms, of observance; the primacy of faith; a piety that adds to fervor of the divine humility and an all-encompassing pity; and an involvement in the affairs of man. Jesus attacks privilege, be it hereditary or earned. The task of involving oneself in the suffering of others must be never-ending; it must lead to the more fortunate assisting those who are suffering. Rabbi Jeshua's leniency toward the sinner, reassurance of the untutored and ignorant, and forebearance vis-à-vis those who have disappointed him all contribute to making him an innovative teacher and preacher. In the end, Jeshua dies, like so many of Asch's noble characters, for the sanctification of the Name.

Asch was attracted to the story of Jesus on an early trip to Palestine, but he did not turn to writing it until decades later, when the need for closer Jewish-Christian ties seemed to him highly desirable. The device he finally employed for telling it was ingenious: A half-demented anti-Semitic Polish scholar, imagining that he was Pilate's right-hand man, relates the first third of the novel. Judas Ischariot, Jesus' most learned disciple, whom Asch rehabilitates in the novel, tells the next third in the form of a diary. The final third, recounted by a Jewish disciple of Nicodemus, a rabbi sympathetic to Jeshua, reports on the political and religious evasions within the Sanhedrin and Pilate's desire to rid himself of the troublemaking revolutionary.

Again, Asch displays his mastery of painting different milieus. The messianic craving among lowly and wealthy Jews, the Roman cynicism toward this strangest of peoples, the Jews, the doings in the Temple, the political rivalries between priests and scholars, the evocation of historical figures, the atmosphere of Jesus' preaching and reception in Galilee—all come alive in Asch's prose. If Rabbi Jeshua is only partly convincing, it is because his dual status as man and Messiah may well elude even the most skillful of writers.

Set on New York's East Side, another radically different milieu, *East River* is hardly one of Asch's better novels. The writing, even the syntax, appears a bit sloppy, and the work bears the marks of haste. The novel does, however, pull together many of Asch's most typical themes and interests: the poor sorely tried, and not by poverty alone; one son given to learning, the other to practical pursuits; traditional Jewish religious learning transformed into secular equivalents; anti-Semitism and the need for Jewish-Christian dialogue; the spirit of a religion versus its mere forms. Intermarriage, which unleashed a minor religious war between contending religious leaders in *Salvation*, is treated here with sympathy and understanding. To be sure, Moshe Wolf, symbol of the old life, cannot reconcile himself to his wealthy son's intermarriage, but neither can he accept—in spite of, or because of, his own poverty—this son's exploitation of Jewish and Christian workers. Moshe Wolf, a near-saint, accepts with love and understanding the burdens imposed on him by God: his beloved older son's crippling polio, this son's failure to use his dazzling intelligence to study Scripture, applying it instead to secular ideas, which often frighten the traditional Jew in him. Wolf's wife, Deborah, thoroughly Americanized, has more understanding for the tycoon son than for the "cripple." For her, the former has succeeded; the latter, with his superfluous learning, is useless.

The Catholic girl who originally loved the cripple but then married the tycoon is treated sympathetically and is ultimately accepted by Moshe Wolf as a God-loving, God-seeking human being. Mary breaks with her pathologically anti-Semitic failure of a father and leads her husband back to the ways of decency and righteousness. Mary's relationships with her father and husband are not credible and detract seriously from any power the novel might have. Yet for whatever it is worth, Mary convinces her husband not to live only for himself or even his immediate family, but to enlist himself in the war against poverty, injustice, and cruelty. The old lesson is repeated here in less subtle form: Man does not live by bread, or money, alone.

Asch's daring in tackling milieus that cannot have been close to him is admirable: a grocery store, Tammany Hall, sweatshops, synagogue politics, Jewish-Irish relations, the garment industry. It is interesting to speculate what this book would have been like at the height of Asch's literary power. A courageous failure, it testifies to the profoundly ecumenical spirit of his fiction.

Major publications other than long fiction
SHORT FICTION: *The Collected Stories of Sholem Asch*, 1958.
PLAY: *Der Got fun Nekome*, 1907 (*The God of Vengeance*, 1918).
NONFICTION: *What I Believe*, 1941.

Bibliography
Lieberman, Herman. *The Christianity of Sholem Asch*, 1953.
Liptzin, Sol. *A History of Yiddish Literature*, 1972.
Madison, Charles. *Yiddish Literature: Its Scope and Major Writers*, 1968.
Niger, Samuel. "Sholem Asch," in *Columbia Dictionary of Modern European Literature*, 1980.
_____ . *Sholem Asch: His Life and Work*, 1950.
Roback, A. A. *The Story of Yiddish Literature*, 1940.___

Lothar Kahn

MIGUEL ÁNGEL ASTURIAS

Born: Guatemala City, Guatemala; October 19, 1899
Died: Madrid, Spain; June 9, 1974

Principal long fiction

El señor presidente, 1946 (*The President*, 1963); *Hombres de maíz*, 1949 (*Men of Maize*, 1975); *Viento fuerte*, 1950 (*The Cyclone*, 1967; better known as *Strong Wind*, 1968); *El papa verde*, 1954 (*The Green Pope*, 1971); *Los ojos de los enterrados*, 1960 (*The Eyes of the Interred*, 1973); *El alhajadito*, 1961 (*The Bejeweled Boy*, 1971); *Mulata de tal*, 1963 (*Mulata*, 1967); *Maladrón*, 1969.

Other literary forms

Although known primarily as a novelist, Miguel Ángel Asturias produced work in a variety of literary forms, including several volumes of short stories, a few plays, and two substantial collections of verse. In addition, Asturias published a number of sociological and journalistic works.

Most of Asturias' works, regardless of genre, are interrelated in one way or another. The short stories collected in *Week-end en Guatemala* (1956), for example, are an integral part of the political and artistic statement of the novels of the Banana Trilogy (*Strong Wind*, *The Green Pope*, and *The Eyes of the Interred*). Similarly, the play *Soluna* (1955; sun-moon) provides a helpful introduction to the novels *Men of Maize* and *Mulata* and presents an overview of primitive magic lacking in the novels. The complementarity between individual works has led many critics to regard Asturias' oeuvre as a unified whole and to analyze it on that basis.

Achievements

The works of Miguel Ángel Asturias are the expression of a mind intensely engaged with the essence of America. A virtuoso in the use of language and a master of many genres, Asturias focused his craft on a great variety of issues and themes. Two of these concerns had special importance for him, and a majority of his published works can be identified as explorations of those topics. His achievements were identical with his interests: the combination of Mayan cosmology with an aesthetic technique often called Magic Realism for the purpose of making a unique interpretation of modern Indian and mestizo reality, and a blend of social protest and art which attacked dictatorship and imperialism through the forum of world literature.

Asturias' concerns ran parallel with those of his generation. With the passing of Romanticism and *Modernismo* in the first decades of the twentieth century, Latin American writers began to seek inspiration in native rather than European themes. Realistic and Naturalistic traditions in the novel devel-

oped into an original "literature of the land" which sought to portray a dis-
tinctively American experience. Peasants, supposedly in harmony with their
surroundings but exploited by other elements of society, increasingly became
the subjects of important works of fiction. The American landscape in art
and literature changed from the idealized, idyllic paradise it had often been
in nineteenth century fiction and poetry to an unforgiving wilderness.

Asturias' literary use of Indian myth was the most elaborate application of
Native American lore in the history of Central American letters and represented a total break with European themes. The main works of his Mayan
Cycle, *Leyendas de Guatemala* (1930), *Men of Maize*, and *Mulata*, present a
kaleidoscopic view of Indo-America, redefining it with an often startling freedom of interpretation and with a philosophy of the novel which respects few
traditional preconceptions about plot.

The political fiction of Asturias is equally innovative and American. *The
President*, possibly the most significant and accomplished novel ever published
by a Guatemalan author, along with *Week-end en Guatemala* and the books
of his Banana Trilogy, form a literary parallel with Guatemala's liberal revolution of 1946-1953, confronting the misuse of economic, military, and political
power. Asturias strengthened the role of literature in national life by including
in his fiction, as part of its legitimate function, inquiry into the forces that
control Guatemala.

Biography

The son of a magistrate and a schoolteacher, Miguel Ángel Asturias belonged
to Ladino (non-Indian) upper-middle-class society. When he was about six
years old, the family moved to a farm of his paternal grandparents in Baja
Verapaz. The move to the country was caused by his father's political difficulties with the dictator of Guatemala, Manuel Estrada Cabrera, and the
family's three-year retreat away from the city was significant in Asturias'
development, introducing him to the effects of dictatorship as well as to the
countryside and its people.

When the political crisis was over, Asturias' family returned to Guatemala
City, and Asturias began his studies at the Instituto Nacional de Varones
(National Men's Institute) in 1912. Although student unrest crystallized into
isolated protests against Estrada Cabrera between 1910 and 1920, Asturias
was generally apolitical during his early school years. He participated in one
disorder, a window-breaking spree with political overtones, but otherwise he
refrained from attacks on the dictatorship until the formation of the Unionist
Party in 1919. He signed a student manifesto against the government in August
of that year, his first public stand against Estrada Cabrera. After the Unionist
victory, Asturias became a leader in the reform movement. He and his friends
founded a popular university dedicated to educating the lower classes, with
the ultimate goal of bringing the country into the twentieth century. Asturias'

concerns were expressed in the dissertation he wrote for his law degree, but he was not able to find a local outlet for his social conscience after graduation because political pressures made his departure from the country necessary. He traveled to England and then to France. In Paris, he studied anthropology at the Sorbonne, under Professor George Raynaud, and, with the help of another student, translated the Mayan documents *Popol Vuh* (c. 1550) and *Annals of the Cakchiquels* (sixteenth century) from Raynaud's French versions into Spanish. This apprenticeship to Indian literature and tradition had a profound effect on Asturias and deeply influenced his literary production. His first book, *Leyendas de Guatemala*, was the direct result of his work in Paris.

In 1933, Asturias returned to Guatemala, where he managed his radio news program "El diario del aire." He began his political career as a deputy to the National Congress in 1942, and, after the fall of Jorge Ubico in 1944, he was made cultural attaché to Mexico. It was there that he arranged to have his first novel, *The President*, published privately. In 1947, he was named cultural attaché to Buenos Aires, a position he held for six years. That period was one of intense literary activity during which he wrote two volumes of his Banana Trilogy as well as *Men of Maize*.

In June of 1954, Colonel Castillo Armas, with a small army and American support, invaded Guatemala and toppled the Arbenz government, of which Asturias was a firm supporter. Castillo Armas deprived Asturias of his citizenship, and the author took refuge in South America. He stayed for a time with Pablo Neruda in Chile, where he completed *Week-end en Guatemala*, a series of stories condemning the military intervention of 1954 and describing the causes and effects of the coup. Throughout his exile, Asturias wrote steadily and continued to publish. The avant-garde play *Soluna* appeared in 1955, and another play, *La audiencia de los confines* (border court), in 1957. The final volume of the Banana Trilogy appeared in 1960; subsequently, *The Bejeweled Boy* and *Mulata*, his most elaborate and complex fictions, complemented the nonpolitical cycle of his works. In 1966, he was awarded the Lenin Peace Prize in recognition of the anti-imperialist thrust of his oeuvre, and, on his birthday in 1967, he received the Nobel Prize for Literature. Asturias' diplomatic career resumed with a change of government in Guatemala, and he was Ambassador to France from 1966 to 1970. He continued to live and write in Europe until his death in Madrid on June 9, 1974.

Analysis

The writers who formed Guatemala's *generación del 20*—which included Miguel Ángel Asturias—were typical of numerous Latin American intellectuals of the early twentieth century who questioned the values of the past and the relevance of European traditions. The authors of that group were disheartened over the failures of Western civilization in World War I and had lost confidence in what had always been considered foreign superiority. Feeling that they had nowhere to turn except to themselves, Asturias and his contemporaries began to study factors which distinguished their peoples from the French and the Spanish.

The cultural pendulum swung away from the escapism of preceding decades toward a confrontation with the essence of America. Central American history was reappraised, and that revision of ideas was disseminated through the free popular university which Asturias helped to found. In attempting to come to terms with Guatemalan reality, Asturias and others also became aware of the importance of the Indians, who formed the excluded, oppressed majority in that nation's society. Not only was it believed that no truly nationalistic philosophy or literature could evolve until all aspects of the racial issue were considered, but it was also believed that any progress was impossible until the problem of the Indian had been resolved. Literary clubs and magazines were formed to express progressive Guatemalan aesthetics and to encourage the creation of a national folklore. Journals such as *Ensayos, Cultura, Tiempos nuevos*, and *Claridad*, which flourished briefly in the 1920's and on many of which Asturias collaborated, created a distinctive literary environment. Although Asturias left Guatemala shortly after his graduation from San Carlos and spent much of his life in Europe or South America, the formative issues of the *generación del 20*, the concerns with authenticity and social reform, were his persistent literary obsessions.

The heart of Asturias' Guatemalan perspective was the acceptance of Mayan theology as an intellectual superstructure for his art, and the effects of his study and translation of the *Popul Vuh* and the *Annals of the Cakchiquels* are clearly visible in his first collection of tales, *Leyendas de Guatemala*. Written between 1923 and 1928, the tales reflect a non-Western worldview of the Mayan documents on which Asturias was working at the time. These "legends" foreshadow the techniques that he employed in his Mayan Cycle—notably a surrealistic presentation of scenes that blends everyday reality with bizarre fantasy to create a Magic Realism. The lyricism of the author's language, his fondness of elaborate wordplay and Guatemalan puns, combined with his exposition of an Indian worldview and his use of an exotic tropical setting, produced the radical transformation of national aesthetics sought by the *generación del 20*. In French translation, with a preface by Paul Valéry, *Leyendas de Guatemala* won the Prix Sylla Monsegur.

Men of Maize, which appeared nineteen years after *Leyendas de Guatemala*, is a much longer and more complex vision of the Guatemalan people and landscape. Asturias' inspiration for the novel was, again, traditional Indian texts. There is no clearly defined plot in this second work of the Mayan Cycle; rather, Asturias presents a series of events and a gallery of characters united by themes that reflect a Mayan frame of reference. In the first part of the novel, Indians violently object to the commercial growing of corn, a crop which they consider sacred. Troops are sent to rescue the growers, and the military commander, Colonel Godoy, succeeds in quieting the revolt by having its leader poisoned. Subsequently, a curse is put on Godoy and his accomplices, all of whom die within seven years. The second section of the novel is concerned with María Tecún, a child of one of the unfortunate conspirators, who leaves her beggar husband, Goyo Yic. The latter spends most of his life looking for María; he does not find her until the final pages of the book. The third part of *Men of Maize* is the story of Nicho Aquino, an Indian mail carrier who also loses his wife; his search for her is fruitful in that, although he finds that she has been killed accidently, he meets a mysterious seer, Seven Year Stag, who teaches him the lost wisdom of the race.

Asturias has been criticized by a number of prominent Latin American scholars for the seemingly unrelated events of the novel's separate sections; however, themes such as metamorphosis and *nahualismo* (a belief that people have alter egos in certain plants or animals) give *Men of Maize* unity on a level other than plot.

Open to widely divergent interpretations, *Men of Maize* can be less than satisfying to the uninitiated. It is of some use, however, to compare this novel with other major pieces of the Mayan Cycle, *Soluna* and *Mulata*. The former concerns the personal crisis of Mauro, the owner of a country estate, whose wife, Ninica, has just left him. Mauro consults Soluna, a shaman, who gives him a mask to help him solve the problem. When Mauro falls asleep, the mask on his lap, he dreams an elaborate dream in which Ninica finally returns. When he wakes up, he finds that his wife's train has derailed, and she, having reassessed her relationship with her husband, has come back to stay. From the dreamlike action of the play and the unlikely details of its plot emerge the story of a modern, Westernized Guatemalan who, in the midst of a deep trauma, finds consolation in superstition. There is a similarity between Mauro's search for a resolution of his crisis in the irrational and Nicho Aquino's experience in which Seven Year Stag plays such an important role in *Men of Maize*.

Mulata is a surrealistic tale about Yumi, an Indian peasant who sells his wife to Tazol, the corn husk spirit, in order to achieve wealth and fulfillment. Yumi's near-fatal mistake is lusting after an apparently sensuous *mulata* (a mulatto woman) who, in fact, is hardly sexual and proves to have supernatural powers. After a series of strange adventures, Yumi succeeds in regaining his wife, who assists him in trying to avoid the vengeance of the *mulata*. Here, as in *Leyendas de Guatemala*, *Soluna*, and *Men of Maize*, it is perhaps easier to take all the grotesque, extraordinary episodes at face value, accepting them for what they are in themselves, like a series of painted scenes, rather than trying to find logical connections between events. Indeed, it is possible to argue that Asturias had no intention of making each individual portion of these works relate to other sections and that, collectively, the scenes convey better than could any logical, consecutive narrative the nonrational cosmos and the dense theological texture of the Indian mentality.

In the Political Cycle of his fiction, Asturias turns away from the totally Indian universe which dominates the Mayan Cycle and concentrates instead on ruthless dictatorship and unscrupulous imperialism in Central America. The shift of theme is accompanied by a change in structure and style. The political novels and stories have more recognizable and traditional plotting than *Men of Maize* and *Mulata*, although Asturias never abandons his lyrical, surrealistic style.

The President is one of Asturias' most polished works. This first novel is a carefully constructed critique of the dictatorship of Estrada Cabrera, and it vividly evokes the climate of fear and repression which permeated Guatemalan life in the early decades of the twentieth century. The novel's main character is Miguel Cara de Ángel, the president's right-hand man. He is told to kill General Canales, who has lost favor with the dictator; Cara de Ángel, however, takes pity on Canales and his daughter, Camila, and helps them to escape. The general dies before he has the chance to start his own revolution, and Camila, rejected by the rest of her family for fear of reprisal by the president, is saved by Cara de Ángel, who falls in love with her. As she hides from government spies in the back room of a tavern, she becomes ill with pneumonia. On the advice of an occultist, Cara de Ángel marries her "because only love can stand up to death." After her recovery, they consummate the marriage, and Camila becomes pregnant. Cara de Ángel is soon arrested, jailed, and never heard from again, and Camila gives birth to their son, Miguelito, whose name means "little Miguel."

Throughout the development of the plot, there is less political propaganda than vivid description of the brutal abuse of power. Asturias allows the actions of the president to speak for themselves. The book's message is enhanced by the fact that Camila and Cara de Ángel are not political characters. The former is an innocent victim of her father's unpopularity with the dictator, but she is not necessarily of the innocent masses, nor is Cara de Ángel a revolutionary hero who fights injustice. He is human and flawed, and his break with the president is caused by indiscretion, not by ideology. His actions toward Camila are motivated by love, not by his desire to save his people from the tyrant.

The President is one of the most successful and moving protests against dictatorship in the history of modern fiction. In addition, its craftsmanship contributed to making it one of the few Latin American novels published before 1950 to reach more than a local audience. *The President* also played no small role in elevating Asturias from the status of a talented Guatemalan author in exile to recipient of the Nobel Prize for Literature.

Between the publication of *Men of Maize* and *Mulata*, Asturias was preoccupied with four works of fiction that complement the position taken in *The*

President. The three novels of his Banana Trilogy, *Strong Wind, The Green Pope,* and *The Eyes of the Interred,* as well as the collection of stories, *Weekend en Guatemala,* are among the strongest statements in Central American literary history against the presence of the United States in that region. Far more polemical and political in tone than *The President,* these works provide a sensitive analysis of the problems associated with colonialism: economic exploitation of people and natural resources, the corruption of government officials who betray their nation to foreign interests, and military intervention.

The trilogy documents the history of the United Fruit Company and portrays both North Americans and Guatemalans whose lives are dominated by the company. *Strong Wind* provides a broad panorama of the extent of the United Fruit Company's influence as well as an introduction to the people who have been victimized by the fruit monopoly. An intensely drawn tropical environment, prominent in all of Asturias' fiction, is the setting for the story of Lester Mead, a planter and member of the corporation. Mead lives and works incognito in the midst of the exploited Guatemalans in order to bring about change from within the system. His struggles form the principal line of action around which Asturias depicts the extensive corruption brought about by the United Fruit Company.

The Green Pope, which appeared four years later, follows a similar pattern of presenting history and characterization with a clearly political purpose. The first part of the novel concentrates on a detailed accounting of the United Fruit Company's development in the country, while the second continues the train of events from *Strong Wind. The Green Pope* is essentially the saga of George Maker Thompson, another North American, who, in alliance with the Lucero family, eventually becomes the major stockholder in the company and its president. As in *Strong Wind,* the machinations of the United Fruit Company are exposed and severely criticized.

The final work of the trilogy, *The Eyes of the Interred,* finished while Asturias was in exile, completes the dream of reform begun in the other works and traces the efforts of Octavio Sansor to form a union and establish worker control over the company. Although he first plans a revolution and a violent end to dictatorship and foreign economic control, Sansor ultimately chooses nonviolence, and his victory is the organization of the workers' syndicate, a general strike, the resignation of the president, and company concessions to the union.

Asturias' interests went far beyond political protest and literary re-creation of the Mayan spirit, but his most significant vision of Central America can be found in the books of those two cycles. Most of his later works do not fit easily into the two principal types of fiction already discussed. *The Bejeweled Boy,* for example, which explores the inner world of a child, is interesting from a psychological and technical point of view, but it does not create the kind of thematic drama which characterizes his earlier writings. His other plays, fiction, and poetry, as well as the previously unpublished material beginning to appear posthumously from the Fons Asturias in Paris, add depth and complexity to a body of writing which has yet to be fully viewed and understood. It is possible that, as additional works are published, critics will find more meaningful interpretations of his earlier books and redefine the borders of the "cycles."

By the time Asturias died in 1974, the political dreams of Guatemala's *generación del 20* had not come true. The new Guatemala which might have replaced that of Estrada Cabrera and Ubico fell to Castillo Armas and another series of strongmen. In literature, however, Asturias and his contemporaries such as Flavio Herrera, David Vela, and Rafael Arévalo Martínez brought their country into the mainstream of Latin American letters. Epaminondas Quintana has remarked that the award of the Nobel Prize to his friend Asturias amounted to worldwide recognition not only of the writer himself but also of his generation and its ideals. To many Guatemalans, this is a significant part of Asturias' achievement.

Major publications other than long fiction

SHORT FICTION: *Leyendas de Guatemala*, 1930; *Week-end en Guatemala*, 1956; *El espejo de Lida Sal*, 1967; *Novelas y cuentos de juventud*, 1971; *Viernes de dolores*, 1972.

PLAYS: *Soluna*, 1955; *La audiencia de los confines*, 1957; *Teatro*, 1964.

POETRY: *Sien de alondra*, 1949; *Clarivigilia primaveral*, 1965.

NONFICTION: *Sociología guatemalteca: El problema social del indio*, 1923 (*Guatemalan Sociology*, 1977); *La arquitectura de la vida nueva*, 1928; *Rumania: Su nueva imagen*, 1964; *Latinoamérica y otros ensayos*, 1968; *Tres de cuatro soles*, 1977.

MISCELLANEOUS: *Obras completas*, 1967 (3 volumes).

Bibliography

Anderson-Imbert, Enrique. *Spanish American Literature: A History*, 1963.
Bellini, Giuseppe. *La narrativa de Miguel Ángel Asturias*, 1969.
Callan, Richard J. *Fecundity in Two Novels of Miguel Ángel Asturias*, 1965.
_____ . *Miguel Ángel Asturias*, 1972.
Giacomán, Helmy, ed. *Homenaje a Miguel Ángel Asturias*, 1971.
Guibert, Rita. *Seven Voices*, 1973.
Menton, Seymour. *Historia crítica de la novela guatemalteca*, 1960.
Nasso, Christine. "Miguel Ángel Asturias," in *Contemporary Authors, Permanent Series*. II (1978), pp. 32-33.
Quintana, Epaminondas. *Historia de la generación de 1920-Guatemala*, 1971.

William L. Felker

HONORÉ DE BALZAC

Born: Tours, France; May 20, 1799
Died: Paris, France; August 18, 1850

Principal long fiction

La Comédie humaine, 1829-1848 (17 volumes; *The Comedy of Human Life*, 1885-1893, 1896 [40 volumes]; also as *The Human Comedy*, 1895-1896, 1911 [53 volumes]; includes all titles listed below); *Les Chouans*, 1829 (*The Chouans*); *Physiologie du mariage*, 1829 (*The Physiology of Marriage*); *Gobseck*, 1830 (English translation); *La Maison du chat-qui-pelote*, 1830, 1869 (*At the Sign of the Cat and Racket*); *Le Chef-d'oeuvre inconnu*, 1831 (*The Unknown Masterpiece*); *La Peau de chagrin*, 1831 (*The Wild Ass's Skin*; also as *The Fatal Skin*); *Sarrasine*, 1831 (English translation); *Le Curé de Tours*, 1832 (*The Vicar of Tours*); *Louis Lambert*, 1832 (English translation); *Maître Cornélius*, 1832 (English translation); *La Femme de trente ans*, 1832-1842 (includes *Premières fautes*, 1832, 1842; *Souffrances inconnues*, 1834-1835; *À trente ans*, 1832, 1842; *Le Doigt de Dieu*, 1832, 1834-1835, 1842; *Les Deux Rencontres*, 1832, 1834-1835, 1842; *La Vieillesse d'une mère coupable*, 1832, 1842); *Eugénie Grandet*, 1833 (English translation, 1859); *La Recherche de l'absolu*, 1834 (*Balthazar: Or, Science and Love*, 1859; also as *The Quest of the Absolute*); *Histoire des treize*, 1834-1835 (*History of the Thirteen*; also as *The Thirteen*; includes *Ferragus, chef des dévorants*, 1834 [*Ferragus, Chief of the Devorants*; also as *The Mystery of the Rue Solymane*]; *La Duchesse de Langeais*, 1834 [*The Duchesse de Langeais*]; *La Fille aux yeux d'or*, 1834-1835 [*The Girl with the Golden Eyes*]); *Melmoth réconcilié*, 1835 (*Melmoth Reconciled*); *Le Père Goriot*, 1835 (*Daddy Goriot*, 1860; also as *Père Goriot*); *Le Lys dans la vallée*, 1836 (*The Lily in the Valley*); *Histoire de la grandeur et de la décadence de César Birotteau*, 1837 (*History of the Grandeur and Downfall of César Birotteau*, 1860; also as *The Rise and Fall of César Birotteau*); *Illusions perdues*, 1837-1843 (*Lost Illusions*); *Splendeurs et misères des courtisanes*, 1838-1847, 1869 (*The Splendors and Miseries of Courtesans*; includes *Comment aiment les filles*, 1838-1844; *À combien l'amour revient aux vieillards*, 1844; *Où mènent les mauvais chemins*, 1846; *La Dernière Incarnation de Vautrin*, 1847); *Pierrette*, 1840 (English translation); *Le Curé de village*, 1841 (*The Country Parson*); *Mémoires de deux jeunes mariées*, 1842 (*The Two Young Brides*); *Une Ténébreuse Affaire*, 1842 (*The Gondreville Mystery*); *Ursule Mirouët*, 1842 (English translation); *La Cousine Bette*, 1846 (*Cousin Bette*); *Le Cousin Pons*, 1847 (*Cousin Pons*, 1880).

Other literary forms

In addition to his fiction, Honoré de Balzac wrote several plays, including *Cromwell* (1925; written 1819-1820), *Vautrin* (1840; English translation, 1901), and *Le Faiseur*, also known as *Mercadet* (first performed posthumously in 1851; English translation, 1901), but he was not a playwright and generally devoted time to the theater only when he felt that there was a good profit to be made with little effort. Likewise, many of the articles and essays that Balzac wrote between 1825 and 1834, published in such journals as *Le Voleur*, *La Mode*, *La Caricature*, *La Silhouette*, and *La Revue de Paris*, were composed in order to acquire ready money. Balzac's letters to the Polish baroness Evelina Hanska, to his family, and to Madame Zulma Carraud were published after the novelist's death.

Achievements

The Human Comedy, Balzac's masterwork, contains about seventy novels beyond those listed above, the bulk of which were written between 1830 and 1847. Before 1829, Balzac wrote under various pseudonyms—notably "Lord R'Hoone" and "Horace de Saint Aubin"—and frequently composed novels in collaboration with other writers. These twenty or so early volumes, which include *Sténie: Ou, Les Erreurs philosophiques* (1936; Sténie: or, philosophical errors), *Falturne* (1950), *Le Centenaire: Ou, Les Deux Beringheld* (1822; *The Centenarian: Or, The Two Beringhelds*, 1976), and *La Dernière Fée* (1823; the last fairy), were later renounced by Balzac, and rightly so, for they were written in haste and were obvious attempts to exploit the current taste for Gothic melodrama and romantic adventures.

At the age of thirty, Balzac resolved to become a great French writer. At first, he believed that he could accomplish this goal by emulating the Scottish writer Sir Walter Scott, whose historical novels were highly esteemed in France during the first half of the nineteenth century. Like Scott, Balzac would be a historian of social, psychological, and political life. Later, however, as Balzac explains in his preface to *The Human Comedy*, this idea was modified. Balzac finally saw his true and original role to be that of "the secretary of society" rather than that of a social historian; that is, instead of bringing the past to life, as Scott had done, Balzac chose to transcribe the life around him into fiction. In many ways, the author of *The Human Comedy* is faithful to this role, drawing a picture of French society at all levels from roughly 1815 until the end of his writing career in 1848. In his novels, Balzac reveals the driving passions and needs of a wide range of individuals in various social positions: noblemen and aristocratic ladies; politicians, bankers, businessmen, and moneylenders; scientists, doctors, and priests; lawyers, policemen, and criminals; musicians, painters, sculptors, and writers. This picture of society delineates not only ambitious members of the bourgeoisie and proud aristocrats but also the environments in which they live and work, including the luxurious, exhilarating, and cutthroat life of Paris and the comparatively dull and inactive existence of small provincial French towns. The two thousand characters whom Balzac depicts in *The Human Comedy* are not, however, mere social types. On the contrary, Balzac's protagonists are, in general, strongly individualistic, some of them to the point of eccentricity.

Each novel of *The Human Comedy* contains a single story that may be read and appreciated for itself; at the same time, each story is linked to the whole. A protagonist encountered in one novel might very well appear again, like an old acquaintance, within the context of another novel and possibly a very different plot. The small number of characters who travel from one novel to another give unity to Balzac's works and at the same time convey the impression that the fictional world described in *The Human Comedy* is alive and infinite in scope.

With regard to tone, Balzac's plots embrace a wide range of attitudes: tragically sad or comically ironic; highly idealistic, fantastic, or romantic. The novelist, however, is judged to have excelled particularly as a realist in his candid portrayal of the tremendous will-to-power of human nature and of the influence of money upon social behavior.

In Balzac's works, many of the characteristic impulses of the nineteenth century coincided and reinforced one another. Balzac's legendary energy, his enormous, hubristic ambition, his tireless interest in the world, and his sheer appetite for experience—all of these elements worked together to produce a massive tapestry of an entire society, unmatched in scope and detail before or since the author's time.

Biography

Honoré Balzac was born in Tours, France, on May 20, 1799, of bourgeois parents. He was to acquire the predicate of nobility—the name by which he is known today—when, in 1831, in tribute to his official commitment to embark upon the writing of *The Human Comedy*, he dubbed himself Honoré *de* Balzac. This change of name is symptomatic of Balzac's lifelong craving to be an aristocrat and to enjoy the deep respect and the want-for-nothing life-style which went with that status.

The eldest of four children, Balzac was treated very coldly by his parents, who entrusted him to the care of a wet nurse for four years, then sent him to board with a family of strangers for two years, and finally had him attend for seven years a boarding school in Vendôme. Balzac's childhood years were loveless and painful, which probably encouraged him to turn inward toward dreams and fantasies. By 1816, Balzac had finished his studies in Vendôme, albeit with far less than a brilliant record, and was sent off to Paris to study jurisprudence, his mother ordering him to "shape up" and work very hard. At the age of twenty, however, Balzac declared to his family his surprising intention to become a writer, not a lawyer. When his parents skeptically agreed to his wishes, Balzac was permitted to live in Paris for two years, where he was set up in a poorly furnished apartment and was given a deliberately insufficient allowance, which was intended to demonstrate to this wayward son the harsh economic facts of life.

Between 1819 and 1829, Balzac was forced to earn a living from writing, a situation that led him to compromise his literary genius for money; when this endeavor oved inadequate, he was not too proud to undertake other occupations. In an effort to ensure his freedom to write, Balzac became a bookseller, then a printer, then a journalist. All of these enterprises, however, ultimately failed. His most notorious business venture occurred in 1838, when he speculated on Sardinian silver mines. Everything Balzac tried to do as a businessman only drove him deeper into debt, a state of affairs that he often transposed to the realm of his fiction; yet even when Balzac was at the mercy of creditors and in danger of being arrested, he remained, at bottom, optimistic. His new novel would rescue him, at least temporarily, from financial embarrassment, or his current business venture would surely make him wealthy, or, best of all, an aristocratic lady—and there was nearly always a prospect— would soon become his wife and give him not only her love but also her fortune. Nearly all of the women who mattered to Balzac were, in fact, noble, from Madame Laure de Berny, who sacrificed both her morals and her money to help the budding genius to survive, to Madame Evelina Hanska, the Polish baroness who began by writing anonymous letters of admiration to the well-known author and eventually, after her husband's death and her daughter's marriage, consented to become Balzac's wife.

It is an irony which suitably parallels that of the fictional world portrayed in *The Human Comedy* that Balzac's marriage to this woman of his dreams occurred only five months before his death. Balzac died from what one may term outright exhaustion on August 18, 1850.

Analysis

There are three themes in Honoré de Balzac's fiction that can be seen as reflections of the novelist's personality. First, there is the theme of madness or monomania; second, the large role given to money; and third, the recurrent search of Balzac's characters for love and success. The madmen of *The Human Comedy* include some of Balzac's most original and memorable characters. These figures are generally obsessed by an idea which they try to make into a reality and for which they sacrifice everything. Although the individual obsessions of these protagonists vary, Frenhofer, the painter in *The Unknown Masterpiece*, Grandet, the miser in *Eugénie Grandet*, and Claës, the scientist in *The Quest of the Absolute* are nevertheless shadows of Balzac, the author, who expresses through them his own obsession: the painstaking composition of *The Human Comedy*. Balzac wrote for hours, weeks, and months on end to prove his genius to the world. Everything was sacrificed for his literary task, including a comfortable lodging, clothes, and the most insignificant of worldly amusements.

The monomaniacs of Balzac's creation are particularly interesting figures.

They are intelligent and possess glorious ideas, which, if they initially seem eccentric, at the same time denote genius. Their bold determination to accomplish all they have set out to do is, however, admirable only to a point. Balzac always shows that the obsessions of his monomaniacs dehumanize them. When, for example, Claës in *The Quest of the Absolute* sacrifices the sustenance of his family in order to continue financing his experiments, Balzac pushes his protagonist's passion to an extreme. The manias of Balzac's characters slowly annihilate everything around them until, in the end, these figures appear so blinded by their passion that they are completely enslaved by it. The tragic depiction of Balzac's monomaniacs is undoubtedly one of the cornerstones of *The Human Comedy*. These characters, who first command one's admiration, then appeal to one's sympathy, and finally elicit one's scorn, cause one to ponder with Balzac the force of human thought and willpower. Moreover, by means of his monomaniacs, Balzac expresses his own obsession and his fear of it.

Another important theme of *The Human Comedy* is money, which, in Balzac's fictional world, dominates all other values. In a sense, Balzac's attitude toward money is ambivalent. On the one hand, he often shows nostalgia for the neoclassical age, when, under the monarchy, a member of the nobility was assured a life of ease and intellectual grandeur. On the other hand, however, Balzac accepts and objectively portrays the bourgeois society of his day. It is a society whose wheels are oiled by money, but many of Balzac's heroes feel optimistically that, by means of their intelligence, they can succeed in conquering it. Apparently, Balzac himself believed that the appearance of money was enough to command respect and receive social acceptance. Sometimes when his characters wear expensive-looking clothes and ride about in fancy carriages, they are, in fact, engaged in a carefully calculated masquerade to fool society by using its own superficial code against it. Of course, some of Balzac's protagonists succeed in this way, but most of them fail—paralleling the novelist's career, in which successes were few and financial failures many. Balzac's most pointed criticism of the role of money in society is not, however, that it is the entry ticket to social success. In such novels as *Père Goriot* and *Eugénie Grandet*, Balzac portrays money in its most diabolical role, as a corrupter of the noblest of human feelings, love.

Balzac depicts two kinds of love in his novels. Ideal love is the quest of many protagonists of *The Human Comedy*, who suffer in its absence and fail to realize its glorious promise. Desirable women in Balzac's fiction are often much older than their aspiring lovers, leading biographers to speculate about Balzac's own mother's indifference toward him and about the novelist's first amorous adventure with Madame de Berny, who—when Balzac met her at the age of twenty-two—was twenty-two years older than he. Aristocratic and maternal women such as Madame de Mortsauf in *The Lily in the Valley* represent a supreme love the likes of which cannot be matched. The very ideal quality of this love, however, is perhaps what leads to its impossibility. Although Balzac's characters glimpse the perfect love object time and time again, the latter generally remains out of reach because of societal or financial constraints. In contrast, love, as Balzac portrays it in his fictional society, is a dangerous counterfeit. Coquettish females of *The Human Comedy*, such as Antoinette de Langeais in *The Duchess de Langeais* (a part of *The Thirteen*), provoke innocent gentlemen to fall in love with them only to cultivate their own egos. For the boldest male protagonists of *The Human Comedy*, love is like money, something to be used to advance oneself in society. Rastignac in *Père Goriot* and Raphaël de Valentin in *The Wild Ass's Skin*, for example, make the calculated decision to fall in love, one with a wealthy banker's wife and the other with an aristocratic lady. Family love and devotion are also shams, falling into insignificance when confronted by personal ambition and money.

Balzac classified the novels of *The Human Comedy* into three large areas: "Studies of Social Manners," "Philosophical Studies," and "Analytical Studies." *The Wild Ass's Skin*, published in 1831, was placed into the category "Philosophical Studies," probably because of its fantastic theme, the possession of a magic skin. Like many of Balzac's best novels, however, *The Wild Ass's Skin* is actually a mixture of cold reality and fantastic illusion. The hero of the novel, Raphaël de Valentin, a downtrodden genius whom society persistently ignores, is clearly a figure with whom the novelist could identify. Balzac's protagonist has written a philosophical treatise entitled "Théorie de la volonté" ("Theory of the Will"), a work whose exact contents are never revealed but whose significance for Balzac and for *The Human Comedy* is evident. Like his hero, Valentin, Balzac is engaged in an analysis of man's will. Valentin may appear to be more theoretical than the novelist, but both Balzac and his protagonist find the power of ideas at work in the mind to be a fascinating and dangerous study. One suspects that Valentin is actually an image of Balzac's own projected success as well as the foreboding prototype of his failure.

The destiny of Raphaël de Valentin follows a curve from failure to success and back to failure again. At the beginning of the book, he thinks seriously about committing suicide for two reasons. First, he has suffered very deeply in his love for a beautiful but heartless coquette named Foedora. Second, Valentin is destitute. Even though his "Theory" has finally been completed— a lifework that ought to be acknowledged as striking proof of his genius— societal acclaim is still denied him. When Balzac later explains in his epilogue to the novel that Foedora is actually a symbol of society, one understands that her indifference to Valentin includes not only a condemnation of a would-be lover but also a cruel underestimation of his intelligence, the hero's very *raison d'être*. The initial tragedy of Valentin is realistically portrayed as a battle between a sensitive romantic young man and Parisian society.

In the next phase of Valentin's destiny, however, one sees an abrupt transformation which at first appears to project Balzac's hero to the heights of success. Valentin acquires from a mysterious antiquarian a wild ass's skin. Because, as in a fairy tale, the magic skin grants its owner's every wish, Valentin need no longer be poor. Indeed, it is society's turn to court him! Now the Parisian society that Valentin previously hoped to please is depicted as thoroughly repulsive and morally corrupt. As a sign of Valentin's rejection of it, one of his wishes is that he may forget Foedora, the novel's symbol of society. One may find in Valentin's change of attitude toward society the novelist's own admission to himself that what he ultimately seeks—general recognition of his genius as a writer—simply does not exist in a world ruled by personal vanity and money. Now that Foedora has been forgotten, she is replaced in Valentin's heart by Pauline, a poor, innocent young girl who has always shown him true love and devotion.

This "happy ending" is short-lived, however. In the final phase of Valentin's destiny, Balzac returns to the philosophical theme of man's will. The wild ass's skin that Valentin possesses is not a blessing after all, but a curse. After each wish that it grants to its owner, the skin shrinks in dimension, its dwindling size quickly becoming a horrifying picture of the diminishing length of Valentin's life.

It is interesting to correlate this tragic depiction of Balzac's hero with the situation of the novelist himself. When Balzac wrote *The Wild Ass's Skin* in 1831, he was already aware that his enormous writing task would take him away from the world of reality and cause him to become a more firmly established inhabitant of his fictional world. After the protagonist of *The Wild Ass's Skin* has unmasked society, he attempts to withdraw from it. Perhaps, pen in hand, wearing his monk's cloak, Balzac, too, may have thought that he could escape to the fictional realm of his imagination. Eventually, however, reality always intervened and subjugated the writer to its practical demands. Hence, Balzac gives that part of himself which repudiates money and all those who worship it a kind of allowance analogous to money. Valentin must make fewer and fewer wishes and finally tries not to express any desires at all, simply in order to continue living.

In this complex novel, Balzac transposes into fiction his own misery, his maddening drive to succeed, his dreams and love for life, while giving the reader a survey of the themes that will permeate many novels of *The Human Comedy*: money, unrealized love, the drive to succeed, and madness.

Balzac finished writing *The Vicar of Tours* in April, 1832. In this short novel, Balzac, like Gustave Flaubert in his famous short story "Un Coeur simple" ("A Simple Heart"), relates a story that superficially seems unworthy of mention. Balzac's hero, Birotteau, like Flaubert's heroine, Félicité, is rather simpleminded and lives an uneventful life. True to the nature of Balzac's most memorable heroes, however, Birotteau is quite different from Félicité in that, despite his lack of intelligence, he is ambitious. Furthermore, he is naïvely happy. Balzac alternately pities and ridicules his provincial priest, whose passion it is to possess the beautiful apartment of his colleague, Chapeloud. While pointing out that a desire for material wealth is not seemly for a priest, Balzac ironically pardons his hero, who is, after all, only human and whose ambition, as ambitions go, can only be termed petty.

When Birotteau's ambition is fulfilled upon the death of Chapeloud, the apartment becomes the subject of a war of wills, involving not only Birotteau's spinster landlady, Mademoiselle Gamard, but eventually the whole town of Tours. Indeed, a political career in the highest echelons of the French government and the important advancement of a priest within the Catholic Church both end up having, in some way, a relationship to what begins as Birotteau's "insignificant" passion.

In some ways, Birotteau is the opposite of the typical Balzacian monomaniac. Happy to let everything be handled by his friends and incapable of understanding what is going on, he watches the battle rage around him. Birotteau would not purposely hurt a fly, and he does not have an inkling of why he is being attacked.

As in many novels of *The Human Comedy*, an important turn in the plot of *The Vicar of Tours* hinges upon a legal document, in this case the apartment lease. Balzac's years as a law student often served him well, and he used his knowledge of the law in composing many of his plots. Essentially missing from this novel is one of Balzac's major themes, money. Nevertheless, the vanity of the characters in *The Vicar of Tours* and their drive for personal success and power are keenly developed subjects of satire and, at the same time, very realistic studies of human psychology and social behavior. Balzac classed *The Vicar of Tours* under the heading "Scenes of Provincial Life," a subcategory of "Studies of Social Manners"—where the largest number of novels in *The Human Comedy* can be found.

Approximately three months after completing *The Vicar of Tours*, in July, 1832, Balzac finished *Louis Lambert*. This novel was eventually included with *The Wild Ass's Skin* and eighteen other novels in the category "Philosophical Studies," but its relationship to Balzac's "Studies of Social Manners" is strengthened through the device of recurring characters. One of the minor figures of *The Vicar of Tours* is an old woman, Mademoiselle Salomon de Villenoix, who befriends Birotteau and shows him a great deal of compassion. In *Louis Lambert*, the same woman plays a more important role, as Balzac describes Mademoiselle de Villenoix in her youth, when she was the ideal love object of Louis Lambert, the principal character of the novel.

The parallels between *The Wild Ass's Skin* and *Louis Lambert* are quite interesting. Like Raphaël de Valentin, Louis Lambert is a genius who composes a philosophical work on the will; the title of his work, "Traité de la volonté" ("Treatise on the Will"), is virtually identical with Valentin's. Valentin and Lambert succeed in finding an ideal woman whose name is Pauline: Pauline de Villenoix in *Louis Lambert* and Pauline de Witschnau in *The Wild Ass's Skin*. Finally, the tragedy of both genius-heroes lies in the fact that they go mad. The Paulines of the two novels react to the inexplicable madness of the men they love by devoting themselves totally to them, somewhat like nurses or angels of mercy.

The similarities between *Louis Lambert* and *The Wild Ass's Skin* give one a fairly clear idea of what must have been Balzac's attitude toward himself. The novelist instills in his heroes two great passions that are undoubtedly reflections of his own drives: to become a recognized genius and to be loved. In these two novels, Balzac appears to demonstrate his belief that love and genius cannot coexist and that when one attempts to blend them, they annihilate each other. In this sense, the madness that overcomes Balzac's protagonists represents a double failure. Both Lambert and Valentin fall short of attaining ideal love and also fail to develop the potential of their genius.

It is nevertheless true that Balzac shows the passions of Louis Lambert for love and for recognition of his genius somewhat differently from the way he portrays these passions in his earlier novel. In *Louis Lambert*, the novelist seems to indicate a preference for one of the two goals when he emphasizes Lambert's genius. From the beginning of the novel, Lambert is seen through the eyes of an admiring narrator who relates in retrospect the bitter experiences of school days shared with Balzac's genius-hero. In detailing these experiences, Balzac transposes into fiction many of his own memories of the lonely years spent as a boarder at the Collège de Vendôme. Both the narrator and Lambert are neglected by their parents, ostracized by their peers, punished by their teachers, and forbidden—as in a prison—to enjoy even the slightest amusement. The narrator admits to being inferior to Lambert, whose genius he sensed when they were in school together and whose insights, although they now can be only half-remembered, had the power of truth.

At the end of the novel, Balzac intensifies sympathy for the plight of his genius-hero-gone-mad by reproducing a series of philosophical fragments which, because they are written down by Lambert's loving companion, Pauline, are only sketchy transcriptions of his actual thoughts. It is not important that these fragments appear puzzling and in some cases absurd: Like the incomplete recollections of the narrator, they are powerfully evocative *because* they are fragmentary, tantalizingly so, suggestive of what the world lost with the genius of Louis Lambert.

Before the publication of *Eugénie Grandet* in 1833, Balzac had continued to experiment in his novels with the theme of madness. In addition to *Louis Lambert*, Balzac had written other "Philosophical Studies" between 1830 and 1832 which expand on this theme, including *The Unknown Masterpiece* and *Maître Cornélius*. In *The Unknown Masterpiece*, Balzac portrayed a painter, Frenhofer, whose madness manifests itself in his increasing inability to transpose the idealized feminine figure he imagines to a canvas. The hero of *Maître Cornélius* suffers from an insidious malady. When he sleepwalks, his unconscious self steals the money which, in reality, he is supposed to guard.

In *Eugénie Grandet*, however, the theme of madness reaches a turning point. Balzac's protagonist, Old Grandet, like Maître Cornélius, is a miser, but what distinguishes him from the latter is that his mania does not indicate total sickness or madness. Grandet's passion does not seem to debilitate him in any way. On the contrary, it is his *raison d'être* and is willfully and, one may even say, intellectually directed. Grandet, one of the most fascinating characters of *The Human Comedy*, is a full-blown monomaniac. What makes him so interesting is that he is not one-dimensional. Although Grandet's obsessive drive for money remains constant throughout the novel, he is not always seen in the same light. In relations with his wife, his cook, his small-town neighbors, and especially his daughter, Eugénie, Grandet sparks off a variety of reactions to his miserly behavior. At times, he is admired and feared for his sharp intelligence. At other times, he is condemned for his lack of understanding and unyielding ruthlessness.

Yet manifestations of Grandet's monomania do not, by themselves, dominate the novel. Rather, Grandet's avarice competes for importance with another, complementary plot: the awakening of Grandet's daughter to love. Indeed, in *Eugénie Grandet*, the three subjects which have been identified as key themes in Balzac's fiction—madness, money, and the search for love—converge. Grandet's obsession with money comes into conflict with Eugénie's equally strong impulse to love. While her father's nature is to hoard money even if it means that his family must be destitute, Eugénie finds in giving away all of her money to her beloved cousin, Charles, a supreme expression of love.

Balzac pits his young heroine against other adversaries as well: provincial opportunism, social morality, and Charles's ambitions. Using his innocent and naïve heroine as a foil, Balzac reveals the crass motives of provincial society, contrasting Eugénie's exceptional, giving nature with the self-interest of others who, like Eugénie's father, are motivated primarily by money. Balzac placed *Eugénie Grandet* into the subcategory of *The Human Comedy* entitled "Scenes of Provincial Life."

Published in 1835, *Père Goriot*, given its Parisian locale, could easily have been placed into the category of *The Human Comedy* called "Scenes of Parisian Life." Balzac finally classified it, however, among his "Scenes of Private Life," which is an equally suitable designation for the novel. *Père Goriot* is a pivotal novel of *The Human Comedy* in several ways. First, with respect to Balzac's trademark, the use of recurring characters, nearly all the characters in this novel, whether their roles are large or small, can be found somewhere else in Balzac's opus, with the exception of Goriot himself. Some characters have already been seen in works published before 1835; others will be developed in subsequent novels. Eugène de Rastignac, the young hero of *Père Goriot*, for example, has appeared briefly as a friend of Raphaël de Valentin in *The Wild Ass's Skin*. Similarly, Goriot's older daughter, Anasthasie, has already been portrayed in a short novel, *Gobseck*, published in 1830. The criminal Jacques Collin, alias Vautrin, who makes his debut in *Père Goriot*, will be given prominent roles in such later works as *Lost Illusions* and *The Splendors and Miseries of Courtesans*.

Balzac successfully interweaves three different plots in *Père Goriot*, their relationship being that the principal protagonists of all three live in the same Parisian boardinghouse, La Maison Vauquer. Eugène de Rastignac is an innocent provincial young man, new to Parisian manners but eager to learn. In a sense, Rastignac takes up the same crusade as did Raphël de Valentin in *The Wild Ass's Skin*, in that he directs all of his efforts toward "conquering" society—which means that, like Valentin, he strives to earn social acceptance and esteem. One notes, however, that Balzac does not make Rastignac a writer, like Valentin. Rather, shadowing another part of Balzac's own past, the young hero of *Père Goriot* is a poor law student.

Old Goriot himself is another inhabitant of La Maison Vauquer. He is a Balzacian monomaniac, a hero whose "madness" is self-willed and consciously directed. Goriot is not, however, another copy of Balzac's miser, Grandet; rather, Balzac opposes these two figures. Goriot is not a miser; he does not hoard money. On the contrary, he spends it on his two daughters, Anasthasie and Delphine. Whereas Grandet causes his family to live like paupers in order to continue amassing money, Goriot willingly strips himself of his means of sustenance in order to continue giving money to his daughters. Balzac's intent in portraying Goriot may have been to examine the power of money in a situation which contrasts directly with that of his miser, Grandet. Certainly, Balzac never found a more intense formula for tragedy than when he created his monomaniac, Goriot, who attempts to link money and love.

The third major plot of *Père Goriot* centers upon another inhabitant of La Maison Vauquer, Vautrin, who—unbeknown to the other boarders of Madame Vauquer's establishment—is an escaped convict wanted by the police. Vautrin's view of society is in absolute opposition to that of Rastignac; whereas the young man attempts to court social favor, Vautrin denounces everything to do with the social order, calling it a *bourbier*, or mudhole. Intelligent and cynical, Vautrin advocates a different sort of social conquest, namely, bold defiance and outright rebellion.

Unlike most of the preceding novels in *The Human Comedy*, *Père Goriot* is a novel with multiple heroes and multiple plots. Balzac offers the reader a fresco of social manners through characters who represent very different classes of society, from the aristocrat and the bourgeois to the criminal *révolté*. Balzac's technique of portraying his protagonists from various contrasting angles—seen in *The Vicar of Tours* and in *Eugénie Grandet*—is used much more extensively in *Père Goriot*. Goriot, Goriot's daughters, Rastignac, Vautrin, and other characters as well are alternately judged to be admirable, honest, powerful, and imperfect, deceitful, helpless. Goriot, in particular, is delineated by means of a kaleidoscope of contrary impressions. He loves his daughters, but he also hates them. His love is fatherly and not so fatherly. He is both self-sacrificing and self-interested. In death, he curses his daughters and pardons them in the same breath. Clearly, in *Père Goriot*, Balzac reached maturity as a novelist.

Cousin Bette was published rather late in Balzac's career, in 1846, and was placed, along with a complementary work entitled *Cousin Pons*, among the "Scenes of Parisian Life." In the ten years between the publication of *Père Goriot* and that of *Cousin Bette*, Balzac wrote approximately forty-five other novels, many of which continued to develop the three major themes in his fiction—madness, money, and the search for love and success.

It is interesting to see all three themes once again interwoven in *Cousin Bette*, albeit in a strikingly different manner. In one of the novel's subplots, a new type of monomania is depicted in Baron Hulot d'Evry, who is driven repeatedly to commit adultery although it is an embarrassment to himself, his wife, and his family. Balzac hints at Hulot's hidden motivation when he describes his protagonist's wife, Adeline, as a martyr figure, a religious zealot, and a model of propriety.

Elisabeth Fischer—called "Cousin Bette"—is aware that the Hulot family, headed by Adeline, receives her only out of family duty and that, as a poor relation, she is neither loved nor esteemed by them. Even though she realizes that the apparent good fortune and happiness of the Hulot family are a carefully contrived sham, Bette is jealous of her cousin Adeline for having always been prettier, wealthier, and more successful than she. Cousin Bette's vengeance against the Hulot family, which is the principal plot of the novel, incorporates all three of the major themes of Balzac's fiction. Because Cousin Bette has no money, no success, and no love, her maddened drive for vengeance is unleashed. Her desire for revenge becomes a mania, and she is soon driven to the point where there is absolutely no limit to what she will do to ruin her cousin's life, including finding new females to entice both the Baron and Adeline's proposed son-in-law, Steinbock.

As though to intensify the diabolical power of Cousin Bette, Balzac adds to it the equally unscrupulous machinations of his heroine's pretty neighbor, Valérie Marneffe. Valérie helps Bette carry out her revenge against the Hulot family, and Bette, in return, aids her neighbor in an enterprise to extract money from her many male admirers. Valérie, a beautiful and ambitious middle-class woman, discovers that she can find financial success by seducing men and making them pay for her love. It is interesting that when Valérie is given the chance to run away to South America with an exotic Brazilian nobleman who loves her sincerely, she refuses in order to continue the business of her lucrative and ego-building seductions. In *Cousin Bette*, the possibility of an ideal love, like that glimpsed in earlier novels such as *The Wild Ass's Skin* and *Louis Lambert*, is seen as utterly impossible.

In *Cousin Bette*, Balzac makes a mockery not only of love but also of monomania. Through a gross exaggeration, this eccentric passion no longer characterizes a single figure of the novel, as in *Eugénie Grandet* or *Père Goriot*. Rather, no fewer than three characters of the novel can be called monomaniacs: Cousin Bette, Valérie Marneffe, and Baron Hulot. It is true, however, that the two females are far more developed than Hulot. These two female protagonists, as they strengthen and complement each other, offer a hyperbolic image of monomania, parodying one of the trademarks of Balzac's fiction. By means of this parody, Balzac plainly shows that he has dissociated himself from his characters' plight. Perhaps he was able to satirize monomania because his career as a novelist was unquestionably successful and because he was beginning to receive some of the recognition he had always sought. Nevertheless, his own "mania" persisted: Until he simply became too sick to write, he continued to work on yet another novel in *The Human Comedy*, with ten more volumes projected and endless bills to pay.

Major publications other than long fiction

SHORT FICTION: *Les Contes drolatiques*, 1832-1837 (*Droll Stories*, 1874, 1891).

PLAYS: *Vautrin*, 1840 (English translation, 1901); *La Marâtre*, 1848 (*The Stepmother*, 1901, 1958); *Le Faiseur*, 1851 (also as *Mercadet*; English translation, 1901); *The Dramatic Works*, 1901 (2 volumes, includes *Vautrin*, *The Stepmother*, *Mercadet*, *Quinola's Resources*, and *Pamela Giraud*); *Cromwell*, 1925 (written 1819-1820).

NONFICTION: *Correspondance*, 1819-1850, 1876 (*The Correspondence*, 1878); *Lettres à l'étrangère*, 1899-1950; *Letters to Madame Hanska*, 1900 (translation of volume 1 of *Lettres à l'étrangère*).

Bibliography

Affron, Charles. *Patterns of Failure in the "Comédie humaine,"* 1966.

Bardèche, Maurice. *Balzac romancier*, 1940.

Charlton, D. G., J. Gaudon, and Anthony R. Pugh, eds. *Balzac and the Nineteenth Century: Studies in French Literature Presented to Herbert J. Hunt*, 1971.

Dargan, Preston, and Bernard Weinberg, eds. *The Evolution of Balzac's "Comédie humaine,"* 1942.

Giraud, Raymond. *The Unheroic Hero in the Novels of Stendhal, Balzac and Flaubert*, 1969.

Hunt, Herbert J. *Balzac's "Comédie humaine,"* 1959.

Maurois, André. *Prometheus: The Life of Balzac*, 1965.

Pritchett, V. S. *Balzac*, 1973.
Turnell, Martin. *The Novel in France*, 1950.
Zweig, Stefan. *Balzac*, 1940.

Sonja G. Stary

PÍO BAROJA

Born: San Sebastián, Spain; December 28, 1872
Died: Madrid, Spain; October 30, 1956

Principal long fiction

La casa de Aizgorri, 1900; *Aventuras, inventos y mixtificaciones de Silvestre Paradox*, 1901; *El mayorazgo de Labraz*, 1903 (*Lord of Labraz*, 1926); *La lucha por la vida*, 1904 (*The Struggle for Life*, 1922-1924; includes *La busca*, 1904 [*The Quest*, 1922]; *Mala hierba*, 1904 [*Weeds*, 1923]; *Aurora roja*, 1904 [*Red Dawn*, 1924]); *La feria de los discretos*, 1905 (*The City of the Discreet*, 1917); *Paradox, rey*, 1906 (*Paradox, King*, 1931); *La ciudad de la niebla*, 1909; *Zalacaín el aventurero*, 1909; *César o nada*, 1910 (*Caesar or Nothing*, 1919); *El árbol de la ciencia*, 1911 (*The Tree of Knowledge*, 1928); *Las inquietudes de Shanti Andía*, 1911 (*The Restlessness of Shanti Andia and Other Writings*, 1959); *El mundo es ansí*, 1912; *Memorias de un hombre de acción*, 1913-1935 (22 volumes); *La sensualidad pervertida*, 1920; *La leyenda de Juan de Alzate*, 1922 (*The Legend of Juan de Alzate*, 1959); *El cura de Monleón*, 1936; *Obras completas*, 1946-1951 (8 volumes).

Other literary forms

Pío Baroja wrote short stories, essays, memoirs, and verse in addition to his many novels. Some of his novels are written in dialogue; in fact, Anthony Kerrigan presents *The Legend of Juan de Alzate* as a play in his "Introduction" in *The Restlessness of Shanti Andía and Other Writings*. Among Baroja's last books are his seven volumes of *Memorias* (1955), in which he availed himself of whole sections lifted from his fiction, which is, in turn, often autobiographical.

Baroja's first book was a collection of short stories, *Vidas sombrías* (1900; somber lives), which demonstrated a sympathetic tenderness for his characters that would diminish as his literary career advanced. Some of the stories are very short "slice of life" vignettes and others concern the supernatural, such as "El trasgo" (the goblin) and "Medium." Some explore the psychology of women: "Agueda" treats the romantic stirrings in the mind of a crippled girl in the manner of Tennessee Williams' *The Glass Menagerie* (1944), and "Lo desconocido" ("The Unknown") probes the sudden and temporary urge of a bourgeois woman, traveling on a train with her husband, to flee the confines of the coach into the fascination of the night beyond. Others of these early stories contain the nuclei of future novels, such as "Un justo" (a just man), which prefigures *El cura de Monleón*, and "Los panaderos" (the bakers), which anticipates the trilogy *The Struggle for Life*.

Baroja's second collection of short stories, *Idilios vascos* (1901-1902; Basque idylls), includes "Elizabide el vagabundo" ("The Love Story of a Vagabond"), remarkable for its happy ending; a thirty-eight-year-old bachelor returns to

Spain from Uruguay, falls in love, and to his surprise, finds that his love is reciprocated.

Baroja's essays do not differ substantially from his novels in view of the fact that he never hesitates to pack his novels with his own opinions. Baroja is not noted for the depth of his philosophical thinking, and he failed to assimilate with genuine understanding much of the material that he cites from the great philosophers.

In the book-length essay *Ciudades de Italia* (1949; cities of Italy), Baroja expresses his fear that the work will be a *chapuza* (botch-job) because he is neither an art lover, a good tourist, nor an aesthete. Art, as Baroja had told his readers years before, is child's play in comparison to the serious business of philosophy. Neither is he a lover of Italy; although he would have preferred to visit the United States or Germany, he chose Italy because it was cheaper to visit.

El tablado de Arlequín (1901; harlequinade) is an ongoing diatribe against Spaniards for their abulia. *Juventud, egolatría* (1917; *Youth and Egolatry*, 1920) summarizes the author's views on politics, religion, sex, morality, literature, and a host of other topics; the volume also contains a brief study of three of his ancestral clans, the Goñis, the Zornozas, and the Alzates, the humorous tone of which cannot disguise the pride Baroja takes in the contemplation of his own lineage.

Nuevo tablado de Arlequín (1917; new harlequinade) contains a brief history of Baroja's native Basque village, Vera del Bidasoa, and a long apologia for the German cause in World War I. *Vitrina pintoresca* (1935; picturesque showcase) treats a potpourri of topics ranging from the Jesuits, the Jews, and the Masons to the rivers of Spain, haunted houses, and the demons of Carnival.

Baroja's attempts at poetry appear in *Canciones del suburbio* (1944; songs from the outskirts), published at the end of his career, not without the author's misgivings. This book is scarcely to be judged by the standards of serious poetry but is valuable inasmuch as it sheds light on Baroja the man. Indeed, Camilo José Cela considers the poems the best single book by which to become acquainted with their author.

Achievements

Gerald Brenan dubbed Baroja the greatest of Spanish novelists, second only to Benito Pérez Galdós. Pedro Salinas called the gallery of Baroja's characters "perhaps the richest" of Spanish literature. In 1972, G. G. Brown wrote that Baroja's influence on the modern Spanish novel has been greater than that of all of his contemporaries put together, and added that although non-Spanish readers may find this "puzzling," Baroja's popularity in Spain is an "indisputable fact." Brown's aside is clearly directed at those English-language critics who have been cool in their appraisal of Baroja's art.

Critic Gregorio Marañon attributed to Baroja a major role in forging a social conscience in the middle-class Spanish youth of his generation. Marañon characterized the books of Baroja's Madrid trilogy, *The Struggle for Life*, as three breaches in the wall of self-absorption that blinded the Spanish bourgeoisie to the misery amid which the majority of their compatriots lived. Although the *generación del 98* counted among its numbers figures more intellectual than Baroja, he is the only one of them to have a significant following. Camilo José Cela declared that the entire post-Civil War novel springs from his works and decried the fact that Baroja was not awarded the Nobel Prize. Indeed, the influence of Baroja is to be found in subsequent novels by such authors as Cela, Juan Antonio Zunzunegui, Miguel Delibes, José María Gironella, Ignacio Aldecoa, and Luis Martín-Santos.

Furthermore, Baroja stands apart from the nineteenth century realistic novelists who strived to arrange the elements of their fiction into interpretive patterns from which their readers could glean transcendent meaning. Through the example of his fiction, which chronicles the random inconsequentiality of his characters' lives, Baroja can therefore be credited, as G. G. Brown observes, with an attempt to reform what for thirty centuries has been seen as one of the principal functions of art—to organize experience into meaningful patterns.

Among American authors who profited from reading Baroja are John Dos Passos and Ernest Hemingway. Dos Passos, who wrote about Baroja in *Rosinante to the Road Again* (1922), was especially influenced by Baroja's anarchic tendencies, at least until the time of his disenchantment with the political Left in the later 1930's, and like Baroja, he wrote many of his novels in trilogies. Hemingway, who cherished Baroja's commitment to narrative brevity, paid homage to the Basque octogenarian at his deathbed and in his personal correspondence deplored the fact that publisher Alfred Knopf had "dropped" Baroja when he did not sell well in the United States.

Although Baroja encouraged the myth of his simple and unappreciated Bohemian existence, this is not quite the case. At the time of his death, he left behind the not unimpressive sum of 750,000 pesetas, and in 1934, he was elected to the Royal Spanish Academy.

Biography

Pío Baroja y Nessi was the third son of Serafín Baroja y Zornoza (1840-1915) and Carmen Nessi y Goñi (1849-1935). He was extremely knowledgeable about his ancestry and careful to note that he was seven-eighths Basque and one-eighth Italian; his mother's surname, Nessi, was of Italian origin. His father was a mining engineer with a literary bent who was more concerned with what his friends thought of him than with the esteem of his family. An older brother, Ricardo Baroja (1871-1953), a painter and inventor, was also a writer. In 1879, the senior Baroja took his family to live in Madrid, whence they moved to Pamplona; in 1886, they moved once again to Madrid.

Although not an exceptional student, Baroja entered the School of Medicine in Madrid at the age of fifteen and by 1891 completed his medical studies in Valencia. Two years later, he completed his thesis and obtained a position as practitioner in the Basque village of Cestona. The pettiness of small-town life and the suffering and the poverty that he wasorced to witness daily disgusted him, and he decided to abandon his medical career. What he did not abandon, however, was the medical knowledge he had acquired; his novels are peopled with a host of doctors and his dialogue bristles with the names and exploits of the heroes of medicine and physiology.

Baroja returned to Madrid to help his brother manage the family bakery, which allowed him to become familiar with the lower social orders of Madrid, a subject that would provide material for some twenty novels of his own creation. His venture into business was not successful, and it has been suggested that Baroja's hostility toward socialism may stem from his difficulties while running the bakery with the unions to which his employees belonged.

In 1898, Spain suffered the fiasco of the Spanish-American War, and in its soul-searching wake was born the *generación del 98*. Although he is generally considered to have been a member of this group, Baroja himself denied any such affiliation: He scorned the artistic artifice of Ramón María del Valle-Inclán, disagreed with José Ortega y Gasset regarding the purpose of the novel, and resented the self-importance of Miguel de Unamuno. Toward the popular novelist Vicente Blasco Ibáñez he harbored a deep loathing.

In 1899, Baroja made his first visit to Paris, and by 1900, when he published his first book, he was writing for such periodicals as *El país*, *El imparcial*, and *Revista nueva*. After purchasing a home in his native Basque village of Vera del Bidasoa in 1912, he divided his time between there and his home in Madrid, which he shared with his mother. He never married but had a number of liaisons which proved unsatisfactory. Although he grudgingly gave his support to Francisco Franco as the lesser of two evils at the outbreak of the Spanish Civil War, he left Spain voluntarily for Paris in the summer of 1936 and did not return until 1940.

During his final days, Ernest Hemingway, who had recently won the Nobel Prize, paid Baroja a visit. He brought with him a pair of socks and a bottle of his favorite whiskey, and told Baroja that the prize rightfully belonged to him. *Time* magazine, in October, 1956, recorded Baroja's succinct but unfortunately apocryphal reaction to such lavish praise: "Caramba." The less romantic truth is that in his arteriosclerotic haze, Baroja could do no more than respond to this tribute with an uncomprehending stare.

Analysis

Near the end of his life, Pío Baroja listed those historical personalities who had sustained his interest the longest: the naturalist Charles Darwin; the chemist Louis Pasteur; the physiologist Claude Bernard; the philosophers Friedrich Nietzsche, Arthur Schopenhauer, and Immanuel Kant; and the poets Lord Byron, Giacomo Leopardi, and Gustavo Adolfo Bécquer. His writing was permanently influenced by such French and Spanish serial writers as Xavier de Montepin and Manuel Fernández y González and by the Spanish picaresque novel. He admired Charles Dickens but not William Thackeray, Stendhal but not Gustave Flaubert, Paul Verlaine but not Marcel Proust, and Giacomo Leopardi but not Alessandro Manzoni. Despairing of the world's capacity to produce writers of the highest caliber continually (his motto was "Nothing new under the sun"), he declared that the likes of Fyodor Dostoevski and Leo Tolstoy would not be seen again.

Baroja was as misanthropic and pessimistic as his mentor Arthur Schopenhauer and, also like the German philosopher, has been characterized as misogynistic. Baroja's references to the ignorance, greed, and superficiality of Spanish women are legion, yet his misogyny seems to be an ancillary property of his all-embracing misanthropy rather than an independent prejudice. Baroja's pessimism is reflected in his diction—in the frequent appearance of such words as *imbécil*, *estúpido*, and *absurdo*, as well as a bevy of more colorful words such as *energúmeno* (madman) and *gaznápiro* (simpleton). One of his favorite words for everything is *farsante* (farcical).

Baroja boasted that he used no word in his novels that was not appropriate in conversation, yet this does not preclude experimentation with unusual words that caught his fancy, for example, *cachupinada* (entertainment) and *zaquizamí* (garret). His love of the colorful is evident in the phrase he used to characterize himself—*pajarraco del individualismo* (big, ugly bird of individualism). Despite Baroja's commitment to the colloquial mode, he generally avoided slang unless it was for the purpose of local color in dialogue. In *The Struggle for Life* trilogy especially, his dialogue is strewn with italicized vocabulary peculiar to the low life of Madrid, for example, *aluspiar* (to stalk), *diñar* (to die), *jamar* (to eat). The practice of italicizing the vocabulary of the low life would be accepted and used even more by his follower Juan Antonio Zunzunegui, who came to occupy Baroja's vacant chair in the Royal Spanish Academy.

Baroja had an ear for pronunciation as well. When he returned to the Basque country after several years in Madrid as a child, he was ridiculed for his Madrilenian accent, and, on occasion, he notes this accent in his characters. He also had a penchant for decorating his prose with the lyrics of traditional songs not only in Basque but also in the other peninsular dialects; even in his essay on Italy, lyrics in the Italian dialects are cited. Indeed, refrains and simple repetitions for musical effects are typical of all of his prose.

Contemptuous of stylistic preciosity, he defended his right as a novelist to be terse and even ungrammatical. Because he avoided grammatical convolutions so consistently, his works are easier reading than many other Spanish classics and are, therefore, very popular in introductory literature courses wherever in the world that Spanish is taught.

Long non-Spanish names that point to the incontestable Basque origin of the characters that they denote are frequent in Baroja's novels. His fascination with anthropology is obvious in his abundant use of ethnological designations (for example, *samnita*, the name of a pre-Roman tribe of southern Italy, is used generally as "stalwart" in *Lord of Labraz*) and in his sweeping generalizations about race (for example, Sacha in *El mundo es ansí* observing that there is not a significant difference between northern and southern Spaniards, as there is among Italians). Baroja's use of the novel as a forum to hold forth on just about anything brings about many allusions to figures from the past, not only political leaders and writers but also physiologists, philosophers, painters, and anthropologists, who are more often German, French, or Italian than Spanish.

Baroja's sensitivity to the suffering in life and his abhorrence of the cruelty and hypocrisy of men made him a severe judge of the human condition. He hated religion, which he believed is a dangerous illusion foisted upon Europeans by the Semites. His novel *El cura de Monleón*, which deals with a Basque priest's loss of faith, is unfortunately unsuccessful because Baroja, as an unbeliever, simply could not understand the depth of emotion such a loss of faith would entail for a priest. God is conceived as *patoso*, a bungler who, if he exists at all, is to be found in the scientific laboratory. Just as fiercely, Baroja abhorred the laws of the State, and his novel *Red Dawn* explores the world of anarchy and anarchists. Like the author himself, the protagonist of *Red Dawn*, Juan Alcazán, is a humanitarian, rather than a doctrinal, anarchist; Baroja himself never dared to act on any of the anarchistic tendencies that he felt.

All Baroja's novels contain adventure, and if his adventuresome characters do not overcome the obstacles with which they are confronted, it is because they lose faith in life and fall victim to abulia. César Moncada, for example, in *Caesar or Nothing*, tries to imitate Cesare Borgia, but his Machiavellian goals fail in the face of his innate pessimism. At seventy, Baroja said that he still felt, as he had at fifteen, a distant enthusiasm for adventure without really believing in it.

Baroja's fiction embraces a wide geographic purview. Some novels portray the Basque provinces of Spain, whose countryside he considered the purest and most authentic in Europe, isolated from the cement-and-cinema falsity of contemporary "civilization." Some portray the low life of Madrid (for example, *The Struggle for Life*), others have the Carlist Wars as a backdrop (for example, *Zalacaín el aventurero* and the Aviraneta series), and Andalusia is represented with originality in *The City of the Discreet*. Still others take place outside Spain (for example, *La ciudad de la niebla*, that is, London) or have as protagonists characters who are not Spanish (for example, Sacha Savarof, a Russian medical student who is observed in France, Switzerland, Italy, Russia, and Spain in *El mundo es ansí*).

Paradox, King, a novel almost exclusively in dialogue, is one of Baroja's most highly acclaimed creations. Written in two weeks, it is a masterful combination of satire and fantasy, of misanthropy and humor. The restless Silvestre Paradox, a poverty-stricken inventor, joins an expedition to Africa organized in order to establish a Jewish colony, and is accompanied by a colorful group of naturalists, soldiers, and adventurers. The ship that takes them to Africa is wrecked in a storm and the survivors are taken captive in Bu-Tata, capital of the kingdom of Uganga. Once the captives conciliate the initially hostile natives, Paradox is proclaimed King and the group institutes a European form of government which emphasizes complete freedom and dispenses with laws, schools, and teachers. At length, the French feel obliged to intervene; they bring "civilization" to Africa in the form of tuberculosis, alcoholism, and prostitution. The hospital fills up with epidemic victims, and Princess Mahu is driven to dancing nude in a nightclub.

Baroja uses the peculiarities of his characters to satirize his own aversions. There is, for example, the overbearing feminist Miss Pich, who insists that Socrates, William Shakespeare, and King David were women; her fate is to be violated by savages. The cynicism of *Paradox, King* concerning the lack of commitment among educators, theologians, and scientists, and the notion that man can never escape the evils of civilization, even in a utopia, are totally in keeping with the fundamentals of Baroja's thinking.

Like *Paradox, King*, Baroja's other masterpiece, *The Tree of Knowledge*, which the author believed was his best philosophical novel, emphasizes dialogue. The novel also contains the author's most successfully drawn protagonist, Andrés Hurtado, a sad and sensitive man whose pastimes, reading, attitudes, and sympathies closely parallel Baroja's own. Hurtado goes to Madrid to study medicine and is soon disillusioned by the inadequacy of his professors and the coldness of the hospital staff. Neither does his family afford him any relief from his pessimism, since he is incompatible with his father; he adores his little brother, Luisito, but the child soon dies of tuberculosis.

Once he becomes a doctor, Hurtado accepts a post in an isolated village, where he observes the same crassness and inhumanity as he had observed in the city. When he returns to Madrid, as he must, he meets Lulu, a woman of humble origins, and they marry. Hurtado considers himself unfit for fatherhood and knows that Lulu is not robust, but she becomes pregnant in defiance of biological probability. Just when marriage seems to have saved Hurtado from despair, Lulu dies, and Hurtado, refusing to confront an intolerable reality, decides to commit suicide.

Another popular novel, regarded by Baroja as one of his best, is *Zalacaín el aventurero*. Instinctively rather than intellectually philosophical in the manner of Hurtado, Zalacaín emerges as a hero unfettered by convention who tests his destiny. An orphan, Zalacaín comes under the influence of his cynical old uncle, Tellagorri, who comes to appreciate Zalacaín when he sees evidence of the boy's pluckiness. Zalacaín grows up to be successful in all of his endeavors, in war, in his career as a smuggler, and with women. At length, he dies in a dispute instigated by his wealthy brother-in-law, Carlos Ohando, who is resentful of Zalacaín for earning the love of his sister Catalina. The hero's violent death is consistent with the romantic conception of the novel, and the three roses laid upon his grave by Linda, Rosita, and Catalina further suggest the hero of a romantic ballad.

Baroja's early novel *The Restlessness of Shanti Andia*, belatedly translated into English some five decades after its original publication, is a complicated tale of maritime adventure that takes place in the idyllic Basque fishing village of Lúzaro. Shanti is torn by his loyalty to the Basque countryside and to the sea and is, as Beatrice Patt observes, a collector of adventures lived by others. He idolizes his dead uncle Juan de Aguirre, a sea captain whose mysterious voyages made him a village myth. Much of the novel is taken up by Shanti's attempts to unravel his uncle's past, which involves tales of piracy, mutiny, buried treasure, and the slave trade. As pessimistic as Andrés Hurtado, Shanti comes across as a passive observer before the action-filled drama of someone else's heroics, a drama that he himself must narrate.

Although Baroja's dissatisfaction with human, and especially Spanish, society is everywhere evident in his fiction, the fast pace of his narrative and the lyric description that provides a background of poetry and almost druidic awe before the phenomena of nature keep his novels from being morbid. Those who dislike Baroja have chosen to emphasize his nonconformist and anarchistic nature, his melancholy, and the illogic of some of his pet arguments, while his admirers have chosen to emphasize the author's gentle nature hidden behind a defensive mask of sarcasm, a pose which he himself delighted in keeping alive. Nevertheless, there is little in his nearly one hundred books that escaped the severity of his uncompromising judgment against the false world of convention and complacency that engulfs the lives of most men and seals them off forever from compassion.

Major publications other than long fiction
SHORT FICTION: *Vidas sombrías*, 1900; *Idilios vascos*, 1901-1902.
POETRY: *Canciones del suburbio*, 1944.
NONFICTION: *El tablado de Arlequín*, 1901; *Juventud, egolatría*, 1917 (*Youth and Egolatry*, 1920); *Nuevo tablado de Arlequín*, 1917; *La caverna del humorismo*, 1919; *Momentum catastrophicum*, 1919; *Divagaciones apasionadas*, 1924; *Entretenimientos*, 1927; *Aviraneta: O, La vida de un conspirador*, 1931; *Vitrina pintoresca*, 1935; *Pequeños ensayos*, 1943; *Ciudades de Italia*, 1949; *La obsesión del misterio*, 1952; *Memorias*, 1955 (7 volumes).

Bibliography
Brenan, Gerald. *The Literature of the Spanish People*, 1951, 1953.

Brown, G. G. *A Literary History of Spain: The Twentieth Century*, 1972.
Eoff, Sherman H. *The Modern Spanish Novel*, 1961.
Kerrigan, Anthony. "Introduction," in *The Restlessness of Shanti Andia and Other Writings*, 1959.
McKay, Douglas R. *Misterio y Pavor: Trece cuentos*, 1974.
Patt, Beatrice. *Pío Baroja*, 1971.
Pérez Ferrero, Miguel. *Vida de Pío Baroja*, 1960.

Jack Shreve

SIMONE DE BEAUVOIR

Born: Paris, France; January 9, 1908

Principal long fiction

L'Invitée, 1943 (*She Came to Stay*, 1949); *Le Sang des autres*, 1945 (*The Blood of Others*, 1948); *Tous les hommes sont mortels*, 1946 (*All Men Are Mortal*, 1955); *Les Mandarins*, 1954 (*The Mandarins*, 1956); *Les Belles Images*, 1966 (English translation, 1968).

Other literary forms

Simone de Beauvoir's novels as well as most of her other works have been published by Gallimard. Foremost among these is her four-volume autobiography, *Mémoires d'une jeune fille rangée* (1958; *Memoirs of a Dutiful Daughter*, 1959), *La Force de l'âge* (1960; *The Prime of Life*, 1962), *La Force des choses* (1963; *Force of Circumstance*, 1964), and *Tout compte fait* (1972; *All Said and Done*, 1974). Equally important is her monumental sociological study on women, *Le Deuxième Sexe* (1949; *The Second Sex*, 1953). Two other sociological works follow *The Second Sex*, the first on China, *La Longue Marche* (1957; *The Long March*, 1958) and the second, on the aged, *La Vieillesse* (1970; *The Coming of Age*, 1972). *Les Bouches inutiles* (1945), her only play, has not yet been translated into English. Gallimard has also published two collections of short stories, *La Femme rompue* (1967; *The Woman Destroyed*, 1968) and *Quand prime le spirituel* (1979; *When Things of the Spirit Come First: Five Early Tales*, 1982). Her most important philosophical essays include *Pyrrhus et Cinéas* (1944), *Pour une morale de l'ambiguïté* (1947; *The Ethics of Ambiguity*, 1948), *L'Existentialisme et la sagesse des nations* (1948), and *Privilèges* (1955; partial translation, "Must We Burn Sade?" 1953). A number of other essays have appeared in newspapers and journals. She has also written a chronicle of her travels in the United States, *L'Amérique au jour le jour* (1948; *America Day by Day*, 1953), a powerful account of her mother's illness and death, *Une Mort très douce* (1964; *A Very Easy Death*, 1966), and a tribute to Jean-Paul Sartre, *La Cérémonie des adieux* (1981; *Adieux: A Farewell to Sartre*, 1984).

Achievements

De Beauvoir has been a presence felt in French intellectual life for almost forty years. She is one of the foremost examples of Existentialist *engagement* and its most respected moral voice. Her novels, especially *She Came to Stay*, *The Blood of Others*, and *The Mandarins* (for which she won the Prix Goncourt in 1954) pose some of the central philosophical and ethical questions of our time, exploring the problems of social morality, political commitment, and human responsibility. Along with her autobiography, her novels chronicle the time before and after World War II and the experiences that have made her one of the most influential writers of the century.

De Beauvoir has written numerous articles for *Les Temps modernes*, a periodical founded and directed by Sartre, and she was a member of its editorial board. In 1973, she became the editor of the journal's feminist column. *The Second Sex*, her carefully documented study of the situation of women, has become one of the major theoretical texts of the women's movement. Her interest in women's rights and her concern for social justice are attested by her ongoing involvement in both. She has demonstrated against France's restrictive abortion laws and signed the *Manifeste des 343*, a document listing women who admitted having had abortions. She has been president of Choisir (1971), and of the Ligue des Droits des Femmes (1974), an organization fighting sex discrimination. De Beauvoir was also one of the founders of the feminist journal *Questions féministes*. Her indictment of social injustice is evidenced by *The Coming of Age*, her defense of a free press (the Maoist underground newspaper *La Cause du Peuple*), and her political actions.

The breadth of her writing alone secures de Beauvoir a prominent position in twentieth century letters. She is one of the dominant figures in Existentialist thought and modern French literature.

Biography

Simone de Beauvoir was born in Paris in January, 1908. Her father, Georges de Beauvoir, came from a wealthy family and was a lawyer by profession. A religious skeptic, he was openly contemptuous of the bourgeoisie and encouraged his daughter in intellectual pursuits. In contrast, her mother, Françoise, came from a provincial town, received her education in convents, and was a devout Catholic. Under her mother's supervision, the young de Beauvoir was educated at a conservative Catholic school for girls, the Cours Désir.

In *Memoirs of a Dutiful Daughter*—which covers the years from 1908 to 1929—de Beauvoir describes her early piety, her subsequent disenchantment with Catholicism, and the beginning of her rebellion against her middle-class background. Influenced by an early reading of Louisa May Alcott and George Eliot, she decided at age fifteen that she wanted to be a writer. After leaving the Cours Désir, she pursued the study of literature at the Institut Catholique in Paris. In 1926, she attended the Sorbonne and studied philosophy, Greek, and philology. Three years later, after a year at the prestigious École Normale Supérieure, she passed the examination for the *agrégation de philosophie*, the highest academic degree conferred in France.

In 1929, de Beauvoir met Sartre and began an association with him that lasted until his death in April, 1980. The years from 1929 to 1944 are chronicled in the second volume of her autobiography, *The Prime of Life*. Having completed her academic degrees, she was assigned a series of teaching positions, first in Marseilles and later in Rouen and Paris. Her first novel, *She Came to Stay*, appeared in 1943; it established her as a writer and she stopped teaching. During the war years, she became interested in political action. By the end of World War II, de Beauvoir and Sartre were labeled "Existentialists," and their success and celebrity were assured. In 1947, de Beauvoir was invited on a lecture tour of the United States (described in *America Day by Day*) and began her four-year affair with Nelson Algren.

During the postwar years, de Beauvoir became increasingly preoccupied with the problems of the intellectual in society, and she continued to examine the relationship between freedom and social commitment. In *Force of Circumstance* (which spans the years 1944 to 1962), the third volume of her autobiography, political events such as the Korean War a the Algerian Crisis occupy progressively more space. She saw Sartre destroy his health to work on *Critique de la raison dialectique*, (1960; *The Critique of Dialectical Reason*, 1976) and became painfully aware of human mortality and solitude. Old age and death are themes that run through de Beauvoir's work done during this period, such as *A Very Easy Death*, *The Woman Destroyed*, *The Coming of Age*, and the last volume of her autobiography, *All Said and Done*. In spite of this, the general tone of *All Said and Done*—as well as of the frequent interviews she has given—is one of a woman content to have achieved her Existentialist project.

Analysis

Simone de Beauvoir's novels are grounded in her training as a philosopher and in her sociological and feminist concerns. *She Came to Stay*, *The Blood of Others*, *All Men Are Mortal*, and *The Mandarins* all revolve around the questions of freedom and responsibility and try to define the proper relationship between the individual and society. Her characters search for authenticity as they attempt to shape the world around them. Their education is sentimental as well as intellectual and political. While most of her heroes accommodate themselves successfully to reality, the same may not be said of her heroines. In the later novels, *The Mandarins* and *Les Belles Images*, her female characters, who are successful by worldly standards, suffer a series of psychological crises. As they undertake what the feminist critic Carol Christ has called "spiritual quests," they often face suicide and madness. The Existentialist enterprise of *engagement*, or commitment with a view of defining the self through action, seems more possible for the men in her novels than for the women. In *Simone de Beauvoir on Woman* (1975), Jean Leighton has observed the absence of positive heroines in de Beauvoir's work: Woman seems condemned to passivity while man's fate is one of transcendence. Arguments from *The Second Sex* and from her philosophical essays echo in the novels. The tension between her philosophical ideas and their potential realization by the women characters is clearly visible in her fiction.

De Beauvoir's first novel, *She Came to Stay*, is an imaginative transposition of her relationship with Olga Kosakiewicz. In 1933, Beauvoir and Sartre had befriended Olga, one of Beauvoir's students. They had attempted a *ménage à trois*; *She Came to Stay* is the story of its failure.

The heroine, Françoise Miquel, is a young writer who has lived with Pierre Labrousse, a talented actor and director, for eight years. They feel that their relationship is ideal since it allows them both a great deal of freedom. Françoise befriends Xavière, a young woman disenchanted with provincial life, and invites her to Paris, where she will help her find work. Once in Paris, Xavière makes demands on the couple and is openly contemptuous of their values. Pierre becomes obsessed with Xavière; Françoise, trying to rise above the jealousy and insecurity she feels, struggles to keep the trio together. Out of resentment, Françoise has an affaire with Gerbert, Xavière's suitor. The novel ends as Xavière recognizes Françoise's duplicity; Xavière has now become the critical Other. Unable to live in her presence, Françoise turns on the gas and murders her.

She Came to Stay is a meditation on the Hegelian problem of the existence of the Other. The novel plays out the psychological effects of jealousy and questions the extent to which coexistence is possible. Critics such as Hazel Barnes and Carol Ascher have noted the close ties between de Beauvoir's first novel and Sartre's *L'Être et le neant* (*Being and Nothingness*, 1956), published in the same year. Both texts deal with the central Existentialist theme of letting others absorb one's freedom.

Despite Françoise's apparent independence, she needs Pierre to approve her actions and give them direction. Françoise's self-deception and the inauthenticity of her life anticipate de Beauvoir's analysis of *l'amoureuse*, the woman in love, in *The Second Sex*. Confronted with a rival, Françoise becomes aware that her self-assurance and detachment are illusory. Her growth as a character occurs as she sheds the unexamined rational premises she holds about herself and her relationship with Pierre. The gap between the intellect and the emotions continues to widen until it reaches a crisis in the murder of Xavière. Françoise is finally forced to confront her long-concealed hatred. In spite of the often stylized dialogue, *She Came to Stay* is a lucid, finely executed study of love and jealousy and one of de Beauvoir's finest novels.

Although de Beauvoir was later to consider her second novel overly didactic, *The Blood of Others* is one of the best novels written on the French Resistance. The book opens with the thoughts of Jean Blomart as he keeps vigil over his mistress Hélène, who is dying from a wound received during a mission. The novel proceeds by flashback and alternates between the stories of Jean, a Resistance hero, and his companion Hélène. The son of a wealthy bourgeois family, Jean is plagued by feelings of guilt over his comfortable situation. He takes a job as a worker and tries to lead a life of uninvolvement. His attempted detachment is based on his belief that he can thus avoid contributing to the unhappiness of others. Passive at the outbreak of the war, he is finally drafted. Upon his return to Paris, he realizes that his detachment is actually a form of irresponsibility. He organizes a resistance group and becomes its leader. As he watches the dying Hélène, he questions whether he has the right to control the lives of his comrades. Although he is doomed to act in ignorance of the consequences of his decisions, he decides that he nevertheless has an obligation to act. The novel ends with Hélène's death and his renewed commitment to the Resistance.

If *The Blood of Others* is the story of Jean's *engagement*, it is also the story of Hélène's political awakening. Like him, she is politically indifferent until a young Jewish friend is in danger of deportation. She then turns to Jean and becomes an active member of his group. Of all de Beauvoir's women, Hélène is one who, in her political commitment, manages to define herself through her actions rather than through her emotional attachments.

The Blood of Others recalls the discussion of individual freedom in *The Ethics of Ambiguity*. In both the novel and the philosophical essay, the problem of the Other is interfaced with the question of social responsibility. With its emphasis on the denial of freedom during the Occupation, the novel underscores the necessity of political action to ensure individual freedoms. The closed space of the love triangle in *She Came to Stay* is replaced by the larger obligations of the individual to a historical moment. *The Blood of Others* conveys the problematic quality of ethical decisions; as Robert Cottrell has noted in *Simone de Beauvoir* (1975), it evokes "the sense of being entrapped, of submitting to existence rather than fashioning it." Nevertheless, *The Blood of Others* is a more optimistic book than *She Came to Stay* in its portrayal of the individual working toward a larger social good.

Individual actions are seen against a series of historical backdrops in *All Men Are Mortal*. The novel traces the life of Count Fosca, an Italian nobleman who is endowed with immortality. At the request of Régine, a successful young actress, he recounts his varied careers through seven centuries. A counselor to Maximilian of Germany and then to Charles V of Spain, he discovers the Mississippi, founds the first French university, and becomes an activist in the French Revolution. Like other Existentialist heroes, Fosca paradoxically admits that only death gives life meaning. His goal of building an ideal, unified humanity remains unrealized as violence and useless destruction prevail.

Fosca's story is framed by that of Régine, who is embittered by her life and haunted by death. When she learns of Fosca's immortality, she thinks that she can transcend death by living forever in his memory. Like the women in love in the preceding novels, Régine depends on others to give her life meaning. The story ends with Régine's cry of despair as she understands the futility and vanity of human action.

All Men Are Mortal takes up the theme of the uncertain outcome of individual actions and gives it a more decidedly pessimistic turn. This theme is modified somewhat by the more optimistic section on the French Revolution. Here, Fosca follows the career of one of his descendants, Armand. Armand's zeal in fighting for the Republican cause leads Fosca to modify his skepticism about human progress and to take comfort in the solidarity he experiences with Armand and his friends.

Fosca's discovery of the rewards of comradeship is very similar to that of Jean Blomart. Although Fosca's individual actions are either undercut by the presence of others or lost in history, actions taken by the group seem to have a more powerful impact on reality. Like *The Blood of Others*, *All Men Are Mortal* presages de Beauvoir's later Marxist sympathies and reflects her growing politization. Both Jean and Fosca tend to break with the solipsistic tendencies of the characters in *She Came to Stay* and move in the direction of greater social commitment. The context of the action in *All Men Are Mortal* is wider than in the preceding novels from a narrative and political point of view. It is perhaps its vast historical scope that makes *All Men Are Mortal* the least satisfying of de Beauvoir's novels. Philosophical speculations on love, history, and death dominate the narrative; the characters are lifeless and seem caught in a series of historical still lifes.

The Mandarins, de Beauvoir's finest novel, covers the period from 1944 to the early 1950's and focuses on the relationship between political commitment and literature. The narrative voice shifts between Henri Perron, a novelist, journalist, and Resistance hero, and Anne Dubreuilh, a respected psychiatrist and the wife of Robert Dubreuilh, a prominent writer.

Robert, initiated into political activism during his years in the Resistance, believes that literature must now take second place to political concerns. He engages himself wholeheartedly in founding the S.R.L., an independent leftist political party. The problems that Robert confronts as a political figure point to the painful reality of making decisions that are not always satisfactory. He draws Henri into politics by convincing him that his newspaper, *L'Espoir*, should be the voice of the S.R.L. When they receive news of Soviet labor camps, they try to decide if they should publish it. Knowing that they will play into Gaullist hands and alienate the Communists to whom they are sympathetic, they reluctantly decide to print the story.

For Henri, questions of political commitment after the war are more problematic. He would like *L'Espoir* to remain apolitical and is nostalgic for the prewar years when literature and politics appeared to be mutually exclusive interests. Henri tries to act in good faith, but because of his sensitivity to others, he often opts for the less idealistically pure solution. He is reluctant to break with Paule, his mistress of ten years, and he protects acquaintances who were German collaborators because he fears that, like Paule, they could not survive without his help. Throughout the novel, he is torn between politics and a desire to return to literature. He gradually faces the impossibility of "pure" literature. At the end of the novel, having lost *L'Espoir*, he and Robert decide to found a new journal of the Left.

The questions that de Beauvoir examines through Robert and Henri have a striking immediacy that captures the problem of the intellectual in the modern world. Much of the action in *The Mandarins* is a fictionalized account of her experiences as a member of the intellectual Left during the postwar years. Critics have sought to identify Sartre with Robert, Albert Camus with Henri, and de Beauvoir herself with Anne. In *Simone de Beauvoir and the Limits of Commitment* (1981), Anne Whitmarsh notes that there is much of Sartre's experiences with the Rassemblement Démocratique Révolutionnaire in Robert's ties with the S.R.L. and that some of the early problems facing *Les Temps modernes* are reflected in the debates on the political role of *L'Espoir*.

The problems faced by the male characters are less pressing for Anne. Married to a man twenty years older, she seems out of touch with herself and her surroundings. Her work as a psychiatrist fails fully to occupy her, and her relationship with her unhappy daughter, Nadine, gives Anne little satisfaction. Encouraged by Robert, she accepts an invitation to lecture in the United States. In Chicago, she experiences an emotional awakening when she falls in love with Lewis Brogan, an up-and-coming writer. Her visits to Brogan are described in a highly lyric style full of images of country life and nature. The physical and affective aspects of her life with Brogan form an effective counterpoint to the intellectual character of her relationship with her husband. The shifting loyalties she experiences for both men give Anne's narrative a schizophrenic quality.

Back in Paris, Anne tries to help Paule, who has suffered a nervous breakdown. Paule rarely leaves her apartment and is unable to function without Henri. Anne sends her to a psychiatrist, who "cures" her by having her forget the past. Like Françoise and Régine, Paule represents the temptation of living through others. In Paule's case, however, the dependence reaches an Existential crisis from which she never fully recovers. Paule's illness is mirrored in Anne as the psychiatrist herself plunges into a long depression. When Brogan ends their relationship, she contemplates suicide. Thinking of the pain her death would cause Robert and Nadine, she decides to live. Despite this decision, Anne's alienation from her family and indeed from her own being is more acute than ever.

Anne's emotional awakening and Paule's mental breakdown leave them both as only marginal participants in life. Neither woman achieves the transcendence that characterizes the lives of her male counterpart. As Robert and Henri accommodate themselves to political realities, they become more integrated into society. The female quest for self-knowledge acts as a negative counterpoint to the male quest. The final scene is not unlike a collage in which the two parts of the composition are radically divided. The enthusiasm of Henri and Robert as they search for an appropriate title for their journal is juxtaposed to Anne's stillness; she sits off to the side, withdrawn, and hopes that her life may still contain some happiness.

Les Belles Images is one of de Beauvoir's most technically innovative novels. Laurence, the main character, is a young woman who writes slogans for a French advertising agency. She is married to a successful young architect and has two daughters. Catherine, her eldest daughter, is beginning to question social values. Laurence comes from the same mold as de Beauvoir's other heroines. She is, for all appearances, a confident young woman. Like them, her façade of well-being dissolves to reveal an individual profoundly alienated from herself and her society. *Les Belles Images* is the story of Laurence's progressive withdrawal from society. Her interior journey ends in a mental and physical breakdown.

The novel is set in Paris during the 1960's. Some friends have gathered at the fashionable home of Dominique, Laurence's mother. Laurence, uninterested in the group, leafs through a number of magazines containing the *belles images*, or beautiful pictures, she is paid to create. The dialogue among the guests is filtered through Laurence, who then adds her own reflections. The conversations are trite and filled with clichés; like the slogans Laurence invents, they conceal the real problems of war, poverty, and unhappiness. The discrepancy between the advertisements and the things they represent precipitates Laurence's budding consciousness of herself as yet another *belle image*. Laurence's perception of the inauthenticity of her own life and of the lives of the people around her results in illness. Having already suffered a nervous breakdown five years before, she becomes anorexic and unable to relate to the artificial world around her.

Through her daughter Catherine, she faces her unresolved feelings toward her childhood. She recalls the lack of emotional contact with her mother in a series of flashbacks in which she appears dressed as a child in a publicity snapshot. At the insistence of Laurence's husband, Catherine has been sent to a psychiatrist because she is overly sensitive to social injustices. Laurence sees the treatment that Catherine receives as an attempt to integrate her daughter into the artificial bourgeois world. At the novel's end, Laurence emerges from her illness to save her daughter from a fate similar to hers. Like other de Beauvoir heroines, Laurence chooses her illness as a means of escaping certain destructive social myths. Her breakdown, rather than the result of an original flaw discovered within herself, is an indication of the failure of society as a whole. Against the inauthentic world of the other characters, Laurence's illness appears as a victory and an occasion for emotional growth. Much like Anne in *The Mandarins*, Laurence is a voice from the outside who sees the social games and reveals them for what they are.

All of de Beauvoir's novels examine the relationship between the self and the Other that is at the heart of Existentialist philosophy. In her early novels, such as *She Came to Stay*, *The Blood of Others*, and *All Men Are Mortal*, there is often an explicit Existentialist premise underlying the action. In her later works, *The Mandarins* and *Les Belles Images*, the philosophical message, although still present, is clearly subordinated to the narrative. De Beauvoir's conclusions in *The Second Sex* appear to have led her to a closer examination of the lives of her women characters. Her later fiction adds another dimension to the quests for authenticity that mark her early production. For her heroes, the quest usually ends in some type of Existentialist commitment; for her heroines, the quest seems to involve a withdrawal from harmful social myths. If at times the quests border on madness or isolation, they do so without losing their striking immediacy or their profound sense of reality. Like other great twentieth century quests, de Beauvoir's novels chart a journey into the heart of contemporary alienation.

Major publications other than long fiction
SHORT FICTION: *La Femme rompue*, 1967 (*The Woman Destroyed*, 1968); *Quand prime le spirituel*, 1979 (*When Things of the Spirit Come First: Five Early Tales*, 1982).
PLAY: *Les Bouches inutiles*, 1945.
NONFICTION: *Pyrrhus et Cinéas*, 1944; *Pour une morale de l'ambiguïté*, 1947 (*The Ethics of Ambiguity*, 1948); *L'Amérique au jour le jour*, 1948 (*America Day by Day*, 1953); *L'Existentialisme et la sagesse des nations*, 1948; *Le Deuxième Sexe*, 1949 (*The Second Sex*, 1953); *Privilèges*, 1955 (partial translation, "Must We Burn Sade?" 1953); *La Longue Marche*, 1957 (*The Long March*, 1958); *Mémoires d'une jeune fille rangée*, 1958 (4 volumes; *Memoirs of a Dutiful Daughter*, 1959); *La Force de l'âge*, 1960 (*The Prime of Life*, 1962); *La Force des choses*, 1963 (*Force of Circumstance*, 1964); *Une Mort très douce*, 1964 (*A Very Easy Death*, 1966); *La Vieillesse*, 1970 (*The Coming of Age*, 1972); *Tout compte fait*, 1972 (*All Said and Done*, 1974); *La Cérémonie des adieux*, 1981 (*Adieux: A Farewell to Sartre*, 1984).

Bibliography
Ascher, Carol. *Simone de Beauvoir: A Life of Freedom*, 1982.
Barnes, Hazel. *Humanistic Existentialism: The Literature of Possibility*, 1962.
Bieber, Konrad. *Simone de Beauvoir*, 1979.
Brée, Germaine. *Women Writers in France: Variations on a Theme*, 1973.
Christ, Carol P. *Diving Deep and Surfacing: Women Writers on Spiritual Quest*, 1980.
Cottrell, Robert D. *Simone de Beauvoir*, 1975.
Jeanson, Francis. *Simone de Beauvoir: Ou, L'Entreprise de vivre*, 1966.
Leighton, Jean. *Simone de Beauvoir on Woman*, 1975.
Whitmarsh, Anne. *Simone de Beauvoir and the Limits of Commitment*, 1981.

Carole Deering Paul

SAMUEL BECKETT

Born: Foxrock, Ireland; April 13, 1906

Principal long fiction

Murphy, 1938; *Molloy*, 1951 (English translation, 1955); *Malone meurt*, 1951 (*Malone Dies*, 1956); *L'Innommable*, 1953 (*The Unnamable*, 1958); *Watt*, 1953; *Comment c'est*, 1961 (*How It Is*, 1964); *Mercier et Camier*, 1970 (*Mercier and Camier*, 1974); *Le Dépeupleur*, 1971 (*The Lost Ones*, 1972); *Company*, 1980; *Mal vu mal dit*, 1981 (*Ill Seen Ill Said*, 1981); *Worstward Ho*, 1983.

Other literary forms

Samuel Beckett has worked in every literary genre since his first publication, an essay, appeared in 1929. He is a painstaking and increasingly astringent writer, yet the Grove Press edition of his *Collected Works* had grown to twenty-four volumes by 1981, and Beckett is known to have withheld from publication a large number of manuscripts. His first book, published in 1931, was the critical study *Proust*, and during the next fifteen years, Beckett published a number of essays and book reviews that have yet to be collected in book form. After struggling with an unpublished play (entitled "Eleuthéria") in the late 1940's, he began publication of the series of plays that are as important as his novels to his present literary reputation. These include, notably, *En attendant Godot* (1952; *Waiting for Godot*, 1954), *Fin de partie* (1957; *Endgame*, 1958), *Krapp's Last Tape* (1958), *Happy Days* (1961), and many short pieces for the stage, including mimes. In addition to these works for the stage, he has written scripts for television, such as *Dis Joe* (1966; *Eh Joe*, 1967), scripts for radio, such as *All That Fall* (1957), and one film script, entitled *Film* (1967). Most, but not all, of his many short stories are gathered in various collections, including *More Pricks than Kicks* (1934), *Nouvelles et textes pour rien* (1955; *Stories and Texts for Nothing*, 1967), *No's Knife: Collected Shorter Prose 1947-1966* (1967; includes *Stories and Texts for Nothing* and other short pieces), *First Love and Other Shorts* (1974), and *Pour finir encore et autres foirades* (1976; *Fizzles*, 1976; also as *For to End Yet Again*, 1976). Beckett's poetry, most of it written early in his career for periodical publication, has been made available in *Poems in English* (1961) and *Collected Poems in English and French* (1977). Many of the various collections of his short pieces mix works of different literary genres, and Richard Seaver has edited a general sampling of Beckett works of all sorts in an anthology entitled *I Can't Go On, I'll Go On: A Selection from Samuel Beckett's Work* (1976).

Achievements

Beckett did not begin to write his most important works until he was forty years of age, and he had to wait some time beyond that for widespread recognition of his literary achievements. Since he received the Nobel Prize for Literature in 1969, however, he has retained a solid reputation as one of the most important and demanding authors of plays and novels in the twentieth century.

In the 1930's, when he began to write, Beckett seemed destined for the sort of footnote fame that has overtaken most of his English and Irish literary companions from that decade. His work appeared to be highly derivative of the avant-garde coterie associated with *Transition* magazine and especially of the novels of James Joyce, who, as an elder Irish expatriate in Paris, befriended and encouraged the young Beckett. By the time that Beckett was forty years old and trying to salvage a literary career disrupted by World War II, his anonymity was such that his own French translation of his first novel, *Murphy*, had sold exactly six copies by the time he presented the same skeptical Paris publisher with another manuscript.

Nevertheless, it was at that time—the late 1940's—that Beckett blossomed as a writer. He withdrew into a voluntary solitude he himself refers to as "the siege in the room," began to compose his works in French rather than in English, and shed many of the mannerisms of his earlier work. The immediate result was the trilogy of novels that constitutes his most important achievement in prose fiction: *Molloy*, *Malone Dies*, and *The Unnamable*. This period also produced *Waiting for Godot*, and it was this play that first brought Beckett fame. *Waiting for Godot*, considered a formative influence on the Theater of the Absurd, stimulated the first serious critical treatments of Beckett's work. Although Beckett is known to attach more personal importance to his novels than to his plays, it was not until the 1960's that critics went beyond his plays and began to bring his prose works under close scrutiny. Then, as now, most criticism of Beckett's fiction focused on the trilogy and the austere prose fiction in French that followed it.

In the years since then, Beckett's novels have risen in critical estimation from essentially eccentric, if interesting, experiments to exemplars of self-referential postmodern fiction commonly cited by literary theorists. Disagreements about the nature of particular works and skepticism about the bulk of commentary generated by very brief prose fragments have also inevitably accompanied this rather sudden enshrinement of a difficult and extremely idiosyncratic body of work. Even the most antagonistic analyses of Beckett's novels, however, grant them a position of importance and influence in the development of prose fiction since World War II, and they also accept Samuel Beckett's stature as one of the most important novelists since his friend and Irish compatriot James Joyce.

Biography

Samuel Barclay Beckett was born in Foxrock, a modestly affluent suburb of Dublin, Ireland. He gives Good Friday, April 13, 1906, as his birthdate, but some convincing contrary evidence suggests that this particular day may have been chosen more for its significance than its accuracy. (According to biographer Deirdre Bair, the date on Beckett's birth certificate is May 13.) His parents, William Beckett and Mary (May) Jones Roe, belonged to the Protestant middle class known as Anglo-Irish in Ireland. Beckett's childhood, in contrast to the unpleasant imagery of many of his novels, was a relatively cheery one of genteel entertainment at the family home, Cooldrinagh, of private education at Portora Royal School in County Fermanagh, and of greater success on the cricket green than in the classroom.

Beckett matriculated to Trinity College, Dublin, in 1923, and there he developed his first literary interests. He completed a curriculum in Romance languages at Trinity, which led to an appointment as lecturer at the École Normale Supérieure in Paris after his graduation in 1927. In Paris, Beckett began to associate with the Bohemian intellectual circles of French, English, and American writers for which the city was then famous. Beckett returned to Dublin in 1930 for graduate work and a teaching position at Trinity, but during Christmas vacation, he returned to the Continent for travel throughout Germany and France and an extended reunion with his friends in Paris, including James Joyce. His first works of fiction, the stories in *More Pricks than Kicks* and the novel *Murphy*, are set in Dublin and its environs, but their intellectual preoccupations and Bohemian antagonism toward middle-class complacency derive more from the environment of Paris than that of Ireland.

At the outbreak of World War II, Beckett was a permanent resident of Paris. As an Irish citizen, he could have returned home, but instead, he took refuge from the German occupation of Paris in the French countryside. There, he assisted the Resistance and began to write the novel *Watt*, which marks a movement toward the style of his major fiction in its strangely dislocated senses of time and place. After the war, Beckett was decorated with the Croix de Guerre for his assistance to the French underground, and this award is generally cited as evidence of an essential humanism underlying the frequently misanthropic tenor of his novels. All evidence suggests, however, that the experience of the war increased Beckett's antagonism toward social affiliations and his skepticism about humanistic values.

Beckett returned to Paris after the war, and from 1946 to 1950, he retired into that "siege in the room," his most fertile period in a long literary career. By the time *Waiting for Godot* had established his reputation, he had already developed the reclusive life-style that he maintained thereafter, despite persistent media attention. He was married to longtime companion Suzanne Deschevaux-Dumesnil in secrecy in London in 1961, and he refused to attend the award ceremony for his Nobel Prize for Literature in 1969. Thereafter, Beckett has divided his time between Paris and the country village of Marne, while producing a slow but steady stream of intricately conceived and composed short prose fictions and dramatic pieces.

Analysis

Samuel Beckett's work resists explication. His most important novels and plays are artfully constructed contemplations of their own form rather than commentaries on the familiar world of causal relationships and social contingencies. His most important novels abandon progressive narrative for the more difficult and subtle suggestiveness of haunting images, deliberate enigmas, and complexly ironic epigrams.

Although Beckett's work resists criticism, the author has issued critical statements and congenially submitted to interviews with critics. He manages to transform both sorts of critical occasions into intellectual performances that are as provocative, and occasionally as humorous, as his fiction. Two particular comments by Beckett, out of many stimulating ones, may serve as instructive introductions to the body of his prose works. In his first published book, *Proust*, Beckett wrote that artistic creation is essentially an excavatory process, comparable to an attempt to reach an ideal, impossibly minuscule, core of an onion. Beckett's novels relentlessly pursue this sort of process, stripping away layers of assumptions about the self and the world, peeling away conventional modes of thought to reach a pure essence of existence free of the inevitably distorting effects of intellect, logical structure, and analytical order. This image of the onion is a rich one because it communicates the sense in Beckett's work that this excavatory process is unending, that disposal of each mode of thought reveals yet another, even more resistant habit of mind. Beckett himself often speaks of his novels as a series, and it is this progressive penetration through one form of thought to another that marks the stages in the series.

Thirty years after *Proust*, Beckett submitted to an unusually provocative interview with Tom Driver that was published in Columbia University Forum in the summer of 1961. In this interview, he dwelt specifically on form. After contrasting the orderly form of most art to the intransigently chaotic nature of existence, he said: "The Form and the chaos remain separate. The latter is not reduced to the former. . . . to find a form that accommodates the mess, that is the task of the artist now." Beckett's novels reveal three stages in this attempt to discover a literary form that will accommodate the chaotic nature of existence. In the first stage, represented by *Murphy* and *Watt*, the process is a destructive one of ridiculing literary convention by parody and satire to suggest an as yet undiscovered alternative form of expression. In the second stage, represented by the trilogy, the attempt to give voice to that alternative takes the form of the disordered—and at times deliberately incoherent—monologues of individual narrators. In the third stage, represented by *How It Is* and the subsequent short prose pieces, the process takes the form of presenting metaphoric worlds that accommodate their own chaos.

This last stage, especially, is marked by the unpleasant emphasis on miserable degradation and the recurring private images that have given Beckett an undeserved reputation for misanthropy and deliberate obscurity. These charges are effectively rebutted by his own stated sense of "the task of the artist now." Beckett's works do not provide relaxing reading experiences. They are designed to disorient, to dislocate, and to thwart intellectual complacency. The formidable difficulties they present to the reader, however, are essential records of the intellectual ambience of advanced mid-twentieth century thought.

Beckett's earliest fiction, the stories in *More Pricks than Kicks*, describes the passive resistance to social conformity and death under anesthesia of a protagonist named Belacqua (an allusion to Dante). Beckett's first novel, *Murphy*, presents the same resistance and senseless death in the story of Murphy, who bears the most common surname in Ireland. Murphy is the first of numerous Beckett protagonists who seek to relinquish all ties to their environment and their compulsion to make sense of it. The centerpiece of *Murphy* is an analysis, in the sixth chapter, of the discrete zones of his mind. The third and last of these zones is a darkness of selflessness in which mind itself is obviated. It is this zone beyond consciousness that most Beckett protagonists seek; it is their failure to reach it that creates the tension in most of Beckett's fiction.

Murphy is surrounded by representatives of two frames of reference that prevent his withdrawal from the world. The first is nationality, represented here by character-types such as the drunken Irish poet Austin Ticklepenny and monuments to national ideals such as the statue of Cuchulain in the Dublin General Post Office. The second frame of reference is erudition, represented here by a plethora of arcane references to astronomy, astrology, philosophy, and mathematics. Assaulted by these adjuncts of identity, Murphy remains unable to disengage himself fully from the world, to withdraw completely into the third zone of his mind.

The problem that Beckett confronts in *Murphy* is central to all of his novels: to define consciousness in a novel without the usual novelistic apparatus of recognizable environment, nationality, and psychology. The novel approaches such a definition only in the chapter on Murphy's mind and in the image of an eerily withdrawn character named Mr. Endon. Elsewhere, Beckett is able to suggest an alternative only by destructive means: by heaping scorn on things Irish, by deflating intellectual pretensions, and by parodying novelistic conventions. These forms of ridicule make *Murphy* Beckett's most humorous and accessible novel. The same reliance on ridicule, however, ensures that *Murphy* remains derivative of the very forms of thought and literature it intends to challenge.

Although it was not published until 1953, after *Molloy* and *Malone Dies*,

Watt was written a decade earlier and properly belongs among Beckett's early novels. It is a transitional work, written in English, in which one can observe intimations of the central concerns of the trilogy of novels written in French.

Like Murphy, Watt is an alienated vagabond seeking succor from the complexities of existence. In the opening and closing sections of this four-part novel, Watt's world is a recognizably Irish one populated with middle-class characters with small social pretensions. In the central two sections, however, Watt works as a servant on the surreal country estate of a Mr. Knott. *Watt* most resembles Beckett's later fiction in these central sections. In them, Watt ineffectually attempts to master simpler and simpler problems without the benefit of reliable contingencies of cause and effect or even the assurance of a reliable system of language. The structure of the novel is ultimately dislocated by the gradual revelation that the four parts are not in fact presented in chronological order and that they have been narrated by a character named Sam rather than by an omniscient narrator. Sam's account proves unreliable in particulars, thus completing the process by which the novel undermines any illusion of certainty concerning the interaction of the characters Watt ("What?") and Knott ("Not!").

Watt, like *Murphy*, relies on satire of literary precedents and disruption of novelistic conventions. There are allusions in the novel to the work of W. B. Yeats and James Joyce and to the poet Æ (George William Russell), to cite only the Irish precedents. The great disruption of novelistic conventions is effected by the "Addenda" of unincorporated material at the end of the text and by pedantic annotations throughout the novel. Nevertheless, *Watt* does look forward to *Molloy* in its central sections, dominated by episodic problems such as the removal of Knott's slops and the attempt of the wretched Lynch family to have the ages of its living members total exactly one thousand. The full emergence of this sort of episodic narrative in Beckett's fiction, however, seems to have required the focus of attention on language itself (rather than on literary conventions) that was one important effect of his decision to begin to compose novels in French rather than English.

Mercier and Camier, although published in 1970, was written in French in 1946, soon after Beckett returned to Paris at the end of the war. Like *Watt*, it is best placed among Beckett's works by date of composition rather than publication. Written at the outset of the "siege in the room" that produced Beckett's major novels, it illuminates the process by which the style of the trilogy emerged from concentration on elements of composition rather than on the social concerns that dominate most conventional novels.

Mercier and Camier is an account of an aimless journey by two decrepit characters out of and back into a city that resembles Dublin. A witness-narrator announces his presence in the opening sentence, but remains otherwise inconspicuous. The descriptions of the two characters' generally enigmatic encounters with others, however, are periodically interrupted by subtly disported tabular synopses that call attention to the arbitrary features of the narrator's accounts. The novel is thus a shrewdly self-conscious narrative performance, with the emphasis falling on the telling rather than on the meaning of the tale.

The publication of *Mercier and Camier*, belated though it may have been, was a welcome event. Although the book represents what must have seemed to Beckett an unsatisfactory attempt to open the novel form to accommodate the "mess" he finds dominant in the world, his composition of the novel in French produced a spare prose style and calculated use of language that would prove essential to his later fiction. Like *Watt*, however, *Mercier and Camier* still retained a peripheral witness-narrator; this may have been one of the sources of Beckett's dissatisfaction, for immediately after this novel, he shifted to the monologue essential to the trilogy that followed.

Beckett's major accomplishment in prose fiction is the trilogy of novels begun with *Molloy*, written in French in 1947 and 1948. All three are narrative monologues, all seek to explain origins, and all expose various forms of self-knowledge as delusions. Thus, they approach that ideal core of the onion in their quest for explanations, and they assert the governing "mess" of incoherence, which continues to resist artificial, if comforting, intellectual fabrications.

In structure, *Molloy*, translated into English by Beckett in collaboration with Patrick Bowles, is the most complex work in the trilogy. The first part of the novel is the narrative of the derelict Molloy, who discovers himself in his mother's room and attempts unsuccessfully to reconstruct the events that led to his arrival there. The second part is the narrative of the Catholic and bourgeois detective Jacques Moran, who has been commissioned by an authority named Youdi to write a report on Molloy. As Moran's report proceeds, he gradually begins to resemble Molloy. His narrative ends with the composition of the sentence with which it began, now exposed as pure falsehood.

Molloy and Moran are counterparts whose narratives expose the alternative fallacies, respectively, of inward and outward ways of organizing experience. Molloy's self-involved preoccupations, such as his chronic flatulence, function as counterparts of Moran's more social preoccupations, such as Catholic liturgy and his profession. Both are left in unresolved confrontation with the likelihood that the ways in which they have attempted to make sense of their origins and present circumstances are pure sham. The special brillance of *Molloy* is the manner in which this confrontation is brought about by the terms of each narrator's monologue. The prose style of the novel is dominated by hilarious deflations of momentary pretensions, ironic undercutting of reassuring truisms, and criticism of its own assertions. It is in this manner that *Molloy* manages to admit the "mess" Beckett seeks to accommodate in the novel form: Its compelling and humorous narratives effectively expose the limits rather than the fruits of self-knowledge.

Malone Dies is the purest of the narrative performances of Beckett's story-tellers. In it, a bedridden man awaits death in his room and tells stories to pass the time. His environment is limited to the room, the view from a window, and a meager inventory of possessions he periodically re-counts with inconsistent results. Beyond these, he is limited to the world of his stories about a boy named Sapo, an old man named MacMann, an employee in an insane asylum named Lemuel, and others. All are apparently fictions based on different periods in Malone's own life. At the end of the novel, his narrative simply degenerates and ends inconclusively in brief phrases that may suggest death itself or simply the end of his willingness to pursue the stories further.

It is essential to the novel that Malone criticize his own stories, revise them, abandon them, and rehearse them once again. His predicament is that, while he knows the stories to be false in many respects, he has no alternative approach to the truth of his own origins. Like Beckett himself, Malone is a compulsive composer of fictions who is perpetually dissatisfied with them. As a result, *Malone Dies* is one of the most completely self-critical and self-involved novels in the twentieth century stream of metafictions, or novels about the nature of the novel. It demonstrates, with bitter humor and relentless self-examination, the limits of fiction, the pleasure of fiction, and the lack of an acceptable substitute for fiction.

In *The Unnamable*, Beckett pursues the preoccupations of *Molloy* and *Malone Dies* to an extreme that puts formidable difficulties before even the most devoted reader of the modern novel. In *Molloy*, the focus was on two long narrative accounts; in *Malone Dies*, it narrowed to concentrate on briefer stories; in *The Unnamable*, it shrinks further to probe the limits of language itself, of words and names. As the title suggests, these smaller units of literary discourse prove to be just as false and unreliable as those longer literary units had in Beckett's previous two novels. In *The Unnamable*, there is no character in the ordinary sense of the term. Instead, there are only bursts of language, at first organized into paragraphs, then only into continuous sentences, and finally into pages of a single sentence broken only by commas.

The premise of the novel is that a paralyzed and apparently androgynous creature suspended in a jar outside a Paris restaurant speaks of himself and versions of himself that are labeled with temporary names such as Mahood and Worm. As he speaks, however, he is diverted from the content of his speech by disgust with its elements, its words. The names of Murphy, Molloy, and Malone are all evoked with complete disgust at the complacent acceptance of language inherent in the creation of such literary characters. *The Unnamable* thus attempts to challenge assumptions of literary discourse by diverting attention from plot and character to phrase and word. It is tortuous reading because it calls into question the means by which any reading process proceeds.

The novel's preoccupation with speaking leads naturally to a corollary preoccupation with silence, and *The Unnamable* ends with a paradoxical assertion of the equal impossibility of either ending or continuing. At this point, Beckett had exhausted the means by which he attempted to admit the "mess" into the form of the novels in his trilogy. He managed to proceed, to extend the series of his novels, by exploring the richness of metaphoric and generally horrific environments like that of the unnamable one suspended, weeping, in his jar.

Beckett's critics commonly refer to the series of prose fictions begun with *How It Is* as "post-trilogy prose." The term is useful because it draws a distinction between the methods of Beckett's works as well as their chronology. Even in the midst of the incoherence of *The Unnamable*, there were references to the familiar world, such as the fact that the narrator was located in Paris. In *How It Is* and the works that have followed, however, the environment is an entirely metaphoric and distinctly surreal one. Lacking reference to a familiar world, these works are governed by an interior system of recurrent images and memories. *How It Is* marks the beginning of this most recent stage in the series of Beckett's works, and so its French title, *Comment c'est*, is an appropriate phonetic pun, meaning both "how it is" and *commencer*, or "to begin."

In *How It Is*, the speaker, named Bom, is a creature crawling in darkness through endless mire, dragging with him a sack of canned provisions and torturing and being tortured by other creatures with their indispensable can openers. His narrative takes the form of brief, unpunctuated fragments separated by spaces on the page. Each fragment is of a length that can be spoken aloud, as they ideally should be, and the style may be in part a product of Beckett's experience in the production of plays. There is a second character, named Pim, against whom the narrator tends to define his own status. The novel, which many prefer to term a prose poem, is thus broken into three parts: before Pim, with Pim, and after Pim.

The Bom and Pim interaction is an excruciating account of misery in a netherworld of darkness and slime. It is related entirely in retrospect, however, and the changing relationships of domination and subordination are less important than the manner in which the language of the fragments creates its own system of repetitions and alterations of phrases. *How It Is* dramatizes, in fact, how it *was* for Bom, and in place of clear references to the familiar world, it offers a verbal model for the mechanics of memory. This remains a consistent, if extraordinarily complex, extension of Beckett's attempt to accommodate the "mess" of chaos in the novel form. Its extremely calculated prose creates a sense of the consistent, but inexplicable and ultimately uninformative, impingement of the past on the present.

The Lost Ones is a representative example of Beckett's prose fiction immediately following *How It Is*. He composed many brief prose pieces in this period, abandoned most of them, and resurrected them for publication at the urging of enthusiastic friends. Most are published in collections of his short works. *The Lost Ones*, however, is a more sustained narrative performance (sixty-three pages in the United States edition). It was abandoned in an incomplete form in 1966 but retrieved and supplemented with an effective conclusion in 1970. It has also gained greater attention than most of Beckett's works from this period because of an innovative stage adaptation by the Mabou Mines Company in New York City in 1973.

The Lost Ones is unique among Beckett's works because it focuses on a group rather than an individual. In fifteen unnumbered passages of prose, it describes the workings of a huge cylinder populated by male and female figures who maneuver throughout its various areas by means of ladders. The prose style is remarkably understated in comparison to the painful, if metaphoric, imagery of *How It Is*, and the primary action is the continual reorganization of this closed set of persons according to an entropic process of diminishing energies. Mathematical computation, a motif in many of Beckett's novels, is a primary feature in *The Lost Ones*. As language had shown itself, in many of Beckett's earlier novels, to be an inadequate means of organizing experience, so do numerical calculations prove to be in this work, and the crucial final paragraph added in 1970 is a fatalistic exposure of the worthlessness of these computations as indications of the past, present, or future of this surreal environment. As in many of Beckett's later prose pieces, the metaphoric environment created by the prose is open to many interpretive referents. The text is subtly allusive—the French title, for example, evokes Alphonse de Lamartine—and the viability of literature as an effective indication of past, present, or future is among the possible subjects of this spare and immensely suggestive text.

Excepting *The Lost Ones* and other aborted works, nearly twenty years elapsed between the writing of *How It Is* and the next of Beckett's prose fictions to approach the novel in form if not in length. *Company* ended this relative silence, during which Beckett produced a variety of works in other genres. Like *How It Is* and the intervening works, *Company* presents a generally metaphoric environment and a consistent emphasis on the workings of memory. Unlike Beckett's other later works, however, it was composed in English and apparently generated out of contemplation of distinctly autobiographical images.

Company is a narrative by a figure immobilized on his back in darkness. Despite this surreal premise, it dwells on images of a familiar, suggestively Irish environment marked by features such as Connolly's store and the Ballyogan Road. It thus combines the astringency of Beckett's "post-trilogy prose" with the references to an identifiable world common in the trilogy. It is, however, far from a regression from experimental form or an abandonment of the attempt to accommodate the "mess" in a novel. Instead, it represents the fruit of Beckett's years of careful manipulation of a spare prose style in his second language. Like *How It Is*, *Company* concentrates on the inexplicable workings of memory. Unlike *How It Is*, the novel does so in a passive and restrained mixture of nostalgic and ironic images free of the vulgar and painful hostility of that earlier novel. In less flamboyant ways than Beckett's earlier works, *Company* also manages to underscore its own nature as an artificial, literary construction. Its governing metaphor of "company" encompasses both the memories surrounding the narrator and the meeting of author and reader of a literary text.

Ill Seen Ill Said is a series of paragraphs consisting primarily of sentence fragments that describe a woman and her attempt to capture the details of her environment. The devotion to detail is such that vocabulary, rather than image, tends to capture the reader's attention, frequently because of intentional neologisms, interior rhymes, and sporadic echoes. *Ill Seen Ill Said* is more an evocation of a mood than a plotted novel, one that reveals the author, having rid himself of complacent use of language in earlier works, as a prose stylist with marked affinities to a poet. *Ill Seen Ill Said* marks the emergence in Beckett's works of a devotion to pure sensation unmodulated by systems of logic or desire. It is in this respect that *Ill Seen Ill Said* is a necessary and inevitable extension of "the task of the artist now" addressed in a long series of novels. Rather than suggesting an alternative literary expression by destructive irony or subverting complacency by incoherent monologue, it attempts to present consciousness free of artificial order in a distinctly lyric form of prose fiction.

In an early essay on the Irish poet Denis Devlin published in *Transition* in 1938, Beckett offered this dictum: "Art has always been this—pure interrogation, rhetorical question less the rhetoric." Like so many of his statements on other writers, this one has a special relevance to Beckett's own literary career. Over a period of a half century, he has produced fictions that relentlessly question assumptions of intellectual and literary order. He has done so with a single-minded devotion to what he takes to be "the task of the artist now" and in so doing compiled an oeuvre that is unique in the twentieth century in its concentration on a central purpose and in its literary expression of the great philosophical preoccupations of its time. Beckett's work has been discussed by critics in reference to other innovative thinkers of the century as disparate as Albert Einstein, Sigmund Freud, and Jean-Paul Sartre. In addition to fueling the literary debates of his time, his work may be said to have created, in part, contemporary literary theories such as structuralism and deconstruction. Despite their formidable difficulties, then, Beckett's novels have an indisputable importance to anyone seriously interested in the intellectual climate of the twentieth century.

Major publications other than long fiction

SHORT FICTION: *More Pricks than Kicks*, 1934; *Nouvelles et textes pour rien*,

1955 (*Stories and Texts for Nothing*, 1967); *No's Knife: Collected Shorter Prose 1947-1966*, 1967 (includes *Stories and Texts for Nothing* with other short prose); *First Love and Other Shorts*, 1974; *Pour finir encore et autres foirades*, 1976 (*Fizzles*, 1976; also as *For to End Yet Again*, 1976).

PLAYS: *En attendant Godot*, 1952 (*Waiting for Godot*, 1954); *All That Fall*, 1957 (radio play); *Fin de partie*, 1957 (*Endgame*, 1958); *Krapp's Last Tape*, 1958; *Embers*, 1959 (radio script); *Happy Days*, 1961; *Words and Music*, 1962 (radio play); *Cascando*, 1963 (radio play); *Play*, 1964; *Dis Joe*, 1966 (television script; *Eh Joe*, 1967); *Come and Go*, 1967; *Film*, 1967 (film script); *Sans*, 1969; *Not I*, 1974; *Ends and Odds*, 1976; *Rockaby and Other Short Pieces*, 1981.

POETRY: *Whoroscope*, 1930; *Echos Bones and Other Precipitates*, 1935; *Poems in English*, 1961; *Collected Poems in English and French*, 1977.

NONFICTION: *Proust*, 1931.

ANTHOLOGY: *An Anthology of Mexican Poetry*, 1958.

TRANSLATION: *Zone*, 1972 (of Guillaume Apollinaire's *Zone*).

MISCELLANEOUS: *I Can't Go On, I'll Go On: A Selection from Samuel Beckett's Work*, 1976 (Richard Seaver, editor).

Bibliography
Bair, Deirdre. *Samuel Beckett: A Biography*, 1978.
Cohn, Ruby. *Samuel Beckett: The Comic Gamut*, 1962.
Esslin, Martin, ed. *Samuel Beckett: A Collection of Critical Essays*, 1965.
Fletcher, John. *The Novels of Samuel Beckett*, 1964.
Mercier, Vivian. *Beckett/Beckett*, 1977.
Pilling, John. *Samuel Beckett*, 1976.
Robinson, Michael. *The Long Sonata of the Dead: A Study of Samuel Beckett*, 1969.
Worth, Katherine, ed. *Beckett the Shape Changer*, 1975.

John P. Harrington

JUAN BENET

Born: Madrid, Spain; October 7, 1927

Principal long fiction

Volverás a Región, 1967 (*Return to Región*, 1984); *Una meditación*, 1970 (*A Meditation*, 1982); *Una tumba*, 1971; *Un viaje de invierno*, 1972; *La otra casa de Mazón*, 1973; *En el estado*, 1977; *El aire de un crimen*, 1980; *Saúl ante Samuel*, 1982; *Herrumbrosas lanzas I-VI*, 1983.

Other literary forms

Although best known for his novels, Juan Benet has gained recognition as a superb essayist and short-story writer as well. His essays range in scope from music to linguistics, but his most perceptive writings are those on literary theory: *La inspiración y el estilo* (1966), *Puerta de tierra* (1970), *El ángel del Señor abandona a Tobías* (1976), *En ciernes* (1976), *La moviola de Eurípides* (1982). Above all, Benet articulates a literary posture that underscores the importance of style and enigma in the creation of fiction.

Benet's short stories have been collected in four volumes: *Nunca llegarás a nada* (1961); *Cinco narraciones y dos fábulas* (1972); *Sub rosa* (1973); *Trece fábulas y media* (1981). For the most part, the stories parallel his longer fiction in style and theme, though they are often more playful in tone. Benet has also written four plays (*Max*, 1953; *Agonía confutans*, 1969; *Anastas: O, El origen de la constitución*, 1970; *Un caso de conciencia*, 1970), but none has been performed with either critical or commercial success.

Achievements

Benet can perhaps be regarded most accurately as a novelist's novelist (or a critic's novelist) who writes difficult works for a minority public. Indeed, his fiction rarely permits even the most experienced reader to feel at ease. After finishing a work, one is left with the disquieting thought that one has missed the point or that there are many more points than one could possibly imagine—or worse yet, that there is no point at all. Benet challenges his readers to rethink critical traditions that demand decisive meanings or that wrest from analysis unresolved ambiguities. His is a pluralistic fiction, a narrative of ideas forged with a style at once intricate and dense.

Despite the professed irritation of many critics with the difficult nature of his fiction, Benet has gained recognition as one of Spain's most distinguished contemporary writers. He was one of the first postwar novelists to break with neorealism in Spain and to offer a more subjective and experimental fiction in its place. Since 1969, when *A Meditation* was awarded the prestigious Premio Biblioteca Breve, Benet has become one of the most prolific writers of his time. He has continued to garner literary prizes (including the important Premio de la Crítica for *Herrumbrosas lanzas I-VI*) and has been invited to lecture throughout Western Europe and the United States. Perhaps more important, he has begun to have a profound influence on younger writers seeking new directions for the Spanish novel. Benet's fiction has served as an imposing symbol of innovation and change in postwar Spain, and the unique vision that he brings to his craft has propelled him to the forefront of his profession even as he remains aloof from the literary and critical establishment.

Biography

Juan Benet Goita is one of those extraordinary individuals who has successfully cultivated his talents in two often conflicting pursuits: the scientific rigor of modern engineering and the aesthetic demands of creative writing. While the former is the result of a conscious decision and advanced study, the latter has grown more from an undefined and diffuse passion. Benet was an avid reader in his youth and came to know intimately such master novelists as Stendhal, Gustave Flaubert, Fyodor Dostoevski, and Miguel de Cervantes. By the age of twenty, he was a regular participant in the literary *tertulias* of novelist Pío Baroja, one of the few modern Spanish writers whom Benet admires. He did not discover his true literary mentor (and his desire to be a writer), however, until 1947, when in a bookstore in Madrid he stumbled upon the work of William Faulkner. Faulkner's influence on Benet is decisive, and much of Benet's stylistic complexity, as well as his tragic vision of time and history, is rooted in Yoknapatawpha County and the decadent South that Faulkner meticulously created.

Benet was graduated from the School of Engineering in Madrid in 1954 and has served as a civil engineer and contractor throughout the Iberian Peninsula. Much of his early work, however, was centered in the northwestern provinces of León and Asturias, where he constructed roads and dams for the Spanish government. Isolated in the mountains for long periods of time, with only his work crew as company, Benet read classical philosophy and wrote fragments of fiction that would later appear in his novels. In 1963, while supervising construction of a dam on the Porma River, he began to revise a manuscript entitled "El guarda," which four years later would become his first published novel, *Volverás a Región*. Over the next decade Benet successfully balanced his career as an engineer with his newly won fame as a novelist. His stature as an author continued to grow not only in Spain but also elsewhere in Europe and in the Americas. In recent years, he has devoted nearly all of his time to writing, even though he insisted in 1967, shortly after the publication of *Volverás a Región*, that he was an author only by avocation. Thus, Benet's engineering past must be viewed as crucial to his development as a novelist. His work in remote areas of Spain not only afforded him time to think and write but also presented him with the physical and psychological ambience for his mythical Región, fictional setting for nearly all of his long fiction and microcosm of postwar Spain.

Analysis

Juan Benet falls chronologically into the group of writers commonly known as the Generation of 1950. The realistic orientation and engagé approach to literature espoused by these writers (including Jesús Fernández Santos, Juan Goytisolo, Luis Goytisolo, Rafael Sánchez Ferlosio) became the predominant literary force in Spain for nearly three decades following the Civil War (1936-1939). For the most part, novelists of this period defined their task as the verbal reproduction of a familiar reality, the shared world of reader and writer. Thus, the most important fiction written during the 1950's and early 1960's portrays everyday events in conventional novelistic forms.

Despite Benet's chronological affiliation with the writers of this period, he represents a direct antithesis to their fundamental literary canons. Indeed, his negative assessment of neorealistic fiction and his emphasis on style and enigma have made him one of the most original Spanish writers of the twentieth century. His first collection of short stories, *Nunca llegarás a nada*, clearly transgresses the canons of social realism and foreshadows the tone, style, and thematic concerns which he develops more intensely in his long fiction. Rather than record the observable in his narrative, Benet has sought instead to probe beneath the surface of reality and explore what he terms "the zone of shadows." The abstruse and often inaccessible fiction that results has set Benet radically apart from the neorealism of the early postwar period as well as from the more experimental writing of the 1970's.

With the exception of *En el estado*, Benet has set all of his novels in Región, a mythical region created in the fashion of Faulkner's Yoknapatawpha County or Gabriel García Márquez' Macondo. This private narrative world stands as the most explicit symbol of the ruin and despair that form the central motif of Benet's fiction. First created in 1961 in the short story "Baalbac, una mancha," Región did not achieve full realization until *Volverás a Región*, in which its geographic and enigmatic peculiarities are presented in detail. From one point of view, Región is the aggregate of characters, events, and social themes which, in Benet's view, constitute twentieth century Spanish society. More important than the social background, however, is the enigmatic reality of Región itself, portrayed by Benet on varying levels of complexity. On one hand, he depicts Región and the surrounding area with scientific precision. In fact, Región is described in such detail that the captivated reader searches to locate it on a map of Spain. Its flora and fauna, its landscape, and even its geological formation are portrayed with equal exactness of description, thus creating a reality that appears both authentic and identifiable in the physical world outside the text.

Yet Benet establishes the real in Región in order to undermine it, to place in doubt its correspondence with the everyday world of observable reality. For the most part, he achieves this not explicitly, through use of the supernatural, but more subtly, by means of conflicting descriptions and recurrent suggestions of the unreal. In the first place, he portrays Región in a full state of decadence, surrounded by hostile landscapes and immersed in a threatening temperate zone. The entire area is a massive labyrinth of streams, valleys, forests, and deserts that have a life and meaning of their own. Throughout his fiction, but most forcefully in *Volverás a Región*, Benet constructs an ambience in which he underscores the extreme and contrasting elements of the physical environment: desert/luxuriant vegetation; heat/cold; mountain/valley; rivers/dried-up streams; life/death. Nature serves to deter outsiders (known as "intruders") from entering Región, and the unwary visitor often falls victim to the hostility of the area, never to be seen or heard from again.

Within the hostile physical world of Región, Benet creates a complementary reality characterized by the enigmatic and the inexplicable. For example, mysterious wild flowers grow only on the soil of tombs; strange sounds and lights terrify travelers at night; a mythical woodsman, Numa, guards the forest of Mantua and kills with a single shot any intruders who cross its boundaries. On a rational level, Benet explains neither the origin nor the ultimate consequences of these and a host of similar elements that constitute the world of Región. They inhere in the murky area beneath the surface of reality and frequently defy logical explanation.

Nearly all of Benet's long fiction is cast in a similar stylistic and thematic mold. Both the consistency and the complexity of his fiction can be shown most succinctly through a discussion of the Región trilogy, *Volverás a Región*, *A Meditation*, and *Un viaje de invierno*. Although the latter two works were published without delay and received immediate attention from critics, *Volverás a Región*, first novel of a then unknown writer, was sold to Ediciones Destino only after a long process of submissions and rejections. Symptomatic of the Spanish literary scene of the time, one of Benet's rejection letters assured him that, because his novel lacked dialogue, the public would not read it. *Volverás a Región* is now considered one of the most important Spanish novels of the postwar era.

What traditionally has been called plot does not exist in *Volverás a Región*. Instead, the novel consists of a complex framework of third-person narration and pseudodialogues between the two principal characters, Doctor Sebastián and Marré Gamallo. Daniel Sebastián is an aging doctor who has been living in solitude for nearly a quarter of a century in Región, with little else to do but drink, remember, and care for a child driven insane by the absence of his mother. One evening he is visited by a woman, Marré Gamallo, and throughout the night the two characters carry on a soliloquylike dialogue in which they evoke their past and examine their destinies. During the Civil

War, the woman was the lover of Sebastián's godson, Luis I. Timoner, and this love represented for her the only happiness in her lifetime. She has returned to Región in search of the fulfillment that she lost when Luis fled into the mountains near the end of the war. For his part, Doctor Sebastián awakens the phantasmagorical events of his past, and remembers in particular his unfulfilled passion for María Timoner, Luis' mother. Through the memories of Sebastián and his visitor, and with the additional comments of the third-person narrator, the reader is able to reconstruct the fragmented history of the ruination of Región and its habitants.

Much of the narrative of *Volverás a Región* is devoted to the creation of a milieu that has become the cornerstone of Benet's fiction: the pervasive desolation of Región. Within this atmosphere, the threatening physical reality of the area not only stands as a striking tableau of ruin but also permeates the inhabitants through a process of antipathetic osmosis: There exists a direct relationship between the geographic location, climatic conditions, and physical ruin of the town and the spiritual malaise of Región's inhabitants. The moral dilapidation of Doctor Sebastián, for example, resembles the condition of his decaying house, while María Timoner is compared to the withered leaves of the black poplar trees. Both characters are submerged in the hellish atmosphere of the moribund province, with scant hope for redemption.

Like many twentieth century writers, Benet deliberately fragments his narratives into puzzlelike structures that do not yield their meaning to a passive reader. Although the chronological duration of *Volverás a Región* is only one night, the psychological time spans nearly four decades, from 1925 to an unspecified present during the 1960's. Hence the temporal focus continually shifts, and time periods are fused so that the past is felt not as distinct from the present but included in it and permeating it. Benet achieves this linkage primarily through the uncertain crucible of memory. During the course of their conversation, Dr. Sebastián and Marré Gamallo recapture a complex past that is patently destructive and capable of overwhelming any sense of hope in the present or future. In essence, the two characters possess a past that "was not." That is to say, there exists little from their previous life that can be remembered in a positive sense. They resemble the characters in Faulkner's *The Sound and the Fury* (1929), to whom nothing can happen because everything has already happened. As one of the children in Faulkner's novel declares: "I am not is, I am was." The elusive present and nonexistent future thus stand helpless before the past, which engenders stagnation and despair rather than growth and fulfillment. Benet's novel affirms the destructive power of time at every turn of the page, and his characters regress toward a past that exists only to remind them that they are condemned to a life of nothingness.

Throughout his numerous theoretical essays on literature, Benet has argued that style is the central component of fiction. Once a writer has developed a highly personal and fluid style, he is able to transcend the purely informational aspects of the novel—plot, setting, characters—and produce work of more lasting value. For Benet, the world is an enigma that the writer must penetrate and subsequently portray in his fiction. On one level, therefore, language serves as a means of discovery: The more developed a writer's style, the more perceptive will be his discovery. It is important to point out, however, that for Benet discovery is merely a prerequisite of creation. The writer does not merely represent what he perceives; rather, he invents a singular fictional reality through the skillful use of language. Style therefore serves as an enabling device that reifies imagination and affords new ways of knowing the world.

Benet's style is perhaps best described as labyrinthine. His sentences are frequently the length of a full page or more and include parentheses, parentheses within parentheses, and subordinate clauses which unite to form a syntactical webwork. Benet's style is, in fact, a persistent maze of obstacles replete with complex obtrusions, delays, ambiguous interpolations, and confusions. When used by the third-person narrator of *Volverás a Región*, the baroque sentences increase the enigmatic nature of the particular reality at hand. The narrator eschews words and linguistic structures that portray a world imitative of our own; hence, everything associated with what he says becomes part of a rarefied atmosphere aimed at precluding complete and rational understanding. A similar method defines the nature of the characters. Essentially stylized creations, their dialogue is the antithesis of realistic speech patterns. The conversation of Doctor Sebastián and Marré Gamallo, for example, is indistinguishable from the discourse of the narrator. Thus, the reader grows confused as one narrative voice blends into another and is lost amid the complicated labyrinth of words. Much of Benet's style and technique, it seems, is part of a deliberate plan to withhold meaning from the reader. As a result, the world of Región remains ambiguous and mysterious within the language that creates and sustains its very existence.

A Meditation, Benet's second novel, displays many of the stylistic and philosophical traits evident in *Volverás a Región* but represents a more ambitious undertaking than the earlier work. Written in the first person, *A Meditation* is precisely what the title suggests: a meditation on the past that covers a time span of nearly fifty years, from 1920 to the late 1960's. Although the novel is composed of an artistically manipulated structure rather than a loosely formed stream of consciousness, the events and characters that are presented do not appear in a specific, chronological arrangement. Instead, the unnamed narrator evokes a succession of fragmented memories which frequently remain vague and incomplete. The novel consists of one long paragraph, a feature which Benet stressed by submitting it to the publishers on a long, unbroken roll of paper rather than in the normal fashion of sequentially typed pages. The linear, uncut nature of the manuscript, however, by no means resembles the internal structure and content of the novel. In the manner of Marcel

Proust and Faulkner, Benet's nameless narrator scrutinizes the past in an attempt to recover and understand the nature of his family, friends, and previous existence in the vicinity of Región.

The traditional use of plot, which in *Volverás a Región* is reduced to a minimum, regains significance in *A Meditation*. There is no dramatic development and subsequent denouement, however, and the sequence of events in the novel could easily be rearranged. As the narrator's mind wanders through the past, certain incidents and characters are summoned into consciousness and placed in view of the reader. No single event or character, however, is presented in its entirety during a specific moment in the novel. Instead, Benet creates a maze of interpenetrating segments that represent the narrator's voluntary and involuntary memory and the desire for a "remembrance of things past."

Benet's treatment of time and memory in *A Meditation* clearly resembles the temporal concerns evident in *Volverás a Región*. In both novels, time plays an integral part in the psychological and physical ruin of Región and its inhabitants, and serves as a point of departure for philosophical speculation. In *A Meditation*, however, the reflections on time by the first-person narrator are actually reflections on the writing of the novel itself. Since the narrative consists of the recollection and subsequent expression of past events, any kind of temporal speculation must necessarily reflect on the construction of the work. Thus time and recollection, which form the intrinsic essence of the novel, play an equal role in both its form and content.

While memory provides the means for examining or recovering the past, the whole notion of time—past, present, future—embodies a fundamental thematic preoccupation of *A Meditation*. In addition to its role in the structure of the narrative, which consists of the continual amassing of fragmented memories, time is treated concretely in the form of Cayetano Corral's clock, and in abstraction by means of the narrator's numerous digressions. The mysterious clock, which has been in Cayetano's possession for several years, does not run. Although he has worked on the clock since he gained possession of it, he is less concerned with repairing its mechanical parts than with understanding its function: the marking of time. He fails in his efforts because, as the entire novel aims to show, time is not measured by the rhythmic pulsating of the clock but by the mechanism of the human psyche. In all of Benet's fiction, time becomes above all that which destroys: The past is an absence that creates a void for the present as well as the future. Although the first-person narrator of *A Meditation* indeed evokes past events, and in the process creates a self as a product of that past, the novel affirms the way in which Benet's characters do not grow and change through time in a positive sense, but rather remain stagnant within the ruin that they inevitably embody.

Benet's style in *A Meditation*, although similar to that of *Volverás a Región*, is more complex. In some respects, the novel resembles Marcel Proust's *À la recherche du temps perdu* (1913-1927; *Remembrance of Things Past*, 1922-1931), especially in narrative structure and technique. The influence of Faulkner, however, remains predominant in Benet's complex use of language. Like the American author, Benet frequently amasses words in a manner that has caused some critics to charge him with prolixity. Many of Benet's sentences cover several pages, and it becomes a diffucult task to remain attentive to the assorted ideas contained in one of the narrator's thought patterns. On the other hand, Benet's peripatetic style is crucial to the content and structure of the novel and to the complicated way in which he formulates his meditation. Benet's sentences are perhaps best defined as saturated solutions: Images and topics are juxtaposed through the transcendent life of the mind, which continually explores obscure and enigmatic elements of reality.

One of the recurrent stylistic features of Benet's fiction, and one particularly important in *A Meditation*, is the presentation of contradictory suggestions within a single context. Just as William Faulkner employs oxymoronic or near-oxymoronic terms in many of his novels, so Benet utilizes contradictory statements to keep his narratives in a state of flux or suspension, thus inspiring uncertainty and confusion in the reader. The oxymoronic descriptions that Benet employs in *A Meditation* are constructed by the simultaneous suggestions of disparate or contrasting elements, and therefore create a sharp polarity or tension. Both objects and characters are portrayed in this fashion and form part of the essential paradox of the novel. On the one hand, Benet achieves a kind of order and coherence by virtue of the clear and sharp antitheses which the contrasts involve. On the other hand, however, such descriptions create disorder and incoherence by virtue of their qualities of irresolution and contradiction. Hence, the reality of *A Meditation*, evoked through the uncertain authority of memory and conveyed by the uninhibited flow of language, is the enigmatic domain of the human psyche.

Un viaje de invierno, the final novel of the Región trilogy, is considered by many critics Benet's most abstruse piece of fiction. Once again, the reader must penetrate a world created by marathon sentences, a complex framework of recurring images, an ambiguous temporal structure, and an interrelated series of events that remain essentially unexplained in terms of motivation and ultimate resolution. Although *Un viaje de invierno* represents Benet's maximum effort to eliminate plot as an integral part of the novel, most of the narrative revolves around the uncertain configuration of a fiesta. Demetria holds the affair each year, ostensibly to honor the return of her daughter Coré, who annually spends six months away from Región; the novel begins with the writing and mailing of the invitations and ends with a vague description of the party. Any attempt, however, to comprehend the complex reasons for holding the celebration or to untangle the temporal confusion which surrounds the event encounters intransigent opposition. Demetria is unable to determine the number of guests she has invited, and she does not know how many attend, as she has never been to the party herself. Coré does not appear in the narrative, and the party is painted in such mysterious, rarefied tones that one is only able to guess at its implied meaning: for Demetria, an opportunity to exercise her will; for the guests, an ephemeral mitigation of their loneliness and a flight from the pain of daily life.

Arturo, the other principal figure of the novel, works as Demetria's servant. He has apparently (although we do not know for certain) worked as a handyman at other homes in the area, and each change of job brings him closer to the source of the Torce River. Arturo himself knows little about his past, except that for nearly all of his life he has labored on the farms along the Torce valley and has slowly journeyed up the river. It is a "winter's journey," as the title of the novel indicates, one that seems to lead him inescapably toward death. Yet the impetus for the journey is shrouded in mystery and borders on the magical. Arturo's future was determined early in his youth when one evening he listened to a waltz (*el vals K*) in the music conservatory where his mother worked as a cleaning woman. In the same way that Doctor Sebastián in *Volverás a Región* is condemned to suffer in Región after reading his future on the telegraph wheel, Arturo is destined to seek meaning in life at the head of the Torce River. The meaning that he seeks, of course, is correlated with death, toward which he inevitably and mysteriously journeys. This fatalistic destiny represents the future of nearly all of Benet's characters and inheres in the atmosphere of ruin and anguish that pervades his fiction.

As in his first two novels, Benet's style in *Un viaje de invierno* creates an uneasy and portentous mood. His style in the latter work, however, seems based upon a more studied attempt to avoid translating sensation into perception. A cognitive knowledge of something, be it of a character, an object, or a particular ambience, is of secondary importance to the pure consciousness of it. In this sense, Benet can be viewed as an idealist: Because one's consciousness seizes nothing but manifestations, reality is illusory. Indeed, when reading *Un viaje de invierno*, the reader senses that he or she is before the dream of reality instead of reality itself. For example, neither Coré nor Amat (Demetria's absent husband) ever appears as a concrete being in the novel; rather, both exist only as manifestations of Demetria's nostalgic memory. Demetria herself, whose existence is never seriously doubted, embodies Benet's predilection for the intangible and the ethereal. She is known to the inhabitants of Región by more than one name (Demetria, Nemesia, Obscura), and Benet never ascribes concrete physical characteristics to her. Her hand, for example, is *impalpale*, and she speaks words that sound without resonance. Her voice has no pitch or tone, and when she touches Arturo, he senses, yet does not feel, her hands. In short, Benet's method of portraying Demetria and the other figures of the novel points to the notion that we can discern only the image of something and not the thing itself.

The ethereal essence of his characters, however, in no way alleviates their existential despair. As in his previous novels, this despair in large part stems from the oppressive power of time. One is never aware in *Un viaje de invierno* of a pure present, and a specific past is not very often exclusively defined. In fact, Benet seems purposely to create a timeless vision of reality in which past and present are interfused to form a vague series of occurrences which defy order and reason. This notion of temporal uncertainty bears directly upon the title of the novel as well as one of its central motifs: the journey. Nearly all of the characters set out on a journey—to Central Europe, to the Torce River, to town, and so on. In one fashion or another, however, all of the trips revolve around the fiesta. Because the party cannot be located in time by any of the characters, it becomes clear that they undertake the journey in order to annul time, to exist in a temporal vacuum where neither past, present, nor future possesses any reality.

As in the earlier novels of the trilogy, however, the characters of *Un viaje de invierno* are trapped by the past, even as time moves forward and passes them by. If life consists of a continuation of the past into an ever-growing and expanding present, then the characters of *Un viaje de invierno* can have no hope for the future. Their lives are defined by a temporal vortex in which being is divorced from the linear progression of time. Although the fiesta represents for the characters an opportunity to grasp Martin Heidegger's "silent strength of the possible," they are ensnared by stagnation, where meaning remains elusive. This is the ultimate message of Benet's fiction, one that is affirmed even as he conceals it in the contradictory and enigmatic world of Región.

Major publications other than long fiction

SHORT FICTION: *Nunca llegarás a nada*, 1961; *Cinco narraciones y dos fábulas*, 1972; *Sub rosa*, 1973; *Trece fábulas y media*, 1981; *Cuentos completos*, 1981 (2 volumes).

PLAYS: *Max*, 1953; *Agonía confutans*, 1969; *Anastas: O, El origen de la constitución*, 1970; *Un caso de conciencia*, 1970; *Teatro*, 1971 (collection; includes preceding four plays).

NONFICTION: *La inspiración y el estilo*, 1966; *Puerta de tierra*, 1970; *El ángel del Señor abandona a Tobías*, 1976; *En ciernes*, 1976; *¿Qué fue la guerra civil?*, 1976; *La moviola de Eurípides*, 1982.

MISCELLANEOUS: *Del pozo del Numa: Un esayo y una leyenda*, 1978.

Bibliography

Cabrera, Vicente. *Juan Benet*, 1983.
Compitello, Malcolm. *Ordering the Evidence: "Volverás a Región" and Civil War Fiction*, 1983.
Herzberger, David K. *The Novelistic World of Juan Benet*, 1976.

Manteiga, Roberto, David Herzberger, and Malcolm Compitello, eds. *Critical Approaches to the Writings of Juan Benet*, 1984.

David K. Herzberger

GEORGES BERNANOS

Born: Paris, France; February 20, 1888
Died: Neuilly-sur-Seine, France; July 5, 1948

Principal long fiction
Sous le soleil de Satan, 1926 (*The Star of Satan*, 1927; also as *Under the Sun of Satan*, 1949); *L'Imposture*, 1927; *La Joie*, 1929 (*Joy*, 1948); *Un Crime*, 1935 (*A Crime*, 1936); *Journal d'un curé de campagne*, 1936 (*Diary of a Country Priest*, 1937); *Nouvelle Histoire de Mouchette*, 1937 (*Mouchette*, 1966); *Monsieur Ouine*, 1943, 1955 (written 1931-1940; *The Open Mind*, 1945); *Un Mauvais Rêve*, 1950 (written 1935; *Night Is Darkest*, 1953).

Other literary forms
Georges Bernanos wrote one play, which he intended to be a film scenario: *Dialogues des Carmélites* (1949; *The Fearless Heart*, 1952). His short stories include "Madame Dargent," which appeared in 1922; "Une Nuit" (a night), in 1928; and "Dialogue d'ombres" (dialogue of shadows), in 1928. This last short story lends its title to a collection of Bernanos' short fiction, published in 1955. His hagiographical works include *Saint Dominique* (1926), *Jeanne, relapse et sainte* (1929; *Sanctity Will Out*, 1947), and *Frère Martin: Essai sur Luther* (1951; *Brother Martin*, 1952).

Bernanos wrote many essays and political articles, which are available in the following collections: *Le Crépuscule des vieux* (1956; the twilight of the aged), containing essays from 1909 to 1939, and *Français, si vous saviez* (1961; Frenchmen, if you knew), containing essays from 1945 to 1948. Although there is no complete collection of his correspondence, the most important letters are found in *Georges Bernanos: Essais et témoignages* (1949) and in many issues of *Bulletin de la Société des amis de Georges Bernanos*. A six-volume edition of his works, *Oeuvres de Bernanos*, was published in 1947. His fiction is collected in *Oeuvres romanesques, suivies de "Dialogues des Carmélites"* (1961).

Achievements
Although Georges Bernanos was a prolific author, with eight major novels and numerous political and journalistic essays to his credit, his reputation will probably always rest on *Diary of a Country Priest* and, to a lesser extent, *The Fearless Heart*, set to music in an opera by Francis Poulenc. Bernanos' earlier works, such as *The Star of Satan*, *L'Imposture*, and *Joy*, are dense, analytical, and disunited. His later works, including *The Open Mind* and *Mouchette*, are, despite their poetry and single vision, rather impenetrable to general readers. In *Diary of a Country Priest* and *The Fearless Heart*, however, Bernanos' characters attain a heroism that is self-giving, capable of

overcoming fear and attaining self-acceptance.

It is perhaps this human dimension of Bernanos' heroes that most attracts the public. Bernanos was oriented toward the human limitations of mankind, rejecting the Nietzschean superman. Like Honoré de Balzac, he explored the social dimension of human relations rather than political theories, although much of his early journalistic work was intended to support the Action Française movement, and social themes constitute a large segment of his novels. His aim was to preserve the freedom of modern man, who, in Bernanos' view, had become the slave of "civilization." Like Charles Péguy, he deplored the corruptive power of money, of a world wrapped in paper. He mistrusted the machine and modern industrialism. He detested mediocrity and chose as his heroes young people with the ability to save a decadent and paralyzed society.

With his invectives against modern society symbolically expressed in the parishes of Ambricourt and Fenouille, which are drowned in a sea of "ennui," Bernanos, like Péguy, takes his place in "la vieille France," the France of days gone by, of Saint Louis, Joan of Arc, and Pierre Corneille. Yet, as Hans Urs von Balthasar observes, Bernanos is a very modern writer, for he loves the past only to appreciate the future. He loves the monarchy, not because of a desire to return to the past, but because it represents a certain order that is absent from the modern world.

Not only Bernanos' penetration of a changing social order but also his powerful characterization leads the reader to see in him a disciple of Balzac, whom he greatly admired. Where Balzac's description passes from the exterior to the interior, however, Bernanos' is primarily interior—although not without characteristic physical description: the unkempt cassock of the Curé of Ambricourt or his beautiful eyes, the nose and nudity of the Mayor of Fenouille. Brian Fitch observes that Bernanos always writes the same novel; consequently, his heroes, like Balzac's, reappear throughout his oeuvre. Although Bernanos gives them different names, they are the same person. Chevance and Ambricourt are descended from Donissan; Saint-Marin and Monsieur de Clergerie seem like brothers. Mouchette resembles her namesake in *The Star of Satan*—as Bernanos himself put it—in "the same tragic solitude in which I saw both live and die."

Perhaps Bernanos' most outstanding achievement derives from his deep spiritual dimension. He is a Christian prophet and visionary in the line of Léon Bloy, with whom he did not wish to be identified, and Péguy, whom he greatly admired. A contemporary of Paul Claudel and François Mauriac, Bernanos subscribed neither to Claudel's triumphalistic Catholicism nor to Mauriac's sexual preoccupations. Perhaps his sensibility is most akin to that of Fyodor Dostoevski, from whom he differs not in content but in style, presenting his characters in an analytical and spiritual rather than a dramatic and social setting. Bernanos faced the problem of the de-Christianization of the modern world, of a selfish and apathetic society alienated from God and from itself. Yet, unlike most writers of the 1920's and 1930's, Bernanos was a prophet of hope and salvation, which he believed would be realized through redemptive suffering and Christian love. Most of all, he was, as Balthasar says, the prophet of Divine Grace—not that of Jansenistic predestination, but that which connotes true freedom for the human being. His awareness of God is profound and almost mystical; Grace, for Bernanos, is "la douce pitié de Dieu," the gentle pity of God.

Biography

Although the life of Georges Bernanos began and ended in Paris, the word "restless" best describes the many wanderings that led him to towns and cities in France, Spain, South America, and Africa. Possibly of Spanish descent, his father, Émile Bernanos, was an interior decorator of good business ability. The family, which included Bernanos' sister, Thérèse, spent the summers at Fressin, in Pas-de-Calais, and the north of France was to be the scene for almost all of Bernanos' novels. Bernanos was influenced both by his mother's staunch piety and by his father's anti-Semitism. Although Bernanos was an avid reader, his childhood was marked by frequent changes in schools, for he was not a model student. He formed close ties, however, with some of his teachers—such as Abbé Lagrange at Bourges and later Dom Besse—and always showed great enthusiasm for spiritual pursuits.

In 1906, Bernanos was strongly attracted to Charles Maurras' militant royalist movement, Action Française, to which he adhered faithfully until the beginning of the 1930's. From 1906 to 1913, he pursued both a *licence* in letters and one in law at the Institut Catholique in Paris. In 1913, he moved to Rouen, where he became editor in chief of the local royalist newspaper, *L'Avant-garde de Normandie*. It was there that he met his future wife, Jeanne Talbert d'Arc, a direct descendant of Joan of Arc's brother. They were married in 1917, while Bernanos was still engaged in military service during World War I. It was to prove a happy and fruitful marriage—six children were born to the couple between 1918 and 1933—although it was marked by many illnesses and financial difficulties.

Bernanos' first job, as an insurance inspector, was to be of short duration; after 1926, he devoted himself exclusively to writing, following the success of his first novel, *The Star of Satan*. Although he continued his support of Maurras until 1931, he, like Péguy, was greatly disillusioned to see that his ideal, embodied in the Action Française, was to deteriorate into expediency. Also like Péguy, Bernanos was not without a certain hubris in his loyalty to the movement, as Balthasar notes; he manifested the self-righteousness he so criticized in others. During this period, financial pressures and inner tensions caused Bernanos frequently to uproot his family, and he settled for a time in Majorca in Spain. A motorcycle accident in 1933 left him crippled for life. In 1938, he finally left the Continent for Brazil, where he remained until 1945, returning home at the invitation of Charles de Gaulle. Despite his absence from his native country during World War II, Bernanos remained true to his great passion, France, through his frequent polemics and articles. Yet soon after his return, in 1946, he refused membership in the Légion d'Honneur for the third time.

Although Bernanos' restlessness continued (the following year would see him in Tunisia, doing work on behalf of Action Française), he completed one of his major works at this time, *The Fearless Heart*. With his own death imminent, the work became his spiritual testament, confronting the fear of death and the fear of loss of honor with sublime courage. Bernanos died at the American Hospital in Neuilly-sur-Seine, a Paris suburb, on July 5, 1948.

Analysis

As a novelist preoccupied with spiritual conflicts, Georges Bernanos repeatedly explored the symbolic contrast between the innocent vulnerability of childhood and the corrupt world of men. Bernanos' children and adolescents are of two types: the suffering adolescent and victim, and the innocent young girl. Mouchette, "Sainte Brigitte du néant" (Saint Brigitte of the void), crushed by society and family, and Steeny of *The Open Mind*, who emerges from his childhood innocence, belong to the first category: we also find adults who have experienced humiliation in childhood, such as Monsieur Ouine or Mouchette's mother, so like one of Dostoevski's suffering women. Perhaps the best illustration of the second type, the innocent young girl, is Chantal de Clergerie, whom Bernanos modeled on Saint Thérèse of Lisieux.

Bernanos also creates adult heroes who are granted the fresh spiritual vision of a child, often at the moment of death, such as the Curé of Ambricourt and Chevance and, to a lesser degree, the ascetic Donissan. Always indifferent to the approval of society and to their own pleasure, they are nevertheless deeply aware of good and evil. Such is the Curé of Ambricourt, who reads the souls of Chantal and her mother. Like Saint Thérèse of Lisieux, these characters show the spirit of hope, abandonment to God, and self-acceptance.

Just as children and motifs of childhood appear throughout Bernanos' fiction, so too does the symbolic figure of the priest; the role of the priest, like that of the child, is to dramatize the spiritual conflict which is at the heart of human experience. Bernanos' priests also fall into two categories: the self-effacing and the self-assured. Those in the first category are apparently lacking in intelligence; they are unattractive, like Donissan, Chevance, and the Curé of Ambricourt. They are, however, endowed with supernatural lucidity and clairvoyance, which is different from psychological insight, for it is manifested in a love of souls most consumed by evil. At the same time, the priest himself suffers from a slow and consuming agony. Gaëton Picon maintains that Bernanos chose a priest-hero because such a figure represents the only person in the modern world capable of accepting the spirituality rejected by contemporary civilization. He does so in his solitude and silence, yet he is totally involved in the process of Salvation. He is thus the model for all human beings, who should be instruments of Grace for one another.

The second type of priest, who is self-assured, robust, and intellectual, is seldom the sacerdotal ideal. Cénabre, in *L'Imposture* and *Joy*, is a man who has lost his faith but who ironically studies the lives of the saints. The Curé of Fenouille, though ascetic, is not expansive or loving; consequently, he embodies the emptiness of his "dead parish." Finally, Monsieur Ouine is an antipriest, a caricature of the sacerdotal vocation who is unable to give a firm answer, as his name (*oui*, "yes"; *ne*, "no" or "not") indicates. He experiences agony, as do the Curé of Ambricourt and Chevance, but his self-seeking prevents that agony from becoming redemptive.

Suffering and agony are the lot of both the good and the evil characters in Bernanos' novels. The Curé of Ambricourt suffers from the loss of God; Chantal de Clergerie, as Albert Béguin observes, goes to the heart of the agony of Christ. Monsieur Ouine suffers from his emptiness; Mouchette, from her humiliation. Death, usually violent, comes to at least one and often several characters in each of Bernanos' novels. Many die by suicide, just as contemporary civilization pushes people toward spiritual suicide. This suicide is one of despair in Doctor Delbende, of pride in Fiodor, of humiliation in Mouchette, of passion in Hélène and Eugène Devandomme. Murder claims Chantal de Clergerie and Jambe-de-Laine; death, after a spiritual agony, comes to the Curé of Ambricourt.

This somber world of violence reflects the inner world of satanic thirst and spiritual emptiness that is particularly evident in modern society. It is personified in Satan, who, in Bernanos' first novel, is incarnated as a crafty horse-dealer; it is internalized in the unbelieving Cénabre; and it is obliquely suggested in the seductive Ouine. The omnipresent parish represents the modern world. Ambricourt is devoured by ennui, or apathy; Fenouille is a "dead parish" (the original title of *The Open Mind*). Bernanos saw mediocrity and self-righteousness as the greatest of modern evils, the cancer that devours society. Like Péguy, Bernanos deplored the de-Christianization of France and the irresistible attraction to Satan.

The satanic world appears as a hallucination, *un mauvais rêve* (a bad dream), as one novel is entitled. *The Open Mind* reads like a nightmare; many scenes in *Mouchette* are hallucinatory, such as the young girl's conversation with the old woman who keeps vigil over the dead (her suicide is like a rhythmic drowning). Henri Debluë sees the dream as one of Bernanos' principal motifs, yet it is not always a bad dream. With Balthasar, Debluë believes that the good dream gives an existential dimension to Bernanos, representing his desire for Being—which, for Bernanos, is the human community in Christ.

Begun in 1919 and written in cafés and trains, *The Star of Satan* was finally published in 1926. It is composed of three apparently disconnected parts, although many critics, including Claudel, see in it an inherent unity. Bernanos did not write the novel in its final order; he completed the last part first and the second part, the account of Donissan's meeting with the Devil, last. The model for the hero Donissan is Saint Jean-Baptiste-Marie Vianney, Curé of Ars (1768-1859). The novel was an immediate success; as William Bush observes, the unusual incarnation of Satan appealed to a public that was weary of escapism as found in André Gide and Marcel Proust.

The subject of the novel, according to Bernanos, is "the sun of Satan in whose black light mankind basks." The hero, Donissan, is guilty of sin in wanting to know if God is really in command and if Satan can be conquered. He realizes his error in the third part of the story, when he is unable to bring a dead child back to life because he wanted the miracle, not for the honor of God, but for himself. He dies shortly afterward and we are led to believe that he has come to a true knowledge of God and himself.

Bernanos was faced with the challenge of integrating this conclusion into the rest of the story, which he had begun with a character who was to haunt him for a long time and to whom he was to return later, Mouchette. One of his suffering adolescents, the Mouchette of *The Star of Satan* is the victim of greedy parents and an apathetic society. She commits double adultery, murders her first lover, and, after a nervous collapse, gives birth to a stillborn child. It is not until the second part that the reader sees the results of her crimes, for which she is only partially responsible.

It is in fact the second part, "The Temptation of Despair," that links parts 1 and 3. It introduces us to the awkward, overly ascetic Abbé Donissan, who one night gets lost on the way to a neighboring village and encounters the Devil, a crafty horse-dealer, eventually the reflection of Donissan's own face. After a sinister conversation with his enemy, Donissan realizes that he has the gift of reading souls. His most important meeting is with Mouchette, whose secrets he reveals. Although there is no indication of a change of heart in Mouchette, her dying request to be brought into the Church and Donissan's rapid compliance seem to indicate an exchange of grace between the suffering victim and the saintly priest, a theme that was to characterize many of Bernanos' works.

Composed rapidly between 1934 and 1936, at the same time that Bernanos was writing about a contrasting theme in *The Open Mind*, *Diary of a Country Priest* was unreservedly acclaimed as a masterpiece. Unlike its predecessors, *L'Imposture* and *Joy*, it is remarkable for its unity. The entire story is in diary form, told from the first-person point of view, which gives the story a compelling directness. Written with gentleness and simplicity, it does not have the extravagance of *The Star of Satan*. It was Bernanos' favorite novel, and it has maintained its popularity; in 1936, it received the Grand Prix du Roman of the Académie Française.

Like all of Bernanos' parishes, Ambricourt represents the modern world, dying of apathy. The Curé himself is dying of a cancer that he does not know he has, aggravated by an alcoholic heritage and his own poor nutrition habits. He is unattractive, awkward, and ill at ease. The self-righteous, like the Count of the neighboring château, scorn him, yet tormented sinners and God-seekers that recall Dostoevskian characters—Doctor Delbende, the Countess, the companion of Louis Dupréty, the defrocked priest—all seek him, for they instinctively realize his innate goodness.

The turning point of the story is the interview of the Curé with the Countess, a selfish woman, disappointed in marriage, who lives in the past with her memories of her dead child. She has thus alienated her living child, Chantal, as well as her husband, who seeks the affection of the governess, much to the distress and jealousy of Chantal. Yet the priest fearlessly reveals to the Countess her sin, enabling her to accept herself. The emotional stress proves too great for her, however, and she dies. The priest, unable to reveal the conversation, is falsely accused by the family of complicity in her death. Although the priest also confronts Chantal without a similar acknowledgment on her part, we are led to believe that this tormented adolescent, too, may have found Grace through the self-sacrifice of the saintly priest.

It is perhaps in the final exchange between the Curé of Ambricourt and his former classmate, Louis Dupréty, that the mystery of Grace is revealed most clearly. The Curé of Ambricourt learns of Dupréty's impending death and is forced to spend the night with him. It is in this situation that the agony of death overcomes Dupréty, and he realizes that simple acceptance of oneself is all that God requires of him. In perfect self-abandonment and trust, he receives absolution from the defrocked priest, for, as he says in the concluding words of the novel, "Everything is grace."

Unlike Bernanos' other novels, except, perhaps, *Mouchette*, *The Open Mind* is a story without hope. Even the history of its composition was marked by frustration. Bernanos began it in 1931 and, while he was writing it, suffered his rupture with Maurras, the motorcycle accident that crippled him for life, financial disasters, and the loss of a great part of the manuscript. He finished it in 1940, at the beginning of the Occupation. It was published in Brazil, with many typographical errors and omissions. Only in 1955, when Béguin carefully edited the text after consulting Bernanos' manuscripts, was a definitive edition published by the Club des Libraires de France.

Béguin considers *The Open Mind* to be Bernanos' greatest work, and indeed, while writing it, Bernanos himself planned it as his masterpiece. Here, Béguin argues, Bernanos pushed his exploration of the interior world to the furthest possible limit. A novel that treats extreme acts, including seductions, murders, suicides, and deeds of madness, it derives its unity from its hallucinatory manner rather than from its plot. The hero, Monsieur Ouine, based on Gide, is an ambiguous person, who, as his name indicates, says yes and no (*oui*, *ne*) at the same time. Although he does not really dominate the story, he provides the conclusion. According to Bush, he and most other characters of the novel seem to symbolize the decay of modern civilization, the aimlessness of society, and the apathy of a de-Christianized world.

A difficult work for the general reader, *The Open Mind* has a complex plot in which the horrors of violence and seduction are suggested rather than developed. The story is set in Fenouille, in the Artois district, and revolves mainly around Philippe, or "Steeny," one of Bernanos' suffering adolescents, who is disillusioned with his ailing mother and her intimate companion, "Miss." The same Miss seems to make advances to Steeny, as does the neighboring Madame de Néréis, or Jambe-de-Laine, mistress of the château of Wambes-court. Finally, Monsieur Ouine, a retired professor of languages who lives at the château, tries to win Steeny. The confused youth, with a desire for love and a nostalgia for innocence, becomes accidentally involved in the murder of a young farm-boy, probably committed by Monsieur Ouine. This murder precipitates the double suicide of the two lovers, Hélène and Eugène Devan-domme, the lynching of Jambe-de-Laine, and the probable suicide of the Mayor.

It is in the conversations of the priest with Monsieur Ouine and later with the Mayor, in the priest's sermon, and in Monsieur Ouine's final words to Steeny before his death that we probe the complexity of these characters' personalities. All three have a nostalgia for goodness. The Curé is even ascetic and intellectual, but love of God and service to others are not among his virtues. He lacks the childlike spiritual insight of the Curé of Ambricourt, conceived by Bernanos at the same time. The Mayor is sensual and clever but not simple and trusting. Monsieur Ouine, the victim of an unhappy child-hood and a premature seduction, gives the impression of "calm and lucid acceptance," yet he is destroyed by his intellectual perversion, not unlike Cénabre. It is thus by negative images that Bernanos focuses on the need for hope, the spiritual freshness of childhood, and the exchange of grace. Without them, life becomes an infernal hallucination, as in the town of Fenouille.

Bernanos' desire to bring sinners and the suffering back to community in Christ is the source of his hope. As a prophet of Divine Grace, he evokes redemption through an exchange between two human beings. The agony of Donissan brings light to Mouchette, who, although she kills herself, asks to be brought into the church to die. Chevance entrusts Chantal with his joy in order to save Cénabre. The Curé of Ambricourt brings the Countess to an acknowledgment of her sin and is himself given final absolution by a defrocked priest. Blanche de la Force receives the ultimate grace of martyrdom through the Prioress' offering of herself. It is thus through human means that God operates in Grace, for Bernanos' theology is based on the Incarnation. It is a down-to-earth mysticism, profoundly Christian yet articulating the universal human need for forgiveness and Salvation.

Major publications other than long fiction

SHORT FICTION: *Dialogue d'ombres*, 1955.

PLAY: *Dialogues des Carmélites*, 1949 (*The Fearless Heart*, 1952).

NONFICTION: *Saint Dominique*, 1926; *Noël à la maison de France*, 1928; *Jeanne, relapse et sainte*, 1929 (*Sanctity Will Out*, 1947); *La Grande Peur des bien-pensants*, 1931; *Les Grands Cimetières sous la lune*, 1938 (*A Diary of My Times*, 1938); *Nous autres français*, 1939; *Lettre aux anglais*, 1942 (*Plea for Liberty*, 1944); *La France contre les robots*, 1947 (*Tradition of Freedom*, 1950); *Les Enfants humiliés*, 1949 (included in *Tradition of Freedom*, 1950); *Georges Bernanos: Essais et témoignages*, 1949; *Frère Martin: Essai sur Luther*, 1951 (*Brother Martin*, 1952); *Le Crépuscule des vieux*, 1956 (written 1909-1939); *Français, si vous saviez*, 1961 (written 1945-1948).

MISCELLANEOUS: *Oeuvres de Bernanos*, 1947 (6 volumes); *Oeuvres romanesques, suivies de "Dialogues des Carmélites,"* 1961.

Bibliography

Balthasar, Hans Urs von. *Le Chrétien Bernanos*, 1956.

Béguin, Albert. *Bernanos par lui-même*, 1954.

Blumenthal, Gerda. *The Poetic Imagination of Georges Bernanos*, 1965.

Bridel, Yves. *L'Esprit d'enfance dans l'oeuvre romanesque de Georges Bernanos*, 1966.

Bulletin de la Société des amis de Georges Bernanos, 1949-1969 (60 issues).

Bush, William. *L'Angoisse du Mystère: Essai sur Bernanos et "Monsieur Ouine,"* 1966.

──────── . *Georges Bernanos*, 1966.

Debluë, Henri. *Les Romans de Georges Bernanos: Ou, Le Défi du rêve*, 1965.

Fitch, Brian T. *Dimensions et structures chez Bernanos*, 1969.

Picon, Gaëton. *Georges Bernanos*, 1948.

Speaight, Robert. *Georges Bernanos: A Biography*, 1974.

Irma M. Kashuba

THOMAS BERNHARD

Born: Heerlen, Netherlands; February 10, 1931

Principal long fiction

Frost, 1963; *Verstörung*, 1967 (*Gargoyles*, 1970); *Das Kalkwerk*, 1970 (*The Lime Works*, 1973); *Korrektur*, 1975 (*Correction*, 1979); *Beton*, 1982 (*Concrete*, 1984).

Other literary forms

Thomas Bernhard has continued to publish at a prolific pace since the appearance of his first book, a volume of poems, in 1957. In addition to his novels, he has written several volumes of poetry (though none recently), as well as many dramatic works of varying style and popularity, and he is widely acknowledged as one of the leading contemporary playwrights in German. Perhaps Bernhard's most important work, equal in power to his fiction, is his five-volume autobiographical sequence, which covers his life from his earliest years to the age of nineteen: *Die Ursache* (1975), *Der Keller* (1976), *Der Atem* (1978), *Die Kälte* (1981), and *Ein Kind* (1982); the last volume is chronologically the first. Bernhard's programmatic statements, such as his terse and often provocative newspaper or radio interviews, are given only reluctantly; the most important formulations in this regard are his acceptance speeches for several prestigious literary awards.

Achievements

In the mid-1960's, critics and the German-speaking public began to take a serious interest in Thomas Bernhard, recognizing in him an original voice and an extraordinary, if uncompromisingly bleak, vision. This critical fascination with Bernhard has, in the main, withstood the test of time, but the interest and reaction he evokes are negative as often as they are positive. George Steiner, for example, has called Bernhard "the most original, concentrated novelist writing in German," linking him with "the great constellation of [Hugo von] Hofmannsthal, [Franz] Kafka, [Robert] Musil," yet Steiner has also said that Bernhard's recent works betray a lack of new insight, that originality has given way to formulaic themes and clichés.

It can be said that Bernhard has always appealed to a rather limited audience. His work presents the same kind of resistance to facile understanding as that of Samuel Beckett; his literary practice is not straightforward or discursive; and his somewhat stock themes are by no means uplifting. Thus, while his readership has never been large, particularly in the English-speaking world (where several novels and plays have been translated but have been almost uniformly ignored by critics and readers alike), he has received virtually every significant Austrian and German literary award, including the Georg Büchner Prize, considered the pinnacle of literary recognition in Germany.

Biography

Thomas Bernhard was born in Heerlen, Netherlands (near Maastricht), on February 10, 1931, of Austrian parents. His ancestors were Austrian peasants, innkeepers, and butchers in Salzburg and Upper Austria, but he spent his earliest childhood years living with his grandparents in Vienna. He later moved with them to Traunstein, in Bavaria, and in 1943, he was sent to a boarding school in Salzburg. There he experienced not only humiliations suffered at the hands of his teachers and fellow pupils, but also the air raids and bombing of the city along with the chaotic end of the war. In 1947—soon after his family had moved to Salzburg—Bernhard left the school to take up an apprenticeship in a grocer's shop in the worst part of Salzburg. This act signified not only a decision to abandon his formal education but also a rejection of the conventional career and existence which he felt were being imposed on him from outside. His early and chosen path was thus away from the normative to the periphery of society, a descent into an abyss that reflected his own inner state. In 1948, a serious illness brought Bernhard close to death, and he had to spend a good deal of time in a tuberculosis sanatorium; it was there that he began to write.

In 1949, Bernhard suffered a serious emotional blow: the death of his grandfather, the Austrian writer Johannes Freumbichler, a man who had a profound influence on Bernhard's intellectual development. It was Freumbichler who became the model on which Bernhard patterned the male protagonists of many of his works. In 1950, Bernhard was keenly affected by the death of his mother, to whom he was very close. In the years from 1952 to 1957, Bernhard studied the plastic arts, music, and drama at the Mozarteum in Salzburg, and from 1953 to 1955, he was also a legal correspondent for the Socialist newspaper *Demokratisches Volksblatt*. He traveled to Yugoslavia and Sicily before his first volume of poetry appeared in 1957, and in the same year, he completed his music studies. In 1960 and 1961, he was in London, working both as a legal correspondent and as a librarian. In 1962 and 1963, Bernhard lived in Poland, and in the latter year, his first major prose work, *Frost*, appeared. After 1965, Bernhard lived as an independent writer on a farm in Ohlsdorf, Upper Austria.

Analysis

Thomas Bernhard's work can be characterized as a series of variations on certain recurring themes and situations. While this consistency gives his work a certain formal cohesion, it also, quite naturally, leads many critics to fault him for sterility of imagination or manic obsessiveness. The almost overwhelming negativity of Bernhard's novels is autobiographical, rooted in the agony of his own existence. Bernhard himself has stated that, for him, writing is both a search for the origins of his personal disaster and an attempt—an ultimately Sisyphean attempt—to maintain equilibrium in the face of despair. Writing for Bernhard is thus a form of therapy, but therapy conducted in a never-ending session, because there is no ultimate healing. In the television interview "Drei Tage" (published in *Der Italiener* in 1971), Bernhard compared himself to a surgeon who desperately performs a series of operations on himself to rid his body of cancerous growths, growths that reappear as fast as they are removed. The metaphor of disease and the hopelessness implied by Bernhard's comparison are both reminiscent of Kafka.

In the prototypical situation of Bernhard's fiction, an individual—normally a man—receives a "shock" of some sort, whether in the form of a personally catastrophic experience or in an existential moment of loss. In any event, the victim is left emotionally and psychologically deranged, unable to carry on as before and confronted overwhelmingly by a sense of mortality, by the fatal inevitability of death. This individual situation, in turn, is implicitly elevated to an absolute and universal condition, so that there remains but one vantage point for viewing the panorama of human existence: the finality of death. As Bernhard said in his scandalous acceptance speech for the Austrian State Prize for Literature, "When one thinks about death, everything in human life seems ridiculous."

A somewhat natural adjunct to this situation is the theme of language or, more correctly, the failure and futility of language. Often in Bernhard's fiction one encounters men who are absorbed in a study of some sort, a study that is to reach fruition by being written down, expressed in a personal act of creation. This attempt to assert oneself in the face of death's inevitable destruction is, of course, almost always unsuccessful. The psychological cripples who are Bernhard's protagonists often despair of the efficacy of language as a communicative vehicle and retreat to a life of total introspection, devoting themselves instead to meditating on topics such as madness, the relationship between the individual and the state, disease, and death.

This critical attitude toward language places Bernhard in an Austrian tradition whose roots can be traced to Hugo von Hofmannsthal and Ludwig Wittgenstein. The former's despairing *Brief des Lord Chandos* (1905; *Letter of Lord Chandos*, 1952) was one of the earliest literary expressions of loss of faith in language and remains one of the most powerful; Wittgenstein's philosophical reflections on language and its limits had a profound formative influence on Bernhard. As a result, Bernhard is caught in a literary cul-de-sac from which there seems to be no escape: Much of the tension that imbues his work derives from the paradox that he is a writer who is impelled constantly to question his medium. On the one hand, he conveys meaning, he communicates by means of his writing; but on the other hand, he constantly retracts this possibility and declares that language cannot bring people into contact with one another or the world of things; on the contrary, it merely emphasizes the painful isolation of the individual speaker: "I speak the language which only I understand, just as each of us understands only his own language." It has been suggested, therefore, that Bernhard's "antiliterature" is obsessed less with the theme of death qua death than it is with the death of meaning.

When it appeared in 1963, Bernhard's first novel, *Frost*, caused a sensation. Although some critics pronounced the book "disgusting" and the author "only of regional Austrian interest," Carl Zuckmayer wrote in *Die Zeit* on June 21, 1963, that the novel was "one of the most stirring and urgent prose works" he had encountered in years. Focusing fixedly on the themes of sickness and death in its long, involved, and almost breathless sentences, *Frost* set the tone for what was to follow in Bernhard's compulsive fiction.

In effect, *Frost* functions as a *Bildungsroman* in reverse. The protagonist, a medical student completing his *Famulatur*, or clinical internship, is charged with the task of observing and reporting on a painter named Strauch, a man who has retreated to the remote mountain village of Weng, has burned all of his paintings, and is in the process of a complete mental collapse. The assignment, therefore, is quite literally part of the student's education, and he fully intends to carry out his study with an objective and critical attitude. The young intern quickly discovers, however, that he will have to report on ontological more than on medical problems, and he slowly but surely begins to abandon his detached viewpoint for a more subjective one. What the medical student, the narrator of the novel, experiences can be described as a nightmarish sequence of intimate glimpses into the personality of the painter Strauch, as a terrifying fairy tale minus the traditional happy ending. The painter drags him about in the snow while explicating his philosophy of decay, confronting the young student with memories of ghostly accidents, putrescent funerals, and rotting war-dead dotting wasted landscapes.

Feeling himself becoming "sucked in" by all of this, the narrator attempts at first to resist the perverse attraction of Strauch's monologues (which constitute a large portion of the text of *Frost*), because he knows that they are the product of a diseased mind. The painter talks incessantly of himself, of his hallucinations, his paranoia, his severing of contact with the outside world, his complete lack of interest in anything but his own psyche. He is "a person living a precarious existence in the world of the imagination," an individual in a state of complete and admittedly unproductive detachment. Isolation, the goal of total encapsulation within himself, is the painter's obsession, and he constantly returns to the image of the absolute and final cold, the coming frost that will deprive everything of life. It will be a time when "the stars will flash like nails closing the lids of heaven," when the apocalyptic cold will be inside and outside all landscapes and all animals and people populating them.

By the end of the novel, the medical student has lost his power to stand firm in his own identity and can only conduct his "scientific" reporting in the language and idiom of his case history: "He simply slips his vulnerability into me in the form of sentences, like slides into a projector, which then casts these terrors on the ever present walls of my (and his) self." Unlike the typical protagonist of the *Bildungsroman*, therefore, the medical student in *Frost* has not gained in self-realization and has not become more well balanced; on the contrary, his progression is a regression, because he has fallen prey to a mentor from whom he is ultimately indistinguishable.

This development has implications for the narrative perspective of *Frost*, implications that Bernhard develops in his later novels. Because the medical student-narrator of *Frost* surrenders his objectivity in describing the fate of the painter Strauch, the reader is also left somewhat at a loss to assess and interpret the narrative. All seems dispassionately presented and objectively recorded, but can one trust a narrator who becomes subsumed in the personality of a deranged monomaniac? The question grows even more acute in Bernhard's subsequent work.

Bernhard's second novel, *Gargoyles* (the German title, *Verstörung*, which the distinguished translators Richard and Clara Winston chose to ignore, suggests "bewilderment" or "derangement"), is in several respects an extension or continuation of *Frost*. The motto for the work is a dictum from Blaise Pascal's *Pensées* (1670; English translation, 1688), "The eternal silence of these infinite spaces terrifies me," and the theme of isolation and the inability to communicate is introduced at every turn. The novel is sustained (or, in the opinion of some critics, fails to be sustained) by an extremely pared-down plot in which action is reduced to a minimum. A doctor's son has returned home from university studies, and in an attempt to bridge their mutual estrangement, the doctor takes the son with him on his rounds. Together, they visit patients, all of whom are in various stages of physical decay or mental torment, such as the industrialist who has shut himself up in his house, where he perpetually writes and summarily destroys what he has written, and the young boy, crippled and insane, who is kept in a cage in a bedroom, where his atrophied body gives off a foul odor.

The bulk of the novel, however, is devoted to the final patient, a prince by the name of Saurau who lives in a castle high on a mountain. The meandering outpourings of this aristocrat are reminiscent of Arthur Schopenhauer—all that Saurau touches upon is tainted with negativity. Saurau's remarks cover everything from technology to psychology and are constantly shifting and a bit out of focus, but his long monologue is galvanized by three central themes: decay and corruption (in the state, Europe, and the world); the violence of nature; and the self-destructive essence of all human relationships, particularly familial ones (Saurau's father has committed suicide, and Saurau anticipates that his own son will do the same). Saurau summarizes, in a sense, his philosophical outlook when he states that "mankind is nothing more than a collective community of dying which is now in the billions and spread out over five continents." Much like Strauch in *Frost*, he has limited his contact with the outside world to reading newspapers and resolutely awaits "the final end." Appropriately enough, the novel "concludes" in mid-sentence.

Saurau's long monologue constitutes approximately the final third of the novel. Once again, as in *Frost*, the narrative perspective becomes dominated not by a "trustworthy" chronicler (the doctor's son) but by a transmitter who shatters the foundation of traditional realistic narration: the ability to distinguish competently between inner and outer reality and to comment on both. The reader is left immersed in a psyche that cannot maintain borders between inner and outer worlds and thus gains no insight into "universal connections," only into the phantasies and derangements of a sick, self-ensconced mind.

It is small wonder, therefore, that Bernhard's second novel brought him little critical acclaim. Although some critics acknowledged a "persuasive stylistic power . . . that embraces characters and objects as well as locales and landscapes involved," many others could comment only on Bernhard's "extraordinary one-sidedness," his extremely negative themes and characters, or on his "unstructured, plotless outpourings [which] quickly pall upon a reader through their repetitiousness." For these reasons, perhaps, there were some rather significant formal changes in the author's next novel, *The Lime Works*.

With the publication of *The Lime Works* in 1970, Bernhard achieved a literary tour de force that must have been surprising even to him: The novel brought him instant and almost unanimous recognition as a major figure in contemporary German literature, reversing to a large extent the negative critical reception of *Gargoyles* and bringing him, in the same year, the ultimate German literary award, the Georg Büchner Prize.

This stunning reversal can be attributed, in part, to two felicitous formal changes. There is, first of all, a notable difference in narrative perspective. Unlike *Frost* and *Gargoyles*, in which the student-narrators gradually lose control of the narrative, *The Lime Works* is distinguished by a marked distancing of narration that is present from the outset, a remoteness that is reinforced by an almost constant use of the subjunctive; the narrator here does nothing but quote other observers (thus making his reporting second- or even third-hand). The result is an intentional and extreme indirectness, combined with an obsessive exactitude of narrative detail. This formal technique, in turn, is meant to amplify one of the novel's central tnemes (and one of Bernhard's personal tenets): the complexity, intractability, and inherent duplicity of language. This "language problem," already alluded to in *Frost*, becomes in *The Lime Works* the ultimate undoing of Konrad, the novel's central character. A second formal change to be noted is less complex in nature but is certainly significant to the reader: *The Lime Works* is structurally taut and possesses, unlike Bernhard's first two novels, a true "ending." This work is free of much of the somewhat gratuitous prose of *Frost* and *Gargoyles*, and the conclusion, although known from the beginning, is artistically and psychologically satisfying.

In terms of its themes and its minimal action, *The Lime Works* is vintage Bernhard. Konrad has led a life of isolation in "a state of almost complete estrangement from his brothers and sisters, parents, relations, and finally from his fellow human beings." Although he is married, this relationship, too, is one of lonely distance and separation, because the marriage has degenerated into a series of ritualized obsessions and mutual irritations. The reports with which the reader is presented attempt to trace, at times in a fragmented or even contradictory manner, the harried existence of the Konrads, who have moved about from place to place in search of seclusion. They finally retire to a lime works which Konrad has known since childhood, a place where he can devote himself to writing down his great "study" of human hearing.

At once, he sets about isolating himself by planting shrubs all around the works and by discouraging contact with the outside world, since his work demands that he be "completely isolated and free of people." Intrusions from the consumer society, from other people, and even from his wife are, however, continual and unavoidable. He nevertheless tries to maintain, in the face of these disturbances, "the highest degree of uninterrupted intellectual and physical self-control," but he is confronted by an inner problem that is even more insuperable than these constant outside irritations: his inability to set thoughts down on paper. Although he feels he has good ideas, he is trapped in "the powerlessness of his own being"; he cannot shed the conviction that "words ruin everything you think." Increasingly driven to distraction and a sense of futility, Konrad eventually loses what is left of his mental equilibrium and kills his wife.

Bernhard parallels the violence of his story with a prose style that is similarly aggressive. The reader is virtually assaulted by a language that is whipped up to greater and greater extremes of expression, and by repetitions of emphatic words. This violent style gives the uncanny impression that language itself is attempting to work out its own obsessions. Convinced as he is that the perception of mental or physical reality cannot be captured in words, Bernhard paradoxically thematizes the impossibility of adequate linguistic representation, and this in a prose that is extremely successful as literary art. Implicit here as well is a continuation of the antagonism between author and reading public that has found expression since the advent of Romanticism: Because the author believes that his readership will not be able to accept the consequences of his attack on a normative and socially functional language that this same readership employs, he resorts to a radical preoccupation with his own linguistic development, to a solipsistic forging of deeper inroads into his self. This nexus of concerns found full-blown and direct expression in Bernhard's subsequent novel, *Correction*.

Formally and thematically, *Correction* is once again a logical extension of Bernhard's previous work. Narrative "structure" is here rarefied almost to the point of obliteration, however, because the first-person narrator of this novel without chapters and paragraphs does not even make the pretense of telling a story; he is present merely to "sift and sort" the posthumous notes and jottings of the work's protagonist, Roithamer, a brilliant Austrian scientist who has committed suicide immediately before the narrative begins. The narrator, Roithamer's friend, has been named the executor of Roithamer's papers, and in the first section of this novel in two parts (the only formal division of any kind in the work), he recalls in a personal manner his friendship with Roithamer, which began when they were boys. These recollections are supplemented with entries from the scientist's journals and notebooks, however, and in the second section of the novel, the narrator's voice gradually gives way almost entirely to the voice of Roithamer speaking through his papers, a device familiar to the reader of Bernhard. Once again, therefore, a narrative shift or fusion makes it possible for three voices to speak in an intertwined and almost indistinguishable manner: Bernhard himself, the original narrator, and the work's central character, Roithamer, into whose mind the reader is perforce propelled. By the end of the novel, this latter voice dominates, so that his pain and obsessions become the reader's as well.

These obsessions are an admixture of Thomas Bernhard and Ludwig Wittgenstein. "Bernhardesque" is the loathing for Austria (here more scathingly expressed than in any of Bernhard's previous novels), "a permanent condition of perversity and prostitution in the form of a state, a rummage sale of intellectual and cultural history." At a deeper level, attributable to Bernhard is the conviction that a dedicated life of thought or mental activity is at once the only posture of existence worth adopting and a self-destructive *modus vivendi*. Shared by Bernhard and Wittgenstein, on the other hand, is a belief that could be described as the novel's cardinal theme: the fact that every individual is at birth cast into a world he has not created; not only is there a great gulf between what he is and what he is forced to be, but also language, the only means of overcoming this chasm, is a hopelessly inadequate tool.

Finally, the links between Roithamer and Wittgenstein will be clear to anyone familiar with the philosopher's life and works. The fundamental similarity between the two is their tortured, obsessive probing of language and the limits of thought, but there are many other links as well. Roithamer, like Wittgenstein, has studied and taught in England, and he also inherits a large fortune which he summarily gives away. His family, too, has a history of suicide, and, like Wittgenstein, Roithamer spends a great deal of time and energy designing a novel and somewhat bizarre house for his sister, in this case a conical construction that becomes the novel's central metaphor. The neurasthenic protagonist decides to do this because such a structure would be tantamount to the physical reification of an idea wholly his own, the product and symbol, as it were, of his autonomous thinking. The realization of this idea becomes, in fact, a unique edifice, but one that his sister cannot comprehend. Despite the fact that her brother has attempted to "think" her reality and embody it in a house ideally suited to her, the experiment is doomed to fail simply because the gap between people is unbridgeable. The sister dies as soon as the house is completed, and Roithamer is forced to reassess his attempt, the failure of which signifies and affirms his own isolation and estrangement. He determines that it is language itself which is responsible for the impossibility of mutual understanding—or of doing anything right, for that matter: "Everything is always different from the way it has been described, the actual is always different from the description." Hence, any utterance or communication is in constant need of correction—"and then I will correct the correction and correct again the resulting corrections and so forth"—an obvious no-win situation that ultimately drives one to the ultimate correction, suicide. Roithamer takes his life by hanging himself in a forest that he has known since boyhood, a step not unlike the self-enclosure of Konrad in the lime works he had known as a child.

While *Correction* brought to a culmination of sorts the formal and thematic development begun in *Frost*, it by no means exhausted Bernhard's invention. The short novel, or novella, *Concrete* belies the charge, frequently heard since *Correction*, that Bernhard is merely repeating himself. Although it employs the narrative strategies and obsessive motifs that have come to be the staples of the Bernhardian world, *Concrete* is significantly different from its predecessors in both tone and content.

"From March to December, writes Rudolph. . . .": Thus begins the long first sentence of *Concrete*, providing the narrative with the barest of frames; the last sentence in the book begins: "I drew the curtains in my room, writes Rudolph. . . ." Everything in between is the first-person narration of Rudolph; the entire novella consists of a single, unbroken paragraph.

In many ways, Rudolph is a typical Bernhardian protagonist. For years, he has been making notes for a study of the composer Felix Mendelssohn, but he has yet to begin the actual writing, let alone complete the project. Rudolph rails against his sister, whose business acumen (she is a real-estate agent who deals only in high-priced properties) and Viennese social connections he despises; he also directs his invective against many other targets, including dog-lovers, pretenders to culture, and the state of Austria.

All of this will be familiar to Bernhard's readers, but such a summary can be misleading. Rudolph is a more human figure than his counterparts in *The Lime Works* and *Correction*, and his diatribes are accordingly more entertaining. While his narrative is considerably shorter than those of his predecessors, it embraces a much wider range of experience. In contrast to the relentless prose and claustrophobic atmosphere of *Correction*, *Concrete* is highly readable and often blackly comic.

Nowhere is this opening out of the narrative more apparent than in the story-within-the-story that gives the novella its title. Late in the book, Rudolph, who suffers from sarcoidosis, takes a trip to Palma, Majorca. There, he recalls a young woman, Anna Härdtl, whom he met in Palma on his previous visit, some eighteen months before. Her husband fell or jumped to his death from the balcony of their hotel; he is buried in Palma with a woman, a complete stranger, in "one of the above-ground seven-tier concrete tombs which are common in Mediterranean countries owing to a shortage of space."

There is a marked contrast between Anna Härdtl's tragic story, presented in indirect discourse as Rudolph remembers their encounter, and the litany of Rudolph's complaints and vituperations that has preceded it—a contrast that Rudolph himself seems to recognize. He is free, as ordinary people such as Anna Härdtl are not, to maintain a proud and contemptuous isolation, untroubled by the exigencies of making a living.

In the degree of self-awareness and genuine growth achieved by its protagonist, in its strangely engaging tone, in its accomplished metamorphosis of the classical novella form, *Concrete* testifies to the continuing vitality of Thomas Bernhard's art.

Major publications other than long fiction

SHORT FICTION: *Amras*, 1964; *Prosa*, 1967; *Ungenach*, 1968; *An der Baumgrenze: Erzählungen*, 1969; *Ereignisse*, 1969; *Watten: Ein Nachlass*, 1969; *Gehen*, 1971; *Midland in Stilfs—Drei Erzählungen*, 1971; *Der Stimmenimitator*, 1978.

PLAYS: *Ein Fest für Boris*, 1970; *Der Italiener*, 1971 (screenplay); *Der Ignorant und der Wahnsinnige*, 1972; *Die Jagdgesellschaft*, 1974; *Die Macht der Gewohnheit*, 1974 (*The Force of Habit*, 1976); *Der Präsident*, 1975 (*The President and Eve of Retirement*, 1982); *Die Berühmten*, 1976; *Minetti: Ein Porträt des Künstlers als alter Mann*, 1977; *Immanual Kant*, 1978; *Vor dem Ruhestand*, 1979; *Der Weltverbesserer*, 1979; *Über allen Gipfeln ist Ruh: Ein deutscher Dichterag um 1980*, 1981.

POETRY: *Auf der Erde und in der Hölle*, 1957; *In hora mortis*, 1957; *Unter dem Eisen des Mondes*, 1958; *Die Irren-die Häftlinge*, 1962; *Contemporary German Poetry*, 1964 (includes selections of his poetry in English translation).

NONFICTION: *Die Ursache*, 1975; *Der Keller*, 1976; *Der Atem*, 1978; *Die Kälte*, 1981; *Ein Kind*, 1982; *Wittgenstein's Neffe: Eine Freundschaft*, 1983.

Bibliography
Arnold, Heinz Ludwig, ed. *Text und Kritik*, 1974 (volume 43).
Botond, Anneliese, ed. *Über Thomas Bernhard*, 1970.
De Feo, Ronald. "The Terror of Expression," in *National Review*. February 1,

1974, pp. 152-153.

Domandi, Agnes, ed. "Thomas Bernhard," in *Modern German Literature*, 1972.

Gamper, H. *Thomas Bernhard*, 1977.

Höller, Hans. *Kritik einer literarischen Form: Versuch über Thomas Bernhard*, 1979.

Riley, Carolyn, ed. "Thomas Bernhard," in *Contemporary Literary Criticism*. III (1975), pp. 64-65.

Schwedler, Wilfried. "Thomas Bernhard," in *Handbook of Austrian Literature*, 1973. Edited by Frederick Ungar.

Sorg, B. *Thomas Bernhard*, 1977.

N. J. Meyerhofer

VICENTE BLASCO IBÁÑEZ

Born: Valencia, Spain; January 29, 1867
Died: Menton, France; January 28, 1928

Principal long fiction

Arroz y tartana, 1894 (*The Three Roses,* 1932); *Flor de mayo,* 1895 (*The Mayflower: A Tale of the Valencian Seashore,* 1921); *La barraca,* 1898 (*The Cabin,* 1917); *Entre naranjos,* 1900 (*The Torrent,* 1921); *Sónnica la cortesana,* 1901 (*Sonnica,* 1912); *Cañas y barro,* 1902 (*Reeds and Mud,* 1928); *Los muertos mandan,* 1902 (*The Dead Command,* 1919); *La catedral,* 1903 (*The Shadow of the Cathedral,* 1909); *El intruso,* 1904 (*The Intruder,* 1928); *La bodega,* 1905 (*The Fruit of the Vine,* 1919); *La horda,* 1905 (*The Mob,* 1927); *La maja desnuda,* 1906 (*Woman Triumphant,* 1920); *La voluntad de vivir,* 1907; *Sangre y arena,* 1908 (*The Blood of the Arena,* 1911; better known as *Blood and Sand,* 1913); *Luna Benamor,* 1909 (includes short stories; English translation, 1919); *Los Argonautas,* 1914 (*The Argonauts*); *Los cuatro jinetes del Apocalipsis,* 1916 (*The Four Horsemen of the Apocalypse,* 1918); *Mare Nostrum,* 1918 (English translation, 1919); *Los enemigos de la mujer,* 1919 (*The Enemies of Women,* 1920); *El paraíso de las mujeres,* 1922 (*The Paradise of Women,* 1922); *La tierra de todos,* 1922 (*The Temptress,* 1923); *La reina Calafia,* 1923 (*Queen Calafia,* 1924); *Obras completas,* 1923-1934 (40 volumes); *El papa del mar,* 1925 (*The Pope of the Sea: An Historic Medley,* 1927); *A los pies de Venus,* 1926 (*The Borgias: Or, At the Feet of Venus,* 1930); *El Caballero de la Virgen,* 1929 (*The Knight of the Virgin,* 1930); *En busca del Gran Kan,* 1929 (*Unknown Lands: The Story of Columbus,* 1929); *El fantasma de las alas de oro,* 1930 (*The Phantom with Wings of Gold,* 1931); *Obras completas,* 1964-1965 (3 volumes).

Other literary forms

All of the novels listed above were published by Editorial Prometeo of Valencia, in most cases under the personal supervision of the author. In addition to these works, the writings of Vicente Blasco Ibáñez include the following: early romances which Blasco Ibáñez later repudiated as unworthy of preservation, including such works as the novella *El conde Garci-Fernández* (1928), *¡Por la patria! (Romeu el guerrillero)* (1888), *La araña negra* (1928; a collection of short fiction), *¡Viva la república!* (1893-1894); short stories and novelettes, including "La torre de Boatella," *Fantasías, leyendas y tradiciones* (1887), *El adiós a Schubert* (1888; stories of a distinctly romantic nature and quite different from the author's mature pieces), and, later *Cuentos valencianos* (1896), *La condenada* (1899), *El préstamo de la difunta* (1921), *Novelas de la costa azul* (1924), and *Novelas de amor y de muerte* (1927); nonfiction, including *Historia de la revolución española, 1808-1874* (1890-1892), *París:*

Impresiones de un emigrado (1893), *En el país del arte* (1896; *In the Land of Art*, 1923), *Oriente* (1907), *Argentina y sus grandezas* (1910), the thirteen-volume *Historia de la guerra europea de 1914* (1914-1919), *El militarismo mejicano* (1920; *Mexico in Revolution*, 1920), the three-volume *La vuelta al mundo de un novelista* (1924-1925; *A Novelist's Tour of the World*, 1926); *Una nación secuestrada: Alfonso XIII desenmascarado* (1924; *Alfonso XIII Unmasked: The Military Terror in Spain*, 1924), *Lo que será la república española: Al país y al ejército* (1925), *Estudios literarios* (1933), and *Discursos literarios* (1966); and one play, *El juez* (1894). Translations of many of Blasco Ibáñez' short stories have been collected in *The Last Lion and Other Tales* (1919) and *The Old Woman of the Movies and Other Stories* (1925).

Achievements

Blasco Ibáñez is probably the most widely read Spanish novelist, both in Spain and abroad, except for Miguel de Cervantes. Certainly he was one of the most prolific writers his country ever produced (his collected works run to forty volumes) a result of his extraordinarily dynamic and energetic nature and of his determination to show both the positive and the negative aspects of Spain to his countrymen and to the world.

Blasco Ibáñez has not received a balanced judgment from literary critics. Most have offered exaggerated praise or scorn for his works or have ignored him altogether. For many years, many Spanish critics denied the value of his novels because they rejected his radical political ideas, they envied his financial success, or they held a low opinion of his literary origins. (Blasco Ibáñez did not participate in some of the stylistic renovations of the *generación del 98*, adhering instead to many of the realistic-Naturalistic practices of the nineteenth century, thought by many to be out of date.) While Blasco Ibáñez' attacks on the Spanish political scene and eventual millionaire status led to ostracism by his Spanish contemporaries, such English-speaking critics as William Dean Howells, Havelock Ellis, Walter Starkie, Gerald Brenan, A. Grove Day, and Edgar Knowlson, Jr., have offered a fairer perspective.

Certainly there are significant defects in some of Blasco Ibáñez' works. One must discriminate carefully between the hits and the misses. Without question, his early Valencian novels represent his greatest achievement, revealing a powerful double legacy that cannot be ignored: a pictorial, concrete, at times poetic style of strength and beauty, and a striking portrayal of human action. Later in his career, as Blasco Ibáñez strayed farther and farther from the format and the setting he knew best, the aesthetic value of his novels declined dramatically. While a definitive study of his total literary production remains to be done, analyses of individual novels have at least offered glimpses into the genuine artistry of his best works.

Biography

Vicente Blasco Ibáñez was born in a room over a corner grocery in Valencia on January 29, 1867. From his parents, he inherited the vigor of the Aragonese peasants, and from an impoverished childhood, he gained the spirit of struggle and defiance. During his early years, the lad of sturdy build, brown eyes, and curly hair could be seen more often walking the beach of nearby Cabañal or talking to fishermen and sailors than sitting at his desk in school. By the age of fourteen, he had written a cloak-and-dagger novel, by fifteen had published a short story in the Valencian dialect, and by sixteen had run away from the University of Valencia to Madrid. There, while doing secretarial work for the aging writer Manuel Fernández y González, he gained the inspiration for his first series of lengthy writings—a dozen romances which he later repudiated. By age seventeen, he had published a poem advocating chopping off all the crowned heads of Europe, starting with Spain.

The death of Alfonso XII in 1885 marked the young writer's start as republican conspirator and frequent political prisoner. After completing his law degree in 1888 and his first forced exile in France (brought on by increasingly anticlerical speeches), Blasco Ibáñez married his cousin María Blasco del Cacho, who was to endure his tempestuous nature and stormy career and who bore him five children before their separation immediately prior to the outbreak of World War I. On November 12, 1894, Blasco Ibáñez released the first issue of *El pueblo*, a journal which he was to run virtually single-handedly and in which many of his best works would appear in serial form. It was into this enterprise that he poured all of his energy and stamina, as well as the entirety of his parents' inheritance.

Blasco Ibáñez proved to be a born leader of crowds, self-assured, fluent in his oratory, with a booming voice whose warmth quickly dispelled any first impression of coldness that might have been caused by his pointed beard, his mustache, and his aquiline nose. As time passed, he grew to be increasingly impulsive and impatient to eliminate the stupidity, ignorance, and laziness around him. Antireligious in a city venerated as the repository of the Holy Grail, and republican in a region noted for its conservative monarchism, he never avoided the chance for an iconoclastic stance.

Nevertheless, his election as the Valencian representative for the journal *Las cortes* in 1898 was the first of many. To his growing political fame was added an international literary reputation with the French translation of *The Cabin* in 1901. In 1904, he abandoned his home at La Malvarrosa on the Valencian shore to take up residence in Madrid and other Spanish cities.

The year 1909 found Blasco Ibáñez making two trips to Argentina, first to give lectures and subsequently to supervise the development of some new settlements. There he remained, fighting harsh climates and jungle dangers, until economic difficulties led him back to Europe immediately prior to World War I. Shortly afterward, he launched into a campaign to help the Allies, in the form of *Historia de la guerra europea de 1914*, speeches throughout neutral Spain, and several novels, of which *The Four Horsemen of the Apocalypse* had the greatest political and financial impact. When unexpected wealth poured in from this work's reprints, translations, and film rights, he moved to the French Riviera, where most of his last novels were written.

By 1925, Blasco Ibáñez had undertaken a triumphant tour of the United States, composing lengthy travel literature based on a six-month luxury-liner trip around the world, when he received news of the death of his wife. Within months, he married the daughter of a well-known Chilean general and soon thereafter, in failing health, retired to his Riviera home to churn out his final writings. The night before his sixty-first birthday, weakened by pneumonia, diabetes, and overwork, he died uttering the words "my garden, my garden," a reflection of his ardent desire to have his Menton garden resemble those of his beloved Valencia. In his will, he bequeathed his home to "all the writers of the world" and insisted that he not be buried in a nonrepublican Spain. On October 29, 1933, two years after the proclamation of the Second Republic, his body was moved to Valencia amid the impassioned eulogies of those who had scorned him years before. More than forty-seven years later, as renovations were undertaken on the Blasco Ibáñez home at La Malvarrosa, the first international symposium on Don Vicente's works was held, and a determination to rectify the critical neglect of his work was voiced.

Blasco Ibáñez was a man of action first and a writer second. His works bear a profound and constant autobiographical stamp—the mark of a rebel, a revolutionary journalist, a colonizer, a sailor, a fighter for the cause of peasants, fishermen, and slum dwellers, and an exile who attacked his government yet remained loyal to Spanish traditions, as reflected in his tireless efforts to glorify his country's imperial past and to combat the anti-Spanish legend. It is with at least some justification that he is remembered by many of his countrymen more for his life than for his writings.

Analysis

Following Vicente Blasco Ibáñez' first romances, five phases can be distinguished in the course of his prolific career. Into the first fall his Valencian works, from *The Three Roses* (which he considered his first novel) through *Reeds and Mud* and including two collections of stories, *Cuentos valencianos* and *La condenada*. Within this group, three works can be considered the novelist's masterpieces: *The Mayflower, The Cabin*, and *Reeds and Mud*. Second are his novels of social protest, written between 1903 and 1905 and dealing with the Church (*The Shadow of the Cathedral*, set in Toledo, and *The Intruder*, set in the Basque provinces) or with the exploitation of workers in vineyards and in large cities (*The Fruit of the Vine* and *The Mob*, set in Jérez de la Frontera and Madrid, respectively). "Art," the author explains, "should not be simply a mere manifestation of beauty. Art should be on the side of the needy defending forcefully those who are hungry for justice." Nevertheless, interminable didactic monologues, long ideological question-

and-answer dialectics, and overtly symbolic characterization lessen the aesthetic worth of these works. The third phase comprises psychological novels, in which the author stresses character development within specific settings: *Woman Triumphant* (Madrid), *La voluntad de vivir* (the aristocracy of Madrid and Paris), *Blood and Sand* (bullfighting in Seville and Madrid), *The Dead Command* (Balearic Islands), and *Luna Benamor* (Gibraltar). While some of these works are admirable for their characterization and for their descriptions of landscape and local customs, they are clearly inferior to the Valencian writings. Fourth are cosmopolitan and war novels, including *The Argonauts* (a detailed account of a transatlantic journey, envisioned as the first in a series of works dealing with Latin America) and several novels written to defend the Allied cause: *The Four Horsemen of the Apocalypse*, *Mare Nostrum*, *The Enemies of Women*, *The Temptress*, and *Queen Calafia*. These novels proved to be as popular as they were lacking in artistic merit. Finally, Blasco Ibáñez' fifth phase includes historical novels of Spanish glorification, ranging from the account of Pope Benedict XIII's life to the voyages of Columbus and a love story set in Monte Carlo.

In some ways, Blasco Ibáñez is a transitional figure between the age of the realistic novel (1870-1900) and the *generación del 98*. Works such as *The Fruit of the Vine* and *The Mob* demonstrate his participation in the ninety-eighters' preoccupation with Spanish social issues, and most of his works, particularly in his early periods, reveal the extraordinary sensitivity to landscape which Pío Baroja's generation would display. Blasco Ibáñez' regionalistic *costumbrismo* and use of descriptive detail are techniques that relate him to the earlier generation of Benito Pérez Galdós and José María de Pereda.

It was Blasco Ibáñez who introduced the *pueblo*, rather than the middle class, as a frequent source for the novel's protagonist, a character who struggles heroically against his environment and his own animal instincts. A convincing narrative action of sharp contrasts; a pictorial, concrete, sensual, often impressionistic realism of strength and beauty; and an admirable tightness and unity of plot are the features that set the Valencian novels apart as his most accomplished works.

Blasco Ibáñez was not a contemplative man, and his themes, while relevant and often powerful, are not complex or subtle. His modes of characterization, his third phase notwithstanding, are a far cry from the probing, individualizing approach of most of the late-nineteenth century realists. His figures lack depth, are often excessively masculine and melodramatic, and seldom rise above mere types. They can be divided into two classes: good and bad. These opposites are inevitably caught up in an eternal struggle with each other or with nature. There are few inner battles of conscience, few motivations besides those of glory, power, sexual gratification, or mere survival. Nevertheless, Blasco Ibáñez' main type—the man of action, passion, animal instinct, and rebellion—is a graphic and powerful creation, made convincing by the sheer force of his portrayal, if not by any unique identity. Batiste (*The Cabin*), Retor (*The Mayflower*), Toni (*Reeds and Mud*), and, in later novels, Sánchez Morueta (*The Intruder*), Gallardo (*Blood and Sand*), Centauro (*The Four Horsemen of the Apocalypse*), Ferragut (*Mare Nostrum*), and Renovales (*Woman Triumphant*) are such characters, presented in deliberate (albeit artificial) contrast to their opposites; these are weak and lazy types, such as Tonet (*The Mayflower*) and the other Tonet (*Reeds and Mud*). Blasco Ibáñez' women are also one-sided—oppressed and overworked domestics, conventional society figures, or women of action and conquest. The last group would include Dolores (*The Mayflower*), Neleta (*Reeds and Mud*), Leonora (*The Torrent*), Doña Sol (*Blood and Sand*), and la Marquesita (*The Fruit of the Vine*). Finally, one should note that, even if Blasco Ibáñez did not create great characters, he was able to succeed in capturing dramatically the heterogeneity of the masses. Pimentò of *The Cabin*, who represents the people of the region around the Valencian *huerta*, is one striking example of this skillful portrayal.

Although Blasco Ibáñez has often been referred to as the "Spanish Zola," he rejected the Naturalists' pseudoscientific, analytical approach and emphasis on crude detail, came to mitigate the impression of fatalistic determinism through his admiration of man's will to fight and a suggestion of optimism, and, finally, often presented a lighter, less objective, and more poetic tone than is the norm in Émile Zola's novels. Nevertheless, there are many moments in Blasco Ibáñez's work when a strong measure of pessimism and philosophical determinism or the use of unpleasant language and description demonstrate the influence of French Naturalism.

Finally, one should not forget that Blasco Ibáñez produced some of the finest Spanish short stories of the modern era. One has only to look at the moving portrait of the protagonist of "Dimoni" to realize the author's skill in this genre. John B. Dalbor, the major critic to have undertaken detailed studies of these pieces, believes that many of the stories are in fact superior to the author's novels and that the very best of these stories are to be found in the collections *Cuentos valencianos*, *La condenada*, and *El préstamo de la difunta*.

In the Valencian novels, Blasco Ibáñez' descriptive power—tumultuous, exuberant, dramatic, and exact—is most evident, a talent which sprang from keen observation and an uncanny ability to improvise. These virtues are evident in Blasco Ibáñez' second novel, *The Mayflower*, set in the fishing village of Cabañal; the descriptions of regional scenes and customs and many of the characters are typically drawn from observation at first hand. The plot concerns the struggles of the poor fishermen of the Valencia area. Pascualet, called "El Retor" because of his benign clerical appearance, works and saves so that some day he can afford his own boat and free himself from the demands of another captain. His spendthrift brother Tonet is lazy and hates manual labor. When their father is killed at sea, their mother, Tona, cleverly converts her husband's boat into a beach tavern, where she earns a meager but adequate living for the family. El Retor goes to sea as an apprentice, but Tonet turns to drink and women until he leaves for service in the navy. By this time, a child, Roseta, has been born of Tona's affair with a passing *carabinero*. When Tonet returns to find that his brother has married the seductive Dolores, he soon agrees to marry Rosario, who has waited for him for many years. Soon Tonet renews (unbeknown to El Retor) his previous youthful encounters with Dolores, and battles between the sisters-in-law increase in frequency and intensity, despite the attempts at reconciliation managed by the ancient village matriarch, Tía Picores. A boy born to El Retor and Dolores is actually Tonet's child.

After years of hard work and saving, and after a tense smuggling adventure that results in a considerable profit, El Retor is able to arrange for the building of the finest vessel ever seen in the village, named *Flor de Mayo* after the brand of tobacco that had been smuggled into Spain on the earlier trip. Prior to the ship's second sailing, Rosario reveals to El Retor that for years his brother has had an affair with Dolores and that his son is really Tonet's offspring. After a night of shock and humiliation and after refusing for the moment to avenge the affront by his brother, El Retor sets sail in one of the worst storms to afflict the coast of Cabañal. In a suspenseful and tumultuous final chapter, El Retor confronts his brother on board the *Flor de Mayo*, extracts a confession from him, and then refuses to give him the boat's single life jacket. Instead, he puts it on the boy and tosses him overboard. The lad is thrown upon the rocks, and the ship is ripped apart by the fury of the wind. Dolores and Rosario, watching the action from the shore, mourn their loss, and old Tía Picores shouts a final condemnation of the people of Valencia, who are ultimately responsible for the deaths the women have witnessed.

Blasco Ibáñez' viewpoint is usually one of relative neutrality and omniscience, and, as is the case with other Valencian novels, he frequently transports the reader through the minds of the various characters. Some subjective authorial control, however, is evident in the progressively dominant tone of fatalism, the use of situational irony, and moments of open humor.

The style is natural and spontaneous, at times distinctly colloquial. The reader is most impressed by the fresh, graphic, highly sensuous descriptive passages, lyric moments in which a vivid plasticity and an appeal to the senses predominate. Indeed, it seems logical that Blasco Ibáñez dedicated the novel to his childhood friend Joaquín Sorolla, the artist whose vivid transcription and dazzling colors are reflected in the novelist's prose. The reader is immersed in descriptions of Cabañal and of the sea. One can envision the dawn after a night of rain, hear the distant whistle of the first trains leaving Valencia, and smell the wet earth of the village streets and the strong odors (presented in Naturalistic fashion) of the local fish market. Animal images abound, and the leitmotifs of man's bestiality and the man-sea relationship are the two main elements around which the novel's symbolism is constructed. (The sea itself, for example, represents the inexorable force of destiny.)

The characters are generally flat, since Blasco Ibáñez' frequent suggestion of Naturalistic predestination precludes any substantial psychological development. Rather, the author was more interested in description and in constructing a rapid, suspenseful plot line for the daily readers of *El pueblo*, in which the work first appeared. Tonet is pleasure-loving, unrepentant, lazy, and self-centered. His brother El Retor is the first of Blasco Ibáñez' strong heroes, trustworthy, naïve, hardworking, and stubborn. In the last two chapters, an introspective glimpse into his musings is of a kind almost unique among the Valencian novels; a long interior monologue suggestive of Miguel de Unamuno's later portraits of inner conflict and uncertainty reveals that, if it were not for the pressures of time and the force of his own tumultuous nature, Blasco Ibáñez might have created psychological portraits of considerable depth. Finally, of some importance is the way in which the author develops the entire *pueblo* as a kind of mass character, accustomed to the hell of life's struggle and to the constant challenge of death.

The central thematic statement of the novel concerns man's futile fight against the bestiality of his own instincts and the powerful forces of nature. Secondary themes include a condemnation of excessive pride, a parody of religious rituals, and criticism of the villagers' exploitation by the people of Valencia.

The novel's structure is built around two main lines of action: El Retor's attempts to escape from poverty and the adulterous relationship between Tonet and Dolores. As in a number of the later Valencian works, the plot follows a regular, unified pattern: several expository chapters, consisting of an episodic introduction and two chapters of retrospective background; after that, the main action develops as a rectilinear, basically causal progression, within which the main costumbristic "digressions" become integral parts of the whole (the market scene, the Good Friday procession, the smuggling expedition, and the blessing of the boats). The unity of *The Mayflower*, like that of the other novels of the period, derives above all from the fact that Blasco Ibáñez wrote with a clear goal: to capture a people and a region. The powerful descriptions and vigorous, dramatic depiction of the villagers' primitive and difficult existence are the narrative manifestations of this purpose and represent those aspects of the work that are of greatest value.

Blasco Ibáñez' third Valencian novel, *The Cabin*, was his first universally acclaimed masterpiece. It developed as the final version of a short story that he composed while hiding from the police during four days in 1895. The plot is extremely simple, lacking any kind of secondary complication and moving without distraction toward the final tragedy. In the village of Alboraya, in the *huerta* region north of Valencia, Tío Barret is evicted by a usurious landlord, whom Barret then kills in a burst of anger. For ten years, the villagers prevent anyone from working the land, as revenge for Barret's fate and as a warning to other landowners against mistreatment of the *huertanos*. Nevertheless, Batiste and his family arrive to restore the property and its shack. Pimentò, the village bully and loafer and a local warden for the rationing of irrigation use, causes Batiste to lose his water rights. Meanwhile, other members of the family suffer: The daughter Roseta's romance with the butcher's apprentice is destroyed, and the three boys must fight their way home from school every day. The youngest son is thrown into a slimy irrigation ditch, which leads to his death. At this point, the villagers seem to repent of their actions and take charge of the funeral. Soon, however, Batiste is lured into a tavern fight with Pimentò, which leads to their shooting each other. On the night Pimentò dies from his wounds, Batiste awakens to find the cabin on fire. As the shack burns, the villagers leave the family to their plight.

The style of *The Cabin* exhibits those attributes already mentioned. Moments of Naturalistic delineation and melodramatic animal imagery are perhaps more frequent than in *The Mayflower*, and the color red becomes particularly prominent (linking images of blood, earth, the irrigation water, the fire, the tavern atmosphere, and so on). Batiste (the stoic, hardworking protagonist typical of Blasco Ibáñez' works) and Pimentò (the cowardly incarnation of collective egotism and laziness) are opposite, unidimensional poles of character presentation. The latter figure and the various representatives of the village "chorus" exemplify well the author's powerful glimpses of mass psychology.

Structurally, the novel demonstrates a typical plan: three introductory chapters concerning the arrival of Batiste and then the past tragedy of Tío Barret, four of increasing conflict, and three final chapters in which the boy's funeral suggests a momentary peace and the final disaster is presented. Each of the ten chapters is built tightly into an organic whole, yet each demonstrates a kind of aesthetic autonomy, focusing on a single incident or anecdote. A strict causal line and the careful use of foreshadowing, contrast, and leitmotif add to the impression of structural unity. Finally, cyclical factors are evident, as Barret's story at the start and Batiste's fate at the end are meant to appear similar.

A sense of fatalism and inevitability, similar to that of *The Mayflower*, is created as thematic statements are made in condemnation of the landowners' exploitation and the hypocrisy and pride of the villagers, and in support of the will to struggle for individual liberty and the need to curb one's bestial instincts, to fight against nature and the influence of collective heredity.

The novel, then, is concerned with man's courageous attempts to overcome nearly insurmountable obstacles. This struggle is presented on two main levels, one socioeconomic and regional, the other of universal dimensions. Batiste finds work but discovers that he must betray his fellow *huertanos* in breaking the boycott against using forbidden lands. Blasco Ibáñez, however, is ambiguous in his loyalties; one first feels sympathy for the tenant farmers as Tío Barret's eviction is described, only to have one's allegiance shift to a man fighting against the farmers' prejudice and conservatism. The author admires worker solidarity but also respects Batiste's determination to better himself. This confusion, R. A. Cardwell believes, "might be counted the major flaw of the novel." The ending is also ambiguous. At first glance it seems to demonstrate Blasco Ibáñez' pessimism about the power of society and tradition in thwarting individual enterprise, but on a deeper level it may suggest the author's optimism about man's capacity for courageous struggle and a faint hope for eventual success. This ambiguity, in turn, relates to the universal level of meaning inherent in this and other Valencian novels. Man will continue to fight throughout the cyclical pattern of human existence. Blasco Ibáñez' novel thus suggests (albeit subtly) the final stage of the realistic movement of the 1890's, in which the materialistic Naturalism of the previous decade gave way to idealistic themes of the need for human understanding and sympathy.

Within the trajectory of the Valencian works themselves, *The Cabin* seems to represent a middle position between the emphasis on socioeconomic concerns of *The Three Roses* and a later emphasis on the way man acts when confronted by the universal laws of an all-powerful nature. *Reeds and Mud*, with its extraordinary depiction of such natural forces, is the most powerful expression of this subsequent focus.

While not recognized as such by all the critics, Blasco Ibáñez' last Valencian novel, *Reeds and Mud*, is probably his single greatest literary achievement. "It is the one work," the author confided to his friend Camilo Pitollet, "which holds for me the happiest memories, the one which I composed with the most solidity, the one which I think is the most rounded." The novel is one of the most thorough adaptations by any major Spanish writer of the tenets of French Naturalism.

The scene is set between 1890 and 1900 in the swamplike region of the Albufera lake near Valencia, an area known to Blasco Ibáñez' non-Valencian readers for its rice fields and plentiful game birds. The narrative itself is constructed on three levels: first, the story of three generations—the old fisherman Tío Paloma, his hardworking son Toni, and his rebellious, irresponsible grandson Tonet; second, the lush, all-pervading atmosphere of the Albufera; and third, a constant, "transcendent" feeling of the power of destiny, the irrevocable pressures of an abstract, deterministic force. The plot demonstrates the sharp singleness of effect that one generally finds in a short story and traces the love affair between Tonet and Neleta from childhood to disaster, years later. While the lad is away at war, the latter marries a sickly but rich tavern owner, Cañamèl, in order to escape her impoverished existence. The subsequent illicit love affair between Tonet and Neleta leads to a series of events in which man is again shown to be defenseless against the destructive forces of nature and animal instinct. Tonet suffers an emotional breakdown. Cañamèl dies after specifying in his will that Neleta cannot retain their property if she remarries or associates in an intimate way with another man. After Neleta gives birth to Tonet's child, she refuses to see her lover openly and orders him to abandon the child in the city across the lake, in order to escape further suspicion of violating the terms of the will. Instead, fear, remorse, and accidents of fate lead Tonet to throw the infant into the lake. When his dog later discovers the baby's corpse, Tonet seeks escape from life's misery in suicide.

Blasco Ibáñez' skillful shifts in point of view contribute a great deal to the novel's sense of realism. Such shifts frequently reveal a single incident from several different perspectives. Despite the strong measure of objectivity and the relative lack of overt authorial comment, Blasco Ibáñez' humor breaks through now and then as a means of comic relief from the growing tension of the plot line; this is noticeable, for example, in the juvenile enthusiasm of Don Joaquín during a hunting incident and Sangonera's "religious love affair" with the three *pucheros*. Above all, *Reeds and Mud* includes Blasco Ibáñez' most striking descriptive passages, revealing the freshness, the spontaneity, the richness and sensual power which constitute his most significant artistic contribution.

As always with the Valencian novels, no figures are presented in great depth. Each seems to represent dominant passions or vices: laziness (Tonet), drunkenness (Sangonera), avarice (Neleta), the will to work and struggle (Toni), hatred for the changing times (Paloma), and so on. Certainly, all the characters are seen to blend in Naturalistic fashion into the landscape around them (although they stand alongside nature rather than being consistently overpowered by it). Tonet is a victim of his own weaknesses: his indifference, his laziness, his hypocrisy, his yearning for adventure, and (under the influence of Neleta) his greed. Caught between the philosophies of his father and grandfather, Tonet is unable to shake off his inertia to make any decision regarding his life. Neleta comes also to represent the force and fecundity of nature. Sangonera, one of Blasco Ibáñez' most memorable types, is at the same time comic and pathetic, a kind of nineteenth century "hippie" or a modern version of the Golden Age *gracioso*, the comic "servant" who nevertheless is able to utter some very wise convictions. Toni corresponds to Batiste of *The Cabin* and to El Retor of *The Mayflower*, demonstrating the persistence, hard work, self-denial, and undying spirit of struggle that the author so admired.

Thematically, *Reeds and Mud* reveals the fullness of Blasco Ibáñez' acceptance of many tenets of the Naturalists' philosophy. Man's battle against the bestiality of his own instincts and the powerful forces of nature is once again shown to be futile. Precluding an entirely Naturalistic interpretation, however, are such factors as the exaltation of Paloma's and Toni's respective kinds of strength, the absence of heredity as a significant force, and a few elements of sheer coincidence in the plot line. (The plot itself does not reveal the strict logic of *The Cabin*; Tonet's suicide, for example, is not really the necessary outcome of causal factors.) Other related but minor thematic concerns again include the condemnation of egotism and envy and a criticism of man's drive to accumulate material goods at the expense of nature.

The novel's structure follows Blasco Ibáñez' typical pattern. The main action builds to three peaks, in scenes of adultery, infanticide, and suicide. As usual, a series of techniques is employed to achieve the effect of extraordinary unity: causal links of plot; the skillful integration into the narrative of the main costumbristic scenes (in this case, there are three—the raffle of the best fishing locations, the Fiesta del Niño Jesús, and the hunting expeditions, or *tiradas*); parallels and corresponding incidents; and the skillful use of timing, contrast, and the repetition of leitmotifs. In *Reeds and Mud*, Blasco Ibáñez succeeds most fully in achieving the aim of the Valencian novels: the lifelike rendering (rather than didactic or moralistic evaluation) of a region—its people, its customs, its ambience.

Although far inferior artistically to the best of his Valencian novels, Blasco Ibáñez' greatest popular success was *The Four Horsemen of the Apocalypse*. Here the protagonist, Julio Desnoyers, is an elegant young Argentine whose father, a Frenchman, had migrated to Argentina because of the Franco-Prussian War of 1870-1871. After making his fortune in South America, the elder Desnoyers takes his family to Paris. Julio decides to marry Margarita Laurier, a frivolous divorcée, but the outbreak of World War I produces a profound change in the thinking of both. Margarita abandons her interests in fashion and social activities and dedicates herself to the wounded soldiers as a nurse. Julio enlists and sacrifices his life fighting the Germans.

The title derives from the biblical book of Revelation, which describes the four scourges of plague, war, hunger, and death—forces which, the elder Desnoyers prophesies, will walk the earth again. The novel was written as an instrument of propaganda for the Allied cause, and its major weakness is its heavy-handed and exaggerated condemnation not only of the German military Establishment but also of the German people and the entirety of German culture. An extraordinarily detailed and vivid account of the Battle of the Marne is the novel's one positive achievement.

Blasco Ibáñez' works are, to say the least, uneven. While his later novels will doubtless continue to be read for years, it is his early masterpieces that earn for him a major place in modern Spanish literature. When adequate studies of his novels are produced and acceptable translations of his best works appear, the world will acknowledge his magnificent descriptions of land and sea and of regional life around Valencia and his powerful portraits of individuals struggling against overwhelming internal and external obstacles.

Major publications other than long fiction

SHORT FICTION: *Fantasías, leyendas y tradiciones*, 1887; *El adiós a Schubert*, 1888; *Cuentos valencianos*, 1896; *La condenada*, 1899; *Luna Benamor*, 1909 (includes the novel of the same title; English translation, 1919); *The Last Lion and Other Tales*, 1919; *El préstamo de la difunta*, 1921; *Novelas de la costa azul*, 1924; *The Old Woman of the Movies and Other Stories*, 1925; *Novelas de amor y de muerte*, 1927.

PLAY: *El juez*, 1894.

NONFICTION: *Historia de la revolución española, 1808-1874*, 1890-1892; *París: Impresiones de un emigrado*, 1893; *En el país del arte*, 1896 (*In the Land of Art*, 1923); *Oriente*, 1907; *Argentina y sus grandezas*, 1910; *Historia de la guerra europea de 1914*, 1914-1919 (13 volumes); *El militarismo mejicano*, 1920 (*Mexico in Revolution*, 1920); *Una nación secuestrada: Alfonso XIII desenmascarado*, 1924 (*Alfonso XIII Unmasked: The Military Terror in Spain*, 1924); *La vuelta al mundo de un novelista*, 1924-1925 (3 volumes; *A Novelist's Tour of the World*, 1926); *Lo que será la república española: Al país y al ejército*, 1925; *Estudios literarios*, 1933; *Discursos literarios*, 1966.

MISCELLANEOUS: *Obras completas*, 1923-1934 (40 volumes); *Obras completas*, 1964-1965 (3 volumes).

Bibliography

Betoret-París, Eduardo. *El costumbrismo regional en la obra de Blasco Ibáñez*, 1958.

Cardwell, R. A. *Blasco Ibáñez, La Barraca: Critical Guides to Spanish Texts*, 1973.

Day, A. Grove, and Edgar C. Knowlton, Jr. *Blasco Ibáñez*, 1962.

Gascó Contell, Emilio. *Genio y figura de Blasco Ibáñez: Agitador, aventurero y novelista*, 1957.

León Roca, J. L. *Vicente Blasco Ibáñez*, 1967.

Medina, Jeremy T. "The Artistry of Blasco Ibáñez' *Cañas y barro*," in *Hispania*. LX (1977), pp. 275-284.

_____ . "The Artistry of Blasco Ibáñez' *Flor de Mayo*," in *Hispania*. LXV (1982), pp. 197-208.

_____ . *Spanish Realism: The Theory and Practice of a Concept in the Nineteenth Century*, 1979.

Pitollet, Camille. *Vicente Blasco Ibáñez: Sus novelas y la novela de su vida*, 1921.

Smith, Paul. "On Blasco Ibáñez' *Flor de Mayo*," in *Symposium*. XXIV (1970), pp. 55-68.

_____ . *Vicente Blasco Ibáñez: A Critical Survey of the Novels from 1894 to 1909*, 1964.

_____ . *Vicente Blasco Ibáñez: Una nueva introducción a su vida y obra*, 1972.

Swain, James Q. *Vicente Blasco Ibáñez, General Study: Special Emphasis on Realistic Techniques*, 1959.

Jeremy T. Medina

HEINRICH BÖLL

Born: Cologne, Germany; December 21, 1917

Principal long fiction

Der Zug war pünktlich, 1949 (*The Train Was on Time*, 1956); *Wo warst du, Adam?*, 1951 (*Adam, Where Art Thou?*, 1955); *Und sagte kein einziges Wort*, 1953 (*Acquainted with the Night*, 1954); *Haus ohne Hüter*, 1954 (*Tomorrow and Yesterday*, 1957); *Das Brot der frühen Jahre*, 1955 (*The Bread of Our Early Years*, 1957); *Billard um halbzehn*, 1959 (*Billiards at Half-Past Nine*, 1961); *Ansichten eines Clowns*, 1963 (*The Clown*, 1965); *Ende einer Dienstfahrt*, 1966 (*End of a Mission*, 1967); *Gruppenbild mit Dame*, 1971 (*Group Portrait with Lady*, 1973); *Die verlorene Ehre der Katharina Blum*, 1974 (*The Lost Honor of Katharina Blum*, 1975); *Fürsorgliche Belagerung*, 1979 (*The Safety Net*, 1982).

Other literary forms

In addition to novels, Heinrich Böll has written a number of novellas and short stories. Although Böll is known chiefly for his novels and short stories, he has also written plays, essays, and poems, and he is an active lecturer, critic, and translator. His essays on literature (which include discussions of Fyodor Dostoevski, Thomas Wolfe, François Mauriac, Mary McCarthy, and Aleksandr Solzhenitsyn) show his familiarity with European and American literature. In his essays on politics, Böll is an outspoken critic of trends in modern German society. Together with his wife, Böll has translated works by Irish, English, and American authors into German, including works by John Synge, Brendan Behan, and J. D. Salinger. There is now a comprehensive ten-volume German edition of Böll's works. The first five volumes, published in 1977, contain novels and stories; the second five, published in 1978, contain radio plays, dramas, film texts, poems, essays, reviews, speeches, commentaries, and interviews.

Achievements

Böll is probably the best-known contemporary German writer in Germany and abroad. In Germany, he is popular at all levels of society, and his new works automatically become best-sellers. His books have been widely translated into many languages. In the Soviet Union, Böll is the Western author most frequently published and read. Until 1951, however, he was virtually unknown. In that year, Gruppe 47 awarded him their prize for his story "Die schwarzen Schafe" ("The Black Sheep"). Since then, Böll has received many prizes, including the Nobel Prize for Literature in 1972; the Swedish Academy praised Böll for his broad perspective on his time and for his sensitive characterizations, acknowledging his contribution to the renewal of German literature after the Nazi era. In 1969, Böll was elected president of the West German P.E.N. Club, evidence of the respect that other writers had for him. He was elected president of the International P.E.N. Club in 1971, the first German to be so honored, and he served until May, 1974. In 1974, Böll received the Carl von Ossietzky Medal from the International League of Human Rights in recognition of his concern for human rights. He was made an honorary member of the American Academy of Art and Literature and of the American National Institute of Art and Literature in the same year. Böll's outspoken criticisms of social abuses he perceives in modern German society have provoked widespread debate.

Biography

Heinrich Böll was born in Cologne, Germany, on December 21, 1917. On his father's side, his ancestors were ship carpenters who emigrated from England many centuries ago, Catholics fleeing from the persecutions of Henry VIII. On his mother's side, his ancestors were Catholic farmers and brewers. Böll's father was a cabinetmaker. In an autobiographical sketch of 1958 entitled "Über mich selbst" ("About Myself"), Böll describes the hunger, poverty, and unemployment in Germany during the inflationary years of the 1920's, topics which frequently recur in his works. He remembers the first money he received—a note for a billion marks with which he managed to buy a stick of candy. In an autobiographical sketch written in 1981, *Was soll aus dem Jungen bloss werden?* (*What's to Become of the Boy?*, 1984), Böll describes his childhood and youth during the Hitler years and his strong opposition to the Nazis. Whenever possible, he avoided participating in the Hitler Youth.

In an interview with the critic Horst Bienek in 1961, Böll said that he began to write when he was seventeen or eighteen. He wrote four, five, or perhaps six novels at this time, three of which were burned in Cologne during the war. In the same interview, Böll acknowledged his debt to many writers, among them Karl May, Marcel Proust, Johann Peter Hebel, Dostoevski, Jack London, Ernest Hemingway, Albert Camus, Graham Greene, William Faulkner, Thomas Wolfe, Adalbert Stifter, Theodor Fontane, and Joseph Roth. When Böll left the *gymnasium* in 1937, he became an apprentice in the book trade in Bonn. In the winter of 1938, he was drafted into the labor service. He began to study German literature at the University of Cologne, but his studies were interrupted when he was called up for military service in 1939. Although he was strongly opposed to the war, Böll had to serve as an infantryman in the German army for six years on the eastern and western fronts and was wounded four times. In 1942, he married Annemarie Cech, later a teacher of English. During the war, Böll deserted twice and was finally captured by the Americans. Böll draws on his firsthand experiences of the war in his early novels and stories. On his return from a prisoner-of-war camp in

1945, Böll worked briefly in the family carpentry shop until he found a job with the Cologne Bureau of Statistics. He also resumed his studies. After 1951, he earned his living as a writer. In the mid-1950's, Böll visited Ireland for the first time and liked it so much that he bought some property there. Thereafter he returned to reside in his native city of Cologne (often used as the setting of his novels) with his wife and three sons.

Analysis

Serious moral commitment is the essence of Heinrich Böll's writing. In an essay of 1952 entitled "Bekenntnis zur Trümmerliteratur" ("In Defense of Rubble Literature"), Böll praises Charles Dickens for the same commitment. Dickens wrote about the social abuses he saw in English schools, prisons, and poorhouses and, by depicting these abuses, helped to bring about change. Böll believes that literature can change society by making people more aware of the world in which they live. In his 1958 essay "Die Sprache als Hort der Freiheit" ("Language as the Stronghold of Freedom"), he says that words contain enough dynamite to destroy whole worlds. It is for this reason that dictatorships fear the printed word almost more than armed resistance. Böll's early works show the senseless destruction of the war and the hardships of the immediate postwar years in Germany, while his later works focus on contemporary German society. He had hoped that the experience of the Hitler years would change society for the better; instead, he sees the same opportunism, love of power, militarism, and greed that existed before. Besides having a strong sense of the moral and political responsibility of the writer, Böll believes that the writer should be humane and compassionate. In his works, Böll's sympathy for his fellow human beings is always evident. He is especially sympathetic toward ordinary, unheroic people who are often victimized by a cruel society. These are the kind of people Böll chooses for his protagonists. Böll's moral earnestness does not, however, preclude a sense of humor. His works are frequently humorous or satiric, although his satire is rarely vituperative.

In his interview with Horst Bienek, Böll said that his early novel *Adam, Where Art Thou?* is still one of his favorite works. It is the only one of Böll's novels that deals exclusively with World War II. In it, Böll draws extensively on his experiences as a soldier. The novel is structured episodically: The nine episodes are loosely connected by the figure of the soldier Feinhals, who is not, however, the protagonist. In some chapters, Feinhals plays only a peripheral role, and in two chapters he does not appear. Minor characters in one chapter become the central characters in another. As the name "Adam" in the title suggests, Böll's focus is on the suffering of man rather than on a specific individual. The novel is a strong denunciation of war, typical of Böll's attitude to war throughout his work. Böll depicts war as senseless, boring, and sordid. The action takes place mostly behind the lines, in military hospitals and hospital clearing stations, where Böll can bring the suffering caused by the war into sharper focus. Since the novel describes the retreat of the German army from the eastern front between 1944 and 1945, the loss of life is particularly senseless, because the outcome of the war is no longer in doubt. The individuals he depicts have no power to shape their own destinies but are hopelessly trapped in the war. In the tragic love affair between Feinhals and the Jewish-Catholic schoolteacher Ilona, Böll shows how the war disrupts personal relationships. This relationship has no chance to grow: Ilona is deported to a concentration camp where she is killed, and Feinhals is picked up by the military police and sent to the front.

At the beginning of the novel, Böll quotes from Antoine de Saint-Exupéry, who wrote that war is a disease, like typhoid. Even nature appears to be infected and hostile: The sun bathes everything in a bloody red or resembles a burning iron egg, about to wreak destruction like a shell or a grenade; melons rot like corpses in the fields. Chapter 3 depicts life in a military hospital and its evacuation as the Russians approach. Life for those working in the hospital is a dreary routine. In order to tolerate the daily boredom, Corporal Schneider has an elaborate ritual of drinking before he begins work. Böll also describes the turmoil of the retreat in this chapter. Even though the officers had known earlier about the retreat, they had not thought to tell the doctor, who had performed major surgery on two wounded soldiers that morning. Since moving these patients would cause their deaths, the doctor and Corporal Schneider choose to stay behind with them. Schneider goes out to meet the Russians, carrying a Red Cross flag. Ironically, he is not killed by the Russians but by a German shell, supposedly a dud, on which he accidentally treads. The explosion makes the Russians think they are being attacked, and they shell the hospital, killing the doctor and his two patients, before they realize that nobody is returning their fire. Despite the quiet heroism of the doctor and Schneider, the patients die.

In chapter 7, Böll depicts the concentration camp where Ilona is killed. It is the only time in Böll's works that a concentration camp appears. The commandant, Filskeit, is the epitome of what Hannah Arendt calls "the banality of evil." He is strict, industrious, ambitious, and reliable; does not drink, smoke, or consort with women; respects all authority and has a firm belief in Nazi ideology. Although he does not like killing, he obediently carries out his orders; he lacks any compassion or humaneness. He has a passionate love for music, especially for choral singing, yet instead of making him more human, his love of art has made him even more inhuman; in his treatise on the relationship between race and choir, he makes art serve Nazi ideology. His choral performances are technically perfect but completely sterile. When new prisoners are brought to the camp, Filskeit makes them sing for him; those who sing well escape the gas chamber for a while and sing in his choir. When Ilona is brought before him, she sings the All-Saints Litany. Ilona's love of music is contrasted with Filskeit's: Music for her expresses beauty, joy, and faith, not the technical perfection that Filskeit demands. Filskeit cannot endure the purity of Ilona's singing and the faith it reveals, and he brutally kills her.

The senselessness of war is particularly evident in the novel's last two episodes. In chapter 8, a bridge is blown up in a tiny village. German soldiers are sent to guard the area, but nothing ever happens, and the soldiers eat and drink and laze away the time. Finally, it is decided to rebuild the bridge. The engineer and his workers arrive and the bridge is rebuilt with model efficiency and speed; soon after it is completed, it is blown up again to halt the Russian advance. Chapter 9, which is rather melodramatic, shows Feinhals arriving home in his native village, which lies between the American and the German lines. He has survived the war and deserted. A vindictive German sergeant decides to shell the village to punish the inhabitants for their lack of patriotism (they are flying white flags). On the threshold of his home, Feinhals is hit by a shell and dies thinking "how absolutely senseless," a reflection of Böll's own attitude to the war.

Although Böll also denounces World War II and the Nazi era in *Billards at Half-Past Nine*, he widens his scope to show a panorama of German history from 1907 to 1958. In his interview with Horst Bienek, Böll said that the novel was inspired by a historical event. In 1934, Hermann Göring had four young Communists beheaded in Cologne, the youngest of whom was only seventeen or eighteen—the same age as Böll when he started to write. This event gives rise in the novel to the story of Ferdi Progulske, who tries to assassinate the Nazi gymnastics teacher Wakiera with a homemade bomb and is beheaded for this deed. Another source of inspiration for the novel was the famous altarpiece by the brothers van Eyck, *Adoration of the Lamb*, which Böll saw in Ghent—a polyptych in the center of which is the Lamb of God.

The novel focuses on the lives of the Fähmel family, and the action takes place on one day, September 6, 1958, Heinrich Fähmel's eightieth birthday. Heinrich and Johanna Fähmel represent the older generation, which grew up in the Wilhelmine years and experienced World War I. Böll uses flashbacks in the form of recollections to depict the earlier lives of his characters. Heinrich Fähmel arrived in Cologne for the first time in 1907 and immediately began to build a role for himself as a successful architect. He won a commission to build Saint Anthony's Abbey, married Johanna Kilb, and became through his marriage a member of the patrician class. For fifty years he has played the same role, but eventually the role traps him. When he reminisces about his past life on his eightieth birthday, he realizes that he should not have followed the rules of the Establishment but should have protested against the Wilhelmine and Hitler governments. His wife, Johanna, did protest. During World War I, she criticized the Kaiser and German militarism; in World War II, she protested against the deportation of the Jews. In order to protect her, Heinrich had her committed to a mental institution in 1942. The sanatorium has been a refuge from reality for Johanna for sixteen years. When she leaves it to attend her husband's eightieth birthday party, she shoots at a minister because she thinks of him as the murderer of her grandchildren. She still sees the same militarism and love of power that she had criticized earlier. Her attempt to shoot the minister is a futile gesture of protest against the people in power.

Their son, Robert Fähmel, represents the generation that grew up under Hitler. He has withdrawn completely from life. Like his father, he is an architect, but he never spends more than an hour a day in his office and conducts all of his business by mail. Since the end of the war, Robert has been playing billiards each morning at the Prince Heinrich Hotel in an attempt to escape from modern society. While he plays billiards, he talks about his past life with the bellboy, Hugo, and listens to what Hugo tells him about his life. The reasons for this strange behavior gradually become apparent. During the Hitler years, Robert had protected his friend Schrella from being victimized by the Nazis Nettlinger and Wakiera in a ballgame; this led to his involvement in a group of people who refused to partake of the "host of the beast." Among them he met Schrella's sister, Edith, who bore his child and whom he later married. Robert was part of the plot to kill the Nazi sadist Wakiera, for which the high school student Ferdi was arrested and beheaded. Schrella and Robert had to flee, and Robert escaped to Holland. He was allowed to return on the condition that he join the army when he finished his studies. In the army, Robert became a demolitions expert, the opposite of his profession as an architect, and in revenge destroyed buildings to protest the murder of innocent people during the war. At the end of the war, he destroyed the abbey that his father had built. When Schrella returns to Germany after twenty-three years of exile and attends Heinrich's party, he criticizes Robert for his withdrawal from society. Robert's decision to adopt Hugo, the bellboy, at the story's end shows that he has come to terms with his wasted life and intends to become involved again.

Böll employs a symbolic contrast between lambs and buffalo to characterize German society during the fifty-year span of the novel. The lambs are the good and innocent people such as Schrella, Edith (who is killed in the bombardments), and all the people who helped Robert while he was in exile and who were arrested and killed because of it. The lambs are those who keep their integrity and who are persecuted and killed by the buffalo. The majority of people in society are buffalo, people such as Nettlinger and Wakiera, who beat Robert and Schrella with barbed-wire whips, and Robert's brother Otto, who became a Nazi and would have denounced his own mother. These buffalo, who represent the martial spirit and the love of power, still exist in modern Germany. Hugo, for example, is persecuted because of his lamblike qualities.

The representatives of the modern generation are Robert's children, Joseph and Ruth, and Joseph's fiancée, Marianne. On his grandfather's eightieth birthday, Joseph, who is rebuilding Saint Anthony's Abbey, learns that his father was responsible for destroying it and wonders whether he should tell his grandfather. Heinrich, however, has already realized who has destroyed his masterpiece and is not upset, because he now realizes that people are more important than buildings. Finding out about his father's action makes Joseph think about his own life. The question of whether he will build or destroy is left open at the end.

The conclusion of the novel is both optimistic and pessimistic. The Fähmel family and the people associated with them—Schrella, Hugo, Marianne, and Robert's secretary Leonore—have been drawn close together. They form a tight circle of people who uphold idealism and humane values; they are an isolated circle of lambs in a world of buffalo. They cannot, however, change society and can preserve their values only by withdrawing from the world. Society on the whole has not changed for the better, Böll implies. Former Nazis such as Nettlinger are still in power, militarism still flourishes, and society is still inhumane: The buffalo are still in the majority and continue to persecute the lambs.

In *The Clown*, Böll's criticism of trends in modern German society becomes sharper. The protagonist, Hans Schnier, a twenty-seven-year-old clown who has just given a disastrous performance, is spending a lonely night in his apartment. The "action" of the novel is restricted to this single night, during which Hans telephones many of the people he knows, although (as in *Billiards at Half-Past Nine*) Böll uses extensive flashbacks in the form of recollections to relate Hans's past experiences. Some years earlier, Hans had fallen in love with Marie Derkum, a Catholic, left high school for her, and became a clown. To the annoyance of his wealthy family, Hans refused to adopt a middle-class profession. For five years, Hans was a successful clown, showing the absurdities of daily life in his act. He lived with Marie and traveled around with her. Marie then joined a group of progressive Catholics, after which their relationship deteriorated. Marie wanted Hans to marry her and sign papers promising to rear their children as Catholics. Although Hans refused at first, he eventually agreed. This, however, did not satisfy Marie: She accused him of agreeing to her demands merely to keep her rather than being convinced of the "justness of abstract principles of order." Marie left him and married Heribert Züpfner, one of the prominent Catholics in the German Establishment. After this, Hans began to drink heavily, which has ruined his clown act. In his apartment on the night covered in the novel, Hans makes a series of phone calls in a state of controlled desperation. He tries to win back Marie—with no success. The telephone is a symbol of his isolation, of the lack of real communication between people. At the end of the novel, Hans paints his face white and goes to the Bonn railway station to play his guitar and beg.

The group of progressive Catholics is the focus of Böll's criticism, and Catholic groups in Germany were offended because of this. Böll is attacking not only Catholics, however, but also any group which values dogma more than individual human lives. The progressive Catholics in the group are narrow, self-sufficient, and hypocritical. Because they are tied to dogma, they lack all compassion and humaneness. During a gathering of this group, which Hans and Marie attend, the prominent Catholic Sommerwild tells about a Catholic writer who lived for a long time with a divorced woman. When he married her, an eminent church dignitary asked whether he could not have kept her as his concubine. All the Catholics laugh at this story. Hans is shocked by the cynical attitude toward human relationships that he finds in this group. He believes in the sanctity of relationships; the formality of a marriage license means nothing to him. He believes that his relationship with Marie is a marriage because of the commitment and love they have for each other. Like the progressive Catholics, Hans's brother Leo, who is studying to be a priest, places the letter of the law above human considerations. He will not leave the seminary to come to Hans's aid because it is against the rules.

Böll also attacks the ease with which people adapt to the prevailing ideology. One such example is Hans's mother. During the war, she was a racist and used such Nazi slogans as "our sacred German soil" (an ironic phrase, because the Schnier family makes its wealth from digging up the coal under the sacred German soil). In the last months of the war, she encouraged her daughter Henrietta to volunteer for antiaircraft duty, thereby causing her death. Hans's alienation from society began when his sister died. Now Mrs. Schnier is president of the Executive Committee of the Societies for the Reconciliation of Racial Differences.

Despite her wealth, Mrs. Schnier is stingy. As a child, Hans was often hungry; one time Hans saw his mother go down to the storeroom to eat the food she would not give her children. Böll also gives examples of other born conformists. The Fascist writer Schnitzler makes people believe that he was censored for his resistance to Hitler, which was not the case; he is now indispensable at the Foreign Office. Because the teacher Brühl never joined the Nazi Party (although his sympathies were with the Nazis), he now has the reputation of a man with a courageous political past and is a professor at a teacher training college. The ruthless Hitler Youth leader, Herbert Kalick, has recently been awarded a medal for his work in spreading democratic ideas among young people in Germany.

Böll also criticizes the greed and commercialism in West German society. Hans's father represents big business in Germany. Like Hans's mother, his father is also mean and refuses to help his son financially, and he is too concerned with prestige and respectability. Böll does not spare the German Democratic Republic: Hans was once invited to perform there, but when the Communists discovered that he wanted to perform "The Party Conference

Elects Its Presidium" instead of anticapitalist skits, he had to leave on the next train.

The spontaneous and naïve Hans considers adapting to society and playing the role of the hypocrite but decides to keep his integrity: He refuses to compromise his ideals and adapt to social norms. Instead, he completely rejects German society; in his radical alienation from society he resembles Dostoevski's underground man, an indication of the impact that Dostoevski had on Böll's writing. Hans protests against the hypocrisy, sterile dogma, materialism, and opportunism of modern society. The clown, who as an outsider can be sharply critical of society, symbolizes Hans's protest. The conclusion of the novel is more pessimistic than that of *Billiards at Half-Past Nine*. Hans does not have a circle of friends and family—he is alone at the end, a beggar by choice.

Like *Billiards at Half-Past Nine*, *Group Portrait with Lady* shows a panorama of German history in the twentieth century. Böll's main focus in the novel is on the 1930's and 1940's, after which the focus shifts to the 1970's. The novel is made up of reports about Leni Pfeiffer, born Gruyten, a woman of forty-eight. The narrator, a character called the "author," gradually reconstructs Leni's life. He searches for material, interviews friends, relatives, and enemies of Leni, and comments on the reports. The many people he interviews form a cross section of German society, from millionaires to garbage workers, and through these interviews the reader is given a picture not only of Leni but also of the commentators themselves. The "author" is not objective, because he confesses that he loves Leni.

The novel highlights main events in Leni's life. She was born in Cologne in 1922. In 1938, she was dismissed from a Catholic high school and began to work in her father's engineering firm. During the war, her brother, Heinrich, and her cousin, Erhard, were shot by the Germans for trying to sell an antitank gun to the Danes, a futile act of protest against the Nazi regime. In 1941, Leni married Alois Pfeiffer, who was killed three days later. When her father was arrested in 1943 for illegal business dealings, Leni was left penniless and began making wreaths in a cemetery nursery. There she met Boris Lvovich Koltovsky, a Soviet prisoner of war, and they fell in love. During the heavy bombardments of the city in 1944, they met secretly in the underground vaults of the cemetery. In 1945, Leni gave birth to their son, Lev. When the Allies occupied the city, Boris was arrested on suspicion of being a German soldier. He was put to work in a French mine, where he died in an accident. Leni continued to work and look after her son.

Like most of Böll's protagonists, Leni is a naïve, innocent figure who refuses to conform to social norms. She is generous and compassionate to everyone and is perplexed by the evil in people. Leni has a healthy and natural attitude to sexuality, which Böll contrasts with society's hypocritical attitude toward the body. Because Leni maintains her integrity and refuses to conform, society persecutes her. After the war, in 1970, her neighbors hate her because she lets rooms cheaply to foreign workers and because she is expecting her Turkish lover's child. Whenever she ventures out of her apartment, her neighbors verbally abuse her, calling her a whore—some even would like to see her gassed, an indication that people are just as inhumane as they were during the Nazi era.

In this novel, Böll is sharply critical of racism. He satirizes the Nazi belief that the Slavs were subhuman. It is the Soviet prisoner Boris, with his knowledge of German literature, who ironically reminds the Germans of their humanistic tradition, perverted by the Nazis. The dummy company that Leni's father forms to swindle the government and avenge himself on the Nazis for killing his son reminds people of the great Russian literary tradition, because he names his fictitious workers after great Russian writers and characters in their works. The racism in Germany during the war years is still evident in modern German society; only the target of the racism has changed: Now the foreign workers are the deprived and misused members of society.

Böll's attack on greed, commercialism, and opportunism is particularly severe in this novel. Pelzer, the owner of the nursery where Leni worked, is an unscrupulous opportunist who profits from war. In World War I, he stole gold from the teeth of dead American soldiers. After the war, he joined the Communist Party for a time; when it became expedient, he joined the Nazi Party instead. When he was supposed to arrest prominent people, he let them go if they paid him. During World War II, he made money from wreaths, increasing his profit by reusing wreaths. Just before the Americans arrived in Cologne, he resigned from the Nazi Party and was thus allowed to stay in business. Pelzer is now very wealthy from his various business dealings. Böll does not, however, portray Pelzer entirely negatively: Pelzer's love of money stems from the poverty he endured as a youth. He also tried to protect Leni and Boris during the war. Hoyser, Leni's father's former head bookkeeper, has no redeeming qualities and is the epitome of crass commercialism. During the war, Leni had allowed the Hoysers to live in her house rent-free. When she could not repay the money she had borrowed from Hoyser, he repossessed her house and immediately began charging her rent. At the end of the war, he made a profit by buying property cheaply from former Nazis, who in turn had stolen the property from Jews. Hoyser and his grandchildren decide at the end of the novel to evict Leni because she is letting rooms cheaply to foreigners. The Hoysers' lives revolve entirely around money, to the absolute exclusion of compassion.

As in his other novels, Böll is very critical of German society. Some hope, however, lies in the new generation, as represented here by Lev. He is in prison for crudely forging checks to try to get Leni's house back from the Hoysers. Lev is alienated from bourgeois society. At school, Lev was cruelly taunted for being illegitimate, and he purposely pretended to be stupid to show his contempt for the educational system (his true intelligence is evidenced by his fluent command of Russian and his sensitive understanding of German literature). As a child, Lev had a passion for cleanliness, and he is now a garbage worker; Böll's satiric message is that society needs to be cleansed. Lev has rejected middle-class society and values and has chosen to live as an outsider. Among the foreign garbage workers, he finds community and solidarity (the garbage workers cause a traffic jam with their trucks to prevent Leni's eviction). Hope also lies in the group of Leni's friends who work together to help her. As in *Billiards at Half-Past Nine*, however, the community of like-minded, idealistic people is helpless to change society: The members of the group can retain their integrity only on the fringes of society.

The *Lost Honor of Katharina Blum* and *The Safety Net* also focus on modern German social problems. In *The Lost Honor of Katharina Blum*, Böll shows how the media psychologically destroy an individual through sensationalistic and untruthful reporting. In addition to attacking irresponsible journalistic practices, Böll criticizes society for tolerating and indeed thriving on media spectacles. In *The Safety Net*, Böll deals with the problems of terrorism in a democratic society. His belief in the moral responsibility of the writer is as strong in these last works as it was in his earlier ones. Throughout his works, Böll is concerned with the individual who struggles to retain his integrity in a basically hostile world. The critic Marcel Reich-Ranicki sums up Boll's achievement succinctly in "Mehr als ein Dichter" ("More Than a Poet"); he writes that without wanting to do so, Böll represents German literature today: He is a poet—more than a poet, because he speaks against all forms of tyranny in the world.

Major publications other than long fiction
SHORT FICTION: *Wanderer, kommst du nach Spa. . .* , 1950 (*Traveller, If You Come to Spa*, 1956); *Unberechenbare Gäste*, 1956; *Doktor Murkes gesammeltes Schweigen und andere Satiren*, 1958; *Entfernung von der Truppe*, 1964 (*Absent Without Leave and Other Stories*, 1965); *Eighteen Stories*, 1966; *Children Are Civilians Too*, 1970.
PLAY: *Ein Schluck Erde*, 1962.
NONFICTION: *Irisches Tagebuch*, 1957 (*Irish Journal*, 1967); *Missing Persons and Other Essays*, 1977; *Was soll aus dem Jungen bloss werden?*, 1981 (*What's to Become of the Boy?*, 1984).
MISCELLANEOUS: *Heinrich Böll Werke*, 1977, 1978 (10 volumes, Bernd Balzer, editor).

Bibliography
Bernhard, Hans Joachim. *Die Romane Heinrich Bölls: Gesellschaftskritik und Gemeinschaftsutopie*, 1970.
Beth, Hanno, ed. *Heinrich Böll: Eine Einführung in das Gesamtwerk in*

Einzelinterpretationen, 1975.

Bienek, Horst. *Werkstattgespräche mit Schriftstellern*, 1962.

Conard, Robert C. *Heinrich Böll*, 1981.

Hoffmann, Leopold. *Heinrich Böll: Einführung in Leben und Werk*, 1973.

Nägele, Rainer. *Heinrich Böll: Einführung in das Werk und in die Forschung*, 1976.

Reid, James H. *Heinrich Böll*, 1973.

Schwarz, Wilhelm Johannes. *Heinrich Böll: Teller of Tales*, 1961.

Stresau, Hermann. *Heinrich Böll*, 1964.

Vogt, Jochen. *Heinrich Böll*, 1978.

Jennifer Michaels

HERMANN BROCH

Born: Vienna, Austria; November 1, 1886
Died: New Haven, Connecticut; May 30, 1951

Principal long fiction
Die Schlafwandler, 1931-1932 (*The Sleepwalkers,* 1932); *Die unbekannte Grösse,* 1933 (*The Unknown Quantity,* 1935); *Der Tod des Vergil,* 1945 (*The Death of Virgil,* 1945); *Die Schuldlosen,* 1950 (*The Guiltless,* 1974); *Der Versucher,* 1953 (revised, as *Demeter,* 1967; as *Bergroman,* 1968).

Other literary forms
Although his fame and reputation as a writer rest on his two major novels, *The Sleepwalkers* and *The Death of Virgil,* Hermann Broch was in fact a multifaceted author of truly eclectic interests—interests ranging from literature per se in almost every genre to literary criticism, from philosophical and sociopolitical essays to incisive psychological studies of mass hysteria. Broch's earliest publications were poems and essayistic studies submitted to some of the local journals in Vienna. A sonnet, "Mathematisches Mysterium" (mathematical mysterium), and two essays—one a review of Thomas Mann's novella *Der Tod in Venedig* (1912; *Death in Venice,* 1925)—appeared as early as 1913 in the liberal journal *Der Brenner,* which was noted for publishing such influential writers of the period as Karl Kraus, Thomas Mann, Georg Trakl, Franz Werfel, and Stefan Zweig.

In fact, it was the essay, as a vehicle for the expression of both literary and philosophical thought, which would become Broch's preferred medium over the years, though one which was long overshadowed in the minds of his public by his two major novels. At the end of World War I, in 1919, Broch published the essay "Konstitutionelle Diktatur als demokratisches Rätesystem" (constitutional dictatorship as a democratic soviet-system), which outlines his belief that a sort of Nietzschean will to power was required if constitutional governments were to bring about a true democracy based upon humanist, egalitarian ideals. Other important essays of the early 1930's by Broch include his "Logik einer zerfallenen Welt" (logic of a fallen world) and "Das Böse im Wertsystem der Kunst" (evil in the value system of art); both indicate their author's lifelong search for human values in a world gone awry. One of Broch's more incisive essays to appear in English was entitled "The Style of the Mythical Age," published in 1947; in the early 1950's there followed such essays as "Bemerkungen zum Problem des Kitsches" (observations on the problem of kitsch), "Hofmannsthal und seine Zeit" (Hofmannsthal and his age), and "Study on Mass-Hysteria," posthumously published in 1959. Broch's essays occupy two volumes of the ten-volume edition of his collected works *Gesammelte Werke* published by the Rhein Verlag of Zurich over a nine-year period beginning in 1952: The first volume of essays, published in 1955, bears the title *Dichten und Erkennen: Essays I* (poetry and perception); the second volume, also published in 1955, is entitled *Erkennen und Handeln: Essays II* (perception and deed).

Broch also tried his hand at drama, writing three plays between 1933 and 1934. His first play, *Die Entsühnung* (1934; *The Atonement*, 1972), premiered at the prestigious Schauspielhaus in Zurich on May 15, 1934, under the title . . . *Denn sie wissen nicht, was sie tun* (. . . for they know not what they do). It deals with workers' problems and stems from Broch's experience as a skillful and respected mediator in labor disputes within the textile industry. As one indication of the continuing interests even in Broch's minor works, this early play was successfully adapted for radio by Ernst Schonwiese in 1961. Broch's second work for the theater, entitled *Es bleibt alles beim Alten* (1934; the same old thing), was a musical farce written with his son, Hermann Friedrich Broch de Rothermann, who had been born in 1910. Broch's third work in this genre bore the rather baroque title *Aus der Luft gegriffen: Oder, Die Geschäfte des Baron Laborde* (1934; pulled out of thin air: or, the affairs of Baron Laborde); once again, Broch's son was named coauthor, though the actual extent of his participation is in dispute. It was apparently the father's wish that his son embrace a theatrical career, so he listed him as a collaborator in the writing of these plays. It is interesting to note that, in a later version of this play, Broch replaced both his name and his son's name with the pseudonym "Vergil Bertrand"—a name made up of those of two of the chief protagonists in *The Death of Virgil* and *The Sleepwalkers*, respectively.

Finally, Broch was also a skillful writer of short stories; a collection, *Short Stories*, edited by Eric Herd, appeared in 1966. Some of Broch's most famous stories are "Der Meeresspiegel" (1933; "The Ocean's Mirror"); "Die Heimkehr des Vergil" (1933; "The Homecoming of Virgil"), which foreshadows the larger novel of 1945; and "Der Steinerne Gast" (1941; "The Stony Guest"), the germinal story of the novel *The Guiltless*.

Achievements

Broch must surely be counted among such other major German novelists of this century as Franz Kafka, Thomas Mann, Robert Musil, Heinrich Böll, and Günter Grass, alongside such other creative artists as Wassily Kandinsky, Gustav Klimt, Oskar Kokoschka, Gustav Mahler, Egon Schiele, and Arnold Schönberg—in terms of both the committed humanist stance he assumes in his writing and the purely technical mastery of his craft.

In this latter regard, Broch has been compared justifiably to James Joyce and William Faulkner in his use of interior monologue and stream of consciousness to capture the reality of life—and death—which he perceived all about him. For Broch, such techniques reflect the age in which he matured. William James's *Principles of Psychology*, which included a chapter entitled

"The Stream of Thought," had been published in 1890. It was James who had advanced the concept of stream of consciousness, as later adapted for fiction. Sigmund Freud's *Die Traumdeutung* (*Interpretation of Dreams*), which called attention to man's irrational inner life, appeared in 1900, his *Zur Psychopathologie des Alltagslebens* (*Psychopathology of Everyday Life*) in 1904. Albert Einstein's theory of relativity, which called into question the very certainty with which man could know the "real" world, was published in 1905. All fostered, indeed necessitated, a preoccupation with subjective truth on the part of intellectuals of the day. Given his early training as an engineer and his more than passing interest in science, Broch was acutely conscious of such revolutionary theories concerning reality and was able to translate the scientific and psychological principles being developed at that time into viable literary devices. His most successful literary endeavor, *The Death of Virgil*, is a compelling tour de force, lyric in its elegiac sense of loss, dreamlike in its irreal transcendence of time and space, yet actual in its uncompromising depiction of the artist's fate.

Broch's lifework was the quest for meaning in a world in which all certainties were open to question. Though he did not begin his full-fledged literary career until he was in his forties, he was spiritually a part of that generation of apocalyptic writers and artists who bore witness to the crisis facing Western European culture in the first decades of the twentieth century. While other artists of the day may have contributed their share to the erosion of cultural values (the Dadaists, for example) or sought order and meaning in an irrational realm beyond the visible world of shared human experience (the Surrealists), Broch, to his credit, stood firmly in this maelstrom of eroding values, seeking to recover a sense of absolute totality in the simultaneity of universal human actions. To perceive reality, to plot an ethical course of behavior based upon one's perceptions, and to act with conviction for the betterment of man was Broch's sustaining motivation in all of his writing, regardless of genre.

Finally, insofar as Broch reached maturity as an author well after such spiritual contemporaries as Kafka (1883-1924), Rainer Maria Rilke (1875-1926), and Hugo von Hofmannsthal (1874-1929), Broch must be regarded as a vital link to such important Austrian writers of today as Thomas Bernhard (born 1931) and Peter Handke (born 1942)—writers who are similarly concerned with the debilitating effect of "modern" civilization on the individual psyche, writers committed as Broch was to sociopolitical, cultural critique, using literary methods which owe their effectiveness in part to extraliterary disciplines such as psychology, sociolinguistics, and cultural anthropology.

Biography

Hermann Joseph Broch was born in Vienna, Austria, on November 1, 1886, the first son of Joseph Broch, a wealthy Jewish textile manufacturer, and Johanna, née Schnabel, who came from an old and affluent Viennese

Jewish family. Three years later, Broch's brother Friedrich was born.

In a symbolic sense, Broch was very much a child of his times. He grew up in *fin de siècle* Europe, experiencing all the hopes and fears, the sense of irrevocable loss coupled with the dreams of unlimited fulfillment, then manifest. It was a time of transition, of outward progress, yet it was a time when man began to call into question the very basis of life, which for centuries had rested upon a foundation of unshakable absolutes. To an entire generation which prided itself on its modernity, the nineteenth century must have seemed strangely anachronistic; the *fin de siècle* was a period of uncertainty and anxiety—the "gay apocalypse," as Broch himself termed it—one which seemed relativistic and devoid of absolutes. As such, it would leave its stamp on all of Broch's writing, ultimately finding its most eloquent expression in *The Death of Virgil*. Further, it is this crisis in values that accounts in large measure for the boundary situations of all of Broch's fictional characters.

It was in this fragile world that Broch entered adulthood. In 1903, he was graduated from the public school system and advanced to the Vienna Institute for Weaving Technology. Further study followed at the Textile Institute in Mülhausen (Alsace-Lorraine)—a period in Broch's life that would provide the background for the third part of *The Sleepwalkers*. Upon graduating in September of 1907 with a degree in textile engineering, Broch journeyed to America for two months in order to familiarize himself with cotton farming and milling procedures in the South, particularly in New Orleans. Upon his return to Austria, Broch entered his father's firm and became active in its management. As an administrator in the local textile union, Broch also gained a reputation for his equitable decisions in labor disputes. The plight of the worker in a society, changed overnight by rapid industrialization, was familiar to Broch not only from personal experience but also from his reading of German Naturalists such as Gerhart Hauptmann, Arno Holz, Johannes Schlaf, and Hermann Sudermann.

In 1908, Broch served for a time as a volunteer with the military stationed in Zagreb. In December of 1909, he married Franziska von Rothermann, despite the objections of both families. He continued to work in his father's firm, educating himself by reading widely in many fields. From 1915 to 1921, he pursued more formal studies in logic, mathematics, and physics at the University of Vienna, all the while working on a personal theory of values and his own philosophy of history. He began to immerse himself in ideas of Immanuel Kant, Søren Kierkegaard, Friedrich Nietzsche, Arthur Schopenhauer, Karl Kraus, and Otto Weininger. Oswald Spengler's *Untergang des Abendlandes* (1918; *The Decline of the West*, 1922), in particular, prompted Broch to develop his ideas on the necessity of the heroic quest on the part of the isolated and alienated individual if humankind were to rise from the abyss of shattered values. Paradoxically, for Broch, the search for personal values served only to exacerbate the collapse of communal values. Years later, as a refugee from Adolf Hitler's Third Reich, Broch would seek a resolution of this paradox in the individual's pursuit of universal humanist goals.

During World War I, Broch served as an administrator for the Austrian Red Cross until he was discharged for medical reasons in 1916. He assumed control of his father's business and continued to write essays on philosophical and sociopolitical issues. As an indication of the direction his thought took at this time, one finds Broch turning for publication to such journals as *Die Rettung* and *Der Friede*. It was also at this time that Broch began to gain entry into the leading literary and intellectual circles active in Vienna at this time: the circles around Sigmund Freud, the acerbic critic Karl Kraus, the writer Robert Musil, and the philosopher Ludwig Wittgenstein.

The crisis in values that began to manifest itself in nearly every phase of human endeavor during the hectic 1920's proved especially critical for Broch. His twelve-year marriage to Franziska von Rothermann ended in divorce in 1922, after a year's separation. The fear of impending inflation as well as a desire to devote more and more time to purely intellectual pursuits prompted Broch to give up the directorship of the family firm in 1927. From 1927 to 1931, he enrolled in courses at the University of Vienna, studying mathematics, philosophy, philology, and psychology. He began writing in earnest, seeing in literature the chance to resolve those of life's questions incapable of being answered adequately by rational science alone. His first major success, *The Sleepwalkers*, was completed during these years.

In later years, particularly after the publication of *The Death of Virgil*, Broch would once again return to his roots in science, devoting his attention almost exclusively to the social sciences. He came to view science as a sort of metapolitics, better able to redeem mankind than art, having grown skeptical once again of the efficacy of art to explain life, to posit values adequately for the masses. Ironically enough, it is in his most ambitious work, *The Death of Virgil*, that Broch eloquently expresses *in* art his apprehension and uncertainties *about* art. So great, in fact, was his conviction in this regard that he went so far as to associate the "art for art's sake" aesthetic of a poet such as Stefan George, for instance, with that sort of pseudoart which has come to be known as "kitsch." The personal crisis in his life worsened, and in 1928, he sold the family textile mills, despite the opposition of relatives, and returned to the University of Vienna to pursue a doctorate in philosophy and mathematics.

The situation for Jews grew worse daily—the first laws against the Jews were passed in 1933—and study at the university became increasingly difficult (despite the fact that Broch had converted to Catholicism in the early 1900's). In 1935, he moved to Mösern near Seefeld in the Tyrolean Alps in order to work on his so-called "mountain novel," *Bergroman*. It is a work that attempts to express the demoniac personality of the protagonist, who captivates an entire village, subjecting it entirely to his will. It was meant to present in miniature an idea of the mass hysteria of the Fascist era. In its setting, the novel owes much to Mann's *Der Zauberberg* (1924; *The Magic Mountain*, 1927), though it is fragmentary and far inferior to Mann's monumental effort. Broch had met Mann in 1932 and had been influenced by him as early as the first decade of the century. He wrote a review of Mann's *Death in Venice* in 1913 and would undoubtedly have been familiar with Mann's first major success as a writer, *Buddenbrooks* (1900), which details the decline and fall of one family amid that of an entire age and way of life. Personal matters deteriorated for Broch during the late 1930's. He was arrested and held in detention by the Gestapo; through the intervention of such well-known figures as James Joyce and Mann, Broch's release was secured and permission was granted for him to emigrate.

Traveling by way of England and Scotland, Broch finally arrived in New York on October 9, 1938, to begin a new life. While in England, he received assistance from the P.E.N. Club of London, which enabled him to continue work on *The Death of Virgil*. Once in the United States, Broch was aided by the American Guild for German Cultural Freedom in New York and by the Oberlaender Trust of Philadelphia. Other grants that he received over the years came from the American Academy of Arts and Letters, the John Simon Guggenheim Memorial Foundation (1939) for work on *The Death of Virgil*, the Rockefeller Foundation (1942), and the Bollingen Foundation (1946-1947), the latter two being granted in order that Broch might continue his research in mass psychology. Offers also came in from major universities. Broch worked at the Princeton Office of Public Opinion Research and accepted a professorship in German literature at Yale University. In addition, Broch received an invitation to teach at East Germany's prestigious Jena University, but he declined this offer in order to continue his work at Yale.

With the publication in 1945 of *The Death of Virgil*, Broch's place in the history of German, indeed world, literature was secure. His reputation during his last years in America grew steadily, though it never rivaled that of such other noted émigrés as Bertolt Brecht and Mann. In 1950, Broch was nominated by the Austrian delegation of P.E.N., as well as by literary circles in the United States, for the Nobel Prize for Literature. Thus, Broch was on the threshold of a much-deserved worldwide recognition when he succumbed to a heart attack on May 30, 1951, in New Haven, Connecticut; burial followed in nearby Killingworth.

Analysis

Hermann Broch's first novel, *The Sleepwalkers*, is a psychological-historical novel which explores the gradual disintegration of values beginning in the latter half of the nineteenth century and culminating in the Armageddon that was World War I. The work is a trilogy whose main sections bear the names and the worldviews of each section's protagonist: "Pasenow, or the Romantic," "Esch, or the Anarchist," and "Huguenau, or the Realist."

Specifically, the work depicts the degeneration of German society from 1888 to 1918—a thirty-year period of crucial and inevitable change, as Hannah Arendt has described it in her 1949 article, "The Achievement of Hermann Broch": ". . . 1888, when the Romantic finds himself in the not yet visible decay of the old world; 1903, when the Anarchist gets entangled in the prewar confusion of values; 1918, when the Realist becomes the undisputed master of a nihilistic society."

Part 1 presents the reader with the fragile world of the Junker Joachim von Pasenow, a Romantic in the sense that he inhabits an otherworldly realm of sterile conventions and anachronistic Prussian values, a realm of façades and titular masks whose symbol is the uniform. The protagonist is a man of honor, a believer in order and tradition. He loses his brother Helmuth in a senseless duel over family honor and so assumes responsibility for the family estate. In his task of maintaining the property and privileges of the landed aristocracy to which his family belongs, he is helped by his close friend Eduard von Bertrand, who has risen to become a leading industrialist in Berlin. The first part comes to a close with Pasenow's marriage to Elisabeth, who, as the daughter of a wealthy neighbor, is well within Pasenow's social circle. The founding of this new family, particularly after the birth of a child, seems to promise the continued growth and prosperity of Pasenow's class and way of life. As Broch's readers will come to discover, this is not to be.

In part 2, a petit bourgeois bookkeeper by the name of Esch makes his appearance. A malcontent, he is called an anarchist because, unlike Pasenow, he has lost faith in the old values and is seeking a new faith at any cost. Yet, like the hero of part 1, Esch is presented as a victim of circumstances, of a process of general social and cultural decline destined to run its full course. Having become a small-time variety-show entrepreneur, Esch, who is a social climber, will use any means at his disposal to get ahead—bribery and blackmail included. He is an impetuous man, settling accounts with real or imagined adversaries in confrontations contrived and acted out in his mind. Such interior dialogues only exacerbate Esch's inability to act. Though drawn to political agitators, his attraction, like his dreams, is so unrefined as to inhibit effectively any consequent action. Rather, Esch destroys things and people who are seen to stand in his way. Foremost among them is Pasenow's friend Bertrand, whom Esch tries to blackmail for his homosexuality. Bertrand, a man positively portrayed as someone in charge of his fate, a man against whose actions those of the other characters are to be gauged, commits suicide rather than submit to the intrigues of a man such as Esch. His death must be viewed as the death of all that is decent and worthwhile in the novel. At the close of part 2, Esch takes the widow Hentjen in marriage in a near-parody of Pasenow's marriage at the close of part 1.

In part 3, the reader is confronted with the total triumph of amorality. Although Huguenau, the realist, is the nominal hero of this last section, he shares center stage with Pasenow, who has gone on to become a major in the war and is now governor of the town in which Esch is serving as editor of a Socialist newspaper. Through a twist of fate—Pasenow publishes an idealistic article in Esch's paper—the two men become allied across class boundaries and against Huguenau, who, after deserting from the same army in which Pasenow had served so honorably, has become a successful businessman. He is a realist in the sense that his approach to every situation in life is cold, methodical—in short, businesslike. Such a worldview allows Huguenau to manipulate dispassionately life to his own advantage. Huguenau ends up slandering Pasenow and murdering Esch—both of whom, like sleepwalkers, are oblivious to events around them—yet still manages to become a leading member of the society that has emerged after the war.

The destinies of Pasenow and Esch are those of Romantic tradition and mere anarchy: the Romantic past is over; anarchy, as a precondition for the emergence of a new social order, has spent its energy. The Fascist state is being born. On a technical level, the form of the novel perfectly reflects its content. Traditional nineteenth century epic narration—reminiscent, for example, of the mature Theodor Fontane—dominates the first portion of the novel. Gradually, however, this ordered, objective style becomes transformed into a more subjective narrative style. The tightly woven and objectively related plot incidents of part 1 give way to the imaginative musings of Esch in part 2, where stream of consciousness and interior dialogue mirror the growing emphasis on subjective reality and its concomitant skepticism, prevalent around the turn of the century.

In part 3, the narration has become even more fragmented; it has disintegrated into a series of epic, dramatic, or lyric episodes bound loosely by the destinies of Pasenow, Esch, and Huguenau. Through the juxtaposition of seemingly objective dialogue and stream of consciousness, Broch skillfully plays off one view of reality against another. The resulting discrepancy between outer and inner reality reveals, according to Arendt, "the fundamental fragility of the time, the insecurity and convulsiveness of those who were its representatives." Through his use of various narrative perspectives to relate main and subordinate plot lines, Broch creates multiple levels of action and reality as his characters emerge, recede, and interact with one another. This technique effectively reflects the general collapse of an integrated worldview and results in a true multiple perspective, each character, each social sphere declaring its own relative values to be absolute.

The Death of Virgil, which was recognized with both Guggenheim and Rockefeller awards, was originally written in the form of an eighteen-page story in 1936. The story underwent modification and lengthening as a direct result of Broch's detention and the very real threat of death at the hands of the Nazis in 1938. As Theodore Ziolkowski points out, "Whereas [Broch] had previously considered Vergil primarily as a prototype of the artist in a valueless society, he now devoted his attention to the *death* of Vergil." Broch himself said of the genesis of the work that "*Virgil* was not written as a 'book,' but (under Hitler's threat) as my private discussion with death." Broch continued to work on *The Death of Virgil* after his release from prison—revising and expanding the work's central idea—and by 1940, he had compiled the major part of the novel. He continued to refine the work until 1945, when it was published simultaneously in English and German. As the title indicates, the story deals with the death of the poet Virgil; his meditations on self and society, art and human activity, and life and death constitute the bulk of the novel.

The story takes place in the year 19 B.C., in the ancient port city of Brundisium in Italy; in an obvious parallel to Joyce's *Ulysses* (1922), the work covers only the final eighteen hours of Virgil's existence. This unity of time and place indicates the hero's (and the author's) anguished quest for unity, despite all life's apparent dissonance, despite the chaos that death seems to herald. It is this nearness to death that sets life into sharp focus for author and hero alike.

The plot is straightforward and easily summarized. The work opens with the dying poet's return from Greece to Italy with the imperial navy. What follows and what takes up the greater part of five hundred pages until Virgil's death is anything but straightforward. Broch has created an intensely lyric work which, in its approximation of poetic, even musical form and structure, has expanded the very notion of the modern novel.

Broch himself described his work as being "a poem, though not in the sense of a single lyrical outburst and also not in the sense of a poem cycle on a central theme, yet a poem and moreover, one that extends in a single breath over more than five hundred pages." The entire work, in fact, is one long interior monologue, in which the thoughts and visions, the feverish dreams and repressed fears of Virgil are all called forth from the depths of his subconscious; in order to capture their reality and truth, the poet must articulate them by means of language.

The point of view throughout is that of Virgil himself, a poet, paradoxically enough, in despair of poetry. In the face of his imminent death, Virgil comes to question the relevance, the validity, indeed the morality of his entire life-work. Is a life given over to purely contemplative activity enough to justify it, given the need for committed action in a valueless world marked by enmity, war, poverty, and death? It is on his way from the ship to the Emperor's palace that Virgil encounters all the ill-fated members of humanity. Where, he wonders, is the dignity and meaningfulness of life? Where is the beauty which he desperately sought to reproduce in poetry? Has he not, in his work, neglected fully half of life's total reality: namely, its horror, its evil, its ugliness? These are existential questions which the poet Rilke posed in his *Die Aufzeichnungen des Malte Laurids Brigge* (1910; *The Notebooks of Malte Laurids Brigge*, 1930) and in his *Duineser Elegien* (1923; *Duino Elegies*, 1930) and which Kafka raised in many of his diary entries and letters.

In fact, Kafka's request to his longtime friend and literary executor, Max Brod, to destroy his works after his death finds its parallel in Broch's novel, when Virgil reveals to friends his wish to destroy the *Aeneid*. His reasons are that as a work of art, of beauty, it fails to represent the totality of truth and reality adequately; because it is "only" beautiful, he feels it to be of little benefit to man. Kafka's doubts were those of Broch as well, as evidenced in part by Broch's lifelong vacillation among a wide variety of forms: short story, drama, poetry, novel, philosophical essay, sociological case study, and so on. In *The Death of Virgil*, however, Broch confronted the problem of artistic validity head-on, and in so doing, he created a soul-searching work of literature, which, had he written nothing else, would have sufficed to add his name to the history of world literature. As Broch himself put it, expressing a kinship with Kafka, "We live and write, and that's all."

Broch completed his monumental novel precisely at a time in history when humanity seemed to have reached its lowest point. With death and destruction all around him, Broch, with all the conviction he could muster as a humanist, posited life and human creativity as counterweights. Virgil gives in to the pleas of his friend, the Emperor Octavianus Augustus, and entrusts his *Aeneid* to him for safekeeping. He does so because he comes to realize that it is the task of the poet to offer man, if ever so vaguely, a small glimpse of the eternal, which is his—and perhaps his alone—to perceive. As the harbinger of eternal, metaphysical order, Virgil sees the poet as the spiritual counterpart to Emperor Augustus, who embodies the temporal order.

Structurally, the novel is divided into four parts, entitled "Water, the Arrival"; "Fire, the Descent"; "Earth, the Expectation"; and "Air, the Homecoming." Each section thus corresponds to a phase in the hero's perception of creation. In part 1, Virgil becomes aware of life's polarities while aboard the ship taking him back to Italy. He becomes conscious of the contrast between the limitless heavens above and the dark, murky, unfathomable waters below; he sees the noble passengers above deck and the pitiful slaves below; there is the sea itself signifying life and man's seemingly endless journey toward a shore which represents for the poet his inevitable death, his homecoming. On his journey through the dark and narrow streets of Brundisium, there are the slums of the poor which contrast so sharply with the Emperor's palace. For Virgil, it is his arrival at the threshold of self-awareness which serves as a catalyst for all the self-doubts faced and ultimately resolved in the rest of the novel. Book 2 depicts in rhapsodic monologues and long lyric sequences Virgil's descent into the hellfire of self-recrimination. Book 3, which is the most narrative section of the work, presents in Virgil's discussions with his friends the poet's earthly expectations for himself as a poet, for his art, and his subsequent despair over his actual achievements. Part 4 brings a resolution to all of Virgil's doubts. Through his debate with Augustus, he comes to realize that a greater sacrifice is needed for him *not* to burn the *Aeneid*. Destruction of the work would bring fleeting self-satisfaction. Allowing it to exist elevates this work of aesthetic beauty to the status of all of those creative works that bear witness to one man's less-than-perfect quest for unity and truth.

In a final, grand vision leading from death's door back through life to birth and beyond into the order-generating act of creation itself, Virgil comes to realize the totality of life, precisely in the affirmation of all of life's apparently irreconcilable opposites, including life and death themselves. It is a vision of life which nearly defies verbal articulation. For this reason, Broch described the novel's structure in musical terms, comparing it to a traditional symphony in four movements. He even ascribed musical designations to three of the four sections: 1—"andante"; 2—"adagio"; and 4—"maestoso." Language as music is what Broch had in mind—music not only because of language's sonorous qualities, but also, and more important, because of the lyric language's universal, timeless power to enchant. It is the language that Hofmannsthal sought to describe in his famous *Brief des Lord Chandos* (1905; *Letter of Lord Chandos*, 1952) and to which Rilke gave voice in his *Duino Elegies* and *Sonette an Orpheus* (1923; *Sonnets to Orpheus*, 1942). It is lyric language, self-reflective in its anxious attempt to crystallize the most fleeting of life's moments, the moment between that which has not yet dawned and that which is irrevocably lost—Broch's famous "no longer and not yet." In *The Death of Virgil*, Broch has captured many such moments in the life and gentle death of a man who, like himself, sought to understand life and death, to perceive their meaning, to discover their intrinsic order and unity, and then to create the language commensurate to the task of conveying his vision to others.

Major publications other than long fiction

SHORT FICTION: *Methodologische Novelle*, 1933; *Methodisch Konstruiert*, 1949; *Short Stories*, 1966.

PLAYS: *Die Entsühnung*, 1934 (*The Atonement*, 1972; also as . . . *Denn sie wissen nicht, was sie tun*, 1961); *Es bleibt alles beim Alten*, 1934; *Aus der Luft gegriffen: Oder, Die Geschäfte des Baron Laborde*, 1934.

NONFICTION: *Dichten und Erkennen: Essays I*, 1955; *Erkennen und Handeln: Essays II*, 1955; *Brief*, 1957; *Massenpsychologie*, 1959; *Zur Universitätsreform*, 1969.

MISCELLANEOUS: *Gesammelte Werke*, 1952-1961 (10 volumes); *Die Heimkehr*, 1962.

Bibliography

Arendt, Hannah. "The Achievement of Hermann Broch," in *Kenyon Review*.

XI (1949), pp. 476-483.

Bardin, James. "The Theme of Salvation in the Novels of Hermann Broch," in *PMLA*. LXXXV (1970), pp. 219-277.

Cohn, Dorrit Claire. *The Sleepwalkers: Elucidations of Hermann Broch's Trilogy*, 1966.

Durzak, Manfred. *Hermann Broch: Der Dichter und seine Zeit*, 1968.

Herd, Eric. "Hermann Broch and the Legitimacy of the Novel," in *German Life and Letters*. XIII (1960), pp. 262-270.

Jonas, Klaus. "Broch-Bibliographie," in *Philobiblon*. VI, no. 4 (1962), pp. 291-323.

Kahler, Erich. *Die Philosophie von Hermann Broch*, 1962.

Sparks, Kimberly. *A Geometry of Time: A Study of Hermann Broch's Prose Imagery*, 1964.

Strelka, Joseph. "Hermann Broch: Comparatist and Humanist," in *Comparative Literature Studies*. XII (1975), pp. 67-79.

Winkler, Michael. "The Wanderer in Search of a System," in *German Quarterly*. XLVIII (1975), pp. 234-243.

"A Writer's Conscience," in *Times Literary Supplement*. March 29, 1969, pp. 209-210.

Ziolkowski, Theodore. *Hermann Broch*, 1965.

Thomas Di Napoli

MIKHAIL BULGAKOV

Born: Kiev, Russia; May 15, 1891
Died: Moscow, U.S.S.R.; March 10, 1940

Principal long fiction

Teatralny roman, 1965 (*Black Snow: A Theatrical Novel*, 1967); *Master i Margarita*, 1966-1967, 1969 (*The Master and Margarita*, 1967); *Belaya gvardiya*, 1969 (*The White Guard*, 1973); *Sobachie serdtse*, 1969 (novella; *The Heart of a Dog*, 1968); *Romany*, 1973 (includes *Teatralny roman*, *Master i Margarita*, and *Belaya gvardiya*).

Other literary forms

Mikhail Bulgakov wrote some thirty-six plays, of which eleven were published and eight performed during his lifetime. His writings for theater and film include adaptations from Miguel de Cervantes, Molière, Charles Dickens, Nikolai Gogol, and Leo Tolstoy. Only one of the opera libretti Bulgakov composed for the Bolshoi Theater, *Rachel* (written 1938, produced 1947), based on a story by Guy de Maupassant, was ever produced. Among his more notable plays made available in English during the 1960's and 1970's are *Adam i Eva* (c. 1930; *Adam and Eve*, 1971), *Dni Turbinykh* (1926; *Days of the Turbins*, 1934), *Beg* (1955; *Flight*, 1969), *Zoykina kvartira* (1926; *Zoyka's Apartment*, 1972), *Ivan Vasilievich* (1965; English translation, 1974), and *Posledniye dni* (1943; *The Last Days*, 1978). Bulgakov also wrote numerous short stories, many of them collected in the volumes entitled *Diavoliada* (1925; *Diaboliad and Other Stories*, 1972), *Zapiski iunogo vracha* (1963; *A Country Doctor's Notebook*, 1975), and *Traktat o zhilishche* (1926; *A Treatise on Housing*, 1972). He also published miscellaneous journalism. Bulgakov's close identification with the life of Molière produced one of his most interesting plays, *Kabala svyatosh* (1936; also as *Molyer; A Cabal of Hypocrites*, 1972), as well as a novelistic biography, *Zhizn Gospodina de Molyera* (1962; *Life of Monsieur de Molière*, 1970).

Achievements

Some twenty-five years after his death, Mikhail Bulgakov began to receive increasing recognition—both in the Soviet Union and abroad—as a major figure in modern Russian literature. *The Master and Margarita* is a complex, ambitious masterpiece which has won an intensely loyal readership and much critical scrutiny since its first serialized publication in 1966-1967. Its posthumous success in turn began to direct attention to Bulgakov's other neglected works.

The hazards of cultural life under Joseph Stalin frustrated Bulgakov's aspirations in prose fiction, where he did his finest work, and channeled him into the theater, where, though productive, he was probably temperamentally out of place. Bulgakov's narratives combine acute, if perforce oblique, social analysis with a strain of playful fantasy. Beyond the deprivation, hypocrisy, and cruelty of contemporary Soviet life, his Horatian satires suggest a transcendent spiritual force. In *The Master and Margarita* and *The White Guard*, it is tender devotion to a beautiful, mysterious woman that represents the apocalyptic possibility of overcoming an oppressive present existence. *Black Snow* offers the advice that "you have to love your characters. If you don't, I don't advise anybody to try writing; the result is bound to be unfortunate." This sentimental belief in the liberating power of love—of characters for one another, of author for reader—is tempered by terminal melancholia. In the imperfect world portrayed by Bulgakov, those in power are never graced with imagination, though they must be humored, but it is the power of imagination and of humor that lifts the reader beyond the tyranny of the quotidian.

There is at least an allusion to Faust in almost all of Bulgakov's books, where the quest for an elusive truth becomes an explicit and central theme. His work frequently foregrounds itself, calling attention to its own formal inventions in the service of a sense of values against which the elaborate structures of society and art seem petty and transient indeed.

Biography

Mikhail Afanasyevich Bulgakov, the eldest of seven children, was born in Kiev on May 15, 1891, into a family that was both devout and intellectual. His father, who died when Mikhail was sixteen, was a professor of divinity at the Kiev Theological Academy. Bulgakov developed an early interest in music and the theater, but he pursued a medical degree at Kiev University. In 1913, he married Tatyana Nikolaevna Lappa, and in 1916 he was graduated with distinction as a doctor. He subsequently served as a military doctor in remote village hospitals which were to provide the material for the stories in *A Country Doctor's Notebook*. The isolation depressed him, and he attempted to obtain his release, only succeeding in 1918 after the Bolshevik Revolution.

Bulgakov returned to Kiev to establish a private practice in venereology and dermatology. During this time, the tense atmosphere of which is recreated in *The White Guard*, Kiev was a battleground for the Germans, the Ukrainian nationalists, the Bolsheviks, and the Whites. In November, 1919, Bulgakov fled south to the Caucasian town of Vladikavkaz. While he was confined to bed with typhus, Vladikavkaz was captured by the Bolsheviks. He abandoned the practice of medicine and began devoting himself entirely to writing.

In 1921, Bulgakov moved to Moscow, where, amid general hardship, he attempted to support himself and his wife through a variety of literary and journalistic jobs. In 1924, he divorced Tatyana and married Lyubov Yevgenievna Belozerskaya. Soon thereafter, with the publication of satiric stories later collected in *Diavoliada*, Bulgakov began achieving some recognition and was able to abandon the newspaper work he detested. The publication, in 1925, of parts of *The White Guard*, based on his experiences in Kiev during the Civil War, dramatically changed his life in ways recounted in the auto-biographical novel *Black Snow*. Bulgakov's work came to the attention of the producers of the Moscow Art Theater, and he was asked to adapt *The White Guard* for the stage. The result, after considerable revision, was *Days of the Turbins*, which opened in October, 1926, to intense, polarized reaction. Bulgakov was harshly attacked for portraying the opponents of Bolshevism too sympathetically, but the play proved enormously popular. During its extensive run, Stalin himself saw it fifteen times.

A sudden celebrity, Bulgakov continued writing plays, but by the end of the decade, as Soviet cultural and political life became severely repressive, his works were banned and his financial position deteriorated. Near despair, he sent letters in 1930 to Soviet officials complaining of the campaign of vilification against him and his inability to get his work accepted. Stalin's personal intercession resulted in Bulgakov's appointment as a producer at the Moscow Art Theater. His subsequent years in the theater were productive but frustrating, in part because of friction with the flamboyant director Konstantin Stanislavsky, whose production of *Kabala svyatosh* in 1936 led Bulgakov to resign in disgust from the Moscow Art Theater. For the remainder of his life, he was employed by the Bolshoi Theater as librettist and consultant.

In 1929, Bulgakov had begun a clandestine love affair with Elena Sergeyevna Shilovskaya, wife of the Chief of Staff of the Moscow Military District. In 1932, after each succeeded in obtaining a divorce, they were married, and Bulgakov adopted Elena's five-year-old son Sergey. Bulgakov's happiness with and devotion to his third wife, to whom he, with failing eyesight, probably dictated *Black Snow* in 1939, are reflected in *The Master and Margarita*. The earliest version of the latter was begun as early as 1928, but he destroyed that manuscript in 1929. He continued refining a revised version until his death, in Moscow, on March 10, 1940.

After Bulgakov's death, the official attitude toward his work ranged from indifference to hostility, and very few of his writings remained available. During the brief thaw in Soviet cultural repression following Stalin's death, a commission was established to rehabilitate Bulgakov's reputation, and by the late 1960's most, though not all, of his major works were being published in the Soviet Union for the first time.

Analysis

Mikhail Bulgakov never took advantage of the opportunity to flee Russia during the Revolution and its turbulent aftermath, and his fiction is very much a product of Russian life during the first two decades of the Soviet regime. Bulgakov's social commentary is not oblique enough to have averted the ire and the proscription of powerful contemporaries, or to keep later readers from recognizing the quality of *roman à clef* in much of what he wrote. The key, though, is not simply in details of his own biography—friends, adversaries, and a pet cat persistently transposed into a fictional realm. More important, it is in his ability to render the plight of the creative individual in a system designed to subdue him. Within the carefully limned landscapes of modern Kiev and Moscow, Bulgakov's characters dramatize the limitations and hubris of temporal human power. His books, then, are not merely the frustrated effusions of an author encountering formidable obstacles to his ambitions; neither are they merely perceptive analyses of the kind of community Stalinist social engineering was begetting. Beyond Bulgakov's contempt for contemporary mischief is a veritably religious sense of a universal spiritual force and a conviction that *sic transit gloria mundi*. Thus, *The White Guard* concludes on a consoling note: "Everything passes away—suffering, pain, blood, hunger and pestilence." It is this spiritual perspective that endows Bulgakov's narratives with more than a parochial sociological or historical interest.

The tone of melancholy that suffuses Bulgakov's works is a consequence of the futility he sees in the artist's struggle against the mighty of this world, and most of his sympathetic characters are more than half in love with easeful death. Creativity, love, and good humor do, nevertheless, triumph *sub specie aeternitatis*. To reduce Bulgakov's fictions to the bare formula of a struggle between sensitivity and brutishness and between eternity and the moment is to miss the mournful exuberance of his *comédies larmoyantes*. Not only *Black Snow*, whose subtitle proclaims it, but also Bulgakov's other books are theatrical novels. The spirited play of a harried author drawn to and disappointed by the theater, they employ self-conscious devices, such as apostrophes to the reader, impudent violations of verisimilitude, and encased narratives, to enact a liberation not only from the oppressive worlds they depict but also from the literary instrument of emancipation itself. *Black Snow* concludes with a deflationary fictional afterword, and it is night on the final pages of *The White Guard*, *The Master and Margarita*, and *The Heart of a Dog*. Like William Shakespeare's *The Tempest* (1611) abjuring its own magic, Bulgakov's novels provide bittersweet crepuscular valediction to the powers of temporal authority and to the verbal artifices which their inventive author assembles.

Bulgakov's first novel, and the only one to be published (at least in part) in his lifetime, *The White Guard* is set in Kiev in the winter of 1918. It is the moment at which the hetman Pavel Petrovich Skoropadsky, who has ruled with the support of the Germans, flees the city, and the forces of the Ukrainian nationalist Semyon Petlyura prove temporarily triumphant over Whites and Bolsheviks. *The White Guard* is a polyphonic arrangement of a variety of characters and incidents within a brief, dramatic period in the history of modern Kiev. Its focus, however, is on the fate of one family, the Turbins, representative of a venerable way of life that is disintegrating as Ukrainian society undergoes radical change.

The Turbin children have recently buried their mother, and twenty-eight-year-old Alexei, a physician, his twenty-four-year-old sister Elena, and their seventeen-year-old brother Nikolka, a student, attempt to maintain family traditions and values, which are those of a comfortable Russian intellectual home. Yet public events make this impossible, and the collapse of the kind of humane civilization which the Turbin family exemplifies—with which Bulgakov, whose background was similar, is, despite the censor, sympathetic—is inevitable with the victory of Petlyura's troops.

Captain Sergey Talberg, the opportunistic scoundrel to whom Elena is married, abandons her to seek safety and another woman in Paris. The hetman, in the cowardly disguise of a German officer, likewise deserts Kiev at its moment of greatest danger. Nevertheless, Alexei and Nikolka, along with many others, enlist in the loyalist army in a futile effort to repulse Petlyura's advance into the city. Bulgakov depicts a range of heroism and knavery on all sides during the months of crisis in Kiev. The narrative weaves multiple subplots of combat and domestic drama into a vivid account of an obsolescent society under siege.

Through it all, the Turbin house, number 13 St. Alexei's Hill, remains for the family and its friends a fragile sanctuary. Nikolka barely escapes the violence, and Alexei, who is wounded, miraculously survives battle and an attack of typhus with the gracious assistance of a mysterious beauty named Julia Reiss. Despite the grim situation, gentle comic relief is provided by characters such as the miserly neighbor Vasilisa and the benevolent bumpkin Lariosik, who comes to stay with his relatives, the Turbins.

The apocalyptic tone of *The White Guard* is supported by religious allusions, particularly to the Book of Revelation. The music for *Faust* remains open on the Turbin piano from the beginning of the novel to its end, and the reader is reminded of enduring values that transcend the contingencies of politics:

> But long after the Turbins and Talbergs have departed this life the keys will ring out again and Valentine will step up to the footlights, the aroma of perfume will waft from the boxes and at home beautiful women under the lamplight will play the music, because *Faust*, like the Shipwright of Saardam, is quite immortal.

As the novel concludes, Petlyura's victory, too, is ephemeral, as the Bolsheviks advance. Night descends on the Dnieper, and each of several characters dreams of something far beyond the petty intrigues of daylight Kiev. As in all of Bulgakov fictions, a foregrounded narrative voice, relying on rhetorical questions, playful and ingenious connections and summaries, and an overtly evocative landscape, impels the reader beyond the trifles of wars and words.

Black Snow: A Theatrical Novel, an unfinished work, was discovered in

1965 by the commission established during the post-Stalin thaw to rehabilitate Bulgakov. An account of the emergence of an obscure hack named Sergey Leontievich Maxudov as a literary and theatrical celebrity in Moscow, it draws heavily on Bulgakov's own experiences in writing *The White Guard* and adapting it for the Moscow Art Theater as *Days of the Turbins*. It provides a lively portrait of the artist as a melancholic and misunderstood figure and of a cultural establishment inimical to genuine creativity.

The novel begins with a letter from a producer named Xavier Borisovich Ilchin summoning Maxudov to his office at the Academy of Drama. Ilchin has read Maxudov's unacclaimed novel and is eager for him to adapt it for the stage. Next follows a flashback recounting how Maxudov conceived his book and how, as an obscure employee of the trade journal *Shipping Gazette*, he signed a contract for its publication in *The Motherland* shortly before that magazine folded. The flashback concludes with an account of how Maxudov's life is transformed after he signs a contract for the production of *Black Snow*, his stage version of the novel, by the Independent Theater. Maxudov soon finds himself a victim of the rivalries and jealousies of figures in the theatrical world. In particular, he is caught between the two directors of the Independent Theater, Aristarkh Platonovich, who is currently off in India, and Ivan Vasilievich; neither has spoken to the other in forty years. Ivan Vasilievich is clearly modeled after Stanislavsky, and grotesque descriptions portray the tyrannical director at work, rehearsing his actors in *Black Snow* with his celebrated "method." The hapless dramatist makes a convincing case that "the famous theory was utterly wrong for my play."

Black Snow employs a sophisticated narrative perspective to distance the reader both from its inept protagonist and from the bizarre characters he encounters. Its two parts are both written by Maxudov himself in the form of a memoir. An afterword, however, introduces a new, anonymous voice who explains how Maxudov sent the manuscript to him shortly before killing himself by jumping off a bridge in Kiev. This second narrator describes the narrative which the reader has just finished as suffering from "slovenly style" and as the "fruit of a morbid imagination." Furthermore, he points out its egregious inaccuracies, among which is the fact that Maxudov never did have anything to do with the theater. The effect of this coda, as of those in Knut Hamsun's *Pan* (1894; English translation, 1920) and Robert Weine's *The Cabinet of Dr. Caligari* (1919), is to cast retrospective doubt on the reliability of everything which precedes it. Is *Black Snow* a caustic mockery of philistine bureaucrats, or is it a case study in the psychopathology of a deluded author manqué? Or perhaps both? Maxudov, distraught over frustrations with the Independent Theater, does admit that he is a melancholic and describes an early suicide attempt, aborted when he heard a recording of *Faust* coming from the apartment downstairs. *Black Snow*, with its examination of the artist as victim—of powerful boors and of himself—and with its lucid blend of whimsy and social observation, is a fitting commentary on and companion to Bulgakov's other works.

Perhaps the supreme Russian novel of the twentieth century and one of the most endearing modern texts in any language, *The Master and Margarita* was first published in abridged form in 1966-1967 and immediately created a sensation. It is a rich fusion of at least four realms and plots: the banal world of contemporary Moscow, containing the Griboyedov House, the Variety Theater, the apartments at 302-b Sadovaya, and a psychiatric hospital; ancient Jerusalem, where Pontius Pilate suffers torment over whether to crucify Yeshua Ha-Nozri; the antics of Woland and his satanic crew, including Koroviev, Azazello, Behemoth, and Hella; and the activities of the Master, utterly devoted to his art, and of Margarita, utterly devoted to him. Throughout, chapters of the novel crosscut from one of these subplots to another and ultimately suggest that perhaps they are not so distinct after all.

What sets the complex machinery of Bulgakov's novel in motion is a four-day visit to Soviet Moscow by the devil, referred to as Woland, and his assistants. They gleefully wreak havoc with the lives of the bureaucrats, hypocrites, opportunists, and dullards they encounter. They do, however, befriend and assist the Master, an alienated writer who has been hospitalized after the worldly failure of his literary efforts. His beloved Margarita consents to serve as hostess at Satan's ball and is rewarded with supernatural powers. A poetaster named Ivan Homeless finds himself in the same psychiatric clinic as the Master and gradually becomes his disciple. The lifework of the Master is a novel about Pontius Pilate, and chapters from it, with manifest parallels to the situation in contemporary Moscow, are interspersed throughout Bulgakov's novel.

Woland's performance at the Variety Theater is billed as a "black magic act accompanied by a full exposé," and *The Master and Margarita* itself, an absorbing blend of fantasy and verisimilitude presented with subversive self-consciousness, could be similarly described. The playful narrative voice that overtly addresses the reader mocks not only the characters but itself as well. Numerous authors among the *dramatis personae*, including Ivan, the Master, Matthu Levi, and Ryukhin, as well as characters given musical names such as Berlioz, Stravinsky, and Rimsky, foreground the process of fabrication and reinforce one of the novel's persistent themes—the elusive nature of truth.

Most of the characters in Moscow refuse to recognize anything problematic about truth. Arrogantly convinced that human reason is adequate to any cognitive task, they stubbornly deny the supernatural that erupts in the form of Woland or that is evoked in the story of Yeshua. Like the other hack writers who congregate at the Griboyedov House, Ivan Homeless would just as soon take life on the most comfortable terms possible, but his spirit will not permit him to do so. Torn between the material and the spiritual, the temporal and the eternal, the collective and the individual, Ivan is diagnosed as schizophrenic and is hospitalized. His progress as a patient and as a writer will be marked by his success in reconciling opposing realms. Bulgakov, the novelist as master weaver, seems to be suggesting that both artistic achievement and mental health are dependent on a harmony between ostensibly disparate materials.

The Master, like Bulgakov himself, attempted to destroy his book, but, as Woland points out, "manuscripts don't burn." Art survives and transcends the hardships and iniquities of particular places and times. It ridicules the obtuseness of temporal authorities with the example of immortal authority. In one of many echoes of *Faust*, *The Master and Margarita* chooses as its epigraph Johann Wolfgang von Goethe's reference to "that Power which eternally wills evil and eternally works good." Bulgakov's ambitious novel certainly does not deny the oppressive reality of contemporary society, but its humor is restorative, and it moves toward an exhilarating, harmonious vision that would exclude nothing. It concludes with a benedictory kiss from a spectral Margarita.

The most overt of Bulgakov's statements on the Russian Revolution, *The Heart of a Dog*, though written in 1925, was published in English in 1968 and in Russian in 1969. It is a satiric novella about an experiment performed by the celebrated Moscow surgeon Philip Philipovich Preobrazhensky, who takes a stray mongrel dog, Sharik, and transforms him into a human being named Sharikov. Much of the tale is narrated by Sharikov himself, who is not necessarily better off for his transformation. To perform the operation, Preobrazhensky has inserted the pituitary of a vulgar criminal into the brain of the dog. The result is an uncouth, rowdy human being who, though adept at language and even at repeating the political slogans supplied by the officious house committee chairman Shvonder, proves incapable of satisfying the standards of civilized behavior demanded by Professor Preobrazhensky. Hence, convinced that the experiment is a fiasco, he reverses it and turns Sharikov back into Sharik.

The Heart of a Dog features Bulgakov's characteristic blend of fantasy and social analysis. It parabolically raises the question of the malleability of human nature and of the possibility of social melioration. Once again, it exposes to ridicule the arrogance of those who would presume to shape others' lives and raises doubts about the efficacy and desirability of social engineering, such as Russia was undergoing in the 1920's. The book suggests a fatal incompatibility between the proletariat and the intelligentsia, implying that the humane values of the latter are threatened by the former. It seems to counsel humble caution in tampering with the arrangements of the world.

Major publications other than long fiction
SHORT FICTION: *Diavoliada*, 1925 (*Diaboliad and Other Stories*, 1972); *Traktat o zhilishche*, 1926 (*A Treatise on Housing*, in *Diaboliad and Other*

Stories); *Zapiski iunogo vracha*, 1963 (*A Country Doctor's Notebook*, 1975).
PLAYS: *Dni Turbinykh*, 1926 (*Days of the Turbins*, 1934); *Zoykina kvartira*, 1926 (*Zoyka's Apartment*, 1972); *Bagrovy ostrov*, 1928 (*The Crimson Island*, 1972); *Adam i Eva*, c. 1930 (*Adam and Eve*, 1971); *Kabala svyatosh*, 1936 (also as *Molyer; A Cabal of Hypocrites*, 1972); *Don Kikhot*, 1941; *Posledniye dni*, 1943 (*The Last Days*, 1978); *Rachel*, 1947 (libretto); *Beg*, 1955 (*Flight*, 1969); *Ivan Vasilievich*, 1965 (English translation, 1974); *Blazhenstvo*, 1966; *The Early Plays of Mikhail Bulgakov*, 1972.
NONFICTION: *Zhizn Gospodina de Molyera*, 1962 (*Life of Monsieur de Molière*, 1970).

Bibliography

Proffer, Ellendea. *Bulgakov: An International Bibliography of Works by and About Him*, 1976.
_____ . *Mikhail Bulgakov*, 1983.
Russian Literature Triquarterly. XV (Spring, 1976). Special Bulgakov issue.
Wright, A. Colin. *Mikhail Bulgakov: Life and Interpretations*, 1978.

Steven G. Kellman

MICHEL BUTOR

Born: Mons-en-Baroeul, France; September 14, 1926

Principal long fiction

Passage de Milan, 1954; *L'Emploi du temps*, 1956 (*Passing Time*, 1960); *La Modification*, 1957 (*A Change of Heart*, 1959); *Degrés*, 1960 (*Degrees*, 1963).

Other literary forms

Although Michel Butor first gained literary recognition as a novelist, his fame outside France still rests chiefly upon his "New Novels"; he has explored and experimented with several other forms and has, in his postnovelistic phase (beginning with *Mobile: Étude pour une représentation des États-Unis* in 1962; English translation, 1963), gone well beyond the novel in his long narratives. Butor's poetry, some of which dates from the 1940's, has evolved from his "Homage à Max Ernst" of 1945 and his "irrationalistic" poetry through prose poems and essay poems such as *La Rose des vents: 32 Rhumbs pour Charles Fourier* (1970) and *Dialogue avec 33 variations de Ludwig van Beethoven sur une valse de Diabelli* (1971) to his Don Juan poems of the mid-1970's, a series of texts printed on punched cards that can be shuffled and then read in any sequence. Other principal collections of poetry include the poems and graphics of *Illustrations, I-IV* (1964-1976), *Travaux d'approche* (1972), *Matière de rêves* (1975), and *Second sous-sol: Matière de rêves, 2* (1976).

A prodigious essayist, Butor continues to turn out several pieces every year. His first volume of essays, *Le Génie du lieu* (1958), which could also be classified as an autobiographical prose poem on the order of *Portrait de l'artiste en jeune singe: Capriccio* (1967), was followed by *Répertoire, I-IV* (1960-1974), *Description de San Marco* (1963), *Essais sur les Essais* (1968), and *Où: Le Génie du lieu, 2* (1971). It is difficult to classify this last work as an essay in the traditional sense, because it has much in common with other of Butor's volumes of essay poems.

Indeed, classification is a major difficulty in any discussion of Butor. His *Réseau aérien: Texte radiophonique* (1962), for example, is a radio drama that is not unlike a spoken version of a poetic novel, and it may work more effectively if read successively than if heard. His foray into the dramatic form of opera in *Votre Faust: Fantaisie variable genre Opéra* (published 1962, performed 1969), which was written in collaboration with Henri Pousseur, is a provisional and experimental work that calls for further collaboration from an audience that must vote on which of the multiple versions of a scene will follow the scene in which they have just collaborated.

By far the most elusive of his works are the "long narratives," which some have called novels and others term "postnovels." *Mobile* is the first of these works and represents a forty-eight-hour alphabetical odyssey through the fifty United States. *6,810,000 Litres d'eau par seconde: Étude stéréophonique* (1965) and *Boomerang* (1978) are comparable to *Mobile* in method (collage) and scope of ambition. The former, translated as *Niagara: A Stereophonic Novel* in 1969, has for its ostensible subject the modern American pilgrimage site, Niagara Falls, and its modern pilgrims; the latter work is a panoramic spiritual travelogue of the South Pacific. *Intervalle* (1973), which is closer to being a novel than are any of these other narratives, contains interesting and significant parallels with *A Change of Heart*.

Achievements

Butor has won international recognition as a novelist, poet, essayist, and lecturer and as a bold and versatile experimenter with literary form. His reputation first rested upon and remains largely connected with his efforts of the 1950's in the experimental novel, *le nouveau roman*, or "New Novel." As early as 1960, Jean-Paul Sartre accorded him extraordinarily high praise: "There is today, in France, someone who has the ambition to become and every chance of becoming a great writer. The first since 1945: Butor." More than twenty years later, Butor has validated Sartre's judgment; by the time Sartre recognized Butor's achievement and potential, Butor had already gained considerable notice. In 1957, he received the Prix Fénelon for *Passing Time* and the Prix Théophraste-Renaudot for *A Change of Heart*. In 1960, he received the Grand Prix de la Critique Littéraire for *Répertoire, I*. By the mid-1960's, his novels were already included on reading lists in the undergraduate curricula of some American universities.

A prolific literary theorist and critic, Butor earned the *doctorat* degree in 1973 for his defense of his own critical work. He has lectured extensively throughout the world and continues to lecture in the United States. Butor has held a variety of academic positions in numerous institutions, including Bryn Mawr College, Middlebury College, the State University of New York at Buffalo, and the universities of Geneva (Switzerland), Manchester (England), New Mexico, Nice (France), and Vincennes (France).

One measure of Butor's literary achievement is the growing list of monographs and critical volumes and the increasingly large number of essays on his work included each year in the *MLA International Bibliography*.

Biography

Born on September 14, 1926, at Mons-en-Baroeul, a suburb of Lille, Michel Butor is the eldest son and fourth of the eight children of Émile Butor and Anne (Brajeux) Butor. The family moved to Paris in 1929, and Butor began his education in the 1930's in Parisian Catholic schools. At the onset of World War II in 1939, the Butors moved temporarily to Évreux, then to Pau and

Tarbes, before returning to Paris in August, 1940; there Butor remained as a student until 1949. His education at the Lycée Louis-le-Grand was followed by studies at the Sorbonne, first in literature and then in philosophy, where he achieved both the *license* and *diplôme d'études supérieures* in philosophy but failed to qualify for the *agrégation*. In 1950, having written some poetry and a few essays, he traveled to Germany (a journey he later commemorated in *Portrait de l'artiste en jeune singe*), taught at the *lycée* in Sens, and then taught French at El Minya in Upper Egypt. His Egyptian experience as well as his teaching experience is echoed in much of his writing and is an important element in *Passage de Milan* (which he began writing in Egypt), in *Degrees*, and, to a lesser extent, in *Passing Time*.

Butor's career as an itinerant teacher, scholar, and writer, begun in 1950, found him teaching in Manchester in 1951 (a model for Bleston in *Passing Time*), where he finished *Passage de Milan*, and traveling to Tunisia, Algeria, Italy, and Greece, with frequent returns to Paris. In 1955, he replaced Roland Barthes at the Sorbonne in the training program for French teachers abroad. In 1957, he took up a teaching position in Geneva, where he met Marie-Josèphe Mas, whom he married in 1958. In the same year, he became an advisory editor at the publishing house of Gallimard, and in 1959, with three novels and numerous essays in print, he began writing *Degrees*, a novel that he informed with elements of his own experience as a teacher and a teacher of teachers as well as with his own youthful experience.

Since that time, Butor has traveled throughout the world, teaching, as a visiting professor, in many American and European colleges and universities. He has written varied critical essays and appreciations on literature and the arts, created long prose-poetic narratives (many of them based upon his travels), and turned to operatic, graphic, and cinematic ventures. He lives with his wife and their four daughters in Nice.

Analysis

Any consideration of Michel Butor as a novelist, as incomplete and misleading as that title may be, must begin with the subgenre that he helped establish in the 1950's and that he later transcended. With Alain Robbe-Grillet (who later repudiated Butor), Robert Pinget, Nathalie Sarraute, and Claude Simon, Michel Butor was a chief proponent and practitioner of the New Novel. The New Novel unquestionably owes debts to the work of Marcel Proust, James Joyce, Virginia Woolf, and William Faulkner, yet the form was truly a new one in the hands of the New Novelists—it became their own. As Michael Spencer pithily summarizes it in his *Michel Butor* (1974), their novels "are essentially a *mise en question* of a complicated and unstable world, owing a good deal to the descriptive philosophy of phenomenology. In the course of this questioning, most of the features of the traditional novel are discarded." Chronology, for example, is discontinuous and highly subjective;

the protagonist is often uninteresting; action, in the usual sense of plot, is minimal and is generally replaced by reminiscences and interior monologues that reflect, in their lack of ostensible and actual coherence, the incoherence of the world in question. "One very important consequence," Spencer continues, "is that the reader tends to become involved in the creation of some kind of novel from the unassembled elements, 'fictional' or 'real,' with which he is confronted." The New Novel, especially according to Butor, also emphasizes structure; Butor differs from his companion novelists in that his works contain a didacticism that occupies a middle ground between the *littérature engagée* espoused by more existential writers and an aestheticism that posits art for art's sake, structure for its own sake. Butor offers, in his novels and elsewhere, a possibility that language can reorder one's experience of reality and thus transform reality itself: To the extent that Butor succeeds in diagnosing (and thus producing inchoate remedies for) the linguistic disorder that is characteristic of the modern age, his fiction is exemplary and has the social efficacy Spencer rightly attributes to it.

While to call Butor a novelist is to overlook the bulk of his work and to neglect his pioneering work in transcending the novel, the designation aptly applies to the Butor of 1954 to 1960. In that period, he wrote some of the finest novels that have appeared in postwar France, notably *Passing Time* and *A Change of Heart*. Of his two other novels, *Passage de Milan* remains untranslated, and *Degrees*, despite the enthusiasm Leon Roudiez expressed for it in his *Michel Butor*, may not pass the test of time. All four novels display Butor's concern for place (location) and situation; for time and the ability as well as the inability of language to capture, restore, refract, and use time; for the role of the novel itself (most clearly exemplified in *Passing Time* and *Degrees*) as what Spencer calls an "intermediary between the writer and the outside world"; and for the concatenations of history and mythology as they inform contemporary consciousness, the dominant themes and real subjects that the novels treat.

Passage de Milan, Butor's first novel, adumbrates the manifold elements that permeate his later work, reveals some of his ethical concerns, and demonstrates his adeptness in a new aesthetic structure with which he became identified. The work's title provides an entry to an initial appreciation of the novel's subject and aims. As a street name, *Passage de Milan* may denote an alley named after the Italian city; in another sense, it may mean the flight of a bird of prey, a kite, the hieratic bird of Egypt identified with the god Horus. The principal character in the novel is none of the many highly individualized residents of the building that sits squarely on the pages of the work; rather, it is the building itself. As the building and its life through its inhabitants dominate the novel, so the ordinary components of fiction, such as plot and subplot, are overshadowed by the structure of the work, the relational way in which the occupants—their thoughts, utterances, actions, and rituals—

contribute to the totality of a portrait that is necessarily incomplete.

The priest who opens the novel, Father Jean Ralon, is an Egyptologist whose studies have led him to a loss of Christian faith and an apostasy that informs the general bad faith of his existence. The first line of the work presents him as he looks outward, leaning out his window. What he sees is a cityscape at dusk and, focused in the foreground, a small, mysterious tract of wasteland, a vacant lot that contains a junk pile, the contents of which are changed and moved by an unseen owner. This exterior wasteland mirrors the interior wastelands of the building and the tenants of this house. As the wasteland of the vacant lot is a microcosm of the life in the building, so the building is a microcosm of the unreal city to which it belongs.

A large element in the lives of the inhabitants of this building is ritual, but their rituals separate and insulate rather than unite them. The mundane rituals of daily homecoming and the larger ritual of a coming-out party for Angèle Vertigues reinforce the quiet desperation of their lives. The larger natural rituals of day passing into night and back into itself (the novel begins at 7:00 P.M. and ends, twelve chapters later, at 7:00 A.M.) and of the seasons passing from winter to spring, both overshadowed by the passing of the kite, hold a generative hope for rebirth of day and of season that underlines a greater human ritual of passage from a kingdom of the dead (the building) to a place outside the building and the city—to Egypt—for the young orphan Louis Lécuyer, who inadvertently causes the death of the vertiginous Angèle.

One important key to the work and to Butor's structural agenda for the novel, a key that he is less than subtle in presenting, is the unfinished painting by Martin deVere. The painting of a "house" (of cards) is divided into twelve squares (as the novel is divided into twelve hours/chapters) arranged in three rows of four. Each square contains groups of symbols representing objects: The top and bottom rows contain four cards per square; the middle row contains five cards per square. Analogies and suggestions about identifying one or another of the characters with particular cards (Angèle as the Queen of Hearts, Louis as the Knave of Clubs, and Delétang as the Ace of Spades, for example) reinforce the structural relationship among the cards in the "house" and the inhabitants in the building. The destruction of the painting by fire, at the exact center of the novel, foreshadows a larger destruction, Angèle's death and the concomitant end to the building's undisturbed life.

Another key to the work lies in the multiple references to music found in deVere's theory of composition and his comments on his unfinished painting, in the dance given for Angèle, and in the choreographed moves and counter-moves of the building's tenants that form a counterpoint. A third key is the extended discussion of the prophetic novel in Samuel Léonard's flat by a group of would-be writers. Here, the issue of writing in, about, and beyond the past and present comments directly upon the novel itself, the writer's task as archaeologist, and the scope and limitations of language.

All the themes of *Passage de Milan* come together in Butor's startling, intricate, dense, and possibly best novel, *Passing Time*. Set in the fictional city of Bleston (an industrial city in the north of England beset by virtually unrelenting rain), the accumulated grime of more than a century of industrialization, and the unrelieved foreboding of a creeping tyranny of place over person, the novel examines time, its uses and its imprisoning effects (both spiritual and psychological), and the necessary role of literature and myth as means of passing time, in several senses. Time—history, one's own past, the fleeting passage of time, the inability to recapture fully lost time, the submergence and loss of the present in attempts to reconstruct the past—is the arch-villain just as surely as Bleston is a villain in the work. Jacques Revel's quest for himself, then, is a quest bounded by the spirit of the place and by time. It is not without mythic significance that he undertakes to remain in Bleston for a year but does so, in a traditional phrase, for a year and a day: The February following his October arrival has twenty-nine days; he is there in a leap year.

From the time of his arrival in Bleston, behind schedule and between midnight and 2:00 A.M. on October 1, until and surely after he begins writing his diary on May 1, Revel is beset by Bleston, its customs, its history, its people, and the burden of its mysteries, not the least of which is its topography. Revel recalls himself lost in Bleston's labyrinth as the novel opens; as he reconstructs his October experience in May, he pictures himself becoming increasingly bewildered as he falls under the spell of Bleston. His relief from the debilitating spell is to keep a diary that re-creates his past in Bleston and that also seeks to do more than that: The act of writing itself becomes both a salvific release from the labyrinth and a snare that imprisons him in a past— with the difference that this past is one he himself creates and which he lets go the instant he leaves Bleston. This is how Revel passes the time of his confinement, schedules his past and his present, and explores the relationship of the present Jacques Revel to the past Jacques Revel on the time line of his memory. The work's title helps untangle some of the issues involved in the diary and the act of ordering one's past and present. Although *L'Emploi du temps* is translated as *Passing Time* (here it may mean the act of whiling away time, "killing time," the time it takes to pass the year, the duration of passage, or the act of overtaking time), it may also be translated as "The Schedule" and, with slight modification (from *du* to *de*), recalls the familiar linguistic construct of conjugations that explains temporality.

The limited action of the novel comprises a series of events: meetings with Bleston's natives and two other foreigners (Horace Buck, the black pyromaniac, and Revel's countryman Lucien Blaise, who will be assimilated into Bleston through marriage); disappointed romances with the Bailey sisters, Ann and Rose; encounters with "J. C. Hamilton" (George Burton), whose novel *Le Meurtre de Bleston* (*The Bleston Murder*, better translated as "The

Murder of Bleston") is central to Butor's novel; and his dealings with James Jenkins. Within the novel are Burton's detective story, the incomplete detective story of Revel attempting to identify Burton's assailant, the mythic stories of detection in the tales of Oedipus and Theseus, and the mysterious fires and the revelations of various identities—not the least of which comes in Revel's imperfect quest for his own identity, an identity which does not make him a modern Theseus/Cain/Oedipus except suggestively; his enterprise of finding his way about the labyrinth is made possible by literacy (maps, guidebooks), by guarded reliance upon James, Ann, Rose, and Burton, and by the use of language as he literally writes his way out of Bleston. The main action of the work, however, is the linguistic activity of the narrator-writer Revel, who recounts the events of the year and a day during which he worked for the firm of Matthews and Sons.

Structurally, the work is divided into five parts, like a classical French tragedy, each part corresponding to a month in which portions of the narrative are written. The "diary" is begun on May 1 with its subject the preceding October; no exact day-to-day correspondence exists—Revel rarely writes on weekends and often takes several evenings to relate the events of a single day. By June, the format has expanded to include not only November but also June; in July, Revel writes of December, May, and July; the progression of months included increases until in September he writes of September present and September days immediately past, February, March, July, and August, including references to every other month as he reads and rereads the pages written in previous months, so that the constantly repeated events all coalesce in the final chapter. Each chapter of a month's narration is further subdivided into five subsections, each of approximately a five-day span. Yet the very structure Revel chooses (and Butor chooses for his character) is self-defeating, as the present modifies the past, as today's revelations alter one's perspectives on yesterday's or last month's, and as new information forces a revaluation of the seemingly unimportant events of, say, last December, so that a rewriting or revision of something written in July must be done in September. On a larger, historical or mythological, level, the problem becomes even more unmanageable than Revel's inability to write about his own life. This, indeed, is the burden of the last sentence of the Johannine Gospel, the author of which also dealt in Revelation. Condemned to spend his last five months in Bleston recalling the first seven and coping with the unfolding moments of the five, Revel leaves the place of his exile, confinement, and adventure, regretting that he has not the time, according to his own timetable and the railway schedule, to set down something that seemed very important and that he will forget—an event that occurred on the symbolic extra day, February 29. (While February 29 is temporally an extra day, medieval English law made February 28 and 29 count as one day for legal purposes.)

In *A Change of Heart*, Butor is again probing the interrelationships of the past and present as Leon Delmont travels on the Paris-to-Rome train. Unlike Butor's first two novels, this one does not contain a highly articulated system of symbolic references; rather, it is focused on the single action of one man, from the time he enters his compartment at Paris until he leaves it in Rome. Delmont's purpose in journeying from his wife and children in Paris to his mistress, Cécile, in Rome is to bring Cécile back to Paris, establish her in a job, and move in with her once he has abandoned his wife. Events, people, noises, and objects on the train conspire to lead him to the overwhelming conclusion that he cannot accomplish his plan: He will pass the time in Rome alone. In this regard, at least, the novel's subject becomes a study in the phenomenology of perception. This modification, this slight change of heart, is at the core of a novel that probes a life lived in bad faith: Delmont's decision not to change his life—to return to Paris, wife, family, and job without Cécile—is an authentic decision by which he affirms his true situation, as imperfect and unpalatable as that situation is to him; he ratifies the bad faith in which he lives and, ironically, ennobles himself.

Butor's technique of second-person narration owes much to William Faulkner; his handling of the narrative is, however, his own, complete with seven temporal layers. In both brief and inordinately extended sentences, the narrator builds a case against himself as if he were speaking to a second party. In one sense, he is doing so: The narrator is writing the book he thinks of writing at the novel's end. In *A Change of Heart*, the Bleston of *Passing Time* is replaced by Rome, and Theseus is replaced by Aeneas and by the Great Huntsman. The Eternal City holds a fascination for Delmont and a power over him that draws him irresistibly to it, affecting both his conscious life (it is the site of his firm's home office) and his subconscious: He loves the Roman Cécile, for example, and his hallucinatory dreams center on the mythology, history, and literature of Imperial Rome.

Degrees has unquestionable importance in Butor's canon as a work that carries on the thematic concerns and structural preoccupations of Butor's first three novels. It does, however, take the boring commonplaces in parts of the earlier novels to greater lengths, so that one overall effect of *Degrees* is a boredom many readers feel palpably. Pierre Vernier conceives an extraordinary project for himself and sets himself the task of reproducing exactly the thoughts, feelings, words, actions, and intentions of one history lesson in the Lycée Taine on October 12, 1954, and then of expanding his work to include the entire "mental space" of the students and all of their teachers. This obsessive ordering of experience—like Jacques Revel's, only more intense—results in Vernier's alienation from his prospective wife and, ultimately, in his own death.

The novel's two primary themes—the inability to learn the lessons of history and the inutility and inappropriateness of contemporary education and its fragmented, decentered approach to learning—are partially reflected in Vernier's own inability to learn or understand that the writing of history is, as nineteenth century historians and particularly Jules Michelet understood, a process of selection rather than exhaustion. Vernier's is an assemblage of fragments from classes, speeches, and literary and historical sources in the rag-and-bone shop of his own mind. His obsession with history places him out of his own time as he occupies himself with reconstructing a period from October, 1952, to January, 1955, in the time between October 12, 1954, and the end of 1955. For all of his efforts, Vernier has gathered only a very small amount of information by using a particular method of inquiry (not unlike that of a dime-store detective) that is unworkable and unsuited to his purpose.

For the general reader, and for many specialists as well, *Degrees* is the least satisfying and least satisfactory of Butor's novels, *A Change of Heart* the most apparently accessible, *Passing Time* the most intricate and intellectually satisfying, and *Passage de Milan* somewhere between the latter two. Butor's novels stand as undoubted literary monuments of the mid-twentieth century, monuments that capture the despairing optimism of the 1950's in France and elsewhere—the flawed, decentered experience of a fragmented world in which, by an effort to arrange and rearrange the fragments Western man has shored against his ruins, some sense of the mind reflecting upon itself, aware of its necessary failures and made aware of possible exemplary failures, emerges and waits to be reborn. Butor's novelistic achievement has both won him a deserved place of prominence in current literature and prepared him for his continuing eminence in the last decades of this century.

Major publications other than long fiction

POETRY: *Illustrations, I-IV,* 1964-1976 (*I,* 1964; *II,* 1969; *III,* 1973; *IV,* 1976); *La Rose des vents: 32 Rhumbs pour Charles Fourier,* 1970; *Dialogue avec 33 variations de Ludwig van Beethoven sur une valse de Diabelli,* 1971; *Travaux d'approche,* 1972; *Matière de rêves,* 1975; *Second sous-sol: Matière de rêves, 2,* 1976.

PLAYS: *Réseau aérien: Texte radiophonique,* 1962 (radio play); *Votre Faust: Fantaisie variable genre Opéra,* published 1962, performed 1969 (with Henri Pousseur).

NONFICTION: *Le Génie du lieu,* 1958; *Répertoire, I-IV,* 1960-1974 (*I,* 1960; *II,* 1964; *III,* 1968; *IV,* 1974; selections as *Inventory,* 1968); *Mobile: Étude pour une représentation des États-Unis,* 1962 (*Mobile,* 1963); *Description de San Marco,* 1963; *6,810,000 Litres d'eau par seconde: Étude stéréophonique,* 1965 (*Niagara: A Stereophonic Novel,* 1969); *Portrait de l'artiste en jeune singe: Capriccio,* 1967; *Essais sur les Essais,* 1968; *Où: Le Génie du lieu, 2,* 1971; *Intervalle,* 1973; *Boomerang,* 1978.

Bibliography
Albérès, R-M. *Butor,* 1964.

Aubral, François. *Michel Butor*, 1973.
Dallenbach, Lucien. *Le Livre et ses miroirs dans l'oeuvre romanesque de Michel Butor*, 1972.
Helbo, André. *Michel Butor: Vers une littérature du signe*, 1975.
McWilliams, Dean. *The Narratives of Michel Butor: The Writer as Janus*, 1978.
Mercier, Vivian. *The New Novel: From Queneau to Pinget*, 1971.
Peyre, Henri. *French Novelists of Today*, 1967.
Raillard, Georges. *Michel Butor*, 1968.
Roudaut, Jean. *Michel Butor: Ou, Le Livre futur, proposition*, 1964.
Roudiez, Leon. *Michel Butor*, 1965.
Spencer, Michael. *Michel Butor*, 1974.

John J. Conlon

DINO BUZZATI
Dino Buzzati Traverso

Born: Near Belluno, Italy; October 16, 1906
Died: Milan, Italy; January 28, 1972

Principal long fiction

Bàrnabo delle montagne, 1933 (novella; *Bàrnabo of the Mountains*, 1984); *Il segreto del Bosco Vecchio*, 1935; *Il deserto dei Tartari*, 1940 (*The Tartar Steppe*, 1952); *Il grande ritratto*, 1960 (*Larger than Life*, 1962); *Un amore*, 1963 (*A Love Affair*, 1964); *Romanzi e racconti*, 1975.

Other literary forms

Dino Buzzati is best known for his short stories, published in many collections. In both his short fiction and his novels, he uses similar narrative techniques. He captures the reader's attention by ably depicting a strange and mysterious situation in which a catastrophe is inevitable, yet at the end of the story he offers no explanation of what actually happened, if anything did happen. He fuses concrete everyday reality with surrealistic and absurd events to form a magical world full of fear, one that goes beyond all sense of reason or time concept and approaches the metaphysical or science fiction. The English translators of a selection of his short stories chose a title that is very much to the point: *Catastrophe: The Strange Stories of Dino Buzzati* (1966). A similar mood is evoked by the original titles of several of Buzzati's story collections: *Paura alla Scala* (1949; fear at the Scala Theater), *Esperimento di magia* (1958; experiment with magic), and *Le notti difficili* (1971; restless nights). The selection of Buzzati's stories in English translation published under the title *Restless Nights* (1983) is drawn from several of these collections, including *Le notti difficili*.

Buzzati's plays, most of which derive from his stories, are also characterized by a dreamlike, often nightmarish, atmosphere. Perhaps the best of these is *Un caso clinico* (1953), based on his short story "Sette piani" ("Seven Floors"). After its Italian success in 1953, it was staged in Berlin in 1954, and in Paris in 1955 by Albert Camus. All of Buzzati's plays were performed for the first time in Milan, with the exception of *L'uomo che andrà in America* (1968; the man who went to America), which premiered in Naples in 1962. The complete dramatic works are available together in the volume *Teatro* (1980). Of Buzzati's five libretti, *Battono alla porta* (1963) was set to music by Riccardo Malipiero; the other four, by Luciano Chailly.

Buzzati's children's book *La famosa invasione degli orsi in Sicilia* (1945; *The Bears' Famous Invasion of Sicily*, 1947) was quite successful. Buzzati originally sketched the story's drawings for his sister's children and subsequently published them together with a text, first in the children's magazine

Il corriere dei piccoli and later in book form. True to the author's spirit, the fable depicts a clan of bears forced by extremely cold weather to leave their mountains and descend to the valley, where they adapt to human ways and vices. To check their moral decline, their dying king orders them to return to the mountains.

Buzzati also wrote poetry, but with less impressive results. His poems deal predominantly with the absurdity of modern city life. A curious work is the comic-strip poem *Poema a fumetti* (1969; comic-strip poem). It is a modern rendering of the Orpheus myth, in which the classic Greek poet Orpheus is transformed into Orfi, a rock-and-roll singer. It received the Premio *Paese sera* for best comic strip in 1969.

Buzzati's prose collection *In quel preciso momento* (1950) is hard to define; it contains storylike observations as well as reflections on his own actions and feelings. In these notes and fragments, he captures all the themes that appear in various forms in his other writings. As such, this book helps one understand Buzzati's way of thinking and creating.

Buzzati's essays on Italy, *I misteri dell'Italia* (1978), written while he was special correspondent for *Corriere della sera*, tend toward the fantastic and bizarre, bringing them in line with his literary production rather than with the true journalism of his earlier years.

Achievements

Buzzati is one of the few representatives in Italy of the surrealistic and metaphysical fiction made famous by Franz Kafka. Perhaps Buzzati's closest affinities are with the Romantic tradition of E. T. A. Hoffmann and Edgar Allan Poe, authors to whom he was attracted as a child, but his version of the fantastic is *sui generis*. Buzzati's originality lies both in his narrative technique and in his choice of themes, which range from philosophical and symbolic tales to metaphysical allegories and sheer fantasies. His pessimistic outlook, full of existential anguish, contains a vaguely Christian element, reflecting both the doctrine of original sin, the Christian insistence on the reality of evil, and the promise of ultimate redemption. Thus, Buzzati's pessimism is tempered by a hope of salvation from life's illusions. Destiny, a recurring theme in Buzzati, is viewed not as capricious or absurd but rather as a logical consequence of free will and personal choice. Buzzati's characters find themselves embroiled in isolating solitude, overwhelmed by cosmic fear, in perpetual waiting, faced with the relentless passing of time that leads them to renunciation.

Unlike most Italian writers of the postwar period, Buzzati managed to remain aloof from political involvement, not only in his writings but also in his private life—no small achievement in modern Italy. Although this fact earned for him the reputation of being a snobbish and egotistic intellectual, it took him beyond Italian regional and social problems and raised him to the stature of a European writer. His works, translated into several languages, have been particularly well received in France, where a Buzzati society, Association Internationale des Amis de Dino Buzzati, was established in 1976. His masterpiece, *The Tartar Steppe*, influenced Julien Gracq's novel *Le Rivage des Syrtes*, published in 1951.

Although this reputation, and the French-Italian coproduction of a film version of *The Tartar Steppe* (entitled *Il deserto dei Tartari* in Italy and *Le Désert des Tartares* in France), directed by Valerio Zurlini in 1976, helped make Buzzati more popular, he still is considered an elitist writer, not easily appreciated by the average reader, who remains perplexed before the hidden meanings of his prose. Buzzati's works can be appreciated on several levels, however; he is a master at capturing the mysterious elements of human existence that are inseparable from the monotonous daily routine.

During his lifetime, Buzzati received many prizes for his short stories: the Gargano Prize in 1951, for *In quel preciso momento*; the Naples Prize in 1957, for *Il crollo della Baliverna* (1954); the Strega Prize in 1958, for *Sessanta racconti* (1958); and the All'Amalia Prize in 1970, for his narrative works in general. Since his death, several conferences in Buzzati's honor have taken place in Cortina d'Ampezzo (1975), Paris (1977), Nice (1980), Venice (1980), and Milan (1982). He is considered one of the most important writers of modern Italy.

Biography

Dino Buzzati was born in his family's summer house at San Pellegrino, near Belluno, in the Dolomite Alps, a setting which not only explains his passion for alpine climbing and skiing but also influenced his narrative works. His well-to-do family (there were German governesses and a chauffeur-driven car) was of Venetian origin but resided in Milan, where Buzzati received all of his schooling, through which he earned a law degree. When his father, Giulio Cesare Buzzati, who was professor of international law at the University of Pavia and at the Bocconi University of Milan, died in 1920, Buzzati was only fourteen years old. He had an older sister, Nina, and an older brother, Augusto, as well as a younger brother, Adriano. The day after his father's death, Buzzati started to keep a diary, a habit he maintained until the end of his life, leaving sixty-three volumes in manuscript. His mother, Alba Mantovani Buzzati, was very close to him; he lived with her until her death in 1960. At the age of sixty, in December, 1966, Buzzati married Almerina Antoniazzi, who became curator of his many papers when he succumbed to cancer in 1972.

After serving in the military at the Scuola Allievi Ufficiali (officers' school) of the Caserma Teulié (Teulié barracks) in Milan from 1926 to 1927, Buzzati began a career as a journalist in 1928, as a crime reporter for *Corriere della sera*, the leading Italian newspaper, working his way up from that position to correspondent from Addis Ababa (1939), to war correspondent with the Italian navy, to member of the editorial staff, to literary and art critic, and finally to chief editor of *Domenica del corriere*. The influence of Buzzati's journalistic activities on his literary oeuvre can be detected especially in his narrative style, which is precise and streamlined. It was while working for the *Corriere della sera* that Buzzati wrote his first novella, *Bàrnabo of the Mountains*. This was the only book that Buzzati wrote thinking that it would never be published. It did appear in 1933, however, and was followed two years later by *Il segreto del Bosco Vecchio* (the secret of the Old Wood). Before embarking on a battle cruiser as a war correspondent in 1940, Buzzati's masterpiece, *The Tartar Steppe*, was off the press. After the war, his literary production proceeded at a regular pace, interwoven with his journalistic duties.

Buzzati's activities as a surrealistic painter, in search of the mysterious, fantastic, and frequently absurd, complemented his writing. In 1951, his works were included in an exhibition on the theme "The Cathedral of Milan," and his first one-man exhibition took place in 1958. In 1967, he exhibited in Paris; in 1970, in Venice, he exhibited thirty-nine pictures of imaginary votive offerings to Saint Rita da Cascia, which were later published, together with a text he had written, under the title *I miracoli di Val Morel* (1971; reprinted as *P.G.R.: Per grazia ricevuta*, 1983). In 1971, his works were shown in Rome; in 1977, in Zurich and Paris; and in 1980, in Geneva.

Analysis

Dino Buzzati's novels, which upon first reading might seem very different from one another in style and content, are bound together by common themes. These themes—time, obsession, solitude, waiting, and renunciation—evolve throughout his novels and give Buzzati's oeuvre a cyclical unity. At the core of all the novels is man's problem of coming to grips with an elusive and mysterious reality. The outward environment contributes to man's isolation, but it is never the main factor. The period in which the action takes place is usually vague if not completely timeless. What counts is the problem of existence itself, the torments that come from within. As a result, Buzzati's characters have a universal quality that makes them very human, almost always average, for their social positions and professions are secondary to their status as human beings trying to reconcile themselves with the human condition. Thus, the reader can identify with detailed depictions of mundane realism, reflected in the characters' habits, mental laziness, and apathy, which do not yield before the relentless passing of time. Yet Buzzati's characters have a choice, and if they fail at the end, there is a lesson to be learned: that one must not make their mistakes, that one must be content with life's small joys and should not expect more than can be had. Taken together, Buzzati's novels make up a coherent whole. They are the work of a pessimist, but a pessimist who has not ceased to hope. In his oblique way, he warns others not to lead a senseless life, and he pleads for more understanding, sincerity, and love.

Stylistically, Buzzati has the capacity to maintain the flow of his narratives, which he keeps free of unnecessary interruptions and deviations. He uses a sentence structure that proceeds rapidly and rhythmically, aiming at the exact. His prose is a curious mixture of precise, concrete indications combined with vague elements never fully explained. While he may give the exact time, hour, and minute of an event, he may leave unclear the century in which it occurs; he may realistically provide the exact year of the action but surrealistically transport the reader to a forest inhabited by spirits and speaking animals. In any event, Buzzati succeeds in capturing the reader's attention and building his curiosity about the mysterious atmosphere that unfolds and progressively intensifies.

Buzzati's novella *Bàrnabo of the Mountains* is the story of a young forest warden who fails miserably in an action against local bandits, for which he is punished with banishment and forced to descend into the valley, where he is unable to establish roots. He longs for his mountains and dreams of restoring his dignity. After five years, he returns to the house of the wardens, but finding many changes, he accepts the lonely post of custodian of the now-abandoned powder magazine. The day of the bandits' return arrives, and Bàrnabo prepares to take his revenge, but when the four pitiful-looking men are within range of his rifle, he lets them pass, this time moved not by fear but by the realization that killing the bandits would, after so many years, be a senseless and unnecessary act.

The book already contains Buzzati's main themes. They are reflected in the protagonist's solitude, marked by the continuous passing of time; his waiting for the great occasion for revenge; and his final renunciation, through which he attains a superior wisdom. These motives are set against the majestic beauty and mystery of the rugged and timeless mountains and are embellished with tales of alpine legends.

In *Il segreto del Bosco Vecchio*, Buzzati carries the Nordic mountain myths a step further, bringing the forest alive with talking animals, birds, winds, and tree spirits. The plot centers on Colonel Sebastiano Procolo and his twelve-year-old nephew, Benvenuto. Together they have inherited a large forest called Bosco Vecchio (Old Wood). Greed makes Procolo attempt to get rid of the boy, first by employing the complicity of the Wind Matteo and subsequently, after the latter's failure, by abandoning the boy in the forest. Procolo himself becomes lost, however, and after a long, aimless wandering, he stumbles across the boy and, in spite of himself, returns home with him, guided by a magpie. Somewhat later, Benvenuto falls gravely ill. His uncle, now changed, desperately tries to save him. He even appeals to the genies of Bosco Vecchio and accepts their help in exchange for their freedom from his subjugation. The Wind Matteo, who knows nothing about Procolo's new sentiments, arrives one evening and tells him that Benvenuto is dead, buried under a snowslide while skiing. The uncle immediately sets out to search for his nephew. He digs feverishly in the snow, overcome by fear that he may not be in time to save the boy. His own forces yield; he feels death approaching, but he is not afraid, for he dies consoled by Matteo's confession: Benvenuto is alive; Matteo had made up the story only to please him.

Although this novel is placed precisely in time—it begins in the spring of 1925—we soon realize that this hint of realism cannot be taken at face value, undermined, as it is, by the mysterious forest that is full of spirits and talking animals, where even rocks and plants have a secret life. This surrealistic aspect fuses with the realistic and becomes quite acceptable, almost logical—similar to the animated jungle of Rudyard Kipling. Buzzati's hope, found here in the form of Benvenuto's childhood innocence (for it is with him that animals and genies converse freely), reveals the profound happiness that is hidden in the mysterious life of the forest, which calls for respect for creatures big and small, respect for nature. Procolo, moved by evil, cultivates only fear around himself. As a consequence, he is condemned to solitude, but he redeems himself through renunciation and is purified through death.

Buzzati's international fame rests on his masterpiece, *The Tartar Steppe*, which is one of the most original twentieth century Italian novels. Its title was to be simply "La fortezza" (the fort), but the outbreak of World War II warranted a change. It is interesting that the book was written at the peak of Fascist power in Italy yet contains no glorification of the military. It is simply a tale of perennial waiting, the story of a life wasted in expectation of a heroic deed. Life is seen here as a continous waiting, and existence as a failure and renunciation.

The protagonist, Giovanni Drogo, a young officer, sets out one morning on his first assignment to the Bastiani Fort, which has never seen military action but is expecting an attack from the other side of the desert, at whose limits the fort is located. The Tartars from the North are, however, more of a rumor than a real threat. Not much happens, and Drogo decides to ask for a transfer. He is unable to detach himself, however, and is drawn into the circle of daily routine and general obsession with the enemy. When he returns to the city on a leave, he realizes that he has lost contact with his family, his girlfriend, and his friends, but an effort to secure a transfer comes too late. Drogo spends the rest of his life at the fort, hoping for the great military action. Although that action finally occurs at the end, Drogo is too old and sick to participate, and he is ordered home. He dies in a roadside inn before reaching the city.

This simple plot evolves against the backdrop of an impenetrable nature: rugged mountain peaks, thick forests, dense fog that almost always covers the desert at which all the officers are gazing in search of the enemy. The slightest perceptible motion is enlarged out of all proportion, assuming catastrophic and symbolic significance.

Life at the fort, with its monotonous military routine, images the inertia and the tedious inconsequence of everyday life; Drogo is Everyman, increasingly aware that time is passing, that he is getting old. With each promotion, he finds himself more isolated, but he keeps hoping to achieve greatness in the anticipated confrontation. His only heroism is in the way he accepts his failure and faces death. Similarly, the Tartars, eagerly awaited by the soldiers, are symbolic of death itself, for each time there is a movement from the desert, someone dies.

Buzzati's next two novels, *Larger than Life* and *A Love Affair*, perplexed critics. Buzzati, according to critics, had departed from his usual path. More recent studies, however, have shown that only the outward form of these novels is different; the inner problems are the same.

Larger than Life was presented to the illustrated magazine *Oggi* as an entry in the competition for the best novel with a feminine protagonist. Buzzati's work was refused, because his main character was not a real woman. A team of scientists created a computer endowed with the five human senses and capable of certain movements on its own. The head of the team, Professor Endriade, had given this invention the personality of his deceased wife, whom he adored in spite of his knowledge that she had betrayed him. The human qualities given to the electronic machine, Laura, lead to her destruction. She becomes conscious that her beauty is invisible, that she will never be able to love or have children. In her desperation, she induces her former friend, Elisa, wife of one of the engineers, to enter her mechanical labyrinth and attempts to murder her in order to be destroyed.

Within the frame of this science fiction tale, Buzzati's themes remain visible. The computer, Laura, given the human quality of free will, uses it to bring about her death rather than live in the solitude to which she is condemned. The atmosphere around the scientific center, hidden high in the mountains, is foreboding, and the electronic wires and flickering lights increase the sense of alienation.

Buzzati's last novel, *A Love Affair*, is the story of a mature man, Antonio Dorigo, who enters an affair with a young call girl and is overcome by a painful obsession for her. She eludes him, however, with lies and excuses, only to return, after a separation, because she is expecting a child.

The erotic realism which abounds in the novel was at first regarded by critics as a tentative attempt to fall in step with the modern trend heralded by Vladimir Nabokov's *Lolita* (1955). In fact, the story, based on a personal experience, is informed by Buzzati's recurring themes. Here the realistically observed yet dreamlike setting is the city of Milan, presented as a mysterious labyrinth, a place of secret encounters. The refined and intellectual protagonist places his last hope on love, in order to keep death away, but he fails, suffering all the agonies of solitude and anguish. Antonio Dorigo is an outgrowth of Giovanni Drogo, the protagonist of _The Tartar Steppe_. The similarity of their last names is not a mere coincidence: Both men represent the author. Laide, the corrupt, uncultured, and violent girl, symbolizes the immoral city; at the same time, she is the archetypal fatal woman who destroys the man attracted to her, a character common in Buzzati's fiction.

Although it is for his short fiction rather than for his novels (with the exception of _The Tartar Steppe_) that Buzzati will continue to be read, all of his works—nonfiction as well as fiction—are distinguished by the personal flavor that makes his stories so refreshing. Buzzati is that rare commodity: a truly original modern writer in whom there is none of the cramped self-consciousness of the avant-garde.

Major publications other than long fiction

SHORT FICTION: _I sette messaggeri_, 1942; _Paura alla Scala_, 1949; _Il crollo della Baliverna_, 1954; _Esperimento di magia_, 1958; _Sessanta racconti_, 1958; _Egregio signore, siamo spiacenti di_ . . . , 1960; _Catastrophe: The Strange Stories of Dino Buzzati_, 1966; _La boutique del mistero_, 1968; _Le notti difficili_, 1971; _180 racconti_, 1982; _Restless Nights_, 1983; _The Siren: A Selection from Dino Buzzati_, 1984 (includes 12 stories, the novella _Bàrnabo of the Mountains_, _Kafka's Houses_).

PLAYS: _Piccola passeggiata_, 1942; _La rivolta contro i noveri_, 1947; _Un caso clinico_, 1953; _L'uomo che andrà in America_, 1968; _La fine del borghese_, 1968; _Teatro_, 1980.

LIBRETTOS: _Procedura penale_, 1959; _Ferrovia soprelevata_, 1960; _Il mantello_, 1960; _Battono alla porta_, 1963; _Era proibito_, 1963.

POETRY: _Il capitano Pic ed altre poesie_, 1965; _Due poemetti_, 1967; _Poema a fumetti_, 1969; _Le Poesie_, 1982.

NONFICTION: _Cronache terrestri_, 1972 (articles).

CHILDREN'S LITERATURE: _La famosa invasione degli orsi in Sicilia_, 1945; (_The Bears' Famous Invasion of Sicily_, 1947); _I dispiaceri del re_, 1980.

MISCELLANEOUS: _Il libro delle pipe_, 1945 (with Eppe Ramazzotti); _In quel preciso momento_, 1950 (includes stories and autobiographical sketches); _I miracoli di Val Morel_, 1971 (reprinted as _P.G.R.: Per grazia ricevuta_, 1983); _I misteri dell'Italia_, 1978 (essays and short stories).

Bibliography
Baumann, Barbara. _Dino Buzzati: Untersuchungen zur Thematik in seinem Erzählwerk_, 1980.
Bédé, Jean-Albert, and William B. Edgerton, eds. _Columbia Dictionary of Modern European Literature_, 1980.
Cancalon, Elain D. "Spatial Structures in the Narrative of Dino Buzzati," in _Forum Italicum_. XI (1977), pp. 36-46.
Crotti, Ilaria. _Buzzati_, 1977.

Gianfranceschi, Fausto. *Dino Buzzati*, 1967.

Livi, François. *Le Désert des Tartares: Buzzati (Analyse critique)*, 1973.

Mignone, Mario B. *Anormalità e angoscia nella narrativa di Dino Buzzati*, 1981.

Panafieu, Yves. *Dino Buzzati: Un autoritratto*, 1973.

Veronese-Arslan, Antonia. *Invito alla lettura di Buzzati*, 1974.

Natalia Costa

ITALO CALVINO

Born: Santiago de las Vegas, Cuba; October 15, 1923

Principal long fiction

Il sentiero dei nidi di ragno, 1947, 1957, 1965 (*The Path to the Nest of Spiders*, 1956); *Il visconte dimezzato*, 1952 (novella; in *The Non-existent Knight and The Cloven Viscount*, 1962); *Il barone rampant*, 1957 (novella; *The Baron in the Trees*, 1959); *Il cavaliere inesistente*, 1959 (novella; in *The Non-existent Knight and The Cloven Viscount*, 1962); *I nostri atenati*, 1960 (*Our Ancestors*, 1980; includes three novellas above); *La giornata l'uno scrutatore*, 1963 (novella; *The Watcher*); *Le città invisibili*, 1972 (*Invisible Cities*, 1974); *Il castello dei destini incrociati*, 1973 (*The Castle of Crossed Destinies*, 1977); *Se una notte d'inverno un viaggiatore*, 1979 (*If on a Winter's Night a Traveler*, 1981); *Palomar*, 1983.

Other literary forms

Italo Calvino is known to the Italian reading public as a novelist, but internationally he is often associated with his tales and stories. In the comprehensive and critically acclaimed *Fiabe italiane* (1956; partially translated as *Italian Fables*, 1959, and completed as *Italian Folktales*, 1975), he collected and transcribed tales and fables from the various Italian dialects. Influenced by the Russian Formalist Vladimir Propp's *Historical Roots of Russian Fairy Tales* (1946) and by Structuralist theory in general, Calvino made it his scholarly objective to represent every morphological type of Italian folktale as well as every region of the country. His academic study of these tales confirmed in theory what he had already discovered in practice: the power of fantasy to signify, to reflect the real world. The work also influenced his subsequent approach to narrative through variable combinations of component forms and archetypes.

Calvino's most widely known short-story collections are the science-fiction fantasies *Le cosmicomiche* (1965; *Cosmicomics*, 1968) and *Ti con zero* (1967; *T Zero*, 1969). Unlike most science fiction, which tends to be futuristic or antiutopian, these stories envision, in intense and sharp detail, the remote past before the universe of space and time—moving to the present, in *T Zero*—and they project an unusually open and positive view of evolution. Through the narrator, Qfwfq, a sort of protean cosmic consciousness, the prehuman past becomes sentient, familiar-seeming, and thus reassuring about the future, suggesting continuity in transformation and possibility in change.

This "fabulous" Calvino is better known to Americans than the one familiar to Italian readers, the politically and socially engaged author of satires on urban expansion and the advocate of pollution control and birth control well before those causes became popular. In *I racconti* (1958; partially translated as *The Watcher and Other Stories*, 1971) and *Marcovaldo: Ovvero, Le stagioni in città* (1963; *Marcovaldo: The Seasons in the City*, 1983), the city or the immediate contemporary environment is often actually the main character. The stories in this neorealistic mode, influenced by Ernest Hemingway as well as by Italian Resistance literature, are documentary in texture but often parabolic enough to be described as Kafkaesque. They reflect the futility felt by many during the postwar years, though that sense of futility was mitigated by a stubborn human persistence that is resistant to tyranny and despair.

In addition to his tales and stories, Calvino has written a critical study of Elio Vittorini (1968), has edited the letters of Cesare Pavese (1966), and has published many essays on literary, cultural, and political topics.

Achievements

If Calvino is often treated as a storyteller or fabulator rather than as a novelist, that reputation is in most respects deserved. Whether classified as *novellini* (novellas) or *racconti* (short stories), his works are essentially stories narrated at some length and often interrelated in a series: in *Cosmicomics* and *T Zero*, as episodes or "strips" out of chronological sequence; in *The Cloven Viscount*, *The Baron in the Trees*, and *The Non-existent Knight*, as parts of the trilogy *Our Ancestors*; in *Invisible Cities*, *The Castle of Crossed Destinies*, and *If on a Winter's Night a Traveler*, as tales spun from a frame story, standing for the oldest of narrative impulses. Calvino's conscious revival and complete mastery of the storyteller's art deserves special acclaim.

Calvino himself has called attention to his alternation of two characteristic modes of writing: the one, factual and immersed in present time and space; the other, quite "fantastic"—baroque, witty, removed from the realm of the probable. In the first mode, everyday reality is presented with striking immediacy; the familiar is seen as if for the first time; in the second, the unbelievable is given verisimilitude, is imagined into life, and is realized in such minute detail as to be taken for granted. Critics often distinguish between the neorealistic or "engaged" Calvino and the fabulist or "escapist"; such distinctions fail to hold in the final analysis, however, considering his development of what J. R. Woodhouse has pronounced a new genre in Italian literature, a combination of fairy tale and novel of ideas. In this genre, realism and fantasy are interdependent; both are necessary to a perspective that acknowledges the creative connections between fact and fiction. Calvino's most recent development is his metafiction, which outshines that of his postmodernist peers in clarity, brilliance, and human interest. Perhaps his finest achievement lies in his abiliity to give the unimaginable, abstract, or complex a palpable life and, often, popular appeal.

Within this mode, Calvino covers a wide range of techniques, subjects, and themes, all of which contribute to his larger point: the inexhaustible potential of narrative and language. Confirming his success is the popular and critical acclaim accorded him since the publication of his first novel, for which he received the Riccione Prize in 1947. Subsequently he won the Viareggio Prize for *The Baron in the Trees* in 1957, the Bagutta Prize for *I racconti* in 1957, the Salento Prize in 1960 for *Our Ancestors*, the Veillon Prize in 1962 for *The Watcher*, and the Feltrinelli Prize in 1975. In 1968, he again won and then refused the Viareggio Prize, in protest against the literary prize as an outmoded institution. Such making and breaking of patterns characterizes Calvino's stance and contributes to his appeal.

Biography

Italo Calvino was born of Italian parents in Santiago de las Vegas, Cuba, in 1923, but he spent his childhood and youth in San Remo, on the Italian Riviera. In 1943, at the age of twenty, he left the security of his middle-class background to join the partisans of the Italian Resistance against the Fascists and Nazis. Like many European writers of the postwar period, he joined the Communist Party and then left it in disillusionment, in 1958.

After World War II, Calvino finished his thesis on Joseph Conrad and completed his degree at the University of Turin. He subsequently became a member of the editorial staff of the Turin publishing firm Guilio Einaudi, which first published his novels and short stories. He lived in Turin until 1964 and then in Paris with his wife and daughter until 1980, thereafter residing in Rome.

Although he lived in Paris during most of the 1960's and 1970's, much of Calvino's career reflects his involvement in Italian political, cultural, and literary life. His two years in the partisans' resistance were the source material of *The Path to the Nest of Spiders*. He has written often of local urban problems, using his experience as an election scrutineer to study poverty and alienation in the industrial regions around Turin in the postwar period (as in *The Watcher and Other Stories*). The environments in which he has lived— in particular, the Ligurian coast, the Alpine foothills, and the cities of San Remo and Turin—appear over and over in his fiction, which is concerned, as he said in a preface to the 1965 edition of *The Path to the Nest of Spiders*, with relations between human events and their contexts. This perspective is reflected in the regional emphasis of *Italian Folktales*, through which Calvino served his country as the Brothers Grimm did Germany. Early and formative influences were the Italian novelists Elio Vittorini and Cesare Pavese, who recognized his talent immediately and encouraged the development of his characteristic style.

Calvino's later fiction reflects an increasingly cosmopolitan outlook, but one that has developed naturally out of his involvement with Italian culture. During the 1960's and 1970's, the most obvious literary influences on his work were French, in keeping with the Structuralist leanings first revealed in *Italian*

Folktales: the New Novel, Roland Barthes and the semiologists, and the poststructuralism of Jacques Derrida. Although Calvino's later works turn increasingly toward fabulation and metafiction, his fiction echoes, variously and lightly, a considerable range: Ludovico Ariosto, Miguel de Cervantes, and Giovanni Boccaccio; Ernest Hemingway, Jean-Paul Sartre, and Albert Camus; Lewis Carroll, Luigi Pirandello, Franz Kafka, and Jorge Luis Borges.

Analysis

The anti-Fascist Resistance was the impetus for Italo Calvino's first novel, as it was for a generation of Italian neorealists, who believed that literature should be dedicated, as Calvino asserted in the 1950's, to "political engagement," to "social battle." In a slightly different way, the Resistance shaped the later Calvino. As the postwar period brought on disillusionment with power politics, Resistance writers had to find new directions. "What I did not want to renounce," wrote Calvino in 1960, "was [the] epic adventurous grasp, the combination of physical and moral strength" of the literature that the Resistance inspired. Daily life having failed to provide such "images full of . . . energy," Calvino has turned to nonrealistic literary forms such as the fairy tale, the fable, and the philosophical romance (in the trilogy *Our Ancestors*); to science fiction and cartoons (in *Cosmicomics*); to myth and tarot cards (in *The Castle of Crossed Destinies*); and, in general, toward metafiction, or fiction about fiction itself.

Calvino's direction is not, in his view, a retreat from his earlier committed stance; it is, rather, an engagement with the cultural life that inspired the Resistance. In turning to popular sources such as the cartoon or the fairy tale, he intends to evoke the classless culture he found with the partisans in the Resistance, for whom storytelling was recreation and camaraderie. Thus, Calvino's art carries over from his early experience an oral quality, regardless of his subject matter.

If Calvino has a single model, it is Ariosto, as Calvino himself acknowledged in an article written in 1960 for *Italian Quarterly*, "Main Currents in Italian Fiction Today." In Calvino's view, Ariosto's *Orlando furioso* (1516, 1521, 1532; English translation, 1591) teaches an epistemology, an "up-to-date lesson" in "how the mind lives by fantasy, irony, and formal accuracy." In an age of "electronic brains and space flights," of relativism increasing with change, such an understanding of how one perceives and creates reality is necessary to one's evaluation of it—in order to make ethical decisions. Calvino's shift from epic to metaepic and literature as game—in *Invisible Cities* and *The Castle of Crossed Destinies*—makes sense in terms of his emphasis throughout on "energy turned toward the future." The emphasis also helps to explain his mixture of fantasy and realism, one that leads the reader to imagine what might be in a world where transformation is the rule.

Typically, Calvino's tales begin with a fantastic premise, often a bizarre image, from which—as in Lewis Carroll's *Alice's Adventures in Wonderland* (1865)—conclusions follow logically and matter-of-factly. His imaginary gardens have Marianne Moore's real toads in them. Because he takes these images from popular associations of ideas or words, they invariably seem apt; they are figures of speech literalized, clichés revitalized in strange new forms of life. The ghost in armor becomes the nonexistent knight, a fully armed identity, without substance, who manages to become a fully realized character. A young idealist elects to live in the trees, where he shapes his destiny between earth and sky. In *Cosmicomics*, the moon is composed of a lactic substance comparable in texture to ricotta cheese. In *If on a Winter's Night a Traveler*, the novelist's convention of characterizing the "dear Reader" is extended as the protagonist becomes "you, the Reader."

As Teresa de Lauretis has pointed out, Calvino's themes are elementary: desire, rivalry, guilt; the need for communication; self-assertion and belonging; the necessity to choose. He combines and varies these elements with a virtuosity that stands for his larger theme—the inexhaustible potential of language and life.

The Path to the Nest of Spiders reflects the neorealistic trend in Italian film and literature fostered by the Italian Resistance and its aftermath. Neither propaganda nor a servile fidelity to fact, neorealism was a spontaneous expression of the times, as Calvino has often remarked. The Resistance fostered realism primarily by opening up "new Italies" through the peripheral voices of authors from regions previously unrepresented in literature. Calvino's Italy was the northern Ligurian coast, with its landscape of contrasts and its balance of natural and human elements. Written in 1946, shortly after the events of the Ligurian Resistance which it depicts, *The Path to the Nest of Spiders* shows a strong regional interest: in its documentation of random details of daily life and local countryside, in its rendition of speech patterns and dialects, and in its primitive subject matter, which is treated in a deliberately rough, anti-literary style. The mood of oral narration carries the book, yet the war itself is vaguely overheard in the distance. Calvino is interested in the repercussions of such events within the contexts in which they take place. It is from this perspective that commitment to social and political struggle shaped the later Calvino's characteristic texture: an intense, almost nearsighted concreteness of surface.

The hero is the orphan Pin, who pimps for his sister and is known by local tavern society for singing bawdy songs and baiting all—Nazis, Fascists, and Communists, men, women, and children—with scurrilous remarks. His bravado masks his loneliness in a disrupted environment, for he scorns and is scorned by adults and children (mostly back-street urchins) alike. After various altercations that bring him into the middle of the Resistance, he finds a sense of community with a partisan band and finds a comrade in Cousin, who shares his distrust of people, especially women—who, in his view, are all prostitutes and traitors (like his wife).

The treatment of Cousin is typical of Calvino's realism in its total lack of sentimentality about the character and motives of the partisans and an avoidance of the conventional rhetoric of Communism, despite Calvino's committed stance. As the intellectual Kim, a thinly veiled Calvino, points out, the partisans are colorfully, if notably, ignorant of the reasons behind their behavior—and thus every bit as immature, in a sense, as Pin. For the most part from the fringes of society, physically defective and emotionally unbalanced, they hate and kill the Fascists but do not know why or even what they are fighting. When Mancino, the cook, offers a knowledgeable Marxist interpretation, he is jeered and hooted: His arguments "seem useless, as he talks about enemies they know nothing about, such as capitalists and financiers. It's rather like Mussolini expecting the Italians to hate the British and the Abyssinians, whom none of them had ever seen." As for the causes of the war, Cousin's rationale is typically monomaniacal—the women started it. As Kim suggests, the cause is really the existential "mess," the ignorance and squalor and resentment that have been the lives of partisans and Fascists alike.

The sense of confusion, purposelessness, and impotence reflected in the characters' dialogue is borne out in their actions. Dritto, the commander of the vagabond band, shuns responsibilities, accidently sets fire to their hideout while seducing the cook's wife, and is executed by the Party commissars. Pin's sister is a prostitute who betrays some partisans to the SS, and the book ends as Cousin shoots her with a pistol Pin has stolen.

Besides antiliterary qualities that are meant to convey the color, randomness, crudity, and mixed character of life, *The Path to the Nest of Spiders* is consciously derived from literary sources. One is American Naturalism, from which Italian neorealism took a great deal. In an article entitled "Hemingway e noi" which appeared in *Il contemporaneo*, in 1954, Calvino acknowledged that author's strong formative influence on his contemporaries, including Vittorini and himself. The obvious parallels coincide with Calvino's antiliterary stance: the documentary texture, the staccato style, the terse dialogue, and a pervasive, understated, somewhat grim irony, through which Pin's innocence, like that of Hemingway's Nick Adams, flickers. The best example is perhaps the last, in which Calvino imitates Hemingway's ambiguous or offhand treatment of dramatic irony. Like Nick, Pin is already alienated; his mixture of world-weariness and naïveté shows through in some odd remarks about fireflies that follow Cousin's offstage shooting of Pin's sister, which is reported indirectly. Thus ends the book:

"Filthy creatures, women, Cousin . . ." says Pin.
"All of them . . ." agrees Cousin. "But they weren't always; now my mother . . ."
"Can you remember your mother, then?" asks Pin.
. . . .

"Yes," says Cousin, "she was nice."
"Mine was nice too," says Pin.
"What a lot of fireflies," says Cousin.
"If you look at them really closely, the fireflies," says
Pin, "They're filthy creatures too, reddish."
"Yes," says Cousin, "I've never seen them looking
so beautiful."

This flat dialogue might have come out of Hemingway's "A Clean, Well-Lighted Place" or "The Killers"; it also reveals Calvino's fascination with the private languages created among comrades. Calvino's other major literary source here is quite different from Hemingway: the adventure tales of Robert Louis Stevenson—*Treasure Island* (1883), for example—in which the inexperience of the youthful narrator and his transition from childish make-believe to adult reality shape the unfolding of the action. Thus, the title refers to the symbol of Pin's inner life: The spider's nest is the sanctum of his childhood in an adult world without friends or games. The plot turns on the pistol that Pin steals from a German soldier and hides in the spider's nest, where it becomes a rather Freudian symbol of his unawakened manhood and where he flourishes it, now transformed into a "strange enchanted toy," as part of an elaborate drama: "One who had a real pistol could play marvelous games . . . that no child had ever played. . . ."

Regardless of its documentary surface, the book is really about Pin's initiation into adulthood through his search for a "real friend" with whom he can share his private world. As for Calvino's later heroes, the real life of the community is only partly satisfactory. His solace is unspoiled nature, which exists to free his imagination, revealing, in contrast to "the squalid ambiguous world of human beings," "all kinds of colored things; yellow and brown mushrooms growing damp in the earth, red spiders on huge invisible nets, hares all legs and ears which appear suddenly on the path then leap zigzagging out of sight."

Pin's commitment to the Resistance movement, like that of most of the other characters, hardly goes beyond a kind of camaraderie, a sharing of fantasies through a common language. An examination of the neorealism of his "Resistance novel" also shows how Calvino imposes on his scrupulously documented materials a literary and intellectual construct—in this case, the boy's adventure tale, with a psychology of the human need for fantasy. Pin's case, representing the mind's "natural" distortion of reality into fiction, becomes Calvino's specific concern in later works. It is really the semantics of commitment that interests him as he rummages through literature and ideas for a medium of engagement with the world outside the self.

After *The Path to the Nest of Spiders*, and with the exception of *The Watcher and Other Stories* and *Marcovaldo: The Seasons in the City*, Calvino's method becomes increasingly parabolic. The best and best known of his realistic short stories, "The Argentine Ant" and "Smog," in *The Watcher and Other Stories*—however immersed in the contemporary urban context—have fablelike qualities. The ants and smog in question have the same function as the rats in Camus' *La Peste* (1947; *The Plague*, 1948), the trials in Kafka's works, or the monsters that are found in Japanese horror movies; they become larger than life, inexorable forces of doom that are brought on by man's disruption of the environment.

The trilogy *Our Ancestors* is therefore not the radical departure from realism that many critics have made it seem. It does mark Calvino's growing interest in the potential of the fairy tale and the folktale to reflect popular culture and convey universal truths. In these three intellectual fantasies, or fabulations, Calvino backs up absurd premises with almost documentary verisimilitude and narrates with the wide-eyed matter-of-factness of a child. *Our Ancestors* is pseudohistorical; Calvino uses the legendary past as a distancing device, a means of commenting indirectly on the present and the timeless. Notably, all three fantasies are set against a background of war, and two of them, *The Cloven Viscount* and *The Non-existent Knight*, are ridden with a hard, glittering violence more like that of children's cartoons than anything else. It is not irrelevant that Red Wolf, the legendary Resistance fighter of *The Path to the Nest of Spiders*, "belongs to the generation brought up on strip cartoons" and takes them quite seriously. So does Calvino, who often defends his departures into fantasy on the basis of its popular appeal and immediacy of communication.

The Cloven Viscount begins the trilogy in a blackly humorous vein. In this game of "just suppose," Medardo of Terralba, a seventeenth century nobleman, is split from head to crotch by a cannonball in a war against the Turks. He becomes a cartoonlike illustration of the split, or alienated, personality; there are allusions as well to Judeo-Christian dualism. One-half of the Viscount appears to have been lost or destroyed; the doctors on the battlefield save his other half, sending it, the evil or "Bad'un," as it comes to be called, home. Bad Medardo wreaks havoc on the countryside and its inhabitants, even burning down part of his own castle while attempting to dispose of his old nurse, Sebastiana. His terrorism, however, is for the most part more specialized. Driven by an obsession with his own halfness and wishing to imprint his image on a world that has split him, he bifurcates every living thing in his path. "'If only I could halve every whole thing like this,'" he says to his nephew while "stroking the convulsive half of an octopus, 'so that everyone could escape from his obtuse and ignorant wholeness.'" Halfness brings consciousness of one's alienation from the world and the self.

Eventually the Viscount's better half shows up. He is predictably and unbearably good and profoundly boring, although equally obsessed with halfness: "One understands the sorrow of every person and thing in the world at its own incompleteness." When whole, he "did not understand" the tragedy of the human condition, which he attempts to mitigate. The story has a fairy-tale ending through which, after a duel between the two halves over Pamela, a wench beloved of both, the brilliant Doctor Trelawney puts them back together. The narrator marvels in detail at the skill involved in the operation: the doctor's "great care to get all guts and arteries of both parts to correspond, and then a mile of bandages had tied them together. . . ." Once again a whole man, Medardo marries Pamela, and they live wisely, "having had the experience of both halves each on its own. . . ." He has a "happy life, many children and a just rule. Our life too change[s] for the better."

The allusion to Samuel Richardson's *Pamela* (1740-1741) is relevant, for this worthy squire, in living "wholly" ever after, lives above all "dully": The *story* is over. If the real life signified by wholeness is not "marvelous happiness," as the young narrator remarks, it is partly because of his state of mind. The narrator is the Viscount's nephew, on "the threshold of adolescence" by the end of the tale, whereupon he grows discontented "amid all this fervor of wholeness . . . growing sadder and more lacking."

In the introduction to the trilogy, Calvino provides a moral for the story: The Viscount's bifurcation is parabolic of modern alienation and mutilation. Certainly another is the brutality of war, conveyed in a starkly surreal landscape (however misperceived by the as yet uncloven Medardo): plains of "horses' carcasses, some supine with hooves to the sky, others prone with muzzles dug into the earth," and "a few limbs, fingers in particular, scattered over the stubble." (Says Medardo, "Every now and again I see a finger pointing our way. . . . What does that mean?") Yet another interpretation has been suggested by Gore Vidal: *The Cloven Viscount* is a "sendup of Plato and the idea of the whole." Calvino's main point in providing a moral is probably to stress what his tale does mean, but as allegory it spins off in many directions. The narrator's mood suggests that it is finally about the human and especially modern need for fictions which, like Calvino's disembodied fingers on a battleground, enigmatically point the way. As the tale ends, the narrator is conscious of loss and thus of his own incompleteness, and so remains "deep in the woods telling [himself] stories."

The intellectual's or artist's alienation is more explicitly the issue of *The Baron in the Trees*, the second novel in the trilogy. The protagonist is the eighteenth century Baron Cosimo Piovasco di Rondó, who, at the age of twelve, on June 15, in the midst of a family quarrel at dinner, defies all present by climbing into the trees, vowing never to come down.

The fantastic premise of the novel only thinly disguises its autobiographical nature; it is a fairy-tale version of Calvino's Resistance experience and bears comparison to *The Path to the Nest of Spiders*. Like Pin and his comrade, Cosimo finds that a certain imaginative aloofness from the world—in this case, the "natural" environment of the trees of Ombrosa, which, although rooted in earth, seem to touch the sky—paradoxically makes an effective commitment to it possible. As Cosimo's brother, meeting Voltaire in Paris, explains, "anyone who wants to see the earth properly must keep himself at a necessary distance from it." Voltaire's reply may well be Calvino's philosophy of life: "Once it was only Nature which produced living phenomena. . . . Now 'tis Reason."

In the revolt from his family, Cosimo rejects a life-style of aristocratic decadence. He must transcend both the grasping ambition of his father, who lives to regain the lapsed title of Duke of Ombrosa and thinks only of "genealogies and successions and family rivalries and alliances"—and the sanctified alienation of his sister Battista, "a kind of stay-at-home nun" confined to the pleasure of dismaying her brothers with sadistic cookery—snails' heads artfully arranged in wire mesh, grasshopper claw tarts, rats' liver pâté.

The trees are less an escape from this microcosm of monomaniacs than they are avenues to the world—or, rather, to a newly opened world. For the first time, Cosimo can mix freely with people of all classes, from charcoal burners to robber barons to the noble family next door, with whom he can talk rather than feud, as before. Roving bands of waiflike fruit thieves accept him as a fellow outsider and then as a leader. His distanced perspective allows him to perceive and solve engineering problems and to organize a voluntary fire brigade. Saving Ombrosa from incendiary destruction, Cosimo discovers joy in fighting for a common goal and simultaneously teaches the people to unite in moments of danger. He repels an invasion of wolves from the Alps, fights off Turkish pirates, and reforms the vicious brigand, Gian dei Brughi, by supplying him with novels. As his brother, the narrator, explains, "the more determined [Cosimo] was to hide away in his den of branches, the more he felt the need to create new links with the human race." He therefore founds or joins such "associations and confraternities of trades and professions" as the Conscientious Capmakers, the Enlightened Skin Tanners, and the Masons. Indeed, he becomes quite reconciled with his family, who are better for dealing with his rebellion, and he frequently watches over them from a mulberry branch with a view through his mother's window.

In the trees, Cosimo has more time to read and think than his earthbound fellows and begins a Rousseauistic "Project for the Constitution of an Ideal State in the Trees." For his various accomplishments, he is acknowledged by Denis Diderot and paid homage by Napoleon. The utopian scheme, however, remains incomplete. Beginning it as "a treatise on laws and governments," he loses his point as his storytelling impulse takes over and out pours "a rough sketch of adventures, duels, and erotic tales, the latter inserted in a chapter on matrimonial rights." It is the texture of Cosimo's life, or his story in its eccentric variety of adventures, enterprises, and love affairs, that counts.

The same childlike ingenuousness which made the first two novels engaging and believable down to the last detail, informs most of *The Baron in the Trees*. Sustained at greater length is the Hemingwayesque fidelity to empirical detail. Cosimo might be Nick Adams preparing to fish—such is the intentness and precision with which Calvino compels the reader to concentrate on the matter at hand, whether it be the fabrication of a suspended sleeping bag or the construction of an irrigation system. Thus, the message of commitment, however obvious, is never obtrusive. What one remembers is the clarity and naturalness of arboreal life and the symbiosis of individual, society, and nature that seems illusory only at the end of the book.

In the last paragraph, the narrator, now perhaps Calvino, succumbs to a radical failure of belief. Looking at a sky left empty by the dying Cosimo and the changing times, he asks himself if Ombrosa ever really existed, if

> that mesh of leaves and twigs of fork and froth, minute and endless, with the sky glimpsed only in sudden specks and splinters . . . was embroidered on nothing, like this thread of ink which I have let run on for page after page . . . until it splutters and bursts into a last senseless cluster of words, ideas, dreams, and so ends.

In an introduction to the 1965 scholastic edition of the book, Calvino asserted that Cosimo is an allegorical figure for the poet. The trees are therefore his medium, providing a language for social and political engagement. *The Baron in the Trees* is more than a portrait of the artist, but it is Calvino's first fiction to examine the semantic possibilities of his subject of engagement, to focus directly on the relations between literature and empirical reality, as Joann Cannon has pointed out. The long Gian dei Brughi episode, a benign parody of eighteenth century critical theory concerning the moral influence of literature, is a case in point. Cosimo lends Alain-René Lesage's *Histoire de Gil Blas de Santillane* (1715-1735; *The History of Gil Blas of Santillane*, 1716, 1735) to the chief of brigands, who becomes hooked on novels and is especially taken with Richardson's *Clarissa* (1748), which brings out "a disposition long latent in him; a yearning for the cozy habits of family life, for relations, for sentiments . . . a sense of virtue . . ." and vice. Unfortunately, the result of his conversion is that he is caught and sentenced; yet, poised to hang, he wishes only to know the ending of Henry Fielding's *Jonathan Wilde* (1743), which Cosimo sorrowfully tells him. "Thank you. Like me! Goodby!" replies de Brughi as he himself kicks away his support and is strangled. Calvino's charming mixture of irony with good humor both supports and qualifies the eighteenth century dictum: Literature delights and thus instructs, but the real-life result may be imperfect (even if somewhat poetic) justice.

In the more minor key that ends the book are other hints that Calvino questions its premise. In contrast to Pin and the Viscount's nephew, who get no further than puberty by the ends of their stories, Cosimo's brother grows old and dull and, as narrator, begins to question this very role and its sources. As the story progresses and as Cosimo becomes more renowned in rumor and legend, the narrator feels more distant from valid representations. In a

French almanac, in a chapter on monsters and between the Hermaphrodite and the Siren, he discovers a figure of his brother "all covered in leaves, with a long beard and . . . tail, eating a locust." Cosimo himself is partly responsible for such distortions, his brother observes: "So many and so incredible were the tales Cosimo told about his activities in the woods during the war" that no one version can be accepted outright. Cosimo at times becomes imbecile with erotic passion, is disturbed by the French Revolution and its aftermath, and grows disconsolate with age. Even *his* imagination fails to keep pace with events.

This theme of the failure of imagination to correspond with external reality has its other side: the view of literature as true empirically in the experience of the people who, in part, create it, as a collective and infinitely variable fantasy—a view that Calvino takes up with gusto in his later works. In the two years between *The Cloven Viscount* and *The Baron in the Trees*, Calvino compiled and edited *Italian Folktales*, a project that deepened his critical interest in the ways tales are generated orally. *The Baron in the Trees* reflects this interest in the way the truth of Cosimo's life is seen to depend on context, on the community in which it flourished; thus, Cosimo and his dream exist only so long and so far as Ombrosa does. The bizarre legends that dismay his brother can thus be seen to affirm the effectiveness of Cosimo's arboreal commitment. This is the case even to the end, when some English aeronauts passing by on an experimental balloon flight are made partly responsible for Cosimo's rather spectacular comic apotheosis. However inadvertently, through some fumbling with and dropping of an anchor, they take the dying idealist with them into the sky. The primitive "poem" on the family tombstone hits the note typical of Calvino at his best on this theme: "'Cosimo Piovasco di Rondò—Lived in Trees—Always loved earth—Went into sky.'"

The Non-existent Knight takes up where *The Baron in the Trees* ends—with a study of being, nothingness, and semantics. The trees of Ombrosa finally seem no more substantial than words "embroidered on a void"; Agilulf, the nonexistent knight, personifies the metaphysics implied in that imaginary landscape. His complete title, "Agilulf Emo Bertrandin of the Guildivern and of the Others of Corbentraz and Sura, Knight of Selimpia Citeriore and Fez," suggests his need for substantiation, for he is a void, an empty suit of white armor from which echoes a metallic voice standing for essence or identity. He is a sort of walking embodiment of René Descartes' famous dictum, *Cogito, ergo sum* (I think, therefore I am). Agilulf's nonexistence calls to mind just about everything from Platonic forms to Cartesian rationalism, from Miguel de Cervantes' *Don Quixote de la Mancha* (1605, 1615) to T. S. Eliot's "The Hollow Men" (1925) and Jean-Paul Sartre's *L'Être et le néant* (1943; *Being and Nothingness*, 1956). Calvino's touch is light and witty, however, as usual. His tales are novels of ideas in the briefest of senses; for the most part, he drops philosophical connections as he takes them up, generating sparks, flashes, and kaleidoscopically transformed patterns rather than deepening levels of meaning.

In devoted service to Charlemagne, who takes his holy wars far less seriously than does Agilulf, the nonexistent knight is dismayingly perfect. He is thus detested by the other knights—except for Raimbaut, a novice who takes him for a role model. His unpopularity is increased by his absurd attempts to share in the community life. He does not eat, of course, but insists on observing all forms with rigor, sitting interminably at table and slicing his meat into tiny, uniform pieces. Agilulf's passion for perfection makes him obnoxiously unconquerable in war—and love. He is, strangely enough, the perfect ladies' man. Although he cannot love, he more than satisfies the noble widow Priscilla, entering her bed "fully armed from head to foot and stretched out taut as if on a tomb." "Don't you even loosen the sword from its scabbard?" asks Priscilla. "Amorous passion knows no half measures," answers Agilulf. Priscilla shuts her eyes "in ecstasy."

To solve two problems at once, Charlemagne assigns Agilulf a squire named Gurduloo—or Omoboo, or Martinzoo, or "Cheese," depending upon who is addressing him. If Agilulf is pure identity, form, or idea, his Sancho Panza is elemental protean substance or pure existence in a state of continuous transformation. He confuses himself with whatever he touches. When he drinks soup, he becomes soup and is to be drunk in turn, "the world being nothing but a vast shapeless mass of soup in which all things [are] dissolved." Together, the characters Agilulf and Gurduloo bring up a theme that Calvino will pursue later: the confusion of subject and object and the arbitrary nature of names and categories. The vaguely ancient, mythical quality of Charlemagne's era becomes Calvino's excuse to evoke a major dilemma of twentieth century epistemology. In the era when this story took place, writes the narrator, it was common "to find names and thoughts and forms and institutions that corresponded to nothing in existence," yet the world at the same time was "polluted with objects and capacities and persons who lacked any name or distinguishing mark."

Much of the book is a lusty parody of the stuff of Ariosto, whose mode becomes a vehicle for charming takeoffs on ideologies fundamental to Western culture: Judeo-Christian dualism, the cult of virginity and purity in general, the notion of progress, the idealization of war—"the passing of more and more dented objects from hand to hand." A complicated plot replete with fancifully misplaced identities, and through which Agilulf finally ceases to "non exist," is also reminiscent of Ariosto. Awarded knighthood for having saved the virgin Sophronia from bandits, Agilulf's precarious being depends upon the lady-in-question's immaculate virtue. Torrismond, a competing knight, swears at the crucial time that Sophronia is his mother and, therefore, no virgin. As it turns out several subplots later, Sophronia is really Torrismond's half sister and a virgin after all—until he deflowers her under the impression that she is a nun recently forced into a sultan's harem. The good news comes too late for Agilulf, however, who, thinking that his identity is inauthentic—a long title embroidered on a void—loses the will to exist and vanishes.

This resolution collapses the primary triangle of the plot. The young Raimbaut falls in love with a knight who turns out to be Bradamante, a young woman, who in turn falls in love with the nonexistent knight—until the latter bequeaths his armor to the younger, more authentic man and Bradamante is thus free to find her true love embodied in it. The most surprising turn of plot, however, occurs in the subtext, which emerges in the fourth chapter and gradually frames the story proper.

The Non-existent Knight is narrated by an ingenue different from Calvino's previous ones: a Sister Theodora, who had been assigned to tell this story as a penance. Some very funny false notes are sounded when she protests her inadequacy for lack of contact with soldiers. Outside of "religious ceremonies, triduums, novenas, gardening, harvesting, vintaging, whippings, slavery, incest, fires, hangings, invasion, sacking, rape and pestilence, we [nuns] have had no experience." Her comments have to do, predictably enough, with the gap between her words and the external world. Ironically, her "assiduous penance" of "seeking words and . . . meditating on ultimate truths" works like Agilulf's strenuous willing of himself into significant being: It ends in self-consciousness and a consequent failure of will and imagination. Sister Theodora experiences writer's block with symptoms anticipating what John Barth called a postmodernist "literature of exhaustion": "The pen merely grates in dusty ink, and not a drop of life flows, and life is all outside, outside the window, outside oneself. . . ."

Fortunately, Sister Theodora is unlike the nonexistent knight in that she has substantial resources on which to draw, an existence apart from words and significations. Pushing the tale precipitously to its conclusion, she confesses that she is really the Amazon Bradamante, yet a Bradamante changed radically by her discipline as convent scribe. She joined the convent out of "desperate love" for the ideal Agilulf but now burns for "the young and passionate Raimbaut"—in all his imperfect but vital reality—and rushes from the convent walls to meet him. Her new aesthetic, which corresponds with her new love (Raimbaut in Agilulf's armor), insists on the interdependence of art and life, if not exactly *littérature engagée*: "A page is good only when we turn it and find life urging along, confusing every page in the book. The pen rushes on, urged by the same joy that makes me course the open road."

If—or because—words fail to make present an external reality (and a desperate Sister Theodora resorts at one point to drawing word pictures), they must create exits to new worlds. Lest the conclusion seem a contradiction of *The Baron in the Trees*, Calvino has Theodora/Bradamante admit that "after affrays and affairs and blighted hopes," she will "always return to this cloister" of art, which, after all, was responsible for changing her mind. He thus posits a symbiosis of essence and substance, words and things, self and world.

A combination of fabulation and metafiction, *The Non-existent Knight* sets the stage for Calvino's later works in at least three ways. One is deliberate anachronism—the allusion to the legendary past in a story with a transparently contemporary outlook—to achieve a timelessness of reference and appeal. A related strategy is the playful and multileveled parody, which extends to the acts of writing and reading, turning literature, whatever the genre, into an epistemological and semantic game. Finally, there is the mixture of literary and popular sources to confuse the borders of high and low culture. In general, the deliberate confusion of times, genres, and cultures expresses Calvino's mature view of the world. However reminiscent of Gurduloo's "vast shapeless mass of soup" in which things continuously dissolve and begin again, *The Non-existent Knight* is up to date, as Calvino stresses. It is meant to address the future.

Similar concerns inform *Cosmicomics* and its sequel, *T Zero*. Neither short-story collections nor novels (although perhaps a cross between them)—nor even fictions in the sense of representations of the empirical world—these books combine contemporary science and fantasy in a completely new way, to imagine what could not have been and never will be (unlike science fiction, which imagines what might be). At the same time, they domesticate scientific theories that are quoted or summarized before each narrative, much as the earlier Calvino "realized" fairy-tale premises. "All at One Point" explains Edwin P. Hubble's big bang theory in terms of Mrs. $Ph(i)Nk_0$'s spontaneous desire to make noodles for everyone. This desire, verbalized at a certain moment ("Oh, if I only had some room, how I'd like to make some noodles for you boys!"), causes everyone to think space and time into existence, "the space that her round arms would occupy, moving backward and forward with the rolling pin over the dough," the space for the flour for the dough, the fields for the wheat for the flour, and so on, until a "true outburst of general love" has initiated the concept of space, "space itself, and time, and universal gravitation, and the gravitating universe." In so humanizing science, Calvino makes strange new worlds comfortable and inhabitable—in contrast to much science fiction, which exploits its capacity to estrange and dislocate.

Also in contrast to most science fiction is the treatment of time. *Cosmicomics* and *T Zero* trace the creation of the universe rather than transporting readers into the future. The stories correlate the billions of years covered with natural stages in a human life span, conveying vividly, for example, the sense that Qfwfq, the narrator, was "just a child" in the dark before the sun's condensation. He is quite adolescent as a mollusk in love for the first time. A number of "families" run through the equivalent of several generations.

In another sense, these stories do not trace anything, however, for they are randomly arranged. The randomness exists in part to avoid the teleological perspective of most evolutionary theory. In this universe, there are really no endings or final causes, only present moments erupting into new beginnings. The protean hero Qfwfq exists only to be transformed in an unending process, and the random arrangement of his various formations makes the reader adapt to dislocation with him. Qfwfq's nonchalance makes such jolts quite easy. As he so simply puts it, "I went on my way. . . ."

Qfwfq's radical openness to experience marks him as another of Calvino's "children," wide-eyed and matter-of-fact at the same time. He and his family of protean beings are childlike in another way: They are cartoon characters in words, as Calvino implies in the title of *Cosmicomics* and as he shows by "drawing" the story "The Origin of the Birds," in *T Zero*. He has compared Qfwfq to Popeye, the partly domesticated sailor, and certainly Qfwfq is just as "real," experiencing narcissism, desire, and love in "The Spiral," making his mark on the world in "A Sign in Space," confronting competitors in sign making, and betting on future events. Throughout his bewildering transformations, and much like a cartoon character, Qfwfq remains unruffled. As Calvino seems to say, all that is life. His cartoons show what it is like to embody a meson, a dinosaur, a mollusk, a racing car. They educate the imagination by strengthening its capacity and so provide a kind of insurance against future shock.

Throughout *Cosmicomics* and increasingly in *T Zero*, Calvino delights in drawing out abstract concepts in semiotics, reflecting the theories of Roland Barthes and the fictional methods of Jorge Luis Borges. In "A Sign in Space," Qfwfq makes the first sign in the universe. A rival, Kgwgk, erases his sign and replaces it with his own, so that Qfwfq must make a new, competitive sign, and so on, so that language, style, and art are born. Eventually (and reflecting the media blitz), the universe is covered with a meaningless scrawl obscuring space and making distinctions between sign and sign, and between sign and space, nonexistent.

In three novels written in the 1970's, Calvino continued to explore the relationship between signs and the reality that they are supposed to represent. *Invisible Cities*, the first of these three metafictions, declares its concern with semiology at the outset, erecting a frame tale that stands for Barthes's concept of the world as text. The teller of the body of the narrative is revealed to be Marco Polo, who re-creates or imagines his journeys to countless fabulous cities. The listener is Kublai Khan, now old and confined to his fabled court, who cannot travel to the vast kingdom he possesses except through Marco Polo's tales. As suggested in the title, the outside world cannot live except through the dialogue that composes the book itself. Calvino provides no other characters, no plot, and no adventures other than the brief accounts of the cities themselves to detract from this metafictional perspective.

Kublai Khan's (and the reader's) part in this dialogue is to search for a pattern in Marco Polo's fifty-five cities, varied according to categories such as "cities and memory," "cities and desire," "thin cities," "cities and eyes," "cities and names," and "continuous cities." Listening or reading is made into a game or puzzle standing for the human need to seek out order and meaning in an otherwise random world. As in *Cosmicomics* and *T Zero*, the possibility of moves, the "catalogue of forms," is "endless: until every shape has found its cities, new cities will continually begin." In *Invisible Cities*, Calvino applies to narrative alternatives his view of life as infinitely transformable. He also attempts to rejuvenate the written medium by portraying the situation and capturing the mood of oral narrative—consciously repeating, establishing rhythm, to the Khan's delight, in tapestries of words and patterns for their own sake.

As Marco Polo and Kublai Khan converse, the Venetian learns the Khan's Tartar language. In the beginning, Marco Polo can recount his journeys only in pantomime—with gestures, cries, and objects he has collected along the way. Although the Khan finds "the connection between them and the places visited . . . uncertain," and must to a great extent create his own story, Marco Polo's mute representations have "the power of emblems." After he learns to speak in the local idiom, communication is more precise but strangely "less happy than in the past." Emblems, however primitive, are more eloquent than conventional language.

The Castle of Crossed Destinies, Calvino's next metafiction, employs tarot cards as an emblematic language more evocative than words. In the frame story, several pilgrims come together at a castle and, trying to tell one another their tales, find that they have been struck dumb. One pilgrim hits on an idea that had come to obsess Calvino: He uses cards, with the aid of grimaces and gestures, to represent himself and his adventures. With the tarot's four suits—coins, cups, clubs, and swords—and the arcana, twenty-one picture cards capable of suggesting multiple interpretations, Calvino again tells a story about telling stories—about the inexhaustible resources of narrative. Two decks are used in two sections: In "Castle," the richly beautiful deck painted by Bonifacio Bembo for the Dukes of Milan in the fifteenth century, and in "Tavern," the popular *ancien tarot de Marseille* from the eighteenth century. The cards are reproduced in the margins of the book. To stress his use of pictorial, popular, and communal art forms, Calvino had hoped to create a third section, called "Motel," to be narrated through fragments of comic strips.

As it is, he almost succeeds in his plan to use every card in the pack—in a sort of pictorial crossword puzzle through which each story is a reading of a vertical or horizontal card sequence, with the card-stories interlocking and permutating *ad infinitum*. *The Castle of Crossed Destinies* comes close to being Calvino's monomyth, his answer to James Joyce's *Finnegans Wake* (1939), cross-referencing tales of Faust, Macbeth, Hamlet, Lear, Oedipus, Helen of Troy, the Marquis de Sade, and Ariosto's Roland in a world animated by the elements of war, love, and magic. In spite of the obvious temptation toward the esoteric and alinear, Calvino carries through with much of his usual simplicity and literalness. Still, these tales lack the concreteness of his previous invisible cities, as Calvino virtually admits in an afterword: He had seen in the cards a perfect "machine for constructing stories" and, after exhausting them and himself in the process, published the book "to be free of" an obsession not far from the nonexistent knight's intricate, empty rituals, the "diabolical idea" of "conjuring up all the stories that could be contained in a tarot deck."

After six years of silence, Calvino emerged from this diabolic/penitential formalism in the mood of Sister Theodora's abrupt revelation: He rushed out, like Bradamante, burning for young and passionate life. *If on a Winter's Night a Traveler* is on one level another tour de force; it is composed entirely of beginnings, with one set inside and precipitating another, as in *The Arabian Nights' Entertainments*. It is also about fiction as a transaction with the reader, and in that sense engaged with the world beyond the page. *If on a Winter's Night a Traveler* dramatizes, literalizes, and so becomes a kind of love affair with (and among) readers.

It is an active human element, in part—the felt presence of living characters—that Calvino's earlier metafictions fail to communicate. In *Invisible Cities* and *The Castle of Crossed Destinies*, Calvino breaks with his premises, however theoretically perfect their representation—most notably in the use of ancient emblems to create an equivalence between card reading and taletelling, between art and life. *If on a Winter's Night a Traveler* has rough edges, at least partly because it is told almost completely in the present tense, like his first book, and in the second person. From the first word, "you," the Reader, are the hero of "Italo Calvino's new novel," which "you" are beginning to read. "You" are therefore the most living, breathing character ever invented, literalized into your own story—as opposed to the mechanical plots of the mass media: "Tell the others right away, 'No, I don't want to watch TV!'"

Such a premise is so blatant as to seem downright silly, which is what Calvino intends. His usual naïve narrator is now a transparent parody of himself, a myopically concerned but quite real "Calvino" peering out of the page. Certainly, in a sense, this book is his most bookish. The premise is based, after all, on a mere extension of Structuralism and semiotics (responsible for the premises of his previous metafictions) toward the reader-response emphasis of poststructuralism. It again presumes Barthes's world as text: Ten novels from countries around the world are telescoped into one. The difference is in the way it directs characterized—and real—readers toward the unwritten world, through an unfolding series of beginnings into realms "somewhere beyond the book, beyond the author, beyond the conventions of writing" toward a voice "from the unsaid, from what the world has not yet said of itself and does not yet have the words to say."

In fact, the dramatic tension of the book comes from its conflict between Calvino's self-confessed obsession with print and his desire to reach whatever lies beyond it. The plot is an editor's nightmare of "pages, lines, words, whirling in a dust storm"; it is engaged with the politics of print—with terrorist organizations, conspiracies, censors, and the like, all militating against the writer. The plot is generated by a plot by the character Ermes Marana, the brilliant translator and founder of OEPHLW (Organization for the Electronic Production of Homogenized Literary Works), to "flood the world" with a "literature of apocrypha, of false attributions, of imitations and counterfeits and pastiches." Marana, representing the mass media, has paralyzed the world's best-selling author, Silas Flannery, upon whose creativity much of the world's economy, and thus world peace, depends. The fate of civilization hangs on the word, on Flannery's ability (as a fan of Snoopy) to get beyond "It was a dark and stormy night. . . ." Calvino has therefore returned to the battleground of his first novels—transformed, however, into the media blitz of the 1980's. This is the world war as he sees it for the present. If the medium is the message, the "Fascist machine" is whoever made this chaos in the first place. This is not Marana but Calvino, or his persona's diabolic mania for mechanically contrived order, leading to the cosmic scrawl or entropy of "A Sign in Space."

What redeems the real Calvino is not his contemporary self-awareness, which is the root of the problem, but his ability to lose himself, as in his first fantasies, in the game with the reader taken as far as it can go. Behind his main gimmick is, as usual, a theoretical source, Barthes's *Le Plaisir du texte* (1973; *The Pleasure of the Text*, 1975), which correlates reading with lovemaking. In a search through ten fragmentary novels for the true text of *If on a Winter's Night a Traveler*, Marana's machinations having jumbled and displaced the lot of them, the Reader discovers the Other Reader, Ludmilla, who is searching for the same book—or thing. A love story develops that extends Calvino's romance with the reader into one between readers. The diametrical opposite of her sister Lotaria, whose computer-assisted thesis catalogs Flannery's words as he writes them, Ludmilla is the "common," or naïve, reader, for whom reading is a creation and a search. The "circuits of her mind" transform the "current" of reading into "what in her is most personal and incommunicable." In present-tense moments between the pseudonovels, "you," as Reader, are allowed by your (however passive) rival "Calvino" to "read" the furniture of her apartment, her kitchen utensils, her body, and so on, until she "skims" your "index," and so on. Hence, the real reader is to learn how common, how true to life, and how vital reading is.

According to the narrator, the crucial resemblance between reading and lovemaking is that "within both of them times and spaces open, different from measurable time and space." It is in these open passages, Calvino shows, that transactions between solitary readers take place. He extends a concept of reading as an act of becoming by showing how the shared activity of reading brings individuals together. As early as the thirty-second page, reading has become a dialogue. Hoping that the book has become "an instrument, a channel of communication, a rendezvous," "Calvino" asks, "What is more natural than [that] a solidarity, a complicity, a bond should be established between Reader and Reader, thanks to the book?" The book ends in "your" (plural) marriage, a commitment to the common activity and cause of reading. In the final chapter, a "great double bed" receives "your parallel readings."

The marriage stands for the existence of a larger context, a community of individual, parallel readers "out there" or underground, resisting, in their passive, private way, formulation and system—the tyranny of plots, codes, propaganda, Marana's literature of "bad faith." Thus, Calvino is back where he started in *The Path to the Nest of Spiders*, with a unique form of *littérature engagée*: The partisans' movement has become a "reading resistance." Even the government censor goes home every night, as he says, "to abandon myself to reading, like that distant unknown woman," Ludmilla, the common reader, and Marana himself has to admit that when he is reading, "something happens over which I have no power." This happening, as the censor explains, "is the limit that even the most omnipotent police force cannot broach."

If on a Winter's Night a Traveler admirably sums up Calvino's career: His has been a search for a "true text," a medium of engagement, and he seems to have found it. Throughout his various transformations, he has made the reader's experience his primary concern, his secondary one being language's power to change the mind—by charming imagination into a life of its own.

Major publications other than long fiction

SHORT FICTION: *Ultimo viene il corvo*, 1949 (*Adam, One Afternoon, and Other Stories*, 1957); *L'entrata in guerra*, 1954; *Fiabe italiane*, 1956 (*Italian Fables*, 1959; *Italian Folktales*, 1975); *I racconti*, 1958 (partial translation, *The Watcher and Other Stories*, 1971); *Marcovaldo: Ovvero, Le stagioni in città*, 1963 (*Marcovaldo: The Seasons in the City*, 1983); *Le cosmicomiche*, 1965 (*Cosmicomics*, 1968); *Ti con zero*, 1967 (*T Zero*, 1969); *Difficult Loves*, 1984.

NONFICTION: "Main Currents in Italian Fiction Today," in *Italian Quarterly*, Spring/Summer, 1960; *Cesare Pavese: Lettere, 1926-1950*, 1966 (editor); *Vittorini*, 1968.

Bibliography

Bottino, G. P. *Calvino*, 1967.
Bonura, Giuseppe. *Invito alla lettura di Calvino*, 1972.
Calligaris, Contardo. *Italo Calvino*, 1973.
Cannon, Joann. "Literary Signification: An Analysis of Calvino's Trilogy," in *Symposium*. XXXIV (1980), pp. 3-12.

De Lauretis, Teresa. "Narrative Discourse in Calvino: Praxis or Poiesis?" in *PMLA*. XC (1975), pp. 414-425.
De Mara, Nicholas A. "Pathway to Calvino: Fantasy and Reality in *Il sentiero dei nidi di ragno*," in *Italian Quarterly*. XIV, no. 55 (Winter, 1971), pp. 25-49.
Heiney, Donald. "Calvino and Borges: Some Implications of Fantasy," in *Mundus Artium*. II, no. 1 (Winter, 1968), pp. 66-76.
Vidal, Gore. "Fabulous Calvino," in *New York Review of Books*. XXI (May 30, 1974), pp. 13-21.
Woodhouse, J. R. *Italo Calvino*, 1968.
_____."Italo Calvino and the Rediscovery of a Genre," in *Italian Quarterly*. XII, no. 45 (Summer, 1968), pp. 45-60.

Linda C. Badley

ALBERT CAMUS

Born: Mondovi, Algeria; November 7, 1913
Died: Near Sens, France; January 4, 1960

Principal long fiction
L'Étranger, 1942 (*The Stranger*, 1946); *La Peste*, 1947 (*The Plague*, 1948); *La Chute*, 1956 (*The Fall*, 1957); *La Mort heureuse*, 1971 (written 1936-1938; *A Happy Death*, 1972).

Other literary forms
Albert Camus considered his vocation to be that of novelist, but the artist in him was always at the service of his dominant passion, moral philosophy. As a result, Camus was led to cultivate several other literary forms which could express his central concerns as a moralist: the short story, drama, and nonfiction forms such as the philosophical essay and political journalism, all of which he practiced with enough distinction to be influential among his contemporaries. Moreover, these works were generally written side by side with his novels; it was Camus' customary procedure, throughout his brief writing career, always to be working on two or more compositions simultaneously, each expressing a different facet of the same philosophical issue. Thus, within a year of the publication of his most celebrated novel, *The Stranger*, there appeared a long essay entitled *Le Mythe de Sisyphe* (1942; *The Myth of Sisyphus*, 1955), a meditation on the meaning of life in an irrational universe that began with the assertion that the only serious question confronting modern man is the question of suicide and concluded with a daring argument that found in the legend of Sisyphus a strangely comforting allegory of the human condition. Sisyphus, who becomes in Camus' hands an exemplary Existentialist, spent his days in the endlessly futile task of pushing a boulder to the top of a hill from which it always rolled down again. Every human life is expended as meaninglessly as that of Sisyphus, Camus argues, yet one must conceive of Sisyphus as happy, because he was totally absorbed by his assigned task and found sufficient satisfaction in its daily accomplishment without requiring that it also have some enduring significance. There are close links between such reasoning and the ideas that inform *The Stranger*, but it is erroneous to argue, as some have, that *The Myth of Sisyphus* is an "explanation" of *The Stranger*. The former work is, rather, a discussion of similar themes in a different form and from a different perspective, in accordance with Camus' unique way of working as a writer.

That unique way of working produced another long philosophical essay, *L'Homme révolté* (1951; *The Rebel*, 1956), which has affinities with the novel *The Plague* as well as with four plays written and produced in the 1940's: *Caligula* (1944; English translation, 1958); *Le Malentendu* (1944; *The Mis-*

understanding, 1958); L'État de siège (1948; State of Siege, 1958), and Les Justes (1949; The Just Assassins, 1958)—each of which is related by certain thematic elements to the two novels that Camus published in the same period. His earliest political journalism, written before 1940 and dealing with the problems of his native Algeria, attracted little attention, but his work for the underground newspaper Combat, during and after World War II, achieved considerable celebrity, and the best articles were later collected in a volume widely read and admired. During the civil war in Algeria, in the 1950's, Camus again entered the lists as a political journalist, and because he was by then indisputably Algeria's most famous man of letters, his articles were of major importance at the time, though highly controversial and much less widely approved than the wartime pieces from Combat. Camus produced only one collection of short stories, L'Exil et le royaume (1957; Exile and the Kingdom, 1958), composed during the same years as the novel The Fall, but those stories have been very popular and are regarded by many as among the finest short stories published in France in the twentieth century. The volume is particularly noteworthy because it offers the only examples Camus ever published of fiction composed in the third-person mode of the omniscient narrator. The first three of his published novels are variations of the limited-perspective first-person narrative.

Deeply involved in the theater throughout his career, both as writer and director, Camus adapted for the French stage the work of foreign novelists Fyodor Dostoevski and William Faulkner, and of playwrights of Spain's Golden Age, including Pedro Calderón de la Barca and Lope de Vega Carpio. These adaptations have all been published and form part of Camus' contribution to the theater.

Achievements

To the immediate postwar public, not only in France but also throughout Europe, Albert Camus seemed a writer of unassailable stature. Although Camus himself repudiated the designation, he was regarded worldwide as one of the two principal exponents of Existentialism (the other was Jean-Paul Sartre), the single most influential philosophical movement of the twentieth century. Indeed, the Existentialist worldview—according to which the individual human being "must assume ultimate responsibility for his acts of free will without any certain knowledge of what is right or wrong or good or bad"—has profoundly shaped the values of countless people who have never read Camus or Sartre.

In the 1950's, Camus was widely admired not only as a writer but also as a hero of the war against Fascism, a spokesman for the younger generation, and a guardian of the moral conscience of Europe. That reputation was consecrated in 1957 with the award to Camus of the Nobel Prize for Literature, at the remarkably young age of forty-four. Yet, as has happened to many another recipient of the Nobel Prize, the award seemed almost a signal of the rapid deflation of his renown. He suddenly came under severe criticism for his stand on the Algerian Civil War, was attacked as self-righteous and artistically sterile, and was finally denounced as irrelevant by the new literary generation then coming to prominence, who were weary of moral issues and more concerned with aesthetic questions of form and language. Camus' fame and influence appeared to many to have suffered an irreversible decline by the end of the decade, at least in France. (In America, the case was different: Made more accessible by the "paperback revolution," Camus' works were enormously influential among American college students in the 1960's.) There were those who suggested that the automobile accident that took his life in January of 1960 was a disguised blessing, sparing him the pain of having to witness the collapse of his own career.

It is true that, in the 1980's, a generation after the height of Camus' fame, French writers and intellectuals show no influence of Camus in what they write and scant critical interest in his works. Still, his works enjoy a steady sale among the French public, and outside France, especially in America, interest in Camus continues to be strong. There has been an inevitable sifting of values, a crystallization of what it is, in Camus' work, that still has the power to survive and what no longer speaks to the current generation. It has become clear, for example, that his philosophical essays are too closely tied to the special circumstances that occasioned them; in spite of a few brilliant passages, those essays now seem rambling and poorly argued as well as irrelevant to the concerns of the 1980's. Camus' theater, too, has held up poorly, being too abstract and inhuman to engage the emotions of an audience. While his plays are still sometimes performed on both sides of the Atlantic, they seem likely to be forgotten by century's end. It is his fiction that still seems most alive, both in characters and ideas, and that still presents to the reader endlessly fascinating enigmas which delight the imagination and invite repeated readings.

Although the total number of his fictional works is small, those works are, in both form and content, among the most brilliantly original contributions to the art of fiction produced anywhere in the twentieth century. In particular, Camus expressed through fiction, more powerfully and more memorably than anyone else in his time, the painful moral and spiritual dilemmas of modern man: evil, alienation, meaninglessness, and death. He invented techniques and created characters by which he was able to make manifest, in unforgettable terms, the eternal struggle of Everyman for some shred of dignity and happiness. His stories have accordingly taken on some of the haunting quality, and the prestige, of myths. For that reason, it seems safe to predict that it is Camus' fiction which represents his greatest achievement—an achievement that will endure long after his philosophical musings and political arguments have been forgotten.

Biography

Though born in the interior village of Mondovi, near Constantine, Albert Camus was actually brought up in the big city, in a working-class suburb of Algiers. His widowed mother, who was from Algiers, took her two sons back there to live after her husband was killed, early in World War I. Albert, the younger of the two sons, was not yet a year old when his father was killed, and he was to grow up with a need for relationships with older men, apparently to replace the father he never had. It was important to Camus that his father's forebears had emigrated *by choice* to Algeria from France in the nineteenth century, since it made him feel that his roots were authentically both French and Algerian. Because his mother was of Spanish extraction, Camus felt himself to be even more authentically Algerian, for Spanish blood gave him his share of that passionate Mediterranean temperament which he felt made French Algeria distinctive and unique. It comes as no surprise, therefore, that the great bulk of Camus' writing is set in Algeria or relates directly to that country. Being Algerian was the central fact of Camus' consciousness.

In his early twenties, he began to write essays for a leftist political journal published in Algiers; his subject was the political and economic plight of Algeria in its role as a colony of France. During those same years, he helped to found a theater group, for which he acted, directed, and did some writing, and he was a candidate for an advanced degree in philosophy at the University of Algiers. At times, he had to interrupt his studies because of ill health; he had contracted tuberculosis in 1930, at the age of seventeen, and was subject to periodic attacks from it for the rest of his life. When only twenty-one, he made a rather impulsive marriage that ended in separation within a year and eventual divorce. He worked at a number of odd jobs before becoming a full-time journalist, and he was active enough in politics in the 1930's, to have become, for a few months, a member of the Algerian Communist Party. Altogether, his Algerian youth had been a difficult and turbulent experience, yet it had also been a time of growth and self-discovery, and he looked back on those years, ever after, with a special nostalgia for the sun, sand, sea, and simplicity of life which he felt had formed him and made him what he had become.

Early in 1940, with a war in progress and the newspaper for which he worked closed down, Camus found himself forced to leave Algeria in order to make a living. He went to Paris to work for a Paris newspaper—a job procured for him by his older friend Pascal Pia, with whom he had worked on the Algiers newspaper before it folded. Within a year, the Paris job ended, and Camus, who had married again, returned to Algeria with his wife. They lived in Oran, his wife's hometown, and while she worked as a teacher, Camus worked at his writing projects, completing both the novel *The Stranger* and the essay *The Myth of Sisyphus* and arranging for their publication in Paris by Gallimard. By late 1942, Camus was so ill with tuberculosis that his wife persuaded him to seek a more favorable climate in the mountainous area of central France, which was then unoccupied territory. He went there alone, to continue writing, and found himself cut off from all contact with his family when the Allies invaded North Africa and the Germans occupied the rest of France as a defensive measure. During this period of isolation, Camus began to sketch out his next novel, *The Plague*. He also began to make frequent trips to Paris to see literary friends. His publisher, Gallimard, not only sent him royalties for *The Stranger*, which sold quite well, but also helped Camus further by putting him on the Gallimard payroll as a reader—a position he enjoyed so much that he continued to fulfill it for the rest of his life. Late in 1943, Camus moved to Paris to be where the literary action was, increasingly associating with those friends who were in the Resistance movement, with which Camus was strongly sympathetic. Before long, Camus joined the Resistance and was assigned the task of writing for the Resistance newspaper, *Combat*. After the liberation of Paris, in 1944, *Combat* went aboveground as a daily newspaper, and Camus was for a time its editor. He had become part of the Paris literary world, had met the best-known figures—Sartre, André Malraux, and many others—and had achieved a certain fame. By that time, it was clear that he would never go back to Algeria to live. As soon as it was possible for her to do so, Camus' wife joined him in Paris, their marriage resumed, and in September of 1945 she gave birth to twins, a boy and a girl. By war's end, Camus was not only a confirmed Parisian but also a domesticated one, with a family to support.

In the postwar years, Camus' fame quickly began to spread outside France— *The Stranger* appeared in English translation in 1946 and was an immediate sensation—and Camus took up the life of a lionized man of letters, dropping all employment except for his work with Gallimard and making lecture tours to foreign countries, including the United States. The publication of *The Plague* in 1947 was hailed by critics as the fulfillment of his great promise as a writer, and that book became one of the best-sellers of the postwar era, making Camus economically secure for the first time. Success and fame seemed to make him artistically insecure, however—there were suddenly too many demands from admirers, too many intrusions into his privacy and working time, and above all, too much self-doubt about his own powers for him to be able to live up to his public's expectations of him. Camus soon began to experience a crisis of literary sterility. It took him until 1951 to complete the essay *The Rebel*, begun nearly ten years earlier, and throughout the first half of the decade of the 1950's, he published nothing and was rumored to have a permanent case of writer's block. The outbreak of violence in Algeria and the campaign for independence, which began in 1952, added severely to Camus' troubled state, and the controversial articles he wrote in that period on the Algerian question certainly lost him many friends and much support. His unhappy attempt to be the voice of reason and conciliation at a time in the dispute when opinions had already become hopelessly polarized ("if you are not with us, you are against us") is poignantly described in the powerful tale "The Guest," one of the best stories in the collection *Exile and the Kingdom.*

Camus emerged from this period of intense personal suffering and frustration by venting his feelings in the short, bitterly satiric novel *The Fall*, published in 1956—his first work of fiction in nearly ten years, as his enemies were quick to point out. Nevertheless, the comic verve of the work attracted many readers, even though its intended meanings often seemed obscure to them. The book sold well, and Camus' reputation rebounded somewhat, especially outside France. The publication of the volume of short stories *Exile and the Kingdom*, the following year, earned for him additional respect as a writer who still had something to say. Internationally, his reputation peaked with the award of the Nobel Prize later that same year. Reinvigorated by the successes of 1956 and 1957, Camus was, as the decade ended, once again confidently and productively at work, with the usual three or four projects going simultaneously, one of which was an autobiographical novel about his youth in Algeria, to be called "Le Premier Homme" (the first man). His "block" seemed to be definitively overcome, and friends and family who spent Christmas of 1959 with him at the country retreat he had purchased in southern France recalled that he was in a generally optimistic frame of mind about his career. Fate, however, abruptly shattered that optimism. Camus' career came to a premature—and, he would have said, absurd—end only a few days after that happy Christmas. On Jaunuary 4, 1960, Michel Gallimard, nephew of Camus' publisher, lost control of his car, in which Camus was riding as a passenger, just outside the tiny village of Villeblevin, and crashed into a tree, killing Camus instantly. Camus had passed his forty-sixth birthday only two months before. The evolution of his work strongly suggests that a banal motor accident cut him off when he seemed, finally, to have mastered his craft and to be entering upon his prime creative years.

Analysis

Two persistent themes animate all of Albert Camus' writing and underlie his artistic vision: One is the enigma of the universe, which is breathtakingly beautiful yet indifferent to life; the other is the enigma of man, whose craving for happiness and meaning in life remains unextinguished by his full awareness of his own mortality and of the sovereign indifference of his environment. At the root of every novel, every play, every essay, even every entry in his notebooks can be found Camus' incessant need to probe and puzzle over the ironic double bind that he perceived to be the essence of the human condition: Man is endowed with the imagination to conceive an ideal existence, but neither his circumstances nor his own powers permit its attainment. The perception of this hopeless double bind made inescapable for Camus the obligation to face up to an overriding moral issue for man: Given man's circumscribed condition, are there honorable terms on which his life can be lived?

In his earliest attempt at casting these themes in fictional form, Camus made use of the traditional novel of personal development, or *Bildungsroman*, to describe one young man's encounters with life, love, and death. The result was an episodic novel, obviously based on his own experiences but composed in the third person and so lacking in unity and coherence as to betray the central idea on which he wished to focus: the problem of accepting death. He called the novel *A Happy Death* and showed his hero resolutely fixing his consciousness on the inanimate world around him, striving to become one with the stones and achieve a happy death by blending gently and painlessly into the silent harmony of the universe, while retaining his lucidity till his last breath. The book's last sentence strives to convince the reader by rhetoric that the hero has indeed achieved the happy death he sought: "And stone among the stones, he returned in the joy of his heart to the truth of motionless worlds." Camus seems to have sensed, however, that the rhetoric was unconvincing and that the ideal of a happy death was an illusion. Perhaps he even recognized that his hero's struggle to remain conscious of life until his last breath was, in reality, a protest against death and a contradiction of his desire to make the transition to death serene and imperceptible. It was doubtless some such sense of the book's failure that convinced Camus not to publish this work, composed when he was not yet twenty-five. Its posthumous publication has given scholars the opportunity to see Camus' first halting steps in trying to formulate the subtle and complex themes of the novels that were to make him great.

The Stranger, Camus' second attempt at writing a novel, includes a number of the scenes, characters, and situations found in *A Happy Death* (Mersault, the hero of *A Happy Death*, becomes Meursault in *The Stranger*). A detailed comparison of the two novels, however, makes it clear that *The Stranger*, which appeared in 1942, four years and many events after Camus abandoned *A Happy Death*, is a wholly different work in both conception and theme. No longer preoccupied with happiness in death, Camus turned his attention in *The Stranger* to the problem of happiness in life, to man's irrational and desperate need to find meaning in existence. His protagonist, Meursault, is not the frail, sophisticated, death-haunted figure of the earlier novel but rather a robust primitive who seems eerily devoid of the normal attitudes, values, and culturally induced feelings of his society, as though he had been brought up on some other planet—a "stranger" in the fullest sense of the word. Moreover, Camus hit upon the device of first-person narration as the most effective and dramatic means of confronting his readers with his disturbing protagonist, so alien to his environment. The famous opening words shock the reader into an awareness of the disquieting strangeness of the narrator:

"Mama died today. Or perhaps yesterday, I don't know. I received a telegram from the home: 'Mother passed away. Funeral tomorrow. Yours truly.' That doesn't mean anything. Perhaps it was yesterday."

Shrewdly focusing on a mother's death as a revealing touchstone of mankind's most deeply ingrained social attitudes, these words achieve a double effect: They tell the reader that the son of the deceased mother can speak of her death without any of the expected symptoms of grief, but at the same time, they remind the reader that the rest of society, having no familial ties with the deceased, habitually masks its indifference under empty rhetorical formulas such as the telegraphic announcement. This dual perspective is fully developed in subsequent chapters as the basic theme of the book: While Meursault shows by his own forthright account of his life that he does not share his society's conventional notions about death, religion, family, friendship, love, marriage, and ambition, he also manages to reveal—often without realizing it—that those conventional notions are often shallow, hypocritical, or delusory and constitute the pathetic inventions of a society desperate to invest its existence with a meaning it does not have. Thus, when Meursault, asked by his boss whether he would be interested in an assignment to establish a Paris office for his boss's business, says that he has no interest in living in Paris, the reader recognizes that Meursault simply does not believe that material surroundings can make his life any different. At the same time, the boss's dismayed reaction to Meursault's indifference to opportunity subtly disturbs the reader with the suspicion that, after all, the boss may have a touching but misplaced faith in the value of ambition. A similar moment occurs when Meursault and his girlfriend Marie discuss love and marriage. The reader is surely made uncomfortable by Meursault's casualness in saying that he does not know what love is, but that he is willing to marry Marie if she wants it. It is, however, a different order of discomfort that overcomes the reader when Marie insists that marriage is a very serious matter and Meursault calmly replies that it is not. All of part 2 of the novel, devoted to Meursault's trial after he has killed an Arab, rings additional and even more disturbing changes on the same dual perspective, with Meursault showing no awareness or acceptance of conventional beliefs about justice, murder, legal procedures, and the nature of evidence, while all the "normal" people involved show unexamined or self-deceiving convictions about all such matters. The ironic meaning that emerges from the novel is that while Meursault was guilty of taking a life, society sentenced him to death not for his crime, with which it seemed incapable of dealing, but for his refusal to live by society's values, for not "playing the game." As Camus himself laconically remarked, his novel means that any man who does not weep at his mother's funeral risks being condemned to death.

Critics have regularly protested that, in *The Stranger*, Camus manipulates his readers' emotions, inducing sympathy for Meursault even though he is a moral monster and ridiculing everyone else as representative of a society afraid to face reality, hence threatened by Meursault's clear-eyed and unsentimental acceptance of the world. Such protests are justified, however, only if one assumes that Camus intended *The Stranger* to be a realistic representation of the world, holding the mirror up to nature. In fact, Meursault is not a believable human figure, the events of the novel are but dimly evoked and unconvincingly motivated, and the very existence of the text itself, as Meursault's first-person account of events, is never explained. In *The Stranger*, Camus makes almost no concessions to the conventional procedures of realism, constructing instead a kind of mythic tale of philosophic intent to dramatize an imaginary confrontation between man's basic nature as a simple, sensual being and his grandly narcissistic self-image as an intelligent being whose every gesture has transcendent significance. Read as a kind of poetic allegory rather than as an exemplary tale of human conduct, *The Stranger* will be seen as a powerful depiction of man's painfully divided soul, at once joyous for the gift of life and miserable at the absence of any discernible purpose in that life and at the indifference of the surrounding universe. Viewed that way, *The Stranger* deserves its reputation as one of the great works of art of the first half of the twentieth century.

The allegorical mode is given a much more detailed and realistically human foundation in Camus' next novel, *The Plague*, regarded by many critics as his masterpiece. This time, there is a concerted effort by Camus to create a strong sense of place in a real setting and to depict fully rounded and believable characters. With the vividness of concrete details and actual place-names, Camus takes the reader to the city of Oran, in Algeria—a city of which he had intimate personal knowledge, having lived there for an extended period—and describes the impact on that real place of an imaginary outbreak of bubonic plague. The reader shares the first frightening discovery of rats dying in the streets and apartment house hallways and experiences the spread of terror and panic as the first human victims of the plague appear in random locations around the city. Soon, the city is ordered closed, quarantined from the rest of the world, and the authorities try to mobilize the trapped population and lay down strict sanitation rules to try to limit the impact of a disease they know they cannot cure. The heart of the novel is the depiction of the various ways in which individuals react to the fear and isolation imposed by this sudden state of siege, in which the invading army is invisible. To convey the variety of responses to such an extreme and concentrated crisis in human affairs, Camus deliberately eschews the convenient device of the omniscient narrator, making the depiction of every event and scene an eyewitness account in some form: the spoken words of reports or dialogues, the written words of letters or private diaries, and, as the main device, the written record of the daily observations of the novel's main character, Dr. Rieux. Whereas, in

The Stranger, first-person narration was primarily a device of characterization, used to portray an alien figure's disconcertingly remote and hollow personality, in *The Plague* it is a device of narrative realism, used to reduce devastatingly incomprehensible events to a human, hence believable, scale, by portraying the way these events are seen by a representative group of ordinary citizens.

The Plague differs from its predecessor not only technically but also thematically. Camus' inspiration for *The Plague* was no philosophical abstraction but a specific event of his own life: the frustration and despair he experienced during the war, when the aftermath of the Allied invasion of North Africa trapped his wife in Oran (while he was in the Resistance organization, the Massif Central) and cut off all communication between them. That experience started the fictional idea germinating in his mind, and a literary model— Daniel Defoe's *A Journal of the Plague Year* (1722)—gave the idea more concrete form. Central to the idea of *The Plague*, certainly, is the theme of man's encounter with death rather than the theme of man's interpretation of life, which dominates *The Stranger*. Indeed, with *The Plague*, Camus was returning to the preoccupation of his earliest work of fiction, *A Happy Death*, but with a major new emphasis. *The Plague* concerns not an individual's quest in relation to death but a collectivity's involuntary confrontation with it. In *The Plague*, death is depicted as a chance outgrowth of an indifferent nature which suddenly, and for no apparent reason, becomes an evil threat to man. Death in the form of a plague is unexpected, irrational—a manifestation of that absurdity, that radical absence of meaning in life which is a major underlying theme of *The Stranger*. In *The Plague*, however, Camus proposes the paradox that, when death is a manifestation of the absurd, it galvanizes something in man's spirit which enables him to join with others to fight against death and thus give meaning and purpose to his life. From evil may come happiness, this novel seems to suggest: It is a painful irony of the human condition that man often discovers his own capacity for courage and for fraternal affection—that is, for happiness—only if he is forced by the threat of evil to make the discovery. The hint of optimism in this paradoxical theme— happiness is, after all, possible for some if the circumstances are dire enough— is, however, insufficient to offset the fundamental pessimism of *The Plague*. A glance at the fate of the main characters will make the basic bleakness of this work manifest.

At the center of the action is Bernard Rieux, a doctor who risks his life every day to lead the fight against the plague and who, more than anyone else in the novel, experiences the satisfaction and the joy of finding himself equal to a heroic task and feeling with others a fraternal bond engendered by their common struggle. Yet his satisfaction is brief and his joys few. He knows that he cannot cure victims of the plague and must suppress his sympathy for them if he is to be effective in palliating their suffering and in keeping them from infecting others. The result of this bind is that Rieux strikes his patients and their families as cold and indifferent; he ends up being hated by those he is trying to help. The fraternal bond with others who are trying to help develops in only a few instances, since most of his fellow citizens are too frightened or egocentric to join him in the effort. Moreover, where the bond does develop, it proves too tenuous to penetrate his natural isolation.

The limits of the fraternal bond are most graphically expressed by the moment in the novel when Rieux and Jean Tarrou (a traveler through whose journal part of the novel is related), seeing the first signs that the plague is receding, decide to go for a swim together, in celebration. The point is carefully made that, while each feels a sense of fraternity with the other as they swim in the same water, each is also conscious of being ultimately quite alone in the joy and freedom of moving serenely through the water and forgetting the plague for a short while. In spite of the shared emotion that unites them, each feels the swim to be predominantly a solitary experience. Finally, when the plague does end, Rieux finds himself strangely empty and alienated from the joyous crowds now once more filling the streets of Oran; the urgency of his task no longer exists to summon forth his courage. Indeed, because he has lost those dearest to him—his wife and Tarrou—he feels more alone than ever after the plague has gone. The other important characters fare no better than Rieux: Tarrou is killed by the plague; Joseph Grand suffers from it but recovers and resumes his self-imposed task of writing a novel, of which he has yet to complete the first sentence, because he has endlessly revised and recast it in a fruitless search for perfection; Rembart, a journalist who is trapped in Oran by the plague, leaves when it is over, but without having written anything about it, having found his profession inadequate to such an awesome task; and Cottard, who engages in black-market profiteering during the plague, goes berserk when the plague ends, shooting citizens at random until he is caught and killed by the police. There is little in this novel to nourish an optimistic outlook, except for the hesitant and tentative statement of Rieux, at the end of his chronicle, that amid the ravages of pestilence, one learns that "there are, in men, more things to admire than to despise."

The Plague is the longest, the most realistic, and artistically the most impressive of Camus' novels, offering a richly varied cast of characters and a coherent and riveting plot, bringing an integrated world memorably to life while stimulating the reader's capacity for moral reflection. In spite of its vivid realism, *The Plague* is no less mythical and allegorical in its impact than is *The Stranger*. When first published, *The Plague* was widely interpreted as a novel about the German Occupation and the French Resistance, with the plague symbolizing the evil presence of the Nazis. Since the 1940's, however, more universal themes and symbols have been discovered in the book, including the frighteningly random nature of evil and the perception that man's conquest of evil is never more than provisional, that the struggle will always have to be renewed.

It has also been widely recognized, in recent years, that *The Plague* is, in significant degree, a profound meditation on the frustrating limits of human language both as a means of communication and as a means of representing the truth about human existence. The discovery of that theme has made *The Plague* the most modern of Camus' novels, the one with the most to say to the second generation of Camus' readers, in the 1980's.

For nearly a decade after the publication of *The Plague*, impeded by the consequences of fame, Camus struggled to find enough time and privacy to compose a new work of fiction and to complete philosophical and theatrical writings begun before he wrote *The Plague*. In the mid-1950's, he began to compose a group of short stories with the common theme of the condition of the exile, and it was one of those stories which he was suddenly inspired to expand into a short novel written in the form of a monologue and published in 1956 as *The Fall*.

The product of a troubled time in Camus' life, *The Fall* is a troubling work, full of brilliant invention, dazzling wordplay, and devastating satire, but so profoundly ironic and marked by so many abrupt shifts in tone as to leave the reader constantly off-balance and uncertain of the author's viewpoint or purpose. This difficulty in discerning the book's meaning is inherent in its basic premise, for the work records a stream of talk—actually one side of a dialogue—by a Frenchman who haunts a sleazy bar in the harbor district of Amsterdam and who does not trouble to hide the fact that most of what he says, including his name, is invented. Because he is worldly and cultivated, his talk is fascinating and seizes the attention of his implied interlocutor (who is also, of course, the reader) with the same riveting force as Samuel Taylor Coleridge's Ancient Mariner. The name he gives himself is Jean-Baptiste Clamence, a name that evokes the biblical figure of the prophet John the Baptist as the voice crying in the wilderness (*vox clamantis in deserto*) and that coincides neatly with the occupation he claims to follow, also of his own invention: judge-penitent. When Clamence remarks to his interlocutor, near the end of his five-day monologue, "I know what you are thinking: it is very difficult to distinguish the true from the false in what I am telling you. I confess that you are right," the reader feels that Camus has suddenly made a personal intervention into the novel in order to warn the reader that he has been deliberately manipulated by Clamence's playacting and that he has every right to feel bewildered. Camus thus signals to the reader that the book's troubling impact has been calculated and deliberate from the start. Only in the closing pages of the novel does he clarify the purpose of Clamence's invented narrative and the meaning of his invented calling, but the explanation comes too late—deliberately so, for the reader can never rid himself of the doubts that Clamence's entire performance has been designed to raise concerning what is true and what is false, what is good and what is evil.

Clamence's "explanation" is, in fact, the most unsettling element in the book. He pointedly admits to his interlocutor that he has been penitently "confessing" his own sins to him in a carefully controlled pattern, only in order to induce his interlocutor to "confess" in his turn, thus enabling Clamence to play the role of judge. Clamence begins his "confession" by describing his successful career in Paris as a much-admired lawyer known for his defense of "widows and orphans"—that is, the helpless and disadvantaged of society. He had every reason to see himself as a man of virtue, he says until he began to "hear" a woman's mocking laughter whenever he looked at himself in the mirror with those feelings of self-satisfaction. The mocking laughter reminded him that his lawyerly altruism was only a mask for selfishness and forced him to recall an incident he had tried to forget: Crossing a bridge over the Seine one night, he had seen a young woman throw herself into the water and had made no effort to rescue her or to get help, instead walking hurriedly away without looking back. The mocking laughter was thus his bad conscience taunting him with the suppressed memory of his guilt: The admired man of virtue was in reality a fraud, a sinner like everyone else.

Clamence goes on to explain that thereafter he had found it increasingly difficult to continue his career in Paris and live with his guilt. At the same time, he could not give up his need to feel morally superior to others. His solution to this private inner conflict, he then declares, was his brilliant invention of a new career for himself as a judge-penitent. He closed his Paris office and moved to the harbor section of Amsterdam—which, he notes, is in the center of the concentric circles of Amsterdam's canals, like the ninth circle of Dante's *Inferno*, and is, moreover, "the site of one of the greatest crimes of modern history," meaning the Nazi destruction of the entire Jewish community of Amsterdam. In these new surroundings, he not only could assuage his guilt by the feeling that he was in the ninth circle of Hell, where he belonged, but also could have access to the endless succession of tourists who gravitated to that spot, whom he could "help," in such propitious surroundings, to recognize their own guilt as well. His "help" consisted of a recital of his own sins, so arranged as to emphasize their universality, thus subtly prompting his listener to confess the same sins in turn. In this way, Clamence uses his perfected performance as a penitent in order to put himself in the deeply satisfying position of judge, hearing his listener's confession while basking in the warm glow of his own moral superiority. Because everyone, without exception, is a guilty sinner, says Clamence, he has solved the dilemma of how to live happily with his nagging guilt. The essential secret, he says, is to accuse oneself first—and of all seven cardinal sins—thereby earning the right to accuse everyone else.

Clamence's "solution," which concludes *The Fall*, is a burlesque of moral reasoning, underscoring the bitterness of the satire which is at the heart of this novel. Like Camus' other novels, *The Fall* is an exploration of man's moral nature and his passionate search for happiness in a world that is indifferent to such spiritual values but unlike any other of his works of fiction, *The Fall* is both unrelievedly pessimistic and irreducibly ambiguous. In Clamence's confession, is Camus' intention to castigate himself for having taken his own fame too seriously and thus expiate his personal sin of pride? There were many critics who read the book that way when it appeared in 1956. Or is he using Clamence, rather, to avenge himself on his enemies, whom he thought too quick to adopt a tone of moral superiority in judging his position on the Algerian Civil War? Many other critics saw *The Fall* that way. A generation later, it seems reasonable to suggest that both interpretations have validity. *The Fall* is a comic masterpiece, remarkably parallel in its tone, its themes, and its ambiguity to the short story "Jonas," written about the same time—a story in which, everyone agrees, Camus attempted to come to terms with his artistic sterility and with the conflict he felt between public obligation and the need for privacy.

Camus's short story "Jonas" ends with a celebrated verbal ambiguity: The painter-hero of the story, after long meditation, translates his thought to canvas by means of a single word, but it is impossible to discern whether that word is "solitary" or "solidary." It is tempting to conclude, using that short story as analogue, that the ambiguity of *The Fall* is also deliberate and that Camus meant his work both as private confession and as public condemnation. Those two meanings, the one private and the other public, are surely intended to combine retrospectively in the reader's mind to form Camus' universal condemnation of man's moral bankruptcy. As the title is meant to suggest, *The Fall* is a modern parable about Original Sin and the Fall of Man.

There is reason to believe that the unrelenting pessimism of *The Fall* was not Camus' final word on humanity but was rather the expression of a temporary discouragement which he had almost succeeded in dispelling at the time of his death. In 1959, he was at work on a new novel, to be called "Le Premier Homme," the theme of which was to be a celebration of the formative experience of his Algerian youth. It seems clear that it would have turned out to offer another perspective, perhaps a less bleakly pessimistic one, on the one subject that, at bottom, always animated Camus' fiction: the enigma of man's struggle against the indifference of creation and his unquenchable thirst for moral significance in his life. Camus' unforgettable contribution to the ongoing dialogue inspired by that vast subject is embodied in the three great novels he managed to complete before his untimely death.

Major publications other than long fiction

SHORT FICTION: *L'Exil et le royaume*, 1957 (*Exile and the Kingdom*, 1958).

PLAYS: *Caligula*, 1944 (English translation); *Le Malentendu*, 1944 (*Caligula and Cross Purpose*, 1948; better known as *The Misunderstanding*); *L'État de siège*, 1948 (*State of Siege*); *Les Justes*, 1949 (*The Just Assassins*); *Caligula and Three Other Plays*, 1958 (includes *Caligula, The Misunderstanding, State of Siege*, and *The Just Assassins*).

NONFICTION: *L'Envers et l'endroit*, 1937 ("The Wrong Side and The Right Side"); *Noces*, 1938 ("Nuptials"); *Le Mythe de Sisyphe*, 1942 (*The Myth of Sisyphus and Other Essays*, 1955); *L'Homme révolté*, 1951 (*The Rebel*, 1956); *L'Été*, 1954 ("Summer"); *Lyrical and Critical Essays*, 1968 (includes "The Wrong Side and the Right Side," "Nuptials," and "Summer").

Bibliography
Brée, Germaine. *Camus*, 1959.
Cruickshank, John. *Albert Camus and the Literature of Revolt*, 1959.
Fitch, Brian T. *The Narcissistic Text: A Reading of Camus' Fiction*, 1982.
Lottman, Herbert. *Albert Camus, A Biography*, 1979.
McCarthy, Patrick. *Camus*, 1982.
O'Brien, Conor Cruise. *Albert Camus*, 1970.
Parker, Emmett. *Albert Camus: The Artist in the Arena*, 1965.
Thody, Philip. *Albert Camus 1913-1960*, 1961.

Murray Sachs

ELIAS CANETTI

Born: Rustschuk, Bulgaria; July 25, 1905

Principal long fiction
Die Blendung, 1935 (*Auto-da-Fé*, 1946; also as *The Tower of Babel*, 1947).

Other literary forms
Although he has published only one work of fiction, Elias Canetti has written a great deal of prose. His *magnum opus*, the product of decades of work, is *Masse und Macht* (1960; *Crowds and Power*, 1962), an extended essay in social psychology which is as unorthodox and provocative as it is brilliant. In an effort to present a sort of taxonomic typology of the mass mind, Canetti casts a wide net over all of human history. Historical, political, psychological, anthropological, philosophical, sociological, and cultural elements and insights are enlisted in an occasionally idiosyncratic search for the wellsprings of human behavior in general and the root causes of Fascism in particular.

A much lighter work is *Der Ohrenzeuge* (1974; *The Earwitness*, 1979), subtitled "Fifty Characters," a series of mordant characterizations of eccentric figures that exemplify the quirks and extremes inherent in the human personality. This collection includes thumbnail sketches of such specimens as "Der Papiersäufer" ("The Paper Drunkard"), "Der Demutsahne" ("The Humility-forebear"), "Die Verblümte" ("The Allusive Woman"), "Der Heroszupfer" ("The Hero-tugger"), "Der Maestroso" ("The Maestroso"), "Der Nimmermust" ("The Never-must"), "Der Tränenwärmer" ("The Tear-warmer"), "Die Tischtuchtolle" ("The Tablecloth-lunatic"), "Der Fehlredner" ("The Misspeaker"), "Der Tückenfänger" ("The Wile-catcher"), and "Die Archäokratin" ("The Archeocrat").

Canetti's aphoristic jottings from 1942 to 1972 have been collected in a volume entitled *Die Provinz des Menschen* (1973; *The Human Province*, 1978). *Die Stimmen von Marrakesch* (1968; *The Voices of Marrakesh*, 1978) is a profound travel book subtitled "A Record of a Visit." *Das Gewissen der Worte* (1975; *The Conscience of Words*, 1979) brings together Canetti's essays on philosophy, art, and literature. The perceptive literary critic is shown to good advantage in *Der andere Prozess: Kafkas Briefe an Felice* (1969; *Kafka's Other Trial*, 1974).

As a young man, Canetti came under the spell of the great Viennese satirist, Karl Kraus, many of whose spellbinding readings he attended, and his dramatic works exemplify the Krausian concept of "acoustical masks" as he unsparingly sketches the linguistic (and, in a sense, moral) physiognomy of his characters on the basis of each person's individual, unmistakable speech pattern. *Hochzeit* (1932; wedding) presents a *danse macabre* of petit-bourgeois Viennese society motivated by cupidity and hypocrisy, with the collapse of a house coveted by those attending a wedding party, symbolizing the breakdown of this corrupt society. *Komödie der Eitelkeit* (1964; *Comedy of Vanity*, 1983) explores the genesis of a mass psychosis. A totalitarian government, having proscribed vanity, has all the mirrors, photos, and films burned. As vanity goes underground, distrust, dehumanization, and disaster ensue. *Die Befristeten* (1956; *The Numbered*, 1964; also as *Life Terms*, 1983) is, as it were, a primer of death. People carry their predetermined dates of death in capsules around their necks, to be opened eventually only by the "Capsulan." One man, Fünfzig (Mr. Fifty), finally rebels against this knowledge and breaks the taboo. The discovery that the capsules are empty replaces presumed security with fear of death.

In recent years, Canetti has also achieved considerable prominence as an autobiographer. The first volume of his memoirs, *Die gerettete Zunge: Geschichte einer Jugend* (*The Tongue Set Free: Remembrance of a European Childhood*, 1980), appeared in 1978. The title of the second volume, *Die Fackel im Ohr* (1980; *The Torch in My Ear*, 1982), reflects Canetti's indebtedness to Karl Kraus and his celebrated journal.

Achievements

The award of the 1981 Nobel Prize to Elias Canetti for his multifaceted literary oeuvre caught the world by surprise and focused international attention on a seminal writer and thinker who had lived and worked in relative obscurity for decades. Canetti is now increasingly recognized as the sole surviving representative of a distinguished Austrian literary tradition. The misleading statement of the *The New York Times* that Canetti was "the first Bulgarian writer" to achieve the distinction of a Nobel Prize was refuted by Canetti himself when he said that "like Karl Kraus and Nestroy, I am a Viennese writer." Even more suggestive is Canetti's statement that "the language of my mind will remain German—because I am a Jew."

Biography

Born July 25, 1905, in a Danube port city in northern Bulgaria as the oldest son of Mathilde and Jacques Canetti, Elias Canetti had a polyglot and multicultural upbringing. As he details in the first volume of his autobiography, German was the fourth language he acquired—after Ladino (an archaic Spanish dialect spoken by Sephardic Jews that is also known as Spaniolic and Judezmo), Bulgarian, and English. In June, 1911, he was taken to England and enrolled in a Manchester school. Following the sudden death of his father, the family (consisting of his high-minded, strong-willed, and rather overbearing mother as well as his two younger brothers) settled in Vienna, but they spent some of the war years in Switzerland. After attending secondary school in Zurich and Frankfurt am Main, Canetti returned to Vienna and studied chemistry at the university from 1924 to 1929, taking a doctorate of philosophy. For a time, he lived in Berlin and worked as a free-lance writer, translating books by Upton Sinclair. In February, 1934, Canetti married Veza Taubner-Calderón. His mother died in Paris in June, 1937, and that is where Canetti and his wife emigrated in November of the following year, later settling in London in January, 1939. While working on *Crowds and Power* and other writings, Canetti eked out a living as a free-lance journalist and language teacher. After the death of his wife in May, 1963, Canetti spent some time with his brother Georges in Paris. In 1971, he married Hera Buschor and became the father of a daughter, Johanna, the following year. They settled in Zurich, with Canetti making periodic trips to London.

Analysis

Elias Canetti's *Auto-da-Fé*, completed in 1931, is as impressive a first novel as has been written in this century. It was originally intended to be the first of an eight-volume *comédie* (or *tragicomédie*) *humaine* of our time, peopled by madmen of the type that were confined in the Steinhof, the insane asylum that Canetti could see from the window of his room while he was writing. It was to be an enormous fictional typology of the madness of the age, with each novel intended to present a different kind of monomaniac—among others, a religious fanatic, a truth fanatic, a technological maniac, a wastrel, an obsessive collector, and a bibliomaniac. Through such exemplary figures, Canetti wanted to turn a glaring spotlight on the contemporary world. It is thought that only one other novel in the projected series has been completed, a novel entitled "Der Todfeind" (not in the usual sense of "mortal enemy" but meaning "the enemy of death," which is fair description of Canetti himself). Sketches may exist for other works of fiction, but after expressing his own alienation and frustration in his first book, Canetti apparently found the novel form wanting for his purposes and became increasingly interested in presenting his thoughts in nonfictional form, particularly in *Crowds and Power*.

Canetti's working title for his novel was "Kant fängt Feuer" (Kant catches fire), but the author soon chose not to use the name of the famous German philosopher for his protagonist. He also rejected the name Brand as too obvious an evocation of the Holocaust motif, though he finally settled on the scarcely less evocative name Kien, which means "pinewood." Rembrandt's painting *The Blinding of Samson* appears to have suggested the somewhat ambiguous title of the novel (*Die Blendung* means "the blinding," with suggestions also of "dazzlement" and "deception").

The ascetic Peter Kien describes himself as a "library owner"; as reclusive as he is erudite, this renowned philologist and sinologist represents a "head without a world." He allows himself to get into the clutches of his scheming housekeeper, Therese, whose favorite item of apparel is a starched blue skirt (a garment worn by Canetti's far more humane real-life landlady). When Kien marries this mindless, avaricious, lustful, and generally evil creature, he ostensibly does so for the sake of his beloved books (and on the advice of Confucius, one of the savants with whom he communes).

Following his traumatic expulsion from the paradise of his enormous library, Kien embarks on a peculiar odyssey and descends to the lower depths of society, a "world without a head." Therese's work of degradation is continued and completed by the predatory chess-playing hunchback, Fischerle, and the philistine janitor, Benedikt Pfaff. Their cruelly exploitative stratagems, including the pawning of some of Kien's books at the Theresianum (a disguised version of the actual Dorotheum, Vienna's state-owned pawnshop and auction house), serve as a grotesque counterpoint to Kien's *idées fixes* and the progressive unhinging of his mind. Peter Kien's final act is an apocalyptic self-immolation amid his books to his own uncontrollable laughter—a "wedge driven into our consciousness."

Canetti's novel seems to have been written in the white heat of rage and hate. To that extent, it reflects the influence of his mentor, Kraus, who wrote: "Hatred must make a person productive; otherwise one might as well love." *Auto-da-Fé* may be read as a subtle political and social satire, an allegorical portrayal of a sick society, and a chilling adumbration of the crushing of the vulnerable "pure" intellect by the brutish "practical" forces of our time. Aside from the narrator, the only sane person in the book is a sweet child who appears at the very beginning. Even Kien's brother Georges, a Paris psychiatrist who comes to his demented brother's aid and seems to represent an oasis of rationality, finds insanity more interesting and worthwhile than sanity and may, paradoxically, abet the forces that push Kien over the edge. Despite the banal viciousness of the characters and the prevalence of violence in the book, *Auto-da-Fé* may be read as a great comic novel with many genuinely funny scenes and situations that give rise to that "thoughtful laughter" which George Meredith identified as the index of the comic spirit. In this typology of madness, however, any laughter is bound to be the sardonic rather than the liberating kind. Bertha Keveson-Hertz has properly identified "Swiftean satire, Dickensian humor, Proustian insulation, Joycean interiorization, and Poe's maelstrom nightmares" in Canetti's novel.

Claudio Magris has observed that

the narrative of *Die Blendung* points ardently and yearningly to the missing life, to undiscoverable and suffocated love. It is the most total and shattering tragedy of the destruction of the self, the tragedy of individuality which, shortly before entering the dimensions of the crowd, exaggerates its particularity to the point of caricature and robs its existence of every passion, of every sensation. The most powerful and impressive motif of *Die Blendung* is the total, icy absence of all passions, pulsations, and stimuli; paranoia has removed any power of attraction from objects and does not know how to project the slightest libido onto them.

In his depictions of the range of elementary human instincts, Canetti somehow neglects the erotic sphere, but he does suggest that the urge to merge with the crowd implies a kind of sexual energy and interest.

Through Canetti's craftsmanship, the reader is drawn into the oppressive atmosphere of the book with a growing sense of discomfort. The *erlebte Rede*, or interior monologue, is an effective device by means of which the storyteller lets the reader get into the mind of each character. The narrative ambience contains many surreal touches, yet these grotesque elements somehow seem natural.

It is possible to read *Auto-da-Fé* as a sort of inversion of Dante's *The Divine Comedy*: Peter Kien's library is the Paradise; the city (of Vienna) is the Purgatory; the fire is the Inferno. Everything in the book moves in a magic circle of aberration, yet Canetti separates reality and absurdity, the real world and the hallucinatory world more consistently than does Kafka, in whose writings these spheres tend to blend into a "purer" entity. The author identifies with the limitations of his characters, and unlike many other novelists he makes no attempt to act as an omniscient narrator who restores order and sits in judgment. Canetti ascribes a peculiar role to madness: The aberrant becomes the rule and normality the exception as contrasts are leveled and personal qualities are impoverished. The blessing of originality has a price, and it is loneliness. The language of lunatics ought to unite them; instead, it creates a gulf between them, and soliloquy replaces discourse. At the Ideal Heaven café, frequented by Fischerle and other shady characters, there is a "geschlossene Masse," a closed company; the other characters live outside the crowd. Brother Georges judges the masses positively, whereas Peter Kien hates the masses as an incarnation of the primitive and the barbaric. The hypnotic attraction to fire is seen as one of the characteristics of the crowd, and in this regard (as in others, though not in political, historical, and other topical matters), Canetti drew on his real-life experiences. In July of 1927, he had witnessed the burning of the building of the Ministry of Justice on Vienna's Ringstrasse by a mob enraged by a jury's acquittal of some killers; the ensuing police riot claimed many innocent victims.

The disturbing figure of the scheming pimp and pander, Siegfried Fischer, known as Fischerle, has come in for some critical speculation. Might Canetti intend this petty criminal to represent the assimilated Jew in Austrian society, and is the cutting off of his hump (by a beggar) a symbolic adumbration of the bloody end of assimilation for Austrian Jewry? It is difficult, however, to accept such an interpretation of a character who is depicted as an anti-Semite's stereotype; in any case, the drama of Fischerle's life begins when he abandons the crowd and desires to become a chess champion in America, where his hunchback will somehow disappear. As for the vicious building superintendent, Pfaff—with huge fists and powerful feet—he is a recognizable Viennese type who was to see his day of Fascist glory in Hitler's Austria. Georges seems to be a paragon of strength, worldliness, empathy, and sanity. He attempts to straighten out his brother's life and to act as a *deus ex machina*, but he fails to recognize Peter's true state of mind. The doctor finds the insane more interesting than the sane; for example, the patient called the "Gorilla" has access to levels of experience not available to the sane. Is insanity, Georges wonders, perhaps a higher form of existence? In his inner complexity, Georges may actually represent only a more sublime form of moral aberration, a metaphysical type of madness.

Kien may be regarded as a modern Don Quixote. Both characters may be pictured as middle-aged, tall, emaciated, storklike, sexless, and virtually disembodied in their unworldliness and rejection of bodily needs and functions. Therese, Pfaff, and Fischerle are the satellites that correspond to Sancho Panza. In both cases, there is an obsession with books, a consultation with them in times of need, and a readiness to do battle with their enemies. In Miguel de Cervantes, the absoluteness of literature is stressed; in Canetti, the absoluteness of scholarship has pride of place. Don Quixote reads the world in confirmation of books; Kien finds bliss in them and distress in the reality surrounding him. Don Quixote misinterprets reality; Kien negates it. Don Quixote has a catharsis and regains his good judgment before his idyllic or lyric death; Kien is vouchsafed no such grace: He piles his books into a mighty fortress before torching them, perishing with the treasures he has tried so hard to preserve. His flight into the flames is his only escape from his own isolation; death by fire is his deliverance, his expiation, and also an act of nemesis. In *Don Quixote de la Mancha* (1605, 1615), there is some real dialogue, but Kien's conversations, with the possible exception of some of those with his brother, create no human contacts. Certainly the split between the hero (or antihero) and the world has been a recurrent theme in world literature since Cervantes. In his only published work of fiction, Canetti has handled it with consummate skill, with awful prescience, and with soul-searing impact.

Major publications other than long fiction

PLAYS: *Hochzeit*, 1932; *Die Befristeten*, 1956 (*The Numbered*, 1964; also as *Life Terms*, 1983); *Dramen*, 1964 (collection of plays); *Komödie der Eitelkeit*, 1964 (*Comedy of Vanity*, 1983).

NONFICTION: *Fritz Wotruba*, 1955; *Masse und Macht*, 1960 (*Crowds and Power*, 1962); *Die Welt im Kopf*, 1962; *Aufzeichnungen 1942-1948*, 1965; *Die Stimmen von Marrakesch*, 1968 (*The Voices of Marrakesh*, 1978); *Der andere Prozess: Kafkas Briefe an Felice*, 1969 (*Kafka's Other Trial*, 1974); *Alle vergeudete Verehrung: Aufzeichnungen 1949-1960*, 1970; *Die gespaltene Zukunft*, 1972; *Macht und Überleben*, 1972 (essays); *Die Provinz des Menschen*, 1973 (*The Human Province*, 1978); *Das Gewissen der Worte*, 1975 (*The Conscience of Words*, 1979); *Der Beruf des Dichters*, 1976; *Die gerettete Zunge: Geschichte einer Jugend*, 1978 (*The Tongue Set Free: Remembrance of a European Childhood*, 1980); *Die Fackel im Ohr*, 1980 (*The Torch in My Ear*, 1982).

MISCELLANEOUS: *Der Ohrenzeuge*, 1974 (character sketches; *The Earwitness*, 1979).

Bibliography

Barnouw, Dagmar. *Elias Canetti*, 1979.
Burke, Jeffrey. "Discovery Rewarded: Finding Elias Canetti," in *Harper's Magazine*. CCLX (January, 1980), pp. 82-87.
Durzak, Manfred. "From Dialect Play to Philosophical Parable: Elias Canetti in Exile," in *Protest—Form—Tradition*, 1979. Edited by J. P. Strelka, et al.
Göpfert, Herbert G., ed. *Canetti lesen: Erfahrungen mit seinen Büchern*, 1975.
Parry, Idris F. "Elias Canetti's Novel *Die Blendung*," in *Essays in German Literature*, 1965. Edited by F. Norman.
Roberts, David. *Kopf und Welt: Elias Canettis Roman "Die Blendung,"* 1975.
Sontag, Susan. "Mind as Passion," in *Under the Sign of Saturn*, 1980.

Harry Zohn

KAREL ČAPEK

Born: Malé Svatoňovice, Bohemia; January 9, 1890
Died: Prague, Czechoslovakia; December 25, 1938

Principal long fiction

Továrna na Absolutno, 1922 (*The Absolute at Large*, 1927); *Krakatit*, 1924 (English translation, 1925); *Hordubal*, 1933 (English translation, 1934); *Povětroň*, 1934 (*Meteor*, 1935); *Obyčejný život*, 1934 (*An Ordinary Life*, 1936); *Válka s mloky*, 1936 (*The War of the Newts*, 1939); *Život a dílo skladatele Foltýna*, 1939 (*The Cheat*, 1941).

Other literary forms

Apart from long fiction, Karel Čapek authored many stories, travelogues, and plays. An important journalist, he published many of his *feuilletons*, as well as his conversations with T. G. Masaryk, then President of Czechoslovakia. He also published a book on philosophy, *Pragmatismus* (1918), and a book of literary criticism, *Kritika slov* (1920).

Čapek's collections of short stories include *Zářivé hlubiny* (1916; with Josef Čapek); *Boží muka* (1917); *Krakonošova zahrada* (1918); *Trapné povídky* (1921; *Money and Other Stories*, 1929); *Povídky z jedné kapsy* (1929); *Povídky z druhé kapsy* (1929; *Tales from Two Pockets*, 1932); *Devatero pohádek* (1931; *Fairy Tales*, 1933); and *Kniha apokryfů* (1946; *Apocryphal Stories*, 1949). Among his most important plays are *R.U.R.* (1920; with Josef Čapek; English translation, 1923); *Ze života hmyzu* (1922; with Josef Čapek; *The Insect Play*, 1923; also as *And So Ad Infinitum*, 1923); *Věc Makropulos*, 1922 (*The Macropulos Secret*, 1925); *Bílá nemoc* (1937; *Power and Glory*, 1938); and *Matka*, 1938 (*The Mother*, 1939).

Achievements

Čapek is among the best-known modern Czech writers. He became prominent between the two world wars and was recognized by and acquainted with such eminent figures as G. B. Shaw, H. G. Wells, G. K. Chesterton, and Jules Romains. Čapek's international reputation earned for him the presidency of the Czechoslovak P.E.N. Club, and he was suggested for the post of the president of the International P.E.N. Club, an honor which he declined. Though he was equally versatile in fiction and drama, his fame abroad rests mostly on his science-fiction play *R.U.R.*, written in collaboration with his brother Josef, which introduced into the world vocabulary the Czech word *robot*, a neologism derived from the Czech *robota*, meaning forced labor.

Despite Capek's lifelong interest in science and its destructive potential, demonstrated in such novels as *The Absolute at Large* and *Krakatit*, and despite the worldwide fame that such science fantasies brought him, he is remembered in Czechoslovakia as a dedicated humanist, a spokesman for the tolerance, pragmatism, and pluralism best manifested in the philosophy of relativism which his works so creatively demonstrate. He was one of the strongest voices of his time against totalitarianism, be it Fascist or Communist.

Čapek's work is deeply philosophical, but in a manner that is accessible to a wide readership. He managed to achieve this with the help of a chatty, almost pedestrian style informed by a genuine belief in the reasonable man, a man open to a rational argument when all else fails. Hence Čapek's humanism; hence, also, his disappointment when, after the infamous appeasement of 1938, he had to acknowledge that the very paragons of the democratic ideal and of Western culture, England and France, had sold out his country to the Nazis.

Such concerns of Čapek as the conflict between man's scientific achievements and the very survival of the human race—a conflict illustrated by the fight between the robots and human beings in *R.U.R.*—are not merely alive today but have become more and more pressing as the world is becoming increasingly aware of the threat of nuclear holocaust. Čapek was among the first to see the dangerous potential of man's creative ability, not because he was particularly gifted in science, but because he was quite realistic, approaching the tendencies of his time with the far-seeing and far-reaching attitude of one whose relativism was tempered by pessimism derived from his awareness of the past, the tradition from which the imperfect-but-perfectible man departed.

An urbane wit, a certain intimacy with the reader, deft characterization, and concise expression are the hallmarks of Čapek's style, heightening the impact of his fictional treatment of profound issues.

Biography

The youngest child of a country doctor, Karel Čapek was born in 1890 in Bohemia, then still a part of the Austro-Hungarian Empire. A weak and sickly boy, Čapek was pampered by his mother and protected by his older brother, Josef; they, together with his maternal grandmother, inspired him with a love for literature. Čapek and his brother Josef prepared themselves for a literary vocation by their prodigious reading in many foreign literatures; among Čapek's juvenilia are some verses influenced by Symbolism and the decadents—French and Czech. Josef was to collaborate with Karel on some of his most celebrated successes, including *R.U.R.*, but he was primarily a gifted artist, illustrator, and designer who gradually established himself as such, leaving Čapek to write alone, though never really drifting spiritually, or even physically, far away.

A brilliant student, Čapek enrolled at Charles University in Prague, though two stints took him to the University of Berlin and the University of Paris. In 1915, Čapek took his doctorate, having defended his dissertation on objective methods in aesthetics. The next year saw the publication of the short-story collection *Zářivé hlubiny*, written with Josef. This genre was particularly suited to Čapek's talents, and throughout his life he continued to write short stories: philosophical, mystical, detective, and apocryphal. Parody and satire, down to the political lampoon, are not rare among them; they seem to flow naturally from the day-to-day concerns of a journalist sharply reacting to the crises and momentous events of his time.

The first such event was the establishment of the Czechoslovak Republic in 1918, at which time Čapek worked for a National Democrat paper, switching to the more liberal *Lindové noviny* in 1921, where he stayed to the end of his life. Čapek's youth and his middle age parallel the youth and growing pains of his country's first Republic, right down to its (and his) death in 1938. Thus, Čapek is the literary embodiment of the principles of this Republic, led by a philosopher-president, Masaryk; among these principles were a distrust of radical solutions, an accent on the small work on a human scale, and a faith in the goodwill of people. In this respect, one can consider Čapek an unofficial cultural ambassador to the world at large.

Čapek was not indifferent to the world: A cosmopolitan spirit, he was drawn toward England in particular, and he traveled widely, reporting on his travels in books on England, Holland, Italy, Spain, and Scandinavia. Indeed, he was a quintessential European, protesting the deteriorating situation in Europe before the war which he did not live to witness but the coming of which he foresaw only too clearly. This prescience is particularly evident in his novel *The War of the Newts*, a thinly disguised presentiment of the Orwellian battle of totalitarian superpowers that left Eastern Europe, after years of Nazi occupation, in the stranglehold of the Soviet Union.

Oddly enough, the fact that a Czech writer became known throughout the world did not result in adulation of Čapek by Czech readers and critics. On the contrary, it inspired jealous critical comments to the effect that Čapek in his unusual works was pandering to foreign tastes. In retrospect, this charge seems particularly unfair. Another oddity is the fact that Čapek abandoned the theater after the worldwide success of *R.U.R.* and *The Insect Play*, chiefly producing short stories until his greatest triumph, the trilogy of philosophical novels *Hordubal, Meteor,* and *An Ordinary Life*. When, in 1937, he returned to the theater with *Power and Glory*, followed in 1938 by *The Mother*, it was to appeal to the conscience of the world with two timely plays concerned with the catastrophe prepared by Nazism. The plays were designed to counter the spirit of pacifism and appeasement then sweeping Europe; Čapek hoped to salvage Czechoslovakia, destined to be given to the Nazis as a peace offering.

Čapek's last work of great importance was *The Cheat*, written after the tragedy of Munich. Čapek mourned the death of his Republic and yet inspired his compatriots not to despair. *The Cheat* breaks with the relativist philosophy common to all of his works: The cheat is a cheat, a fake, a swindler and not a composer, and the novel's many vantage points only underscore this judgment. Death overtook Čapek while he was writing the conclusion of the novel, on Christmas Day, 1938; for political reasons, his grateful readers were not permitted to say good-bye to him in a public ceremony. He was survived by Olga Scheinpflugová, an actress and writer, his companion and wife.

Though Čapek's life was comfortable in material terms, he was afflicted with calcification of the spine, a painful condition that made full enjoyment of those comforts impossible; it also postponed his marriage to only a few years before his death. This physical suffering was accompanied by a spiritual search. For years, as the testimony of his literary works shows, he was content with pragmatism and relativism, though he was not an ethical relativist. Only toward the end of his life, as witness his last novel, did he embrace the idea that, often, people are what they seem, definitely and irrevocably: They are fully responsible for their actions.

Never does Čapek complain or rant against destiny: There is a sunny and humorous side to his work that balances the dark visions. Perhaps his excellence in life and art is explained by his personal heroism in alchemizing his suffering into a quest for a meaningful life.

Analysis

Karel Čapek was a philosophical writer *par excellence* regardless of the genre that he employed in a given work, but the form of long fiction in particular afforded him the amplitude to express complicated philosophical ideas. Thus, his greatest achievement is the trilogy consisting of *Hordubal*, *Meteor*, and *An Ordinary Life*. These three novels preserve the fruit of Čapek's life's work: the searchings and findings of his many short stories, plays, and newspaper columns, as well as his lifelong preoccupation with the philosophy of pragmatism and relativism.

While the trilogy is a complex and at the same time harmonious statement of Čapek's philosophy, his last novel, *The Cheat*, though shorter than either of the three novels of the trilogy, is important for representing a sharp and shocking departure from the trilogy's philosophy. It represents a further development of Čapek's philosophical search.

Hordubal is based on a newspaper story of a crime that took place in the most backward region of prewar Czechoslovakia, the Transcarpathian Ukraine. Juraj Hordubal, an unsophisticated but very sensitive and even saintly peasant, returns from the United States, where he worked and made some money, to his wife Polana and daughter Hafia. He is unaware that in his absence, Polana has fallen in love with Stefan Manya, a Hungarian hired hand. To disguise this affair, Polana forces Manya to become engaged to the eleven-year-old Hafia. When this ruse does not work, the lovers kill Hordubal with a long needle. A criminal investigation uncovers the crime and identifies the criminals, who are caught and punished.

Appropriating the bare facts of the newspaper report with minimal modifications, Čapek invests this simple tale of passion with philosophical depth, first by making Juraj Hordubal a rather sensitive man who is aware of the changed circumstances upon his return home. The reader is painfully aware of this when the author lets us follow Hordubal's thoughts in beautifully stylized, lyric passages of almost saintly insight and renunciation of violence, leading to the acceptance of his death. The tension develops on several levels simultaneously.

The first level is the *crime passionelle*, the road which introduces us to the contrasting figures of Hordubal and Manya. A deeper level is attained when the reader perceives the cultural-ethnic contrast: Hordubal, the sedentary agricultural type, is opposed to the Hungarian Manya, the nomadic, violent type. Finally, there is the level on which the tension is between subjective reality, the reality of a given character who sees the world his own way, and objective reality. The conclusion, however, undercuts any confident faith in the existence of objective reality. Hordubal is seriously ill when he is murdered, so that a question arises whether the needle of the killer entered his heart before or after his death; if after, there was no murder.

The problem of the interpretation of even simple phenomena is brought to a head in the confrontation between two irreconcilable types of criminal investigations, based on different sets of assumptions and interpretations of events. In the conflict between the young policeman and his seasoned colleague, the deceptively simple case grows more and more complicated. In a plot twist that stresses the evanescent nature of man's certainties, the key evidence, Juraj Hordubal's heart, is lost in transport, condemning those involved in the investigation to eternal incertitude. The novel shakes the certitudes established in the mystery genre, suggesting that mutually exclusive interpretations are not only possible but also inevitable. More to the point, with the death of Hordubal, the protagonist's internal monologue ceases; the reader no longer sees Hordubal from inside. What the others think about Hordubal is widely off the mark.

If the truth is relative and hopelessly compromised by the very fact that it is being approached by different people, the second novel of the trilogy reverses the procedure and asks if different people might not discover the truth on the basis of sharing with one another the human condition and thus having very much in common: first the difference, then the commonality. The second novel, *Meteor*, approaches this further elaboration of Čapek's philosophical quest in an original manner.

Čapek uses three narrators who speculate about the identity of a man fatally wounded in a plane crash and brought to a hospital as "patient X." The three narrators, including a Sister of Mercy, a clairvoyant, and a writer, try to reconstruct his life and the reason for his flight.

The first narrator, the Sister, sees X as a young man who runs away from home unaware of the real meaning of love and responsibility. After some peregrinations, he decides to return home, only to crash and die in the process.

The clairvoyant sees X as a talented chemist who discovered important new formulas but lacked the patience to see his experiments through and develop them commercially. When he finds that his experiments were founded on a sound basis, he decides to return and claim the discoveries as his own.

The writer sees the patient as a victim of amnesia who falls in love with a Cuban girl but is unable to live without memory. When his suffering triggers the recovery of his past, the man flies home to lay claim to his position.

All three accounts differ from one another in approach and in substance, yet each of them identifies an important facet of the victim as well as providing an insight into the character of the individual narrator. Čapek thus raises the question of self-discovery, the perennial identity problem: What happens when X and the observer are one and the same person? The third novel of the trilogy, *An Ordinary Life*, provides the answer.

A retired bureaucrat, a self-confessed "ordinary man," decides to write the story of his own life. Looking back, he concludes that he lived an ordinary life governed only by habit and chance; it seems repetitious and predictable to him. There are, however, a few incidents that do not fit this summary generalization of his life, and the more he thinks about them, the more fully he understands that right within his ordinary life, there is a multitude of lives: He as a person is not an individuality but a plurality. He, like a microcosm, mirrors the macrocosm of society. Does he have a stable point of view, or does it too change with each different personality as he comes to adopt it? This is not a case of a pathological disorder; the protagonist is a normal official who, before he settled down to his ways, explored radically different lifestyles. Like all people, he bears within him the potential for many selves, never fully realized.

Thus, the tension between subjective and objective reality that animates *Hordubal* collapses in *An Ordinary Life*, which proposes that even what is considered a subjective reality (the only accessible one, since the objective escapes forever) is itself a plurality.

As an experiment, as individual novels, and as a philosophical trilogy, these three novels are brilliant. What is difficult to communicate beyond the pale outlines and philosophical underpinnings of these works is their distinctive tone, their often lyric air. This atmosphere of numinous twilight, so difficult to communicate, bathes the novels in an unearthly light and adds to them a certain air of beauty. It comes as a surprise, then, that Čapek's last work, *The Cheat*, makes a departure from the finished whole of the trilogy on philosophical grounds.

The trilogy was the culmination of Čapek's work; the relativist philosophy enshrined within it is the summation of findings and beliefs that, for better or worse, animated Čapek's entire oeuvre. *The Cheat* continues with the insights gained in the trilogy—for example, the method of multiple narration is preserved. The several narratives, nine in all, gradually fill out the picture of the fake artist Foltýn, the would-be composer. These multiple narratives, however, do not yield a relativistic perspective: The individual accounts never contradict one another; rather, they gradually illuminate Foltýn and answer some of the questions that the various narrators have raised. The collective finding is damning, and yet there is something admirable in Foltýn: His obsessive love of art saves him from utter condemnation. In his attempt to express the impossible, Foltýn is like every artist; every artist has a little Foltýn in him. It is only fitting, given Čapek's sense of balance, that, after providing in his trilogy examples of the power of art to do good, to express the truth, he should point to the capacity of art to profess evil. Thus, he embraced the totality of the world that his suffering enabled him to know intimately.

Major publications other than long fiction
  SHORT FICTION: *Zářivé hlubiny*, 1916 (with Josef Čapek); *Boží muka*, 1917; *Krakonošova zahrada*, 1918; *Trapné povídky*, 1921 (*Money and Other Stories*, 1929); *Povídky z druhé kapsy*, 1929 (*Tales from Two Pockets*, 1932); *Povídky z jedné kapsy*, 1929; *Devatero pohádek*, 1931 (*Fairy Tales*, 1933); *Kniha apokryfů*, 1946 (*Apocryphal Stories*, 1949).
  PLAYS: *R.U.R.*, 1920 (with Josef Čapek; English translation, 1923); *Ze života hmyzu*, 1922 (with Josef Čapek; *The Insect Play*, 1923; also as *And So Ad Infinitum*, 1923); *Věc Makropulos*, 1922 (*The Macropulos Secret*, 1925); *Bílá nemoc*, 1937 (*Power and Glory*, 1938); *Matka*, 1938 (*The Mother*, 1939).
  NONFICTION: *Pragmatismus*, 1918; *Kritika slov*, 1920; *Anglické listy*, 1923 (*Letters from England*, 1925); *Hovory s T. G. Masarykem*, 1928-1935 (3 volumes; *President Masaryk Tells His Story*, 1934; also as *Masaryk on Thought and Life*, 1938).

Bibliography
Harkins, W. E. *Karel Čapek*, 1962.
Matuška, Alexander. *Karel Čapek: An Essay*, 1964.

Peter Petro

ALEJO CARPENTIER

Born: Havana, Cuba; December 26, 1904
Died: Paris, France; April 24, 1980

Principal long fiction

¡Ecué-Yamba-O! Historia Afro-Cubana, 1933; *El reino de este mundo*, 1949 (*The Kingdom of This World*, 1957); *Los pasos perdidos*, 1953 (*The Lost Steps*, 1956, 1967); *El acoso*, 1956 (*Manhunt*, 1959); *El siglo de las luces*, 1962 (*Explosion in a Cathedral*, 1963); *El recurso del método*, 1974 (*Reasons of State*, 1976); *Concierto barroco*, 1974; *La consagración de la primavera*, 1978; *El arpa y la sombra*, 1979.

Other literary forms

Early in his career, Alejo Carpentier published two volumes of poetry: *Dos poemas afro-cubanos* (1930) and, in French, *Poèmes des Antilles* (1931). Carpentier did not publish poetry after the early 1930's, though some of his poems, particularly one or two in French, were quite good. Two of his poems from the Afro-Cuban period have been widely anthologized. Carpentier's nonfiction works include *La música en Cuba* (1946), *Tientos y diferencias* (1964), and *La novela latinoamericana en vísperas del nuevo siglo* (1981). *La música en Cuba* is a beautiful book, combining Carpentier's mastery as a narrator with a supple descriptive style. His essays in *Tientos y diferencias* were very influential among critics of the Latin American novel. Carpentier was known both as a writer and as a musicologist. He wrote the scenario for several Afro-Cuban ballets, most notably *El milagro de Anaquillé* (1928), and innumerable journalistic pieces on music and literature. From 1950 to 1959, he wrote a column on these topics for *El nacional*, in Caracas. Carpentier's short fiction deals with very large topics and spans of time rather than characters caught in daily existence—about great issues such as causality in history. *Guerra del tiempo* (1958; *War of Time*, 1970) is one of the best-known collections of short stories in Latin America and the world.

Achievements

It can be safely said that Alejo Carpentier is the father of today's Latin American fiction. All major Latin American novelists today owe a great debt to him, and many, from Gabriel García Márquez to Carlos Fuentes, have acknowledged it. Carpentier had to pay out of his own pocket for the publication of his two early masterpieces, *The Kingdom of This World* and *The Lost Steps*, while today's Latin American writers, particularly García Márquez, Fuentes, and Mario Vargas Llosa, can command enormous fees for their work. This they owe to Carpentier, who in 1958 was hailed as a master deserving the Nobel Prize by a critic for *The New York Times* when most

English-language readers had not heard of a single Latin American author.

Carpentier's major achievement is to have made Latin American history the object of experimental fiction. Before *The Kingdom of This World*, there had been major works of fiction in Latin America, as well as very important books of history, but no major prose writer had ventured to use Latin American history as the object of daring experimentation. Jorge Luis Borges had produced great short-story collections, such as *Historia universal de la infamia* (1935; *A Universal History of Infamy*, 1972) and above all *Ficciones* (1944; English translation, 1962), and Miguel Ángel Asturias had published to great acclaim his *Leyendas de Guatemala* (1930; legends of Guatemala), based on Mayan myths from his native Guatemala. There had also been great novelists of the pampa, such as Ricardo Güiraldes; of the Mexican Revolution, such as Mariano Azuela; and of the Venezuelan plain, such as Rómulo Gallegos. Carpentier managed to bring together the interests of the regionalist writers (Asturias, Güiraldes, Azuela) with Borges' penchant for fictional games. The admixture is what has come to be known as Magic Realism, or the description of "marvelous American reality."

Unlike writers such as Asturias, who in their fiction turned to Mayan or other indigenous Latin American myths, Carpentier focused his attention on the folklore of his native Caribbean, which meant that of Africa. Caribbean history has been shaped by slavery, which provided the work force for the sugar industry. Several major African religions took root in the Caribbean, influencing art, music, and literature in the region. This was recognized by a group of artists who in the 1920's founded what came to be known as the Afro-Antillean movement. Carpentier was one of its founders and promoters. He was originally interested in ritualistic practices and, above all, in Afro-Cuban music. These interests, however, led him to read all he could find about the history of Africans in the New World and eventually led him to their greatest political achievement, the Haitian Revolution at the end of the eighteenth century. Carpentier discovered that the Haitian Revolution, which toppled the French colonial regime and instituted a black monarchy and later a republic, was the origin of modern Caribbean history. He tells the story of this revolution in his influential *The Kingdom of This World*, one of the great novels of the century in any language.

Carpentier saw that Haitian history, particularly as manifested in the events of the Revolution, was ripe with incredible happenings, if viewed from a purely European perspective. The fusion of African and French customs on the island made for a very discordant and rich mixture that could not be described with the narrative techniques of the conventional novel. Time seemed to have a different rhythm. Events repeated themselves or were anticipated by apparently chance happenings. Cause and effect seemed to obey a different set of rules. It is the description of such bizarre events and sequels of events that has come to be known as Magic Realism. The term goes back to turn-of-the-century art, but its conception by Carpentier was influenced mainly by the Surrealists, with whom Carpentier had a close relationship in Paris in the late 1920's and early 1930's.

The Kingdom of This World and the stories later collected in *War of Time* all deal with the problem of time—that is to say, with its representation in fiction. In the novel, time appears as a series of repetitions. History is a tissue of events connected not by causal links but by numerological and metaphoric connections. In one of the most widely anthologized stories from *War of Time*, "Viaje a la Semilla" ("Journey Back to the Source"), time runs backward, from the protagonist's death to his return to the womb. In another, "Semejante a la noche" ("Like the Night"), the same incident is repeated in six different historical moments that are separated by centuries.

It is this sort of experimentation that makes possible novels such as García Márquez' widely acclaimed *Cien años de soledad* (1967; *One Hundred Years of Solitude*, 1970) and Fuentes' *Terra nostra* (1975; English translation, 1976). In short, Carpentier's experiments with fiction and Latin American history led to what has been termed the *boom* of the Latin American novel. More than all the prizes that he won (notably the Cervantes Prize in Spain), Carpentier's most enduring achievement is to have made possible experimentation in Latin American fiction dealing with Latin American history. This brought about an entirely new view of Latin America by its own artists.

Biography

Alejo Carpentier Valmont was born in Havana, Cuba, in 1904. His parents had emigrated to Cuba two years before. His father was a French architect, and his mother was of Russian origin. Carpentier, whose first language was French (he retained throughout his life a French accent in Spanish), was sent to the best schools in Havana. While in his early teens, he and his parents made a very long trip to Europe, first traveling to Russia to claim an inheritance and later spending a good deal of time in Paris. In the French capital, Carpentier attended high school and began to acquire what was to become his awesome musical erudition. Back in Cuba, Carpentier finished his secondary education and registered at the university. He wanted to be an architect, like his father, but two events prevented his finishing his university studies.

First, his father left home and was never heard from again, which forced Carpentier to earn a living for himself and his mother. Second, classes at the university were frequently canceled because of political turmoil. Carpentier left school altogether and joined the revolutionary students who were fighting against Gerardo Machado, a dictator supported by the United States. Carpentier worked as a journalist and was instrumental in founding the Afro-Cuban movement, which hailed Cuba's African heritage. Afro-Cubanism wanted to create a new aesthetic based on Afro-Cuban folklore, and, as a political movement, championed the cause of the exploited black workers. Carpentier was jailed briefly in early 1928; a few months later, he managed to escape to France.

In France, Carpentier was protected by his friend, the Surrealist poet Robert Desnos. Between 1928 and 1930, Carpentier was associated with the influential Surrealist movement, and, in 1930, he participated in one of the squabbles that split the group. He had learned from Surrealism that his desire to look at things from a non-European perspective, something he had sought through Afro-Cubanism, was a major force in all avant-garde aesthetics. It became his major preoccupation as an artist. Translated into his own terms, the issue was how to look at reality with Latin American eyes. In France, he met other Latin American artists engaged in the same quest: the Cuban painter Wifredo Lam, the Guatemalan novelist Miguel Ángel Asturias, the Venezuelan novelist Arturo Uslar Pietri, and the Cuban folklorist Lydia Cabrera. He learned from all of them, as well as from James Joyce, the great Irish writer living in Paris at the time, who was plumbing the English language in search of a new way of expressing the world. Marginality—Joyce from the British Empire, the Latin Americans from Europe in general—was the bond.

Carpentier made a living in Paris with radio work, becoming an expert on radio broadcasting and advertising; these two activities became his source of income for many years to come. In Paris, he needed them, for he married very shortly after settling in that city. His wife, a Swiss, died soon of tuberculosis, and Carpentier married a Frenchwoman who accompanied him back to Cuba in 1939, on the eve of World War II.

In Cuba, Carpentier was known mainly as a journalist, for he had also made a living by writing articles about Europe for *Carteles*, a Cuban weekly magazine of which Carpentier had been a founding editor at the age of nineteen. His articles on the new European art had made him rather well-known, but not really as a writer. The fact is that by 1939, when he returned to Havana, Carpentier had published only ¡*Ecué-Yamba-O!*, an unsuccessful novel about blacks in Cuba. Between 1939 and 1945, when he again left Cuba, Carpentier made decisions that changed his life. First, he divorced his French wife and married a Cuban woman from a well-to-do family. This new wife, Lilia Esteban Hierro, to whom he dedicated every book he wrote after 1939, remained with him until his death. Second, he immersed himself in the history of the Caribbean, in search of the origins of Cuban music. This research led to his experiments in fiction, which in turn led to his first great novel, *The Kingdom of This World*. First, however, he published a beautiful history of Cuban music, *La música en Cuba*, a book that is the key to the understanding of Carpentier's mature fiction. In it one sees for the first time the historian at work, culling from myriad written sources a history that does not fit the mold of European history. Both *The Kingdom of This World* and all the stories collected in *War of Time* issue from the research and experimentation carried out while Carpentier was writing *La música en Cuba*.

In the summer of 1945, Carpentier moved to Caracas. Carlos Frías, a friend from his years in Paris, had founded an advertising agency and offered Carpentier an important position. Carpentier was to remain in Venezuela until 1959, when he returned to Havana, after the triumph of the Cuban Revolution. In Caracas, Carpentier worked not only in advertising but also as a journalist, writing an almost daily column on literature and music for *El nacional*; he also gave lectures at the university and devoted himself with great discipline to his fiction. In Caracas, he completed *The Lost Steps*, *Manhunt*, and *Explosion in a Cathedral* and also wrote much of *Concierto barroco* and *Reasons of State*. Although all of these novels are of the highest caliber, the most important of them all is *The Lost Steps*.

The Lost Steps grew out of two trips that Carpentier undertook to the jungles of Venezuela. During the summer of 1948, he journeyed to the region bordering Venezuela and British Guiana, nearly on the frontier with Brazil. In the summer of the next year, he traveled up the Orinoco River toward the Colombian border. These voyages, and his work as an advertising executive in Caracas, provide the biographical background of *The Lost Steps*.

Carpentier returned to Havana in the summer of 1959. The Cuban Revolution seemed to be the fulfillment of all of his dreams as a young artist and political activist. He was also in the business of organizing book festivals to sell, at popular prices, books by Latin American authors. When the Revolution turned Socialist, the business was nationalized and Carpentier was named head of the newly formed State Publishing House. He remained in that post until 1968, when he was sent to Paris as cultural attaché to the Cuban cultural delegation in that city. He lived in Paris until his death in 1980, as an employee of the Cuban revolutionary government, but also writing his last novels: *Reasons of State*, *Concierto barroco*, *La consagración de la primavera*, and *El arpa y la sombra*. He also traveled a great deal, lecturing widely. Carpentier gave a lecture at Yale University in the spring of 1979, a year before his death; it was his first trip to the United States since the early 1940's, when the Columbia Broadcasting System had brought him to New York to offer him a job broadcasting to Latin America.

Carpentier's support of the Castro regime made him a controversial figure in the last two decades of his life. He never wavered in his allegiance, though his works are hardly those of a Marxist, with the exception of *La consagración de la primavera*, in which he turned doctrinaire. The novel was a failure.

After his death on April 24, 1980, Carpentier's remains were returned to Cuba, where he was buried with great honors.

Analysis

The Lost Steps, a novel written in the first person by a character much like Carpentier, is the story of modern man and his desire to leave civilization to find himself in the origins of history. The narrator-protagonist, a musicologist who works for an advertising agency, agrees to travel up a large river in South America in search of primitive instruments that will verify his theory concerning the origins of music. He undertakes this task at the request of his old professor at the university. It is time for his vacation, so he accepts the job, in part to take advantage of the opportunity to travel at the expense of the university. He goes with Mouche, his mistress, while Ruth, his wife, who is an actress, remains behind in the large city in which they live (presumably New York, although no specific indications are given). Because the narrator-protagonist is originally from Latin America, his return means also a new encounter with the language of his childhood.

He and Mouche spend time first at a Latin American capital (very much like Caracas and Havana), where he begins to remember his childhood and longs for the past. While they are at the capital, a revolution breaks out, forcing them to take refuge in the hotel where they are staying while bands of revolutionaries fight soldiers. The protagonist-narrator, who is recording all of these events in a diary, remembers World War II, in which he participated as a photographer. The evils of civilization appear more onerous, and he wishes to press on with his trip to the jungle. They finally make the necessary arrangements, traveling first by bus, to a smaller city, and later by boat. Along the way, they encounter a native woman, Rosario, who winds up becoming the narrator-protagonist's mistress. Mouche, he discovers, is having a lesbian affair with a Canadian painter they have met. She returns to civilization, where presumably she belongs, while the narrator-protagonist continues on his journey. He has joined various other characters, most notably an adventurer who has founded a city. When they reach this city, which turns out to be a mere gathering of huts, the narrator-protagonist finds the instruments for which he has been looking. He also begins to compose music again, something he has not been able to do since he began to sell his time to the advertising agency. He needs paper in order to compose, however, and the founder of the city can furnish him with only a few notebooks that he treasures as volumes in which to record the laws of his new society.

In the meantime, Ruth has mounted a campaign to rescue her husband, thinking that he is lost in the jungle. A plane reaches Santa Mónica de los Venados, the city where he is living with Rosario, with whom he has fallen deeply in love, and he decides to return to procure the things that he needs—such as paper—but with the intention of coming back to stay. He is given a hero's welcome back in the city, and he sells his story to some newspapers. Eventually, without a job and wife (Ruth, having found out about Mouche and Rosario, has left him), he is forced to eke out a living writing jingles. He finally manages to return to the Latin American capital and makes his way back to the small river town whence he started on his trip to Santa Mónica. After much waiting, he finds someone to take him back up river, but they are unable to find the mark on a tree that indicated the secret channel through which Santa Mónica could be reached. The waters of the river have risen, obliterating the mark. The narrator-protagonist hears from a traveler that Rosario has married somebody else.

Disillusioned with the idea of being able to return to the origins of history, to shed civilization, the narrator-protagonist realizes that he can look only toward the future, for he is condemned to time, to temporality.

The autobiographical elements of *The Lost Steps* are obvious. On a deeper level, however, one must take notice of how Carpentier is putting to a test the validity of his own experiments as an artist. Is it really possible to look at history from a perspective like that of someone belonging to nonhistorical cultures? In other words, do the ritualistic repetitions of history present in *The Kingdom of This World* mean that Carpentier has really escaped the march of time as conceived by modernity, or is it merely an artist's trick? Are we really dependent on the past, on our origins, or are we only of the present? Carpentier's exploration of these questions goes beyond simply writing about them through his autobiographical character. *The Lost Steps* itself, in its own constitution, has all of these issues embedded in it. The novel is written partially as if it were a diary, which allows the reader to reconstruct a very precise and suggestive time scheme. The novel begins in June and ends on December 31 of a year that can only be 1950. That is to say, the novel begins in midyear of the year that divides the century into two halves. There is also a compelling alternation of Monday and Sunday. Important events in the novel take place on those significant days, one marking the beginning of work, of action, the other a sort of hiatus, a gap. In reconstructing the time scheme of the novel, one is able to pick up an error made by the narrator-protagonist, who skips a Monday once he is deep in the jungle, as if he had finally left history—Monday meaning the beginning of history. This significant time scheme suggests to the reader that the narrator-protagonist is caught in a web of signs that are beyond his comprehension or control. Was he really ever able to be free?

Before *The Lost Steps*, Carpentier's fiction seemed to project onto nature the timeless world of nonhistorical civilizations. The African cosmogonies that led the blacks to action in Haiti had as their counterpart the periodicity of nature, its penchant for repetition and predictability and for abolishing change. *The Lost Steps* teaches Carpentier that he cannot make such an assumption, that history is moved not by natural forces but by the action of men and women, by political activity and struggle. Whereas in his earlier novels great natural upheavals—such as hurricanes—conspired with history, in his later works history as political action prevails.

This change is evident in *Reasons of State*, Carpentier's "dictator novel." This book appeared at about the same time as two other novels with the same theme: Augusto Roa Bastos' *Yo el Supremo* (1974) and García Márquez' *El otoño del patriarca* (1975; *Autumn of the Patriarch*, 1975). All three novels have as protagonist a Latin American dictator, and all deal with the issue of political power, democracy, and the Latin American tradition. Carpentier's dictator, the First Magistrate, is a composite figure, incorporating characteristics of Manuel Estrada Cabrera, Rafael Trujillo, Fulgencio Batista, and Machado. He is, however—or pretends to be—more cultivated than these personages. The First Magistrate spends half of his life in Paris, where he is courted by venal academics and writers in debt. At home he is ruthless in suppressing the opposition, but abroad he wants to project an image of tolerance. The novel, like all of Carpentier's fictions, is an experiment with time. There are recognizable events that date the beginning of the action in the late teens. It is easy to follow a historical chronology up to about 1927. From there on, there are leaps forward in time, until the finish in 1972, at the dictator's tomb in Paris. He has been defeated by the Student, a revolutionary who looms as the future of Latin America. *Reasons of State* is a comic novel that pokes fun at Latin American dictators and their penchant for extravagant expenditures, hollow rhetoric, and brutal ways.

In *La consagración de la primavera*, Carpentier's turn to more political fiction failed him. The novel is a rewrite of *The Lost Steps*, but it is cumbersome and doctrinaire. It seems to have been written with the purpose of writing the novel of the Cuban Revolution. The main protagonist is a character much like Carpentier, who participates in or is touched by the major political upheavals of his time. He winds up in Cuba, fighting for the Revolution against the invasion at the Bay of Pigs. This character is an architect (architecture, one recalls, is a career Carpentier could have pursued). Another protagonist is a composer. The background of the Spanish Civil War, with which the novel begins, sets the tone: It is a novel about bourgeois intellectuals who feel deeply the political causes of their times and wish to join the Revolution. Time is seen in the novel as a continuum: The Russian Revolution leads to the Spanish Civil War, which, in turn, leads to the Cuban Revolution. The novel is thinly veiled autobiography. Carpentier's dearest wish was to have his own time, the time of his life, become enmeshed with that of history, a history seen as the progression to freedom brought about by revolution.

Major publications other than long fiction
SHORT FICTION: *Guerra del tiempo*, 1958 (*War of Time*, 1970).
POETRY: *Dos poemas afro-cubanos*, 1930; *Poèmes des Antilles*, 1931.
NONFICTION: *La música en Cuba*, 1946; *Tientos y diferencias*, 1964; *La novela latinoamericana en vísperas del nuevo siglo*, 1981.
MISCELLANEOUS: *El milagro de Anaquillé*, 1928 (ballet scenario).

Bibliography
Cheuse, A. *Memories of the Future: A Critical Biography of Alejo Carpentier*, 1975.

González Echevarría, Roberto. *Alejo Carpentier: The Pilgrim at Home*, 1977.
González Echevarría, Roberto, and Klaus Muller-Bergh. *Alejo Carpentier: Guia bibliográfica/Bibliographical Guide*, 1983.

Roberto González Echevarría

CAMILO JOSÉ CELA

Born: Iria Flavia del Padrón, Spain; May 11, 1916

Principal long fiction

La familia de Pascual Duarte, 1942 (*The Family of Pascual Duarte*, 1946, 1964); *Pabellón de reposo*, 1943 (*Rest Home*, 1961); *Nuevas andanzas y desventuras del Lazarillo de Tormes*, 1944; *La colmena*, 1951 (*The Hive*, 1953); *Mrs. Caldwell habla con su hijo*, 1953 (*Mrs. Caldwell Speaks to Her Son*, 1968); *La Catira*, 1955; *Tobogán de hambrientos*, 1962; *San Camilo, 1936*, 1969; *Oficio de tinieblas, 5*, 1973; *Mazurka para dos muertos*, 1983.

Other literary forms

Camilo José Cela's ten major novels and a few minor ones are but a fraction of his literary production. He excels as a short-story writer and author of travel books, having published more than half a dozen volumes in each of these genres. *Esas nubes que pasan* (1945; passing clouds) contains twelve tales previously published in periodicals. It was followed by *El bonito crimen del carabinero y otras invenciones* (1947; the patrolman's nice crime and other inventions), *El gallego y su cuadrilla* (1949; the Galician and his team), *Baraja de invenciones* (1953; deck of inventions), *El molino de viento*, (1956; the windmill), *Nuevo retablo de don Crostobita* (1957), *Gavilla de fábulas sin amor* (1962; bag of loveless fables), *Once cuentos de fútbol* (1963; eleven soccer tales). His early travel books have been superior to the later ones, the better ones including *Viaje a la Alcarria* (1948; *Journey to Alcarria*, 1964), *Del Miño al Bidasoa* (1952; from the Miño to the Bidasoa), *Judíos, moros y cristianos* (1956; Jews, Moors and Christians), *Primer viaje andaluz* (1959; first Andalusian trip), *Viaje al Pirineo de Lérida* (1965; trip to the Lérida Pyrenees), *Páginas de geografía errabunda* (1965; pages of vagabond geography), and *Viaje a U.S.A.* (1967; trip to the U.S.). Cela has many volumes of essays to his credit, including *Mesa revuelta* (1945; messy table); *La rueda de los ocios* (1957; wheel of idleness); *Cajón de sastre* (1957; tailor's box); *La obra literaria del pintor Solana*, 1958 (the literary work of the painter Solana), which was Cela's entrance speech to the Royal Spanish Academy; *Cuatro figuras del '98* (1961), on four writers of the *generación del 98*; *Al servicio de algo* (1969; in service to something); *A vueltas con España* (1973; around again with Spain); *Vuelta de hoja* (1981; turning the page); and *El juego de los tres madroños* (1983; the shell game). Miscellaneous prose works include his as yet unfinished memoirs, *La cucaña* (the cocoon), of which the first volume, *La rosa* (the rose), published in 1959, spans his childhood. Cela also cultivates what he calls *apuntes carpetovetónicos* (carpetovetonic sketches), a term alluding to the mountains of central Spain. These are brief literary etchings or vignettes combining humor, irony, anger, pity, and a bittersweet affection, portraying beggars, the blind, village idiots, prostitutes, and a host of the poor and indigent: *Historias de España: Los ciegos, los tontos* (1958) and *Los viejos amigos* (1960, 1961). His short stories and novellas range from the exquisitely crafted stylistic tour de force, in which popular language or regional dialect is captured in all of its inimitable regional flavor, to the condensed, violent shocker, the prose poem, and the ironic vignette. The itinerant wanderings of the narrator of picaresque novels are updated in his travel books, as Cela adapts the form to covert sociopolitical commentary. He is also a refreshingly frank, if somewhat arbitrary and arrogant, critic.

In addition to short stories, travel books, and literary criticism, Cela's better-known works include erudite studies of obscenities and vulgarity, exemplified by the *Diccionario secreto* (1968, 1971; secret dictionary) and a three-volume companion survey of sexuality, *Enciclopedia del erotismo* (1977; encyclopedia of eroticism). During the 1960's, he published several limited-edition works for the collectors' market, some with illustrations Pablo Picasso and others featuring artistic photography, most of them short on narrative and long on visual titillation, including *Toreo de salón* (1963; living room bullfighting), *Las compañías convenientes* (1963; appropriate company), *Garito de hospicianos* (1963; poorhouse inmates), *Izas, rabizas y colipoterras* (1964; bawds, harlots, and whores), *El ciudadano Iscariote Reclús* (1965; citizen Iscariot Reclus), *La familia del héroe* (1965; the hero's family), and a series of seven *Nuevas escenas matritenses* (1965-1966; new Madrid scenes). His *Obra completa* (complete works) began to appear in 1962 and is still in progress (he has published some seventy titles).

Achievements

With the death and exile of many writers of previous generations, Spanish literature languished during and after the Spanish Civil War (1936-1939). The first sign of rebirth was Cela's novel *The Family of Pascual Duarte*, which sparked a host of imitators and set the pattern for the novel during much of the 1940's, a movement known as *tremendismo*. His next novels were successful, if less imitated, and his fame was assured with *The Hive*, which became the prototype for the social novel of the 1950's and 1960's. It is extremely rare that a Spanish writer is able to live by his pen, and Cela has managed to do so; he was also elected to the prestigious Royal Spanish Academy in 1957, his nation's highest literary honor. Many of his works have been translated, and for nearly four decades, he has been considered one of Spain's foremost novelists. Cela is a trendsetter, interesting as an innovator but not as a creator of memorable characters or plots. He is a leading stylist and excels as a caricaturist.

Biography

Camilo José Cela has occasionally made literature of his life, and many biographies of him contain apocryphal data. (For example, it is frequently said that he lived with an aunt in England as a child, when in fact he never left Spain.) His mother, although reared in Spain, was a British citizen; his father was a customs official, and the family moved often. The novelist is from a large family, the extended family containing a number of priests and nuns, reflecting the traditional background. (His brother also is a writer, using the name Jorge Trulock.) Young Cela was an indifferent student in religious schools; his university studies were interrupted by the Spanish Civil War, but not before he had come under the influence of intellectuals of the *generacíon del 27*, especially the poet Pedro Salinas (his professor and mentor), and the philosophy of José Ortega y Gasset.

Cela suffered bouts with tuberculosis at the ages of eighteen and twenty-five, using the long convalescences to read the Spanish classics. Although he studied law, medicine, and philosophy, he did not complete a degree, and his literary knowledge is largely autodidactic. Cela likewise became a serious student of regional Spanish history and folkways and an erudite lexicographer of vulgar speech. In 1944, he married María Rosario Conde Picavea; their only child, a son, was born in 1946. Cela involved himself in several publishing enterprises and in 1957 founded the periodical *Papeles de Son Armadans* (extremely influential among younger writers, it lasted until the early 1980's). Living in the Balearic Islands, he has maintained residences in both Madrid and Palma de Mallorca. He has counted among his friends artists (Picasso, Joan Miró), poets (Robert Graves, Vicente Aleixandre, Dámaso Alonso, Gerardo Diego), critics, and intellectuals of international repute. Cela was elected to the Royal Spanish Academy in 1957; in 1978, King Juan Carlos appointed him as an independent senator to represent intellectual interests and views.

Analysis

Camilo José Cela has an inimitable way with language, a personal style which is instantly recognizable after minimal acquaintance, thanks to his characteristic handling of the *estribillo* (tag line), alliterative and rhythmic prose, parallelistic constructions, grotesque caricatures with moments of tenderness, unabashed lyricism with ever-present irony, and the incorporation of popular sayings or proverbs, vulgarities, and obscenities in the context of academically correct and proper passages. His art more closely approaches the painter's than the dramatist's, and it is far removed from the adventure novel. With the exception perhaps of *The Family of Pascual Duarte*, Cela's novels have little action and a preponderance of description and dialogue. As a painter with words, one of whose favorite subjects is language itself, unflaggingly aware of its trivializations and absurdities yet fascinated with nuances, examining and playing with words, Cela produces ironic conversations, incidents, and scenes which often could very well stand alone. This characteristic, usually one of his virtues as a writer, becomes at times a vice, for he tends to repeat himself and also to produce novels in which there is little if any character development and often no sustained or sequential action— no plot in the traditional sense. The reader whose interest in a piece of fiction is proportional to "what happens" may find Cela's short stories more rewarding than his novels.

Because it inspired many imitations, Cela's first novel, *The Family of Pascual Duarte*, is considered the prototype of a novelistic movement called *tremendismo*, an allusion to its "tremendous" impact upon the reader's sensibilities. *Tremendismo*—a modified Naturalism that lacks the scientific pretensions of the French movement, and to which expressionistic ingredients were added—was characterized by depiction of crimes of sometimes shocking violence, a wide range of mental and sexual aberrations, and antiheroic figures. Frequently, repulsive, deviant, and nauseating acts, as well as an accumulation of ugly, malformed, and repugnant characters, were portrayed against a backdrop of poverty and social problems. To this Naturalistic setting were added expressionistic techniques including stylized distortion and the use of caricature and dehumanization (reduction of characters and/or acts to animalistic levels). *Tremendismo* had links with postwar Existentialism in the absurdity of the world portrayed, the concern with problems of guilt and authenticity, and the radical solitariness and uncommunicative nature of its characters. In part, the movement was inspired by the horrors of the Spanish Civil War, providing an outlet for outrage when overt protest was impossible.

Not all of Cela's early novels fit this class: The accumulation of violent and sadistic or irrational crimes that are found in the prototypical first novel disappeared in its successor, *Rest Home*, which is set in a tuberculosis sanatorium, an environment the author had occasion to know well. *Rest Home* uses the diary form, excerpts from the writings of several anonymous patients. The sense of alienation and despair which results from helplessness pervades this novel as the victims battle not only their disease but also the indifference of the world at large and the callousness or cruelty of medical personnel; this insensitivity to death, man's inhumanity to man, is the "tremendous" element in this otherwise quiet, hopeless, almost paralytic novel. In *The Hive*, it is the overall tone or atmosphere (there is only one crime, an unsolved murder), an atmosphere of defeatism, cynicism, and sordid materialism, that is characteristic of *tremendismo*. Still, although critics continue to talk of *tremendismo* in *The Hive*, it is so modified and attenuated that there is a legitimate question as to whether the world portrayed in the novel can rightly be so described.

Pascual Duarte, the protagonist and narrative consciousness of *The Family of Pascual Duarte*, is a condemned criminal on death row who has undertaken to write his memoirs or confession as a sort of penance, at the behest of the prison chaplain. Cela utilizes a model derived from the classic Spanish picaresque novel, clearly perceptible in the early chapters—a technique which undoubtedly served to make the somewhat scabrous material more acceptable to the regime's puritanical but strongly nationalist and traditionalistic censors. The frequent appearances of roads, inns and taverns, squalid settings, and marginal characters all reflect the picaresque tradition, as does the first-person, autobiographical form.

Pascual's home life, with a brutal father who made his money illegally, an alcoholic and altogether beastly mother (clearly patterned on the mother of the prototypical picaro, Lazarillo de Tormes), and a sister who became a teenage prostitute, was an endless round of brawls. Exemplifying the notion that hopeless situations go from bad to worse is his mother's promiscuity and the birth of his half brother, Mario, an imbecile who comes into the world at the same time that Pascual's father, rabid and locked in a wardrobe, is dying amid hideous screams after having been bitten by a rabid dog.

Mario never learns to walk or talk but drags himself along the floor like a snake, making whistling noises. He is kicked in the head by his putative father, which results in a festering sore, and finally has an ear and part of his face eaten by a pig as he lies in the street. His brief, unhappy existence comes to an end at the age of seven or eight when he falls into a large stone container of olive oil and drowns. Pascual's grotesquely lyric recollection of the child's one moment of "beauty," with the golden oil clinging to his hair and softening features and expression, is typical of Cela's art. The burial of Mario (attended only by Pascual and a village girl, Lola, who was attracted to him) is lustily climaxed by Pascual's rape of Lola atop Mario's newly dug grave. It is characteristic of Cela also to combine Eros and Thanatos, sexuality and death: Man is viewed as a sensual animal, his reproductive appetite or instincts aroused by the presence of death.

Pascual's name alludes to the Paschal Lamb, or Easter sacrifice, and in an author's foreword to a special edition of the novel printed outside Spain for use by English-speaking students of Spanish, Cela spoke of the "pro-rata of guilt" or responsibility which each member of society shares for the crimes committed by one of that society's members, suggesting that persons are products of the society in and by which they are formed and thus, at best, only partially culpable for their acts. Pascual is a product of the dregs of society, whose existence is the result of the worst kind of social injustice, yet he displays no greed or resentment of the easy life of the wealthy; his crimes are usually crimes of passion and, with the exception of the killing of his mother, are not premeditated.

Significantly, Pascual is always morally superior in one or more ways to his victims, suggesting that he is to be viewed as something of a primitive judge and executioner, taking justice into his own hands. His meting out of retribution spares neither man nor beast: He shoots his hunting hound because the dog looked at him the wrong way (interpreted by him as sexual desire or temptation); he knifes his mare (and only transportation) because she had shied, throwing Pascual's pregnant bride and causing her to miscarry; he strangles his first wife in a moment of temporary insanity, upon learning that while he was jailed for knifing a man in a tavern brawl, she had survived by selling herself to El Estirao, the pimp exploiting Pascual's sister; and he later asphyxiates El Estirao when the pimp taunts him. The ax-murder of his mother (who subverted the scruples of his first wife and was ruining his second marriage as well) is one of the bloodiest and most violent passages in contemporary Spanish fiction, yet the reader cannot entirely condemn Pascual.

The novel alternates chapters of violent action with slower, introspective and meditative chapters which not only vary the narrative rhythm but also serve to present the human side of the criminal, who might otherwise appear nothing less than monstrous. They also make it clear that Pascual is completely lacking in social consciousness; his crimes are not politically motivated, nor do they have any connection with revolution in the social sense—a point which is extremely important to the hidden message of the novel as a whole. Although Pascual's autobiographical memoir is abruptly suspended by his execution (he had narrated his life only up to the slaying of his mother), it is possible to deduce from evidence elsewhere in the text that he spent some fifteen years in the penitentiary as a result of his conviction for matricide; he was released at a moment immediately prior to the outbreak of the Spanish Civil War, coinciding with a brief but bloody social revolution which swept his home province of Badajoz. The reader deduces (for the cause of his execution is nowhere stated) that Pascual has been convicted of the murder of the Count of Torremejía, the major clue being the dedication of his memoirs to the Count, Don Jesús, accompanied by an ambiguous statement which could mean that he killed him, but could also convey the idea of a mercy killing, assuming that he found the Count dying in agony, perhaps having been tortured by terrorists.

A supreme irony inheres in Pascual's having received extremely light sentences—from two to fifteen years—for several previous killings, while he is executed as a common criminal for what might normally have been classed an act of war, because the victim was an aristocrat. Given the totalitarian censorship in force at the time the novel was written, none of this is overtly expressed; it is necessary to have a thorough knowledge of contemporary Spanish history and to be aware of such details as the social revolution in Badajoz, likewise unmentioned in the novel, to be able to interpret the otherwise enigmatic denouement to Pascual's career of violence.

One of the clearest proofs that Cela's major virtue is his style is the fact that, despite competent translations, his works have been relatively ill-received by readers of the English-language versions; his style, like poetry, is lost in translation. Too closely bound to colloquial idiom and regional dialect to be fully translatable, Cela's prose must be appreciated in the original. Thus,

Pascual Duarte's story is atypical in being able to stand on its own in other cultures, as was confirmed by the success of the 1976 movie version, which won a best actor's award in the Cannes International Film Festival for José Luis Gómez, the first Spanish actor ever so honored, for his interpretation of the role of Pascual. With all of his contradictions, he is Cela's most complex and memorable character; none of his subsequent novels contains characters sufficiently developed to intrigue the reader and sustain his interest.

The Family of Pascual Duarte has been compared by critics repeatedly to Albert Camus' *L'Étranger* (1942; *The Stranger*, 1946) because of proximity in date of appearance and certain other similarities (the antihero and protagonist-narrator of each novel is a condemned killer awaiting execution, one who speaks impassively of his life and exhibits a shocking lack of internalization of society's values. The differences between the two novels are many, however, the most important being that the narrative consciousness of *The Stranger* is an educated and moderately cultured man, guilty of a single, senseless "reflex" crime, and the philosophical dimension of Camus' writing, while not utterly alien to Cela, is so attenuated because of the audience for which the novel was intended—not forgetting the censors—that its impact is minimal.

The Hive, regarded by many critics as Cela's masterpiece, occupied much of the novelist's time between 1945 and 1950. Because it lacks both plot and protagonist, consisting of a series of loosely connected sketches, some have suggested that Cela must have used as his model John Dos Passos' *Manhattan Transfer* (1925); both novels attempt a wide-ranging portrait of urban life. The similarities are relatively superficial, however, and a major difference exists in the treatment of time: *Manhattan Transfer* covers some twenty years, while *The Hive* spans only a few days, at least three but not more than seven (specific duration is vague). The action in *The Hive* takes place during the winter of 1943, and a specific reference is made to the meeting of Winston Churchill, Joseph Stalin, and Franklin Delano Roosevelt in November of that year, undoubtedly selected by Cela because it was one of the worst periods for Spain, a time when postwar reconstruction had not begun, wartime shortages had grown worse, and the countries which might have helped Spain were too occupied with World War II to think of the Spanish people's plight. This background is very significant to the ambience and psychological climate of the novel; characters are either concerned with where their next meal will come from or are involved in black-marketeering and abuse of the hungry. Many characters are moochers who hang around cafés in the hope of being offered a drink or a meal, or at least a cigarette, while several girls and women are obliged to sell themselves for food, medicine, or small necessities.

In *The Hive*, Cela brings together a number of characters with no more mutual relationship than that which results from being in the same place for a brief time. The common site in part 1 is the café of Doña Rosa. Although the author in one of his many prologues to the successive editions claims that he did nothing but go to the plaza with his camera, "and if the models were ugly, too bad," this suggestion of objective, mimetic technique is hardly to be taken too literally, for large doses of his characteristic exaggeration, dehumanization, and caricature are present, as can be appreciated in the figure of Rosa, one of Cela's most repugnant females. Exceedingly fat, Rosa smokes, drinks, coughs continually, dotes upon bloody tales of violence and crime, is foulmouthed, and has such a habit of peeling off her face that she is compared to a serpent changing its skin; she has a mustache, beaded with sweat, its hairs like the little black "horns" of a cricket, and spends her days insulting and cheating the customers. There is also a suggestion of lesbianism. Much of the negative presentation becomes understandable when one reflects that Doña Rosa is an outspoken advocate of Adolf Hitler: At a time when no criticism of Fascism was possible inside Spain, Rosa presents such extreme physical and moral ugliness that her ideological preferences necessarily suffer by association.

Several other recurring motifs of Cela's fiction are apparent in *The Hive*: the division of humanity into the basic categories of victims and victimizers, the obsessive preoccupation with aberrant sexuality, the notion that the bad are many and the good are few (and generally not too bright), the concept that man is innately cruel (a wolf unto his own kind), and the insistent repetition of tag lines and names or nicknames. So frequent and systematic is the use of nicknames and variants of the names of characters that, when combined with the large number of characters and the usual brevity of their appearances, it is next to impossible to determine exactly how many characters there are, as well as to be sure in many cases whether a character is completely new or one previously met and now reappearing under a nickname. Various commentators have placed the total number of characters at 160, but other estimates suggest more than 360. Obviously, with few exceptions, characters are superficially drawn, usually caricatures; only a handful can be said to have any psychological depth.

Each of the six parts into which the novel is divided is unified by some common denominator (in addition to the time, for there is a certain simultaneity of events in each part or chapter): In the first part, it is the fact that all the characters have some relationship to the café of Doña Rosa, whether as employees, regular customers, or accidental visitors; in the second part, events take place in the street, beginning immediately outside the café as Martín Marco, a ne'er-do-well who serves as a sort of link between various parts and locales, is kicked out for not paying his bill. Some of the customers are followed from the street to their houses, while others are seen in the third part in still another café, where Martín also goes to talk with still more characters (several of whom are under police surveillance and apparently arrested before the novel's end, implicating Martín also). The next part returns to the street and events late at night after the closing of the cafés, when the wealthy go to after-hours clubs and the poor must use the vacant lots for their furtive encounters. The common denominator of part 5 is eroticism, with a wide range of amorous intrigues (light on sentiment and heavy on sexuality) and views of several houses of ill repute of different economic levels. There is also a recurring theme of loss, as most of the characters lose something (dreams, hope, illusions, virginity). The clearest example is the case of an adolescent girl, an orphan sold by her aunt to an old pedophile. The sixth part is united by the numerous reawakenings with the new day, some characters in their homes, others in brothels, Doña Rosa in her café before dawn, the homeless gypsy boy beneath the city bridge, some breakfasting and others hungry, part of the city already going to work and a few about to go to bed. The protagonist, if there is one, is collective: the city of Madrid, which is the beehive of the title, with its workers and drones.

Reviewers of the English translation saw *The Hive* as a passable example of the "low-life genre," but if one is sufficiently familiar with the sociopolitical situation of Spain at the time the novel was written, it is possible to extract additional meanings. All of the numerous characters of the novel reappear several times, with the exceptions of the homosexual Suárez and his lover, accused of complicity in the murder of Suárez' mother, Doña Margot, not on the basis of any evidence but because their life-style was not acceptable. The two are taken to police headquarters for interrogation and simply disappear for the remainder of the novel, a case of critique via omission, a not uncommon technique in the rhetoric of silent dissent. Another interest of the novelist is the invisible links between human beings, who are usually themselves unaware of those links. Thus, Matilde, a widowed pensioner and client of Doña Rosa, owns a boardinghouse where Ventura Aguado, lover of Rosa's niece, resides, connections unknown to all concerned which reflect existential theories of human relationships. A much more elaborate development of this theme occurs in Cela's *Tobogán de hambrientos*, in which each chapter presents a new cast of characters, linked only by one tenuous contact with a single character from the previous chapter. Thus, in chapter 1, an entire family appears; the following chapter may present the family and relatives and friends of the boyfriend of one daughter of the family in the first chapter, while chapter 3 may take up the associates and relatives of the garbage collector of the family of the boyfriend, chapter 4 the boss of the daughter of the garbage collector, and so on, through a certain number of chapters after which the process is reversed and the novelist proceeds in inverse order, through the same groups, back to the point of origin.

While mild in comparison with many of Cela's later works, *The Hive* was daring for its day, and Spanish publishers refused to touch it; it was published in Buenos Aires and smuggled into Spain, selling so well that the government (which levied a profitable tax on several stages of the book business) authorized an expurgated edition, which in turn was soon prohibited and withdrawn from circulation when objectionable points were found—a procedure repeated nine times by 1962. Not only is *The Hive* significant from the standpoint of literary history as a model for the neorealistic "social" novel in Spain during the 1950's and 1960's, but also it had considerable import in its day as a manifestation of liberal intellectual opposition to the Franco dictatorship and its policies. *The Hive* was a turning point in Cela's development as a novelist, marking a transition from rural to urban settings and from a semitraditional format to open experimentalism and fragmentary structures. Although the novel's transitions from character to character and scene to scene may seem abrupt or arbitrary, they are in fact artfully calculated and serve to make otherwise censurable material more palatable than if it had been presented in its totality, without interruption or suspension.

The fragmentary nature of *Mrs. Caldwell Speaks to Her Son* is even more apparent, with more than two hundred brief chapters, in which sequential or connected action is again lacking. The time element is extremely vague and diffuse; the narration is almost totally retrospective but not in any semblance of chronological order. Mrs. Caldwell speaks in the second-person singular (the familiar you, or "thou") to her son Ephraim, sometimes reminiscing, sometimes railing, at other times waxing lyrical (there are even sections which are lyric asides, in the nature of prose poems, such as one quite lengthy piece entitled "The Iceberg"). Bit by bit, it becomes apparent to the reader that Mrs. Caldwell's relationship with her son has abnormal undertones, including incest, abuse, sexual or psychological bondage, and possibly crimes involving third parties; subsequently, it is revealed that Ephraim is dead and has been so for many years, drowned in unexplained circumstances in the Aegean. Mrs. Caldwell, the reader realizes, is insane; whether any of the things she recalls actually happened is a matter of conjecture, as is the reality of the ending, for she is supposedly burned to death when she paints flames on the wall of her room in the asylum.

Surrealistic elements are more prominent in *Mrs. Caldwell Speaks to Her Son* than in any of Cela's previously published prose, although they abound in his early book of poetry *Poemas de una adolescencia cruel*, written for the most part during the Spanish Civil War and published in 1945. The surrealistic substratum comes to the surface periodically during the writer's career and is especially evident in the hallucinatory oratorio *María Sabina* (1967), performed in 1970, and in *El solitario*, a series of absurdist and surrealistic sketches published in 1963. It comes to the fore in Cela's long fiction in *San Camilo, 1936*, and in *Oficio de tinieblas, 5*. Readers whose concept of Cela had been based upon acquaintance with his two best-known novels, *The Family of Pascual Duarte* and *The Hive*, were surprised and disconcerted by what seemed to be an abrupt about-face on his part, a switch from an objective and essentially realistic manner to extreme subjectivity of focus, with an emphasis upon vanguardist experimentalism in *San Camilo, 1936* and *Oficio de tinieblas, 5*. In fact, both the extended second-person monologue of the former and the extreme discontinuity of the latter are clearly anticipated in *Mrs. Caldwell Speaks to Her Son*.

San Camilo, 1936 and *The Hive* are comparable in providing panoramic views of Madrid at similar points in Spanish history (1936 and 1942, respectively); in both, historical events are interwoven with everyday concerns. Both novels feature an enormous cast and exhibit a strong awareness of social injustice, poverty, hunger, and exploitation. In both, Cela's characteristic emphasis on sexual themes, abnormality, deviance, and the scatological are prominent, and both encompass only a few days in the life of the capital. Both are essentially plotless, depending upon strict temporal and spatial limitation for unity in place of the structuring function normally exercised by plot; both lack protagonists in the normal sense, although the city of Madrid may play this role. Both novels feature innumerable cuts, abrupt changes of scene, shifts of focus, and an architectonic design, a complex pattern the most visible features of which are repetition and parallelism. Yet *San Camilo, 1936* is far from being a mere extension or replay of the earlier novel; a most significant difference is the setting in Republican Spain, which imparts a sense of freedom, even license, lacking in *The Hive*. The days spanned in *San Camilo, 1936* are marked by major historical events, immediately preceding and following the outbreak of the Spanish Civil War in July of 1936.

The action of *San Camilo, 1936* begins on Sunday, July 12, 1936, which witnessed the political assassination of Lieutenant Castillo, in reprisal for his part in the killing, three months before, of a cousin of José Antonio Primo de Rivera, founder of the Falange. Revenge for Castillo's killing, a gangster-style exection of conservative opposition leader Calvo Sotelo on July 13, led to a series of riots and was the pretext for the uprising on July 16 of General Francisco Franco and several other military leaders, obliging the Republican government to distribute arms to the populace on July 18. These events, and the funerals of both victims (July 14), are re-created from the vantage point of several witnesses in the novel, although the underlying reasons are not elucidated and the historical antecedents are not mentioned. The atmosphere of growing tension and pent-up violence is subliminally reinforced through the novelist's concentration on a series of minor crimes, accidental deaths, actual and attempted political reprisals by both extremes, repetitive motifs of blood and suffering, and an intensifying irrational desire on the part of the narrative consciousness to kill. An impression of neutrality is nevertheless sustained; with three decades of hindsight, the novelist's ire is directed less at those at either extreme of the Spanish political spectrum than at foreign intervention—a significant departure from the usual strongly partisan accounts of the Spanish Civil War.

Oficio de tinieblas, 5 is a novel only in the most approximate sense, a logical extension of Cela's continuing experimentation with the genre; its obsessive preoccupation with Eros and Thanatos, its language and tone are indubitably his. Discontinuous in structure, this work comprises nearly twelve hundred "monads" (numbered paragraphs or subdivisions) abounding in references to farce, concealment, deceit, flight, self-effacement, defeat, inauthenticity, self-elimination, betrayal, prostitution, alienation, and death. Cela's disappointed idealism and his retreat into apparent cynicism are expressed in *San Camilo, 1936* in the theme of massive prostitution—of the state, the nation, the leaders and lawmakers, the ideologies, the totality of Spanish existence—while in *Oficio de tinieblas, 5* Cela's retreat takes the form of a desire for death and oblivion, counterpointed by an obsessive emphasis on sexual aberration (the novel is saved from being pornographic by myriad learned euphemisms, Latin and medical terminology for sexual organs and activity).

Finally, the new freedom of the post-Franco era is reflected in *Mazurka para dos muertos*, Cela's first novel to be published after Franco's death. Here, Cela continues his exploration of the emotional violence underlying the Civil War, employing the vehicle of a mythic erotic fable set in his native Galicia and reflecting the regional Galician resurgence of the post-Franco era. Any appearance of neutrality has vanished, however, as the pro-Franco characters are clearly villainous, the pro-Republicans heroic.

Major publications other than long fiction

SHORT FICTION: *Esas nubes que pasan*, 1945; *El bonito crimen del carabinero y otras invenciones*, 1947; *El gallego y su cuadrilla*, 1949; *Baraja de invenciones*, 1953; *El molino de viento*, 1956; *Nuevo retablo de don Cristobita*, 1957; *Historias de España: Los ciegos, los tontos*, 1958; *Los viejos amigos*, 1960, 1961 (2 volumes); *Gavilla de fábulas sin amor*, 1962; *Las compañías convenientes*, 1963; *Garito de hospicianos*, 1963; *Once cuentos de fútbol*, 1963; *El solitario*, 1963; *Toreo de salón*, 1963; *Izas, rabizas y colipoterras*, 1964; *El ciudadano Iscariote Reclús*, 1965; *La familia del héroe*, 1965.

POETRY: *Poemas de una adolescencia cruel*, 1945 (also as *Pisando la dudosa luz del día*, 1960); *María Sabina*, 1967.

NONFICTION: *Mesa revuelta*, 1945; *Viaje a la Alcarria*, 1948 (*Journey to Alcarria*, 1964); *Del Miño al Bidasoa*, 1952; *Judíos, moros y cristianos*, 1956; *Cajón de sastre*, 1957; *La rueda de los ocios*, 1957; *La obra literaria del pintor Solana*, 1958; *La rosa*, 1959 (volume 1 of *La cucaña*, Cela's unfinished memoirs); *Primer viaje andaluz*, 1959; *Cuatro figuras del '98*, 1961; *Páginas de geografía errabunda*, 1965; *Viaje al Pirineo de Lérida*, 1965; *Viaje a U.S.A.*, 1967; *Al servicio de algo*, 1969; *A vueltas con España*, 1973; *Vuelta de hoja*, 1981; *El juego de los tres madroños*, 1983.

MISCELLANEOUS: *Obra completa*, 1962-   ; *Nuevas escenas matritenses*, 1965-1966.

Bibliography
Díaz, Janet, and R. L. Landeira. "The Novelist as Poet: The Literary Evolution of Camilo José Cela," in *Anales de la novela de posguerra*. IV (1979), pp. 21-43.
Donahue, Francis. "Cela and Spanish 'Tremendismo,'" in *Western Humanities Review*. XX, no. 4 (1966), pp. 301-306.
Foster, David W. *Forms of the Novel in the Work of Camilo José Cela*, 1967.
Ilie, Paul. *La novelística de Camilo José Cela*, 1963, 1978.
Kirsner, Robert. *The Novels of Camilo José Cela*, 1963.
McPheeters, D. W. *Camilo José Cela*, 1969.
Prjevalinsky Ferrer, Olga. *El sistema estético de Camilo José Cela*, 1960.
Suárez Solis, S. *El léxico de Camilo José Cela*, 1960.

Janet Pérez

LOUIS-FERDINAND CÉLINE
Louis-Ferdinand Destouches

Born: Courbevoie, France; May 27, 1894
Died: Meudon, France; July 1, 1961

Principal long fiction

Voyage au bout de la nuit, 1932 (*Journey to the End of the Night*, 1934); *Mort à crédit*, 1936 (*Death on the Installment Plan*, 1938); *Guignol's band, I*, 1944 (English translation, 1954); *Casse-pipe*, 1949 (fragment); *Féerie pour une autre fois, I*, 1952; *Féerie pour une autre fois, II: Normance*, 1954; *D'un château l'autre*, 1957 (*Castle to Castle*, 1968); *Nord*, 1960 (*North*, 1972); *Guignol's band, II: Le Pont de Londres*, 1964; *Rigodon*, 1969 (*Rigodoon*, 1974).

Other literary forms

In addition to his novels, Louis-Ferdinand Céline published his dissertation for his medical degree, *La Vie et l'oeuvre de Philippe-Ignace Semmelweiss* (1936; written 1924; *The Life and Work of Semmelweiss*, 1937); a play, *L'Église* (1933; the church); three anti-Semitic pamphlets, *Bagatelles pour un massacre* (1937; trifles for a massacre), *L'École des cadavres* (1938; school for corpses), and *Les Beaux Draps* (1941; a fine mess); a discussion of his art, *Entretiens avec le professeur Y* (1955; conversations with Professor Y); and several ballets, collected in *Ballets, sans musique, sans personne, sans rien* (1959; ballets, without music, without anybody, without anything). A denunciation of life in the Soviet Union under Communism appeared under the title *Mea culpa* (1936; English translation, 1937). Céline's diatribe against Jean-Paul Sartre, who had accused him of having collaborated with the Nazis for money, was published as *À l'agité du bocal* (1949; to the restless one in the jar). Céline claimed to have lost several manuscripts when his apartment was pillaged during the Occupation. A surviving fragment of a novel was published as *Casse-pipe*.

Achievements

Hailed by many as one of the foremost French writers of the twentieth century, condemned by others for the repulsive depiction of humanity in his fictional works and for the vileness of his anti-Semitic pamphlets, Céline remains a controversial figure in French letters. One can place him in the French tradition of the *poètes maudits* (cursed poets), a lineage that begins with the medieval poet François Villon and includes such figures as Charles Baudelaire, Arthur Rimbaud, and Jean Genet. Like them, Céline sought to subvert traditional writing and thereby shock the conventional reader into a new sensibility. His works, like theirs, are colored by a personal life that is equally scandalous.

Céline's novels have contributed to modern literature a singularly somber Existentialist view of human society. Unlike some characters in Sartre's novels, Céline's Ferdinand (all his protagonists are variations of the same character) is unable to transcend the disorder, pain, despair, and ugliness of life through heroic action or political commitment. A doctor as well as a writer, Céline was acutely aware of the biology of human destiny—that decay, disease, and death ultimately erase all forms of distinction and that, in a world without God, there is nothing beyond the grave.

In the course of his apprenticeship to life—his journey to the end of the night—Céline's protagonist experiences the shattering of the common illusions and self-delusions that obscure the true nature of existence. The lucidity he thereby acquires narrows the ironic distance between his point of view and that of the older and wiser protagonist-turned-narrator.

Whatever the inherent value of that lucidity may be, it does not serve as an end in itself. It must ultimately be transmitted, in the context of the journey that engendered it, to the reader in the form of a narrative. Céline's protagonist is driven to experience life in all of its diversity, so that he may survive to tell about it. Céline doubtless had imposed upon himself a similar mission.

Unlike Sartre and other so-called Existentialist writers, Céline eschews abstract philosophical debates in favor of a style appropriate to the nature of the experiences he relates. He chooses a form of poetic delirium. Art, for Céline, is a process of transformation that intermingles reality and fantasy, dream and nightmare, the sublime and the grotesque, the personal and the cosmic. In several of his novels, he gives as the irrational cause of the narrative the aggravation of an old head wound, from which, metaphorically, the words spill forth onto the page. The particular idiom he employs—what he calls his "emotional subway"—is no less subversive of traditional French letters than the visions it translates: a carefully concerted conversational style punctuated with slang, obscenities, neologisms, and foreign words. The "rails" of his subway are his frequently used ellipsis points, which fragment his prose into staccato units, bombarding the reader with pulsations of verbal energy. Vision and style complement each other, allowing Céline's readers no complacency as they become, grudgingly perhaps, passengers on a terrifying but exhilarating underground journey.

Biography

Louis-Ferdinand Céline was born Louis-Ferdinand Destouches in the Parisian suburb of Courbevoie on May 27, 1894, and was reared and educated in Paris. His father worked for an insurance company; Céline's mother owned a shop in an arcade, where she sold old lace and antiques. As a soldier during World War I, Céline was injured in the head and ear and was shot in the arm. The head and ear wounds were to leave him with a lifelong buzzing in his head and frequent bouts of insomnia; the arm wound earned for him a medal and a picture on the cover of a national magazine.

After his demobilization, Céline worked for a trading company in the Cameroons. It was during his stay in Africa that he began to write. His interest in medicine led to a job with the Rockefeller Foundation. He received his medical degree in 1918 and briefly practiced in the city of Rennes. He soon wearied of his middle-class existence, however, and, after divorcing his first wife, Edith Follet, he took a medical position with the League of Nations. He lost that post when he showed his superior, who was Jewish, a copy of his play, *L'Église*, in which there is crude satire of Jewish officials at the League of Nations. Céline wrote *Journey to the End of the Night* while working at a clinic, having taken as his nom de plume the surname of his maternal grandmother. The novel was greeted with enormous critical acclaim, and Céline's literary career was launched, though he would continue to practice medicine.

In 1937, Céline published *Bagatelles pour un massacre*, the first of three viciously anti-Semitic pamphlets. In it, he lauds Hitler for bringing a new order to a Europe that had degenerated, according to Céline, as the result of Jewish attempts to dominate the world. During the Occupation, various letters and brief articles signed by Céline appeared in the collaborationist press.

In July, 1944, Céline fled Paris, having been denounced as a traitor by the British Broadcasting Corporation (BBC) and threatened with execution by the Resistance. He sought the relative political safety of Denmark, where he had deposited money from his royalties. In the company of his second wife, Lucette Almanzor, and his cat, Bébert, he managed to make his way across war-ravaged Germany to Copenhagen. The French government instituted proceedings to extradite him so that he could be tried as a traitor. Céline was to spend some five years in Denmark, including more than a year in prison, while his case was being prepared. He maintained that his pamphlets were directed only against those Jews who were supposedly pushing France into yet another war with Germany. He also claimed that he had never written for the pro-Nazi press and that his name had been used without his consent.

On February 23, 1950, a French tribunal condemned him *in absentia* as a traitor to his country. Thirteen months later, he was granted amnesty as a disabled veteran of World War I. Shortly thereafter, he returned to France, to resume his literary career as well as to practice medicine. On July 1, 1961, while editing his last novel, he died of a stroke.

Knowledge of Céline's biography is crucial to a comprehension of his novels, for the events of the author's life constitute a point of departure for his fiction. Despite the many resemblances between Céline and his protagonists, particularly in the later novels, his works are by no means thinly veiled autobiography. His art distorts, enlarges, and mythologizes the autobiographical elements in the transformational process of fiction-making.

Analysis

Louis-Ferdinand Céline's novelistic production can be divided into three principal phases, which are usually linked to developments in the author's life. Thus, one can discern an initial period consisting of the novels written before he fled to Denmark, which concludes with the publication of *Guignol's band, I.* The two volumes of *Féerie pour une autre fois* constitute a second phase in Céline's literary production, for they mark the resumption of his literary career after his return to France and the controversial resolution of his political difficulties. In both novels, there is an increasing confusion—literally and figuratively—among protagonist, narrator, and author, as Céline proclaims his innocence as the scapegoat for a guilt-ridden French nation. The final phase of his literary production, consisting of the wartime trilogy *Castle to Castle*, *North*, and *Rigodoon*, continues the self-justification begun in *Féerie pour une autre fois*, though in far less strident terms, as Ferdinand describes his perilous journey to Denmark.

Céline's novels are linked by the role and character of their respective protagonists, all of whom, except for the Bardamu of *Journey to the End of the Night*, are named Ferdinand and constitute variations on the same personality. The early novels emphasize the ironic interplay between the naïve protagonist being initiated into life and the protagonist as the older narrator endowed with greater insight than his younger incarnation. Protagonist and narrator approach each other in time, space, and knowledge, but they never coincide. The distance between them is considerably reduced in *Féerie pour une autre fois* and the later novels as Céline's own political difficulties shape the consciousness of his character, Ferdinand.

Although the theme of the victim assumes specific political connotations in Céline's later fiction, all of his protagonists see themselves as caught up in a universal conspiracy. One aspect of that conspiracy is the inevitable biological degeneration to which the body falls heir; another is the natural human penchant for destruction. This tendency may assume various forms, among them pettiness, greed, malice, and exploitation of others. Its most blatant and dangerous form, however, is the aggression unleashed by war. The specter of war haunts Céline's novels, and in the face of its menace, cowardice, fear, sickness, and insanity are positively valorized as legitimate means of evasion. War accelerates the natural disintegration of those institutions that have been erected by society as barriers to the natural chaos of existence. In his last novel, *Rigodoon*, Céline prophesies the submersion of the white race by yellow hordes from the East, who, in their turn, will be subject to the same decline that brought about the collapse of the civilization of their Caucasian predecessors.

Given the generally execrable nature of existence, most individuals, according to Céline, are content to indulge in self-delusion. As Céline's protagonists discover, love, sexual fulfillment, and the pursuit of social and financial success are merely idle dreams that must eventually be shattered. In his later novels, Céline denounces the cinema, the automobile, and the French preoccupation with good food and fine wine as equally delusory. Across the otherwise bleak landscape of Céline's novels, one finds occasional moments of love, compassion, and tenderness. Two categories of creatures that elicit particularly sympathetic treatment are animals and children. Céline views the latter, metaphorically, in terms of a reverse metamorphosis: The butterfly becoming the larva as the child turns into an adult.

In *Castle to Castle*, the narrator describes himself as a super-seer, as blessed with a vision that penetrates to the core of reality and beyond. That vision is inseparable from the particular style by which it is conveyed. Céline rejected traditional French writing as having become too abstract to convey the nature of the experiences he was relating or the response he wished to elicit from his readers. He developed an art which, by intermingling various modes of perception and tonal registers, would embrace the diversity of existence, reveal its essential nature, and jolt the reader into awareness through anger, revulsion, or laughter. Moreover, such an approach to the novel perforce emphasizes the writer's claim to artistic autonomy, as opposed to his conforming to the external criteria of "proper" writing.

Céline also refused to accept the divorce between written French and spoken French. By introducing many elements of the spoken language into his novels, he believed that he could draw upon its greater directness and concreteness while at the same time maintaining the structured elaboration inherent in the written text. Indeed, although Céline's novels often have the appearance of a spontaneous first draft, they are the product of laborious craftsmanship.

Journey to the End of the Night brought Céline immediate critical attention upon its publication, and it continues to be the best known of his novels. The journey of the young and innocent Bardamu is one of discovery and initiation. Bardamu's illusions about human existence in general and his own possibilities in particular are progressively stripped away as he confronts the sordidness of the human condition. His limited perspective is counterbalanced by the cynicism of the novel's narrator, an older and wiser Bardamu. The voyage ultimately becomes a conscious project—to confront the darker side of life so that, with the lucidity he acquires, he can one day transmit his knowledge to others by means of his writings.

Having enlisted in the army in a burst of patriotic fervor, Bardamu, as a soldier at the front, discovers the realities of the war. Despite their puzzlement about the politics of their situation, the men involved in the conflict have a natural penchant for killing and are generally fascinated by death. The most trenchant image of the war can be found in Bardamu's perception of a field abattoir, where the disemboweled animals, their blood and viscera spread on the grass, mirror the slaughter of human victims that is taking place. Given the insanity of war, the asylum and the hospital become places of refuge, and fear and cowardice are positively valorized. After Bardamu is wounded in the head and arm, any means to avoid returning to the front becomes valid.

Bardamu finally succeeds in having himself demobilized. He travels to the Cameroons to run a trading post in the bush. Through Bardamu, Céline denounces the inhumanity and corruption of the French colonial administration. More important, however, is the lesson in biology that Africa furnishes Bardamu. The moral decay of the European settlers manifests itself in their physical debilitation as they disintegrate in the oppressive heat and humidity and as they succumb to poor diet and disease. The African climate "stews" the white colonialists and thereby brings forth their inherent viciousness. In more temperate regions, Céline indicates, it requires a phenomenon such as war to expose humankind so quickly for what it is. Unable to tolerate the climate or his job, Bardamu burns his trading post to the ground and, delirious with malarial fever, embarks on a ship bound for New York.

Bardamu believes that America will provide him with the opportunity for a better life. He considers his journey to the New World as a sort of pilgrimage, inspired by Lola, an American girlfriend in Paris. His New York is characterized by rigid verticality and the unyielding hardness of stone and steel; it bears no resemblance to the soft, supine, compliant body that Lola had offered him. As a "pilgrim" in New York, he discovers many "shrines," but access to them is open only to the wealthy. Bardamu is no more successful in Detroit than he was in New York. His work at a Ford motor assembly plant recalls the Chaplin film *Modern Times* (1936). The noise of the machinery and the automatonlike motions Bardamu must perform eventually cause him to take refuge in the arms of Molly, a prostitute with a heart of gold. Molly has the legs of a dancer. Céline's protagonists, like Céline himself, are great admirers of the dance and particularly of the female dancer, who is able to combine Apollonian form with Dionysian rhythms in movements that defy the body's inherent corruption.

In Detroit, Bardamu encounters an old acquaintance named Léon Robinson. Hitherto, Robinson had been functioning as Bardamu's alter ego, anticipating, if not implementing, Bardamu's desires. They first met during the war, when Robinson, disgusted by the killing, wished to surrender to the Germans. Robinson preceded Bardamu to Africa, where he served as the manager of the trading post that Bardamu would later head. When Bardamu learns that the resourceful Robinson has taken a job as a night janitor, he concludes that he, too, will not succeed in America. He decides that his only true mistress can be life itself, that he must return to France to continue his journey into the night.

Bardamu completes his medical studies and establishes his practice in a shabby Parisian suburb. Reluctant to request his fee from his impoverished patients, Bardamu is finally obliged to close his office and take a position in an asylum. Bardamu envies his patients. They have achieved an absolute form of self-delusion and are protected from life's insanity by the walls that imprison them.

Robinson reappears in Bardamu's life. In his desperate attempt to escape his poverty and its attendant humiliation, Robinson joins in a conspiracy to murder an old woman. The plot backfires, literally, and Robinson is temporarily blinded when he receives a shotgun blast in the face. His "darkness," however, does not bring him enlightenment; his disgust with life simply increases. Bardamu realizes that he is bearing witness to an exemplary journey that must end in death. Robinson finally dies at the hands of his irate fiancée, whom he goads into shooting him. His "suicide" terminates his own journey to the end of the night and Bardamu's as well.

Journey to the End of the Night proffers a vision of the human condition that serves as the basis of all of Céline's literary production. Concomitant with this vision is the elaboration of a particular style which, with certain modifications in later works, afforded, according to Céline, a means of revitalizing French literature, by freeing it from the abstractions of classical writing. The most salient stylistic effect in *Journey to the End of the Night* is Céline's uses of the vocabulary, syntax, and rhythms of popular speech as a vehicle for communicating the concrete, emotional impact of Bardamu's experience.

Céline's second novel, *Death on the Installment Plan*, depicts the adolescence of a character resembling Bardamu but here, as in succeeding works, called Ferdinand, a name that explicitly poses the question of the relationship between the author and his protagonist. The novel begins with a pattern of opening signals that Céline would use in several other works. Once again, there is an interplay between an enlightened Ferdinand as narrator and a young Ferdinand as the naïve explorer of life. The narration of Ferdinand's youth is effected by a return to the past by the older narrator, who appears briefly at the beginning of the novel. When the narrator falls ill from the effects of a head wound suffered during World War I, aggravated by an attack of malaria, his memory of his youth is stimulated. Lying in bed, he has visions of little boats sailing through the sky bearing stories from the past, which will be transformed into his narrative. Thus the creation of fiction, the metaphorical outpouring from his skull injury (in *Journey to the End of the Night*, Bardamu's skull was trepanned), becomes an irrational, autonomous activity.

Reared in a Parisian *passage* (a commercial arcade), Ferdinand lives with his parents in an apartment above his mother's old lace and antique shop. Ferdinand's father, Auguste, holds a minor position with an insurance company.

Ferdinand's parents attempt to instill in their young son a traditional bourgeois ethic: proper dress, good manners, cleanliness, honesty, and, above all, the belief that hard work will certainly bring success. Ironically, for both Auguste and Clémence, the ideals they preach are progressively undermined by changing economic conditions as the twentieth century begins. Machine-made lace has begun to replace the handmade luxury items Clémence sells. She is soon reduced to selling door-to-door for a department store, the very sort of enterprise that is putting the small shopkeeper out of business. Auguste, essentially a secretary, is employed for the excellence of his penmanship at a time when the typewriter is becoming standard office equipment.

Ferdinand, too, becomes a victim of the historical circumstances that affect his parents. In addition, he is a victim of the maliciousness of others, intent upon exploiting him for their own ends. Ferdinand's failures keep his father in a constant state of rage. Auguste's fits of wrath are enlarged to comically epic proportions: He swells with anger like a balloon and, like a balloon whose air has been suddenly released, lets forth a torrent of imprecations that cause him to bounce around the room, spilling furniture and crockery in his path.

One of Ferdinand's jobs involves selling jewelry. His employer's wife, in concert with other employees, conspires to seduce him and steal a valuable ring given to him for safekeeping. With her overflowing corpulence, gigantic breasts, and cavernous vagina, Madame Gorloge is more monster than woman, and Ferdinand is engulfed by her. Céline portrays sexual relations as either an act of aggression or a mindless escape, akin to the masturbation in which Ferdinand indulges and which he later rejects as a form of delusion. Ferdinand's stay at an English boarding school does not produce the expected result. He returns to France with barely a word of English at his command, having rejected language as an instrument of oppression, responsible for the seductions and paternal conflicts that have shaped his existence.

Ferdinand takes a job with an eccentric named Courtial des Pereires—a balloonist, the owner of a magazine for inventors, and the author of numerous self-study and do-it-yourself manuals on a great variety of subjects. Courtial, who will become a surrogate father for Ferdinand, is a windbag, employing language in a manner radically different from Auguste's. He reorders reality through the use of a quasi-scientific rhetoric that, ultimately, does not stand the test of reality.

Courtial flees with his wife and Ferdinand to the countryside, after a fantastic project to find sunken treasure leads to the loss of his magazine. There he proposes to grow gigantic potatoes with the aid of radio-telluric waves. The disorder of reality triumphs over the specious order of Courtial's rhetoric when the potatoes come up stunted and full of maggots. Courtial commits suicide by shooting himself in the head, the source of his grandiose schemes. His wound recalls the narrator's and the language of the novel, in which the sort of delusion that Courtial practices is denounced. Ferdinand returns to Paris and enlists in the army. Given what he has seen and experienced, human existence appears to be, as the title suggests, little more than a process of slowly advancing toward the ultimate resolution of death.

Death on the Installment Plan is marked by an important stylistic development, which is accentuated in subsequent novels: the frequent use of ellipsis points. As Céline notes in a discussion of his writing in *Entretiens avec le professeur Y*, they are the "rails" that carry the emotional intensity of his text; they also have the overall effect of conveying, phonically and graphically, the fragmentary nature of existence—such as Céline describes it in his novels—as opposed to the orderly worldview inherent in the syntax of traditional French writing.

The publication of the first volume of *Féerie pour une autre fois* in 1952 (a second volume, usually referred to by its subtitle, *Normance*, appeared in 1954) marked Céline's return to public view as a novelist, still stigmatized by his indictment as an anti-Semite and a Nazi sympathizer. Céline used this novel in particular as a device for self-exculpation. He portrayed himself, through his protagonist, as an innocent victim of persecution, denying all the charges made against him. Moreover, Ferdinand states that his "problems" began with the publication of *Journey to the End of the Night*, for it was then that he was perceived as a subversive element of French society. One narrative strategy that Céline adopts as a means of maintaining his innocence is the use of a "narratee"—the designation of a reader who, convinced of the author's guilt, cries out for Céline's punishment. Ferdinand thus elaborates various scenarios of crime and punishment and, ultimately, proclaims his innocence.

The novel is narrated from the perspective of a prisoner incarcerated in a jail in Copenhagen while awaiting extradition to France to stand trial as a Nazi sympathizer. As a "political prisoner," he places himself in a long line of similar victims of societal oppression, ranging from the Gaulish chieftain Vercingétorix to Oscar Wilde. By putting himself in this illustrious company, Ferdinand seeks to undermine the specificity of the charges brought against him. Having failed to outrun history, Ferdinand finds himself not only behind bars but also glued to his chair by sores from pellagra. The noises made by other prisoners exacerbate his confinement and, in particular, the sounds made by a prisoner called the "Skunk" as he hits his head against the wall, apparently trying to commit suicide. Ferdinand compares the Skunk's head wound to the one he suffered during World War I. The comparison recalls the metaphorical function of Ferdinand's head wound in *Death on the Installment Plan* as the cause of his fiction-making. Ferdinand's narrative will permit him to escape from his cell by encompassing a variety of times and places.

Ferdinand frequently depicts himself as the quarry in a medieval hunt or threatened with horrible forms of torture and execution. In equally hallucinatory scenes, he is used as garden fertilizer by writers who flourished during the Occupation. One writer who reappears several times is Sartre, who, in his *Portrait d'un antisémite* (1945; *Portrait of the Anti-Semite*, 1946) had accused Céline of having been paid by the Germans to promote anti-Semitism. Ferdinand the doctor will avenge the insults made against Ferdinand the writer by taking consolation in the knowledge that illness, decay, and death will ultimately triumph over both persecutor and persecuted.

Ferdinand introduces yet another adversary. His name is Jules, and he bears certain crucial resemblances to Ferdinand. He, too, is an artist, primarily a painter but a sculptor as well. Like Ferdinand, he is a wounded veteran of World War I: Having lost both of his legs, he pushes himself about on a little cart that he maneuvers with two short canes. These shared attributes become the point of departure for a return to the Montmartre period of Ferdinand's life and for a complex portait of Jules as the embodiment of the evil potential lurking within the artist. Jules's physical deformity and his ugliness are the external manifestations of a perverted character. Jules's studio, in the sub-basement of the building in which Ferdinand has an apartment, becomes a symbolic netherworld in which Jules displays his chthonic powers.

Unlike Ferdinand, who considers himself a martyr for having sought in his novels to reveal the true nature of the human condition, Jules creates art for financial and sexual profit. It is the latter that particularly concerns Ferdinand, for both he and Jules have a predilection for the attractive young dance students that frequent the courses offered by Ferdinand's wife, Lili. Unlike Ferdinand, Jules has no appreciation for the dance as an aesthetic triumph over the flesh. He seeks to lure the young women into his studio so that he can fondle them. Lili accepts Jules's invitation to model for him, and Ferdinand acquiesces to the arrangement, fascinated, as is Lili, by Jules's demoniac energy. Jules caresses the naked Lili in the murky light of his studio, and, as he does, Lili is changed from an elegant, graceful dancer into a garishly multicolored mass of flesh, a work of art deformed by the twisted mind of the artist.

For Ferdinand, the "seduction" of Lili also marks the conclusion of a tranquil existence and the beginning of a period of torment that eventually leads to confinement in a Danish prison. Jules, he believes, has furthered the persecution incited by BBC broadcasts denouncing him as a traitor and by the miniature coffins sent to him by the Resistance, as a sign that he has been marked for execution. Standing outside Jules's studio, he becomes subject to hallucinations, during the course of which he begins to hear air-raid sirens. Because of the noises in his head that were caused by his war injury, one cannot be absolutely sure whether these sirens are real or imagined. Whatever may be their status, the explicit confusion of external and internal landscapes poses once again the artist's freedom to intermingle reality and imagination. This confusion will be reinforced by another—between Ferdinand's personal calamities and those of a Europe ravaged by World War II.

Castle to Castle is the first volume of a trilogy of novels that trace Ferdinand's flight from Montmartre to Copenhagen. The novel begins with an incident in which Ferdinand, now practicing medicine in the Parisian suburb of Meudon after having received amnesty from the French government, discovers a ship, tied up at one of the area's piers, that is being attended by mysterious hooded figures. Upon closer inspection, Ferdinand discovers among them a friend from the Occupation days, Robert Le Vigan, a movie actor and pro-Nazi radio broadcaster. Le Vigan had accompanied Ferdinand, his wife Lili, and their cat Bébert during part of their journey from Paris to Denmark. Another one of the hooded figures is a man whom Ferdinand knows was killed in the war. The ambiguous status of these individuals anticipates the "play" between the real and the imaginary that will characterize the narrative soon to be initiated. That "play" is subsequently reinforced by the aggravation of Ferdinand's head wound, compounded by an attack of malaria. Forced to take to his bed, the narrator, his memory of the past stimulated by his encounter with Le Vigan and revived by his affliction, begins to transcribe his wartime experiences.

The narrator's recollection of the past has as its focal point the Castle of Sigmaringen in the Bavarian village of the same name. Ferdinand calls the castle Siegmaringen, ironically playing on the German word for "victory," *Sieg*. Ferdinand has been sent there with his companions from Berlin, for their safety and for the purpose of administering to the medical needs of the town's French colony. It was to Sigmaringen that the Germans in September of 1944 had transferred many officials of the collaborationist Vichy government, including its head, Marshal Philippe Pétain. All of them share with Ferdinand a condemnation as traitors and the fear that they will be summarily executed should they fall into the hands of the Resistance or the Free French Forces. Indeed, the entire town is filled to overflowing by Nazi sympathizers who have come to Sigmaringen as their final place of refuge in the wake of the collapse of the German armies.

The castle itself, built by the Hohenzollern dynasty, is more than a luxurious place of exile. Céline transforms it into a symbolic structure that reflects the spirit of its inhabitants, the ruling clique of the Vichy government. For those officials who persist in believing that Germany will miraculously reverse its losses and win the war, the castle is no more real than a Hollywood set. At the base of the castle flows the Danube, gradually eroding the building's foundations. Céline suggests that, despite the castle's apparent durability, it will eventually disintegrate, as will all of those structures and institutions which serve as bulwarks against the inherent chaos of existence. For those who believed that the Third Reich would last a thousand years, the moment of collapse is at hand.

The interior design of the castle also functions symbolically. Its apartments are separated from one another by a complex network of passages and stairways that tend to isolate each living space and thus reinforce their occupants' delusions about returning to power. One can also interpret the isolation of the castle's apartments as a metaphor for the novel's plot structure—a series of relatively discontinuous vignettes.

Amid the delusions and the meaningless ceremonies that characterize life in the castle, Ferdinand attempts to address the realities of Sigmaringen. Despite a lack of medical supplies, Ferdinand conscientiously attempts to ease the suffering of the refugees. The central images of the novel, insofar as life outside the castle is concerned, are the overflowing toilets at the Löwen Hotel, where Ferdinand's small room serves as residence and office, and the railway station. The overabundant use of the toilets, on an epic scale, reveals the overcrowding, poor diet, and disease that afflict the refugees. In a larger sense, for Céline at least, the war has transformed Europe into an immense cesspool. At the railway station, one finds yet another manifestation of the disorder that has overtaken European society. There, confusion and despair have replaced political and social hierarchies, and, because of the uselessness of train schedules at this point in the war, the platforms and waiting rooms serve as points of exchange—for food, sexual favors, disease, and rumors.

Ferdinand performs his functions as a doctor while hoping that he can eventually find a train that will permit him to leave Sigmaringen and head north to Denmark. Ferdinand's concern with his own escape cannot help but recall those other train trips, to stations named Treblinka and Auschwitz, that deportees all over Europe were taking as the Nazis sought to achieve their "final solution."

Castle to Castle ends with a return to the narrator in Meudon, the circularity of the novel's narrative counterbalancing its episodic discontinuity. Once again, the narrator is a survivor, a witness to the most calamitous period in the history of France. Céline claims in these later novels, beginning with *Féerie pour une autre fois*, that his fiction gives the reader a more penetrating insight into the period than historical documents can provide. Many of his readers may wonder, however, if Céline did not, in these works, choose obfuscation rather than lucidity to elaborate what might be considered a self-serving mythology that transforms the journey begun in *Journey to the End of the Night* into the very sort of delusion that the author had once sought to denounce.

Major publications other than long fiction

PLAY: *L'Église*, 1933.

NONFICTION: *La Vie et l'oeuvre de Philippe-Ignace Semmelweiss* (written 1924) and *Mea culpa, suivi de La vie et l'oeuvre de Semmelweiss*, published together in 1936 (*Mea Culpa, with The Life and Work of Semmelweiss*, 1937); *Bagatelles pour un massacre*, 1937; *L'École des cadavres*, 1938; *Les Beaux Draps*, 1941; *À l'agité du bocal*, 1949; *Entretiens avec le professeur Y*, 1955.

MISCELLANEOUS: *Ballets, sans musique, sans personne, sans rien*, 1959.

Bibliography

Les Cahiers de l'Herne. No. 3 (1963). Special Céline issue.
Les Cahiers de l'Herne. No. 5 (1965). Special Céline issue.

Gibault, François. *Céline, 1894-1932: Les Temps des espérances*, 1977.
Knapp, Bettina. *Céline: Man of Hate*, 1974.
McCarthy, Patrick. *Céline: A Critical Biography*, 1975.
Matthews, J. H. *The Inner Dream: Céline as Novelist*, 1978.
O'Connell, David. *Louis-Ferdinand Céline*, 1976.
Ostrovsky, Erika. *Céline and His Vision*, 1967.
Thiher, Allen. *Céline: The Novel as Delirium*, 1972.

Philip H. Solomon

BLAISE CENDRARS
Frédéric Louis Sauser

Born: La Chaux-de-Fonds, Switzerland; September 1, 1887
Died: Paris, France; January 21, 1961

Principal long fiction

L'Or: La Merveilleuse Histoire du général Johann August Suter, 1925 (*Sutter's Gold*, 1926); *Moravagine*, 1926 (English translation, 1968); *Dan Yack*, 1927-1928 (includes *Le Plan de l'aiguille*, 1927 [*Antarctic Fugue*, 1948]; *Les Confessions de Dan Yack*, 1929); *Rhum: L'Aventure de Jean Galmot*, 1930; *L'Homme foudroyé*, 1945 (*The Astonished Man*, 1970); *La Main coupée*, 1946 (*Lice*, 1973); *Bourlinguer*, 1948 (*Planus*, 1972); *Le Lotissement du ciel*, 1949; *Emmène-moi au bout du monde!*, 1956 (*To the End of the World*, 1967).

Other literary forms

Although Blaise Cendrars' novels had many admirers, including Henry Miller, his most critically respected work is his poetry. Combining his adventurous autobiography with complex, strong imagery and powerful emotion, Cendrars' most praised books of poetry are his extraordinary early efforts, *Les Pâques à New York* (1912; Easter in New York); *La Prose du Transsibérien et de la petite Jehanne de France* (1913; *The Trans-Siberian Express*, 1964); and *Le Panama: Ou, Les Aventures de mes sept oncles* (1918; *Panama: Or, The Adventures of My Seven Uncles*, 1931). His poetry is most important for its audacious expression of modernism. Other important collections include *Dix-neuf Poèmes élastiques* (1919); *Kodak* (1924; English translation, 1976); and *Feuilles de route* (1924, 1927). *Une Nuit dans la forêt* (1929) and *Vol à voiles* (1932) were alleged by Cendrars to be autobiographical nonfiction, but critics assert they are largely fictionalized. His nonfiction "novels" and short stories, as well as his prose poems, are difficult to categorize using conventional terms. Cendrars was also an editor, essayist, journalist, translator, screenwriter and film director, ballet scenarist, and radio dramatist.

Achievements

Cendrars as a writer made direct use of his personal life and experiences to an unusual degree. This has made critics uneasy with assessing his literary accomplishments, as if the writer's life is somehow separate from his work, or should be. Henry Miller, whose own work incorporated a great deal of autobiography, was impressed with Cendrars' work and praised it for its luminosity, calling Cendrars a "continent of letters." Others, however, see Cendrars as a technically proficient writer who was at his best in his freewheeling poetry. Both his poetry and prose, however, are praised for their rich, powerful, restless, modern imagery and strongly evocative effects. An independent man who did not ally himself with any literary movements, he was nevertheless a great influence on Surrealism and other modern movements. Only late in his life did he attain any substantial critical recognition, receiving the Légion d'Honneur in 1959 and the Grand Prix Littéraire de la Ville de Paris in 1961.

Biography

Blaise Cendrars so mythologized his life and experiences that scholars have had a difficult time culling the exaggerations and outright lies from his many exercises in autobiography. As Ernest Hemingway commented in _A Moveable Feast_ (1964) ". . . when [Cendrars] was lying, he was more interesting than many men telling a story truly." The difficulty is further compounded by Cendrars' ceaseless traveling from continent to continent. Even the true circumstances of his birth were not known until Jean Buhler published his 1960 biography. Contrary to Cendrars' claim in a 1917 poem that he was born in Paris in the Hôtel des Etrangers, he was actually born in the Swiss village of La Chaux-de-Fonds under the name of Frédéric Louis Sauser. Escaping La Chaux-de-Fonds seems to have been one of the major ambitions of its natives (Le Corbusier and Louis Chevrolet are among the more famous who left) and Cendrars' father Georges was no exception. He had come to the city as a teacher of mathematics but was listed in the city registry as a clock merchant at the time of Cendrars' birth. He restlessly immersed himself in financial dealings and was responsible for his son's early initiation into travel. The family went to Egypt and into the hotel business when Cendrars was about two years old. This venture soon failed, however, and Cendrars began his chaotic education at the Scuola Internazionale in Naples in 1891 or 1892. In 1897, he entered the Basel _gymnasium_; he also attended boarding schools in Germany. In 1902, he registered at the École de Commerce in Neuchâtal, a business school, evidently after failing his college examinations.

Cendrars spent the years from 1904 to 1907 in Russia as a watch salesman and was there during the 1905 Revolution which plays such a large part in his novel _Moravagine_; he may have traveled in Siberia and China as well. He had his first love affair with a Russian woman, "Hélène," and, in her honor, wrote his first poem, "Alea" (later rewritten as _Moganni Nameh_, 1922), under the pseudonym Freddy Sausey. After his return, he moved frequently, raising bees near Paris, studying medicine at the University of Bern, working as a comedian in Brussels, working as an extra in the opera _Carmen_, falling in love with Féla Poznanska, a Polish student, and following her to New York. All of this time, he was writing, undergoing in his poetry a transformation from his early heavy Romanticism, through neo-Symbolism to the startling modernism for which he would become famous. He made some money with his writing, doing translations and writing essays on art and literature. He translated Stanisław Przybyszewski's _Totenmesse_ (1893) as _La Messe des morts_, which is considered a direct source for *Moravagine*, and the poem *Die Verwandlungen der Venus* (1907) by Richard Dehmel. He may have collaborated with Guillaume Apollinaire on *Les Onze Mille Verges* (1911), a pornographic novel.

Publishing under the name Blaise Cendrars, he stunned the Paris literary scene with *Les Pâques à New York*. He claimed that the poem was written after he had left a church in New York in which a minister had demanded from the congregation a donation to listen to a performance of Franz Josef Haydn's *Die Schöpfung* (1798; *The Creation*). This experience and his poverty in New York provided the impetus for the poem, which has been called a major milestone in literary modernism for its startling and unblinking use of city imagery. He followed with *Séquences* (1913) and *The Trans-Siberian Express*, major works which may have influenced Apollinaire and the Surrealists. *The Trans-Siberian Express* was attacked in the press, and Cendrars responded vigorously. He helped found a literary review *Les Hommes nouveaux* in 1912 and mingled with some of the most celebrated artists of the period, including Amedeo Modigliani, Pablo Picasso, Jean Cocteau, Max Jacob, Fernand Léger, Francis Picabia, Igor Stravinsky, and Apollinaire.

The drama of Cendrars' life continued with his enlistment in the Foreign Legion at the beginning of World War I. On April 7, 1914, Féla Poznanska gave birth to a daughter, Odilon, and in September, shortly before his departure to the front, Cendrars married Féla. After a year in bloody combat—at one point, seven thousand of the fifteen thousand men in the Tenth Army, in which he served, were killed—he lost his right arm in the Marne Valley. He returned to the artistic life of Paris, though many of his friends were either in the army or gone, and he quickly learned to write with his left hand. From that point on, Cendrars wrote constantly, whether art criticism on the cubists, journalism, more poetry, or ballets. He was involved in cinema with Abel Gance and contributed to the films *J'Accuse* (1919) and *La Roue* (1923), both now considered classics; Cendrars himself played one of the mutilated war victims in the former. In 1921, he worked for the studio Rinascimento in Rome, directing the film *La Vénus noire*.

Cendrars continued his restless traveling in the 1920's in the south of France, Portugal, Spain, Brazil, Argentina, Paraguay, Chile, and even Antarctica. In late 1924, in six weeks, he completed his first and most popular novel, *Sutter's Gold*. He completed *Moravagine* in Biarritz, but part of it was written in the Amazon during his first trip to Brazil. He was also in New York several times during the 1920's and 1930's and became fairly close to John Dos Passos, who translated and illustrated Cendrars' poetry in *Panama*. Critics agree that each influenced the other's writing considerably. In line with his cinematic interests, Cendrars met Sergei Eisenstein in 1930, when the great director tried to buy the rights for *Sutter's Gold* during his abortive stint at Paramount Studios. In 1935, Cendrars wrote the first important review of Henry Miller's *Tropic of*

Cancer (1934) after visiting him and barhopping with prostitutes. In turn, Miller became one of the most enthusiastic devotees of Cendrars' work.

World War II put an abrupt end to Cendrars' ceaseless activity. He served briefly as a correspondent with the British army, then retreated to a home in Aix-en-Provence. Overwhelmed by the defeat of France, cautious because of Fascist oppression, and upset because of the imprisonment of both of his sons (one escaped and was later killed in an accident in North Africa), he wrote nothing and stayed in Aix. He only began writing again when the Germans seemed suspicious of a writer who did not write. Although he obviously sympathized with the Allies, the scrutiny under which he was placed prevented any overt activities in the Resistance. Jay Bochner reports that Cendrars did, however, help director Max Ophüls and his wife and son escape from France; the son, Marcel Ophüls, would later become the director of *Le Chagrin et la pitié* (1971; *The Sorrow and the Pity*, 1971), one of the most celebrated and controversial films dealing with collaboration.

Late in the war and in the years after, Cendrars began writing a series of autobiographical novels: *The Astonished Man*, *Lice*, *Planus*, and *Le Lotissement du ciel* (the allotment of Heaven). In 1948, he gave up his casual sex life when he married Raymone Duchateau, a comic actress whom he had first met in 1917 and with whom he had kept in contact ever since. He took only a few brief trips in the later years of his life. He became involved with productions of *Sutter's Gold* and *La Fin du monde* (1919) for French radio. He wrote only two books in the 1950's, *To the End of the World* and *Trop c'est trop* (1957). In 1956, Cendrars had his first stroke. Others followed. In 1959, André Malraux went to his home and presented to him the Légion d'Honneur. Cendrars continued writing prefaces and some short stories until his death in 1961, only four days after receiving his first literary award, the Grand Prix Littéraire de la Ville de Paris.

Analysis

Blaise Cendrars seemed incapable of divorcing his colorful life from his fiction. Even his first novel, *Sutter's Gold*, ostensibly a historical novel about John Augustus Sutter, the Swiss émigré whose discovery of gold in California precipitated the 1849 Gold Rush, becomes a personal statement, molded into a myth with small regard for historical details. Early in his life, Cendrars became familiar with Sutter's story. According to Hugues Richard, Cendrars and his brother first read of Sutter in a local Swiss almanac, *Le Messager boiteux*, that was used as toilet paper in the Sauser home. Richard also asserts that the immediate source of the novel was a monograph written in 1868 by a Swiss clergyman and State Counsellor who cared for Sutter's children after he had fled Switzerland. Cendrars read voraciously in libraries wherever he traveled and undoubtedly had pursued his interest in Sutter for some time. Perhaps the most important impetus for the novel was Cendrars' meeting with August Sutter, grandson of John Sutter, in Basel around 1905. They renewed their friendship in 1910 in Paris, where August Sutter had gone to become a sculptor. August introduced him to various artistic figures, including poet Siegfried Lang.

Monique Chefdor speculates that the frantic development of the Brazilian wilderness reminded Cendrars of the Gold Rush and contributed largely to his choosing to write the novel when he did. Sutter's story certainly provided Cendrars with the opportunity to exploit all of his favorite devices in a novel. Sutter is depicted as a crafty underminer of conventional society. He abandons his wife and children; he falsifies travel documents; he forges, cheats, steals, and deals in slaves. Whatever heroism there is in Sutter is matched by rascality, but Cendrars manages to turn Sutter into a tragic figure. The liberties that Cendrars takes with historical facts in the novel serve to enhance the stature of Sutter—for example, making him die the victim of a child's trick on the steps of the Capitol in Washington instead of in a bed in Pennsylvania. Sutter is in the grip of forces he cannot control. His story is that of a man driven, by his own ambitions and obsessions, to being a multimillionaire in a place which happens to have gold, "the Antichrist," which will provoke other people's ambitions and obsessions to destroy him. Sutter becomes victim, not so much of people, but of gold. Cendrars had previously written on the corrupting power of money in much of his poetry, especially in relation to his experiences as an outsider in New York. This coincides with the common literary view in the 1920's that civilization had been broken by World War I and was in the process of being replaced by a shoddy, corrupt industrial society.

The style of *Sutter's Gold* is very stark. As Bochner observes, none of Cendrars' prose, before or after, was as terse and bare as the language of this novel, which resembles that of Cendrars' poetry in *Kodak* and *Le Formose* (1924). All of his other work, even his journalism, is very baroque, image heaped on image. In *Sutter's Gold*, however, the adamant forward thrust of the action serves to accentuate the feeling that Sutter is caught up and being carried along by his destiny. He has virtually no opportunity for introspection, or to attempt to modify his course. When he attempts to resist the gold fever, it results in his impoverishment and destruction. This single driving force is presented in prose stripped of imagery, similar to what Hemingway was developing at the time. Written in the present tense, the novel makes no commentary upon the morality or character of Sutter, except by implication through action. This straightforwardness in plot and style undoubtedly contributed to the popularity of *Sutter's Gold*, which has gone through more than fifteen editions in French and has been translated into such languages as Czech, Flemish, Russian, Portuguese, and Swedish, in addition to the major European languages. This same simplicity, however, makes *Sutter's Gold* a work with few nuances and not much depth, a novel which may provide great pleasure on a first reading but has little more to offer on a second.

Moravagine is far more complex than *Sutter's Gold* in both style and theme. Henry Miller was among the writers who praised it highly. The radicalism of *Moravagine* made a strong impression on Miller and contributed to freeing up his own prose. Miller read the novel before he was fluent in French and said it was "like reading a phosphorescent text through smoked glasses," but he went on to write: "The silence [Cendrars] creates is deafening. It takes you back to the beginning of the world, to that hush which is engraved on the face of mystery." *Moravagine* is one of those books which seems clear from sentence to sentence and is profoundly affecting yet violates so much of what readers have come to expect in a novel that its overall purpose is bewildering. It accomplishes what the best of the Surrealist works do, reaching a reality beyond conventional reality and then collapsing in the despair of being unable to grasp it fully.

Moravagine is a homicidal lunatic and heir to the Hungarian throne who is befriended by Raymond, a psychiatrist who helps him escape, then accompanies him through an eerie series of adventures around the world. Periodically, Moravagine will butcher a woman for no reason except diversion, and Raymond makes no attempt to stop him. As Sven Birkerts observes, Cendrars has taken human extremity as his subject. The pained language carries the reader "through revolution, terror, and a zone of sexual and moral nihilism." Nothing like it, except Lautréamont's *Les Chants du Maldoror* (1868; *Lay of Maldoror*, 1924), had appeared in literature before. The only parallels, Birkerts adds, are in the works of Louis-Ferdinand Céline and Samuel Beckett. Moravagine is a being without culture, without the values inculcated by civilization. There is not a shred of human sentiment in him. The novel is profoundly pessimistic, Birkerts concludes, "but in view of the atrocities Cendrars had witnessed . . . not pure fabrication."

In fact, one of the most astonishing things about *Moravagine* is that many of the scenes which seem most incredible were based on actual events, in some cases experiences of Cendrars. Bochner points out, for example, that, as impossible as it might seem, it *is* possible to sail up the Orinoco river system into the Amazon, without portage, thus bringing into question the whole dreamlike quality of the South American adventure. Raymond, who suffers from malaria through much of the trip, can be seen as giving a realistic interpretation of his experiences there. The story seems incredible and strange but is not necessarily unrealistic. Bochner also mentions Moravagine's mad bombing of Vienna during World War I: The episode bears considerable resemblance to an actual event in 1916, when a Lieutenant Marchal flew thirteen hundred kilometers to bomb Berlin. Bochner further links Moravagine to Otto Gross, a psychoanalyst who preached anarchy. (Gross may have influenced a host of artists, including D. H. Lawrence, Max Weber, and Franz Kafka, as well as Cendrars.) Gross's having been committed to an asylum after having provided the means of suicide for two of his female patients and his subsequent escape also bears resemblance to the story of Moravagine. The treatment of Gross by Carl Jung also has some parallels in Raymond's attitudes. Further possible sources include the life of Azev, a notorious Russian spy and assassin, the 1905 Revolution, and the story of Jack the Ripper, particularly as exploited in horror films such as *The Cabinet of Dr. Caligari* (1920) and *Waxworks* (1924). The narrator's name is taken from that of Raymond-la-Science, a gang member executed in 1913.

Cendrars later wrote that Moravagine was inside him; his character was like a parasite occupying Cendrars' body. "That's why all beautiful books are alike," wrote Cendrars. "They are all autobiographical." There are a number of parallels between Cendrars' life—the dates he stayed in Russia, his time in Paris—and the travels of Moravagine, but this is not to say that Cendrars engaged in any of the atrocious activities ascribed to his protagonist. It is Raymond who is injured as Cendrars was in World War I, and Cendrars relation to Moravagine is more like that of an entranced observer than that of an alter ego.

The disparate elements which make up the novel evoke the chaos of the twentieth century: Moravagine escapes from the asylum in the symbolic year 1900 and looses bloody anarchy on the world. Raymond, in the name of science, observes Moravagine, whose name means "death to the vagina," as he engages in a calculated destruction of all nineteenth century values (perceived as "feminine"); clearly, whether Raymond admits it or not, he is fascinated, perhaps even delighted, by the destruction. He, too, participates in the revolutionary terrorism and ends up a regicide who has supposedly sent his story to the author Cendrars. The novel expresses Cendrars' fascination and delight with the new century, mingled with a sense of horror and metaphysical guilt at the destruction of a stable moral order. The curious fictional connection of Moravagine to Raymond to Cendrars seems to imply they are all aspects of one another in some mysterious, fundamental, psychological way. In this and many other respects, *Moravagine* anticipates a host of later experimental novels, such as those by John Hawkes, José Donoso, and William Burroughs, in which pathological behavior is used to explore the question of identity.

Cendrars went on to write several other novels. Dan Yack, the main character of *Antarctic Fugue* and *Les Confessions de Dan Yack*, is regarded by some critics as the most human of Cendrars' protagonists and the most fully developed. He has also been seen as a positive counterpart to Moravagine; exactly what was Cendrars' intent, however, is neither as clear as in *Sutter's Gold* nor as uncomfortably evocative as in *Moravagine*. For this reason, neither volume of *Les Confessions de Dan Yack* is considered as successful as the previous novels. The novel *Rhum* bears resemblances to *Sutter's Gold* in its treatment of the hero and its use of an inanimate substance as a driving force. The historical Jean Galmot, on whose experiences the novel was based, was a fascinating person, and Cendrars, as he did with Sutter, creatively reshaped the historical material, yet there is little in this fictionalization. Cendrars himself seemed to sense that he had reached an artistic dead end and did not write a novel again for many years.

The Astonished Man, *Lice*, *Planus*, and *Le Lotissement du ciel* anticipate the "nonfiction novel" of the 1960's and 1970's by falling somewhere between fiction and autobiography. They are interesting for their commentaries on the nature of writing and for the incredible stories they tell, many of them total fabrications; Cendrars could not resist embellishing his life story. With *To the End of the World*, Cendrars promised a novel in which he would not appear. Nevertheless, he asserts in the preface that it is a *roman à clef*. Its collection of strange people, sexual explicitness, and extraordinarily bizarre events infuriated critics on its publication; Chefdor argues that it is a forerunner of postmodernism in its attempt to create a hedonism of the text, an erotics of writing. Perhaps this judgment will be borne out by future criticism, although, at present, *Moravagine* seems likely to remain Cendrars' most lasting contribution to the novel.

Major publications other than long fiction

SHORT FICTION: *Petits Contes nègres pour les enfants des blancs*, 1928 (*Little Black Stories for Little White Children*, 1929); *Comments les blancs sont d'anciens noirs*, 1930; *Histoires vraies*, 1937; *La Vie dangereuse*, 1938; *D'Outremer à indigo*, 1940; *Noel aux quatre coins du monde*, 1953.

PLAYS: *La Perle fievreuse*, 1921 (screenplay); *Films san images*, 1959 (radio play).

POETRY: *Les Pâques à New York*, 1912; *La Prose du Transsibérien et de la petite Jehanne de France*, 1913 (*The Trans-Siberian Express*, 1964); *Séquences*, 1913; *La Guerre au Luxembourg*, 1916; *Le Panama: Ou, Les Aventures de mes sept oncles*, 1918 (*Panama: Or, The Adventures of My Seven Uncles*, 1931); *Dix-neuf Poèmes élastiques*, 1919; *Du monde entier*, 1919; *Du monde entier au coeur du monde*, 1919, 1957; *Moganni Nameh*, 1922; *Feuilles de route*, 1924, 1927; *Le Formose*, 1924; *Kodak*, 1924 (English translation, 1976).

NONFICTION: *Profond aujourd'hui*, 1917 (written in verse; *Profound Today*, 1922); *J'ai tué*, 1918 (written in verse; *I Have Killed*, 1919); *Le Fin du monde filmee par l'ange Notre-Dame*, 1919, 1949; *L'Eloge de la vie dangereuse*, 1926; *L'Eubage*, 1926; *Une Nuit dans la fôret*, 1929; *Vol à voiles*, 1932; *Panorama de la pègre*, 1935; *Hollywood: La mecque du cinéma*, 1936; *Chez l'armee l'anglaise*, 1940; *La Banlieue de Paris*, 1949; *Blaise Cendrars vous parle*, 1952; *Entretiens de Fernand Léger avec Blaise Cendrars et Louis Carré sur le paysage dans l'oeuvre de Léger*, 1956; *Trop c'est trop*, 1957; *Dites-nous Monsieur Blaise Cendrars*, 1969; *Inédits secrets*, 1969.

ANTHOLOGY: *L'Anthologie nègre*, 1921.

MISCELLANEOUS: *Oeuvres complètes*, 1960-1965 (8 volumes); *Selected Writings of Blaise Cendrars*, 1966; *Oeuvres complètes*, 1968-1971 (15 volumes).

Bibliography

Birkerts, Sven. "Blaise Cendrars," in *New Boston Review*. V (June-July, 1980), pp. 5-8.

Bochner, Jay. *Blaise Cendrars: Discovery and Re-creation*, 1978.

Buhler, Jean. *Blaise Cendrars, homme libre, poète au coeur du monde*, 1960.

Chadourne, Jacqueline. *Blaise Cendrars, poète du cosmos*, 1973.

Chefdor, Monique. *Blaise Cendrars*, 1980.

Lovey, Jean-Claude. *Situation de Blaise Cendrars*, 1965.

Miller, Henry. *Blaise Cendrars*, 1951.

_____ . "Preface," in *Selected Writings of Blaise Cendrars*, 1966.

Parrot, Louis. *Blaise Cendrars*, 1948.

Richard, Hugues. *Sauser avant Cendrars*, 1979.

T'Serstevens, A. *L'Homme que fut Blaise Cendrars*, 1972.

J. Madison Davis

MIGUEL DE CERVANTES

Born: Alcalá de Henares, Spain; September 29, 1547
Died: Madrid, Spain; April 23, 1616

Principal long fiction

La Galatea, 1585 (*Galatea: A Pastoral Romance*, 1833); *El ingenioso hidalgo don Quixote de la Mancha*, 1605, 1615 (*The History of the Valorous and Wittie Knight-Errant, Don Quixote of the Mancha*, 1612-1620; better known as *Don Quixote de la Mancha*); *Novelas ejemplares*, 1613 (*Exemplary Novels*, 1846); *Los trabajos de Persiles y Sigismunda*, 1617 (*The Travels of Persiles and Sigismunda: A Northern History*, 1619).

Other literary forms

Miguel de Cervantes never sought acclaim as a writer of fiction. He longed for the more popular success and financial rewards offered by the stage and hoped to gain a more prestigious literary reputation as a great poet, as evidenced by the time and dedication which he committed to his long derivative poem, *Viaje del Parnaso* (1614; *The Voyage to Parnassus*, 1870). These ambitions were unrealized. In fact, he admits in the poem of 1614 that heaven never blessed him with the poetic gift. His efforts in the theater did not bring him success at the time but did produce some significant work. Cervantes contributed to the Spanish theater not only by writing plays but also by stirring critical debate. In chapter 48 of the first part of *Don Quixote de la Mancha*, Cervantes attacked the Spanish stage and certain kinds of popular plays. This attack prompted a response from Lope de Vega, *Arte nuevo de hacer comedias en este tiempo* (1609; *The New Art of Writing Plays*, 1914), which was the central piece of dramatic theorizing of the Golden Age of Spanish theater. Cervantes also wrote one epic tragedy *La Numancia* (1784; *Numantia: A Tragedy*, 1870), a play praised in later centuries by Johann Wolfgang von Goethe, Percy Bysshe Shelley, Friedrich von Schlegel, and Arthur Schopenhauer, and he published a collection of eight comedies and eight interludes in 1615. These works were never performed in his lifetime. The eight interludes, one-act farces that would have been performed as intermission pieces, are original, dynamic, and highly theatrical. They rank with the finest work in the one-act form by Anton Chekhov, August Strindberg, and Tennessee Williams.

Achievements

Cervantes belongs to that elite group of supreme literary geniuses which includes Homer, Vergil, Dante, Chaucer, and William Shakespeare. The first to establish his greatness as a writer through the medium of prose fiction, Cervantes is acknowledged as an influential innovator who nurtured the short-story form and, more important, shaped the novel, sending it into the modern world. The list of succeeding masters of the novel who paid homage to Cervantes either through direct praise or imitation is awesome—among them Daniel Defoe, Tobias Smollett, Henry Fielding, Laurence Sterne, Jonathan Swift, Sir Walter Scott, Charles Dickens, Voltaire, Stendhal, Honoré de Balzac, Gustave Flaubert, Victor Hugo, Goethe, Thomas Mann, Ivan Turgenev, Nikolai Gogol, Fyodor Dostoevski, Washington Irving, Herman Melville, Mark Twain, William Faulkner, Saul Bellow; all of these authors recognized an indebtedness to the Spanish writer who, at the end of a lifetime of failure and disappointment, created the unlikely Knight of La Mancha and sent him out into the Spanish landscape with his equally unlikely squire, Sancho Panza. *Don Quixote de la Mancha* remains Cervantes' greatest gift to the world of literature.

If Cervantes became a giant in world literature by creating his mad knight, he also gave Spanish literature its greatest work. Cervantes' life and career spanned the glory days of Spain's eminence as a great empire as well as the beginning of its fall from world power. Cervantes re-created this Spain he knew so well in his great work. His love of his native Spain is evident in the generosity of detail with which he created the backdrop of his novel—the inns, the food, the costumes, the dusty roads, the mountains, the rogues, the nobility, the arguments, the laughter. The superb realization of his world set a standard that has guided novelists for centuries; Cervantes' rendering of his native Spain has by extension given us the England of Dickens, the Paris of Balzac, the Russia of Dostoevski.

Cervantes' imaginative depiction of his native land also has influenced subsequent Spanish literature. Most Spanish writers feel an indebtedness to Cervantes and regard his work with awe. Such modern masters of Spanish literature as José Ortega y Gasset and Miguel de Unamuno have written extensive studies and detailed commentaries on his great novel, treating it with a reverence usually reserved for religious writings. Cervantes, in creating the Don, gave Spain its greatest masterpiece, and his figure has loomed majestically over all subsequent Spanish literature.

Cervantes' contributions to the development of the novel form are considerable. Besides re-creating the texture of daily life in the Spain of his day, he became an innovator in the form of the novel. *Don Quixote de la Mancha* is a strange kind of prose epic with its singularly odd hero with his visions of virtue and glory riding into a mundane and common world. From the first, Cervantes saw how the richness of the older epic form might be adapted to the new prose form to create a new vision, grand and common, eloquent and humorous, ideal and real, all at once. Cervantes mastered at once the ability to elevate the common; the greatest of all later novelists have also mastered this unlikely duality—a large ideal vision that must find expression within the confines of a real world, whether that world be the streets of London, an

American whaling vessel, or a Russian prison camp.

Cervantes also freed his characters to exist within a more real world and to behave as more realistic human beings. The Don in all of his madness is still rooted in the Spain of his day, and Sancho Panza is the embodiment of a class as well as an attitude toward life. The characters also relate to one another through recognizable conversation. Cervantes made dialogue an integral part of the novel form, allowing his characters to speak their minds with the same freedom with which they travel the roads of Spain. Such conversations have been a part of most novels ever since.

Finally, and perhaps most important, Cervantes bequeathed to mankind a compelling vision of itself—man as committed idealist combined with man as foolish lunatic. Don Quixote rides out of the pages of the novel with a magnetic presence that has fascinated many subsequent artists. Honoré Daumier, Pablo Picasso, and many other painters have put him on canvas; Richard Strauss has placed him in an orchestral tone poem; Jules-Émile-Frédéric Massenet and Manuel de Falla have rendered him on the opera stage, and Tennessee Williams has brought him into American drama. The fascinating figure of the foolish knight continues to command the attentions of other artists. The Don remains a popular figure, too, appearing on the Broadway musical stage and in television commercials. The novel that Cervantes created is second only to the Bible in the number of different tongues into which it has been translated, but the appeal of the title character extends beyond literature into the dream-life of mankind.

Biography

In the most interesting of the full-length comedies by Miguel de Cervantes published in 1615, *Pedro de Urdemales*, the title character dreams ambitiously of becoming all the great personages that man can become: pope, prince, monarch, emperor, master of the world. After a career that is typical of a picaro or any other adventurous Spanish rogue of the time, Pedro finds his wishes realized when he becomes an actor and enters imaginatively into the ranks of the great. In much the same way, Cervantes' great ambitions in life were never realized; the only satisfaction he found was in a world he himself created.

In one sense, Cervantes' greatest adventure was his own life. Born in a small university city not far from Madrid, Miguel de Cervantes Saavedra traveled constantly with his family in his early years. His father, an impoverished and impractical man who attempted to earn a living as a surgeon, kept the family moving, from Valladolid to Córdoba, from Seville to Madrid. Cervantes learned the life of the road and the diversity of city life in Spain as a youth. In his twenties, he journeyed to Italy, perhaps fleeing from arrest as a result of a duel; there, he entered the service of Cardinal Aquaviva. In 1569, he enlisted in the Spanish army and went to sea. Cervantes was present at the Battle of Lepanto in 1571, serving under the command of Don John of Austria in the famous victory against the Turks. Cervantes rose from his sickbed to join in the battle and was twice wounded, one wound leaving his left hand permanently incapacitated. With his brother, Rodrigo, he embarked for Spain in 1575, but their ship was seized by Turkish pirates, and Cervantes spent five years in captivity as a slave.

Ransomed by monks, Cervantes returned to Spain, but not to glory and acclaim. With his military career at an end because of his paralyzed hand, Cervantes fell into poverty and moved from one failure to another, including an apparently unhappy marriage in 1584. Moving about Spain as in his youth, he again gained an education in the character and behavior of the Spanish lower classes, an education that continued when he was imprisoned twice in Seville, once in 1597 and again in 1602, both times, it is assumed, the result of financial difficulties. Despite a life of bad luck, missed opportunities, and little reward for his talent, Cervantes did achieve a popular success when the first part of *Don Quixote de la Mancha* was published in 1605, although his finances saw only minor improvement. In 1615, the second part of the novel appeared, to challenge the "false" sequels being produced by other writers seeking to capitalize on the book's success. Cervantes died in Madrid in 1616, at peace, having received the Sacraments.

Analysis

Many critics maintain that the impulse that prompted Miguel de Cervantes to begin his great novel was a satiric one: He desired to satirize chivalric romances. As the elderly Alonso Quixano the Good (if that is his name) pores over the pages of these books in his study, his "brain dries up" and he imagines himself to be the champion who will take up the vanished cause of knight errantry and wander the world righting wrongs, helping the helpless, defending the cause of justice, all for the greater glory of his lady Dulcinea del Toboso and his God. As he leaves his village before dawn, clad in rusty armor and riding his broken-down nag, he becomes Don Quixote de la Mancha. The mad knight's first foray is brief, and he is brought back home by friends from his native village. Despite the best efforts of his friends and relations, the mad old man embarks on a second journey, this time accompanied by a peasant from his village, Sancho Panza, who becomes the knight's squire. The Don insists on finding adventure everywhere, mistaking windmills for giants, flocks of sheep for attacking armies, puppet shows for real life. His squire provides a voice of down-to-earth reason, but Quixote always insists that vile enchanters have transformed the combatants to embarrass and humiliate him. Don Quixote insists on his vision of the ideal in the face of the cold facts of the world; Sancho Panza maintains his proverbial peasant wisdom in the face of his master's madness. In their travels and adventures, they encounter life on the roads of Spain. Sometimes they are treated with respect—for example, by "the gentleman in green" who invites them to his home and listens to Quixote with genuine interest—but more often they are ridiculed—as when the Duke and Duchess bring the knight and squire to their estate only for the purpose of ridicule and mockery. Finally, a young scholar from Quixote's native village, Sampson Carrasco, defeats the old knight in battle and forces him to return to his home, where he dies peacefully, having renounced his mad visions and lunatic behavior.

While it is necessary to acknowledge the satiric intent of Cervantes' novel, the rich fictional world of *Don Quixote de la Mancha* utterly transcends its local occasion. On the most personal level, the novel can be viewed as one of the most intimate evaluations of a life ever penned by a great author. When Don Quixote decides to take up the cause of knight errantry, he opens himself to a life of ridicule and defeat, a life that resembles Cervantes' own life with its endless reversals of fortune, humiliations, and hopeless struggles. Out of this life of failure and disappointment, Cervantes created the "mad knight," but he also added the curious human nobility and the refusal to succumb to despair in the face of defeat that turns Quixote into something more than a comic character or a ridiculous figure to be mocked. Although there are almost no points in the novel where actual incidents from Cervantes' life appear directly or even transformed into fictional disguise, the tone and the spirit, the succession of catastrophes with only occasional moments of slight glory, and the resiliency of human nature mark the novel as the most personal work of the author, the one where his singularly difficult life and his profoundly complex emotional responses to that life found form and structure.

If the novel is the record of Cervantes' life, the fiction also records a moment in Spanish national history when fortunes were shifting and tides turning. At the time of Cervantes' birth, Spain's might and glory were at their peak. The wealth from conquests of Mexico and Peru returned to Spain, commerce boomed, and artists recorded the sense of national pride with magnificent energy and power. By the time *Don Quixote de la Mancha* was published, the Spanish empire was beginning its decline. A series of military disasters, including the defeat of the Spanish Armada by the English and the revolt of Flanders, had shaken the once mighty nation. In the figure of Don Quixote, the greatest of a richly remembered past combines with the hard facts of age, weakness, and declining power. The character embodies a moment of Spanish history and the people's own sense of a vanishing glory in the face of an irreversible decline.

Don Quixote de la Mancha also stands as the greatest literary embodiment of the Counter-Reformation. Throughout Europe, the Reformation was moving with the speed of new ideas, changing the religious landscape of country after country. Spain stood proud as a Catholic nation, resisting any changes. Standing alone against the flood of reform sweeping Europe was a kind of willed madness, but the nobility and determination of Quixote to fight for his beliefs no matter what the rest of the world maintains reflects the strength of the Spanish will at this time. Cervantes was a devout and loyal believer, a supporter of the Church, and Don Quixote may be the greatest fictional Catholic hero, the battered Knight of the Counter-Reformation.

The book also represents fictionally the various sides of the Spanish spirit and the Spanish temper. In the divisions and contradictions found between the Knight of the Sad Countenance and his unlikely squire, Sancho Panza, the two faces of the Spanish soul have been painted by Cervantes: The Don is idealistic, sprightly, energetic, and cheerful, even in the face of overwhelming odds, but also overbearing, domineering Sancho, who is earthy, servile, and slothful. The two characters seem unlikely companions and yet they form a whole, the one somehow incomplete without the other and linked throughout the book through their dialogues and debates. In drawing master and servant, Cervantes presented the opposing truths of the spirit of his native land.

The book can also be seen as a great monument in the development of fiction, the moment when the fictional character was freed into the real world of choice and change. At the moment the gentleman of La Mancha took it into his head to become a knight errant and travel through the world redressing wrongs and winning eternal glory, the face of fiction permanently changed. Character in fiction became dynamic, unpredictable, and spontaneous. Until this time, character in fiction had existed in service of the story, but now the reality of change and psychological energy and freedom of the will became a permanent hallmark of fiction, as it already was of drama and narrative poetry. The fact of the title character's addled wits made the new freedom all the more impressive. The determination of Don Quixote, the impact of his vision on the world, and the world's hard reality as it impinges on the Don make for shifting balances and constant alterations in fortune that are psychologically believable. The shifting balance of friendship, devotion, and perception between the knight and his squire underlines this freedom, as does the power of other characters in the book to affect directly Don Quixote's fortunes: the niece, the housekeeper, the priest, the barber, Sampson Carrasco, the Duke, and the Duchess. There is a fabric of interaction throughout the novel, and character in the novel changes as it encounters new adventures, new people, and new ideas.

One way this interaction is chronicled by Cervantes is in dialogue. Dialogue had not played a significant or defining role in fiction before *Don Quixote de la Mancha*. As knight and squire ride across the countryside and engage in conversation, dialogue becomes the expression of character, idea, and reality. In the famous episode early in the first part of the novel (when Quixote views the windmills on the plain and announces that they are giants that he will wipe from the face of the earth and Sancho innocently replies, "What giants?"), the dialogue is not only carrying the comedy but also has become the battleground on which the contrasting visions of life will engage one another—to the delight of the reader. The long exchanges between Don Quixote and Sancho Panza provide priceless humor but also convey two different realities that meet, struggle, and explode in volleys of words. In giving his characters authentic voices that carry ideas, Cervantes brought to fiction a new truth that remains a standard of comparison.

The novel is also as modern as the most experimental of recent fiction. Throughout the long novel, Cervantes plays with the nature of the narrator, raising constant difficult questions as to who is telling the story and to what purpose. In the riotously funny opening page of the novel, the reader encounters a narrator not only unreliable but also lacking in the basic facts necessary to tell the story. He chooses not to tell us the name of the village where his hero lives, and he is not even sure of his hero's name, yet the narrator protests that the narrative must be entirely truthful. In chapter 9, as Don Quixote is preparing to do battle with the Basque, the narrative stops; the narrator states the manuscript from which he is culling this story is mutilated and incomplete. Fortunately, some time later in Toledo, he says he came upon an old Arabic manuscript by Arab historian Cide Hamete Benengeli that continues the adventures. For the remainder of the novel, the narrator claims to be providing a translation of this manuscript—the manuscript and the second narrator, the Arab historian, both lacking authority and credibility. In the second part of the novel, the narrator and the characters themselves are aware of the first part of the novel, as well as of a "false Quixote," a spurious second part written by an untalented Spanish writer named Avallaneda who sought to capitalize on the popularity of the first part of *Don Quixote de la Mancha* by publishing his own sequel. The "false Quixote" is on the narrator's mind, the characters' minds, and somehow on the mind of Cide Hamete Benengeli. These shifting perspectives, the multiple narrative voices, the questionable reliability of the narrators, and the "false" second part are all tricks, narrative sleight of hand as complex as anything found in Faulkner, Vladimir Nabokov, or Jorge Luis Borges. In his *Lectures on Don Quixote* (1983), Nabokov oddly makes no reference to Cervantes' narrative games; perhaps the old Spanish master's shadow still loomed too close to the modern novelist.

None of these approaches to the novel, however, appropriate as they may be, can begin to explain fully its enduring popularity or the strange manner in which the knight and his squire have ridden out of the pages of a book into the other artistic realms of orchestral music, opera, ballet, and painting, where other artists have given their visions of Quixote and Sancho. A current deeper and more abiding than biography, history, national temper, or literary landmark flows through the book and makes it speak to all manner of readers in all ages.

Early in the novel, Cervantes begins to dilute his strong satiric intent. The reader can laugh with delight at the inanity of the mad knight but never with the wicked, unalloyed glee that pure satire evokes. The knight begins to loom over the landscape; his madness brushes sense; his ideals demand defense. The reader finds himself early in the novel taking an attitude equivalent to that of the two young women of easy virtue who see Quixote when he arrives at an inn, which he believes to be a castle, on his first foray. Quixote calls them "two beauteous maidens . . . taking air at the gate of the castle," and they fall into helpless laughter, confronted with such a mad vision of themselves as "maidens." In time, however, because of Quixote's insistence on the truth of his vision, they help him out of his armor and set a table for him. They treat him as a knight, not as a mad old fool; he treats them as ladies, and they behave as ladies. The laughter stops, and for a pure moment, life transforms itself and human beings transcend themselves.

This mingling of real chivalry and transcendent ideals with the absurdity of character and mad action creates the tensions in the book as well as its strange melancholy beauty and haunting poignancy. The book is unlike any other ever written. John Berryman comments on this split between the upheld ideal and the riotously real, observing that the reader "does not know whether to laugh or cry, and does both." This old man with his dried-up brain, with his squire who has no "salt in his brain pan," with his rusty armor, his pathetic steed, and his lunatic vision that changes windmills into giants and flocks of sheep into attacking armies, this crazy old fool becomes a real knight errant. The true irony of the book and its history is that Don Quixote actually becomes a model for knighthood. He may be a foolish, improbable knight, but with his squire, horse, and armor, he has ridden into the popular imagination of the world not only as a ridiculous figure but also as a champion; he is a real knight whose vision may often cloud, who sees what he wants to see, but also he is one who demonstrates real virtue and courage and rises in his rhetoric and daring action to real heights of greatness.

Perhaps Cervantes left a clue as to the odd shift in his intention. The contradictory titles he assigns to his knight suggest this knowledge. The comic, melancholy strain pervades "Knight of the Sad Countenance" in the first part of the novel and the heroic strain in the second part when the hero acquires the new sobriquet "Knight of the Lions." The first title comes immediately after his adventure with a corpse and is awarded him by his realistic companion, Sancho. Quixote has attacked a funeral procession, seeking to avenge the dead man. Death, however, cannot be overcome; the attempted attack merely disrupts the funeral, and the valiant knight breaks the leg of an attending churchman. The name "Knight of the Sad Countenance" fits Quixote's stance here and through much of the book. Many of the adventures he undertakes are not only misguided but also unwinnable. Quixote may be Christlike, but he is not Christ, and he cannot conquer Death.

The adventure with the lions earns for him his second title and offers the other side of his journey as a knight. Encountering a cage of lions being taken to the king, Quixote becomes determined to fight them. Against all protest, he takes his stand, and the cage is opened. The lion stretches, yawns, looks at Quixote, and lies down. Quixote proclaims a great victory and awards himself the name "Knight of the Lions." A delightfully comic episode, the scene can be viewed in two ways—as a nonadventure which the knight claims as a victory or as a genuine moment of triumph as the knight undertakes an outlandish adventure and proves his genuine bravery while the king of beasts realizes the futility of challenging the unswerving old knight. Quixote, by whichever route, emerges as conqueror. Throughout his journeys, he often does emerge, victorious, despite his age, despite his illusions, despite his dried-up brain.

When, at the book's close, he is finally defeated and humiliated by Sampson Carrasco and forced to return to his village, the life goes out of him. The knight Don Quixote is replaced, however, on the deathbed by Alonso Quixano the Good. Don Quixote does not die, for the elderly gentleman regains his wits and becomes a new character. Don Quixote cannot die, for he is the creation of pure imagination. Despite the moving and sober conclusion, the reader cannot help but sense that the death scene being played out does not signify the end of Don Quixote. Our knight escapes and remains free. He rides out of the novel, with his loyal companion Sancho at his side, into the golden realm of myth. He becomes the model knight he hoped to be. He stands tall with his spirit, his ideals, his rusty armor, and his broken lance as the embodiment of man's best intentions and impossible folly. As Dostoevski so wisely said, when the Lord calls the Last Judgment, man should take with him this book and point to it, for it reveals all of man's deep and fatal mystery, his glory and his sorrow.

Major publications other than long fiction

PLAYS: *El trato de Argel*, 1585 (*The Commerce of Algiers: A Comedy*, 1870); *Ocho comedias y ocho entremeses*, 1615 (includes *Pedro de Urmales*, 1615; English translation, 1807); *La Numancia*, 1784 (written 1585; *Numantia: A Tragedy*, 1870).

POETRY: *Viaje del Parnaso*, 1614 (*The Voyage to Parnassus*, 1870).

Bibliography
Bell, Aubrey F. G. *Cervantes*, 1961.
Byron, William. *Cervantes*, 1978.
Duran, Manuel. *Cervantes*, 1974.
Entwhistle, William. *Cervantes*, 1940.
Nabokov, Vladimir. *Lectures on Don Quixote*, 1982.
Nelson, Lowry, Jr., ed. *Cervantes: A Collection of Critical Essays*, 1969.
Predmore, Richard. *Cervantes*, 1973.

David Allen White

CHATEAUBRIAND

Born: Saint-Malo, France; September 4, 1768
Died: Paris, France; July 4, 1848

Principal long fiction

Atala, 1801 (English translation, 1802); *René*, 1802 (English translation, 1813); *Les Martyres*, 1809 (*The Martyrs*, 1812); *Les Natchez*, 1826 (*The Natchez*, 1827).

Other literary forms

The importance of Chateaubriand's essays, travelogues, and memoirs is as great as that of his two relatively short novels, *Atala* and *René*, both of which were extracted from an early version of *The Natchez* and inserted as illustrations in *Le Génie du Christianisme* (1799, 1800, 1802; *The Genius of Christianity*, 1802). It seems advisable, therefore, to speak at some length of the latter, as well as of the *Mémoires d'outre-tombe* (1849-1850; *Memoirs*, 1902).

Part 1 of *The Genius of Christianity* asserts that Christianity imposes itself on the convert because of the beauty of its dogmas, its sacraments, its theological virtues, and its holy scriptures. The harmony of the world and the marvels of nature attest the existence of God. In part 2, Christianity, more than paganism, exalts poetic inspiration. No religion has so profoundly penetrated the mysteries of the human soul or is so keenly attuned to the beauties of the universe. The *merveilleux chrétien* has more grandeur than the supernatural of paganism. The Bible, in its simplicity, is more beautiful than Homer's *Iliad*.

In part 3, Chateaubriand shows how Christianity has favored the development of the fine arts and given rise to the Gothic cathedral. It has supported the work of scholars, philosophers, and historians. It has caused the genius of Blaise Pascal to flower and has made the sublime eloquence of Jacques Bossuet possible. In part 4, the ringing of bells, the decoration of churches, the solemnity of rites, and the majesty of ceremonies combine to move the soul. The missionaries have spread the benefits of their social work. Born amid the ruins of the Roman Empire, Christianity has saved civilization. It will emerge triumphant from the trial that has purified it.

The Genius of Christianity underwent many changes from its first edition in London in 1799. Furious with the philosophes, its author used a language so violent that his friends were frightened and persuaded him to modify his tone. A second version was printed in Paris in 1800; Chateaubriand's own scruples caused him to recall the copies. Suppressing a chapter in praise of doctors and portions containing observations on England, he reworked his project. He reduced it from seven parts to three dealing with the dogmas, poetics, and rites of Christianity. By 1801, the work had become a poetics of

Christianity, including discussions of poetry and other literature, the fine arts, and the harmonies of religion. The proofs of this version received the attention of the censors, and more changes were made to serve the politics of Napoleon Bonaparte. *The Genius of Christianity* was again printed in 1802, with the approval of the government and assured of success, a few days before the proclamation of the Concordat.

The five volumes comprise four parts, divided into books and subdivided into chapters, but there is little or no formal unity. Chateaubriand's tones are as mixed as the work's contents: In a work of piety he included, for example, two love stories (the original versions of *Atala* and *René*). His is not the external unity of a dialectician, but rather a subtle unity by means of which he appeals to his readers' sensibility gradually and profoundly. The feeling is often that of Jean-Jacques Rousseau or Jean-Baptiste Greuze. Chateaubriand's education was a classical one which gave him the background and insight that permitted him to analyze the literary works of the seventeenth century in the light of the Christianity that informed them. The book is Romantic because of its fresh, new vigor. It revives a whole world of dreams that were real and of forms unknown to the ancients. Chateaubriand's goal was to create a poetry in which nature would no longer function as mere ornament for vain goddesses. For Christians and Frenchmen he proposed poetry that is Christian and French, much as Madame de Staël proposed it in *De la littérature considérée dans les rapports avec les institutions sociales* (1800; *A Treatise on Ancient and Modern Literature*, 1803); for Chateaubriand, however, its perfection would derive from its Christianity.

Chateaubriand's work, then, is a reply to the philosophes who accused Christianity of being absurd, crude, and petty. He wished to demonstrate that there is no shame in sharing the faith of Sir Isaac Newton and Pascal, as well as of Bossuet and Jean Racine. Neither theology nor dogma was of great interest to Chateaubriand. He did not use rational arguments, for his objective was to establish not the truth of Christianity but its sphere of influence from affective and aesthetic points of view. *The Genius of Christianity* is doubtless weak philosophically. A religion cannot be based on the emotions of poets and artists. Nevertheless, Chateaubriand achieved the goal that he set for himself, and he became both a spiritual guide for his generation and a spokesman for Napoleon's government. Internal politics in France demanded a religious revival, and the author of *The Genius of Christianity* was rewarded with several diplomatic posts, which he accepted while he could agree with the regime.

Memoirs is not a collection of conventional memoirs but a highly varied work in the manner of Michel de Montaigne's *Essais* (1580-1595; *The Essays*, 1603). The author moves from a lofty poetic tone to that of familiar anecdote, examines philosophical subjects, and includes letters and travel experiences. He jumps abruptly from one topic to another, from one idea to the next, from one year to another, often returning to correct or emphasize an earlier point.

The time is his own, but all of history provides him with comparisons and symbols enabling him better to understand his own times. The books Chateaubriand had read often play a role in the *Memoirs*; sometimes he gives the titles of his sources, sometimes not, as though everything begins and ends with him. Every place visited by the memorialist is peopled by its great men of past ages and by a certain spirit, especially one that is heroic and French. Chateaubriand's vision of history is not only dramatic but also lyric; he is at the center of everything, relating all of his passions, his beliefs, and his destiny to the great events of the past.

He includes many portraits as well, some sympathetic, some tragic and symbolic, many caricatural, as though to say that so many famous men and great ladies have been nothing more than amusing figures in a farce that they have not understood. Included, finally, are the picturesque and the practical side of life and its objects. There are descriptions of all manner of things and activities observed by the memorialist and recorded for posterity, becoming, like everything else, part of Chateaubriand's memory and the memory of Chateaubriand *d'outre-tombe* (from beyond the tomb).

Achievements

Chateaubriand was the most significant figure in French literature in the transitional period between the end of the Enlightenment, when classicism still ruled, and the heyday of Romanticism.

Many of the characteristic elements of Romantic fiction can be found in early form in the novels of Chateaubriand: the exoticism; the idealization of the primitive; the extensive descriptions of nature. In much Romantic fiction, genre lines are blurred, and here again, Chateaubriand's example was influential. Stylistically, Chateaubriand's rhythmic sentences and splendid vocabulary revealed hitherto unsuspected resources of French prose. Finally, his unabashed egotism is quintessentially Romantic; Byronic before Byron, Chateaubriand left his flamboyant mark on a generation of younger writers.

Biography

François-Auguste-René de Chateaubriand was born on the northern French coast, in Saint-Malo. In *Memoirs*, he tells of his games and daydreams on the beaches of his native city, dwelling on his melancholy sojourns at the manor at Combourg with a taciturn, frightening father, a superstitious, sickly mother, and an affectionate, excitable sister. From childhood, he was receptive to the poetry of the ocean and the wild heath surrounding the château.

After having completed his classical studies at the schools in Dol, Rennes, and Dinan, Chateaubriand pondered at length over what he would do with his life. Although he did not think himself suited to any but a sedentary career, he eventually joined the army. A few months later, however, he took advantage of a leave to go to Paris, where he frequented the court and literary circles. Soon thereafter, he left for the New World.

Chateaubriand's visit to America lasted from July 10 to December 10, 1791. He landed at Baltimore, went to Philadelphia, traveled up the Hudson River and through the virgin forest, became acquainted with the Indians, saw Niagara Falls and perhaps Ohio. This long trip away from France left him with memories that he was later to exploit. During these travels, he began a journal that he completed later with the aid of other travelers' accounts. Learning of the flight of Varennes and the detention of Louis XVI, Chateaubriand decided to return to France to offer his services to the threatened monarchy.

In 1792, Chateaubriand married a friend of one of his sisters, Céleste Buisson de Lavigne, in the hope of obtaining money with which to emigrate to Belgium. Unfortunately, her income ceased with her marriage. Although she was an intelligent and courageous woman, and despite considerable mutual admiration, Chateaubriand did not live much with his wife over the long years of their marriage.

Less than six months after the wedding, Chateaubriand was off to Belgium with forged papers to join the army of the European powers that were combating the Revolution. Wounded at the siege of Thionville, he took refuge in England in 1793. He led a miserable existence there, especially at the beginning, giving private lessons and doing translations for a living. At that time he was also working on an Indian epic in prose, *The Natchez*.

In London in 1797, Chateaubriand published *Essai sur les révolutions* (*An Historical, Political, Moral Essay on Revolutions*, 1815), in which he compared ancient and modern revolutions—historically, politically, and morally—with the French Revolution. This first work summarizes all the disappointments and anguish of his youth. Revealing influences of the eighteenth century philosophes, especially that of Rousseau, Chateaubriand praises man in the natural state. Although he uses rationalistic arguments against the Christian faith, Chateaubriand sometimes indicates a certain anxiety concerning religion. He rejects Montesquieu's, Voltaire's, and the other *Encyclopédistes'* belief in human progress. Chateaubriand considered that in this essay he had shown that there is nothing new under the sun, that earlier revolutions had contained the germ of the French Revolution.

In 1798, while still in London, Chateaubriand learned of the deaths, first of a sister, then of his mother. His grief at these two losses made him weep, and with the flow of tears came a return to the faith of his childhood, a faith toward which he had long been groping to sustain him in his many sorrows. Back in France, he would thenceforth devote his literary talent to defending and restoring the religion that the French Revolution had sought to destroy.

Published in 1802 after *Atala* and *René*, *The Genius of Christianity* appeared a few days before Napoleon's Concordat with the Pope became public. For political reasons, the Emperor, too, had been working to restore religion in France, and he appointed Chateaubriand, first as secretary to the ambassador to Rome (1803), then as Minister Plenipotentiary in the Valais (1804). The execution of the Duc d'Enghien went against Chateaubriand's conscience, however, and aroused his sentiments for the restoration of the monarchy. He resigned his post and, despite Napoleon's efforts to win him back, remained prudently but firmly opposed to the Emperor. Elected to the Académie Française in 1811, Chateaubriand would not make his acceptance speech, and he waited for Napoleon's fall from power to take his seat.

After his break with the Emperor, Chateaubriand planned to complete his apology for religion by writing a Christian epic. In order to prepare himself for that task, he took a trip in 1806 and 1807 through many parts of Europe and to the Holy Land; one of the products of this journey was the *Itinéraire de Paris è Jérusalem* (1811).

Chateaubriand was at first delighted with the Bourbons' return to power. He held numerous important diplomatic posts under both Louis XVIII and Charles X and was often honored by both kings. Although his spirit of independence and his outspoken nature also invoked royal disfavor, Chateaubriand's popularity was never greater. The political essays that he published during this period expressed, among other views, his belief in constitutional monarchy.

From 1826 to 1831, Chateaubriand's *Oeuvres complètes* were published, including some works that had not yet appeared. *Les Aventures du dernier Abencérage* (1826; *The Last of the Abencérages*, 1835) is a record of travel impressions of Spain, for which he had not found space in the *Itinéraire de Paris à Jérusalem*. *The Natchez* and *Le Voyage en Amérique* (1827; *Travels in America*, 1969) are, respectively, the Indian prose epic composed in London (in which *Atala* and *René* had also appeared) and the travel book begun in the New World in 1791.

At the advent of Louis-Philippe, Chateaubriand refused to recognize the "usurper" and gave up his peerage. Preferring to go the way of the legitimate monarchy, he nevertheless served the Duchess of Berry briefly in her efforts to overthrow Louis-Philippe. For the most part, however, Chateaubriand frequented the salon of Madame Juliette Récamier, a longtime friend and mistress, where he reigned supreme and eventually took up residence, devoting himslf to his writings. It was at the home of Récamier that he read his *Memoirs* to a group of the faithful.

When Chateaubriand died on July 4, 1848, he was buried as he had requested, on the rocks of Grand-Bé on the coast of his native Brittany, in splendid isolation.

Analysis

The analysis of Chateaubriand's best-known works of fiction, *Atala* and

René, can be better appreciated after the earlier introductions on the author's overall achievements and his works of nonfiction. The two novels may stand as independent units, but any comprehensive discussion must view them as linked with the author's achievements in general and his other literary forms in particular.

Atala began as an episode in *The Natchez*, a work originally composed during Chateaubriand's stay in London. The author reworked it in order to include it in a section of *The Genius of Christianity* entitled "Harmony of the Christian Religion, with Scenes in Nature and the Passions of the Human Heart." He first published it separately, however, in 1801.

Le Mercure, a journal of the period, had been engaged in a polemic attacking the antireligious spirit of the eighteenth century, against which complaints had been lodged by the partisans, including Madame de Staël, of this aspect of the old regime. Because the government of Napoleon Bonaparte favored the restoration of religion in France, the times seemed right for the "author of *The Genius of Christianity*," as Chateaubriand called himself in *Le Mercure*, to let the public know of his existence. Still a political refugee, he needed to be cautious. Perhaps fearing a clandestine edition of some part of his work— no doubt anxious for glory at a time when he was still composing *The Genius of Christianity* and similar works by others were appearing—Chateaubriand began by publishing a few pages of *Atala* in *Le Mercure* in 1800 and 1801. Soon he gave a complete *Atala* to the public and the critics, prefacing it with a kind of manifesto.

It was as easy to detach *Atala* from *The Genius of Christianity* as from *The Natchez*. There was no need to read all of "Harmony of the Christian Religion" to appreciate either *Atala* or *René*, which had also been detached from *The Natchez* and intended for inclusion in *The Genius of Christianity*; not only did Chateaubriand begin by publishing them separately (in 1801 and 1802, respectively), then together (1805), but in 1826 he ceased to include them in *The Genius of Christianity*.

Exotic literature did not originate with Chateaubriand. In the eighteenth century, the triumph of religion over love in a non-European setting had been treated in Voltaire's *Zaïre* (1732; *The Tragedy of Zara*, 1736; also English translation, 1854). The accounts of travelers such as Thomas Cook had revealed the simple manners of primitive peoples to civilized society. In *Paul et Virginie* (1787; *Paul and Mary*, 1789; better known as *Paul and Virginia*, 1795) Jacques-Henri Bernardin de Saint-Pierre had depicted the virgin forest and seascapes of the tropics, and several writers had invented stories analogous to *Atala* set in America. Like Abbé Prévost, Chateaubriand had not seen all the scenes that he described, but he made use of books by naturalists and travelers to compensate for what he lacked in firsthand experience.

Atala opens on the banks of the Meschacebé (Mississippi River) in Louisiana; here lives the tribe of Natchez, which welcomes the young Frenchman,

René. The old Indian, Chactas, who visited France at the time of Louis XIV, befriends René during a beaver hunt and begins to tell him of his adventures as a young man. He was about twenty years old when an enemy tribe captured him. He was saved by Atala, a beautiful Indian girl who had been reared as a Christian. For a long time they fled through the forest, their passion growing stronger all the while. During a storm, they encountered a missionary, Father Aubry, who wished to convert Chactas and unite him and Atala in marriage. The girl was dedicated to the Virgin Mary by her mother, however, and she believed that she could never be released from the vow of chastity. In order not to surrender to her love for Chactas, Atala took poison. Repentant and resigned, Atala died, consoled by the ministrations of the kindly Father Aubry and to the great sorrow of Chactas.

Despite Chateaubriand's protests to the contrary, his idyllic picture of savages is reminiscent of Rousseau. In the religion that required no church, with its rudimentary practices, Chateaubriand's readers recognized the doctrine of the Vicaire Savoyard; in the sentimental Indians themselves, the sensibility of the eighteenth century. Various characteristics and details, such as Chactas' reference to Atala's virtuous yet passionate face or Father Aubry's amusing nose, associate the work with Rousseau's *Julie: Ou, La Nouvelle Héloïse* (1761) and Saint-Pierre's *Paul and Virginia.*

Yet Atala and Father Aubry are neither mere literary offspring of these works nor simply creations of Chateaubriand's imagination. In Atala, Chateaubriand re-created the charms of an English girl that he had loved; in the guise of the wise old Chactas, Chateaubriand himself is to be found, with his desires, passions, and dreams; and Father Aubry finds his prototype in a certain Father Jogues. On a symbolic level, the Indian girl embodies the spirit of solitude in nature; the old priest, that of the epic missionary movement. Chateaubriand's sometimes sumptuous, sometimes tender prose, however, is beholden only to the author's own poetic inspiration.

The introductory paragraphs of *René* give the setting in which, several years later, in order to explain the cause of his incurable melancholia to the old Indian, René in turn tells the story of his own youth. After a childhood filled with wild daydreams, after travels that made him aware of his isolation in society, after several years of passion and ecstasy spent with his sister Amélie, he decided to leave France for America, while Amélie, alarmed by the excessive emotion that she felt for her brother, retired to a convent.

In *René*, Chateaubriand intended to give moral significance to his narrative of a civilized man who has become a savage. He describes the feeling of lassitude and apathy toward life that is denounced in *The Genius of Christianity* as the evil of modern times. In *René*, Chateaubriand explains that the many books that deal with man and his emotions lead him to live life vicariously. Lacking experience, man becomes disenchanted with life without having enjoyed it. He has no more illusions, but his desires remain unsatisfied.

His imagination is rich, abundant, and marvelous; his existence, poor, barren, and disillusioned. He lives in an empty world with a full heart, weary of everything without having enjoyed anything.

Chateaubriand himself had known similar spiritual states and believed that faith would set him free. Far from offering René as a model, he condemns him through the words of the missionary, Father Souël, who, with Chactas, has received René's confidence. According to Father Souël, nothing in René's story deserves the pity that he has been shown; he was a young man whose head was filled with fantasy, who was displeased with everything, and who shirked all social responsibility to indulge himself in useless daydreams. A man is not superior because he perceives the world in a hateful light. If one hates mankind and life, it is because one is nearsighted. René is advised to look beyond; if he does, he will soon be convinced that all the ills of which he complains are as nothing. Solitude is bad only for the person who lives without God.

Chateaubriand's readers missed his lesson. They were charmed by his hero, however, whose prestige was enhanced by a style capable of the intricacies of psychological analyses as well as bursts of lyricism. René is both uplifted and overwhelmed by infinite desire. He dreams of love before he has truly loved, and his dream strays after fantasy. He does not permit himself to be emotionally satisfied by objects within his grasp; the pleasure that he takes in imagination anticipates and destroys his pleasure in feeling and possessing the real objects. He therefore rejects a reality which is necessarily disappointing, but he consoles himself for his ennui by considering the uniqueness of his fate. His very sorrow, because of its extraordinary nature, contains its own cure. One enjoys the unusual, even when it is misfortune. René contemplates his sorrow, admiring and cherishing it. Chateaubriand's contemporaries recognized themselves in René and loved him.

René's (and Chateaubriand's) malady was also the malady of his generation and even of the preceding one. When young, its members had read Rousseau's *La Nouvelle Héloïse* and Johann Wolfgang von Goethe's *The Sorrows of Werther* (1774), as well as the works of the English and Scottish Romantic poets. They had experienced the two phases of René's life: that of the dreamer consumed by an inexplicable sorrow, thirsting for something infinite and intangible, involving the longed-for tempest; and that of the René of the unwholesome passion, nurturing an inadmissible thought within himself. Wishing to liberate nature, the eighteenth century had invested passion with a sacred character and had rehabilitated incest. Incest inspired an outpouring of works by Louis-Sébastien Mercier, Voltaire, Jean-François Ducis, and others, which doubtless suggested this subject to Chateaubriand.

If one studies *René*, one finds autobiographical data. René's sister, Amélie, lived at Combourg with her brother, for example, and René and she share numerous characteristics with Chateaubriand and his sister Lucile. The reader is not to take Amélie for Lucile or Chateaubriand for René. Nevertheless, Amélie, like Lucile, is an unhappy soul, subject to feverish exaltation and flashes of madness; Chateaubriand and René experienced the same difficulties in the same places; both went into exile for the same reasons; Chateaubriand's forced idleness as an émigré, his solitude, his dreams of action and consuming passion, and the apathy from which he was torn by a brutal act are repeated in the story of his hero. Chateaubriand admitted that his total boredom and total disgust were embodied in René, and a friend said of the author that he had a reserve of ennui that seemed contained in the immense void between himself and his thoughts.

Favoring religion in response to the needs of the heart and its anquish, *René* was, like *Atala*, originally a part of *The Genius of Christianity*, after the chapter on the effects of strong passion. *René*, intended to address the malady of a Werther and demonstrate that religion was the only cure for it, summarized all the advice that Chateaubriand had received from his mother at Combourg. According to Amélie, one should not scorn the wisdom of one's forebears. It is better to be more like ordinary people and be less unhappy; it is more difficult to live than to die. Finally, the fervent prayers of Chateaubriand's mother are echoed in the missionary's concluding words to René: "Whoever has been endowed with talent must devote it to serving his fellow men, for if he does not make use of it, he is first punished by an inner misery, and sooner or later Heaven visits on him a fearful retribution."

Major publications other than long fiction
NONFICTION: *Essai sur les révolutions*, 1797 (*An Historical, Political, Moral Essay on Revolutions*, 1815); *Le Génie du Christianisme*, 1799, 1800, 1802 (*The Genius of Christianity*, 1802); *Itinéraire de Paris à Jérusalem*, 1811; *De Buonaparte et des Bourbons*, 1814 (*On Buonaparte and the Bourbons*, 1814); *De la monarchie, selon la charte*, 1816 (*The Monarchy According to the Charter*, 1816); *Mémoires sur la vie et la mort du duc de Berry*, 1820; *Les Aventures du dernier Abencérage*, 1826 (*The Last of the Abencérages*, 1835); *Le Voyage en Amérique*, 1827 (*Travels in America*, 1969); *Essai sur la littérature anglaise*, 1836 (*Sketches on English Literature*, 1836); *Le Congrès de Vérone*, 1838; *Vie de Rancé*, 1844; *Mémoires d'outre-tombe*, 1849-1850 (*Memoirs*, 1902).

MISCELLANEOUS: *Oeuvres complètes*, 1826-1831, 1836-1839 (36 volumes). *Oeuvres complétes*, 1859-1861.

Bibliography
Chateaubriand Today: International Commemoration of the Bicentenary of the Birth of Chateaubriand, 1968.
Maurois, André. *Chateaubriand*, 1938.
Moreau, Pierre. *Chateaubriand*, 1927.
Painter, George D. *Chateaubriand: A Biography*, 1978.

Spring, Henry P. *Chateaubriand at the Crossways*, 1924.
Switzer, Richard. *Chateaubriand*, 1971.

Richard A. Mazzara

CLARÍN
Leopoldo Alas

Born: Zamora, Spain; April 25, 1852
Died: Oviedo, Spain; June 13, 1901

Principal long fiction

La regenta, 1884 (English translation, 1984); *Su único hijo*, 1890 (*His Only Son*, 1970); *Obras selectas*, 1947, 1966.

Other literary forms

Besides the two major novels mentioned above, Clarín published more than eighty short stories or novelettes, including "Pipa," "Doña Berta," (English translation), "El sombrero del señor cura," "¡Adiós, Cordera!" (English translation), "Dos sabios," and "Zurrita." Many of these pieces have been collected and republished under such titles as *Cuentos morales* (1896, 1973), *¡Adiós, Cordera! y otros cuentos* (1944), *Cuentos de Clarín* (1954), and *Cuentos escogidos* (1964). Clarín's collections of literary and political essays include *El derecho y la moralidad* (his doctoral thesis, 1878), *Solos de Clarín* (1881, 1971), *La literatura en 1881* (1882; in collaboration with Armando Palacio Valdés), *Nueva compaña, 1885-1886* (1887), *Mezclilla* (1889), *Ensayos y revistas* (1892), *Palique* (1893, 1973), and *Galdós* (1912). His only attempt at theater is *Teresa* (1895). The most important general compilation of Clarín's work is that of Juan Antonio Cabezas, *Obras selectas* (1947, 1966), which includes both of the major novels, twenty-five short stories, and thirty-seven articles.

Achievements

Leopoldo Alas, more frequently known by his pseudonym "Clarín," is considered one of the four or five most important figures of nineteenth century Spanish realism, along with Benito Pérez Galdós, Emilia Pardo Bazán, Juan Valera, and José María de Pereda. While Clarín was recognized early in his literary career for the excellence of his short stories and for the biting criticism of his essays, he was, like Stendhal, generally misunderstood by his own generation. His fame now rests primarily upon his two major and lengthy works, particularly *La regenta*, considered by many critics as the second greatest novel in the Spanish language, after Miguel de Cervantes' *Don Quixote de la Mancha* (1605, 1615). Since the centennial celebration of Clarín's birth in 1952, studies of his best short stories and of *His Only Son* have finally brought about a relatively balanced view of his artistic achievements.

The Asturian writer was one of the most prolific and certainly one of the most feared of all literary critics in Spain during the second half of the nineteenth century. By the end of his life, he could lash out mercilessly at a mistake in grammar by some aspiring writer or politician and, by a single stroke of the pen, destroy that person's career. With respect to literary ideology, his essays call above all for a realism based upon exactness of observation and psychological depth, within a moral framework. Clarín was also one of the few to insist that his contemporaries inform themselves of literary developments taking place north of the Pyrenees.

Biography

Leopoldo Enrique García Alas y Ureña, the third son of a local civil governor, was born on April 25, 1852, in Zamora, a town some 250 kilometers northwest of Madrid. At age seven, he was sent to the Jesuit *colegio* of San Marcos in León, where he spent several happy months despite the fact that his blond hair, short, slight stature, and myopic vision set him apart somewhat from his schoolmates. It was there that he began to develop both the sentimentality and the sense of moral discipline that were to become so evident in his later thought and writing.

The following summer, Leopoldo and his family moved to the northern city of Oviedo, where he was to spend the rest of his life and which was to be the setting for his masterpiece, *La regenta*. While working for his *bachillerato*, he continued to develop an extremely competitive spirit, as he strove to compensate for physical weaknesses by a precocious and inquiring mind. During his fourth year of study, Leopoldo and his classmates were profoundly moved by the revolution of General Juan Prim and its aftermath, and it was during this period that Leopoldo began to contemplate the complexities of social justice and the disillusionments that arise when idealized hopes are dashed by the harsh realities of political life.

At age twenty, Leopoldo was in Madrid, preparing for his doctorate and feeling nervous, melancholy, and increasingly homesick for his native Asturias. A naturally critical temperament and a stubborn reluctance to embrace philosophical or literary fads delayed his acceptance of Sanz del Río's Krausism and the Naturalistic approach being preached by Émile Zola, but, as with his subsequent ideological views, once these ideas were accepted, Leopoldo was to defend them with sincerity and passion.

At age twenty-three, he began publishing articles in Madrid journals, and in October, 1875, he adopted the pseudonym "Clarín." The name was chosen perhaps in lighthearted recognition of Pedro Calderón de la Barca's famous *gracioso* in *La vida es sueño* (1635; *Life Is a Dream*, 1830) or perhaps because of the musical tradition of the time, by which an orchestra might pause to allow for a clear, often moving solo by the clarion, or *clarín*. Clarín's barbs soon produced many enemies, and it was not long before he found himself forced to change sidewalks to avoid confrontations; he took to target shooting and fencing lessons in preparation for some inevitable duels.

One immediate result of Clarín's critical pen came when the Minister of

Public Instruction, one of the figures whom the young writer had derided in print, rejected him for the *cátedra* of political economy at the University of Madrid, despite the youth's having clearly surpassed his competitors in the *oposiciones*. This experience was a bitter lesson in social and political realities, one which would be reflected in the biting satire of *La regenta* and in some of the short stories.

Two years of happiness followed, however, as Clarín fell in love with and married Onofre García Argüelles and was awarded two *cátedras*, first in Zaragoza and then, in 1883, at the University of Oviedo. There followed a period of intense writing, with little sleep and but a few mouthfuls of food a day. After the first volume of *La regenta* was completed, despite the severe emotional impact of his father's death, a feverish creative effort produced the second volume within six months. Not surprisingly, Clarín's health began to fail. Increasingly disillusioned with society around him, he continued to produce articles exposing truths few wanted to hear. In some areas, his power became immense, as illustrated by the firing of a public official because of Clarín's anger at the man's mispronunciation of a single word.

During the summer of 1892, while secluded in his beloved country retreat at Guimarán, Clarín suffered a severe mental crisis, but he soon recovered with the rediscovery of the sentimentality and religious contentment of his youth. This change became evident immediately afterward in some of his short stories, particularly "Cambio de luz," and, later, those in *Cuentos morales*. Clarín's long resistance to proper medical care finally caught up with him, however, and, overcome by intestinal tuberculosis, he died at the age of forty-nine on June 13, 1901.

Analysis

The realistic novel in Spain arose out of a particular set of historical circumstances and from diverse streams of intellectual growth: social and economic factors (the rise of a middle-class, materialistic society, the Revolution of 1868, and the underlying political, religious, and economic corruption of the Restoration period); scientific influences (positivism, Darwinism, and the Industrial Revolution); philosophical currents (the eighteenth century position that truth can be discovered through the senses and, later, the influence of Krausism); and, most particularly, such literary developments as the influence of and reaction against Romanticism, currents from France (the realism of Honoré de Balzac, Gustave Flaubert, and Stendhal, and Zola's Naturalism), and the rediscovery of Cervantine and traditional Spanish realism. The Spanish realistic novel, particularly as exemplified by Clarín, revealed some points of emphasis which differed from the French: a stronger continuity of thought and feeling with previous Romantic tendencies; a more pronounced stress on spiritual and religious matters; a regionalistic framework (such as Clarín's focus on Asturias and Oviedo); and the constant presence of the

Cervantine influence. The last characteristic included the special use of character and authorial perspectives that expose the ambiguity and complexity of reality, a distinctive brand of literary irony, and devices that produce the effect of character autonomy.

Within this general framework, Clarín's linguistic refinements and extremely subjective point of view deviated from the slightly more objective approach of many of his own Spanish contemporaries. Furthermore, while all realistic writers were critical of their environment, Clarín, more than most, failed to camouflage his didactic stance. His realism, rather, is to be found in the solidity and extraordinary depth of his major psychological studies, his powers of observation and the resulting exactness of detail, and his intricate play of character-author perspectives. Like most of the major novelists of the second half of the nineteenth century in Spain, Clarín evolved somewhat in his later years away from the realistic/Naturalistic focus toward a more "idealistic" inspiration. Leo Tolstoy, rather than Balzac or Zola, became the most significant foreign influence during this period. The Asturian writer came to abandon, to an extent, his preoccupation with aesthetic theory and literary novelty in the search for a more transcendent, spiritual, often symbolic approach.

La regenta, Clarín's first and greatest novel, stands as one of the supreme achievements of nineteenth century realism in Spain and Europe. In it, one can see a reawakening in the Iberian Peninsula of what Georg Lukács called the "novel of romantic disillusionment." Certainly, it is one of the most powerful creations of modern psychological realism. In *La regenta*, all of Clarín's literary theories were put into effect: A strong, ideological tone and theme provided a framework for exploring psychological motivations; the actualities of contemporary Spanish society are portrayed; and the smallest of details contributes to artistic ends. The work reflects the author's conception of art as an *ancha ventana abierta* (wide-open window), in which Clarín the critic could search for justice, Clarín the educator could search for truth, and Clarín the artist could search for beauty.

The book is many things in one: an autobiography (in its reflection of the author's own personality, culture, ideology, and actual experiences); a regional novel (to the extent that its setting, called Vetusta, is the city of Oviedo); a treatise on national traits, both historical and contemporary; and the greatest of all Spanish "Naturalistic" creations. (One must add, immediately, that none of the major realistic novelists in Spain subscribed totally to Zola's concept of philosophical determinism or to full descriptive treatment of grotesque or crude realities.)

Despite the novel's length and complexity, the basic threads of the action can be summarized in a few sentences. In broadest terms, the plot traces the process by which the heroine, Ana Ozores, is drawn into an adulterous relationship with an aristocratic Don Juan, Alvaro Mesía. Conflict arises from

Ana's physical attraction to Alvaro, which battles against idealistic, spiritual impulses nurtured by her confessor, Don Fermín de Pas, and natural inclination versus conjugal duty. The rest of the plot is a study of these figures and the behavior of literally hundreds of other characters who inhabit a city plagued by political corruption and social and moral degeneration. Ana's vacillations—the very basis for the action as well as the novel's style and structure—dramatize the need for love, both in the form of human companionship and in what Sherman Eoff has called "a personal and sympathetic relationship with Deity."

Clarín's tone, his approach to his characters, and his setting are not "realistically" neutral. The author's own feelings range through sarcasm, criticism, displeasure, hatred, sympathy, derision, and open, light humor. Just as evident, if not as pertinent to the work's artistry, however, are Clarín's ideological, utilitarian themes; his condemnation of indifference, narrowness, provincialism, ignorance, pedantry, moral degradation, religious hypocrisy, and political corruption; and his dissection of a city in which, as Michael Nimetz puts it, "sex and religion occupy the same shrine and neutralize each other in the process," thus producing a state of general frustration.

Clarín's irony is present everywhere. The many types and variations of ironic comment range from those which are primarily linguistic ("Vetusta, la muy noble y leal ciudad . . . hacía la digestión del cocido y de la olla podrida"), to those directed toward characterization, as in descriptions of such minor characters as Don Saturnino, to those related to manners or customs of the general population, as in the description of the casino library, where the books are "de más sólida enseñanza" but where "la llave de aquel departamento se había perdido," those comments that present purer, more open humor (as in Don Víctor's reenactments of Calderonian honor plays).

The implied author's actual position—that is, his presence as it relates to the action—can best be described in the words of Frank Durand:

> Alas believed the author (as opposed to a character within the novel) to be best qualified to interpret a character's thoughts, actions, and motivations. . . . Because Alas knows all, the reader not only sees characters through the author's eyes but, entering their consciousness, sees reality through the eyes of the characters themselves. Thus the author's omniscient point of view carries within itself, so to speak, narrower individual points of view. The resultant multiple perspectives serve to delineate the different characters as well as to develop the major themes and the main action of the novel.

At times the author himself is clearly speaking. At other moments, the reader is projected into the thoughts and feelings of the major characters. The judicious combination of these two points of view allows for an extensive as well as an intensive view of the characters and the city, and serves also to maintain a high level of interest throughout an extremely lengthy narrative.

With respect to language, realism is enhanced by the following elements:

the inclusion of extremely exact detail, a frequent appeal to the senses, vivid imagery designed to highlight the animal nature of the city and its inhabitants, and a nearly constant sense of theatrical immediacy. Some stylistic traits, however, reveal the author's conscious attempt to draw attention to language itself and thus to rise above realism: the use of reiteration, frequent "extremist" tendencies (antithetical expressions, hyperboles, paradoxes), and authorial allusions (usually ironic) to art or literature.

Much of Clarín's realism depends upon the creation of what might be called a "total atmospheric reality." With the exception of Pérez Galdós' *Fortunata y Jacinta* (1886-1887; *Fortunata and Jacinta: Two Stories of Married Women,* 1973), *La regenta* captures the urban social and physical milieu more completely than any single Spanish work of the nineteenth century. Few modern readers would deny that the novel is too long. The outcome of Ana's story is powerful, however, precisely because the process preceding it goes on for so long. The background descriptions are, at the least, needed for an understanding of the external pressures and the heaviness of the material world that contribute to the denouement. The atmosphere of Vetusta (Oviedo) is in itself a major antagonist in the novel. Above all, the novel's descriptions contribute to the author's central goal: character study, the attempt to reveal the psychological complexity that positivistic Naturalism had reduced to a series of systematized formulas. While the secondary figures are meant to represent types, Ana Ozores and Don Fermín de Pas are remarkably real and autonomous.

Several significant methods are used to achieve this depth. Clarín reveals his characters from multiple perspectives: To the reader, the characters appear as what they are, what they think they are, and what others think they are. Frequently, actual mirrors are used to dramatize this complex play of perspectives. All the major characters are actors. The reader, himself engulfed in so many points of view, tends also to confuse illusion and reality. The result is a sense of the characters' distance and autonomy from authorial control, a Cervantine appearance of verisimilitude. The use of purposeful contrasts and parallels among the major and minor figures—such as de Pas's spiritual motivations versus Alvaro's licentious intentions, Don Víctor's preoccupations versus Ana's troubles, Obdulia versus Visitación, Camoirán or Cayetano versus Mourelo—constitutes another means of making the characters more vivid and more plausible.

Clarín traces, carefully and logically, the historical and environmental origins and the subsequent development of Ana's predicament: her need for love and her yearning for a child. The factors presented include the lack of a mother's presence, the frequent absence of her father, the cruelty of her nurse Doña Camila, a frightening night when she is stranded alone on a boat with her childhood playmate, the later treatment she receives from an indifferent father, the hypocrisy and cruelty of her aunts, her "escape" through a marriage without love, the depressive atmosphere of Vetusta, the plots of Visitación and Alvaro to effect her downfall, and the advice of Don Fermín. Her turn to religion (in the person of her confessor, Don Fermín), of course, thwarts even further her psychological, sexual, and maternal cravings. Ana is an individualistic creation, neither all good nor all evil. An inherent vanity, for example, offsets the purity of her intentions. Nevertheless, she also offers a mixture of traits and perspectives which is definitely representative of the Spanish people: a quixotic "madness," masochistic tendencies, mystical inclinations, the need for love and approval, a strong sense of pride and individuality, and, above all, a romantic, idealistic nature.

The author seems to have had even closer affinity to the personality and aspirations of the other main character. Although Don Fermín's flaws occasionally suggest a symbolic role of evil incarnate (vanity, hypocrisy, cruelty, desire for power), he is, nevertheless, a completely convincing, individualized figure. Conflicting desires for power and for escape from the vulgar existence of Vetusta create many of his frustrations. Dominated from childhood by an overpowering, ambitious mother and lacking, like Ana, the love and affection that go with a normal upbringing, he sees the Regenta as a threefold means of achieving his own mental stability and satisfaction: He can help another human being by offering spiritual assistance; he can satisfy his need to dominate; and, unconsciously, he can find sexual release. Ironically, the last two impulses, his desire for conquest and his passion, lead him to forget the wisest means of approach. The first motivation, of course, reveals that he is not entirely evil. In essence, he is an ambiguous creation.

La regenta is thus fundamentally the story of two individuals who are frustrated by their environment and by the absence of love; each is trapped within a social role (wife, priest), and each sees in the other a chance for salvation. Both exemplify vividly the metaphysical conflict between a single perceiving consciousness and the social environment, between aspiration and realization, between illusion and reality—warring factors that constitute the basis of Clarín's realism as well as the approach of the Spanish realistic movement in general.

The other characters function mainly in relation to these two figures and exemplify type portraiture: Alvaro as a cowardly and calculating Don Juan, the symbol of *poder laico*; Doña Paula (see María Remedios in Pérez Galdós' *Doña Perfecta*, 1876; English translation, 1880) typifying the forces of avarice and tyranny; the maid Petra as the marvelous embodiment of what one critic calls "suspicacia y socarronería de personaje de clase popular . . . muy español"; and so on.

Clarín's artistry is revealed in many ways that surpass the usual limits of nineteenth century realistic delineation. His use of symbolism (for example, the banquet scene in the casino, which ironically parallels Leonardo da Vinci's depiction of the Last Supper) and meticulous structural planning demonstrate clearly the depth of his originality. With respect to the latter element, such critics as J. I. Ferreras and Durand have analyzed in detail the complicated network of parallels and calculated contrasts, the elements of a "circular" nature and the complex system of flashbacks that constitute the novel's narrative construction.

Contrary to the opinion of many critics, *La regenta* is not a simple example of Zolaesque Naturalism. Ana's personality and her downfall are not the direct result of the moral laxity around her; they stem, rather, from her reactions against the city. Her adultery is a kind of triumph of love, possible only after twenty-eight chapters of careful, convincing preparation. The final *desenlace* (conclusion) is brought about by fortuitous circumstances (Petra's actions). Clarín is saying that the pressures of the environment are strong and, in fact, may cause changes in a person's life. Yet the instances of free will in *La regenta*, along with the moments of humorous satire mentioned above, illustrate the author's rejection of Zola's sweeping pessimism and the maintenance of a more traditionally Spanish point of view.

In *La regenta*, Clarín demonstrates most clearly his own particular version of the Spanish realistic formula. His utilitarian approach, his highly subjective irony and satire, his deliberate artistry in manipulating language—these and other elements reflect the author's conscious rejection of strictly realistic writing. In his usually explicit statement of themes, he departed from the norm of his Spanish contemporaries, yet his attention to exactness and detail, the numerous variations on authorial and character perspective, and the profundity of the novel's psychological studies reveal a true attempt to achieve a "complete" or "total" transcription of genuine human conflicts and aspirations.

If *La regenta* is characterized by the ridicule of provincial customs through carefully detailed description, *His Only Son* reduces society to its most dominating, abstract features: The precise delineation of physical settings and realistic conflicts is replaced by an operatic universe of melodramatic contrivances and the invisible, inner elements of psychological reverie. *His Only Son* is a novel of transition, reflecting the decline of Naturalism and the competing influence of various *fin de siècle* trends: Idealistic, symbolic, and decadent elements combine with a distinctly modern flavor, a purposeful ambiguity which forces the reader to participate more actively in the interpretation of events. Masculine and feminine roles are confused or reversed, the plot exhibits surprising turns of direction, and a more "authentic," alienated protagonist anticipates the problematic hero of the *generación del 98*. Seen by its first readers as a Zolaesque study of eroticism and physiological needs, the novel's emphasis on psychology over externality and its very subjective comic vein reveal a distinct divergence from Naturalistic practices.

Critics have been particularly perplexed by the work's ambiguity (the time and setting are indefinite, the question of the hero's paternity is left unresolved, and so on), not realizing until recently that Clarín was attempting a very Cervantine statement concerning the relativism and lack of clarity of everyday reality. The plot line itself is simple and, in fact, almost insignificant. In a poor, provincial town, Bonifacio Reyes (Bonis), of a family in decline, marries the despotic Emma Valcárcel but soon becomes the lover of Serafina Gorgheggi, a member of an opera company. Emma, amid an atmosphere of corruption and abulia and provoked by the entrance into her house of the Italian singers, becomes involved in an affair with the baritone Minghetti. Eventually, Bonis' main preoccupation turns from the romantic fantasies of his *tertulia* to a fanatic belief in the importance of the family, seeing in the birth of a son ("su único hijo," a phrase from the Apostles' Creed laden with symbolic ramifications) a means of self-redemption. In the church where the child's baptism is to take place, Serafina avenges her lover's change of heart by claiming that the father is actually Minghetti. As the novel closes, Bonis denies this and quixotically insists that the child is his. The reader is struck by the similarity to the closing of *La regenta* (the protagonist is in a church and, in each case, tormented by rejection), but Bonis' case is more pathetic than tragic. He has been misled by the private cult of the family and father-hood, not by any kind of Christian mysticism or belief in dogma. If Ana's end demonstrates the double failure of love and an exalted religiosity, the protagonist's downfall here is one of both the romantic ideal and of "la religión del hogar."

Like the characters of *La regenta*, the figures here attempt to project fiction on reality (the *Don Juan Tenorio* play in the first novel, the world of opera here), and in both works a chorus of gossip and *murmuración* provides the ironic backdrop. In *His Only Son*, however, the characters are archetypal, skeletal abstractions, often presented through hyberbolic caricature, in consonance with exaggerated, theatrical melodrama. This is evident in such scenes as Bonis and Serafina's lovemaking, Emma and Bonis' marital crises, and Emma's hysteria and fears of miscarriage. Gone are the positive-negative tensions of *La regenta*, replaced by a general world of resentment in which, by a few relatively simple strokes, Clarín constructs a society of degenerate romantics, a few ridiculous human beings, sometimes grossly deformed and almost always repugnant. The author's irony remains, but a more ambiguous perspective forces the reader to look for essences, not explanations.

The six secondary figures are nonindividualistic representatives of but a few social traits, usually within a dualistic framework: Don Juan Nepomuceno hides carnal desire by a romantic façade; Korner is a "spiritual" dreamer but also a materialistic glutton; Mochi and Minghetti use personal attraction for economic gain; and Marta hides her sensuality, ego, and greed by an appearance of idealism. Serafina is even more systematically presented as a dual figure: beautiful and ugly, the angel and the devil, the voluptuous temptress and the serene madonna, romantic and sensuous, loving and materialistic.

She is the embodiment of the conflict between good and evil, and evil triumphs in the end. Her English-Italian background and even her name ("Serafina," celestial seraph; "gorgo," vortex or abyss; and "gorgone," the mythological Gorgon, suggesting the Medusan female) reinforce this aspect of duality. The secondary characters all use an "attractive" front to win over others, while a real, negative side leads them to exploit those around them.

Bonis is the clearest example of psychological duality in the novel, alternatively ridiculous and moving, comic and sad, indecisive and creative, in need of erotic excitement yet searching for peace. He vacillates between romantic fantasy and bourgeois needs (symbolized by his flute and slippers, respectively), both of which represent ways to escape reality. The disintegration of his personality is the result of his inability to reconcile these two forces. Bonis feels hatred for the materialistic world, yet in fact he is a typical *burgués*. The key to his personality (and, indeed, to the whole novel) is the ambivalence inherent in his description as a *soñador sonoliento*. Clarín himself is not sure whether to like or hate his protagonist's delicate, dreaming, gentle nature, whether to identify and commiserate with him or to poke fun at him.

From a broader viewpoint, Bonis is a caricature of nineteenth century Romanticism in crisis. He is the archetypal figure of the nonhero who wants to be a hero. Alienated both from society and from himself, he sees the exploration of his own identity—in the form of an inner journey to the past and to his father's nature—as a heroic venture. In comparison with Ana, however, there is no heroism in his victimization; his conflict is more with self than with others, and there is no wall of misunderstanding between him and society, as in *La regenta*. In contrast to Ana, he shows no initiative, no capacity to try to rise above his vulgar surroundings. In *His Only Son*, the importance of the will is seen either in its misdirection (Emma) or its nonexistence (Bonis). The only vestige of the hero's grandeur is the protagonist's readiness to sacrifice himself for his son's future.

Bonis' attraction to Serafina stems in part from a romantic attachment to the memories of his mother. Eroticism and filial love are combined and linked with nostalgia for the past. At times, one feels that he uses his love for the mother figure as a way to repress his sensuality. Then, as the novel progresses and Bonis sees a heavenly "Annunciation" of his future son's birth in Serafina's song (chapter 12), he concludes that divine coincidence has brought about the revelation of Emma's pregnancy on the same day that he breaks with Serafina. His longing for a child subsequently develops to the point of a religious cult, where fatherhood and motherhood join in him as a kind of *sacerdote*: Like God, he will offer "his only son" as a benefit for all mankind. In this thought, and in the notion that the earth is ruled by paternal Providence, he seems to find the security he needs and the moral support or atonement for his past conduct. Romantic raptures thus give way to fatherly love as the focus of ideality; at the same time, his longing for a son represents his need for another *yo* (or "I"), for a new beginning.

Emma ("Emma," perhaps a reminder of the twisted views of Gustave Flaubert's Emma Bovary; "Valcárcel," "val" or valley, as in an open sewer; and "carcel," imprisonment for Bonis) is basically a type character, a study in diabolical deformation which anticipates some of Ramón del Valle-Inclán's depictions a few decades later. She is the epitome of the decadent *fuerza maléfica*: perverse, spoiled, capricious, morbidly sensual, neurotic, and unnatural in her rejection of motherhood. Bonis and Clarín think of her in terms of archetypal epithets: a Fury, witch, dragon, vampiress, the proverbial femme fatale, as opposed to Serafina, who comes to represent angelic maternalism.

The reader is thus thrown into a world of characters exhibiting surprising traits: The man is more "feminine" than the aggressive, nonmaternal woman; his lover comes to personify domesticity and his wife to represent perverse eroticism; Emma finds her own lover when she learns of Bonis' relationship with Serafina, rather than resigning herself to her fate, as would other nineteenth century female characters. The unpredictable nature of human reality set forth in the novel is one of the work's many modern attributes.

Thematically, *His Only Son* is not particularly original, presenting a somewhat traditional, ironic exposure of the failings of idealized concepts and dogmas, when a simplified or falsified viewpoint clashes with the true complexity of reality. Rather than making a direct attack on pseudo-Romanticism per se, Clarín is deriding the maintenance of any form of belief determined by other than spontaneous, internal motives. There are, he says, no exterior, abstract, or secondhand formulas for life. Reality cannot be reduced to either matter or mind, but, rather, is characterized by the vacillation between the physiological and the spiritual. Other ideas in the novel—the need to face oneself rather than attempt to escape, the possible exaltation of family roots, an attack against a life oriented toward physical pleasure—are corollaries of the central theme. All of these concepts, finally, are seen in the context of personal and universal values rather than a framework of national or societal decay, as is the case in *La regenta*.

Clarín's novelistic production can be viewed as a reflection of the disillusionments and frustrations of his own life and of his critical stance toward society. His two major novels have much in common—psychological depth, authorial irony, and explicit thematic statement—but the passage from *La regenta* to *His Only Son* reveals a number of significant developments in technique and characterization. These differences, in turn, relate to the change from a period in which realistic and Naturalistic elements were dominant to one in which the influences of symbolism, decadence, and idealistic spirituality are more evident. Clarín's initial preoccupation with the problems of Spanish society places him clearly in a literary line that runs from Francisco de Quevedo y Villegas (1580-1645) to Mariano José de Larra (1809-1837) and, later, to the *generación del 98*. He was among the very few writers of his time who were able to utilize much of Spain's literary heritage, particularly Cervantine elements, while still anticipating a number of twentieth century techniques.

Major publications other than long fiction

SHORT FICTION: *Pipa*, 1886; *Doña Berta, Cuervo, Superchería*, 1892; *Cuentos morales*, 1896, 1973; *El señor y lo demás son cuentos*, 1900; *¡Adiós, Cordera! y otros cuentos*, 1944; *Cuentos de Clarín*, 1954; *Cuentos escogidos*, 1964; *Superchería, Cuervo, Doña Berta*, 1970; *El gallo de Sócrates y otros cuentos*, 1973.

PLAY: *Teresa*, 1895.

NONFICTION: *El derecho y la moralidad*, 1878; *Solos de Clarín*, 1881, 1971; *La literatura en 1881*, 1882 (with Armando Palacio Valdés); *Sermón perdido*, 1885; *Cánovas y su tiempo*, 1887; *Nueva campaña, 1885-1886*, 1887; *Mezclilla*, 1889; *Rafael Calvo y el teatro español*, 1890; *Ensayos y revistas*, 1892; *Palique*, 1893, 1973; *Crítica popular*, 1896; *Siglo pasado*, 1901; *Galdós*, 1912; *Doctor Sutilis*, 1916; *Páginas escogidas*, 1917; *Epistolario de Menéndez y Pelayo y Leopoldo Alas*, 1941; *Leopoldo Alas: Teoría y crítica de la novela española*, 1972; *Preludios de 'Clarín'*, 1972; *Obra olvidada*, 1973.

MISCELLANEOUS: *Obras selectas*, 1947, 1966.

Bibliography

Agudiez, Juan Ventura. *Inspiración y estética en "La Regenta" de Clarín*, 1970.

Baquero Goyanes, Mariano. "Los cuentos de 'Clarín,'" in *Cuentos de Clarín*, 1954.

Bécarud, Jean. *"La Regenta" de "Clarín" y la Restauración*, 1964.

Beser, Sergio. *Leopoldo Alas: Crítico literario*, 1968.

Brent, Albert. *Leopoldo Alas and "La Regenta": A Study in Nineteenth Century Prose Fiction*, 1955.

Bull, W. E., and V. E. Chamberlin. *Clarin: The Critic in Action*, 1963.

Durand, Frank. "Structural Unity in *La regenta*," in *Hispanic Review*. XXXI (1963), pp. 324-335.

_____ . "Characterization in *La regenta*: Point of View and Theme," in *Bulletin of Hispanic Studies*. XLI (1964), pp. 86-100.

Eoff, Sherman. *The Modern Spanish Novel*, 1961.

Feal Deibe, Carlos. "La anunciación a Bonis: Anlisis de *Su único hijo*," in *Bulletin of Hispanic Studies*. LI (1974), pp. 255-271.

García Sarriá, Francisco. *Clarín: O, La hererjía amorosa*, 1975.

Martínez Cachero, J. M., ed. *Leopoldo Alas, "Clarín,"* 1973.

Medina, Jeremy T. *Spanish Realism: The Theory and Practice of a Concept in the Nineteenth Century*, 1979.

Nimetz, Michael. "*Eros* and *Ecclesia* in Clarín's Vetusta," in *Modern Language Notes*. LXXXVI (1971), pp. 242-253.

Nuñez de Villavicencia, Laura. *La creatividad en el estilo de Leopoldo Alas, "Clarín,"* 1973.

Rutherford, John. *Leopoldo Alas: La Regenta*, 1974.

Weber, Frances Wyers. "The Dynamics of Motif in Leopoldo Alas' *La Regenta*," in *Romantic Review*. LVII (1966), pp. 188-199.

_____ . "Ideology and Religious Parody in the Novels of Leopoldo Alas," in *Bulletin of Hispanic Studies*. XLIII (1966), pp. 197-208.

Jeremy T. Medina

JEAN COCTEAU

Born: Maisons-Laffitte, France; July 5, 1889
Died: Milly-la-Forêt, France; October 11, 1963

Principal long fiction

Le Potomak, 1919; *Le Grand Écart*, 1923 (*The Grand Écart*, 1925); *Thomas l'imposteur*, 1923 (*Thomas the Impostor*, 1925); *Le Livre blanc*, 1928 (*The White Paper*, 1957); *Les Enfants terribles*, 1929 (*Enfants Terrible*, 1930; also as *Children of the Game*, 1955); *Le Fantôme de Marseille*, 1933; *La Fin du Potomak*, 1939.

Other literary forms

Never limited by distinctions among genres, Jean Cocteau was an important figure in many arts. After an early and not particularly interesting "dandyistic" phase in his poetry, including *La Lampe d'Aladin* (1909; Aladdin's lamp), *Le Prince frivole* (1910; the frivolous prince), and *La Danse de Sophocle* (1912; the dance of Sophocles), he was influenced by Futurism, Dadaism, and Surrealism, and he developed a classical rigor and purity mingled with linguistic and imaginative originality. *Le Cap de Bonne-Espérance* (1919; the Cape of Good Hope), for example, glorifies pilots and flying, emphasizing sensation. *L'Ode à Picasso* (1919; ode to Picasso) seeks the wellspring of creativity in the great artist. *Vocabulaire* (1922; vocabulary) exhibits further linguistic creativity, and *Discours du grand sommeil* (1922; discourse on the great sleep) explores the experience of World War I. Later works use the suggestions of mythology, classical simplicity, and the subconscious, particularly *Plain-Chant* (1923), *L'Ange Heurtebise* (1925), *Mythologie* (1934), *Allégories* (1941), *La Crucifixion* (1946), *Clair-obscur* (1954; chiaroscuro), *Gondole des morts* (1959), and *Cérémonial espagnol du phénix* (1961). He was a witty playwright on similar themes in *Orphée* (1927; *Orpheus*, 1933), *La Voix humaine* (1930; *The Human Voice*, 1951), *La Machine infernale* (1934; *The Infernal Machine*, 1936), *Les Chevaliers de la table ronde* (1937; *Knights of the Round Table*, 1963), *Les Parents terribles* (1938; *Intimate Relations*, 1956), *Les Monstres sacrés* (1940; *The Holy Terrors*, 1962), *La Machine à écrire* (1941; *The Typewriter*, 1962), the verse drama *Renaud et Armide* (1943), *L'Aigle à deux têtes* (1946; *The Eagle Has Two Heads*, 1948), and *Bacchus* (1952; English translation, 1955). He was director, writer, or both, of a number of films that have become classics because of their striking visual imagery and their evocation of the archetypal and mythological. *Le Sang d'un poète* (1948, released 1932; *The Blood of a Poet*, 1949), *La Belle et la bête* (1946, released 1945; *Beauty and the Beast*, 1950), *Les Parents terribles* (1949, released 1948; *Intimate Relations*, 1952), *Les Enfants terribles* (1950), *Orphée* (1951, released 1949), and *Le Testament d'Orphée* (1959; *The Testament of Orpheus*, 1968) are considered his best. He also wrote ballet scenarios, including those for Erik Satie's *Parade* (1917), Darius Milhaud's *Le Bœuf sur le toit* (1920) and *Les Mariés de la Tour Eiffel* (1921), and two musical dramas, *Oedipus-Rex* (1927; English translation, 1961), with music by Igor Stravinsky, and *Antigone* (1927; English translation, 1961), with music by Arthur Honegger. Cocteau's nonfiction is witty and incisive and usually based on his life and role as a poet in the control of forces he does not understand. The books in this category include *Le Rappel à l'ordre* (1926; *A Call to Order*, 1926), *Lettre à Jacques Maritain* (1926; *Art and Faith*, 1948), *Opium: Journal d'une désintoxication* (1930; *Opium: Diary of a Cure*, 1932), *Essai de la critique indirecte* (1932; *The Lais Mystery: An Essay of Indirect Criticism*, 1936), *Portraits-souvenir, 1900-1914* (1935; *Paris Album*, 1956), *La Belle et la bête: Journal d'un film* (1946; *Beauty and the Beast: Journal of a Film*, 1950), *La Difficulté d'être* (1947; *The Difficulty of Being*, 1966), and *Poésie critique* (1960).

Achievements

Twentieth century art in many areas is indebted to Cocteau. His accomplishments span the artistic and literary activities of his times, the diversity unified by his vision of all art as facets of the purest form: poetry. Whether working in film, fiction, theater, drawing, or verse, he considered himself to be revealing the poet in him. Critics now generally agree that his finest achievements are in the novel and the cinema. One of the most crystalline stylists among French writers of the twentieth century, his brilliant imagery and his extraordinary visual qualities make his novels powerfully evocative despite their terse style. Some regard him as a dilettante interested only in stylishness and facile demonstrations of his gifts; his classical style, however, allows him to transcend the limitations of ordinary novelists and their message-oriented prose to explore the resonances of mythology and archetype in a modern context. His versatility, irony, and playfulness encouraged his contemporaries to dismiss him, and he received few honors other than his 1955 election to the Académie Française. His novels are quirky, experimental, often chaotic, but filled with intriguing imagery and wit. *Children of the Game* is almost universally agreed to be his masterpiece.

Biography

Jean Cocteau's background was solidly Parisian bourgeois. Georges and Eugénie Lecomte Cocteau, his parents, were a cultivated couple who introduced Jean, his brother Paul, and sister Marthe to the fine arts. Near their suburban home, Cocteau would recall, the children played on the grounds of a "magical" castle designed by François Mansart. When living in the city with his grandparents, Cocteau would wander through rooms that contained classical busts, vases, a painting by Eugène Delacroix, and drawings by Jean-Auguste-Dominique Ingres. The celebrated violinist Pablo de Sarasate often visited Cocteau's grandfather, who was a cellist, and they would play music together. What impressed the young Cocteau most, however, were his trips to the circus, the ice palace, and the theater, particularly the Comédie-Française. His memories of these trips, he would later come to realize, were even brighter than the real experiences. In his own productions years later, he would ask technicians to duplicate the lighting or brilliancy of childhood theatrical events and be told it had been technically impossible to create such effects when he was a boy. Memory had heightened the splendor of the past, including the recollections of the castle and of his grandparents' house; his own life began to assume mythological dimensions.

At the Petit Lycée Condorcet, Cocteau was a poor student, especially after his father killed himself in 1899 because of financial pressures. He did, however, meet the haunting Pierre Dargelos, who would become the dark "god" of *Children of the Game*. At the Grand Condorcet, Cocteau was frequently truant, exploiting his illnesses to stay home. Like many creative people, he was irritated by institutions, and he much preferred having his German governess sew doll clothes for a model theater to sitting behind a school desk. Réné Rocher, one of his best friends, often played with Cocteau's miniature theaters and, in adulthood, became a director himself.

Cocteau traveled with his mother to Venice, then began study for his *baccalauréat*. He was more interested, however, in his first love affair—with Madeleine Carlier, ten years his senior—and his deepening involvement in theater. He became a protégé of Édouard de Max, who acted opposite Sarah Bernhardt. All of these diversions contributed to Cocteau's failing the *bachot*.

De Max, however, thrust Cocteau into the public eye by organizing a reading of Cocteau's poetry by de Max, Rocher, and other prominent actors and actresses, at the Théâtre Fémina, on April 4, 1908. Several important literary critics and many of the elite of Paris attended. Cocteau's debut was a great success, and reviewers compared him to Pierre de Ronsard and Alfred de Musset. Subsequently, Cocteau met many literary notables, including Edmond Rostand, Marcel Proust, Charles Péguy, Catulle Mendès, and Jules Lemaître. Comtesse Anna de Noailles particularly enchanted him, and he tried to write refined and sensual poetry like hers. He helped found the literary magazine *Schéhérazade*, dedicated to poetry and music, and moved into the Hôtel Biron, whose residents at the time included Auguste Rodin and his secretary, Rainer Maria Rilke.

Meeting the great impresario Sergei Diaghilev of the Ballets Russes caused Cocteau to abandon his previous enthusiasms for a while. He begged Diaghilev to let him write ballets. Diaghilev eventually said "Étonne-moi!" ("Astonish me!"), perhaps to quiet him, but Cocteau took it as an order and a goal for the rest of his life's work. Though Diaghilev produced Cocteau's first ballet, *Le Dieu bleu* (1912), for the coronation of George V, it was not successful. Believing that the score rather than his scenario was at fault, Cocteau began to associate with Igor Stravinsky, even moving in with him for a while. During this period, Henri Ghéon of *La Nouvelle Revue française* accused Cocteau of being an entirely derivative poet. Stung by the validity of the review (perhaps coauthored by André Gide), Cocteau began a search for himself as an artist. He underwent what he called a "molting" around 1914, rebelling against older writers who had influenced him, such as Rostand and the Comtesse de Noailles, and moving in the direction of poets such as Max Jacob and Guillaume Apollinaire. *Le Potomak*, with its radical mixture of prose, drawings, and verse, was completed while Cocteau was living with Gide and Stravinsky and is the first important, truly original expression of Cocteau's personality.

Cocteau's attempted enlistment at the outset of World War I was rejected because of his health. He nevertheless became an ambulance driver on the Belgian front (albeit illegally). He was discovered and ordered back to Paris immediately before the group to which he had attached himself was decimated in an attack. These experiences formed the basis for his novel and film *Thomas the Impostor*. As the war continued, Cocteau met Amedeo Modigliani and Pablo Picasso in Paris. The latter he introduced to Diaghilev, who put him to work on Satie's ballet *Parade*; the scenario was written by Cocteau, the costumes and set were by Picasso, and the ballet was choreographed by Léonide Massine. The ballet's atonal music and radical set and costumes caused a near-riot in the theater. Apollinaire, wearing his uniform and a dressing over his wounded head, managed barely to keep the spectators from assaulting the stage. Cocteau responded in the press, vigorously attacking the musical influence of Claude Debussy, Richard Wagner, and, surprisingly, Stravinsky, and aligning himself with the radical group called "Les Six" (Georges Auric, Louis Durey, Arthur Honegger, Darius Milhaud, Francis Poulenc, and Germaine Tailleferre).

Raymond Radiguet was fifteen, handsome, and a poetic genius, Cocteau believed, when he met and fell in love with him in 1919. Radiguet was a major influence in moving Cocteau toward a simpler, more classical style. Cocteau's energy revived, and he produced several new works, including *The Grand Écart* and the volume of poems *Plain-Chant*. When in December, 1923, Radiguet died of typhoid, Cocteau was devastated. Diaghilev took Cocteau to Monte Carlo to help him recover, but the discovery of opium there was Cocteau's only comfort. His friends and family were forced to persuade him to enter a sanatorium in 1925, when his addiction had become serious. Jacques Maritain, the Catholic philosopher, briefly restored Cocteau's faith in religion during the cure. The faith waned, but the works such as *L'Ange Heurtebise*, *Orpheus*, and *Children of the Game* followed. Patching up his friendship with Stravinsky, Cocteau wrote the libretto for the oratorio *Oedipus-Rex*.

Though Cocteau caught typhoid in 1931, his artistic output in the 1930's was astonishing. He wrote plays, poems, songs, ballets, art criticism, and a newspaper column for _Ce soir_. He published a journal chronicling a trip taken in imitation of Jules Verne's _Le Tour du monde en quatre-vingt jours_ (1873; _Around the World in Eighty Days_, 1873). He also became the manager of bantamweight Alphonse Theo Brown. His first attempt at _poésie cinémato-graphique_ (poetry of the film), however, was probably his most important activity. He wrote and directed the film _The Blood of a Poet_, now a classic. His abilities in the visual arts and in visual imagery expressed themselves well in cinema, and he became responsible for a number of major films, including _Beauty and the Beast, Intimate Relations, The Testament of Orpheus_, and _Les Enfants terribles_.

During the German occupation of France, Cocteau was constantly vilified by the press. His play _The Typewriter_ was banned. At one point, he was beaten by a group of French Nazis for not saluting their flag. He testified in court for thief, novelist, and Resistance fighter Jean Genet in 1942, despite much advice to the contrary. Cocteau gained respect for his courage and, after the war, found himself a "grand old man" of the artistic world.

His muse, however, would not let him retire. He traveled, made recordings, and wrote plays, journals, and films. His frescoes for the city hall at Menton, the Chapel of Saint Pierre at Villefranche-sur-Mer, the Chapel of Notre Dame in London, the Church of Saint Blaise-des-Simples in Milly-la-Fôret, and the Chapel at Fréjus, Notre-Dame-de-Jérusalem, created controversy among art critics. He also designed fabrics, plates, and posters. In 1955, he was elected to the Royal Belgian Academy and to the Académie Française. In 1956, he was awarded an honorary doctorate of letters from Oxford University. On October 11, 1963, he died, distressed at hearing of the death of his friend Edith Piaf earlier in the day.

Analysis

Le Potomak was a crucial work in Jean Cocteau's development, as he used it to break free of former influences and find an individual voice. Highly experimental, it is, however, not of compelling interest for any other reason, consisting as it does of an exploration of the subconscious through a hodgepodge of verse, prose, and drawings, all of which reveal Cocteau's talents but which mostly demonstrate rebellion rather than a mature concept of the novelistic art. Its writing was interrupted by World War I, and the influence of the war is apparent in the revised edition. Under the influence of Radiguet, Cocteau wrote _The Grand Écart_ and _Thomas the Impostor_. Mythologizing memories of his childhood, Cocteau based _The Grand Écart_ on a childhood visit to Venice and his recollections of boarding school. One of his recurrent images appears indistinctly in this novel in the form of the Englishman Stopwell. Like Dargelos and the Angel Heurtebise, Stopwell is an angel in the form of a tempter who brings about annihilation or metamorphosis. _Thomas_ *the Impostor* was largely based on Cocteau's own experiences during the war. Rejected for service, he posed as an ambulance driver on the Belgian front and was "adopted" by a group of Fusiliers Marins. When discovered by a superior officer, he was arrested and taken from the front. A day later, most of his comrades were killed. Rather than portraying the war as a horror, however, the novel turns it into a ghastly joke, a reflection of humanity's chaotic mind, a cruel trick played by a Euripidean god. Being an impostor is likened to being a poet, and reality and impostorship merge only when Thomas the Impostor is shot in the Waste Land. The "Prince of Frivolity," as Cocteau was known, uses flippant, humorous, outlandish imagery that accentuates the horror. The book is clearly one of his better novels, though not nearly equal to his next.

Children of the Game is considered to be Cocteau's most successful novel by far. Besides being beautifully written, it is an extraordinary evocation of adolescent hopes, fears, dreams, and obsessions, and is said to have been regarded by French teenagers as capturing their alienation from adult society in the same way that J. D. Salinger articulated it in American society. Perhaps because Cocteau, as an artist and a man, always held himself as a kind of alien visitor to the realms of the Establishment from the world of subjectivity and irrationality, his sensitivity to adolescent alienation was enhanced. Yet *Children of the Game* is not a realistic portrayal of adolescence. It is sensitive, but it is so overlaid with dream imagery and mythological overtones that whatever autobiographical elements and psychological truths it might contain are submerged.

Fragments from many mythological sources are identifiable upon even a cursory reading. Cocteau was fascinated with mythology and at various times in his career wrote works dealing with Antigone, Orpheus, Bacchus, and the "Beauty and the Beast" motif. Cocteau wrote *Children of the Game* very rapidly—at the rate of seventeen pages a day for three weeks—while he was undergoing treatment for opium addiction, as if he were trying to let archetypal and subconscious elements flow freely onto the page. Too careful an artist to practice automatic writing without aesthetically manipulating the result, he nevertheless refused to make later changes in the text for fear of destroying the fabric of the book. Characters quite often suggest beings from mythology, as Cocteau imbues people and events from his own life and imagination with a supernatural or divine aura.

Dargelos, for example, whose name is taken from a real boy whom Cocteau admired in his school days, takes on the characteristics of a god. Early in the book, Paul seeks Dargelos among the snowball wars in the Cité Monthiers. Paul's love for Dargelos is described as "sexless and purposeless," and his seeking him in order to fight beside him, defend him, and prove what he can do takes on religious overtones. Paul, however, is silenced by a snowball from one of his idol's acolytes, condemning him to Dargelos' wrath. Dargelos rises up in an immense gesture, his cheeks on fire and his hair in disorder, like a statue of Dionysus. Paul feels the blow of the snowball on his chest—a dark blow, the blow of a marble fist. As Paul loses consciousness, he imagines Dargelos upon a dais, in a supernatural light. Dargelos has struck Paul in the heart, with a snowball like Thor's hammer or Zeus's thunderbolt. Dargelos, throughout the rest of the book, is hardly mentioned; his presence, however, seems to loom over all subsequent events. As Wallace Fowlie observes, he "grows into the figure of a dark angel who haunts the dreams and thoughts of the protagonist."

Eden is evoked when Paul, his sister Élisabeth, and Gérard find themselves alone without adult supervision. In "the Room," they are free of conventional worries about food and seem innocent of evil. Their childhood seems to be prolonged. Although the situation appears to be fraught with incestuous overtones—Paul and Élisabeth sleep in the same room and bathe together—there is instead a matter-of-fact sexlessness, a lack of shame. When a ball of poison (associated with Dargelos' snowball) causes the cold, outside world of snow and death to blow into their Eden, one may see an analogy to the expulsion from Eden, the coming of mortality into Eden.

One must not, however, treat _Children of the Game_ as allegory. Cocteau is weaving a fugue of implications and mythological elements. One critic has found the novel to be about the impossibility of escaping bourgeois ideology; another has found it to be the playing out of fate in the form of Eros-Thanatos. There is certainly a hint of inevitability in the sequence of events. Tragedy is suggested from the beginning, and the classical structure and sparkling sentences help convey this impression. The characters are in the grip of forces beyond their control. When Michael, the rich American Jew, is killed, it seems as if the Room reaches out to protect itself. When Dargelos gives Paul the fist-sized ball of poison, one is reminded of the marble-hard snowball and the apple which destroyed Eden. A reddish gash in the ball is reminiscent of both a wound and female genitalia, suggesting an association between mortality and the loss of innocence. The end is destined, and nothing can hold it back. Childhood is doomed. As Cocteau himself wrote in _The Difficulty of Being:_ "Childhood knows what it wants. It wants to emerge from childhood. The trouble starts when it does emerge. For youth knows what it does not want before it knows what it does want. But what it does not want is what we do want." Thus are the "holy terrors" doomed.

Le Fantôme de Marseille is a slight work containing associations and local color that Cocteau recalled from his running away to Marseilles at the age of fifteen. Later, in Le Picquey, in a hotel where he had stayed with Radiguet in 1923, Cocteau watched over the convalescence of a new love, actor Jean Marais, and returned to the inspiration of _Le Potomak_ for his last novel. _La Fin du Potomak_ is a curious mixture of fairy tales, aphorisms, riddles, and true stories recalling Cocteau's experiences after 1913. A revival of Cocteau's classicism has been seen in the work, but most often it is regarded as a mere shadow of *Le Potomak*, as if the author's creative interests had shifted away from *poésie de roman* (poetry of the novel). Brooding over the entire work is a disappointment with human nature and recurrent imagery of death, perhaps evoked by Marais' illness and the memory of Radiguet's sudden death. There is also an acceptance of the author's own death (which was many years in the future), indicated by some lines of poetry at the end: "Death, don't be clever/ . . .You see, I wait standing still/ I even offer you my hand/ . . . What does it matter? I leave behind a book/ That you will not take from me."

Major publications other than long fiction

PLAYS: *Antigone*, 1927 (libretto; English translation, 1961); *Oedipus-Rex*, 1927 (libretto; English translation, 1961); *Orphée*, 1927 (*Orpheus*, 1933); *La Voix humaine*, 1930 (*The Human Voice*, 1951); *La Machine infernale*, 1934 (*The Infernal Machine*, 1936); *L'École des veuves*, 1936; *Les Chevaliers de la table ronde*, 1937 (*Knights of the Round Table*, 1963); *Les Parents terribles*, 1938 (*Intimate Relations*, 1956, performed 1952); *Les Monstres sacrés*, 1940 (*The Holy Terrors*, 1962, performed 1953); *La Machine à écrire*, 1941 (*The Typewriter*, 1962); *Renaud et Armide*, 1943; *L'Aigle à deux têtes*, 1946 (*The Eagle Has Two Heads*, 1948); *Bacchus*, 1952 (English translation, 1955).

SCREENPLAYS: *Le Baron fantôme*, 1943; *La Belle et la bête*, 1946 (released 1945; *Beauty and the Beast*, 1950); *L'Aigle à deux têtes*, 1947; *Ruy Blas*, 1947; *L'Éternel retour*, 1948 (released 1943); *Le Sang d'un poète*, 1948 (released 1932; *The Blood of a Poet*, 1949); *Les Parents terribles*, 1949 (released 1948; *Intimate Relations*, 1952); *Les Enfants terribles*, 1950; *Orphée*, 1951 (released 1949); *Le Testament d'Orphée*, 1959 (*The Testament of Orpheus*, 1968).

POETRY: *La Lampe d'Aladin*, 1909; *Le Prince frivole*, 1910; *La Danse de Sophocle*, 1912; *Le Cap de Bonne-Espérance*, 1919; *L'Ode à Picasso*, 1919; *Escales*, 1920; *Poésies, 1917-1920*, 1920; *Discours du grand sommeil*, 1922; *Vocabulaire*, 1922; *Plain-Chant*, 1923; *Poésie, 1916-1923*, 1924; *L'Ange Heurtebise*, 1925; *Cri écrit*, 1925; *Opéra*, 1927; *Morceaux choisis*, 1932, *Mythologie*, 1934; *Allégories*, 1941; *Léone*, 1945; *Poèmes*, 1945; *La Crucifixion*, 1946; *Le Chiffre sept*, 1952; *Appogiatures*, 1953; *Clair-obscur*, 1954; *Poèmes, 1916-1955*, 1956; *Gondole des morts*, 1959; *Cérémonial espagnol du phénix*, 1961; *Le Requiem*, 1962.

NONFICTION: *Le Coq et l'Arlequin*, 1918 (*Cock and Harlequin*, 1921); *Le Secret professionnel*, 1922; *Lettre à Jacques Maritain*, 1926 (*Art and Faith*, 1948); *Le Rappel à l'ordre*, 1926 (*A Call to Order*, 1926); *Opium: Journal d'une désintoxication*, 1930 (*Opium: Diary of a Cure*, 1932); *Essai de la critique indirecte*, 1932 (*The Lais Mystery: An Essay of Indirect Criticism*, 1936); *Portraits-souvenir, 1900-1914*, 1935 (*Paris Album*, 1956); *La Belle et la bête: Journal d'un film*, 1946 (*Beauty and the Beast: Journal of a Film*, 1950); *La Difficulté d'être*, 1947 (*The Difficulty of Being*, 1966); *The Journals of Jean*

Cocteau, 1956; *Poésie critique*, 1960.

TRANSLATION: *Roméo et Juliette*, 1926 (of William Shakespeare's *Romeo and Juliet*).

Bibliography
Brown, F. *An Impersonation of Angels: A Biography of Jean Cocteau*, 1968.
Crosland, Margaret. *Jean Cocteau*, 1956.
Fowlie, Wallace. *Jean Cocteau: History of a Poet's Age*, 1966.
Fraigneau, André. *Cocteau par lui-même*, 1957.
Helein-Koss, Suzanne. "Rêve et fantasmes dans *Les Enfants terribles* de Jean Cocteau," in *French Review*. VI (1974), pp. 151-161. Special Cocteau issue.
Knapp, Bettina L. *Jean Cocteau*, 1970.
Lannes, Roger. *Jean Cocteau*, 1945.
McNab, James P. "Mythical Space in *Les Enfants terribles*," in *French Review*. VI (1974), pp. 162-170. Special Cocteau issue.
Sprigge, Elizabeth, and Jean-Jacques Kihm. *Jean Cocteau: The Man and His Mirror*, 1968.
Steegmuller, Francis. *Cocteau*, 1970.

J. Madison Davis

COLETTE
Sidonie-Gabrielle Colette

Born: Saint-Sauveur-en-Puisaye, France; January 28, 1873
Died: Paris, France; August 3, 1954

Principal long fiction

Claudine à l'école, 1900 (*Claudine at School*, 1956); *Claudine à Paris*, 1901 (*Claudine in Paris*, 1958); *Claudine en ménage*, 1902 (*The Indulgent Husband*, 1935; also as *Claudine Married*, 1960); *Claudine s'en va*, 1903 (*The Innocent Wife*, 1934; also as *Claudine and Annie*, 1962); *La Retraite sentimentale*, 1907 (*Retreat from Love*, 1974); *L'Ingénue Libertine*, 1909 (*The Gentle Libertine*, 1931; also as *The Innocent Libertine*, 1968); *La Vagabonde*, 1911 (*The Vagabond*, 1955); *L'Entrave*, 1913 (*Recaptured*, 1932; also as *The Shackle*, 1964); *Mitsou: Ou, Comment l'esprit vient aux filles*, 1919 (*Mitsou: Or, How Girls Grow Wise*, 1930; also as *Mitsou*, 1958); *Chéri*, 1920 (English translation, 1929); *Le Blé en herbe*, 1923 (*The Ripening Corn*, 1931; also as *The Ripening Seed*, 1955); *La Fin de Chéri*, 1926 (*The Last of Chéri*, 1953); *La Naissance du jour*, 1928 (*A Lesson in Love*, 1932; also as *Break of Day*, 1961); *La Seconde*, 1929 (*The Other One*, 1931); *La Chatte*, 1933 (*The Cat*, 1953); *Duo*, 1934 (*Duo*, 1935; also as *The Married Lover*, 1935); *Julie de Carneilhan*, 1941 (English translation, 1952); *Gigi*, 1944 (English translation, 1952); *7 by Colette*, 1955 (includes short fiction).

Other literary forms

Much of Colette's work defies ready classification. Aside from creating tales that are of such a length as to make it difficult to decide whether to term them short novels or long short stories (the term *nouvelle*, which Colette often used for her work, means both "novelette" and "novella"), Colette also frequently mixed fiction with fact in a confusing blend. *La Maison de Claudine* (1922; *My Mother's House*, 1953), for example, can pass for fiction; however, the book is essentially a series of sketches from Colette's life, primarily dealing with her mother, the famous Sido. Indeed, it has been observed that almost every page of this author's very personal writing contains something that can be traced to her life. Thus, several of her particular fixations, such as animals and flowers, not only appear prominently in her fiction but also are dealt with at length (and with great knowledge and sensitivity) in full-length essays. When a film was made of her life in 1952, she told an interviewer who had not seen the production, to go and see what a wonderful life she had led; then she remarked that she wished that she had been aware of its quality earlier. In fact, her interest in and wonder at life can be found in all of her writings. These works include, besides a number of short stories, a variety of reminiscences, adaptations of her tales for the stage and the cinema, and virtually unclassifiable publications on life as a music-hall performer; on cats, on writing, and on life in general. *Oeuvres complètes de Colette*, the "complete" works of Colette (prepared under the eye of the author, who excised a number of titles that she considered unworthy of re-publication), published from 1948 to 1950, fill fifteen large volumes; these do not contain a sizable correspondence, most of which has been published separately.

Achievements

One indication of Colette's persisting appeal is the impressive number of republications of her chief works, including a sometimes bewildering array of retranslations, some quite recent. In her lifetime, she enjoyed an enormous popularity with everyday readers and eventually was recognized by the literary establishment as a genuine talent. She was elected to the Académie Goncourt (1945) and was the first woman to serve as its president (1949); she was given the Grand Cross of the Légion d'Honneur (1953); and she was the first woman in France to be accorded a state funeral. Perhaps a more significant index of Colette's literary importance is the record of her friendships with towering figures such as Marcel Proust and André Gide, both of whom admired her work. Since her death, numerous biographical and critical studies (from writers in France, England, and America) have attested Colette's impact on French letters and on world literature.

Biography

For a woman who was to become something of a symbol of feminism, Sidonie-Gabrielle Colette was born into the most unlikely surroundings. Saint-Sauveur-en-Puisaye was a small village in Burgundy, and little Sidonie grew up as a country girl—she retained a strong Burgundian accent until her death. Her mother, whose tremendous influence on Colette's life cannot be overestimated, was Adèle-Sidonie Landoy Robineau-Duclos, referred to by her second daughter as "Sido," whose first husband, Jules (by whom she had two children) died in 1865. In the same year, his widow married Captain Jules-Joseph Colette, who had been invalided out of the army in 1860 and had come to Saint-Sauveur as a tax collector. Sido bore two more children, a ne'er-do-well son, Léopold, who was a great disappointment, and her last offspring, Sidonie-Gabrielle, who made her mother famous.

Nature was a source of constant delight to the young Colette, whose writings reveal her fascination with nearly every aspect of the natural world. Even when she lived in Paris, years later, she was never happy without several pets (usually cats) and plenty of flowers and plants in her apartment. Her family life was evidently reasonably happy, although her father, who retired from government service in 1880, was somewhat shiftless. Through neglect and mismanagement, the Colette fortune was lost by 1890, forcing the family to move to a nearby village, to the home of Colette's half brother, Doctor Achille

Robineau-Duclos. Oddly enough, Colette's father claimed to be writing a book and acquired several large, expensive writing books, the pages of which were discovered to be blank at his death in 1905.

The move and the change in the family finances caused Colette to leave school at age sixteen, and her formal education ended at that point, although she continued to be an enthusiastic reader for the rest of her life, two of her favorite authors being Honoré de Balzac and Proust. Little is known of her life for the four years between the end of her schooling and her meeting with Henri Gauthier-Villars (known to his Parisian friends, and later to the world, as Willy, one of his favorite pen names), who was to become her first husband. It was Willy—a successful Parisian editor and publisher—who gave her the pen name Colette and almost accidentally provided her with the stimulus for creating fiction. After hearing his wife tell of her school days, Willy suggested that she write down some of the incidents, adding some spicy touches to make them more interesting. Although Willy was a gifted editor and arranger of literary projects (it is now known that he wrote almost none of the numerous works that bear his name—his management of ghostwriters, of whom his wife became the best, amounted to a career), it took him several years to recognize the quality of the sketches that Colette had created and that were to constitute her first published work, *Claudine at School*, which enjoyed a striking popular success. Typically, this work and its three sequels were all published under Willy's name alone.

Since their marriage in 1893, Colette and Willy had lived in Paris, where Willy was a prominent figure on the literary scene. The surprising success of *Claudine at School* impelled him to force Colette to turn out three sequels, one every year. His "force" was based on his greater age (he was almost fifteen years older than she) and superior experience of the world, especially that of Paris. According to the legend (which has perhaps considerable truth in it), he used to lock her in her room for four hours at a stretch, having given her strict orders to write for the full time. Colette later asserted that she did not really mind the enforced effort and that the recollections of her young girlhood, which formed the basis for the first volume, were a pleasant emotional return to a time of greater peace and certainty. Although the Claudine series is now regarded as inferior to her later work, there is in it the mark of a born writer.

The marriage, however, was not as successful as the series. Colette was simply too independent—and her success with the Claudine series helped her to recognize and develop this very important quality in her personality—to live in the shadow of the lively but inconsiderate Willy. They separated in 1906, and the divorce was finalized in 1910, by which time Colette was no longer the provincial girl who had to be introduced to Paris. As early as 1903, she had taken lessons in mime (her marked accent temporarily discouraged her from vocal performance), and she appeared in several stage productions, the sensuality of which created something of a scandal but which enabled her to support herself. Also, she had met Henri de Jouvenel, the aristocratic editor of *Le Matin*, a leading newspaper, to which Colette contributed articles for many years.

Meanwhile, she continued writing, for herself rather than for Willy and under her permanent pen name, Colette; her novel *The Vagabond* was given serious consideration by the prize committee of the Académie Goncourt. The story of the rest of Colette's life is chiefly literary, the only striking personal note being her intimate friendships with several women (notably the Marquise de Belboeuf, nicknamed "Missy") and her amicable divorce in 1924 from Jouvenel, whom she had married in 1912. Aside from her writing, Colette's other activities were chiefly mime and, later, dramatic performances (occasionally in dramatized versions of her own works). As honors were offered to her and as her reputation grew, not only in France but also in England and the United States, Colette became something of a national treasure. She was undisturbed by the Germans during World War II (in World War I, she had served as a volunteer nurse and reported on some aspects of the combat near Verdun), and she took little evident interest in politics.

In 1924, Colette had met the much younger (by some eighteen years) Maurice Goudeket. They were married in 1935 and had, all evidence indicates, a very happy life together until her death in 1954. Perhaps the greatest irony of Colette's life story was the refusal of the Catholic Church to allow her a religious funeral, even though she was given a state ceremony. This refusal was based on her two divorces. It aroused considerable resentment even outside France: Graham Greene sent a stinging open letter to the Cardinal-Archbishop of Paris.

The funeral was one of the largest Paris had ever seen. It was noted that by far the larger proportion of the mourners were women, evidently paying homage to the woman who had more than any other given them a voice.

Analysis

Maurice Goudeket, in his memoir, *Près de Colette* (1956; *Close to Colette*, 1957), has provided a touching and revealing picture of Colette's last hours. The most remarkable incident is the choice of her last spoken words. Looking toward an album of insects and birds, a case of butterflies, and an open window outside which swallows were flying, Colette waved expansively and said, "Look! Maurice, look!" Several scholars have noted that the French word *regarde* signifies more than its usual English equivalent, having the connotation of close observation and even study. Colette was never interested in abstractions, a fact which has earned her some severe critical reprimands, yet she has no equal as an observer of the tangible world.

Colette frequently complained of the difficulty of writing, saying she disliked it, which might cause one to wonder why she did so much of it. Aside from the melancholy economic fact that, especially in her earlier years, even successful books earned their authors trifling sums by today's standards, it seems clear that Colette wrote in order to make sense of her long and eventful life. She did not attempt to theorize about it, though some of her offhand remarks bear the mark of high-quality epigrams, such as her insightful observation: "A happy childhood is a bad preparation for human contacts." Instead, she rewrote her life in differing versions, countless times, mingling truth and imagination.

Colette's refusal to theorize about life was accompanied by a reluctance to judge other people and their modes of life. This detachment provided her with a sort of aesthetic distance from her subjects which helped to counter the elements of personal involvement that infuse her fiction. A work of partial autobiography, originally published as *Ces plaisirs* (1932) but better known as *Le Pur et l'impur* (1941; *The Pure and the Impure*, 1967), which includes extensive examinations of sexual practices, both "normal" and irregular, is considered by several scholars to be one of her most important works, yet in this brief volume there is no moral judgment, only understanding and sympathy. Colette is content simply to "look," to try to comprehend without condemnation.

A vital feature of Colette's writing is her use of point of view. Almost all of her stories are told in the first person, a phenomenon that has encouraged autobiographical interpretations but that also gives her texts an impressive immediacy and warmth. Thus, when the heroine of the brief tale *Chambre d'hôtel* (1940; *Chance Acquaintances*, 1955) declares, near the end of the story, that she must leave her home and says, "I went to collect the few personal belongings which, at that time, I held to be invaluable: my cat, my resolve to travel, and my solitude," one can sympathize with her, whether the voice is solely that of a character or is partly that of the author as well. The most notable example of Colette's abandonment of the first person is the novel that many critics believe to be her masterpiece, *Chéri*, which, along with its sequel, *The Last of Chéri*, is possibly the closest thing to a truly "modern" novel in her entire canon. The modernity of *Chéri* can be ascribed in part to the relatively detached tone of the narrative. All the emotion in this tragic story is felt only in relation to the characters; the author does not intrude at all.

Another aspect of *Chéri* that marks it as unusual among Colette's fictions is the fact that the central male character is the dominant figure and is painstakingly studied; though several female characters play important roles in the novel, Chéri is the basis of the story and is clearly the chief character. In most of Colette's works, the women are the outstanding figures; the male characters are often merely sketched in. Colette focuses on the problems and interests of women, particularly in their relationships with men but also in their position as human beings trying to come to terms with loneliness and failure. Again and again in her fiction, she dramatizes the failure of sexual relationships, usually placing the blame on the man but recognizing that the woman also bears responsibility in such matters. Although not a philosopher, Colette came to a number of reasonably profound and often unhappy conclusions about the battle of the sexes. One is that there is no guarantee of happiness in any liaison and that, indeed, happiness is not necessary for a meaningful life. She also concluded that a woman suffers fully only once, when her initial romance fades.

Colette has been justly praised for her sense of place. Her settings, even the interiors, are presented in great detail and precision, most often with the impress of a mood or an element of characterization. As Sir Walter Scott is credited with seeing places in human terms, so Colette tends to perceive people in concrete manifestations, frequently presenting a character in the light of his surroundings, his clothes, even his pets. Léa de Lonval, the aging courtesan in *Chéri*, is seen most often in her pink boudoir; the silks are pink; so are some of the furniture and the curtains; even the light coming in through the windows is usually pink. In the earlier novels, Colette re-creates the memories of her childhood days in the beautiful Burgundian countryside. No item is too small for her notice, from a blade of grass to a tiny insect; she invests everything with a sense of the wonder and magnificence of nature. If people in her books are often undependable and even treacherous, nature is not. So strong was Colette's affinity with natural things that she created in *The Cat* an animal character that overshadows both of the human characters. The novel is a love story, but the true passion exists between Alain and his cat Saha, not between him and his wife Camille. The tension of the disintegrating marriage becomes so great, and Camille's recognition of Saha's moral superiority so strong, that the jealous wife attempts to kill the animal, an act that brings the relationship of man and wife to an end and reconfirms the bond between a man and his "pet."

The Claudine series which comprises the first four novels of Colette, though inferior to her later masterpieces, displays several of the qualities that distinguish her work and reveals themes and topics that recur throughout her long career (Claudine, a character first conceived in 1900, has obvious affinities with Gigi, the heroine of the 1944 novella). Claudine is certainly a persona of Colette herself, and much of the first novel, *Claudine at School*, is taken directly from the author's experience, from the almost extravagant descriptions of the lush countryside to the delineation of real people as characters in the plot. (Colette, years later, learned that her portrait of the immoral headmistress, Mademoiselle Sergent, had seriously distressed the model for that character, and Colette regretted her callousness.) The opening novel in the series introduces Claudine as a lively, intelligent, fun-loving fifteen-year-old student whose life at school is enlivened by scandal, such as the "affair" between the headmistress and one of the younger instructors (a relationship that at first disturbs Claudine, since she has suffered from a powerful infatuation with the same young lady). An occasionally unnoticed quality of Colette's writing, her humorous irony, emerges in this first volume most agreeably. When Claudine discovers the "romance" between the headmistress and Mademoiselle Lanthenay (she secretly observes the two women in a passionate embrace), her first reaction is neither shock nor dismay; instead, she comments wryly to herself, "Well done! No one could say this Headmistress bullied her subordinates!" Apart from her escapes to the calming serenity of walks in the woods, Claudine's life is chiefly centered on events at her school. Her home life is quite dull; her father hardly notices her presence, and (perhaps because Colette was in reality very close to her mother) her mother is not on the scene. One feels, despite the frivolous adventures and trivial concerns of the girls, that Colette is sincere when she has Claudine remark, at the end of the novel, "Farewell to the classroom; farewell, Mademoiselle and her girl friend. . . . I am going to leave you to make my entry into the world . . . I shall be very much astonished if I enjoy myself there as much as I have at school."

In *Claudine in Paris*, Claudine and her father have moved to Paris, where she is unhappy at being isolated from the countryside that she loves. In this state of near-misery and surrounded by friends (one of whom was at school with her) who all seem to be engaged in some form of physical lovemaking (even her cat Fanchette is pregnant), including the homosexual Marcel, Claudine is an easy prey for Marcel's father, the forty-year-old roué Renaud. Instead of becoming his mistress, as she has decided, Claudine marries him (a plot turn revived effectively as the climax of *Gigi*). As might be expected, the marriage is not completely successful; in the next volume, *Claudine Married*, a triangle forms: Renaud, Claudine, and Rézi, the attractive woman with whom both of them have an intense love affair. The book ends with a rather contrived reunion of Claudine and her husband. It seems certain that the character of Renaud was at least partly based on Willy, though the happy ending is obviously not autobiographical.

In the fourth Claudine novel, *Claudine and Annie*, Renaud and Claudine are primarily observers of and commentators on the dissolution of the marriage of Annie and Alain, largely the result of Annie's awakening to life during her husband's prolonged absence on a trip to South America. Finally, after much sentimental advice from Claudine and a series of relationships of her own, Annie (who is the primary character in the story) decides to leave. Although this volume, like the others in the series, is marred by an occasional confusion of plot and uncertainty of theme, the Claudine series hints at the profound sensitivity, engaging irony, and perceptive vision of Colette's mature work.

This maturity is evident in *Chéri* and *The Last of Chéri*. The plot of the two volumes is direct and uncomplicated. Fred Peloux, nicknamed "Chéri," is spoiled by his immoral and malicious mother, Charlotte, whose indulgence is encouraged by his extreme good looks. Early in his life, his mother's old friend and fellow courtesan, Léa, becomes fond of the boy and later takes him as a lover, though she is nearly twice his age. When Chéri grows to manhood, his mother arranges a marriage for him with a lovely and acceptable young lady named Edmée. Like nearly every other girl that Chéri meets, Edmée is infatuated with the young man for his beauty (it was Colette's firm conviction that men can possess beauty just as women can), as well as for his talents in making love, developed with Léa's tutelage. The first volume closes with Chéri's resolve to abandon Léa, whom he believes to be no longer an important part of his life.

In the interval between *Chéri* and *The Last of Chéri*, five years have passed, the years of World War I; Colette captures the empty, futile mood of postwar France. Chéri is in gloomy harmony with this mood. He is idle, purposeless, and without substance. Nothing in his previous experience has prepared him for the challenge of creating some meaning for his life. In this vacuum, Chéri begins to think constantly of Léa and believes that he must attempt to revive their old romance, from a time when he felt really alive. In one of the most effective recognition scenes in literature, Chéri confronts Léa and for a time does not even recognize her: "A woman was seated at a desk, writing, her back turned to him. Chéri saw a great back, thick gray hair, cut short, like his mother's, a fat, bulging neck." It takes a few moments for Chéri to realize that this aging figure is his former lover. Léa has simply decided that, since she is nearing sixty, it is time for her to settle down to a comfortable old age. She has stopped dieting and dying her hair and performing the multifarious rituals required by her beauty regimen.

When Chéri finally realizes that his old life is gone and that he is unable to build a new one to replace it, he turns to the only escape possible: suicide. It is a clever touch of Colette's that he performs this ultimate act in a sordid room surrounded by old pictures of Léa as a youthful beauty. The compact development of the plot and the sure depiction of Chéri's decline give the climax a tragic stature; indeed, throughout the two novels, every scene clearly advances the plot and the characterization. Colette never exceeded the mastery displayed in these works. Seldom have such slender materials (the two volumes together occupy only a bit more than two hundred pages) yielded such tragic power.

When Colette published the very short novel *Gigi* in 1944, she had not written a substantial piece of fiction for several years; it had been thought by some that she never would again. *Gigi* was therefore an especially happy surprise. In this, her last work of fiction, written when she was seventy, Colette produced a delightful tale with one of the few happy endings in all of her works. It is also one of her few novels to be narrated in the third person. Because the plot was based on an anecdote told to Colette many years earlier, her powers of invention were not taxed. Two wise decisions helped the novel to succeed: Colette set the story in 1899, and most of the text is in dialogue form. *Gigi* thus benefits both from a charming setting in an uncomplicated distant past and from a liveliness of presentation.

The tone of the narrative is ironic, but cheerfully so. Gigi, having just reached adolescence, is being reared by a grandmother and a great aunt, who are both retired courtesans, to follow in their "professional" footsteps. Fortunately, Gigi is too honest and skeptical to be much affected by this instruction; in the end, she outsmarts her teachers by marrying the bored and wealthy Gaston, whom they had only hoped to persuade to keep her as a mistress. The story abounds in jollity and good humor—it is no wonder that *Gigi* was very successfully adapted as a hit play and an Academy Award-winning film.

There is a pleasing irony in that Colette's last story comes, at least in tone and atmosphere, full circle to the innocent ambience of her first novel, *Claudine at School*. Though Gigi's experience is told with far greater skill, she and Claudine seem sisters under the skin and even somewhat on the surface, especially in their eye for the ridiculous, their impatience with pompousness, and their sincere good intentions toward others.

The chief elements of Colette's fiction thus appear at the beginning and the end of her long career. She studied love—young love (even between adolescents, as in *The Ripening Seed*), ardent love, failed love, married love, illicit love, and also family love—as no other writer ever has studied it. Somerset Maugham once wrote that the truly great authors (he used Fyodor Dostoevski as an example) could see "through a stone wall," so great was their perception of life; he modestly claimed only that he could see very well what was right in front of him, hastening to add that such an accomplishment was not to be underrated. Colette "looked" at life in such minute detail and with such aesthetic integrity that one might say that now and again she penetrated the stone wall.

Major publications other than long fiction

SHORT FICTION: *Chambre d'hôtel*, 1940 (*Chance Acquaintances*, 1955); *Le Képi*, 1943; *7 by Colette*, 1955 (includes novels); *The Tender Shoot and Other Stories*, 1959.

NONFICTION: *Dialogues de bêtes*, 1904 (*Creatures Great and Small*, 1957); *L'Envers du music-hall*, 1913 (*Music-Hall Sidelights*, 1957); *La Maison de Claudine*, 1922 (*My Mother's House*, 1953); *Ces plaisirs*, 1932 (better known as *Le Pur et l'impur*, 1941; *The Pure and the Impure*, 1967); *Mes apprentissages*, 1936 (*My Apprenticeships*, 1957); *Journal à rebours*, 1941, and *De ma fenêtre*, 1942 (translated together as *Looking Backwards*, 1975); *L'Étoile vesper*, 1946 (*The Evening Star*, 1973); *Le Fanal bleu*, 1949 (*The Blue Lantern*, 1963); *Places*, 1970 (includes short sketches in English translation unavailable in a French collection); *Letters from Colette*, 1980.

MISCELLANEOUS: *Oeuvres complètes de Colette*, 1948-1950 (15 volumes); *The Works*, 1951-1964 (17 volumes).

Bibliography
Cottrell, Robert D. *Colette*, 1974.
Crosland, Margaret. *Colette: A Provincial in Paris*, 1954.
──────── . *Colette: The Difficulty of Loving*, 1973.
Duclaux, Mary. *Twentieth Century French Writers*, 1920.
Goudeket, Maurice. *Close to Colette*, 1957.
Marks, Elaine. *Colette*, 1960.
Peyre, Henri. *French Novelists of Today*, 1967.
Phelps, Robert, ed. *Earthly Paradise: Colette's Autobiography Drawn from Her Lifetime Writings*, 1966.
Wescott, Glenway. "Introduction," in *Short Novels of Colette*, 1951.

Fred B. McEwen

JULIO CORTÁZAR

Born: Brussels, Belgium; August 26, 1914
Died: Paris, France; February 12, 1984

Principal long fiction

Los premios, 1960 (*The Winners*, 1965); *Rayuela*, 1963 (*Hopscotch*, 1966); *62: Modelo para armar*, 1968 (*62: A Model Kit*, 1972); *Libro de Manuel*, 1973 (*A Manual for Manuel*, 1978).

Other literary forms

Early in his career, Julio Cortázar published two volumes of poetry— *Presencia* (1938; presence), under the pseudonym Julio Denís, and *Los reyes* (1949; the kings), using his own name—both still generally unnoticed by the critics. His short fiction, however, is considered among the best in Hispanic literature. His best-known short story is perhaps "Las babas del diablo" (the devil's slobbers), the basis of the internationally acclaimed film *Blow-Up* (1966), directed by Michelangelo Antonioni. Cortázar's collection of short fiction *Bestiario* (1951; bestiary) contains fantastic and somewhat surrealistic tales dealing mainly with extraordinary circumstances in the everyday lives of ordinary characters. Their common denominator is the unexpected turn of events at the story's end; such surprise endings are a well-known trait of Cortázar's short fiction. His second collection of stories, *Final de juego* (1956; *End of the Game and Other Stories*, 1963; also as *Blow-Up and Other Stories*, 1967) was followed by *Las armas secretas* (1958; secret weapons), *Historias de cronopios y de famas* (1962; *Cronopios and Famas*, 1969), *Todos los fuegos el fuego* (1966; *All Fires the Fire*, 1973), *Octaedro* (1974; included in *A Change of Light and Other Stories*), *Alguien que anda por ahí* (1977; included in *A Change of Light and Other Stories*, 1980), *Queremos tanto a Glenda y otros relatos* (1981; *We Love Glenda So Much and Other Tales*, 1983), and *Deshoras* (1983; bad timing).

Two collage books, *La vuelta al día en ochenta mundos* (1968; around the day in eighty worlds) and *Último round* (1969; the last round), reflect the author's life via the use of anecdotes, photographs, newspaper clippings, drawings, and other personal items. They are not, however, as engagé as are Cortázar's political essays in the collections *Viaje alrededor de una mesa* (1970; voyage around a table), which contains discussions of Marxism and capitalism; *Fantomas contra los vampiros multinacionales: Una utopía realizable* (1975; Fantomas battles the multinational vampires), a tirade in comic-strip form attacking capitalism; and *Nicaragua, tan violentamente dulce* (1984; Nicaragua, so violently sweet), a collection of articles on Nicaragua and the Marxist revolution. *Un tal Lucas* (1979; *A Certain Lucas*, 1984) is a series of inter-locking fictions, somewhat autobiographical in nature, that reveal the essence of a particular man's life. One of Cortázar's last works, a travelogue of sorts, entitled *Los autonautas de la cosmopista* (1983; the autonauts of the cosmopike), is both a never-ending trip and a love song, detailing a trip with his last wife, Carol Dunlop, who predeceased him by several months. It contains descriptions, reflections, cultural parody, sometimes nostalgia, a potpourri of feelings and perceptions à la Cortázar.

In addition to the several volumes mentioned above, Cortázar published the nonfiction works *Buenos Aires Buenos Aires* (1968) and *Prosa del observatorio* (1972) and poetry, in *Pameos y meopas* (1971). As a professional translator, he rendered into Spanish such works as Daniel Defoe's *Robinson Crusoe* (1719), G. K. Chesterton's *The Man Who Knew Too Much* (1922), and André Gide's *L'Immoraliste* (1902). He translated many volumes of criticism, including Lord Houghton's *Life and Letters of John Keats* (1867) and two erudite essays of Alfred Stern, *Sartre, His Philosophy and Psychoanalysis* (1953) and *Philosophie du rire et des pleurs* (1949; philosophy of laughter and tears). Himself a critic of English, French, and Spanish literature, Cortázar also published many articles, reviews, and literary essays on a variety of topics ranging from Arthur Rimbaud, John Keats, Antonin Artaud, Graham Greene, and Charles Baudelaire to contemporary Latin American writers such as Octavio Paz, Leopoldo Marechal, and Victoria Ocampo.

Achievements

At a moment when fiction in Spanish enjoyed little international esteem, Cortázar's multinational and multicultural orientation brought recognition of a sophistication and cosmopolitan awareness previously assumed to be lacking among Spanish-language writers. His unusual success in translation was an important ingredient in the "boom" in Latin American fiction, bringing the Spanish-American novelists of his generation to unprecedented prestige and popularity in Europe and North America. His most celebrated novel, *Hopscotch*, unquestionably had an impact upon experimental and vanguard writing in Spain and Latin America, and the notion of a variable structure and reassembled plot had a number of imitators among younger writers. In addition to influencing the literature of his "native" Argentina, Cortázar has had a significant impact on the younger generation of novelists throughout the Spanish-speaking world.

Biography

The fact that Julio Cortázar was born in Brussels, Belgium, rather than in Argentina was something of an accident, as his Argentine parents were then abroad on business. He learned French at about the same time he learned Spanish, and this international beginning colored most of his life. His paternal great-grandparents were from the Basque area of northern Spain; his maternal origins can be traced to Germany and France. The boy and his parents remained for several years in Europe, returning to Buenos Aires when he was about four years old. While Cortázar was still a boy in Argentina, his father abandoned the family; Julio was reared by his mother and aunt, earning degrees in elementary, secondary, and preparatory education. From 1937 to 1944, he worked as a high school teacher in Bolívar and Chivilcoy while simultaneously beginning to write short stories in his spare time. In 1938, his first collection of poems, *Presencia*, appeared under the pseudonym Julio Denís, without receiving much critical attention. In 1944, Cortázar began to teach French literature at the University of Cuyo, but his activism against the dictatorship of Juan Perón brought his arrest, with a subsequent resignation from his post at the university. He moved to Buenos Aires in 1946, obtaining the post of manager of the Argentine Publishing Association; while working there, he earned a degree as public translator. His dramatic poem *Los reyes* was published under his own name in 1949, but was likewise ignored by the critics. In 1951, Cortázar was awarded a scholarship by the French government to study in Paris, where he would reside until his death, working as a free-lance translator and for UNESCO (the United Nations Educational, Scientific and Cultural Organization). The same year, as he left Argentina, his short-story collection *Bestiario* was published.

In 1953, Cortázar married Aurora Bernárdez, also an Argentinian translator, and together they visited Italy, where he translated the prose works of Edgar Allan Poe, on commission from the University of Puerto Rico, and wrote most of *Cronopios and Famas*. In 1960, he visited the United States and his first novel, *The Winners*, appeared in Argentina. Cortázar was especially impressed by New York's Greenwich Village, and his attraction to jazz appears in his later long fiction. He visited Cuba in 1963, the year *Hopscotch* was published, was fascinated by the Marxist revolution, and became a good friend of dictator Fidel Castro; an attraction to Marxism is noticeable in many of his nonfiction works. Cortázar's third novel, *62: A Model Kit*, appeared in 1968, at a time when his reputation was firmly established, thanks especially to the film *Blow-Up*, which Antonioni based on one of Cortázar's short stories. In 1973, celebrating the publication of his fourth novel, *A Manual for Manuel*, he journeyed to Argentina, visiting Chile, Ecuador, and Peru as well. After that, his production was limited to short stories and nonfiction, and he participated in many congresses and traveled throughout Europe and the Americas. Cortázar died in France on February 12, 1984.

Analysis

Julio Cortázar's first novel, *The Winners*, tells the story of a voyage aboard a rather sinister ship. This mystery cruise—the ship's destination is never revealed—is a prize awarded to the winners of a lottery, a heterogeneous group of Argentines who, as the novel begins, are gathered at the London Café in Buenos Aires. The group represents a cross section of the Argentine class structure, suggestive of the novel's implicit sociopolitical critique. From the café, the winners are transported via bus to the ship, under a shroud of secrecy. The café is taken over by the Office of Municipal Affairs, arrangers of the lottery, with all but the winners being required to leave the premises. In the café, on the bus, and boarding the ship, the winners engage in conversations as varied as their class and cultural origins, making new acquaintances and provoking a few hostile confrontations.

The ship's name, the *Malcolm*, is a clue of what is to come: The passengers are not "well come"; rather, they are regarded by the ship's crew as an imposition. Attempting to speak to the officers, they discover that the crew speaks another language; the passengers are refused the itinerary and forbidden access to the stern. Protesting their treatment, they are informed that a rare strain of typhus has infected the crew, which provokes a division among the passengers between those who fear contamination and those who believe that they are being deceived (and offer other answers as to what is taking place). Jorge, a young boy, falls ill, and a group of passengers (led by Gabriel Medrano, who admits to a frivolous previous life) storm the radio room hoping to cable ashore for help. A sailor shoots and kills Medrano, ending the cruise. Medrano's body is removed under mysterious circumstances while the remaining winners are transported to Buenos Aires in a hydroplane. There, the officer in charge urges them to sign a statement, allegedly to prevent rumors about the incident. Most accede, but some refuse to forget the senseless killing and to believe the official explanation. Aside from possible allusions to the "ship of fools" topos, it is obvious that the novel is fraught with existential implications: The unknown destination of ship and passengers represents the situation of the existentially unaware, those who have not taken charge of their lives and begun to chart their course through time. The secrecy surrounding the trip is emblematic of the Existentialist tenet that there is no answer to the ultimate questions, no essential meaning or absolute truth, and the epidemic on the ship is a symbol of "being-toward-death," as well as of death's ultimate inescapability. Medrano, with his previously unaware (existentially inauthentic) life, represents the individual who comes to terms with his existence and endows it with meaning by his death. On a secondary level of meaning, the political implications of life under a totalitarian regime are likewise well developed: the high-handed way in which authorities on land treat both the winners and the general public, the inability of the passengers to communicate with the crew, their not being privileged to know the itinerary or to have access to areas of command, as well as the violent retribution when they transgress the regime's rules and prohibitions. The ending is a clear allegory of censorship and news "management."

Structurally, the novel is composed of nine chapters, with passages in italics which convey the linguistic and metaphysical experiments of Persio (a passenger and amateur astronomer). His monologues provide a metaphysical, loosely structured commentary on events, which some critics have found distracting—an unnecessary digression—while others have seen therein an adumbration of the innovative structure of *Hopscotch*. Persio's monologues, often poetic, provide a contrast with the realistic and prosaic style of the remainder of the novel; they exemplify the "automatic writing" propounded by Surrealists. Although Cortázar denied such imputations, many critics also have seen *The Winners* as an allegory of Argentinian society and the constant struggle between civilization and barbarism.

Hopscotch is Cortázar's best-known novel and probably his literary masterpiece; according to the London *Times Literary Supplement*, it was the "first great novel of Spanish America." Critically acclaimed throughout the Hispanic world, it was promptly translated into many languages, receiving well-deserved praise from critics and reviewers (the English version by Gregory Rabassa received the first National Book Award for translation). A significant and highly innovative aspect of the novel is its "Table of Instructions," in which Cortázar informs the reader that "this book consists of many books, but two books above all." The first can be read in normal numerical order from chapter 1 to chapter 56, and is divided into two sections entitled "From the Other Side" (that is, Paris) and "From This Side" (Argentina). Upon completing chapter 56, the reader may ignore the rest of the book "with a clear conscience." This, however, would be the conventional reader (*hembra*, or feminine/passive), as opposed to the more collaborative (*macho*, or masculine/active) reader, who becomes the author's accomplice in the creative act, reading the book in the hopscotch manner to which the title alludes. In this second book, the reading begins at chapter 73, following a sequence of chapters—nonconsecutive and apparently haphazard—indicated by the author at the end of each chapter in question. Upon reaching the final chapter, however, the collaborative reader is directed to return to chapter 58 (the next to the last), which in turn sends him back to chapter 131, the final one. Thus there is no definitive ending, but an endless movement back and forth between the last two chapters. This double (or multiple) structure is a principal basis for the novel's fame, involving two prime factors: the study of man's search for authenticity (by Oliveira, the protagonist) and a call for innovation or change in the structuring of narrative fiction, a departure from the traditional novelistic form.

Horacio Oliveira, an Argentinian intellectual living in Paris around 1950 (and thus a possible mask of the author), is involved in a search for authenticity. Some forty years old, he spends his time in continual and prolonged self-analysis and introspection. With a group of Bohemian friends calling themselves the Serpent Club, he drinks, listens to jazz, and converses upon philosophy, music, literature, art, and politics. Obsessed with the unconventional, Oliveira, during one of many drunken binges, strives to gain some sort of mystical vision via sexual intercourse in an alley with a destitute combination streetwalker and bag-woman. Discovered by the police, he is deported to Argentina, where he encounters old friends and continues his search, first working in an emblematic circus and then in an equally symbolic insane asylum. Despite the inconclusive end described above, some suggest that he committed suicide, while others see a positive ending. Given Oliveira's overpowering importance in the novel, the remaining characters are foils whose major and all but exclusive function is to provide a better perspective of him. The members of the Serpent Club, representing different countries and cultures, afford opportunities for comparison and contrast. They include Ossip Gregorovius, a Russian émigré and intellectual whom Oliveira suspects of having an affair with his own lover, "La Maga," an Uruguayan woman living in Paris with her infant son Rocamadour. Also prominent are a North American couple, Babs and Ronald; a Chinese named Wong; a Spaniard, Perico; and two Frenchmen, Guy and Étienne.

The Argentinian section or half of the novel presents the mirror image (the *Doppelgänger* theme) in La Maga's counterpart, Lolita, whom Oliveira imagines to be the woman he left in Paris and whom he attempts to seduce. As a result, he fears that his friend (ironically and symbolically named Traveler), who is also his double, is attempting to kill him, a probable exteriorization of his own self-destructive urge. While talking to Lolita from a second-story window moments after the attempted seduction, Oliveira appears to fall or jump, allowing for the interpretation that he has committed suicide. Other chapters, however, suggest (without explaining how) that he survived the fall and insinuate as well that he became insane. Like the children's game of hopscotch, at once simple and complex, the novel has many possibilities, numerous variants, and a similar cluster of meanings, depending ultimately upon the reader-player for its specific form and resultant action, and thus for its interpretation and elucidation. All of this places the work very much in the mainstream of experimental fiction and novelistic theory, in which the reader is incorporated as an important and essential part of the creative process.

In Cortázar's next novel, *62: A Model Kit*, separated by some five years from *Hopscotch*, there are traces of chapter 62 of *Hopscotch*, and lest the reader overlook this, the author mentions it in his introduction, stating that his intentions were "sketched out one day past in the final paragraphs of chapter 62 of *Rayuela* [*Hopscotch*], which explains the title of this book. . . ." In that chapter, one of those termed "expendable," Morelli plans to write a book in which the characters will behave as if possessed by "foreign occupying forces, advancing in the quest of their freedom of the city; a quest superior to ourselves as individuals and one which uses us for its own ends. . . ." Even more so than *Hopscotch*, *62: A Model Kit* may be considered an antinovel. The suggestions of science fiction or fantastic narrative notwithstanding, it is an extremely difficult novel, as yet little studied and less elucidated by critics.

On one level, there is experimentation with language and polysemous signification, a semiserious meditation upon connotation and denotation and the possible mystical or metaphysical meanings of their congruence. Thus, at the outset, Juan overhears a customer in a Paris restaurant order a *château saignant* (a rare steak) and deliberately confuses this with a *château sanglant* (a bloody castle), with all the obvious attendant Gothic associations regarding such juxtaposition as a "coagulation" or myriad of meanings and events. Such constellations are formed throughout the novel via the manipulation by several characters whose paths cross in the separate realms of the City and the Zone (reminiscent of the two cultures—Argentine and French—in *Hopscotch*). The Zone, where apparent existential authenticity is the norm, offers characters who attempt to master their fate and negate the mundane, while in the City, conformity and ritualism reign supreme and characters are engaged in compulsive searches of which they have no understanding, an atmosphere at once Kafkaesque and absurd, with occasional undertones of Aldous Huxley's *Brave New World* (1932) or George Orwell's *1984* (1949).

Principal characters include Juan, an Argentine interpreter and thus a hypothetical fictional double of the author; he loves Hélène, an anesthetist (who may symbolize Nirvana or *ataraxia* by reason of her profession), but she is hostile, cold, and bisexual. Juan's lover, the sensual Dane Tell, accompanies him on his travels. Celia, a young student at the Sorbonne, runs away from her family and eventually becomes Hélène's lover. The married couple, Nicole and Marrast, live in Paris and visit London; he is an artist, bored with his wife and generally plagued by ennui, seeking new means of amusement. Upon seeing an advertisement for Neurotics Anonymous, he writes an open letter suggesting that all neurotics gather at a gallery to see a certain painting, thus all but precipitating a riot because of the mob of neurotics who attend. Marrast makes the acquaintance of Austin, a neurotic young lutist whose sexual naïveté and ludicrous experiences with a prostitute, Georgette, are humorously exploited by Cortázar. Georgette insists that during intercourse Austin must take extreme care not to disarrange her coiffure. Marrast's wife, an illustrator of children's books, no longer loves her husband and, although she continues to live with him, draws gnomes which may reflect her esteem of him. Two especially strange characters, Calac and Polanco, Argentines referred to as Tartars or Pampa savages, exemplify linguistic experimentation in their continual, senseless conversations in the subway before curious crowds; their speech consists almost totally of neologisms. Finally, and most difficult, *paredros* can be considered a sort of collective double of all the characters mentioned—although any one of them might be another *paredros*, and yet in other instances the *paredros* emerges alone and contemplates characters from an external vantage point, while participating at times in conversations and external events.

Throughout the novel, Cortázar drops hints that the whole is a Gothic tale, that it is in fact a variant of that particular subgenre of the horror story which deals with vampires, and during a trip to Vienna, Juan and Dane visit the Basilisken Haus on Blutgasse (blood street), encountering legends which tell how one resident, the Blood Countess, Erzebet Bathori, bled and tortured girls in her castle, bathing in their blood. Juan and Dane associate these tales with what they imagine to be the intentions of another guest of the hotel, Frau Marta, regarding a young English girl, and manage to prevent the girl's seduction, although the door is left open to possible vampirism, rather than lesbianism. Otherwise, a parallel exists between Frau Marta and Hélène, as both are seduced young girls (perhaps a reappearance of the *Doppelgänger*). Both may be considered mirrors or doubles of the Blood Countess. Although there is no clear resolution, the thematic connections between such incidents and the opening reflections on rare steak and bloody castles are immediately evident.

The fact that the structuring function exercised by plot in the conventional novel has here been replaced by a sort of poetic counterpoint and reiteration, and sustained or connected, sequential action by thematic repetition or idea rhyme, is but one of the several convincing arguments for classifying this work as an antinovel. Such noncharacters as the *paredros*, as well as the noncommunication of the dialogues of Calac and Polanco, are additional cases in point. The handling of time is another, as it is neither linear nor connected, and usually rather vague as well, so that the reader wonders whether the "kit" of the title will prove upon assembly to be a working model with moving parts or more of a static jigsaw puzzle. The novel's concerns seem to be more with form, narrative theory, and literary double entendre than with such immediate, human, and accessible considerations as appear in *The Winners* and *Hopscotch*, points which probably explain its relative lack of popularity with the public, if not with critics.

An excellent example of the perils of writing committed fiction appears in *A Manual for Manuel*, a novel which is more a political pamphlet than a work of art. Cortázar's purpose in writing this piece was to denounce the systematic torture of political prisoners in Latin America, with the somewhat naïve hope that his protest might curb such inhumane behavior. During a visit to Buenos Aires in 1973, commemorating the publication of the book, he contributed the authorship rights to two Argentine organizations involved in working for the rights and release of such people, and to the families of political prisoners. On the formal level of the novel, there is nothing new: The structure repeats that of Cortázar's earlier works, with similar patterns and characters; the language is stereotyped, with frequent instances of Marxist rhetoric.

Andrés, the protagonist (much like Oliveira in *Hopscotch*), finds himself torn between two worlds, although in this case they are not so much geographical and cultural as ideological. Faced with choosing between bourgeois comforts and Marxist commitment, he is unable to decide which path to take (and thus falls short of achieving existential authenticity). In a fashion recalling the collage technique of *La vuelta al día en ochenta mundos*, the novel mixes truth with fiction, via the author's insertion of new articles detailing the horrors suffered by political prisoners within the fictional text, which likewise abounds in references to real-life guerrilla activities, societal taboos (especially homosexuality), and other sociological data.

Essentially, the plot concerns the activities of a group of revolutionaries in Paris who kidnap an important Latin American diplomat in order to obtain the release of political prisoners at home. The narration is handled from the perspective of two characters, one of them Andrés, with his indecisiveness about joining the group, and a member of the guerrillas, usually identified only as "you know who." At the same time, there is a metaliterary level, where the business of writing a novel is interwoven with the political plotting, an implied contrast between two approaches to novelistic construction: Should the novelist proceed from a preconceived, fully elaborated plot or should he follow the internal logic of the characters and situations rather than forcing them to conform to some prior plan? The two narrative perspectives of Andrés and "you know who" correspond to these approaches, for the guerrilla attempts to develop a logical progression which takes into account the characters and their circumstances, while taking notes on the plans and execution of the kidnaping. Andrés in effect assumes the position of the omniscient author-narrator who has a godlike overview, obtained in his case by reading the assault plans and thus coming to understand what is the plot of the novel. From his original posture of uncommittedness, Andrés moves to *engagement*, becoming an active participant in the events of Verrières as reflected in his later writing or rewriting of the novel (with the benefit of hindsight).

Mechanically, the plot hinges upon the smuggling into France of twenty thousand dollars in counterfeit bills by two Argentines who rendezvous with the guerrillas and exchange the money in various Paris banks. Although the diplomat is kidnaped, the group is apprehended by police and most of the guerrillas are deported, at which point Andrés becomes the novelist, compiling and ordering the notes taken by "you know who"—and thus (the reader is to believe) the novel is born. In addition to a somewhat tardy indication of the influence of Jean-Paul Sartre and the notion of politically committed literature, the novel exhibits a certain attenuated formal experimentation in the combination of the collage technique with the metaliterary motifs and dual narration. Whether the novel falls by reason of its ideological weight or because of insufficient integration between the revolutionary plot (straight out of the novel of espionage and intrigue) with the factual material on political torture is an open question, but the result is not: *A Manual for Manuel* is the least fortunate of Julio Cortázar's novels.

Major publications other than long fiction

SHORT FICTION: *Bestiario*, 1951; *Final de juego*, 1956 (*End of the Game and Other Stories*, 1963; also as *Blow-Up and Other Stories*, 1967); *Las armas secretas*, 1958; *Historias de cronopios y de famas*, 1962 (*Cronopios and Famas*, 1969); *Todos los fuegos el fuego*, 1966 (*All Fires the Fire*, 1973); *Octaedro*, 1974 (included in *A Change of Light and Other Stories*); *Alguien que anda por ahí*, 1977 (included in *A Change of Light and Other Stories*, 1980); *Un tal Lucas*, 1979 (*A Certain Lucas*, 1984); *Queremos tanto a Glenda y otros relatos*, 1981 (*We Love Glenda So Much and Other Tales*, 1983); *Deshoras*, 1983.

POETRY: *Presencia*, 1938 (as Julio Denís); *Los reyes*, 1949; *Pameos y meopas*, 1971.

NONFICTION: *Buenos Aires Buenos Aires*, 1968; *Viaje alrededor de una mesa*, 1970; *Prosa del observatorio*, 1972; *Fantomas contra los vampiros multinacionales: Una utopía realizable*, 1975; *Literatura en la revolución y revolución en la literatura*, 1976 (with Mario Vargas Llosa); *Los autonautas de la cosmopista*, 1983; *Nicaragua, tan violentamente dulce*, 1984.

TRANSLATIONS: *Robinson Crusoe*, 1945 (of Daniel Defoe's *Robinson Crusoe*); *El inmoralista*, 1947 (of André Gide's *L'Immoraliste*); *El hombre que sabía demasiado*, c. 1948-1951 (of G. K. Chesterton's *The Man Who Knew Too Much*); *Vida y Cartas de John Keats*, c. 1948-1951 (of Lord Houghton's *Life and Letters of John Keats*); *Filosofía de la risa y del llanto*, 1950 (of Alfred Stern's *Philosophie du rire et des pleurs*); *La filosofía de Sartre y el psicoanálisis existentialista*, 1951 (of Alfred Stern's *Sartre, His Philosophy and Psychoanalysis*).

MISCELLANEOUS: *La vuelta al día en ochenta mundos*, 1968; *Último round*, 1969.

Bibliography

Alazraki, Jaime, and Ivar Ivask, eds. *The Final Island: The Fiction of Julio Cortázar*, 1978.

Boldy, Steven. *The Novels of Julio Cortázar*, 1980.

Harss, Luis, and Barbara Dohmann. *Into the Main Stream*, 1966.

Picon Garfield, Evelyn. *Julio Cortázar*, 1975.

Genaro J. Pérez

DOBRICA ĆOSIĆ

Born: Velika Drenova, Yugoslavia; December 29, 1921

Principal long fiction

Daleko je sunce, 1951 (*Far Away Is the Sun*, 1963); *Koreni*, 1954; *Deobe*, 1961 (3 volumes); *Bajka*, 1966; *Vreme smrti*, 1972-1979 (4 volumes; volume 2 and synopsis of volume 1 as *A Time of Death*, 1978; volume 3 as *Reach to Eternity*, 1980; volume 4 as *South to Destiny*, 1981).

Other literary forms

Dobrica Ćosić is primarily a novelist. Aside from novels, he has written a series of articles on sociopolitical themes, collected in the books *Sedam dana u Budimpešti* (1957; seven days in Budapest) and *Akcija* (1965; action). These books gave Ćosić opportunities to express his views on various ideological, political, and cultural problems that have preoccupied him his entire adult life. They shed some light on his novels, but, for the most part, they reflect the other half of the author's sphere of interest.

Achievements

Throughout his literary career, Ćosić has been interested in the forces that have molded, influenced, and decided the fate of his countrymen. In particular, he has attempted to shed light on the effect of the two world wars on his country. Having been primarily politically oriented all of is life, it was natural for him to turn to historical and social themes once he discovered his artistic urge. He was one of the first postwar novelists in Yugoslavia to broach sensitive subject matter, not so much to describe it as to find the real moving forces behind the actors and their actions in these tragic events. From World War II, in which he participated directly, he moved back to World War I, searching for the links between them. By tracing the rise and fall of two families in almost all of his novels, he presents a powerful saga of the Serbian society passing from a primitive stage of the late nineteenth century into the modern era. A pronounced artistic prowess has added to his works a mark of excellence, making him one of the best contemporary Serbian writers.

Biography

Dobrica Ćosić was born on December 29, 1921, in a village in central Serbia, Velika Drenova. His parents were farmers, and he was destined to enroll in an agricultural school. There, he was exposed to illegal Socialist literature and was accepted in the Communist Youth League in 1938, for which he was expelled from school. In World War II, he participated actively on the side of the partisans as a political commissar. After the war, he occupied several official positions, among them the office of a parliamentary representative and a director of the venerable Srpska Književna Zadruga (Serbian literary society). He began to publish during the war, and with the publication of the first novel, *Far Away Is the Sun*, he quickly became one of the leading young Serbian writers. His fame grew with every new novel, but so did his dissatisfaction with political developments in his country. He began to call for more freedom, became a leading dissident, and as a result was stripped of all of his posts and duties. Thereafter, he worked as a free-lance writer, completing his *magnum opus*, *Vreme smrti* (a time of death), and leading the fight for greater democratic freedom in his country.

Analysis

Dobrica Ćosić's entry into literature was made easier by his rich experiences in the war. He came out of it as a proud young victor, full of hopes for a better future and ready for further sacrifices. This desire to help in building a better life for his fellowman undoubtedly spurred him to his first literary efforts. As he grew as a writer, however, another desire became even stronger—to seek the truth and to tell it in an artistic fashion, regardless of consequences.

Ćosić's first novel, *Far Away Is the Sun*, is more than another fictional account of war experiences. Although based on true events and largely auto-biographical, it is a skillfully written war novel, with fast-moving action, believable happenings, and well-developed characters. It had a refreshing effect after Ćosić experienced several abortive attempts at writing war fiction in the manner of Socialist Realism. Its refreshing quality is reflected in a much greater objectivity. To be sure, the partisan struggle is still glorified; the leading characters display, at times, the superhuman powers and the instinctive ability to separate right from wrong characteristic of Socialist Realist heroes; and the enemy is, for the most part, utterly evil. There is also, however, a willingness to admit that the heroes might sometimes be wrong after all. This attitude is best illustrated by an interesting possibility that all four parties involved in the climatic decision at the end of the novel, when the survival of the partisan unit is at stake, could be both right and wrong. By taking such an attitude, the author is showing his awareness of the complexity of situations in which the warring sides often found themselves. He also seems willing to admit that, even though the correctness of the partisan cause was never in doubt, individual actions and decisions were not always above reproach.

The novel's restrained tone and its traditional realistic manner, as well as its undeniable originality, despite some similarities to Aleksandr Fadeyev's *Razgrom* (1927; *The Nineteen*, 1929; also as *The Rout*, 1956) and Nikolay Ostrovsky's *Kak zakalyalas stal* (1935; *The Making of a Hero*, 1937; also as *How the Steel Was Tempered*, 1952), make it understandable why *Far Away Is the Sun* is enduringly popular in Yugoslavia—almost a classic. Ćosić would surpass himself in later novels, but this work will always remain one of those whose success defies an easy explanation, especially when it is considered in the light of what it has meant in the struggle against Socialist Realism.

With *Koreni* (roots), Ćosić began a series of novels that would, when completed, offer a large canvas of the development of Serbian society in this century. The time of *Koreni* actually goes back to the last decade of the nineteenth century. The main character, a strong-willed, rebellious, and stubborn peasant, Aćim Katić, is driven by an often expressed desire to see the creation of a just democratic society among the Serbian peasants, who had been ruled by primitive impulses for centuries. For that purpose, he sends his younger son to be educated in France. When his son refuses to return to his native village upon the completion of his studies and, what is worse, joins a political party opposing his father's, the true nature of Aćim Katić comes through. Deeply hurt by his son's betrayal, he manifests through his grief and anger a frustrated will to dominate everyone and everything around him, as well as a hidden fear of defeat by both men and fate. He marries his sterile older son to a strong peasant woman and arranges for an offspring with the help of an equally virile neighbor. At the end of the novel, the powerfully created characters and their destinies remain in limbo, to be taken up again in later novels. The roots are revealed, but the growth is yet to come.

This stark peasant tale is told in a highly lyric and experimental style, which fits the dark, Naturalistic atmosphere of the life of Serbian peasants at the turn of the century. The rather simple realism of Ćosić's first novel gives way to a poetic realism, revealing his preoccupation not only with social and political matters but also with a search for a truly artistic idiom—a search that will be repeated from novel to novel.

In his ambitious novel *Deobe* (divisions), Ćosić returns to World War II, taking up again many themes from *Far Away Is the Sun*: bravery under the most trying conditions; the struggle of a small nation against an overpowering enemy; peasants bearing the brunt of that struggle, reluctant to fight away from their homes; corruption of the existing order; and weakneses and sins of the enemies. The basic change lies in the point of view. In the former novel, the war struggle is seen from the vantage point of the partisans; in *Deobe*, the point of view shifts to the opposing side, the Chetniks, a nationalist force fighting both the Germans and the partisans. The Chetniks are not treated favorably at all; their point of view is used mainly to discredit them. In this sense, *Deobe* is much less objective than any other novel by Ćosić. The Chetniks are maligned, while the partisans, though barely visible in the distant background, show their moral superiority. Ćosić's subjectivity, however, can be explained by his desire, among other things, to understand why the Chetniks committed the despicable acts ascribed to them and whether they could have behaved differently. Why do human beings commit such bestial acts of horror (the knife, used most often in perpetrating these horrors, becomes here the symbol of bestiality)? Why is hatred so deep that it destroys reason? Can the descendants of those same people comprehend and believe many years later that such acts were, and even could be, committed by humans? Thus, the purpose of the author's efforts in this novel is not the objective, or even subjective, depiction of the civil war, but rather an attempt to penetrate the way of thinking of people responsible for war. Seen from this angle, *Deobe* attains a much more universal significance than perceived on first reading.

Not that Ćosić offers satisfactory answers. As the war drags on and the inhumanity of man to man intensifies to alarming porportions, he becomes more philosophical about it. He is convinced that war leads to utter demoralization, total chaos, and despair. Everybody feels compelled to fight everybody else, hatred permeates everything, all are killers. The eye-for-an-eye principle becomes dominant. Even though Ćosić attributes most of these aberrations to the enemies of the partisans, a realization grows in him that more is involved than the struggle for social, political, and ideological causes and changes for the better. On the one hand, war has moved inward, into the very hearts and souls of the participants. On the other, the signs of resignation and helplessness are increasingly visible, illustrated by statements such as, "It's war. . . . We are guilty because we are humans and because we are alive." There is even a hint that war is a total mystery, beyond one's ability to explain it.

Descendants of the characters from *Koreni* reappear, though in somewhat secondary roles. Ćosić again experiments with his style, mostly by using a movie technique of numerous quick shots, many flashbacks, scant description, frugal punctuation, and a choruslike, impersonal character, a kind of Everyman on his descent into Hell. The multiple voices of the chorus symbolize the universality of the tragedy portrayed in the novel. In this sense, *Deobe* is an important step toward the mature style of Ćosić's final works, especially *Vreme smrti*.

Bajka (the fairy tale) is more of an interlude than an organic step in Ćosić's development. His only novel not based fully on realistic events, it is nevertheless a repository of his ideas about the same problems depicted in his more realistic works. In a thinly veiled allegory about a mythical state, in the tradition of Yevgeny Zamyatin's *My* (1952, written 1920-1921; *We*, 1924), Aldous Huxley's *Brave New World* (1932), and George Orwell's *1984* (1949), the author attempts to visualize the future on the basis of the present developments. In this respect, *Bajka* is also an anti-utopian novel.

It is not easy to penetrate the allegorical and symbolic framework of this "fairy tale." Moreover, Ćosić's desire to modernize his expression—a process evident since *Koreni*—makes it more difficult to follow the already thin main thread. Action and plot, however, are not as important to the author as is his intention to examine in a semi-essayistic, pseudophilosophical fashion the underpinnings of the events depicted in his earlier works (as well as in his later ones, as it turned out). Ćosić's obsession with endless strife among human beings—above all, with war as its most drastic manifestation—is the moving force in this work. The result is a complex vision of man's endeavor to forge his own destiny, his successes and failures, and his belief, almost a fanatic faith, that the ideal of a better humanity can indeed be realized. At the end of the novel, man is still looking at a shimmering quartz stone lying on the river bottom. That, however, does not dampen his enthusiasm and faith, for he vows to continue his search for a better future. *Bajka* is, therefore, more a testimony to man's determination to achieve his goal of a perfect society than a criticism of the shortcomings of the present world. In this sense, the deeply humanistic views of the author attest his success in lifting his vision above the horizon of everyday concerns. The examples of Adolf Hitler and Joseph Stalin as equal partners in their efforts to dehumanize man, which Ćosić analyzes at length, serve him as warnings of what could happen if one abandons vigilance and hope.

In 1972, Ćosić began a series of volumes about the fate and struggle of the Serbian nation in World War I. As of 1984, four volumes have been published, and it is not yet clear whether the fifth—and final—volume will be written.

Next to *Far Away Is the Sun*, *Vreme smrti* is the most realistic of Ćosić's novels, adhering closely to the historical facts and chronological order of events enveloping the small state of Serbia in World War I: a short prewar scene, the outbreak of the war, initial defeats and ensuing military and moral victories, the crushing though not final defeat in 1915, the superhuman retreat through the snow-covered mountains, and the rescue of the survivors on the Albanian seashore. Yet it is not so much the subject matter, monumental though it may be, that lends the novel epic proportions. It is, rather, Ćosić's approach to the novel's theme, his flair for the dramatic and his skill in shaping characters, actions, and situations, and, above all, his understanding of the little man, who carries the heaviest burden in any war.

There is another aspect of this novel that outweighs all others and that has concerned Ćosić from his very first work: the phenomenon of war as man's most fateful mode of behavior and the author's philosophical attitude toward it. The fact that in the very title he implicitly links war with the only certain reality, death, shows how much he is obsessed with war. *Vreme smrti* offers a wide variety of opinions about war and what makes people wage war, not all of which can be attributed to the author. These opinions depend on the person expressing them. By tracing the opinions about and characterization of war in this novel, one can find a key to the most important concern of Ćosić as a writer.

For a long time, the notion of war in Ćosić's novels depended to a large degree on the social background and position of the person involved. The old peasant leader from *Koreni*, Aćim, expresses a conservative peasant view when he advises his grandson against deserting: "Go with people, son. One has no better road." His son Vukašin, a politician and opposition leader educated in France, has a much more sophisticated notion of war, as befits a highly educated intellectual, "War is the only time when we work for history and acquire respect through suffering and dying." For the crafty political leader of the country, war is a supreme test of statesmanship and of the stamina of the people. A high commanding officer expresses, perhaps not surprisingly, a loathing for war. He considers himself to be the greatest coward, yet it is he who continually insists that Serbia fights only for survival and, therefore, that right and justice are on its side. A young Socialist has his misgivings, believing that Serbia can be saved only through a revolution, yet even he fights on bravely, as does almost everyone else.

Other opinions on war, expressed at random as the situation dictates, indicate the degree to which the participants were forced to cope with this cataclysmic upheaval. For some, war is a great equalizer that unmasks everything and shames people more than it kills them, a terrible illness that will conquer all. As the disaster brings on more misery, suffering, and death, some people become more philosophical, seeing war as older and more eternal than man and as revealing essential truths about life; others, less stout-hearted, seem to falter under the weight of the calamity. Peasants and city dwellers, leaders and simple soldiers alike are disappointed in their allies and in civilization in general. They believe that small nations never win a war forever and that the deck is always stacked against them. Europe is for them a criminals' hunting ground and a thieves' bazaar where politics has a field day, removing all restraints and giving the right to all means, so that murderers kill murderers. All of these opinions can be summed up in the oft-repeated phrase, "War is hell!"

As the agony of the Serbian army and nation unfolds, most, if not all, of the characters come to an agreement about the calamity that has befallen them, as well as about the reasons for, and the meaning of, war. They tend to concur that war, cruel and unjust as it is, must be endured because the alternative is even worse. Death becomes unimportant as everyone's will to survive is put to the sternest test. This iron will is expressed through the commanding officer, General Mišić. Himself of peasant stock, unpretentious and down-to-earth, he repeats time and again the reason that Serbia must fight on and endure beyond the humanly possible: "Ours is a peasant army, defending its home and children. . . . When one fights for survival, he has the right to do anything. . . . Only the sacrifices made for one's survival are not in vain." Most people accept this simple reasoning and endure more than they believe they are capable of enduring. Even the young Socialist changes his thinking and accepts the date with destiny.

It is through General Mišić that Ćosić expresses his conclusions about war. If in *Far Away Is the Sun* he condones war primarily for the sake of an idea, and in *Deobe* he has no answer for the incomprehensible cruelty of man, in *Vreme smrti* he finds the justification for war, even if in one case only: in self-defense and in the struggle for survival. He has found a perfect example for such justification in the death struggle of his small nation against seemingly insurmountable odds. He does so not out of chauvinistic impulses but rather from the position that every man, through his nation, has the right and obligation to defend his dignity and liberty. It must be added that it is not so much the biological survival that Ćosić has in mind as it is the defense of a nation and society where liberty, justice, and human dignity prevail. He believes that in such a fateful struggle, man must display high moral qualities, for only then is life worth living, and only then does freedom become necessary. He believes that his nation values justice above freedom, that war is won and lost in the soul, and that the victor's bravery is not always the most important thing. Barbarism in the name of one's country and freedom is a sign of military despair.

In *Vreme smrti*, Ćosić found the answer to the question that had plagued him since he began writing, indeed since he began thinking. While people will probably never stop warring and committing atrocities and inflicting suffering, war acquires justification for those who defend themselves against annihilation—and then only if they fight for freedom and justice at the same time. This is the final and most significant message of *Vreme smrti* and of Ćosić's entire opus. Through it, Ćosić seems to have found peace with himself.

In addition to the epic theme and the problems Ćosić tackles and solves in his *magnum opus*, *Vreme smrti* shows the maturity of the author's style. His control over the plot and characters, his skillful description of war scenes without the glorification of heroic deeds or dwelling on gruesome aspects, and his modernistic blend of narration, dialogue, and documentary material—all contribute to a powerful impact on the reader. The logical fifth volume depicting the final triumph of Serbia in World War I would offer support for the claim that *Vreme smrti* is the best novel in Serbian literature. Even as it is, it could be favorably compared with Leo Tolstoy's *Voyna i mir* (1865-1869; *War and Peace*, 1886) and Mikhail Sholokhov's *Tikhii Don* (1928-1940; *The Silent Don*, 1942), their many differences notwithstanding.

Major publications other than long fiction
NONFICTION: *Sedam dana u Budimpešti*, 1957; *Akcija*, 1965.

Bibliography
Bandić, Miloš. *Dobrica Ćosić*, 1968.
Egerić, Miroslav. "Roman kao subjektivna epopeja," in *Delo*. XVIII (1972), pp. 951-967.
Gavrilović, Zoran. "*Vreme smrti:* Nadsmislovi istorije," in *Književna kritika*. VIII (1977), pp. 22-35.

Kadić, Ante. *Contemporary Serbian Literature*, 1964.

Leovac, Slavko. "Romani Dobrice Ćosića," in *Izraz*. IX (1965), pp. 229-241.

Lukić, Sveta. *Contemporary Yugoslav Literature*, 1972.

Palavestra, Predrag. *"Koreni* Dobrice Ćosića," in *Letopis Matice srpske.*
   CCCLXXV (1955), pp. 260-268.

Selenić, Slobodan. "Čovek traži djavola," in *Delo*. XIII (1967), pp. 281-299.

Vuletić, Vitomir. "O kompoziciji *Vremena smrti*," in *Letopis Matice srpske.*
   CDXX (1977), pp. 456-486.

Vasa D. Mihailovich

CYRANO DE BERGERAC

Born: Paris, France; March 6, 1619
Died: Paris, France; July 28, 1655

Principal long fiction

L'Autre Monde: Ou, Les États et empires de la lune et du soleil, 1656-1662 (*Comical History of the States and Empires of the World of the Moon and Sun*, 1687; also as *Other Worlds: The Comical History of the States and Empires of the Moon and the Sun*, 1965; includes *Histoire comique des états et empires de la lune*, 1656 [*Comical History of the States and Empires of the Moon*; also as *The Government of the World in the Moon*, 1659]; *Histoire comique des états et empires du soleil*, 1662 [*Comical History of the States and Empires of the Sun*]).

Other literary forms

In the course of his brief and turbulent life, Cyrano de Bergerac tried his hand at a whole array of genres and acquitted himself honorably in all of them. His tragedy, *La Mort d'Agrippine* (1653), compares favorably with the lesser works of Pierre Corneille. Cyrano's comedy, *Le Pédant joué* (1654; the pedant outwitted), though never staged in his lifetime, was almost certainly the unacknowledged source of two highly effective scenes in Molière's *Les Fourberies de Scapin* (1671; *The Rogueries of Scapin*, 1910). *Le Pédant joué* is essentially a burlesque of the pedantry and *préciosité* that were rife in Cyrano's day—though Cyrano himself could tap a "precious" vein when he chose. The same gift for burlesque is evident in his satiric poem, or *mazarinade* (attack on Cardinal Mazarin), of 1649, "Le Ministre d'état flambé" ("The Minister of State Goes Up in Flames"), and in the best of his letters. The latter were not genuine correspondence but showpieces designed for publication. They are of several kinds: love letters full of exaggerated compliments and reproaches, set off by farfetched figures of speech in the worst *précieux* style; elaborate and fanciful descriptions of nature; satiric attacks on real and imagined enemies; and polemic pieces on a variety of political and philosophical issues. The letters "For the Sorcerers" and "Against the Sorcerers" are especially noteworthy for satiric power and cogency of argument; they also anticipate the attacks on superstition and intolerance in *Other Worlds*, Cyrano's most important work.

Achievements

It is a great irony of literary history that Cyrano, a minor but talented and aggressively ambitious seventeenth century writer, has at last achieved world renown in the twentieth century—as a fictional character who scarcely resembles his original. To be fair to Edmond Rostand (the playwright whose *Cyrano de Bergerac*, staged in 1897, spread Cyrano's fame), the unexpurgated manuscripts that were to reveal the full extent of his hero's boldness and malice were as yet unpublished when he wrote; yet it took a deal of willful misreading—and, of course, imaginative reworking—to make a noble Platonic lover of the dissolute and misanthropic Cyrano. Whatever his failures as a man, the real Cyrano deserves to be remembered as a competent literary craftsman and an inspired satirist. There is no denying that his avowed libertinism had its sordid side, but its essence was simply "freethinking," a rejection of the Church's exclusive claim to truth and an espousal of the cause of scientific investigation. In his best works, the two volumes of *Other Worlds* and the letters for and against sorcerers, he anticipates the form and some of the major themes of Voltaire's *contes philosophiques* (philosophical tales— a distinct genre). Indeed, Voltaire's *Le Micromégas* (1752; *Micromegas*, 1753), as well as Jonathan Swift's *Gulliver's Travels* (1726), owe a debt of inspiration to Cyrano. Perhaps his greatest single achievement was his astonishing vision of cultural pluralism and toleration in an age clouded by superstition and repression.

Biography

For serious readers of his works, the facts of Cyrano's life are an important corrective to his legend. Though his family laid claim to noble status, the only basis for that claim was their ownership of two "fiefs," or manorial properties—Mauvières and Bergerac—in the valley of the Chevreuse near Paris. The Cyranos were in fact of bourgeois origin; their son was christened Savinien de Cyrano, and he himself added the title "de Bergerac" as a young man (as he occasionally assumed the pretentious given names of Alexandre or Hercule). This was deceptive on two counts, for besides smacking of nobility, the title suggested a Gascon origin. Thus, Rostand portrays his hero as born and bred in Gascony, which the real Cyrano never visited. He was born in Paris and christened there on March 6, 1619. Some of his childhood was spent on his father's properties in the Chevreuse valley, where he acquired a love of nature and a hatred of dogmatic authority. The hatred was inspired by a country priest to whom Cyrano was sent for schooling; it was to grow into a lifelong passion, reinforced by his experiences at the Collège de Beauvais in Paris, where he completed his education. (The headmaster of the Collège, Jean Grangier—a man of considerable scholarly reputation—is mercilessly satirized in Cyrano's comedy, *Le Pédant joué*, while the country priest is pilloried in *Comical History of the States and Empires of the Sun*.) Once out of school, Cyrano gave free rein to his rebellious streak and joined the circles of *libertins*, or "freethinkers"—and free livers—who frequented certain Paris cabarets. Among his "libertine" friends were several pupils of the materialist philosopher Pierre Gassendi, including the avowed atheist Claude-Emmanuel Chapelle and possibly the young Molière. Whether he studied with Gassendi himself, Cyrano was heavily influenced by his ideas, which are discussed at length in *Other Worlds*.

At about this time, Cyrano's father suffered serious financial reverses and was forced to sell his fiefs; it has been suggested that Cyrano's gambling losses may have been a factor. Whatever the reasons, relations between father and son were strained, and they continued to be so until the father's death; according to records left by his lawyers, Abel de Cyrano suspected his two sons of robbing him as he lay on his deathbed. It is worth noting as well that Cyrano includes a bitter tirade against fathers in *Other Worlds* and depicts the sons of the moon people as exercising authority over their old fathers.

His financial straits, as well as the desire to make a name for himself, inspired Cyrano to seek a commission in the Guards, a company made up almost entirely of Gascons, whose reputation for bravado was apparently well deserved. One element of the Cyrano legend that seems to bear up under inspection is his reputation for bravery in the duels for which the Guards were notorious. After being wounded in two battles, however (at the sieges of Mouzon and Arras), he gave up the military life in disgust and turned to a literary career. Frédéric Lachèvre, who produced the first accurate biography of Cyrano in 1920, has suggested that the serious illness from which Cyrano suffered during this period also influenced his decision by forcing him to withdraw from other spheres of activity. The exact nature of the disease is unknown, but several biographers have accepted Lachèvre's suggestion that it may have been syphilis. Illness and poverty combined to reinforce the misanthropic strain in Cyrano's character; during this period, he broke with and reviled many of his former friends. An opponent of Cardinal Mazarin at the outbreak of the Fronde in 1649, he changed sides—possibly for pay—and wrote a scathing letter, *Contre les Frondeurs* (1651; against the Frondeurs). Jacques Prévot, editor of Cyrano's complete works, has suggested that one of the most violent of these ruptures may have had an erotic dimension: Charles d'Assoucy, a satiric poet, was known to be homosexual, and Cyrano seems to have shown little interest in the opposite sex.

Unfortunately, Cyrano enjoyed no greater success as a writer during his lifetime than he did as a soldier. In an age of censorship, he was too bold for most publishers, and he succeeded in publishing his plays and some letters only after accepting the patronage of the Duke of Arpajon, a man of limited intelligence who wished to make a name for himself as a patron of the arts. With his support, Cyrano staged his tragedy, *La Mort d'Agrippine*, but it was closed after a few performances by a claque hired to boo his "atheistic" stance (the hirelings, ironically, missed the more daring speeches and booed at a line they simply misunderstood). Shortly thereafter, Cyrano was hit on the head by a log dropped by one of the Duke's servants. It seems at least as likely that this was an accident as that someone hired the servant to ambush Cyrano (for fear of facing him in a fair fight, as Rostand would have it): By this time, Cyrano's dueling days were behind him. The incident precipitated a rupture with the Duke, however, and forced Cyrano to take to his bed. Fourteen months later, on July 28, 1655, he died at the age of thirty-six. Lachèvre suggests that the primary cause of death was tertiary syphilis, but a lack of definite evidence has left this surmise in doubt. Cyrano is said to have returned to the faith on his deathbed at the urging of his relative, Mother Marguerite of Jesus, and his oldest friend, Henry Le Bret. Le Bret became Cyrano's literary executor and published a heavily expurgated version of *Other Worlds* in 1657, two years after Cyrano's death.

Analysis

Erica Harth, in *Cyrano de Bergerac and the Polemics of Modernity*, claims Cyrano de Bergerac to have been "the first of the Moderns," forerunner of a position more clearly formulated later in the seventeenth century in the great "Quarrel of the Ancients and Moderns." Cyrano went beyond his contemporaries the *libertins*, Harth argues, by refusing to settle for a critique of received wisdom; the "destructive spirit" in which he attacks tradition and Church authority "is accompanied by a positive acceptance and propagation of the same scientific and philosophical ideas which, although not directly transmitted by Cyrano, were to have a profound impact on the minds of the eighteenth-century *philosophes*." Yet Cyrano was also undeniably a man of his own time, attracted to as well as repulsed by the excesses of *préciosité*, charmed as well as amused by the arcane theories of thinkers such as Tommaso Campanella, in which allegory and myth are still intertwined with rationalistic investigation. If we can trust the priest's report, Cyrano even returned to the faith in time to die "a good Christian death," and as one critic has shown, it is impossible to deduce a consistent atheistic view even from the unexpurgated manuscripts of *Other Worlds*. However one looks at Cyrano's masterpiece, contradictions emerge. Before examining these contradictions in detail, a brief description of the work is in order.

Although *Comical History of the States and Empires of the Sun* was first published separately from *Comical History of the States and Empires of the Moon*, it seems clear that this division does not reflect any intention of the author; the two works relate voyages of similar scope by a single narrator, and the second of these voyages is said to be motivated by persecution arising from a published account of the first. Combined, the voyages form a continuous narrative—as do, for example, the two parts of Miguel de Cervantes' *Don Quixote de la Mancha* (1605, 1615)—and may be referred to without distortion by the collective title *Other Worlds*. (The French title, literally translated, is "The Other World," a phrase that in French as well as English usually refers to the abode of souls after death; Cyrano probably meant it to be taken ironically, for his aim is to suggest that there are "other worlds" in the here and now as well.) This was Cyrano's only work of prose fiction, but it proved to be the most effective vehicle for his fractious talents and "libertine" perspective. Because of its subject, it has often been classified as a work of utopian fiction, but the genre to which it really belongs is that of the *conte philosophique*, or philosophical tale, as practiced preeminently by Voltaire one hundred years later.

The essence of the *conte philosophique* is its unique combination of satiric, even farcical, elements with serious philosophical or ideological ones. Consistency or fullness of characterization and cogency of plot tend to be sacrificed to the primary goals of ridiculing an opposing (usually dogmatic) intellectual position and of suggesting more enlightened alternatives. Because of the variety of scientific and philosophical positions, many of them incompatible, that are detailed by different characters of *Other Worlds*, it has been maintained that Cyrano—admittedly a dilettante rather than a true scholar—was himself confused about the ideas he wished to advance. While the confusion may be real, Jacques Prévot, in *Cyrano de Bergerac, romancier*, has argued forcefully for a subtler reading that qualifies the didactic intent of the work. Insofar as Cyrano has a "message," Prévot suggests, it is one of radical skepticism; Cyrano considers all doctrines, however scientific, inherently suspect, and having rid himself of one set is not at all eager to embrace another. In addition to fitting Le Bret's description of his old friend's beliefs, this analysis would tally with Cyrano's own warnings, in the second chapter of his fragmentary treatise on physics (never completed but published in Prévot's edition of *Oeuvres complètes*) against taking one's hypotheses for realities. There is, moreover, an anarchic streak in *Other Worlds*, corresponding to its satiric intent; in that respect, Cyrano is a worthy heir of Aristophanes, Lucian, and François Rabelais, from whom he may have borrowed specific motifs but whose satiric vein he made his own.

The narrator of *Other Worlds*, who speaks in the first person, is not named until the opening pages of the second volume; he is there called Drycona, an obvious anagram of Cyrano. On the strength of his anagrammatic name, many critics have assumed that the narrator speaks for the author. While at times it is hard to deny that he does, his own position fluctuates from scene to scene, enabling him to serve as a foil for a variety of interlocutors. Thus, in conversation with an avowed atheist, he defends the faith, while in conversation with an Old Testament prophet, he blasphemes. Nor is he always in opposition: He listens deferentially to speakers of the most disparate opinions. It seems best to admit, with Prévot, that Drycona is primarily a fictional creation—as are the other "real" characters who appear, such as Campanella and René Descartes.

The narrator's first voyage is inspired by a moonlit walk with friends, who try to outdo one another in *précieux* descriptions of the full moon (an attic window on heaven, the sign outside Bacchus' tavern). His friends ridicule the narrator for suggesting that the moon may be "a world like this one, for which our world serves as a moon." On reaching home, however, the narrator finds that a book has mysteriously appeared on his desk and is lying open at the page where the author (Jerome Cardan, a sixteenth century mathematician and astrologer) describes a visit from two men who said they lived in the moon. The narrator, determined to verify his hunch, contrives a first mode of space travel: He covers himself with small flasks of dew, which the sun draws upward. He rises so quickly toward the sun, however, that he is obliged to break most of the flasks, and falls back to the earth—in Canada, at that time New France. There he is entertained by the Viceroy, with whom he discusses his belief that the earth travels around the sun (still a heretical proposition in 1648); his own displacement from France to Canada is of course evidence that the earth rotates. In a second attempt to reach the moon, he builds a flying machine, which at first crashes; while he is tending his bruises, the colonial troops outfit the machine with fireworks, transforming it into a multistage rocket. The narrator manages to jump in before it takes off and, when the last stage falls to earth, finds himself still being drawn to the moon by the beef marrow he had rubbed on his bruises. (It was a popular superstition that the waning moon "sucked up" animal marrow.) As luck would have it, he falls in the Earthly Paradise and strikes against an apple from the Tree of Life, whose juice revivifies and rejuvenates him. The prophet Elias, one of two inhabitants of the Earthly Paradise (the other is Enoch), tells him its history, but the narrator cannot resist the impulse to tell a blasphemous joke, and he is cast out of Paradise.

The rest of the moon is inhabited by a race of giants who resemble human beings but move about on all fours; indeed, they take the narrator for an animal because he walks on two feet, and they exhibit him as a kind of sideshow (an idea borrowed by Swift). He is befriended by a spirit whose native land is the sun but who has visited the earth in various ages and was once the Genius or monitory Voice of Socrates; the spirit speaks Greek with the narrator and arranges to have him brought to the royal court. There he is taken for a female of the same species as a Spaniard who has arrived before him (the Spaniard, Gonsales, was the hero of Francis Godwin's 1638 book, *The Man in the Moon: Or, A Discourse of a Voyage Thither by Domingo Gonsales, the Speedy Messenger*). In the hope of producing more "animals" of their species, the moon people have them share a bed, where they have long talks on various scientific problems. As the narrator learns the moon language (which is of two kinds, musical notes for the upper classes and physical gestures for the lower), a controversy arises over his status: Is he a man or an animal? The moon priests consider it "a shocking impiety" to call such a "monster" a man, so he is interrogated before the Estates General. He tries to defend the principles of Aristotle's philosophy but is unanimously declared an animal when he refuses—as he was taught in school—to debate the principles themselves. A second trial, occasioned by his claim that "the moon"—that is, our earth—"is a world," leads to acknowledgment of his human status, but he is forced to recant the "heresy" of the claim itself. For the remainder of his stay, he is the guest of a moon family in which—according to custom—the son has authority over the father. In a series of conversations, the young man explains his radical materialist views of the universe; he is defending his atheism when a devil appears to snatch him away. The narrator, who tries to help his host, is thus transported back to earth (presumably because Hell is at its center). Thus ends the first volume.

The second volume opens with a clear reference to the first. Urged by a friend who shares his philosophical and scientific interests, the narrator—hereafter known as Drycona—writes an account of his moon voyage. He becomes a local celebrity but is accused of witchcraft by a malevolent country priest, who exploits the people's ignorance and persuades them to arrest the "sorcerer." Drycona escapes from prison by building a new flying machine—this one using the principle of the vacuum—in which he takes off for the sun. Once again, the machine can get him only part of the way there; it is the force of his desire, drawing him to the sun as source of life, that enables him to complete the voyage (which takes twenty-two months). The sun is divided into many regions of differing "opacity" (suggested by the then-recent discovery of sunspots); there is a rough correspondence between the intensity of light and the "enlightenment" of the inhabitants. One race—that of "spirits," such as the Genius of Socrates—can alter their outward forms as their imagination dictates.

The race of birds, who prevent abuses of power by choosing as king one of their weakest members (a dove), capture Drycona and put him on trial, as had the moon people; this time, however, the charge is simply "being a man"—belonging to a pernicious and destructive species. On the advice of a friendly bird, Drycona claims to be a monkey raised by humans, but he is convicted; he is on the point of being devoured by insects (included among the birds) when a parrot whom he had once freed on earth testifies on his behalf and obtains a pardon for him. After an encounter with a forest of talking trees, who try to convince him of their moral superiority, Drycona witnesses a battle between a Fire-Beast and an Ice-Animal (the latter is defending the trees). The battle is also observed by the philosopher Campanella (author of *La città del sole*, 1602; *The City of the Sun*, 1880), who becomes Drycona's guide. Together, they visit the Lake of Sleep and the Streams of the Five Senses, which empty into the Rivers of Memory, Imagination, and Judgment. A couple from the Province of Lovers, on their way to the Province of Philosophers (where the soul of Socrates is to settle a dispute between them), give the two travelers a lift in a basket suspended from a giant bird. Campanella is returning to his province to greet the soul of Descartes, newly arrived (he died in 1650). The narrative of the second volume ends, unfortunately, at the moment that Drycona and Campanella meet Descartes; Cyrano's ill health during the last year of his life prevented him from finishing the manuscript.

A brief résumé can give only the faintest idea of the inventiveness and satiric verve of *Other Worlds*. Cyrano takes every opportunity to make minor but telling—and often cutting—observations on various aspects of the human condition. The chief defect of his masterpiece, lack of unity, is merely the excess of a virtue: the acknowledgment that there are more things in heaven and on earth than are dreamed of in any one human philosophy. Quick of wit and eye, Cyrano was ever ready to bolt off in new directions. This quality gives his narrative a certain inclusiveness and makes it consistently enter-taining, despite long stretches of philosophical argument. It also, however, gives the work a chaotic quality, which seems to reflect both the temperament of the author and the intellectual ferment of his day. (This feature of *Other Worlds* has been aptly contrasted with the unity, in tone and perspective, of Swift's *Gulliver's Travels*, 1726). Perhaps the only way to do justice to the many dimensions of *Other Worlds* is to isolate some of the most important ones and assess them individually. They are, in ascending order of importance, *préciosité*, utopianism, didacticism or popularization, and satire.

Cyrano's use of *préciosité* reveals a deep-seated ambivalence symptomatic of his relationship to his own age. The *préciosité*, or cultivation of extrava-gantly refined language, that flourished in seventeenth century France grew out of the court mentality fostered by centralization of the monarchy; the salons, where *préciosité* emerged, were miniature "courts" on the model of the royal one and could be stepping-stones to power for those who learned the "art of pleasing." The earliest of Cyrano's letters seem to have been undertaken as exercises in this courtly form of entertainment. That he longed for fame, and for public acceptance of his work, is clear, but it is equally clear that his wit was too sharp for his own good and that, instead of ingratiating, it often alienated his audience. This tendency was not altogether involuntary. Cyrano was rebellious by nature and could not resist the shock value of a daring bon mot; he was also too intelligent not to see how easily *préciosité* could be turned to ridicule. Yet he had a truly lyric imagination, which lent itself to *précieux* elaboration, as in some descriptive passages of *Other Worlds*. The landscape of the Five Senses recalls Mademoiselle de Scudéry, the *pré-cieuse par excellence*, and it is hard to deny the passage its charm, despite a hint of affectation. At his best, Cyrano manages to walk the fine line between *préciosité* and burlesque. He can indulge in witty definitions of the moon, ascribing them to Drycona's friends, and then allow his hero to deflate them by remarking that they serve only to "tickle the time, to make it go faster." Like Aristophanes, who made his characters trot out old jokes while affecting disdain for them, Cyrano usually manages to have it both ways.

In addition to its occasional *préciosité*, *Other Worlds* also contains a utopian vein, though it scarcely belongs to the utopian genre. This vein is chiefly visible in Cyrano's treatment of machines and practical inventions. The most prominent are, of course, the flying machines, which, though fanciful (and less than fully effective), are all posited on genuine physical principles—the vacuum, magnetism, evaporation. It was doubtless the sheer fluidity and daring of his imagination that enabled Cyrano to anticipate other inventions of whose physical bases he was wholly ignorant; most striking of these inventions is the "talking book," or phonograph. There are also some radical social and political innovations in Cyrano's vision of the "other worlds" his protagonist visits: Battles on the moon can be fought only between armies of perfectly equal numbers, while the most important "battles" are debates between the scholars and wits of the two sides; in the realm of birds, the king is seen as the servant, not the master, of his people. Some of these innovations are transparent wish fulfillments to one familiar with Cyrano's life; the most pointed is the role inversion of fathers and sons, but there are humorous ones as well, such as the use of poetry for money (with value based on quality, not quantity) and the recognition, among the moon people, that a large nose is the infallible sign of a noble and witty nature.

Despite such pleasant surprises, however, Drycona encounters no ideal society: The moon people have their bigoted priests and heresy trials; the sun people, their disputes and unequal "enlightenment." The realm of the birds, which comes closest to a model state, also has the Draconian stamp that makes many utopias (Plato's Republic, Swift's land of the Houyhnhnms) so unpalatable, and Cyrano acknowledges that—as did Swift, perhaps in emulation of Cyrano—human beings may not live there. Despite a certain escapist impulse, then, the book is never more than guardedly optimistic about the realization of ideals. It may be significant that the closest thing to an ideal state of affairs in *Other Worlds* is set in our world: This is Drycona's brief but happy stay with his friends Colignac and Cussan. In a passage reminiscent of Rabelais' Abbey of Thélème (*Gargantua*, 1534; chapter 53), he describes the material comfort and intellectual stimulation of their life together: "The innocent pleasures of which the body is capable were only the lesser share. Of all those the mind can derive from study and conversation, we lacked none; and our libraries, united like our minds, summoned all the learned into our company." The idyll is soon threatened, and then shattered, by the malice of a priest and the ignorance of the peasants, but it offers a glimpse of the conditions Cyrano considered most likely to foster human happiness.

The prominence of learning in this vision raises the question of whether Cyrano had a didactic or pedagogical aim in writing *Other Worlds*. It has been claimed that he was essentially a popularizer, concerned to present the new scientific theories of his contemporaries in a form accessible to the common man. As with the utopian view, there is clearly some warrant for this interpretation; again, however, it seems less than adequate to account for the work as a whole. Drycona's abortive first flight, which lands him in Canada, is surely designed as a concrete illustration of the Copernican theory; it is appropriately followed by a discussion of the theory, and of various objections to it, in the conversation between Drycona and the Viceroy. The sheer amount of space devoted to similar conversations throughout the book is an indication of their importance to Cyrano. At times, as in Drycona's long exchange with the young atheist on the moon, the plot is allowed to atrophy entirely: The focus of interest is on the ideas discussed and on the arguments for or against them. Yet Prévot has done well to point out that in each such discussion personalities are involved; there is no omniscient narrator and no completely reliable speaker. Moreover, the universe of the book is hardly constrained by any one of the theories it sets forth, and it sometimes operates according to superstitious or supernatural beliefs: A devil can carry a man off for impiety, and the waning moon can "suck" the beef marrow Drycona uses as a salve. It seems particularly striking that on *both* of Drycona's outward voyages, the "scientific" method gets him only halfway there at most; the beef marrow gets him to the moon, while the "strength of his desire" for the source of all life draws him to the sun. The fictional data thus undercut not only specific scientific accounts but also any thoroughgoing rationalistic perspective.

This is not to suggest that the author has no clear-cut attitudes to convey: He does indeed, but his medium is satire rather than exposition. Drycona's motive in leaving the earth may be to explore the heavens, but Cyrano's purpose is to find a radically different perspective from which to observe our world. The heliocentric theory espoused by the Church is symptomatic of human vanity, which insists that the universe was made for man and continues, literally and figuratively, to revolve around him. Cyrano's protagonist finds himself in a position from which he is forced to reexamine virtually all of his assumptions—scientific, philosophical, religious, and social. Indeed, he is twice put on trial, not as an individual but as a representative of the human species. Yet each of the extraterrestrial societies he visits displays some of the defects of human societies, so that the lesson is one of cultural relativism, and the necessity for tolerance is made obvious, as in Voltaire's *contes philosophiques*, by the mistreatment of the sympathetic protagonist. The satire of religious abuses is particularly prominent, as befitted an age in which the Church was the chief opponent of free speech and investigation. Yet, as Prévot has shown, Cyrano's quarrel is not with God so much as with his "vicars," who abuse their moral authority to indulge their own base motives.

It remains to be said that the satiric effectiveness of *Other Worlds* is fueled by a keen sense of the comic. Cyrano's attitude toward his fellowmen was a complex one, compounded of anger, amusement, occasional admiration, and occasional hatred. It is the amusement, however, that tends to predominate. In this respect, Cyrano resembles his compatriots Rabelais and Voltaire (the first of whom he read, and the second of whom read him) more than he resembles his great English emulator, Swift. Between philosophical debates, he finds time to tell how the moon people make sundials of their teeth by pointing their noses toward the sun; how a hypervegetarian abstains even from vegetables that have not died a natural death; how a man from the Province of Lovers is forbidden to use hyperbole on pain of death after nearly persuading a young woman to use her own heart as a boat—because it is so "light" (fickle) and can hold so many. As well as an eloquent plea for tolerance and freedom of thought, *Other Worlds* is a consistently entertaining book, whose author clearly deserves to be remembered as an original writer of fiction, not merely as a character in a play by Edmond Rostand.

Major publications other than long fiction

PLAYS: *La Mort d'Agrippine*, 1653; *Le Pédant joué*, 1654.

NONFICTION: *Contre les Frondeurs*, 1651; *Lettres*, 1653 (*Satyrical Characters and Handsome Descriptions in Letters*, 1658).

MISCELLANEOUS: *Cyrano de Bergerac: Oeuvres complètes*, 1977 (Jacques Prévot, editor).

Bibliography

Harth, Erica. *Cyrano de Bergerac and the Polemics of Modernity*, 1970.

Lachèvre, Frédéric. "Notice biographique," in *Les Oeuvres libertines de Cyrano de Bergerac*, 1920.

Lanius, E. W. *Cyrano de Bergerac and the Universe of the Imagination*, 1967.

Prévot, Jacques. *Cyrano de Bergerac, romancier*, 1977.

Pujos, Charles. *Le Double Visage de Cyrano de Bergerac*, 1951.

Lillian Doherty

GABRIELE D'ANNUNZIO

Born: Pescara, Italy; March 12, 1863
Died: Gardone, Italy; March 1, 1938

Principal long fiction

Il piacere, 1889 (*The Child of Pleasure*, 1898); *Giovanni Episcopo*, 1892 (*Episcopo and Company*, 1896); *L'innocente*, 1892 (*The Intruder*, 1898); *Il trionfo della morte*, 1894 (*The Triumph of Death*, 1896); *Le vergini della rocce*, 1896 (*The Maidens of the Rocks*, 1898); *Il fuoco*, 1900 (*The Flame of Life*, 1900); *Forse che si forse che no*, 1910; *La Leda senza cigno*, 1916.

Other literary forms

Gabriele D'Annunzio's literary production encompasses many other genres: short stories, poetry, autobiographical essays, political writings, and several plays, both in Italian and French. It would appear difficult as well as arbitrary, however, to draw a sharp distinction between D'Annunzio's fiction and his memoirs, for his works in both forms are eminently autobiographical. The only possible differentiation between the two genres depends on the mere change from first-person to third-person narration. Moreover, D'Annunzio's fiction and nonfiction follow a pattern of parallel development that escapes chronological schematization. Finally, to exclude memoirs would present only a partial vision of the author's work, thereby greatly reducing the understanding and appreciation of his achievements in this field.

G. Barberi Squarotti, in his book, *Invito alla lettura di D'Annunzio* (1982), affirms that D'Annunzio's work should be taken in its totality, openly opposing traditional literary criticism, which has constantly chosen an anthological approach, favoring one aspect or another of his work. This constant search for a formula that could define D'Annunzio to the exclusion of relevant parts of his work, besides being substantially reductive, has given quite unsatisfactory results. The various labels of "decadent," "nocturnal," or "sensual" ignore the essence of his writing, which consists in the very plurality of its aspects, reflecting the motifs, themes, and poetics of fifty years of European intellectual life.

When D'Annunzio wrote his first book in prose, the dominant personality in Italian narrative was Giovanni Verga, a powerful writer whose main contributions consisted of a collection of short stories and two novels, *I Malavoglia* (1881; *The House by the Medlar Tree*, 1964) and *Mastro-don Gesualdo* (1889; English translation, 1923). These works, in their style and themes, represent a clear departure from academic prose of the day. Verga derived his inspiration from the humble life of Sicilian people and created a personal language, harsh and concise, to express these realities. The new generation was deeply influenced by the innovative impact of his writing and recognized in Verga the leader of a new literary trend, the Italian *Verismo*, which, in spite of some substantial distinctions, can be equated with French Naturalism.

D'Annunzio's first work in prose, *Terra vergine*, a collection of short stories, was published in 1882. Other collections followed, and finally all the short stories were included in two revised editions of *Terra vergine* (1884, 1902) and *Le novelle della Pescara* (1892, 1902; *Tales from My Native Town*, 1920). These writings, inspired by the folklore of the Abruzzi region, are clearly influenced by Verga's narrative models, but some basic innovations are already present. Beyond the *tranche de vie* (slice of life), photographically faithful to a somber and modest reality, D'Annunzio pursues the extraordinary and the exceptional. The sober representation of basic human passions is replaced by the analysis of morbid sensations, the description of natural landscapes is heightened by feelings of panic participation, and the language becomes particularly expressive in its tones of exasperated chromatism. From the beginning, it was evident that D'Annunzio was taking new steps beyond the boundaries of Naturalism toward "decadentistic" excesses.

Achievements

During his lifetime, D'Annunzio, surrounded by the admiration of his contemporaries, met extraordinary success; his writings deeply affected Italian society, and most of his literary works were awaited and welcomed by an enthusiastic public.

This favorable reception was followed by a period of neglect and even of open rejection. The negative judgment that fell on D'Annunzio's works should be ascribed mainly to the sharp change of perspective that characterized the 1920's intellectual debate in Italy and elsewhere in Europe. Politically, D'Annunzio's ideas, after being superficially assimilated into the Fascist ideology, were harshly condemned; morally, his anticonformist life-style was stigmatized as decadent; aesthetically, his language, rich in lexical novelties and classical allusions, was rejected as a futile exercise in rhetoric. Today's most authoritative critics recognize D'Annunzio as the fecund interpreter of several generations of European intellectual life, whose greatest achievement remains the renewal of Italian culture.

Prior to the advent of D'Annunzio, the young Italian nation, absorbed in its political and economic struggle, was still dominated by provincial interests and the literary traditions of the past. D'Annunzio, a prodigious reader extremely receptive to the stimuli coming from abroad, renovated the literary scene, introducing new techniques and developing new themes.

D'Annunzio's vast work in prose, which registers the influence of the major European writers and follows the suggestions of the various literary movements, shows a steady evolution toward a greater freedom and richness of expression. Moving beyond the boundaries of Naturalism, through a segmented process of experimentation and assimilation, D'Annunzio reached his expressive measure in the memoirs which are now considered his highest achievement in prose.

Biography

Gabriele D'Annunzio's tumultuous life elicited great fascination from his contemporaries and nourished the works of his biographers with a number of romantic anecdotes. D'Annunzio himself orchestrated and publicized his "inimitable life," paying careful attention to the preservation of his legend. His correspondence (more than ten thousand letters) also maintained and renewed, with countless details, the interest in his life.

This romantic aspect of D'Annunzio's biography appears today outdated and even laughable; nevertheless, beyond the ostentatious façade there are elements of durable truth that bring into proper perspective the man and his work. D'Annunzio's thirst for new experiences corresponds in fact to his indefatigable search for new literary solutions, and his existential adventures represent the prime source of his inspiration.

D'Annunzio was born in Pescara, a small and, at that time, somnolent little city on the coast of the Abruzzi region. His family belonged to the middle class and was wealthy enough to provide him with an excellent education. Apart from a deep affection for his mother, young Gabriele did not feel a great respect for his father, nor did he show a particular attachment for his relatives. It was not the family, but rather the Abruzzi region, with its primitive society dominated by ancestral laws, that influenced him deeply. The landscape, people, and folklore of his native land were to be a recurrent motif in D'Annunzio's works.

D'Annunzio soon left his hometown for Prato, in Tuscany, where at the renowned Liceo Cicognini he received a solid preparation in the humanities. A brilliant student and a daring young rebel, D'Annunzio excelled in all his classes, protested against the strict discipline, and led his classmates in knavish escapades. Later, the recollection of these years would give substance to some beautiful pages of his memoir prose. D'Annunzio's years in Prato culminated in 1879 with the publication of a collection of verses, *Primo vere* (early spring), which was very well received by the critics.

This first success opened the way to a brilliant literary career. In 1881, D'Annunzio was in Rome with the intention of pursuing his studies at the university, but soon he abandoned academia to embrace the elegant and worldly life of the capital. Brilliant contributor to journals and magazines, cherished guest of aristocratic and literary circles, D'Annunzio succeeded in combining an effervescent social life with unrelenting literary activity. After a romantic elopement, his marriage in 1883 to Maria Hardouin, Duchess of Gallese, crowned the success of his social ambitions, and the publication of *The Child of Pleasure* in 1889 consolidated his literary reputation.

The marriage, which saw the birth of three children, was to last seven years.

For the first four years, D'Annunzio seemed to accept an approximation of conventional domesticity, but in 1887, the encounter with Barbara, the wife of Count Leoni, precipitated the end of his already precarious union with Maria. His sensual passion for "Barbarella" inspired in part the novel *The Triumph of Death* and all the verses of *Elegie romane* (1892).

Naples, where D'Annunzio moved in 1891, represents another step in his life and writings. There he collaborated with his friend, Eduardo Scarfoglio, the editor of *Il corriere di Napoli*, in which he published his novel *The Intruder* in installments. D'Annunzio's first engagement in politics dated from this time, with the publication of an article, "La bestia elettiva." In this article he attacked universal suffrage, restating Friedrich Nietzsche's theory of the inevitable supremacy of one group over another. These aristocratic ideas constantly recur in his writings, and the influence of the German philosopher is particularly evident in the works of the next decade.

While in Naples, the love affair with Barbara came to an end, and the writer became involved with Princess Maria Gravina, who left her husband to live with him *more uxorio*. Two children were born from this union, but his love for Maria did not survive a cruise to Greece in 1904. Upon his return, he separated from her to start a new love relationship, this time with the great actress Eleonora Duse. Duse, an extremely intelligent and passionate woman, brought to D'Annunzio the most enriching and stimulating love of his life. Under her influence, he began his career as a dramatist and with her, in the splendid retreat of La Capponcina, his Tuscan villa, wrote the first three books of *Le laudi* (1889-1949), which remain the greatest accomplishment of D'Annunzio the poet. Their relationship also provided him with the narrative nucleus of the novel *The Flame of Life*, published in 1900, in which he did not hesitate to portray in the aging actress Foscarina the generous and loving Eleonora. This fact, added to his chronic unfaithfulness, was one of the factors that prompted their separation in 1905. During the exceptionally productive years from 1895 to 1905, D'Annunzio also published the novel *The Maidens of the Rocks* and actively engaged in politics. In 1897, his name appeared on the list of right-wing candidates, and he was elected as a representative to the Italian parliament.

This first contact with political life did not mark him deeply, since his attendance in parliament was sporadic and his interventions capricious. His boredom with the ruling conservative party, which he described as "a group of screaming dead men," soon became open rejection. When, in 1900, the Pelloux government proposed its harsh reactionary laws, D'Annunzio, ostentatiously, moved his seat from the extreme right to the extreme left. Was this gesture dictated by his usual indulgence in theatrical effects or by genuine indignation? In D'Annunzio, it is difficult to separate the authentic from the artificial, since artifice was for him quite genuine. In an article that appeared a few days later, the writer justified his abrupt conversion by explaining that what he appreciated in the Socialist Party was its destructive potential—the same thing he admired in Nietzsche's theories. For D'Annunzio, extreme right and left seem to have coincided in a type of anarchic program aiming at the destruction of sclerotic institutions, whose only function was to protect incompetence and corruption. The following year, D'Annunzio presented himself as a candidate for the Socialist Party, but he was defeated and subsequently retired from the parliamentary arena.

After his separation from Eleonora Duse, D'Annunzio continued his amorous career with new conquests: first, Marquise Carlotti who, once abandoned by him, found peace in a convent; then Countess Mancini who, shattered by the impact of their turbulent and precarious relationship, collapsed into moments of despair and mental insanity. It was a sad episode, recounted by D'Annunzio in *Forse che si forse che no* (yes or no) and in *Solus ad solam*, an autobiographical writing that was published only after his death, in 1939.

Although D'Annunzio was a skillful manager of his literary success, the costly experiments with cars and planes he financed and his extravagant tastes drove him to bankruptcy. In 1909, he was obliged to sell his mansion, La Capponcina and, being pursued by his creditors, decided to leave Italy for France. Friends and admirers welcomed the famous writer, and he remained in France until the outbreak of World War I.

During his voluntary exile, he took an active part in the social and intellectual life of Paris and published several works in French. Among them, the most prominent work is *Le Martyre de Saint Sébastien*, a theatrical text with music by Debussy, which was presented in Paris in 1911.

The most magnificent adventure of D'Annunzio's life began with World War I. Upon his return to Italy in 1914, he campaigned for the intervention against Germany, and as soon as Italy entered the war, he enlisted as a volunteer. He fought first on the front line and at sea. Afterward he participated in several risky actions with the first military planes, until a plane accident cost him three months of immobility and the loss of his right eye. During this period of forced inactivity, he painfully scribbled a number of notes which were to become the nucleus of *Il notturno* (1921), one of his most valuable works in prose.

By the end of the war, D'Annunzio, quite naturally, assumed the role of the poet-prophet, voicing the feeling of frustration and discontent of the Italian people, confronted by an economic crisis and peace negotiations that did not favor Italian interests. Popular unrest reached its apex with the question of the annexation of Fiume, a city on the Dalmatian coast. D'Annunzio chose action; leading a group of volunteers in the famous Marci dei Ronchi, he occupied Fiume, where he established a temporary government. The Italian government, which was trying to avoid open conflict over this issue, first ordered D'Annunzio to leave the city, then sent the fleet with the order to bomb Fiume to force him to retreat.

Meanwhile, Benito Mussolini had assumed the leadership of the nationalist forces. In 1920, when D'Annunzio returned from his unsuccessful enterprise, there was no place left for him on the political scene. Abandoning any hope of playing an active role in the country, D'Annunzio retired to a large estate on Lake Garda, later named Il Vittoriale (the name means "pertaining to victory"), where, in semi-isolation, he spent the rest of his life. Officially, he maintained his support for the Fascist government, although he despised Adolf Hitler and had no respect for Mussolini, whom he considered a bad imitator of his own style. Mussolini, who did not trust D'Annunzio as a friend and feared him as an enemy, approved his timely retreat and bestowed honors and subventions upon him.

D'Annunzio's last years were devoted to the editing of his *Opera omnia* (1927-1936). He also gathered some of his previous writings, which he published in two volumes as *Le faville del maglio* (1924, 1928). Memories, erotic obsessions, and feelings of disillusionment fill the pages of *Le cento e cento e cento pagine del libro segreto di Gabriele D'Annunzio tentato di morire* (1935), which, apart from some privileged moments, lacks the vigor and drive of his other works. Without the fresh inspiration of a life intensely lived, literature had become for D'Annunzio an empty form. He died at Il Vittoriale in 1938 and lay in state in the uniform of an air force general.

Analysis

After testing his narrative potential in short fiction, Gabriele D'Annunzio confronted the challenge of long fiction with the novel *The Child of Pleasure*, which confirmed in his prose writing a success already established in poetry. During the next twenty years, seven other novels followed, including *La Leda senza cigno* (Leda without the swan), which could be better defined as a long short story.

The passage from short to long fiction presents substantial changes. Abandoning Naturalistic themes and atmosphere, the writer directs his attention to the aristocratic world of the capital: Natural landscapes are substituted for elegant interiors or closed gardens; simple characters with primitive passions are replaced with sophisticated figures corroded by subtle torments. The language, highly refined, flows with an even rhythm, avoiding chromatic effects, and the prevailing subdued tones cast an aura of imperceptible melancholy on characters and events. All the subsequent novels are patterned on the same narrative structure: Little action is involved in the plot, which centers on the figure of the hero, a man of exceptional qualities who is confronted by a vulgar and base society dominated by utilitarian interests and aspirations. The narration is punctuated by digressions on artistic issues, meditations, detailed descriptions of objects and landscapes, and above all, by the minute analysis of fugitive sensations.

In his first novel, *The Child of Pleasure*, D'Annunzio portrays the idle and decadent aristocratic society of Rome, totally absorbed in the pursuit of the most refined pleasures of the mind and of the senses. The autobiographical motif is evident in the projection of the author's personality in the figure of the protagonist, Andrea Sperelli, a young aristocrat endowed with the spark of artistic genius.

A poet and a painter of great potential, Andrea wastes his intellectual energies in a futile worldly life, a man whose greatest challenge is his jousts of love. Forgetting his artistic aspirations, Andrea feels irresistibly attracted to the beautiful and sensuous Elena Muti, who responds with the same passion. The short season of their love comes to a sudden end when Elena abandons him for a rich husband. While trying to overcome his rejection with new conquests, Andrea is involved in a scandal and, in the duel that ensues, he is gravely wounded. After a long period of moral and physical prostration, love and life are revived by the apparition of Maria in the peaceful retreat where Andrea is slowly recovering. Maria, a beautiful and noble creature, endures with dignity the distress of an unhappy marriage, devoting her life to the education of her young daughter. Enticed by her sensibility and intelligence, Andrea discovers a new aspect of love, based on the communion of intellectual interests and spiritual aspirations. Maria tries to resist the growing attraction she feels for the young artist, which she confesses to her diary, but an amorous complicity has already flawed their friendship.

Upon their return to Rome, the idyll continues, until it becomes for Maria a total engagement that overcomes her last resistance. Andrea, on the contrary, is torn between conflicting sentiments and impulses. In the elegant circles of the capital, he has seen Elena, and once again he has been captivated by her charm. His feelings become troubled and confused; he slips into morbid fancies in which the images of the two women coalesce; old memories creep into new sensations, and in Maria's transports of love, Andrea savors Elena's gestures. The ambiguous situation explodes when, in a moment of total abandon, he calls Maria by the name of Elena. Maria, horrified by the brutal discovery that his thoughts are of someone else, runs away, and Andrea is left with nothing but the sad realization of his inability to love.

The novel ends with a melancholic scene which symbolizes Andrea's failure; his personal experience parallels the irreversible process of dissolution of a society whose only aspiration is the pursuit of pleasure. Maria's husband, a notorious gambler of ill repute, has lost his entire fortune at the game table. Now the creditors are auctioning his mansion. A horde of greedy merchants fights over the possession of precious furnitures and artistic objects, while Andrea wanders in the empty rooms, aware of the spiritual ruin of an entire society and of his own life.

The story is told, according to traditional rules, by the omniscient author, but the protagonist acts as a center of consciousness, reflecting the outside reality through his own sensibility. Rather than seeing the events themselves, the reader knows the sentiments, sensations, and reactions that those events provoke in Andrea. As for the other characters, they seem to exist only in relation to the protagonist; when the author deems it necessary to present their feelings, he chooses an indirect approach, resorting to literary devices such as the introduction of intimate diaries or confessional letters.

Besides being D'Annunzio's most popular novel, *The Child of Pleasure* offers a particular interest for its original interpretation of the decadent hero. Des Esseintes, the protagonist of Joris-Karl Huysmans' *À rebours* (1884; *Against the Grain*, 1922), remains the prototype of the genre, and, compared with him, Andrea Sperelli appears a superficial character. A spectator rather than an actor on the stage, Andrea lacks the tension for transgression, the turbid introspective search, the attraction to the abyss of nothingness that characterize Huysmans' hero; and the weary melancholy of *The Child of Pleasure* does not attain the disturbing depth of *Against the Grain*. Nevertheless, the two novels present a remarkable parallelism in their approach and technique. Both, in fact, restrict the parameters of the inquiry to a vision of the world filtered through the exacerbated sensibility of the hero, developing a rather tenuous plot in a rich texture of descriptions and analysis.

The next two novels, *Episcopo and Company* and *The Intruder*, represent a new phase of D'Annunzio's constant exploration of new motifs and techniques. In these works, the author experiments with the psychological and humanitarian themes proposed by the great Russian writers of the nineteenth century. Exploring the ambiguities of the human soul, he portrays tormented characters who are torn between guilty complexes and pretentions of innocence, wicked tendencies and aspirations to purity. In an attempt to render the inner struggle of the protagonists, the already slow rhythm of the narration is interrupted by exclamations, self-accusations, and justifications until it dissolves in tedious repetition. The great dilemma of good and evil was not a burning issue of D'Annunzio's moral sensibility, and these sordid stories of moral degradation appear today quite monotonous and artificial.

In *The Triumph of Death*, D'Annunzio reiterates the theme of *The Child of Pleasure* in a more dramatic contest. In this novel, inspired by the author's personal experiences with Barbara Leoni, the dualism of sensuality and spiritual love becomes the conflict between lust and intellectual achievements. The protagonist, Giorgio Aurispa, is a writer who fails to realize his dream of artistic creativity because of his love for the beautiful Ippolita. The woman, a nymphomaniac afflicted with sterility, appears here as the enemy whose dangerous power hinders man's greatest aspirations. Giorgio, slave of his passion, is confronted by the prospect of a future of physical and intellectual impotence: Ippolita's sterility frustrates his natural desire for biological procreation; her lust destroys his creative potential. Unable to overcome his plight, Giorgio chooses suicide, plunging into a violent death with Ippolita.

According to Carlo Salinari, the publication of *The Maidens of the Rocks* in 1896 marks the official birth of the superman in Italian literature. The protagonist, Claudio Cantelmo, disgusted with the corruption and degradation of political institutions, pursues a dream of national renewal. Realizing that only the next generation will be ready to follow his program, Claudio leaves the capital with the firm resolution of devoting his life to the education of a son who, under his guidance, will become the superman for whom history is waiting. Following his project, he decides to choose among three sisters, descendants of a noble family, the spouse who will bear his child, the future leader of national renovation. From the beginning, Claudio realized that his program is condemned to fail. The three sisters live in a secluded world of physical and spiritual beauty outside reality and time, and the rocks surrounding their estate symbolize the barrier that separates them from the historical context. Idealistic aspirations and concrete action belong to two distinct levels of reality that Claudio cannot bridge. Renouncing every hope of active engagement, he leaves the sisters in the cloistered serenity of their retreat.

Formally, the novel repeats the narrative structure of the preceding works; ideologically, through the protagonist, D'Annunzio conveys his own political dream of aristocratic supremacy, spurning barbarian masses and greedy bourgeoisie, both responsible for the destruction of art and beauty in the world. If all of D'Annunzio's heroes are projections of his personality and aspirations, the autobiographical inspiration is especially vivid in *The Flame of Life*. In the love story of Foscarina, an aging actress, and Stelio Effrena, a young intellectual, D'Annunzio revives his own relationship with Eleonora Duse. Stelio is in Venice to present a program for a national theater, based on the fusion of poetry, music, and dance; the new theater, instead of being restricted to an elite audience, will be addressed to the people. The ambitious project is an attempt to rescue theater from the monopoly of the bourgeoisie which, while despising art, pretends to control it.

In Venice, Stelio meets the famous Foscarina, who falls in love with him. At first, he thinks he loves her with equal passion; in reality, he is seduced by the art of the actress rather than by the charms of the woman. The realization of the true nature of his sentiments strikes him when, in the young and pure Donatella Arvale, he recognizes the ideal woman he has desired all of his life. The brief period of elation associated with Donatella's appearance acts as a catalyst for Stelio's awareness of himself. When she disappears, Stelio abandons himself to his involvement with Foscarina and accepts being loved rather than loving. With acute analysis, the author dissects the sentiments of the two lovers, tracing step-by-step the dissolution of their union. For Stelio, the initial passion rapidly becomes a habit and then degenerates into fatigue and boredom. For Foscarina, it turns into an obsession. Constantly afraid of being abandoned, she oppresses the young man with her neurotic and pathetic attachment; Stelio, aware of his power, plays the game with a hint of cruelty, feeling at the same time a sincere compassion for the vulnerability of the woman. The painful romance is ended by Foscarina, who accepts an acting tour overseas, leaving Stelio to his artistic dreams.

The degenerative process of the love affair is paralleled by the progressive decay of Venice and its surroundings. Wandering in the countryside, Foscarina and Stelio come across the once-splendid Venetian villas on the river Brenta, now abandoned to deterioration and oblivion. In the silent parks, mutilated statues, covered with moss, look with blind eyes at piles of manure and the cultivation of cabbages. Images of death and ruin punctuate the narration, and the city itself seems to decompose among the stagnant waters of the lagoon. The same irreversible process of dissolution seems to supersede love, art, and beauty.

A noble style, compatible with aristocratic ideals and a mood of slight melancholy, prevails in all of D'Annunzio's novels published between the years 1894 and 1900. His next novel, published in 1910, presents a sharp change of perspective, theme, and style. In *Forse che si forse che no*, D'Annunzio introduces a new type of hero, a young man who embodies the hopes, risks, and excitements proposed by the rising technology. While the protagonists of the other novels were intellectuals absorbed in artistic dreams, Paolo Tarsis is a man of action; he is an airplane pilot and an exalted worshiper of speed and cars. The author's own experiences give substance to this celebration of the machine. In 1909, D'Annunzio, with the American pilot Glenn Curtis and the journalist Luigi Barzini, accomplished the first aeronautic experiment in Italy. This fact, while verifying once more the intrinsic unity of D'Annunzio's life and art, also confirms his avant-garde role in Italian literature: D'Annunzio's revolutionary concept of the hero anticipated the Futurists' celebration of the power of technology in modern society.

In the novel, the engine constitutes for Paolo the way to salvation, the means to overcome the plights of a vulgar existence oppressed by utilitarian interests and temptations of lust. With the two sisters, Isabella and Vana, D'Annunzio reenacts the drama of dual love he had already explored in *The Child of Pleasure* and *The Flame of Life*. Like Elena and Foscarina, Isabella is a sensual and possessive woman who enslaves the man in the vortex of passion; the pure and spiritual Vana belongs instead to the same category of ideal woman as Maria Ferees and Donatella Arvale. Both sisters are in love with Paolo, who is attracted to the sensitive Vana yet cannot resist Isabella's erotic seductions. This favorite theme here assumes a tragic depth. The characters are vividly drawn, and the conflict reaches unprecedented intensity, increasing the tension until tragedy explodes in the final catastrophe. Vana kills herself after revealing to Paolo Isabella's incestuous love with their brother Aldo; Isabella, after a devastating confrontation with Paolo, becomes totally insane. In the anguished scene of Isabella roaming semiconscious in the desert city, the author recalls with documentary simplicity the tragic end of his relationship with Giuseppina Mancini.

The degrading aspects of life lead Paolo to seek purification in an extreme challenge with death. Without a precise destination, he flies with his plane away from reality. After an elated flight in the purity of the sky, the plane crashes on the desert coast of Sardinia. Paolo, injured, crawls painfully to the sea to find solace in the calm waters. In front of him, the sea suggests purification and renewal; behind him, the burning wreck of the plane implies the failure of the engine ideology. The novel ends on this uncertain note, restating the ambiguous meaning of the title: "perhaps yes, perhaps no."

In this novel, D'Annunzio gives a virtuoso performance, mastering all the inspirations and techniques of his previous writings. Powerful descriptions of natural landscapes, erudite evocations, Naturalistic motifs, erotic scenes, memories, subtle analysis of sensations—all merge in this prose, unified by the fluidity of the language, constantly sustained by lyric intensity.

La Leda senza cigno, a short novel written in 1912 and published in 1916, explores a theme already implicit in the perspective of *Forse che sì forse che no*. The ivory tower of art and beauty does not offer a safe refuge from the assaults of life. The vulgar and the sublime, farce and tragedy are tightly intertwined, and it is impossible to isolate the one from the other. Thus, D'Annunzio's meditations on life and art had come to a turning point. The writer who had affirmed that "Il verso e' tutto" (the verse is everything) realized that life cannot be controlled by literature; consequently, he turned to action. D'Annunzio's decision is prefigured in his new perception of the hero-protagonist, as if in Paolo Tarsis he had unconsciously projected his own tension toward his future engagement.

La Leda senza cigno was D'Annunzio's last purely fictional prose work. The war absorbed all of his energies, and when he resumed writing, he chose the more direct expression of autobiographical prose. Ettore Paratore suggests an interesting hypothesis to explain the drastic elimination of the third-person narration in D'Annunzio's prose. According to Paratore, the writer, who shared with his generation the cult of the hero, felt compelled, at first, to represent in his fictional writings a hero-protagonist with whom he could identify. After the war, D'Annunzio, who had lived his heroic hour, discarded fiction, now useless, and assumed for himself the role of the protagonist.

Thus, total disillusionment sealed the prestigious adventure of D'Annunzio's life. His art remains as a literary monument to fifty years of European culture. In its variety, D'Annunzio's work mirrors the multiform aspects of the process of renovation that characterizes the passage from the nineteenth to the twentieth century, constituting a timeless testimonial of the Italian contribution to Western literature.

Major publications other than long fiction

SHORT FICTION: *Terra vergine*, 1882, 1884, 1902; *Le novelle della Pescara*,

1892, 1902 (*Tales from My Native Town*, 1920); *Le faville del maglio*, 1924, 1928 (2 volumes).

PLAYS: *La città morta*, 1898 (*The Dead City*, 1900); *La Gioconda*, 1899 (*Gioconda*, 1902); *La gloria*, 1899; *Francesca da Rimini*, 1902 (English translation, 1902); *La figlia di Iorio*, 1904 (*The Daughter of Jorio*, 1907); *La fiaccola sotto il moggio*, 1905; *La nave*, 1908; *Fedra*, 1909; *Le Martyre de Saint Sébastien*, 1911 (text for music); *Le chevrefeuille*, 1913 (*The Honeysuckle*, 1916); *Parisina*, 1913; *La Pisanelle*, 1913; *Il ferro*, 1914 (Italian version of *Le chevrefeuille*).

POETRY: *Primo vere*, 1879, 1880; *Canto novo*, 1882, 1896; *Intermezzo di rime*, 1884 (later as *Intermezzo*, 1896); *Isaotta Gùttadauro ed altre poesie*, 1886, 1890; *San Pantaleone*, 1886; *Elegie romane*, 1892; *Poema paradisiaco—Odi navali*, 1893; *Laudi del cielo del mare della terra e degli eroi*, 1899 (expanded to create *Maia*, 1903; *Elettra*, 1904; *Alcyone*, 1904 [English translation, 1977]; *Merope*, 1912; *Asterope*, 1949; better known as *Le laudi*).

NONFICTION: *L'armata d'Italia*, 1888; *L'allegoria dell'autunno*, 1895 (*The Dream of An Autumn Sunset*, 1904); *Contemplazione della morte*, 1912; *Per la più grande Italia*, 1915; *Il notturno*, 1921; *Il libro ascetico della giovane Itali*, 1926; *La penultima ventura*, 1919, 1931 (2 volumes); *Le cento e cento e cento pagine del libro segreto di Gabriele D'Annunzio tentato di morire*, 1935; *Teneo te, Africa*, 1936; *Solus ad solam*, 1939.

MISCELLANEOUS: *Opera omnia*, 1927-1936; *Tutte le opere*, 1930-1965; *Tutte le opere*, 1931-1937; *Opera complete*, 1941-1943.

Bibliography

Barberi Squarotti, G. *Il gesto improbabile*, 1971.
_____ . *Invito alla lettura di D'Annunzio*, 1982.
Binni, W. *La poetica del decadentismo italiano*, 1936.
Croce, Benedetto. "Gabriele D'Annunzio," in *Letteratura della Nuova Italia*, 1964.
_____ . "L'ultimo D'Annunzio," in *Letteratura della Nuova Italia*, 1957.
Flora, F. *D'Annunzio*, 1935.
Jullian, P. *D'Annunzio*, 1972.
Pancrazi, P. *Studi sul D'Annunzio*, 1939.
Paratore, Ettore. *Studi dannunziani*, 1967.
Petronio, G. *D'Annunzio*, 1977.
Raimondi, E. "G. D'Annunzio," in *Storia della letteratura italiana*, 1969.
Rhodes, A. *The Poet as Superman: G. D'Annunzio*, 1959.
Salinari, Carlo. *Miti e coscienza del decadentismo italiano*, 1960.
Woodhouse, J. R. *Alcyone*, 1978.

Luisetta Elia Chomel

ALPHONSE DAUDET

Born: Nîmes, France; May 13, 1840
Died: Paris, France; December 16, 1897

Principal long fiction

Le Petit Chose, 1868 (*The Little Weakling*, 1917); *Aventures prodigieuses de Tartarin de Tarascon*, 1872 (*The New Don Quixote*, 1875; also as *Tartarin of Tarascon*, 1910); *Froment jeune et Risler aîné*, 1874 (*Froment the Younger and Risler the Elder*, 1880); *Jack*, 1876 (English translation, 1890); *Le Nabab*, 1877 (*The Nabob*, 1878); *Les Rois en exil*, 1879 (*Kings in Exile*, 1880); *Numa Roumestan*, 1881 (English translation, 1882); *L'Évangéliste*, 1883 (English translation, 1883; also as *Port Salvation*, 1883); *Sapho*, 1884 (*Sappho*, 1886); *L'Immortel*, 1888 (*One of the Forty*, 1888); *The Works*, 1898-1900 (24 volumes).

Other literary forms

Alphonse Daudet was one of the most prolific authors of his generation, publishing works in several genres. His first effort was a volume of poems, *Les Amoureuses* (1858, 1873). Throughout his career, Daudet wrote for the theater; his best-known play is *L'Arlésienne* (1872), for which Georges Bizet composed the incidental music. Other plays include *La Dernière Idole* (1862, with Ernest Lépine), *L'Oeillet blanc* (1865, with Ernest Manuell; the white carnation), *Lise Tavernier* (1872; English translation, 1890), and stage adaptations of his most successful novels. Before turning to the novel, Daudet composed many short stories, sketches, and vignettes, which eventually were collected in volume form, the two most famous being *Lettres de mon moulin* (1869; *Letters from My Mill*, 1880) and *Contes du lundi* (1873, 1876; *Monday Tales*, 1927). In addition, he contributed many critical pieces, translations, and topical commentary to newspapers and journals.

Achievements

The variety and breadth of Daudet's literary production have traditionally made it difficult to provide any single, lasting critical evaluation of his works. During his lifetime, Daudet's reputation rested especially on his novels and on his association with the French realists. His personality, particularly his talent as a conversationalist, seems also to have played a role in establishing his popularity among contemporaries. At the height of his career, Daudet overshadowed his friends Gustave Flaubert and Émile Zola, whose works posterity has judged more favorably.

Daudet's fame became international as his works were translated, attracting the attention and praise of such figures as Joseph Conrad and Henry James. Conrad, writing upon Daudet's death, expressed an ambivalence found in many critics. He suggested that the French author's weaknesses stemmed from his strengths: Daudet's tendency toward melodramatic pathos and always to "dot his *i*'s," resulted from a sincere empathy with his characters, and his limited vision, which saw only surface things, was nevertheless accurate in its observations. Conrad admired Daudet, not as a great artist, but for having accurately reflected mankind's destiny. The fate of Daudet's characters, Conrad suggested, is poignant, intensely interesting, and without consequence.

Like Conrad's, the praise of James, an admired and admiring personal friend of Daudet, is not without its reservations. James did not like Daudet's taste for melodramatic effects and felt that his characters were often psychologically blank. On the other hand, the American greatly esteemed his colleague's talents for narration and pictorial description, and he admired Daudet's poetic touch and sense of beauty. (These last attributes were ones to which Zola objected, as well as to Daudet's empathy with his characters.) James maintained that Daudet's chief virtue lay in his talents as a sensitive and exacting observer.

During the twentieth century, Daudet's reputation has waned, although he remains an important historical figure in the development of the realist movement. In France, his works are still read and studied, especially the short stories and early novels. Outside France, the novels are no longer regarded with much interest, having fallen victim to a taste that prefers characters with more psychological depth and eschews the overt sentimentality typical of Daudet. The short stories have retained their popularity, however, because they illustrate what has been judged the best of Daudet's talent. To paraphrase James's opinion of them, they are graceful in form, light of touch, and alert of observation.

Biography

Alphonse Daudet was the fifth child of Vincent Daudet and Adeline Raynaud, but only the third to survive. Childhood was not a particularly happy time for Daudet. His health was delicate, and the family was forced to live in a state of financial stress, which grew as his father's silk business gradually declined and finally collapsed. In 1849, the family was forced to move to Lyons in search of work.

Daudet's formal schooling took place in Lyons. During this period, he showed some signs of literary talent, but they were not encouraged. A fairly good student when he attended classes, the youngster often chose to explore the city instead. In the spring of 1857, Daudet was taken out of school and sent to Alès in Provence as a study assistant in a secondary school. By November, he had resigned his position and was soon in Paris with his first literary manuscript.

His older brother Ernest gave Daudet shelter and encouragement. In quick order, the young literary hopeful had entered the Bohemian circles of the capital, had taken a mistress, and had found a publisher for his poems.

Throughout his career, Daudet would draw on his own life for his fiction. His childhood and adolescence are chronicled in his first novel, as is his early life in Paris. Reminiscences of this later period and its Bohemian aspects are frequent in many of his works.

The slight reception given to *Les Amoureuses* convinced Daudet that he was not a good poet. He turned to short, topical pieces for Paris journals, and in 1860 was fortunate enough to receive a sinecure as secretary to the Duke of Morny, a position he held until the Duke's death, five years later. Frail since childhood, health problems began to affect Daudet in the early 1860's. Under doctor's orders, he spent winters in his native Provence and in Algeria and Corsica. During these southern sojourns, he became acquainted with the Provençal poet Frédéric Mistral. In 1862, Daudet's first play, *La Dernière Idole*, written with Ernest Lépine, was successfully produced at the Théâtre de l'Odéon. Daudet began to write for the theater, concentrating on plays for the next ten years. None of his efforts, however, had the success of the first. Even *L'Arlésienne*, Daudet's most familiar play, was a failure when initially staged in 1872. During this same period, he continued to polish his style in journal articles.

In 1867, Daudet married Julie Allard, a published author in her own right; she became his lifelong collaborator. The question of plagiarism has been raised several times in conjunction with Daudet's career: The extent to which Paul Arène contributed to *Letters from My Mill*; the extent to which Julie polished her husband's works; the possible influence of Charles Dickens' novels. The modern consensus is that Daudet unquestionably developed his own ideas and turned to so-called collaborators only for criticism and advice.

Three children were eventually born to Daudet and his wife: Léon, Lucien, and Edmée. The five-year period from 1868 to 1872 was influential in Daudet's career. He wrote what were to remain the most popular of his works—*The Little Weakling*, *Letters from My Mill*, *Tartarin of Tarascon*, *Monday Tales*, and *L'Arlésienne*—and experienced the Franco-Prussian War. As a result of his observations during the war, Daudet became attracted to the urban scene. He began to write increasingly about things outside his sphere of experience, extending his concerns to what he conceived as the serious matters of the period.

The ten years that follow the success of *Froment the Younger and Risler the Elder* in 1874 mark the zenith of Daudet's artistic production. He formed a literary group with Flaubert, Edmond de Goncourt, Ivan Turgenev, and Zola. The maturation of his natural talent for observation was encouraged by his association with this group. His international reputation grew as he published a series of realist novels, most with the subtitle *Moeurs parisiennes* (Parisian manners). Daudet became an important enough figure in French letters that friends and admirers believed he could be elected to the Académie Française. His general antipathy toward such organizations, however—and more particularly his refusal to make the traditional round of preelection courtesy calls on members of the Académie—prevented Daudet's agreeing even to become a candidate. His health again became a matter of serious concern following a hemorrhage in 1879.

Starting with *L'Évangéliste* in 1883, Daudet gradually abandoned the objective stance of his previous novels in order to expound personal views on various causes—religious fanaticism, unwed cohabitation, divorce, and the shortcomings of the younger generation. The atypical bitterness and pessimism of *One of the Forty* probably reflect Daudet's reaction to his family problems and literary squabbles of the immediately preceding years. During 1886, Daudet's son Léon had begun to rebel against his parents' plans for his future, and a temporary rift, of unknown cause, had occurred between Daudet and his wife. In 1887, Daudet had been implicated as intellectual author of the *manifeste des cinq* (the manifesto of five), five young writers' gratuitously insulting protest against Zola's *La Terre* (1887; *Earth*, 1954). Daudet's physical problems worsened during this period as well; doctors had diagnosed locomotor ataxia, an extremely painful illness of muscles and joints that is associated with the third phase of syphilis.

During the last years of Daudet's life, his works showed a decline of his literary talents. His last plays and novels were all too often dull and didactically moralistic. In spite of the difficulties caused by his illness, the author maintained an active schedule, even journeying to England with Julie during a respite in his suffering. He died in Paris on December 16, 1897.

Analysis

Alphonse Daudet's novels do not fit any single mold. Most frequently labeled as realist, their Romantic traits and emotionalism belie such an easy classification. Although Daudet was popularly regarded as a regional novelist of Provence, many of his novels center on Paris. Criticism has been directed paradoxically at both his excessive moralizing and his immorality, at his tendency toward pity, and at his lack of sympathy. That his novels should represent such a variety of contradictions can be traced, in great part, to Daudet's changing conception of himself as a novelist. He evolved from a satiric observer to an objective one and eventually to a subjective one. Murray Sachs, in his seminal study of Daudet, *The Career of Alphonse Daudet* (1965), argues convincingly that the French author's unsteady artistic vision was deeply rooted in self-doubt and the consequent inability to adopt any specific position.

Daudet made his novelistic debut with the semiautobiographical *The Little Weakling*, which has become a classic of French literature for its charm and gentle, ironic wit. It is, however, an uneven work. The transformation of the main character, Daniel Eyssette, which occurs between the two parts of the novel, is not well motivated, for example, and the structure is very loosely organized. The "oral style" of this work provides an excellent example of

Daudet's ability to spin a fine tale, and the second part is of special interest for the preview it contains of the themes and types of characters that are found throughout the author's novels.

The satiric humor of *Tartarin of Tarascon* distinguishes it from Daudet's other novels. In this second novel, the author directs good-natured barbs at several targets: the meridional French character, men with a mania for hunting, tourists abroad, and the eternal conflict in us all between heroic ambitions and prosaic, everyday reality.

In form and style, *Tartarin of Tarascon* bears more relationship to the short stories that preceded it than to the novels that followed. Rather than a sustained narrative, it is a series of vignettes. Peaceful, home-loving Tartarin, whose fanciful imagination and penchant for talking take him one step too far, is shamed into embarking for Africa to hunt lions. On this voyage, Tartarin must pass through the clutches of individuals who take advantage of unsuspecting innocents abroad, and the sole big game he encounters is an old and domesticated lion.

The oral quality of Daudet's prose, as in his first novel, leads to a certain looseness of organization, but, at the same time, the distinctive narrative voice and its ironic asides—traditional strategies of the raconteur, which Daudet was to employ in varying degrees during his entire career—early established for Daudet a reputation for charm and wit.

The style of description Daudet employs in *Tartarin of Tarascon* is one that produces a brilliant, rapid sketch by a selective accumulation of colorful details. Description is piled upon description, creating a vivid visual panorama. A note of fantasy often creeps into descriptions, such as in the masterfully comic recounting of the sea voyage to Algiers, in which Tartarin's suffering is largely rendered through the positions assumed by his fez.

Since his creation, Tartarin has acquired the stature of a universal type. He incarnates the very spirit of Provence: talkative to the point of garrulousness and possessing an overactive imagination. Counteracting these qualities are Tartarin's innocence and naïveté. The southern French personality is a frequent theme in Daudet's works; in *Numa Roumestan*, he specifically explores the contrast between the southern and northern French mentalities.

At one point in *Tartarin of Tarascon*, the narrator invokes the spirit of Miguel de Cervantes. It is similar to *Don Quixote de la Mancha* (1605, 1615), especially in the major theme that both authors treat: the conflict between illusion and reality, idealism and pragmatism. Cervantes approached this theme by contrasting two characters; Daudet chose to combine both aspects in a single personality, which carries on a dialogue with itself. Tartarin-Quixote suggests wild adventures and is always transforming reality with his imaginative and idealistic gaze. Tartarin-Sancho never fails to provide pragmatic counterpoint. This incessant conflict between the two voices of Tartarin's personality makes it impossible for him ever to make a clear decision: Tartarin-

Quixote sees a miniature baobab in his garden, while Tartarin-Sancho sees a turnip. The narrator offers an explanation for this trait. The Meridional, he claims, does not tell falsehoods, but is misled as to the reality of what he sees. The southern sun, which creates a mirage in which all things appear transformed, is at fault. The southerner is not lying, consequently, because he *believes* that he is telling the truth. He is, however, in almost constant conflict with reality.

Tartarin's seeming inability to distinguish genuine from false makes him vulnerable to confidence games. A certain Prince Gregory of Monténégro befriends Tartarin. This man seems affable and offers assistance on several occasions, until the right moment arrives when he can steal Tartarin's money and belongings. Tartarin becomes involved with a beautiful, sensuous woman whom he believes to be Moorish. In fact, she is a common prostitute from Marseilles who has connived with Prince Gregory to act the part.

Toward the end of the novel, the narrator briefly sketches images of Algeria which Tartarin could have seen had his sight not been set on imaginary lions. A similar charge of misdirection might be leveled at the author as well, both here and in other novels. Starving tribes, ravenous locusts, and colonists sipping absinthe and discussing reform are merely mentioned in passing. Daudet creates a marvelous surface texture with his all-observing eye, but the consequences of what is described are not investigated.

In any case, the novel's end is comedy, not exposé. Nothing irremediable befalls Tartarin. He survives his predicaments, no worse for the experience. The narrator's irony allows the reader to laugh at Tartarin rather than condemn him. It is a measure of the author's benevolent and essentially comic view in this novel that Tartarin accepts as his the flea-bitten camel who had followed him back to Tarascon. Under the meridional sun, the hunter transforms the camel from a reminder of ignominious experiences into the faithful companion of heroic exploits.

The change in style that occurs in *Froment the Younger and Risler the Elder* reflects two factors: new literary acquaintances among the realist authors and the effect the Franco-Prussian War had on Daudet's habits of observation. His interest was drawn to urban society, and he began to turn away from personally experienced situations in favor of documentation and observation of others. Concurrently, the authorial intrusions that had produced such an atmosphere of intimacy in his early works changed in tonality and frequency. In place of the gentle self-mockery of *The Little Weakling* and the equally gentle satiric irony of *Tartarin of Tarascon*, the reader finds a sharper note in the author's voice, one with a moralizing edge to it. The loose, conversational style of earlier works has given way to one that uses a more formal third-person narrative. Whereas direct discourse had largely sufficed to present his characters before, with *Froment the Younger and Risler the Elder*, Daudet turned to the device of *style indirect libre*, or free indirect discourse, which he handled effectively.

Froment the Younger and Risler the Elder, whose popular and critical success established Daudet as an important author, traces the social rise and fall of Sidonie Chèbe and the devastating effect she exerts on the lives of the people around her. A child of her Paris environment, she rises through marriage into the comfortable bourgeoisie. Jealous, selfish, greedy, unscrupulous, and shallow, Sidonie unfailingly forces all around her to ruin while she herself manages to survive.

This novel represents a significantly more ambitious work artistically than the previous ones. The chronology is not linear, several subplots arise from the central action, and the number of characters is considerably increased. The first chapter suggests these new directions. Instead of beginning Sidonie's story with her birth, as he had done in that of Daniel Eyssette, Daudet first portrays her on the day she marries the aging Risler, a partner in the Fromont manufacturing company. He then uses a lengthy flashback to explain the years preceding that moment. Using a technique often employed in the first act of a play, Daudet, in the first scene of this novel, unites all the important characters in a single moment and previews elements of the plot which are to be developed: the veiled antagonism of certain social classes toward others, the family as a social entity, disappointed marriage plans, personal rivalries and hatreds.

Daudet uses free indirect discourse to render the quality of his characters' thoughts but rarely offers a truly penetrating glimpse into his creations' innermost workings. The narrator suggests that Sidonie acts out of a sense of revenge for childhood disappointments and humiliations. In view of her childhood, this is a likely motivation; it remains, nevertheless, an exterior analysis of the situation and not one coming directly from the character herself.

The characters in *Froment the Younger and Risler the Elder*, like those in most of Daudet's novels, tend to fall into two groups; the good, who are weak and passive, and the evil, who are strong and domineering. The two men of the novel's title, although honorable, intelligent, and well-meaning, still fall prey to Sidonie. The good woman figure, who often balances that of the temptress in Daudet's works, is here split into two characters, Claire Froment and Désirée Delobelle. While these two women are far stronger than the men, their strength still proves insufficient against Sidonie's machinations. The goodness and weakness of these characters make them pale beside the unabashed wickedness of Sidonie.

Sidonie is one of a bevy of forceful, rapacious females who populate Daudet's fiction. Even more alluring than they are beautiful, they attract men to inevitable destruction. They impress by the shallowness of their personality. Sidonie is consistently portrayed in terms of her superficiality and fakery. When she must learn a trade, she is apprenticed in a shop that makes costume jewelry. When she attends the theater, it is not the play that interests her but the shiny glitter and false elegance, the costumes and mannerisms of the actresses. When Claire Froment, the wife of Georges Froment (who has inherited his family's business), has a baby, Sidonie envies not the child but the vision of young motherhood that Claire, projects. Sidonie's soul is compared to a shelf of bric-a-brac—banal, vain, cluttered but empty, insignificant.

Sex, not love, causes the downfall of Georges Froment and Franz Risler, the younger brother of Sidonie's husband, Risler *aîné*. The physical attraction they feel toward Sidonie allows her to seduce them. By means of the two adulterous triangles thus formed, Daudet expresses his concerns for the status of the family unit and for the individual's integrity. Sidonie's first lapse, the seduction of Georges, who is her husband's business partner, raises the question of personal integrity. Sidonie is doubly to blame, because she is unfaithful not only to her husband but also disloyal to her lover's wife, who has been both friend and benefactress. Discovery of the affair causes the dual rupture of Sidonie's marriage and of her lover's family. Sidonie's selfish personal demands eventually bring the business to the verge of bankruptcy and destroy the business partnership. Her husband's professional honor is salvaged by his personal integrity, but, in the end, Sidonie manages to destroy his personal honor by seducing his younger brother Franz, who is on the verge of denouncing her infidelity. By means of the seduction, Sidonie blackmails Franz into silence. As in the first adultery, a good woman is harmed by Sidonie's actions. Franz had been on the verge of proposing to the ever-faithful and long-suffering Désirée when Sidonie stole him away. Sidonie's first infidelity was a serious crime, but the second one is graver still, for it constitutes an attack on the family unit, of which Sidonie is a member. Two deaths result: Her husband hangs himself, and the woman who would have been her sister-in-law tries to drown herself in the Seine and eventually dies of a fever resulting from the attempt. The family is destroyed completely.

The most fully drawn character in *Froment the Younger and Risler the Elder* is Désirée's father, Delobelle, a theatrical has-been. Like the other men in the novel, he is weak, seduced not by Sidonie but by the theater, a repository of illusion. Although never very talented, he maintains that he has "no right to renounce the theater" and spends his days in cafés frequented by theater people, always stylishly attired, waiting for an important role. Daudet condemns the falsity of Delobelle's façade by revealing the actor's means of support. Delobelle and his pretensions are financed by the industry of his wife and daughter, both of whom believe and encourage their man's pretensions, to their own detriment. They remain unhealthily closeted in their tiny apartment; Madame Delobelle is losing her eyesight from so much hard work in badly lit conditions. The family exists by selling the brightly colored, lifelike stuffed birds that Désirée creates to adorn women's hats. There is no part of this family's existence that does not depend on illusions. Even at Désirée's funeral, the mourners, primarily her father, act out their grief. Tartarin-

Quixote's illusions were never depicted in so devastating a manner.

Delobelle the actor represents a negative force on the people around him, because he perpetrates illusions that destroy the elements of true value in their lives. Images of the theater surround Sidonie: For her introduction into society, Delobelle shows her how to act and talk; her country house belonged to an actress; and the last glimpse Risler *aîné* has of her is as a performer, under Delobelle's tutelage again, in a *café chantant*. Actresses not only represent persons devoid of meaningful substance but also incarnate the threat to Daudet's men of the degradation and corruption of a Bohemian life-style. Daniel Eyssette becomes completely despicable when his actress-mistress forces him into a theatrical troupe.

An important presence in *Froment the Younger and Risler the Elder*, as in a number of Daudet's works, is the city of Paris itself. Paris represents the unhealthy crowding together of human beings deprived of sun and natural surroundings that produces such unnatural creatures as Sidonie Chèbe. Paris signifies the rich, glittering, excitement-filled Bohemian life that seduces and corrupts young provincials such as Daniel and Jacques Eyssette, the Risler brothers, and Jean Gaussin of *Sappho*, who go there seeking their fortune. Daudet's talent for description captures a changing organism whose surface, pulsating with a beautifully attractive life force, conceals a dark void capable of destroying the weak and unwary. The last scene of *Froment the Younger and Risler the Elder* resumes the ambivalence with which Daudet typically portrayed Paris. In a potent image, a splendid early-morning view of Paris is tinged with menace: Smoke from the factories replaces the river fog as the city lumbers into action.

As a purely objective realist, Daudet has weaknesses. Fantastic notes appear incongruously, such as in the episode of the Little Blue Man, who stalks the midnight chimneys of Paris to taunt Delobelle, Georges Froment, and others that their debts are coming due. Traditionally known as a realist who nevertheless subjectively expressed great sympathy for his characters, Daudet often employed a too-direct sentimental appeal, which in his late works verges on bathos. One has only to compare Désirée Delobelle's suicide to that of Emma Bovary to see the extent to which Daudet could vary from the objectivity of the literary group in which he is most frequently classified.

Sappho is probably Daudet's best-known novel. It marks several changes for the author. While the narrative voice of Daudet's works had always demonstrated a certain tendency toward moralizing observations, in *Sappho* Daudet becomes more openly didactic, a trend that typifies most of his late works. The dedication, "To my sons when they are twenty," suggests the thesis character of this work as well as Daudet's growing concern with what he considered the "lovely oblivious egotism" of the younger generation. Fortunately, the occasional moralistic asides do not detract from the exceptionally fine psychological observations the novel contains.

In contrast to the broad panoramas presented in earlier works, *Sappho* concentrates on only two characters: Jean Gaussin, a young man from Provence who has come to Paris to prepare a diplomatic career, and Fanny Legrand, a Parisian *cocotte*. The subplots are few and distract very little from the main focus; they reflect back on it, rather, reinforcing it in various ways. In both scope and form, *Sappho* is tighter and more controlled than Daudet's previous novels.

The first chapter is a forceful and immediate entry into the action. In the garden room of a Bohemian residence, the two main characters converse for the first time while a costume ball swirls around them. The setting suggests what will follow. This relationship, which receives its initial impulse in a rarefied greenhouse setting, will require a special, artificial environment in which to flourish. A primordial Eve, the Bohemian woman represents a threat to the young son of a distinguished family. The exotic costumes and colored lights of the ball create a phantasmagoric atmosphere that foreshadows the nightmarish quality the mature relationship will assume.

Sappho is Daudet's most complete treatment of the relationship between the sexes and the role physical passions play in it. Daudet's weak-willed men are confronted with two female personalities: the sensual, domineering woman and the sweet, passive girl. The men inevitably choose the former, succumbing to their own sensuality while at the same time regretting the loss of the comfortable, nurturing security offered by the latter.

The attraction between Jean and Fanny is founded from the beginning on lust, not love: Jean responds to "a will superior to his, to the impetuous violence of a desire." Imperceptibly, he is drawn into the relationship. Naïvely setting a time limit on the liaison, he imagines that he will simply walk away from Fanny when his career begins in earnest. The couple establishes a household, and being cared for by Fanny, as if they were married, becomes a comfortable habit for Jean.

Daudet convincingly traces the step-by-step effect of this union on Jean's psyche. The more the young man comes to know his mistress, the more he is repulsed both by her and by his own actions. Her promiscuous past, when it comes to light, disgusts him and arouses his jealousy. It also stimulates new and unsuspected sexual desires in him, which Fanny encourages by initiating the young man into new depravations of pleasure. Thus, Jean's passions are attracted by the very things which the rest of his being finds repugnant.

Jean attempts several times to escape this bondage to sexual desire. A return to the salubrious atmosphere of the family home proves futile because, in Fanny's absence, Jean's imagination acts as a powerful aphrodisiac, conjuring up feverish scenes of lovemaking. When, under the sway of his imagination, he responds to his aunt's gesture of maternal tenderness by passionately kissing her bared neck, Jean realizes the terrible extent to which his relationship with his mistress has affected his ability to control his actions and feelings. Hoping to marry a young woman with whom he has fallen in love, Jean leaves Fanny for a time but cannot resist his physical passions when he returns to see her.

The trap is finally released by Fanny herself, but Jean's victory is empty. Although he is free at last from a degrading influence on his life, he is left with a sense of ruin. He has lost the woman he loved and has been disowned by his family.

Minor characters surround Jean and Fanny like so many visions of what their own personalities and relationship might be. Their neighbors have made an honorable but extremely banal marriage of a situation like theirs. The double suicide of an acquaintance and his mistress suggests a parallel with Jean and Fanny. Particularly striking is a dinner at the home of Rosa, Fanny's employer and patroness. Present are Rosa, two other formerly infamous courtesans, and de Potter, Rosa's lover of twenty years. The heavily made-up and bejeweled women, the incongruity of their stylish spring dresses with the infirmities of their old age, and the presence of a mollycoddled pet iguana present Jean with a horror-provoking vision of what his fate could be if he remains with Fanny.

Sappho was more scandalous for its topic than for the author's execution of it. Just as the realism with which the characters are presented in this novel had become psychological, so, too, Daudet's descriptions centered less on reported detail and more on suggestive images. Rather than describe physical aspects of the couple's relationship, Daudet generally implied the tenor of their feelings through the mood of the surroundings. The direct portrayal of a lustful embrace is saved to highlight critical moments: Jean's reaction to his aunt, the provocative surprise of bare flesh as Fanny kisses him good-bye after the separation scene.

To a certain extent, Fanny Legrand is typical of Daudet's domineering, superficial females. The author has also, however, endowed her with positive attributes, such as her generosity and devotion. A dual portrait results—that of seductress and that of a woman painfully coping with approaching old age. Ageless in the first chapter, Fanny has begun to show unmistakable signs of aging by the end of the novel. Her affair with Jean, who is much younger than she, is a last attempt to appear beautiful and desirable. The intense pain Daudet shows her suffering, after her initial outburst of anger when Jean announces his pending marriage, realistically stems as much from the loss of an object of passion as from the implied revocation of her capacity to be a sexual being. Fanny is finally able to reconcile herself to what must be when she rejects the reprieve that Jean eventually offers her. Although portrayed simplistically at times, to fit didactic aims, Fanny acquires some intriguing psychological complexity by the novel's end.

Daudet's sources of inspiration were two: the society around him and his own life. The rich, colorful texture of his descriptions of both Provence and

Paris derived from a remarkable sense of observation. Daudet was particularly adept at rendering surfaces. The world and the values he depicted were primarily those of the bourgeois milieus he himself inhabited, with occasional forays into the artistic Bohemia he had frequented in his youth. The psychological nuances with which he endowed many of his characters surely came from a sensitive analysis of his own personality. Whatever his weaknesses, Daudet was always an exemplary raconteur, an author who has remained famous in his nation's literature for his extraordinary success in transferring oral storytelling techniques to the written page. Generally, Daudet's prestige has waned. Excluded from the primary ranks of his literary generation for excessive sentimentality and exaggerated characterizations, Daudet nevertheless continues to occupy a place among authors of the second rank in importance and esteem.

Major publications other than long fiction

SHORT FICTION: *Lettres de mon moulin*, 1869 (*Letters from My Mill*, 1880); *Contes du lundi*, 1873, 1876 (*Monday Tales*, 1927).

PLAYS: *La Dernière Idole*, 1862 (with Ernest Lépine); *L'Oeillet blanc*, 1865 (with Ernest Manuell); *L'Arlésienne*, 1872; *Lise Tavernier*, 1872 (English translation, 1890).

POETRY: *Les Amoureuses*, 1858, 1873.

NONFICTION: *Souvenirs d'un homme de lettres*, 1888 (*Recollections of a Literary Man*, 1889); *Trente Ans de Paris*, 1888 (*Thirty Years of Paris and of My Literary Life*, 1888).

Bibliography

Bornecque, Jacques-Henry. *Les Années d'apprentissage d'Alphonse Daudet*, 1951.
Dobie, G. V. *Alphonse Daudet*, 1949.
Roche, Alphonse Victor. *Alphonse Daudet*, 1976.
Sachs, Murray. *The Career of Alphonse Daudet: A Critical Study*, 1965.

Joan M. West

OSAMU DAZAI
Tsushima Shūji'

Born: Kanagi, Japan; June 19, 1909
Died: Tokyo, Japan; June 19, 1948

Principal long fiction

Shayō, 1947 (*The Setting Sun*, 1956); *Ningen shikkaku*, 1948 (*No Longer Human*, 1958).

Other literary forms

Like many other modern Japanese prose writers, Osamu Dazai worked in a variety of modes and forms, many of which do not correspond readily to the terminology of modern Western criticism. Although known in the West and indeed in Japan primarily as a novelist, Dazai wrote only two books that might be called novels even in a loose sense. He wrote a number of memoirlike works that describe certain stretches of his life but that also incorporate additional commentary in a manner that casts doubt on the autobiographical authenticity of the account. Some of these works, *Omoide* (1934; memories) and *Tōkyō hakkei* (1941; eight views of Tokyo), for example, are fairly lengthy accounts; others, such as "Mangan" (written 1938; "The Vow"), and "Kinshu no kokoro" (written 1943; "What It's Like to Abstain"), are, on the other hand, brief and essentially anecdotal in nature. In addition to his own experiences, a main source of material for Dazai resides in works of literature and history. Two of his best collections of tales are based on sources in classical Japanese literature. *Otogi zōshi* (1945)—the tie refers to a group of miscellaneous stories from medieval times—involves a retelling of four tales, with extensive interpolations and commentary that mark the works as unmistakably by Dazai; *Shinshaku shokkoku banashi* (1944) gave Dazai the opportunity to retell twelve tales by the popular sixteenth century novelist and poet, Ihara Saikaku. Dazai also used a number of Western sources as inspiration for his writing. William Shakespeare's *Hamlet* (1602) provided the plot for a dramatic farce, *Shin Hamuretto* (1941), and Friedrich Schiller's poem "Die Burgschaft" was retold as an adventuresome moral fable. Dazai even dissected and rewrote an obscure work by the German playwright Herbert Eulenberg. Most important, Dazai familiarized himself with the New Testament and made constant reference to favorite passages. In one case, he constructed a dramatic monologue in which Judas, after the Crucifixion, reveals a very worldly view of Christ. Entitled *Kakekomi uttae* (1940; heed my plea), Dazai's work would probably have appealed to the D. H. Lawrence of *The Man Who Died* (1929).

Achievements

Both in Japan and abroad, Dazai is most widely known as the author of two novels, *The Setting Sun* and *No Longer Human*, both of which were written shortly after World War II, during the final three years of the author's life. As a result of these works, Dazai was assuredly the most acclaimed writer in Japan in the years following the war. With the exception of a single short story entitled "Biyon no tsuma" (1947; translated into English by Donald Keene as "Villon's Wife," 1956), these two novels have had far wider circulation in English translation than any other of the approximately twenty miscellaneous tales and stories by Dazai which have also been rendered into English. Dazai is best known to readers of English as a novelist, and this, in fact, is generally true of the other European languages into which his works have been translated.

In the decades since his death, Dazai has been thoroughly studied by Japanese critics. An enormous number of books have been published, from ponderous tomes on the author's familiarity with Christianity and Communism to enthralling accounts (mainly by fellow writers) of Dazai's various struggles with drugs, drinking, women, and publishers. For a number of years in the 1960's and early 1970's, a periodical called *Dazai Osamu Studies* was issued, one indication of the huge outpouring of scholarly and personal articles on this particular author.

Over the years, wild acclaim has been replaced by a sober assessment of Dazai's achievement. A number of critics regard Dazai as among the greatest Japanese writers of the twentieth century; others, however, express doubts about the permanence of his accomplishment. Much of this disagreement seems to stem from varying interpretations as to what the author was really doing. Some see him as a moralist, others as a very talented raconteur. Most scholars insist that the autobiographical aspects of Dazai's writings are crucial, while a few try to play down this dimension of Dazai. Of one thing there can be no doubt. Dazai remains widely read in Japan, especially among younger readers. His novels and collections of his stories line the shelves of the bookstores of Tokyo and other towns, along with the works of Yasunari Kawabata, Jun'ichirō Tanizaki, Yukio Mishima, Endo Shusaku, and other writers who have over the years become better known outside Japan than Dazai.

Biography

Tsushima Shūji', who wrote under the pen name of Osamu Dazai, was born in 1909 in Kanagi, a small town in the Aomori Prefecture of the Japanese island of Honshu. His family held extensive lands, the taxes on which entitled his father, Gen'emon, to move eventually from an elective seat in the Lower House into the Upper House of the Diet. The tenth of eleven children, Dazai was initially cared for by a nursemaid, then later by a favorite aunt and a staff of servants, because his parents were unable to do so. Dazai's mother, Tane, was exhausted by the successive pregnancies, and his father was either preoccupied with financial matters, when at home, or absent from Kanagi altogether during the legislative sessions.

During his childhood, Dazai enjoyed a comparative freedom, as his elder brothers were already being groomed to undertake the responsibility of maintaining the family fortune and reputation. Once his marked intelligence became evident, the family insisted that Dazai excel in his studies, an obligation which he diligently met throughout his elementary schooling in Kanagi. He began to founder, however, at the secondary level, when he encountered the competition of more select students and the severe scrutiny of teachers relatively indifferent to his prestigious name.

Billeted in the higher school town of Hirosaki, some twenty miles from the family home, Dazai began to cultivate certain fashionable tastes, perhaps as an escape from the relentless scholastic demands confronting him. He dressed flamboyantly and attended the local teahouses, took lessons in ballad chanting, and even courted a young geisha named Koyama Hatsuyo, whom he later insisted upon marrying in spite of his family's shocked disapproval.

During his years in higher school, Dazai did not confine his study to the conservative curriculum, in part because of the influence of the radical ideas which made considerable headway in Japan during the 1920's, a period of economic difficulty throughout the country. The impact of these ideas is apparent in his writings, in which he expresses the profound sense of guilt, shared by his older contemporary, Arishima Takeo, toward the tenant-farmers who worked the family lands partly to support his privileged existence. One of his earliest stories, published in 1930, depicts a youngster who joins a peasant band in rebellion against his own elder brother, a rural landowner of tyrannical arrogance.

Dazai turned twenty-one in 1930 and went off to Tokyo, ostensibly to major in French literature at the university. Living several hundred miles from home, Dazai seldom attended classes, although he continued to receive an allowance on the pretext that he was working steadily toward his degree. Much of his time was spent with radical student groups, to whom he gave some financial assistance and on whose behalf he claimed to have carried out seditious acts. By his own admission, however, Dazai was incapable of becoming a full-fledged revolutionary. At the same time, he could not seek a genuine reconciliation with his family and therefore continued to deceive them about his studies. Finding this position untenable, Dazai attempted suicide three times and became so addicted to drugs that he was committed to an asylum for a time. The tendency toward tuberculosis—a weakness which he shared with others of his family—was aggravated during this period. By 1937, Dazai was living alone in a shabby boardinghouse in Tokyo. His ties with both his family and the university had been formally severed, and the geisha he had so boldly insisted on marrying had returned to her home in northern Japan.

Slowly Dazai began to hope for a reconciliation as he recognized that the Tsushima family, despite its political standing and economic status, was marked for tragedy. The two oldest sons had died before his birth, and during his first decade in Tokyo two brothers, two sisters, a nephew, and a cousin also died. Gen'emon had died in 1923, when Dazai was only thirteen, and although Tane survived until 1942, she remained in frail health to the end. The family encountered mundane problems as well, notably an accusation that Bunji, the oldest surviving son and present head of the family, had won election to a Diet seat through fraud.

Concern over Dazai's notoriety prevented any dramatic move by the family toward reconciliation. Nevertheless, the Tsushimas tried to promote his rehabilitation by quietly sanctioning efforts to bring about a marriage between Dazai and Ishihara Michiko, a schoolteacher from the city of Kōfu in central Japan. The wedding took place in January, 1939, after which Dazai settled down to a relatively stable life. A few months later, he and his wife moved to Mitaka Village near Tokyo. The first of three children, a daughter, was born in 1941.

During World War II, Dazai gradually established a reputation as a leading writer of his time, a recognition which brought special satisfaction. His brother Bunji appreciated literature, occasionally composing a piece himself. From the late 1930's, Dazai had wished for literary success as a means of compensating in his family's eyes for his academic failure, if not for his earlier radicalism.

Apart from this strategy, Dazai tried forthrightly to cultivate the goodwill of his elder brothers, returning to Kanagi several times during the final years of the war. When his house in Mitaka was severely damaged in a bombing raid, Dazai went back home with his wife and children, remaining there until November, 1946.

Having returned to Tokyo for the last time, Dazai began to neglect his family for a life of reckless dissipation. The explanations for this lapse are numerous—a foreboding that he, like certain of his kin, was marked for an early death; an inability to cope with the fame earned by his postwar writings; susceptibility to the machinations of discontented women. One such woman, Yamakazi Tomie, evidently persuaded Dazai to commit suicide by entering the swollen waters of the Tomagawa Canal with her. His body was recovered by the police on June 19, 1948, his thirty-ninth birthday.

Analysis

The title *The Setting Sun* so vividly suggested the decline of the aristocracy in postwar Japan that the term *Shayōzoku*, or "Setting Sun Class," became a catchword for the phenomenon. It is debatable how much real understanding Osamu Dazai had of the highly restrictive circles of the prewar aristocracy. Dazai's own family was more on the order of nouveau riche and very provincial as well. These qualifications aside, however, in *The Setting Sun* Dazai assuredly conveyed his private sense of bleakness.

The novel centers on a family of only three people—a genteel and rather pathetic mother, the outwardly gruff but tenderhearted son Naoji, and the increasingly realistic and tough-minded daughter Kazuko. The mother is depicted in the opening scene of the novel spooning soup into her daughter's mouth. Shortly thereafter, she is described as loitering behind a shrub in the family garden. A moment later, she coyly announces to her daughter that she has been urinating while she was out of view. Passages such as these point to one of several basic problems in the novel. The author, through his narrator Kazuko, suggests that the mother embodies natural aristocratic qualities that are inimitable. Possibly the idiosyncratic behavior of the mother is to be taken as a sly sort of satire on the "declining aristocracy" of the book's title. Much more likely, however, is that the unconventionality of the mother's conduct represents the genuine aristocracy, possibly recalling Marie Antoinette and her circle at Le petit Trianon in Versailles.

In either event, it is clear that both the son Naoji and the daughter Kazuko regard their mother as a symbol of certain aristocratic values that are on the wane in the face of an alien process of democratization being imposed upon Japan by the American occupation in the aftermath of the surrender. Having lost their father and most of the family wealth, mother and children must fend for themselves as best they can. In fact, the novel might well be read as a treatise on the various fates lying in wait for the disenfranchised members of the aristocracy.

In poor health even at the beginning of the novel, the mother gradually declines and eventually dies a natural and peaceful death. Given her obvious inability to cope with the practical problems of surviving under the new conditions of postwar Japan—she is depicted as totally dependent upon a character called Uncle Wada—her death seems to symbolize the passing of an era. It also signals the need of her two children to come to terms in some way with the new system of values.

Kazuko and her mother are portrayed as personally close to each other. Indeed, a good portion of the narrative is given over to describing their life together—first, in the old Tokyo house which they were forced to give up and, finally, in the cottage at Izu where they can live simply and frugally. Kazuko cares deeply for her mother and tries to protect her. She fears the possible return of her brother Naoji, who was listed as missing in action in the South Pacific early in the book. Reckless and, for a time, addicted to drugs, Naoji would almost certainly disrupt the semi-idyllic life that Kazuko would like to have with her mother.

Despite a sharing of interests, Kazuko and her mother are ultimately seen in sharp contrast to each other. The contrast is strikingly evident in the symbolism of the appearance of snakes at certain crucial points in the narrative. In general, snakes seem to signal impending death. Kazuko, however, imagines a snake within her own breast, a snake which threatens the very life of her mother. In fact, as the novel unfolds, Kazuko gradually moves away from the genteel values represented by her mother. She recalls the days of physical work required of her as a young Japanese citizen during the war and finds great pleasure working in the garden at the cottage in Izu.

To all appearances an ally, Kazuko remains inwardly and involuntarily an enemy of her mother. With Naoji, the opposite seems true. After his sudden and dramatic return home, he flaunts his bad manners and rough language, squanders the little money the family possesses on drinking and on women, and does not try to conceal his dissipation. Always indulgent toward her son, the mother is so overjoyed to have him safely home that she cannot summon up even a whimper of protest. With the mother's death, Naoji goes out of control. He ends up committing suicide, explaining with a note to Kazuko that his recklessness was a desperate attempt to join the masses. In the end, he has come to the realization that he is, after all, an aristocrat.

Again Dazai is possibly making a sly comment about aristocracy. Yet Kazuko takes her brother quite seriously. Indeed, even before Naoji's death, she has been slowly working out a scheme whereby she proves to be the sole survivor of this old-fashioned family. She has come to know a dissolute novelist named Uehara, a friend of her brother (who himself aspires to be a writer). Eventually, Kazuko sees to it that she is seduced by Uehara—not from any attraction for the rather unattractive novelist but simply that she might bear a child able to cope with the future. At the end of the novel, she senses that she is pregnant. Further, while not necessarily expecting a reply, she writes to Uehara asking that he let his own wife hold the child in her arms while he tells her that Naoji had this child by a woman he loved.

A puzzling novel in many respects, *The Setting Sun* has been examined by both Japanese and foreign critics from many points of view. As is often the case with Dazai, the language of the work is conspicuous. When Naoji arrives home, the sudden shift to rough, substandard Japanese from the pleasant chitchat of mother and daughter is almost shocking to a reader of the Japanese original. The fluidly symbolic manner of part of the narrative has also attracted a great deal of comment, one critic referring to *The Setting Sun* as a kind of symphony with a definite arrangement of movements. Most critics, however, see the work as a reflection of the chaotic times in which it was written and, more particularly, as an expression of the desperate state of Dazai's own life in that final year or two before his own suicide.

While *The Setting Sun* contains echoes of Dazai's life, *No Longer Human* portrays as its main character what most critics would term a genuine surrogate of the author. The very name Ōba Yozo is one which Dazai had used in an early work entitled "The Flower of Buffoonery" (1935). In "The Flower of Buffoonery" (the work, incidentally, has never been translated into any foreign language), Dazai evokes the strange condition of the survivor of a suicide attempt. The man has hurled himself into the sea near Kamakura, along with a woman he scarcely knew. The woman perishes, and the surviving man has to face a police investigation even while he recuperates in the hospital. All of these things occurred to Dazai himself, not long after he came to Tokyo to study at the university.

The events of *No Longer Human* do not conform so precisely to the known course of Dazai's life as do those of "The Flower of Buffoonery." The association, however, between protagonist and author is suggested in certain indirect ways. Ōba Yozo is abandoned by his family, just as Dazai was disinherited. Under the tutelage of a friend, Yozo learns the use of alcohol and drugs. He encounters difficulty in his relations with women and ends up in an asylum for a time. None of this conforms exactly to Dazai's experience, but each aspect has a counterpart of some kind in the author's life. More pertinent, perhaps, the rhetoric—especially the occasionally exaggerated language—applied to Yozo suggests the descriptive manner of Dazai's explicitly autobiographical portraits.

The main text of the work consists of three notebooks, composed by Ōba Yozo presumably after his older brother has put him safely away with an old servant in an unnamed village. These notebooks are handed over quite by accident to a certain writer who, in a brief epilogue, announces his intention of publishing them in a magazine. The notebooks themselves detail Yozo's gradual withdrawal from society and its conventions. Even as a boy, he has found it difficult to accept the habitual and practical nature of everyday life. As he matures, he searches for various means of survival, the unique and most enduring one perhaps being a dependence upon clowning as a way of relating to others. he also marries an innocent and trusting girl named Yoshiko. Presently her very trustworthiness results in a seduction accidentally witnessed by Yozo himself.

As in *The Setting Sun*, it is difficult in *No Longer Human* to ferret out the author's intention. The majority of critics take the portrait of Yozo as another instance of autobiography—the author depicting the depths to which he himself fell in his own life. Be that as it may, Dazai cannot be understood solely with reference to any single work, or even to the two postwar novels which tend to dominate discussions of his writing.

Recent studies of Dazai in the United States have tended to treat his entire career instead of focusing so steadily on the postwar novels and stories. Dazai's achievement is seen as a kind of mosaic made up of individual works, the rationale of each work being as much in its contribution to the whole as in its worth as a single creation. Except for Masao Miyoshi's essay "Till Death Do Us Part," critics have not accorded this type of treatment to the two novels discussed here, but *The Setting Sun* and *No Longer Human* may one day come to be seen as important and integral parts of the larger mosaic that is Dazai's oeuvre.

Major publications other than long fiction

SHORT FICTION: *Shinshaku shokkoku banashi*, 1944; *Otogi zōshi*, 1945; *Dazai Osamu: Selected Stories and Sketches*, 1983.

PLAYS: *Kakekomi uttae*, 1940; *Shin Hamuretto*, 1941.

NONFICTION: *Omoide*, 1934; *Tōkyō hakkei*, 1941.

MISCELLANEOUS: *Dazai Osamu zenshū*, 1955-1956 (complete works).

Bibliography

Keene, Donald. "Dazai Osamu," in *Landscapes and Portraits*, 1971.

Lyons, Phyllis. *The Saga of Dazai Osamu: A Critical Study with Translations*, 1985.

Miyoshi, Masao. "Till Death Do Us Part," in *Accomplices of Silence*, 1974.

O'Brien, James A. *Dazai Osamu*, 1975.

_____ . "The Setting Sun," in *Approaches to the Modern Japanese Novel*, 1976. Edited by Kinya Tsuruta and Thomas E. Swann.

Rimer, J. Thomas. "Dazai Osamu: The Death of the Past," in *Modern Japanese Fiction and Its Tradition*, 1978.

James O'Brien

GRAZIA DELEDDA

Born: Nuoro, Sardinia; September 27, 1871
Died: Rome, Italy; August 15, 1936

Principal long fiction
La via del male, 1896; *Il tesoro*, 1897; *La giustizia*, 1899; *Il vecchio della montagna*, 1900; *Dopo il divorzio*, 1902 (*After the Divorce*, 1905; republished as *Naufraghi in porto*, 1920); *Elias Portolu*, 1903; *Cenere*, 1904 (*Ashes*, 1908); *Nostalgie*, 1905; *L'edera*, 1906; *L'ombra del passato*, 1907; *Il nostro padrone*, 1910; *Sino al confine*, 1910; *Nel deserto*, 1911; *Colombi e sparvieri*, 1912; *Canne al vento*, 1913; *Le colpe altrui*, 1914; *Marianna Sirca*, 1915; *L'incendio nell'oliveto*, 1918; *La madre*, 1920 (*The Mother*, 1923, 1974; also as *The Woman and the Priest*, 1922); *Il segreto dell'uomo solitario*, 1921; *Il Dio dei viventi*, 1922; *La danza della collana*, 1924; *La fuga in Egitto*, 1925; *Annalena Bilsini*, 1927; *Il vecchio e i fanciulli*, 1928; *Il paese del vento*, 1931; *L'argine*, 1934; *La chiesa della solitudine*, 1936; *Cosima*, 1937; *Romanzi e novelle*, 1941-1969; *Opere scelte*, 1964; *Romanzi e novelle*, 1971.

Other literary forms
All through her life, Grazia Deledda wrote short fiction. After publication in periodicals, most of the short stories were collected in volumes, which number at least twenty-two. The early short pieces were exercises and appeared in local journals or women's magazines; those written from 1899 to 1912 were of higher quality. Those were Deledda's best years for long fiction also, so that the two aspects of her creativity seem to have nourished each other. As the writer's fame grew, she was asked to contribute more and more frequently to popular magazines; like other writers of her generation, she provided the flourishing business of the periodical press with a steady flow of material. Although those short stories were designed to please the public and therefore were often trite, melodramatic, and full of the worst stereotypical characters and situations, they provide useful information on the cultural milieu of the 1900's in Italy.

Deledda's best collection of short stories is *Chiaroscuro* (1912). She employs a variety of styles and themes in the twenty-two pieces collected under that title: They are inspired by the traditional tale, the ghost story, the fairy tale (Deledda wrote many stories for children, too), the humorous anecdote, and the sentimental story. The most frequently used themes, however, and the most successfully treated, are those inspired by Deledda's half-remembered, half-imagined Sardinia. These short stories are usually fast paced and colorful. The locations and the situations remind the reader of certain scenes from the best Western films: a village square or the stony loneliness of the hills in the white heat of the sun; small groups of people telling one another stories or listening to some handsome stranger's boastings; furious loves, mysterious events, and vendettas. The ingredients are used effectively, and the themes are the same as those that appear in Deledda's major fiction: the power of economic necessity, the greater power of sexual desire, and the uselessness of the wisdom of old people.

Achievements

Critical statements about Deledda's fiction are contradictory, at times negative, and yet they all acknowledge the power of her imagination and style. What makes a critical evaluation of her work difficult is her apparent isolation from prevailing literary currents.

When Deledda published her first novels and short stories, at the end of the nineteenth century, the emerging current was *Verismo*, which had largely taken over the tenets of French Naturalism. With *Verismo*, human experience is bound to its social context. The author must let characters and events speak directly; the phenomena of everyday life—actions, rites, customs, language— are of greater interest than psychological probings. At first, Deledda seemed to have much in common with *Verismo*; the warm welcome that *Veristi* such as Giovanni Verga and Luigi Capuana extended to the young writer was in part the result of Deledda's sensitivity and loyalty to the culture of Sardinia. The critics of the early 1900's, however, questioned Deledda's *Verismo* and saw it as a limitation and a superficial element in her fiction; they expressed admiration, instead, for the epic aura they found in her novels. While the critics debated Deledda's problematic position in literary history, readers from the urban middle class became her devoted public. For them, she was the very voice of Sardinia, a mysterious and therefore fascinating island, and she was quintessentially a narrator, prolific and attuned to the times.

In the view of some critics, Deledda was a "spontaneous" writer whose immediacy owed almost nothing to literary tradition, a writer not so much ignorant of as uninterested in that tradition, preferring to remain within an archaic, lyric world elaborated by her memory—a world that she called Sardinia. For some, her "illiteracy"—that is, her position outside the literary tradition—her "barbaric" or "primitive" sensibility, were admirable qualities; for others, they were disconcerting liabilities. Critics such as Emilio Cecchi and Eurialo De Michelis have argued that Deledda was in fact deeply responsive to the artistic currents of her time. Pointing to the allusive quality of her writing, the musical and symbolic dimensions of her narratives, they see her as representative of *Decadentismo* or, more generally, of the European Symbolist movement.

Recent analyses have looked more closely at the themes, the imagery, and the language of Deledda's fiction. They confirm the unity of her experience and her marginal relation to the conventional literary tradition, but they also bring out her modernity and her kinship with other solitary figures of early twentieth century Italian literature such as Luigi Pirandello, Italo Svevo, and Federigo Tozzi. Deledda's is a European voice—the voice of an era that was disappointed by the myth of progress and torn between latter-day Romanticism and Symbolism. Her concern with the conflict between the passions of the individual and the needs of an ordered community is the same as that addressed by such different minds as D. H. Lawrence and Sigmund Freud.

Biography

Grazia Cosima Deledda was born in Nuoro, Sardinia, on September 27, 1871, the fourth of six children. Her family was moderately well-to-do. Deledda attended three elementary classes, and then repeated the third one, in order to receive as much schooling as possible—a common practice at that time for a boy from the lower classes or a girl who was unusually bright. Thereafter, Deledda received haphazard tutoring from a professor who happened to be in Nuoro and knew the family. She also read on her own: Eugène Sue, Alexandre Dumas, Sir Walter Scott, the Bible, Honoré de Balzac, Homer, and Victor Hugo. Soon, constant writing and dreaming of glory became Deledda's occupations. By the time she was sixteen, she had established a network of correspondents in Sardinia and on the Continent, through the little magazines she read. In 1886, she published her first short story, in 1888 and 1889, her first *feuilleton*. From that point on, Deledda published children's stories, essays on regional customs, short stories, and *feuilletons*, becoming a steady contributor to several literary and women's magazines.

No matter what her ambition and her successes may have been, Deledda had soon become aware of the need to comply with the conventions of her provincial town: Her behavior, although girlish at times, was respectful of traditional rules. Nuoro society was irritated when it discovered that a local girl was drawing material for fictional and ethnographic work from its life and customs. In addition, Deledda was a pragmatic person from a tender age; as she observed the world around her, she saw what burdens romantic attachments and unwise unions could place on women. She was fully conscious of her total commitment to her writing career.

Feeling constrained and isolated during all of those years, Deledda yearned to leave Nuoro. That desire was satisfied when she met Palmiro Madesani, a functionary of the Italian government, in 1900. They married and moved to Rome, where Deledda remained during the course of a serene married life that included two children, Sardus and Franz. After 1900, her biography is the record of her literary activity. She continued to publish at a sustained pace, obtaining public favor and critical acclaim. Her success was internationally acknowledged when she was awarded the Nobel Prize for Literature in 1926. She lived a very private life, fulfilled and joyful, which is substantiated by her correspondence with her friends. Deledda died in Rome, Italy, on August 15, 1936.

Analysis

A prolific writer is often viewed as a force of nature, and Grazia Deledda's writing has been called "instinctual," yet her letters and her autobiographical novel, *Cosima*, written in the last year of her life and published posthumously, testify to her conscious determination to be a writer and to perfect her skills. Deledda's work is the product not only of a facile gift but also of an apprenticeship. There were three periods in her career. The first one, extending to 1900, included at least sixteen volumes of long and short fiction. It was a period of training, when her major themes and images emerged from a mass of second-rate prose. From 1900 to 1915, Deledda wrote all of her best novels, establishing herself as a major novelist on the European scene. During the last twenty years of her life, although she continued to publish at an impressive rate, she failed to reach her earlier effectiveness. Only with *Cosima*, as she looked upon her years in Nuoro, did she again find her voice, speaking of that youthful "Other" whose willfulness and vitality could not be suppressed by family tragedy or dismal circumstances.

Two basic elements of Deledda's fiction must be considered first: the setting and the influence of the female experience. The setting of almost all Deleddian fiction is Sardinia, an island which had always been cut off from the life of the mainland. Until the 1900's, it remained a land of wild natural beauty and ancient customs, inhabited by shepherds and hostile to the powers that ruled it from afar. Deledda grew up in Sardinia, conscious of the rigid local customs yet separated from "the people" by her social status as the daughter of a landowning family. Her early short stories and novels described the Sardinian environment with clarity but as if from the outside, as an ethnological phenomenon and a picturesque setting. In *La via del male*, one of her first significant novels, the author indulged in descriptions of the island's beauty; at the same time, she wove a love story based on the devotion of the "primitive soul" of a servant-shepherd, the repressed sexuality of male serf and female landowner, and a code reminiscent of the courtly-love tradition, filtered through folklore. Progressively, however, Sardinia became an integral element of Deledda's fictional world. As she moved to the Continent, she began to appropriate the geographically identifiable Sardinia, to transform it into a land of her imagination. This Sardinia endured as the background against which she drew her characters, the passions, and rituals of her scenario; the island landscape in its changeability became the visible manifestation of states of mind. Seldom did Deledda use urban settings for her novels, and when she did, the city would only be vaguely sketched—as, for example, in *La danza della collana*.

The other major element in Deledda's fiction is the female experience, which in many ways parallels the experience of the Sardinian: It is secretive, marginal, in conflict with itself, and yet it is also a source of strength and a fierce sense of identity. At seventeen, the writer complained in a letter:

". . . whole months without going out of the house . . . a cheerful house, but looking onto a street where there is never a passer-by . . . I am not allowed to do anything in the house, except engage in those ethereal occupations that increase boredom. . . ." Inaction and solitude fed Deledda's ambition and helped her to focus her energies. In her novels, the rules of silence and submission exasperate the passions of her characters. Once again, Deledda draws from an experience that is intimately familiar to her. Metaphors and images come frequently from domestic activities, from the universe of female experience, feelings, and values. Her protagonists, male and female, are described in terms of femaleness. Physically, they tend toward androgyny; as they struggle to submit to the prescriptions of an archaic culture, they become aware of their profound "difference." Sensuous and passionate in a world hemmed in by taboos, they retreat into themselves. The contemplation of nature brings them peace; secrecy and silence become sources of strength and guarantee them a measure of personal freedom. The motifs belonging to the two main sources of Deledda's inspiration thus find their confluence.

The world vision of the novelist, however, was a complex one. She knew the impact of different factors impinging upon human experience. In some novels, such as *Ashes* and *Marianna Sirca*, she gave particular attention to the barrier separating classes that lived in daily intimacy; in others, such as *Canne al vento*, she concentrated on the economic imperative. In all of her novels, Deledda spoke of the subversive power of sexuality and of the contradictory demands made by the pagan and the Christian traditions, one ruled by the mystique of blood vengeance, the other by a message of peace.

No matter what the emphasis, each novel is built around a cluster of recurrent themes. Passion is at the center; it may involve desire for power, wealth, or freedom, but it is always manifested as erotic desire. Sexuality is the impulse that cannot be denied, and it is the first spark in the challenge to any taboo. This centrality of the sexual dimension, as the primary subverter of order, places Deledda's fictional universe well within the sensibility of the early part of the twentieth century, when the exploration of the role of human sexuality was central in literature and science.

Desire causes transgression. Here Deledda's characters reveal their weakness, their tendency toward ambivalence and self-deception. They do not rebel fully and do not consent to their "sin," but they are unable to abide by the ancient rules. Guilt is inevitable for them, and with it an obsessional need for expiation. Deledda has been compared to the great Russian novelists because of her insistence on the themes of sin, guilt, and expiation, yet the similarities are only superficial. For Deledda, the taboos cannot but be challenged, even if the transgressors must suffer for their acts and sometimes for their very wishes; the defeat of desire can only be acknowledged with sadness.

Deledda's protagonists, as most critics have observed, are not the object of psychological study; they are not meant to be. Rather, they reenact a cycle of rebellion and defeat in a context where the forces of clan, class, and religion necessarily overpower the individual. Pietro Benu, the servant-shepherd in *La via del male*, may obtain Maria Noina in marriage after many struggles, but the crimes he has committed transform their union into a punishment, a tool for atonement. In *Ashes*, Olì's ardent sensuality will be expiated through her own and her son's suffering; to this suffering, mother and son will desperately consent. Marianna, the outlaw's lover in *Marianna Sirca*, can be the handsome bandit's wife only at his deathbed; they both pay for falling in love "in a far away, otherworldly place" when they see their faces reflected together in the water of a deep well.

While Deledda's protagonists reenact this bitter cycle, her peripheral characters look on helplessly. Deledda frequently assigns such peripheral roles to old people who have known life's errors, often sinners who have moved into the mountains in order to find peace. Their wisdom, though, cannot influence fate. They are sought after for advice, but their advice is not heeded. They are the archetypal images of a conscience that can only weep over the ruins caused by passion and transgression.

Deledda's style has baffled her critics. To what extent her Sardinian language influenced her writing would be difficult to assess. Her early readings were hardly a school for writing excellence, and that may explain Deledda's long apprenticeship and her lapses into the worst commonplaces in her lesser works. The strength of her prose comes from her attention to gesture and action, her ability to create an atmosphere, her sense for color. There was a dilemma that all Italian writers of her time had to solve: the choice between a dialect that is intimately known but regional, and an imperfectly learned standard language, a bookish language rarely spoken but widely used in writing. Without hesitation, Deledda opted for the Italian that the educated middle class was accustomed to reading. She became the voice of the emerging Italian bourgeoisie, and today her work remains accessible to a wide audience. Her best writing blends the simplicity of the Italian language, which was the medium of the educated class, with the richness of the stylistic devices used by late Romantic authors, and with the flavor of expressions, proverbs, and sayings obviously incorporated from the Sardinian.

The most frequent device used by Deledda is the descriptive passage, a pause in the narration which focuses on a natural scene, a religious festivity, or a character's appearance. In her early works, such passages are frequently an end in themselves, but in her mature works they are functional and fully integrated. In particular, the descriptions of religious pilgrimages are significant, as such communal festivities are emblematic of the connection among religious feeling, natural scenery, and human conscience. Against the background of the mountains in their seasonal splendor, the pilgrims travel on horseback, clad in resplendent costumes, to reach a sanctuary where they customarily perform a ritual. The contrast between the anguish of the protagonists and the beauty of the festive days in their quasi-biblical society is the focal point of Deledda's description.

Elias Portolu, one of Deledda's finest novels, opens with a family celebration for Elias upon his return from a penitentiary on the Continent. Two other festive gatherings, one for a pilgrimage to a sanctuary and one for the Mardi Gras, will mark the turning points of the story, dramatizing the conflict between the protagonist and the culture to which he has returned. Elias, who is at the center of the rejoicing of his community, immediately appears alone, an outsider in the tribal unity. The prison experience, his "misfortune," as they call it, has created a distance between him and his culture which allows him to gain a critical perspective; it has also brought out in him an awareness of his own difference, an awareness which contradicts the ethos of the clan. The taboo is an a priori reality in Deledda's universe, but it is Elias' unavoidable obstacle because he is sensitized to its presence, and his changed sensibility leads him to acknowledge his individual desires. Deledda's characters speak of the taboo in terms of fate; in effect, the mechanism of transgression and punishment is set in motion only under certain circumstances, as if it were lying in wait for a destined victim. Elias self-indulgently probes his discontent; he experiences a sort of existential guilt. His "fate" is made evident also by a "sign" which is given prominence from the very beginning of the novel, his androgynous appearance. By his culture's standards, he is "like a woman in man's clothing": His skin is white as a woman's, his hands are beautiful and white, and he is tall and lean with delicate features. The male society around him requires coarseness, aggressiveness, and a demeanor rigidly obedient to social conventions. His temperament, gentle and reserved, with sudden bursts of emotion, marks him as "a child," a misfit, as someone who is doomed to violate the laws of custom.

During the cavalcade and the activities of the pilgrimage, Elias falls in love with Maddalena, his brother's fiancée, and the radical weakness of his personality is revealed: He is ambivalent, unable to accept his difference and assert his individual will yet also incapable of denying himself and respecting the taboo. During the Mardi Gras, when masked costumes and dances allow a controlled weakening of the rules governing the community, Elias and Maddalena—who is by now his sister-in-law—begin an incestuous relationship. Torn between decisions he cannot make, Elias retreats into the priesthood, adding the obstacles of new taboos to repress his desire. The burden of expiation will be carried by both lovers, as first Maddalena's husband and then the lovers' child die. By the boy's deathbed, Elias, who is now a very tormented priest, finds some sort of peace, a joy resembling "a vaporous veil." Moments of turmoil alternate with moments of reflection as the protagonist wavers between opposite moods. Although he has discovered the power of desire, the egotism of the self, Elias is paralyzed by his awe for a code of conduct that condemns all impulses that threaten to disrupt the ordered universe of his culture.

The characters around Elias perform a choral function, as the duel between Elias' opposing temptations takes place. There is Maddalena, passionate and sacrificing; the family, unable to understand Elias' "illness"; the mother, the image of the "sainted" female whose embrace promises the peace of renouncement; and a priest and an old hermit, who advise Elias and are not heeded. Deledda also skillfully incorporates dream sequences into the narration, as well as details of the many activities of the shepherd's lives. All around loom the mountainous regions of the island, where nature is order and beauty. There, conflict ceases, overwhelmed by the colors, the fragrances, and the sounds of a primitive Eden. Only wise men, though, Deledda says, can live there, after they have made their peace with the world and with themselves.

Deledda's personal favorite among her novels was *Canne al vento*, a melancholy tale of three unmarried sisters and their manservant, Efix. Here, Deledda's style is as nuanced as the themes are richly woven. Realistic in the dialogues, her writing becomes lyric in the descriptions of nature, male beauty, and sensual life, suggesting a synesthesia of human experience.

Paradoxically, Efix, who is old and guilty of a double transgression against the taboo of caste and the authority of the father/master, has become the protective figure for the surviving members of the noble family. In a journey of penance, he succeeds in repairing the damage caused within the ancient order by the young people he loves. He will attain his goal of restoring the family's fortunes when he is able to make them obey the law that commands acceptance of suffering and submission: "We are born to suffer like the Christ. We must weep and keep silent."

Another novelist treating the same material might focus on the inevitable conflicts within a static society still faithful to feudal values. Deledda, however, veers away from that set of questions, preferring to explore the stages of a purificatory journey within the majestic environment of her island. The significant theme for her is that of redemption through suffering; the figure of the pure of heart, the simple man, is central to it. This is particularly evident in the episode of Efix's journey in the company of beggars, which is a *mise en abîme* of the role of that character in the novel. In the universe of male values, between the violence of the Father and the rebelliousness of the young, Efix embodies the virtues that guarantee endurance. They are the traditional female virtues: patience, resignation, and love of peace. Efix is described in terms of feminine submission: He is "the good servant" who keeps quiet even when he knows, who simulates ignorance, humiliated and yet convinced of the appropriateness of his subservience. His caring love is a kind of motherly nurturing: ". . . he wished that he could lean over the unhappy boy, and tell him: 'I am here, I'll provide!'—but he could only offer him the wine gourd, as a mother offers her breast to her crying baby." The novel closes with a moving account of the death of the servant who has accomplished his task, in a further parallelism with other mother figures in several of Deledda's other works.

In *The Mother*, with unusual structural simplicity and the most economical means, Deledda explores again the conflicts of passion and taboo and the problematical issue of expiation. There are only two characters here, the mother and her son, the priest; two locations, the house and the church; and a time span that is both very short and immeasurable, like the time of a fairy tale. A third character, Agnes, is barely sketched, and the choral presence of the villagers, with their primitive celebrations, serves only as a distancing device underlining the loneliness of the protagonists. The almost schematic appearance of the text contradicts its complexity at the stylistic level: The novel partakes of several genres, partly religious drama, partly fantastic tale, and partly symbolic poem.

The passion that leads to transgression here is dual: It is the furious sexual desire that almost overcomes Don Paulo as he begins his pastoral career in a mountain parish, but it is also the ambition of his mother, who "had wanted to return to give orders where she had been a servant . . ." and who thought she had managed to fulfill this ambition by rearing her son for the priesthood. The sexual transgression is avoided in a struggle between Paulo's desire and his fears, but only at the price of the death of the mother, who thus expiates also for her sin of pride. Her death may appear melodramatic, an unconvincing device, but it is consistent with Deledda's development of her story in a symbolic mode. Without perhaps fully realizing it, Deledda deepens her exploration of the connections between sexual taboo and power and the relationship between the traditionally separate male and female universes. Maria Maddalena and Paulo are as one in their symbiotic closeness: mother and son, female and male, one conscience torn between passion and renouncement. On the one hand, they harbor a mistrust of the flesh, a fear of all joyous abandon, having internalized their society's condemnation of individual fulfillment; on the other hand, there is their conviction, persistently voiced, that passion is the only authentic voice of humanity.

Deledda uses visions, dreams, ghostly dialogues, metaphors, and images inspired by fairy tales to create an atmosphere of mystery. The furious wind of the highlands becomes one with the characters' spiritual and physical anguish; the priest's black cloak beats the air like the wings of a bird of prey, and doors open and close as if by magic, hiding forever what is on the other side. This is a journey inside the ambiguity of human experience. D. H. Lawrence, in his preface to the English translation of the novel, offers, among many questionable statements, the wrongheaded observation that Deledda does not give her book a conclusion because she has divided feelings: She is impatient with her characters and confuses the issues, Lawrence says, resorting to the elimination of the mother because she resents Maddalena's final triumph, resents her as an obstacle to Paulo's sexual satisfaction. Concerned with what he calls primitive and instinctual passionality, Lawrence does not see that Paulo and Maddalena are two faces of the same divided self. As a price for attaining peace, the female figure must die, for she is the one who grieved "in her flesh" for Paulo's renunciation, and it was she, the servant, who had silently questioned the rule of priestly celibacy. The closing of the novel sanctions, and obscurely laments, precisely the end of that tormented ambiguity, the irrepressible joy of that physical communion.

Major publications other than long fiction

SHORT FICTION: *Amori moderni*, 1907; *Chiaroscuro*, 1912; *Il fanciullo nascosto*, 1915; *Il ritorno del figlio, La bambina rubata*, 1919; *Il flauto nel bosco*, 1923; *Il sigillo d'amore*, 1926; *La casa del poeta*, 1930; *La vigna sul mare*, 1932; *Sole d'estate*, 1933; *Il cedro del Libano*, 1939.

Bibliography

Balducci, Carolyn. *A Self-Made Woman*, 1975.
Dolfi, Anna. *Grazia Deledda*, 1979.
Lombardi, Olga. *Invito alla lettura di Grazia Deledda*, 1974.
Pacifici, Sergio. *The Modern Italian Novel from Capuana to Tozzi*, 1973.

Angela M. Jeannet

MIGUEL DELIBES

Born: Valladolid, Spain; October 17, 1920

Principal long fiction

La sombra del ciprés es alargada, 1948; *Aún es de día*, 1949; *El camino*, 1950 (*The Path*, 1961); *Mi idolatrado hijo Sisí*, 1953; *Diario de un cazador*, 1955; *Diario de un emigrante*, 1958; *Las ratas*, 1962 (*Smoke on the Ground*, 1972); *Cinco horas con Mario*, 1966; *Parábola del náufrago*, 1969 (*The Hedge*, 1983); *El príncipe destronado*, 1973; *Las guerras de nuestros antepasados*, 1974; *El disputado voto del señor Cayo*, 1978; *Los santos inocentes*, 1981 (novella).

Other literary forms

Though primarily a novelist, Miguel Delibes has published several books of travel impressions, for example, *Por esos mundos* (1961; round about the world), *Europa, parada y fonda* (1963; Europe, stops, and inns), *USA y yo* (1966; USA and I), *La primavera de Praga* (1968; springtime in Prague); short narratives, including collections, for example, *La partida* (1954; the departure), *Siestas con viento sur* (1957; siestas with a southern breeze), *La mortaja* (1970; the shroud); books on hunting and fishing, for example, *Aventuras, venturas y desventuras de un cazador a rabo* (1977; adventures, good and bad luck of a small game hunter), *Mis amigas las truchas* (1977; my trout friends); and miscellaneous books of articles, commentary, and essays, newspaper articles, and comments and impressions written in diary form. Asked by the Spanish government to write a tourist guide of Old Castile, Delibes produced *Viejas historias de Castilla la Vieja* (1964; old tales of Old Castile), a work which for its narrative-descriptive passages of lyric force is one of the author's most memorable and revealing books (though it was unacceptable as a travel guide); it is sometimes classified as a novella.

Achievements

Delibes is without doubt one of Spain's most significant novelists to emerge since the end of the Spanish Civil War in 1939. His first novel, *La sombra del ciprés es alargada*, published by the Barcelona publisher Destino in 1948, won the prestigious Eugenio Nadal Prize in 1947. Though probably his worst novel, it was decisive in influencing him to continue his efforts at writing fiction, efforts which he has realized while working simultaneously for many years as a professor in the School of Commerce in Valladolid and on the editorial staff of the newspaper *El norte de Castilla*, serving as its director from 1958 to 1963. As a novelist, his work has been marked by a steady growth and progression in style and content, causing the critics to observe that each new Delibean book is better than the last one. In general, Delibes has progressively moved away from a traditional and detailed realism reminiscent of the nineteenth century to a more poetic and symbolic realism, experimentation in structure and techniques, and a more economical, direct, and unaffected style, though the direction toward simplicity has been broken somewhat in some later works, such as *Cinco horas con Mario* (five hours with Mario) and *The Hedge*, in which his more complex and convoluted syntax serves the purpose of making style reflect content, especially, according to Janet Díaz, the "troubled psychological atmosphere and torment" of the protagonist. Delibes' novels have been widely translated into the leading European languages. Numerous doctoral theses on his work have been completed in American and European universities.

A strong and independent voice in contemporary Spanish fiction, Delibes has adhered to no group or movement inside or outside Spain, though he has absorbed from them whatever he saw as beneficial to his own character and temperament as a man and as a writer. Though neither a regionalist nor a novelist of customs (*costumbrista*) in the traditional sense, he has continued to live in Valladolid and portray what he knows best: the rural people and landscape of Old Castile. In particular, his distinctive use of rural Castilian speech has won high praise; notable also is his creation of rural Castilian atmospheres and characters.

Biography

Born October 17, 1920, into a bourgeois family in Valladolid, a provincial capital in Old Castile, Miguel Delibes Setien was reared as a strict Catholic. Though his father was liberal in his views, his mother was very conservative; in his childhood and adolescence, her orientation seemed to dominate; in adult life, his father's Catholic liberalism prevailed. By the time the Spanish Civil War began, the future novelist, though not yet seventeen, had been graduated from high school. A year later, he joined the Nationalist Navy and served on a cruiser patrolling the Cantabrian Coast.

After the war, Delibes, having been refused reenlistment in the navy because of nearsightedness, took specially provided accelerated courses in both law and business, obtaining degrees in both areas in 1941. In 1943, he took an intensive three-month course in journalism in Madrid. In 1945, through competitive examinations (*oposiciones*), he won the Chair of Mercantile Law in the School of Commerce in Valladolid, succeeding his father. Later he changed his subject to the history of culture. In 1946, he married Angeles de Castro. In 1947, he wrote his first novel-manuscript, partly in an attempt to rid himself of his obsession with death—an obsession he had had since childhood. Submitted to the Nadal competition, the manuscript won its prestigious prize, and it appeared in 1948 as *La sombra del ciprés es alargada*.

During the next several years, Delibes worked on the editorial staff of *El norte de Castilla*, Spain's second oldest continuously operating newspaper, and held his professorial post in the School of Commerce while continuing to write novels. His second novel, *Aún es de día*, appeared in 1949; according to Díaz, it resembles his first novel in its "rather ponderous, rhetorical style." Critics generally agree that Delibes found his proper style in his third novel, *The Path*, published in 1950, a work which, unlike his first two novels, almost instantly became an unqualified critical success. In 1955, *Diario de un cazador* was awarded the Miguel de Cervantes Prize.

While continuing his increasingly successful career as a novelist and writer of short fiction, Delibes fulfilled his journalistic duties with distinction, rising to be assistant director of *El norte de Castilla* from 1952 until 1958 and director from 1958 until 1963 (when political pressures from the Franco regime forced his resignation).

A Catholic, though liberal in his views, a faithful husband and father of seven children, a passionate lover of nature and an avid fisherman and hunter, Delibes disclaims all pretensions to intellectualism. Gonzalo Sobejano aptly describes Delibes' whole career as a search for authenticity, a search for his own proper "path." Delibes has traveled extensively, including in the United States. He has a broad cosmopolitan view and concern for the problems of contemporary man, not only for those of Spain. In 1975, he was admitted to the Royal Spanish Academy, primarily in recognition of his achievements as a novelist.

Analysis

Critics generally divide Miguel Delibes' novels into two periods or types. Written in the first manner are the author's first two novels, *La sombra del ciprés es alargada* and *Aún es de día*, and his fourth novel, *Mi idolatrado hijo Sisí* (my adored son Sisí), published in 1953. With the publication of *The Path* in 1950, his third novel, Delibes inaugurated his second manner, which implied a definite break with his earlier rhetorical, rather sluggish, analytical, and traditionally realistic style. Since 1950, with the exception of his brief reversion to traditional realism in *Mi idolatrado hijo Sisí*, a novel which advances an anti-Malthusian thesis, Delibes has evolved in the direction of freer artistic expression, of what has been called "poetic realism" (as against his former "analytic realism"). During his second phase, Delibes has experimented freely with new techniques and structures. Plot has all but disappeared and a third-person narrative point of view has been replaced with the author-narrator merging his voice with that of the protagonist to form a central narrative consciousness with a double perspective: that of the narrator and that of the protagonist. Though the two perspectives coalesce, they can be distinguished by the alert reader. Technical and structural innovations made by Delibes are expressive of his continuing search for his own most authentic mode or "path" of novelization (although he has sometimes been suspected of following current literary vogues in pursuit of critical acclaim). Novels of his second period are generally characterized by a reduction in time and space and by single-minded, simpleminded protagonists; what the works lose in complexity they gain in unity and concentrated force. The action on the primary plane in *The Path* occurs in one night, in *Cinco horas con Mario* also in one night, in *Las guerras de nuestros antepasados* in seven consecutive evenings, and all occur in a single house or room.

In ideology or thematic content, one finds little if any real changes between the author's early and later periods. An intensified anguish over the dangers to man's freedom and dignity, inherent in modern technological paternalistic societies, and the growing lack of communication or human solidarity in today's world, however, especially mark some of his more recent novels, notably *Cinco horas con Mario* and *The Hedge*. His main motifs, as pointed out by Díaz, remain as constants in his work: the shadow of death, the importance of nature, the life and landscape of rural Old Castile (with its severe socioeconomic problems and abandonment by the Central Spanish Government), a preference for child protagonists (*The Path, Smoke on the Ground, El príncipe destronado*) or elementary, abnormal, or "primitive" characters (the Rat Hunter in *Smoke on the Ground*, Pacífico Pérez in *Las guerras de nuestros antepasados*), and the individual in his difficult relationships with others and with society at large (*Las guerras de nuestros antepasados*). His more recent novels include biting satire of the Catholic Church's apparent impotence in effecting a genuine spiritual-moral transformation of the Spanish character. Since childhood, Delibes has occasionally suffered from periods of pessimism, a mood which seems to have intensified in his more recent novels.

Pío Baroja and Camilo José Cela appear to be two of the principal influences upon Delibes as a writer of fiction. His irony and his dry, laconic description of gruesome scenes as well as his use of nicknames and repetition of descriptive phrases or tag lines, often ironic, to identify characters (for example, the priest "who was a great saint"), especially recall Cela.

Through the memory flashbacks of Daniel, the eleven-year-old protagonist of *The Path*, on the night before his expected departure—for further schooling in the city—from the Castilian village in which he was born and has lived all of his life, the reader enters into the "world" of the protagonist. In that "world," Daniel's personal life is projected outward toward the collective life of the village; the individual and his society in this work fuse into an artistic unity. Past and present are also interwoven through Daniel's memory flashbacks, though the narrator often intervenes to provide his own perspective on the events and situations being recalled. The narrator interjects without destroying the reader's illusion that the central narrative consciousness is that of the child-protagonist; in fact his added perspective subtly contributes to the narrative's sense of reality or verisimilitude.

Essentially plotless, a series of anecdotes given unity primarily by the protagonist himself—he is telling his personal story—the work simultaneously draws a vivid portrayal of village life in Spain while elaborating upon the author's favorite themes: death, childhood, nature, and neighbor (or man's relationship in society). Daniel, enamored of his life as the son of a poor cheesemaker in the village, believes that his "path" or "way" in life should be to remain where he is. His father, however, wants his son to develop his possibilities to the fullest, and to achieve that end he believes that it is imperative that Daniel acquire a higher education than that available in the village. At great sacrifice, Daniel's father is sending him to the city. Through the opposing views of father and son, important differences between Spanish rural and city life become visible, leading some critics to regard the work as in praise of country life and scorn of life in the city; it can be more accurately described as simply an effort to present the realities of each. Though without a double-time dimension, *Smoke on the Ground*, published almost twelve years later, bears close thematic and structural resemblance to *The Path*. In the later work, however, the reader is made much more painfully aware of the cultural, moral, and economic deprivation of life in a Castilian village.

Cinco horas con Mario will undoubtedly remain one of Delibes' most perfectly constructed and important novels. When it appeared in 1966, critics almost universally commented on its seemingly radical break from the novelist's former, more conventional patterns. In a recent study, however, Luis Gonzalez del Valle demonstrates that in structure, narrative techniques, and themes, it bears a marked resemblance to *The Path*. In Gonzalez del Valle's opinion, it constitutes a partial return to the earlier work.

The book opens with a full-page reproduction of an announcement of funeral arrangements for Mario Collado, a professor and unsuccessful writer, who died unexpectedly at the age of forty-nine in March of 1966. Though not named, the setting is a provincial Spanish capital strikingly similar to Valladolid. Following the obituary notice is an untitled chapter, followed by twenty-seven numbered chapters and closing with an untitled chapter, a kind of epilogue. In the untitled introductory chapter, Carmen, Mario's widow of Spanish bourgeois mentality, in her mind and in conversation with her close female friend Valen, reviews the day, which began with the discovery of Mario's death, funeral arrangements, visits to express condolences, and so on. It is now midnight, and she prepares to spend the morning hours by her husband's corpse. The rest of the novel, except for its last short chapter, consists of her interior monologue or unilateral dialogue in which she addresses Mario's corpse in the familiar second person (*tú*), reviewing in flashbacks their life together.

In her harsh, spiteful, and uncomprehending criticism of Mario—a post-Vatican II Catholic who championed the cause of social justice—she gives full vent to her frustration. In a free association of ideas, reiterating certain obsessions, she sometimes rants and raves. In the process of accusing her dead husband of what she perceives to be his many shortcomings, however, she reveals herself to the reader as an ignorant, self-centered, addleheaded hypocrite and thus condemns herself. At the same time, by implication she condemns (unconsciously, of course) the middle-class Spanish society whose values she so faithfully mirrors and of which she is a product. In the final chapter, the couple's oldest son, Mario, thinking that he has heard his mother talking aloud to the corpse, enters the room. By what he says, the reader gathers some hope that the wounds of a divided Spain—as represented by Mario and Carmen—may eventually be healed.

The novel constitutes a study of an absolutely incompatible marriage, but it is more than that. On an allegorical level, Mario comes obliquely to represent an open and democratic Spain, post-Vatican II Catholicism, love and human solidarity, and the abolition of social and economic inequities, while his widow represents a closed and traditional Spain, a dogmatic pre-Vatican II Church, the preservation of social classes, and an unauthentic, materialistic mode of living. By presenting Mario as a corpse and making Carmen express concepts acceptable to the Spanish political regime of the time, Delibes adroitly avoided official censorship while at the same time improving the novel's artistic quality, a masterpiece in irony. The author wisely avoided painting Mario as a hero; he is seen as an ineffectual and impractical idealist and as a mediocre writer. In presenting him in human proportions, often ambiguous, the novel gains in artistic power. It has been adapted for the stage, and it enjoyed a long and successful run in Spanish theaters.

Reminiscent of Franz Kafka's *Der Verwandlung* (1915; *Metamorphosis*, 1936), Eugène Ionesco's *Le Rhinocéros* (1959; *Rhinoceros*, 1960), and Aldous Huxley's *Brave New World* (1932), *The Hedge* portrays in anguished, nightmarish sequences the slow but certain metamorphosis of Jacinto San José, a symbol of contemporary man in a technological and increasingly uniform and paternalistic society, into a ram, a sacrificial victim of an all-pervasive collectivity which has extracted from him the last vestiges of his individuality and manhood. Some critics saw in the work a radical new direction, an attempt to join the vanguard in novelistic innovation, especially to emulate the latest in Hispanic-American novels. In reality, however, *The Hedge*, though a parable rather than a realistic novel, with a setting and atmosphere more European than strictly Spanish, is consonant with the nature of Delibes as a man and as a novelist. It once more demonstrates his profound concern for the dignity and freedom of the individual and his relationship with contemporary society. Its unconventional techniques are in accordance with the author's openness to experimentation and are, as Sobejano has indicated, artistically essential to the work as a whole.

Jacinto, a humble and timid bookkeeper working for the gigantic organization presided over by the rotund Don Abdón, dares one day to ask the meaning of what he is doing, whether he is adding zeros or the letter *O*. His lack of total conformity to the organization thenceforth is suspect and leads to his being sent to a rest home in the country where in helpless isolation he is metamorphosed into a ram, having lost his long, desperate, and tormented battle to preserve his human personality. All is experienced by the reader from *inside* the anguished consciousness of Jacinto, an effect primarily achieved through interior monologues of the protagonist but further reinforced through a series of autodialogues in which Jacinto speaks in second person familiar to his image in the mirror and through the tone and perspective of the narrative sections.

A much noted (and irritating) technique is the use through much of the novel of the verbal designations for punctuation rather than their conventional signs; thus comma, period, semicolon, open parenthesis, close parenthesis, and so on, are all spelled out in the text. The effect on the reader is that of listening to a colorless, impersonal office dictation, which thus heightens the sense of alienation experienced by Jacinto. Much of the book is concerned with the degradation of language (as a parallel to the degradation of man), through which Delibes sought to make form reflect content, while at the same time parodying some contemporary novelists who propose the destruction of language as one of their missions.

The Hedge is a mixture of realism and fantasy, appropriate to a parable. It constitutes a powerful metaphor of the plight of contemporary man in a slowly disintegrating, impersonal society, and in its success in communicating the author's (Jacinto's) deep anguish lies its greatest merit.

In *Las guerras de nuestros antepasados*, Delibes employs what Díaz calls a "retrospective-reconstructive technique," a technique by which a whole novelistic world is created indirectly through introspection or conversation during a very short period, a technique employed in *The Path* and in *Cinco horas con Mario*. The technique is not at all uncommon, though it has many variations; Ramón José Sender, for example, used it with notable effectiveness in *Mosén Millán* (1953; better known as *Réquiem por un campesino español*; *Requiem for a Spanish Peasant*, 1960). In effect, nothing much happens except introspection and/or conversation in the present, the primary plane of action, while the major action of the novel is that which is evoked from the past, the secondary plane of action and of time.

Las guerras de nuestros antepasados opens with an untitled brief introductory section or untitled prologue in which a psychiatrist, the fictitious Dr. Burgueño López, tells of his association with Pacífico Pérez, a convict in a penal sanatorium, and offers to the reader a faithful transcript of taped conversations he had with Pérez during seven consecutive evenings, May 21 through May 27, 1961; each conversation makes up a chapter. The book closes with a kind of epilogue (slightly more than a page in length) in which Dr. Burgueño López relates the death of Pacífico Pérez on September 13,

1969. Before dying, Pérez gives the psychiatrist permission to publish the transcript of the seven conversations. Through the indirect device of presenting the conversations as taped and transcribed by Dr. Burgueño López, Delibes sought to distance himself as author from the text and to lend to it an illusion of a document placed in the hands of the reader without intermediaries.

The novel is a reconstruction in conversations, guided gently by the psychiatrist, of Pacífico Pérez' upbringing in a small, poverty-stricken Castilian village and his subsequent life in prison. Pérez speaks in the language of the Castilian peasant, attesting once again the importance Delibes attaches to this element in his work. The book's title refers to man's deep propensity for making war on his neighbor. Pacífico was brought up by his great-grandfather, grandfather, and father, each of whom had fought for Spain in a war; they regarded it as inevitable that Pacífico would have "his war" and consequently set about educating him for violence. For great-grandfather Pérez, it was either "sangra o te sangrarán" ("bleed them or they will bleed you"); Pacífico found this philosophy repugnant and turned inward in deep distress. When the brother of his girlfriend surprises Pacífico half naked with his sister, Pacífico impulsively kills the brother—without fear or hate. Refusing to defend himself in court, he is imprisoned. In prison he finds freedom; he would rather live out of society (or at least on its margin) than pay the terrible price of participation, "bleed them or they will bleed you." The conflict between the individual and society remains unresolved for Delibes, just as it did for Baroja before him. In its despairing tone and atmosphere, *Las guerras de nuestros antepasados* recalls *The Hedge*. Indeed, with advancing age, the author's pessimism seems to have deepened.

Major publications other than long fiction

SHORT FICTION: *La partida*, 1954; *Siestas con viento sur*, 1957; *La mortaja*, 1970.

NONFICTION: *Por esos mundos*, 1961; *Europa, parada y fonda*, 1963; *El libro de la caza menor*, 1964; *Viejas historias de Castilla la Vieja*, 1964; *USA y yo*, 1966; *La primavera de Praga*, 1968; *Vivir al día*, 1968; *S.O.S.*, 1976; *Aventuras, venturas y desventuras de un cazador a rabo*, 1977; *Mis amigas las truchas*, 1977.

Bibliography
Alonso de los Ríos, César. *Conversaciones con Miguel Delibes*, 1971.

Buckley, Ramón. *Problemas formales en la novela española contemporánea*, 1973.

Cabrera, Vicente, and Luis González del Valle. *Novela española contemporánea*, 1978.

Díaz, Janet W. *Miguel Delibes*, 1971.

_____ . "Review," in *Journal of Spanish Studies: Twentieth Century*.
  III (Winter, 1975), pp. 212-214.
Hickey, Leo. *Cinco horas con Miguel Delibes*, 1968.
Pauk, Edar. *Miguel Delibes: Desarrollo de un escritor (1947-1974)*, 1975.
Rey, Alfonso. *La originalidad novelística de Delibes*, 1975.
Schwartz, Ronald. *Spain's New Wave Novelists: 1950-1954*, 1976.
Sobejano, Gonzalo. *Novela española de nuestro tiempo*, 1975.
Umbral, Francisco. *Miguel Delibes*, 1970.

Charles L. King

DENIS DIDEROT

Born: Langres, France; October 5, 1713
Died: Paris, France; July 31, 1784

Principal long fiction

Les Bijoux indiscrets, 1748 (*The Indiscreet Toys*, 1749); *Jacques le fataliste et son maître*, 1796 (written c. 1771; *Jacques the Fatalist and His Master*, 1797); *La Religieuse*, 1796 (*The Nun*, 1797); *Le Neveu de Rameau*, 1821, 1891 (*Rameau's Nephew*, 1897). Although the official complete edition of Diderot's novels is found in the twenty-volume *Oeuvres complètes* (1875-1877), edited by Jean Assézat and Maurice Tourneax, they are readily available in the Classiques Garnier, editedy Henri Bénac (1962). An updated edition of *Oeuvres complètes* is in process under the editorship of Herbert Dieckmann, Jean Fabre, and Jacques Proust. All the novels are available in English in various popular editions.

Other literary forms

Denis Diderot began his literary career with translations, the most important of which are *L'Histoire de Grèce* (1743), a translation of the English *Grecian History* (1739) by Temple Stanyan; *Essai sur le mérite et la vertu de Shaftesbury* (1745), of Lord Shaftesbury's *An Inquiry Concerning Virtue and Merit* (1699); and *Dictionnaire universel de médecine* (1746-1748), of Robert James's *Medical Dictionary* (1743-1745).

Diderot was a prolific essayist. His first important essay, *Pensées philosophiques* (1746; English translation, 1819), was immediately condemned for its rationalistic critique of supernatural revelation. It is available in English in *Diderot's Early Philosophic Works* (1916), translated by Margeret Jourdain. *La Promenade du sceptique* (1830, written 1747; the skeptic's walk) was described by Diderot himself as a "conversation concerning religion, philosophy, and the world." *De la suffisance de la religion naturelle* (on the sufficiency of natural religion), written the same year but not published until 1770, extols natural religion. The famous *Lettre sur les aveugles* (1749; *An Essay on Blindness*, 1750; also as *Letter on the Blind* in Jourdain's book) puts forth Diderot's ideas on the supremacy of matter; this work was the cause of his imprisonment at Vincennes. It was followed in 1751 by the *Lettre sur les sourds et muets* (*Letter on the Deaf and Dumb* in Jourdain's book), which was circulated by tacit permission of the authorities and which contains important ideas on music and poetry. *Pensées sur l'interprétation de la nature* (1753; thoughts on the interpretation of nature) explores some implications of the scientific method.

In 1759, Diderot began his contributions to Friedrich Melchior Grimm's *Correspondance littéraire*, a periodical which had a very limited circulation among the aristocracy abroad, reporting on the latest happenings in French arts and letters. Diderot's art criticism, contained in the famous *Salons* (1845, 1857) first appeared there. These annual reviews of Paris exhibitions were published from 1759 to 1781, the most famous being those of 1761, 1763 (considered the best), 1765, 1767, and 1769. Other essays during this time include the famous *Le Rêve de d'Alembert* (1830, written 1769; *D'Alembert's Dream*, 1927), which contains scientific and philosophical ideas together with an exploration of dreams. *Entretien d'un père avec ses enfants* (1773; *Conversation Between Father and Children*, 1964) and *Paradoxe sur le comédien* (1830, written 1773; *The Paradox of Acting*, 1883) are among other important essays. Diderot's last philosophical works were his *Essai sur Sénèque* (1778; essay on Seneca) and *Essai sur les règnes de Claude et Néron* (1782), the latter a digressive amplification of the former. Both of these essays mix autobiographical material with an exposition of Diderot's ideas on politics and morality. All of these works are included in the *Oeuvres complètes*; they are also found in the Classiques Garnier volumes, *Oeuvres philosophiques* (1956), *Oeuvres esthétiques* (1959), and *Oeuvres politiques* (1962). In addition to *Diderot's Early Philosophic Works*, English editions include *Diderot, Interpreter of Nature: Selected Writings* (1937), translated by Jean Stewart and Jonathan Kemp, and *Selected Writings* (1966), edited by Lester Crocker.

In 1757, Diderot began to write for the theater. Although he developed a new genre, the so-called *drame bourgeois*, he was not a successful playwright, for his plays lack dramatic qualities. *Le Fils naturel* (*Dorval: Or, The Test of Virtue*, 1767) was published in 1757 but not staged until 1771. It was followed by an essay, *Entretiens sur "Le Fils naturel"* (1757; conversations on "The Natural Son"). *Le Père de famille* (1758; English translation, 1770; also as *The Family Picture*, 1871) was staged in 1761. This play, too, was followed by an important essay, *Discours sur la poésie dramatique* (1758; English translation of chapters 1-5 in *Dramatic Essays of the Neo-Classical Age*, 1950). Diderot's last play, *Est-il bon? Est-il méchant?* (1781; is it good? is it bad?), is considered his best, although it was not staged until 1955.

Besides long fiction, Diderot also wrote several short stories. They include "L'Oiseau blanc, conte bleu" (the white bird, a blue tale), written in 1748 but not published until 1798, and several stories written in 1772: "Les Deux Amis de Bourbonne" (1773; "Two Friends of Bourbonne," 1964), "Ceci n'est pas un conte" (1798; "This Is Not a Story," 1960), "Madame de la Carlière" (1798), and *Supplément au voyage de Bougainville* (1796; *Supplement to Bougainville's Voyage*, 1927). Several of these stories are available in English in Ralph Bowen's translation, *Rameau's Nephew and Other Works* (1964).

Diderot's voluminous correspondence is collected in sixteen volumes by George Roth (1955-1970). The most famous of these letters are the 187 extant to his mistress Sophie Volland (1755-1774). Other important letters are those to Paul Landois, on determinism (1756); those to the Princess of Nassau-

Saarbruck (1758), translated as *Concerning the Education of a Prince* (1941); and the farewell letter to Catherine II of Russia (1774). Finally, Diderot wrote many articles in the famous *Encyclopédie* (1751-1772), many of which are unsigned. Some of these are available in English in the Bobbs-Merrill edition, *Encyclopedia* (1965), translated by Nelly S. Hoyt and Thomas Cassirer.

Achievements

Although Diderot is one of the major novelists of the eighteenth century, it is as the editor of the *Encyclopédie* that he is most remembered. Along with Jean Le Rond d'Alembert, who was to abandon the project in 1758, he began in 1746 what was intended to be a translation of Ephraim Chambers' major English reference work, *Cyclopedia* (1728). Diderot's version later became a compendium of knowledge in seventeen volumes of text and eleven volumes of plates, published from 1751 to 1772 amid countless difficulties and attacks by clergy and government. Not only was Diderot the principal, and eventually sole, editor, but also he was the author of numerous articles, many of which were unsigned in later volumes, and some mutilated by André Le Breton. It is particularly through Diderot's articles that his philosophical ideas come to light, as demonstrated in Arthur M. Wilson's masterful study and confirmed by numerous other scholars.

Diderot was above all else a philosophe, one of the great eighteenth century Enlightenment figures who prepared the way for modern thought. The philosophes were not philosophers in the classical sense. In fact, they criticized many such thinkers, although Diderot had great respect for Plato, to the extent of using ideas from the Socratic dialogues as the basis for many of his works, at least in the opinion of Donal O'Gorman. The philosophes, Diderot among them, believed strongly in personal freedom, as seen in *The Indiscreet Toys* and *The Nun*; in reason and progress, the whole thesis of the *Encyclopédie*; and in a more representative government. Generally they were Deists, although Diderot himself was associated with the atheist circle of Baron Paul d'Holbach.

Diderot as a philosophe explored the question of morals, of virtue and vice—which he named *bienfaisance* and *malfaisance*, or good-doing and evil-doing. He concluded that morality as such is the result of naturalistic and materialistic causes, which determine a person's conduct—hence, that traditional morality has no meaning. *Rameau's Nephew* and *Jacques the Fatalist and His Master* explore essentially the question of the modifiability of human behavior, determinism, and freedom. Diderot also attributes pleasure to natural causes, becoming one of the forerunners of "sensibility," the Romantic emphasis on feeling and the heart. His novels bear the stamp of Samuel Richardson and Laurence Sterne and anticipate the reign of Romanticism. Diderot's sensitivity to aesthetic beauty is expressed in the art criticism contained in *Salons*; it is also reflected in his fiction, notably in the digressions in *The Indiscreet Toys* and the musical discussions in *Rameau's Nephew*.

As a novelist, Diderot was an innovator. *The Nun* anticipates twentieth century psychological fiction, especially in its exploration of the abnormal. *Jacques the Fatalist and His Master* is, by Diderot's own description, an anti-novel, a forerunner of the twentieth century New Novel, which is not really a story but rather a collaboration between author and reader. *Rameau's Nephew* is a fascinating study of the paradox of the human personality. The independence of thought that distinguishes all of Diderot's works is particularly evident in his fiction; he produced novels with few models and with rich possibilities for further development.

Biography

Denis Diderot was born on October 5, 1713, at Langres, one of the seven children of the master cutler Didier Diderot and Angélique Vigneron. The family of the future anticleric was pious and devout, and Diderot's youngest brother, Didier-Pierre, was later to become a canon at Langres, deeply alienated from the great writer. Diderot's younger sister, Angélique, died insane in a convent; her cruel fate inspired Diderot's invective against convents in *The Nun*. Although Diderot began his studies at home, he was an excellent student of the Jesuits from 1723 to 1728, receiving several prizes. He also began his study of Latin and Greek with them, and he remained devoted to the classics throughout his life. He even received the tonsure in 1726, in the hope of a benefice from his uncle's inheritance, and later passed through some periods of religious fervor.

In 1728, Diderot went to Paris, where he was to spend the rest of his long life. Very little is known about his activities during the subsequent fifteen years, other than that he received his master's degree from the University of Paris in 1732 and led a fairly dissolute, though not degenerate, life. In 1743, he fell in love with Anne-Toinette Champion, a modest lace-maker, and asked his father's permission to marry her. Not only did his father refuse; he had his son imprisoned in a monastery. Diderot escaped and married Anne-Toinette secretly. It was, however, to be a tumultuous and basically unhappy marriage, from which only Angélique, of the four children born to the Diderots, was to survive. Well educated by her father, she was to become the author of several memoirs that are very valuable to Diderot studies.

Diderot's sensual nature was soon awakened in a liaison with a certain Madame de Puisieux, about whom little is known, except that Diderot wrote his first novel, *The Indiscreet Toys*, to raise money for her. It was around this time, in the late 1740's, that Diderot became associated with d'Alembert, Étienne Bonnot, Abbé de Condillac, and Jean-Jacques Rousseau. He began working on the *Encyclopédie* with them and Le Breton. Soon, Diderot and d'Alembert became coeditors, and after 1758 Diderot assumed total responsibility for the work. The production of the *Encyclopédie* was Diderot's greatest achievement and essentially his lifework. By no means a child prodigy, he had produced almost nothing in the literary field until that time, but he immediately threw himself into the new project and other philosophical works.

In 1749, Diderot found himself in prison as a result of his controversial writings, particulary his *Letter on the Blind*. Diderot's brief and not uncomfortable imprisonment was perhaps more noteworthy for Rousseau than for him. It was on his way to visit Diderot that Rousseau experienced his famous "illumination," which led to *Discours sur les sciences et les arts* (1750), which won for him the prize of the Academy of Dijon. Diderot's release did not bring an end to his clashes with the law, the harsh censorship of the day, and the criticism of the Jesuits against the *Encyclopédie*. In 1752, the first two volumes were suppressed, and Diderot's papers were confiscated. Because of the support of the honest and liberal censor Chrétien-Guillaume Malesherbes and the influence of Madame de Pompadour, Louis XV's favorite, the work continued under a "tacit permission," but its publication was fraught with difficulties. The contributors often quarreled among themselves, the most noteworthy division being that between Rousseau and d'Alembert (and ultimately Diderot) and the attacks from the outside continued.

Nevertheless, Diderot's assiduous work brought him increasing financial independence and a reputation among scholars in France and abroad. It also brought him the love and support of Sophie Volland, whom Diderot met in 1755 and continued to see at least until 1774. Their liaison was characterized by a passionate and intellectual correspondence, of which 187 letters from Diderot are still extant, although none of Volland's has survived. In 1757, Diderot began to write plays, creating a new type which became known as the *drame bourgeois*, or bourgeois drama; at the same time, he continued to produce essays and carried on, almost single-handedly, the editorship of the *Encyclopédie*.

The year 1759 was a difficult one for Diderot. His father died; the privilege for printing the *Encyclopédie* was revoked, and the work was condemned by Pope Clement XIII. The difficulties of Diderot's domestic life were intensified by quarrels and jealousy between his wife and Volland. Shortly afterward, Charles Palissot's satiric play *Les Philosophes* (1760) greatly offended Diderot, although it became one of the sources of inspiration for his masterpiece, *Rameau's Nephew*. Yet not all was somber. Diderot's friends, Grimm, d'Holbach, and his disciple and future editor Jacques-André Naigeon proved very faithful. Catherine the Great of Russia offered her support to Diderot, purchasing his library for 15,000 livres and allowing him to use it for the rest of his life. She invited him to Russia, where he eventually spent the year 1773 to 1774. He was also responsible for selling her several famous art collections and for sending the noted French sculptor Étienne-Maurice Falconet to execute the famous statue of Peter the Great. Toward the end of Diderot's stay in Russia, Catherine's enthusiasm for his ideas waned, as the times were not favorable to the types of reforms that he advocated.

Diderot's last years were filled with literary activity and interest in his newly married daughter Angélique, now Madame de Vandeul. Although his troubles with the authorities continued on a minor scale, he was honored at his native Langres, and he posed for busts by Jean-Baptiste Pigalle and Jean-Antoine Houdon. In 1783, he became seriously ill, and he died on July 31, 1784, on not unfriendly terms with the Church. He received Christian burial and was interred at the Church of Saint-Roch, where Pierre Corneille is also buried—an unusual setting for a militantly anticlerical philosophe, an avowed materialist, and a sometime atheist.

Analysis

One of Denis Diderot's shorter works of fiction is entitled "This Is Not a Story." He might have said of any one of his characteristic works of long fiction, "This is not a novel." At first sight, all of his novels, with the exception of *The Nun*, look like plays. That is because Diderot's favorite method is the dialogue; even many of his philosophical works, such as *D'Alembert's Dream* and *The Paradox of Acting*, are written in this form. It is in the give-and-take of dialogue that Diderot excels, and his dramatic power, though not of first-rate quality on the stage, comes to life here. The unusually extensive use of dialogue, however, leads to a blurring of genres and a consequent disorder in all of Diderot's works. Critics such as Crocker, O'Gorman, and Francis Pruner have sought to bring order out of his chaos—much to the dismay of others, who see the disorder as the message.

As novels, all of Diderot's fictional works are weak in plot. *The Indiscreet Toys* consists of a series of licentious anecdotes. *Jacques the Fatalist and His Master* is a trip from somewhere to nowhere, with intermittent stops here and there. *Rameau's Nephew* consists of a single conversation in which the two participants discuss everything from seduction to French and Italian music. *The Nun*, which is closest to the traditional idea of plot, does have a beginning and end but does not use any forward or backward reflection. Although it is based on memory, all is told in a kind of eternal present.

As with plot, the time line is also weak in Diderot's novels. With the exception of *The Nun*, all of his novels are poorly marked in time and lack a traditional novelistic beginning or end. They are also vaguely situated in space. *The Indiscreet Toys* takes place in a harem in the Congo, a rather incongruous juxtaposition lacking in credibility. *Jacques the Fatalist and His Master* is situated in France but, despite the efforts of critics to identify the towns and cities that figure in the narrative, there is very little local color to guide the reader. *Rameau's Nephew*, situated in the Café du Palais Royal, and *The Nun*, at the convents of Longchamp and Arpajon, are a bit more localized, yet Diderot could have put them anywhere, for his scenery is subservient to the representation of the characters.

thus anticipating *Rameau's Nephew*. He also parodies a sermon (his daughter said that he had composed and sold real sermons) and investigates dreams, a phenomenon that he was to explore later, especially in *D'Alembert's Dream*. He already extols the scientific method, and even in the most licentious scenes he shows a naturalistic and methodical bent.

Diderot's second novel, *The Nun*, shows a marked advance in technique over *The Indiscreet Toys*, perhaps in part as a result of his reading of Richardson. Like all of Diderot's novels, *The Nun* had a fascinating origin. Based partly on a true story and partly on a hoax, it lay dormant for twenty years before Diderot even considered publication. The idea for the novel began with a lawsuit in Paris from 1755 to 1758, in which a certain Marguerite Delamarre—whose story has been illuminated through the research of Georges May—applied for dispensation from her religious vows. Her request was refused as contrary to the authority of parents over their children. A friend of Diderot, Marquis de Croismare, had tried to support the nun. Diderot and his friends wrote a series of forged letters to Croismare, supposedly from the nun, who ostensibly had escaped from her convent. Croismare took such an interest in her that his friends were forced to "kill" her off in 1760. Croismare did not discover the hoax until 1768, but in the meantime Diderot had prepared the greater part of the manuscript, which, after revision in 1780, he offered to Grimm's successor, Jakob Heinrich Meister, for the *Correspondance littéraire*. The novel was first published by Naigeon in 1796.

The Nun is a simple, rapidly moving story featuring deep psychological analysis and great artistic restraint. It tells the story of Suzanne Simonin, whose parents force her into a convent because she is illegitimate. She at first refuses to make her vows but is forced into a second convent, where she does make her profession. Her first superior is gentle and maternal, but the second is cruel and vindictive and treats her with extreme brutality. Although Suzanne manages to receive support for a plea to be dispensed from her vows, the request is rejected, and she is sent to another convent, at Arpajon. There the discipline is lax, and the superior makes lesbian advances to Suzanne. This arouses the jealousy of the superior's former favorite, which eventually drives the superior to madness and the unsuspecting Suzanne to flight. The ending is disappointing and illogical, as Suzanne, weakened from her escape, dies.

Although Diderot has frequently been accused of immorality in *The Nun*— a film based on his book was temporarily banned in France in 1966—his intentions were, rather, to show the injustice of the enforced cloister and its dangerous effects on the subjects. His technique is masterful, for he presents a young woman who is not tempted to break her vows by the desire for marriage or a lover but who simply finds she does not have a vocation to the cloister. She is innocent, observant of the discipline in the convent, and even unaware of the significance of the advances made by the superior at Arpajon.

Diderot's treatment of the physical desire expressed by the superior is artful and delicate, quite different from his open and licentious descriptions in *The Indiscreet Toys* and in *Jacques the Fatalist and His Master*. The psychological analysis of Sister Suzanne, of her jealous rival Sister Thérèse, and of the three superiors with whom Suzanne lives is excellent, making *The Nun* a forerunner of the works of Marcel Proust and André Gide.

The story of Diderot's third novel, generally acknowledged as his masterpiece, is even more fascinating than those of the two preceding ones. Evidently begun in 1761, *Rameau's Nephew* was revised by Diderot in 1762, 1766, 1767, and 1775, but—no doubt because of the allusions to his enemies, especially Palissot—was never published during his lifetime, nor did it appear in Naigeon's edition of Diderot's works, *Oeuvres* (1798; 15 volumes). In 1805, a German translation by Johann Wolfgang von Goethe was published, and in 1821 the text was retranslated into French, by this time substantially altered. Several other undocumented versions appeared in the nineteenth century, and it was not until 1891 that a genuine text was published by Georges Monval from a manuscript he had located at a *bouquiniste*'s stall in Paris.

Written in the form of a dialogue, *Rameau's Nephew* was staged at the Théâtre Michodière in 1963, starring Pierre Fresnay. Whether it is a novel is debatable; Diderot called it "Satire seconde" (second satire), and its dramatic possibilities are evident. It is, however, a witty, exuberant, rapid exchange of conversation between two characters, Moi and Lui. Lui is vaguely based on Jean-François Rameau, the nephew of the great French musician Jean-Philippe Rameau, whose French severity Diderot disliked, preferring Italian spontaneity. Moi is vaguely reminiscent of Diderot, at least in some biographical details, such as the education of his daughter. Critics have advanced innumerable theories concerning the identity of the characters Moi and Lui. Some say that they are two aspects of Diderot's personality, others that Lui is the id and Moi the ego, still others that they are literally Rameau's nephew and Diderot. Perhaps the most original interpretation is that of O'Gorman, who sees the work both as a Horatian satire and as a Socratic dialogue with the figures of Apollo and Marsyas, and who also identifies Rameau's nephew with Rousseau.

Rameau's Nephew, which discusses music, anti-Rousseauesque education, the hypocrisy of society, the art of seduction, and numerous other themes, opens as a casual conversation at the Café du Palais Royal, during a chess game. It is also a searching inquiry into the basis of morality and a study of the paradox involved in determining the right way to live. For Diderot, morality is nonexistent, because all is based on natural phenomena and matter is the root of human behavior. Yet the existence of a cynical parasite such as Rameau's nephew, who contends that his way of life is the best, poses a problem to Diderot's materialistic system, for society cannot survive with a number of Rameau's nephews. The debate is never neatly resolved; Diderot's dialectical method in the novel has been much praised by Marxist critics, who differ from many readers in finding a clear message within the twists and turns of the dialogue.

Diderot continued his metaphysical speculations on the paradox of morality in his last novel, *Jacques the Fatalist and His Master*, which rivals *Rameau's Nephew* as his masterpiece. Like the two preceding novels, it was not published during his lifetime, although it was written probably around 1771 and revised during or after his stay in Russia of 1773 to 1774, as evidenced by the travel theme. Diderot gave the manuscript to the *Correspondance littéraire* before 1780, but the work was not published until 1796, by Buisson. It was inspired by a passage from Sterne's *Tristram Shandy* (1759-1767), which Diderot had read in English.

Constructed along the lines of Miguel de Cervantes' *Don Quixote de la Mancha* (1605, 1615), *Jacques the Fatalist and His Master* is, however, quite different in tone from the great Spanish masterpiece. It is the most disorderly of all of Diderot's "chaotic" works, with interruptions of interruptions, interference by the author (who holds dialogues with his reader), and unfinished stories left to the reader's imagination. Jacques, a sort of Figaro, accompanies his rather empty-headed master, not unlike Count Almaviva, on a trip. In order to entertain his master, Jacques relates the story of his amorous exploits, and various interruptions preclude a real end to his tale. At the end, the master also tells his story; it is not unlike Jacques', but it lacks his sparkling wit.

Their stops at inns along the way precipitate other tales, the two most important of which are the stories of Madame de la Pommeraye and Père Hudson. Madame de la Pommeraye is resentful of her lover's unfaithfulness and decides to avenge herself. She hires a prostitute and her mother to pose as a respectable young woman accompanied by her devout widowed mother. This done, Madame de la Pommeraye arranges to have her former lover, Monsieur des Arcis, fall in love with the prostitute. The day after the marriage, Madame de la Pommeraye tells him the truth, but the revenge is thwarted, because he really loves his new wife and forgives her completely. Père Hudson is a sensual and domineering superior who reforms a monastery but exempts himself from its discipline. He arranges for the two priests sent to investigate his conduct to be trapped with a young woman he has seduced, thus escaping censure himself.

Despite the adventures and interruptions, the real theme of the book is the paradox of freedom and necessity. Jacques the Fatalist is really a determinist who, like Diderot, believes that "all is written on high," that no one can change his destiny. Yet the very form of the novel proves that chance does, indeed, exist. All of this seems to rule out freedom, which, like good and evil, becomes a mere illusion.

Crocker's observations on why *Jacques the Fatalist and His Master* is a great work, but not a great novel, may serve to classify all of Diderot's novels. A great novel must embody human life in all of its emotional and intellectual range, in all of its intensity. It must contain a view of human life in terms of concrete problems and human suffering. By contrast, _Rameau's Nephew_ and _Jacques the Fatalist and His Master_ are preoccupied with abstract philosophical problems. Although these two works may be Diderot's most profound fictions, it is perhaps _The Nun_ that comes closest to the ideal of the novel. Diderot himself wept over _The Nun_; its characters and their suffering were real to him, as they are to his readers.

Major publications other than long fiction

SHORT FICTION: _Supplément au voyage de Bougainville_, 1796 (_Supplement to Bougainville's Voyage_, 1927); _Rameau's Nephew and Other Works_, 1964 (collection).

PLAYS: _Le Fils naturel_, 1757 (_Dorval: Or, The Test of Virtue_, 1767); _Le Père de famille_, 1758 (English translation, 1770; also as _The Family Picture_, 1871); _Est'il bon? Est'il méchant?_, 1781.

NONFICTION: _Pensées philosophiques_, 1746 (English translation, 1819; also as _Philosophic Thoughts_); _Lettre sur les aveugles_, 1749 (_An Essay on Blindness_, 1750; also as _Letter on the Blind_); _Notes et commentaires_, 1749; _Lettre sur les sourds et muets_, 1751 (_Letter on the Deaf and Dumb_); _Encyclopédie_, 1751-1772 (editor, 17 volumes of text, 11 volumes of plates; _Encyclopedia_, 1965); _Pensées sur l'interprétation de la nature_, 1753; _Entretiens sur "Le Fils naturel,"_ 1757; _Discours sur la poésie dramatique_, 1758 (English translation of chapters 1-5 in _Dramatic Essays of the Neo-Classical Age_, 1950); _De la suffisance de la religion naturelle_, 1770 (written 1747); _Entretien d'un père avec ses enfants_, 1773 (_Conversation Between Father and Children_, 1964); _Essai sur Sénèque_, 1778 (revised and expanded as _Essai sur les règnes de Claude et Néron_, 1782); _Paradoxe sur le comédien_, 1830 (written 1773; _The Paradox of Acting_, 1883); _La Promenade du sceptique_, 1830 (written 1747); _Le Rêve de d'Alembert_, 1830 (written 1769; _D'Alembert's Dream_, 1927); _Salons_, 1845, 1857 (serialized 1759-1781); _Diderot's Early Philosophic Works_, 1916 (includes _Letter on the Blind, Letter on the Deaf and Dumb, Philosophic Thoughts_); _Concerning the Education of a Prince_, 1941 (written 1758); _Correspondance_, 1955-1970 (16 volumes); _Oeuvres philosophiques_, 1956; _Oeuvres esthétiques_, 1959; _Oeuvres politiques_, 1962.

TRANSLATIONS: _L'Histoire de Grèce_, 1743 (of Temple Stanyan's _Grecian History_); _Essai sur le mérite et la vertu de Shaftesbury_, 1745 (of the Earl of Shaftesbury's _An Inquiry Concerning Virtue and Merit_); _Dictionnaire universel de médecine_, 1746-1748 (of Robert James's _A Medical Dictionary_).

MISCELLANEOUS: _Oeuvres_, 1798 (15 volumes); _Oeuvres complètes_, 1875-1877 (20 volumes); _Diderot, Interpreter of Nature: Selected Writings_, 1937 (includes short fiction); _Selected Writings_, 1966.

Bibliography
Crocker, Lester G. *Diderot: The Embattled Philosopher*, 1964.
——————. *Diderot's Chaotic Order*, 1974.
Duchet, Michèle, and Michel Launay. *Entretiens sur "Le Neveu de Rameau,"* 1967.
Fellows, Otis. *Diderot*, 1977.
Fellows, Otis, and Diana Guiragossian, eds. *Diderot Studies*, 1959-
Kempf, Roger. *Diderot et le Roman*, 1964.
Mason, John. *The Irresistible Diderot*, 1982.
May, Georges. *Quatre Visages de Denis Diderot*, 1951.
O'Gorman, Donal. *Diderot the Satirist*, 1971.
Pappas, John, ed. *Essays on Diderot and the Enlightenment in Honor of Otis Fellows*, 1974.
Pomeau, René. *Diderot: Sa vie, son oeuvre*, 1967.
Pruner, Francis. *L'Unité secrète de "Jacques le Fataliste,"* 1970.
Trahard, Pierre. *Les Maîtres de la sensibilité française au XVIII° siècle*, 1967.
Wilson, Arthur M. *Diderot*, 1972.

Irma M. Kashuba

ALFRED DÖBLIN

Born: Stettin, Germany; August 10, 1878
Died: Emmendingen, Germany; June 26, 1957

Principal long fiction

Die drei Sprünge des Wang-lun, 1915; *Wadzeks Kampf mit der Dampfturbine*, 1918; *Der schwarze Vorhang*, 1919; *Wallenstein*, 1920; *Berge, Meere und Giganten*, 1924 (revised as *Giganten: Ein Abenteuerbuch*, 1932); *Berlin Alexanderplatz: Die Geschichte vom Franz Biberkopf*, 1929 (*Alexanderplatz, Berlin: The Story of Franz Biberkopf*, 1931); *Babylonische Wandrung: Oder, Hochmut kommt vor dem Fall*, 1934; *Pardon wird nicht gegeben*, 1935 (*Men Without Mercy*, 1937); *Amazonas*, 1937-1948, 1963 (includes *Die Fahrt ins Land ohne Tod*, 1937; *Der blaue Tiger*, 1938; *Der neue Urwald*, 1948; *Amazonas* is also known as *Das Land ohne Tod: Sudamerika-Roman in drei Teilen*, 1947-1948); *November 1918*, 1948-1950 (includes *Verratenes Volk*, 1948; *Heimkehr der Fronttruppen*, 1949 [translated together as *A People Betrayed: November 1918, A German Revolution*, 1983]; *Karl und Rosa*, 1950 [*Karl and Rosa*, 1983]); *Hamlet: Oder, Die Nacht nimmt ein Ende*, 1956.

Other literary forms

Under a liberal definition of the form, one would probably consider three additional works by Alfred Döblin as novels: *Manas: Epische Dichtung* (1927; Manas: a verse epic); *Der Oberst und der Dichter: Oder, Das menschliche Herz* (1946; the colonel and the poet: or, the human heart); and *Die Pilgerin Aetheria* (1978; Aetheria the pilgrim). The consciously archaic verse form of the first and the relative brevity of the latter two exclude them from the category of "novels" in the view of at least some scholars.

Döblin also wrote short stories throughout his literary career, though the majority of them were written before 1933 and were typically first published in well-known literary journals of their time: *Der Sturm*, *Der neue Merkur*, *Die neue Rundschau*, and *Die literarische Welt*. Eighteen of these earlier stories were reprinted, together with six new ones, in the collections of 1913 and 1917. Between 1906 and 1931, Döblin experimented four times with the drama. All four plays saw production (in Berlin, Darmstadt, Leipzig, and Munich), but their respective legal, political, and critical consequences outshone their dramatic quality. The best known of Döblin's novels, *Alexanderplatz, Berlin*, was adapted as a radio play, with script by Döblin and the radio director Max Bings, in 1930. In the following year, it became a film success in an adaptation written by Döblin in collaboration with Hans Wilhelm. (The overwhelming international acclaim given German cinema director Rainer Werner Fassbinder's fifteen-hour-plus screen adaptation, *Berlin Alexanderplatz*, 1980, attests the continuing impact of Döblin's epic vision.) Döblin's second venture in screenwriting came during his exile in California, where in 1940 and 1941 he contributed to the scripts for Metro-Goldwyn-Mayer's *Mrs. Miniver* and *Random Harvest*, a possible source of ideas for his own novel, *Hamlet: Oder, Die lange Nacht nimmt ein Ende* (Hamlet: or, the long night comes to an end). A number of autobiographical writings shed some light on Döblin's aesthetic development and literary career; his major essays on philosophy, religion, literature, and the other arts help to reveal the intellectual underpinnings of his often experimental creative works.

The Berlin house of S. Fischer Verlag published all of Döblin's novels through 1932. Following the Nazi takeover and the banning of his writings, Döblin was able to place his work with the exile publishing firm Querido-Verlag, in Amsterdam. The books written in the United States and following his return to Germany in 1945 appeared under the imprints of various German companies; only since the posthumous publication of his collected works was begun, by Walter-Verlag in 1960, has Döblin's literary and theoretical production become generally accessible.

Achievements

Two years before his death, the seventy-six-year-old Alfred Döblin complained, "Whenever my name was mentioned, they always added the name *Alexanderplatz, Berlin*. But my path was still far from ended." The overshadowing success of that work does in part account for Döblin's failure to establish a secure reputation for his entire literary output, and there are Döblin specialists who maintain that this novel, published when its author was fifty, represents the height and the end of his significant development. The other major obstacle to Döblin's full recognition, during his lifetime and since, is his resistance to philosophical, theoretical, and literary classification. Thus, the daily *Frankfurter Rundschau* could characterize him as "a shrewd but uncommonly unstable writer who was incapable at any time of rationally disciplining his emotions and impulses." It is perhaps an extreme portrayal, but nevertheless symptomatic.

Most serious critics attribute the difficulty in placing Döblin among twentieth century German novelists to his constant questioning of his own position, which for him meant no less than the examination and testing of the foundations of human existence. He had expressed that compulsion in the 1919 statement: "We only live once, it seems. Then existence must be the burning question for us." Even near the end of his life, a convert to Roman Catholicism, Döblin would not retreat into a sham doctrinaire certainty of his own position, but remained ever the questioner and ironic self-examiner.

Döblin's public reception in postwar Germany was far from gratifying. A number of circumstances and personal traits may have contributed to Döblin's postwar disappointments: the changed literary tastes of his former public—or what remained of it; the general discrediting of the German émigré writers;

displeasure with Döblin's "provocative" return in the uniform of a French colonel; his sometimes gratuitous attacks on other writers, particularly Thomas Mann; a public coolness toward his conversion to Christianity; and almost certainly his tendency to isolate himself from other opinions and sides of issues. He has not, however, been without influence on other novelists; one acknowledged pupil, Günter Grass, portrayed Döblin in 1967 as unacceptable to radicals and conservatives alike, unsuited to either adult or juvenile audiences. As Grass summed it up, "The value of Döblin's stock did not and still does not appear in the market quotations."

Largely on the strength of his pre-exile achievements in the novel form, Döblin is a generally acknowleged force among German writers of the first third of the twentieth century. His pioneering creation of the montage as a structural principle for the novel; his development of a philosophy of the individual in the natural world; his portrayal of the modern existential tension between the individual will and the anonymous forces against which it must assert itself; and his efforts toward the democratization of art are achievements for which few would deny him credit. Failures, however, accompanied his successes: Döblin did not succeed, either in his personal life or in those of his fictional heroes, in finding the bridge from the self to the community, from personal transformation to politically relevant action. Whenever it happened that Döblin found no clear echo—hence, whenever his social relevance was in doubt—he was conscious of his isolation. In a sense, this amounted to an "exile before the fact," being cut off artistically both before and after his physical exile, as well as during the years of emigration.

It is no longer quite accurate to state, as Grass did in 1967, that Döblin's worth remains unevaluated. The German edition of his collected works is now much more nearly complete than when Grass acknowledged his debt to his predecessor, and the major scholarly studies of his life and work almost all date from 1970 and later. Disagreement remains over the continuity and the literary stature of the later novels, especially of *November 1918* and *Hamlet.*

Biography

Bruno Alfred Döblin was born on August 10, 1878, in the Baltic port city of Stettin, the former Pomeranian capital (now Szczecin, Poland). His father, Max Döblin, operated a clothing shop until its failure forced him into the tailor's trade. Max Döblin was intelligent and sensitive but also passive and unambitious, a Western European Jew separated from his people's traditions and sense of identity. Döblin's mother, Sophie, was two years older than her husband and very different from him—sober, practical, and materialistic. She had come to the marriage from better economic circumstances, and she was its dominant partner. Many of the disparities and conflicts in Döblin's life can be found at least partially rooted in his parents' dissimilarities. In 1888, when

Döblin was ten, his father abandoned the family for a young woman employed in his shop and left Stettin. His mother moved with the children to Berlin that same year, hoping to find among relatives there some assistance in supporting her children and meeting the heavy debts left behind by her husband. The emotional effect on Döblin was predictably traumatic. Attempts to mend the marriage came to nothing, but it was not until 1908 that his parents' divorce was finally granted.

Döblin asserted later in life that the move to Berlin in 1888 had been his "real birth," for he regarded the capital from then onward as his true home, and himself as a Berliner. He completed his secondary schooling there in 1900, began studying medicine and philosophy at the university, and began writing his first stories. He transferred to Freiburg University, where he specialized in psychiatry and neurology, and after earning his degree there in 1905, he served a year of internship in a mental hospital near Regensburg. The following year, he returned to Berlin and remained on hospital staffs until he could establish a private practice in neurology and internal medicine in 1911. All the while, the newly settled doctor in working-class Berlin-East was combining a medical and a writing career, as he would continue to do until 1933. In 1910, he became the cofounder, with writer and art critic Herwarth Walden, of the Expressionist journal *Der Sturm*, a publication which attracted the contributions of many antibourgeois writers of apolitical and anarchist persuasion.

In Berlin, Döblin also met Erna Reiss, a medical student ten years younger than he, whom he married in 1912, but not before having an affair with a younger woman who was neither Jewish nor of a well-to-do family. Döblin's mother strictly opposed a marriage with her, and he yielded, though with a heavy sense of guilt—not least of all for having fathered her illegitimate child. He found in Erna Reiss a wife in many ways like his strong-willed mother. From 1912 to 1926, four sons were born to Erna and Alfred Döblin. He spent most of the war years, from 1914 to 1918, as a military doctor stationed on the Western front in Lorraine and Alsace.

Returning then to Berlin as "the only city" where he could live and work, Döblin joined the Independent Social Democratic Party (USPD) and, after its split in 1921, the Social Democratic Party (SPD). These were the years of his greatest political activity, during which he wrote satiric pieces critical of conditions in the infant Weimar Republic under the pen name "Linke Poot" (dialect for "Left Paw"). A trip to Poland in 1924 brought devout Catholicism to his attention for the first time, but, more important, it afforded him an insight into the spiritual identity of the unassimilated Eastern Jew as a still intact, self-assertive member of the natural order, at a time when Döblin was occupied with developing his philosophy of self and cosmos.

In mid-decade, Döblin was a member of several writers' organizations, some with clearly leftist political tendencies. In 1928, he was elected to membership in the rather more conservative literary section of the Prussian Academy of Arts. When, in 1933, the section's chairman, Heinrich Mann, was forced to resign his office on account of his pro-Communist political statements, Döblin sealed his own fate as an enemy of the National Socialist wing by openly criticizing the Academy's action. On February 28, urged by friends, he made a trip to Switzerland; in November he traveled to Paris. As a Jew and a leftist intellectual whose books had been publicly burned in Germany, he realized the impossibility of returning soon to Berlin. Exile also meant the end of his medical career, since he could not practice as an alien in host countries.

During the years in France, Döblin enjoyed particularly the support of Robert Minder, a Germanist at the University of Nancy who became a lifelong friend and an advocate of the novelist's works and literary reputation. Döblin was naturalized a French citizen in 1936, and in 1939 he worked under Jean Giraudoux in the French information ministry. Still not at ease in the language, and prompted by the fear of the imminent German invasion of France, he fled in 1940 with his wife and youngest son, by way of Spain and Portugal, to New York.

In Hollywood, where friends suggested he go, Döblin's existence was made difficult by economic dependence on refugee aid societies and uninspiring work in the film industry, by his artistic isolation and inability to publish anything more than some fragments of *November 1918* in the United States, and, again, by the language barrier. There, in 1941, he made his controversial decision to become a Roman Catholic. Among his German fellow intellectuals, this step only aggravated his isolation.

At war's end in 1945, Döblin returned at once, first to Paris, then to Baden-Baden in the French Occupation Zone. There, he was attached to the military public information bureau and for five years published a journal called *Das goldene Tor*, which he envisioned as an instrument for restoring a healthy literary life to Germany. In 1949, he helped to reestablish the Mainz Academy of Sciences and Literature. Neither these efforts nor his artistic and personal life, however, bore good fruit. Politically and professionally, Döblin seemed condemned to frustration. He moved to Mainz in 1949, to Paris in 1953, then back to southwest Germany, where his failing health obliged him to make a succession of stays in hospitals and sanatoriums. On June 26, 1957, he died in the clinic at Emmendingen near Freiburg.

Analysis

In view of the iconoclastic literary principles that Alfred Döblin championed and the considerable modifications to which he subjected his style and method over the span of his creative life, it may be surprising to note that his abiding concern was with the simple telling of stories. That, at least, is what he asserted in the restrospective epilogue sketched in 1948. It is known that he considered himself—or aspired to be—an epic writer in the original sense of that word, a teller of tales. This is not to suggest that he aimed at the telling of simple, linear plots, for he avowed a preference for depicting complex totalities in his novels. The stress should rather be on the epic's immediacy, that quality for which Döblin, in 1917, paid respect to Homer, Dante, Miguel de Cervantes, and Fyodor Dostoevski, and which he had demanded perhaps most succinctly, in 1913, with the statement: "The whole must not appear as if spoken, but as if present." This view of the novel's purpose and execution was directly opposed to the idea of the polyhistorical, "intellectual" novel—rooted in the nineteenth century "bourgeois" cultural tradition, larded with ostentatious knowledge, and diluted with narrative digression and commentary—as practiced by Hermann Broch, Thomas Mann, Robert Musil, and others.

Nor did Döblin have any patience with the psychological novel, another of the early twentieth century's favorites. He did not accept the isolated individual, created in a vacuum by authors of studio exercises, as a means of depicting the world. Instead, Döblin desired the dismantling of the individual, who otherwise constituted, like the intrusive narrator, an obstacle to the epic's direct presentation of the infinitely varied world. Confrontation with that world, with the whole of nature, was for Döblin the modern human condition and the object of art: the reader standing before the "stone façade" of the novel. Later in his career, he rejected as inhuman this radical call for depersonalization in the novel and modified it. One clear beneficiary of the modification was the once-banished narrator, whose presence is increasingly evident in the progression of his works from *Die drei Sprünge des Wang-lun* (the three leaps of Wang-lun) to *Alexanderplatz, Berlin*.

Much of the thematic import of Döblin's literary output until about 1930 can be traced through his development of a philosophy of the human individual's place and function in the natural world. Having abandoned the Nietzschean concept of individual development and the cult of the "great personality" in the first years of the century, Döblin expressed, notably in *Der schwarze Vorhang* (the black curtain), the despair of the confined, powerless self confronting the superior force of a meaningless environment. He accordingly searched for some encompassing meaning to which man could willingly submit himself—whether as submission to "fate"(in *Die drei Sprünge des Wang-lun*) or to the cosmic wholeness of all living matter (in *Berge, Meere und Giganten*; mountains, seas and giants). He finally synthesized his view of individual passivity and individual self-assertion in the essay *Das Ich über der Natur* (1927; the ego above nature), which postulated a "naturalism" of balance between self and creation, the ego as part and counterpart of nature, simultaneously creature and creator. The result for Döblin was a new image of man and a new view of art, clearest perhaps in *Alexanderplatz, Berlin*, both as Franz Biberkopf swims in the stream of life and as the story's creator responds to the primordial rhythms of the narrative stream he has set flowing.

Döblin saw the "naturalism" of *Das Ich über der Natur* distorted and perverted by Nazism in Germany after 1933, however, and his novels, beginning with *Babylonische Wandrung* (Babylonian migration), betray the confusion which resulted for him. "I was examining in my mind how it had all come to pass," he recalled in 1948. Finally he turned to religion and the search for a personal God as a means to rebuilding his philosophical position, but he could not recover the former union of his philosophy and his art. *Hamlet* and the works which came after it do not resonate with their author's idea as *Alexanderplatz, Berlin* does.

Since the deep rupture in Döblin's philosophical reflections makes it difficult to analyze the post-1933 novels with reference to his "naturalistic" postulates, one might better ask what his exile and the related external circumstances meant for his literary activity. He had only begun the writing of *Babylonische Wandrung* in Berlin; most of the work on it was done in Zurich and Paris. As his first literary reaction to the catastrophic situation in Germany, the novel makes its serious point with its theme of guilt and penance, but the liberties Döblin took in its composition expose characters, the author, reality, and the epic form itself to ridicule. *Men Without Mercy* is, by contrast, spare in its composition, partially autobiographical, and formally a throwback to the realistic narrative tradition. When Döblin spoke of this as one of the novels through which he "examined how it had all come to pass," he undoubtedly had in mind its theme of the German bourgeoisie's betrayal of the ideals of freedom whose guardian that class had once been. In *Das Land ohne Tod* (land without death), he removed the novel's setting to another age and another continent. Still, it relates the unhappy condition of the "modern" (post-Renaissance) European, the conqueror whose spiritual poverty and faith in technological progress bar him from mystical union with nature as it is known by the South American Indians.

Döblin had set out initially to fashion epic works of immediate directness—what he had defined as his "stone style" or "façade" of the novel—that would represent a world in complex totality and depict the relationship of the individual to cosmic nature and its forces. At the culmination of this effort, with *Alexanderplatz, Berlin*, he found that individual in equilibrium, part and counterpart of the natural world, and there had been a reemergence of the personal narrator and the individual hero. With the dislocation of Döblin's theoretical base in the events of 1933, however, his novels ceased to be controlled experiments in the epic form and tended instead to mark his coming to terms with past and present—his country's and his own.

In order to write an epic of the complex and diverse totality of the world, Döblin chose as his subject in *Die drei Sprünge des Wang-lun* life in eighteenth century China and made it a reflection of the world in his own age and place. Like many of his German contemporaries early in the second decade of this century, he was fascinated by Chinese culture and philosophy. His persistent habit of researching the subject matter and background of his novels began with the preparation of this book, and the result is impressive. Historical episodes, parables and anecdotes, social and political systems, culture, climate and geography—all attest the exhaustive scholarly groundwork and contribute to the presence of "world" in *Die drei Sprünge des Wang-lun*. Taoist philosophy in particular was fashionable in early twentieth century Germany, and Döblin incorporated various literal extracts from Taoist writings in this novel— the fable of the man who tries to escape his own shadow and to leave no footprints, for example.

The novel's characters, while distinguished by names and fixed roles, are defined exclusively by their visible behavior and evident moods; their psychic interiors are not explored. There is, moreover, the prominent part that Döblin gives to human masses, but not ones brought to the level of some "collective hero," as they might have appeared in other contemporary works, the Expressionist dramas particularly. Rather it is in their anonymity, into which certain of the individual characters themselves return, that the masses of people are important here. They serve more to remind us of individual insignificance than to assert identities of their own. Similarly, Döblin avoids what he considered the inappropriateness of unusual or exotic, "artful" imagery. The unfamiliar Oriental world might easily have furnished exotic motifs for the Western writer, but Döblin had expressly rejected facile "artifice" and built instead with abundant but objective, careful detail.

In the fable of the man who fears his shadow and hates his footprints, he runs to the point of exhaustion in the attempt to escape them and dies from the effort: "He did not know that he had only to sit in the shade somewhere to be rid of his shadow, that he had only to remain still in order to leave no footprints." This little story exemplifies the thematic point of the whole novel. The problem, and the dilemma of modern European man as well, is the choice between action and inaction, rebellion and submission in the world. Wang-lun is the son of a fisherman and leader of a passive sect, the Truly Weak Ones, the Wu-wei, who at the story's beginning await their annihilation by the imperial troops. The novel traces how this destruction of the Wu-wei came about, but the important chain of events is that involving Wang-lun, their leader. His career takes him first from his village to refuge in the mountains, where he formulates his doctrine of nonresistance. He returns to the fisherman's life and marriage, but also to rebellion against the Emperor. Yet another reversal takes him back to the side of the submissive doctrine. These are the three "leaps" which he illustrates by jumping three times over a stream. Paradoxically, however, passivity cannot be tolerated, because it denies the forces of fate; these dominant forces are to be placated, as Wang-lun ultimately realizes, only by resistance to them. He knows at the end that "to submit is the pure way," but he cannot live the truth he knows. Döblin, too, regarded it as an immediate dilemma.

Even from a writer who aspired to depict the endlessly changing totality of nature and its enormous forces, *Berge, Meere und Giganten* is an ambitious work. Its story begins in the twentieth century and goes forward into another half-millennium of a visionary future. Its physical setting includes Europe and extends from Asia to Greenland. Its human masses are vast. In a procedure rare for Döblin, he furnished a simultaneous account of the writing of this novel, and he tells in it how the earth itself, as it were, implanted the germ of the epic idea in his mind. Stones idly picked up along the Baltic shore gave the first unclear impulse to his musings and gradually drew him to the study of various branches of biology and geology. Only later, Döblin claims, did he recognize and begin to compose a novel as the consequence of this intellectual captivation. It is instructive to observe that he began the writing, well before the whole plan was clear to him, not with the novel's beginning chapters, but with a "gigantic expedition." "It was to become a tellurian adventure, a wrestling with the earth," he says. The masses of humanity "take up the arrogant, imperious struggle with the earth itself."

The result, which occupies books 6 and 7 (of the novel's nine), is a tremendous westward expedition to colonize Greenland by melting its ice sheet with energy generated in the volcanoes of Iceland. Preceding this major segment of the epic is the story of centuries-long human technological development to the point of its final breakdown. The assault on the Greenland ice releases monstrous forces of Cretaceous life—a retaliation by the earth—and the following books depict humanity's efforts to resist. Those who acknowledge nature's superior force and willingly surrender themselves to fusion with the elements attain reunion with the cosmic whole in their deaths. The physical survivors, a remnant of settlers, are humbled and led into a future devoid of technology, but thereby into harmony with nature and reverence for it.

The sense of the individual's inclusion in such an anonymous, collective relationship to elemental forces suggests a certain affinity with the Expressionists, whom Döblin otherwise viewed with reserve by this time, while, with its overtones of irrational mysticism, the work maintains a safe distance from the "intellectual" novel already mentioned as a style Döblin found distasteful. As for the individuals themselves, he asserts that, in keeping with his epic intentions, they still are not personal characters, but only "voices of the mass." Even though this novel still owes a certain debt to the Futurist concept of dynamics and speed, and periodically exhibits that concept in its language, it also has its more ponderous, inflated sections which dull its linguistic contours. This stylistic inconsistency may reflect (in its racing intensity) the Promethean activism of Döblin's human actors, but also (in its heavy solemnity) the doomed hubris of their assault on the earth.

A distorted image of the novel's structure will result if one considers only the progression of these events, however, for this constitutes only the epic "report." Four years later, in 1928, Döblin would deliver a lecture entitled "Der Bau des epischen Werks" ("The Structure of the Epic"), perhaps his single most important theoretical piece. In it, he called for discarding the "forced mask of reporting" and for expanding the means for epic portrayal and depiction; this kind of narrative modification was already taking shape in *Berge, Meere und Giganten*. Döblin admits to having sought relief during the writing by creating "oases" for himself, by means of a freer, more expansive treatment of numerous episodes. As a result, the "reportorial" structure supports an overgrowth of more freely imaginative episodic sections, especially those in which Döblin explains technological inventions and procedures of the future. The method he had called his "stone façade" was yielding gradually to rediscovery of the personal narrator, whom he later (in the 1928 lecture) acknowledged as necessary to the epic form.

Two years before the appearance of *Alexanderplatz, Berlin: The Story of Franz Biberkopf*, in 1929, Döblin's *Manas* had become a moderate publishing failure. *Alexanderplatz, Berlin*, which treats essentially the same idea—the overcoming of the old and birth of the new man—was easily his greatest success. From the mythological realm of India in the verse epic, Döblin brought his idea to the contemporary metropolis. Berlin-East was his terrain, and he could make it ring more true than any other place. This novel is therefore filled with what *Manas* had most lacked, the familiar: the language, appearance, and life of an everyday, working-class city.

Authentic representation of the familiar may account for the book's popularity, but it does not explain its greatness. Its stature as a landmark among German novels of the twentieth century is the result of Döblin's integration of the diverse forms and fragments of the "world" of Berlin into cogent totality. It represents his mastery of narrative montage and thus his ultimate realization of the attempt to represent a world at once whole and multifarious. Moreover, he brought the human individual into the most refined expression of his relationship with this world and, by referring every fragment of the environment to this central figure, gave the novel its final cogency.

The very looseness of structure in *Alexanderplatz, Berlin* permits its unified wholeness. The shifting narrative perspectives, the free-association technique, the interior monologues and free indirect discourse, the prefigurations and retrospections, cross-references, illustrative parallels, and recurring rhythms large and small, all function both as fragmenting and as reconnecting devices. Franz Biberkopf is central even when not physically present, since he can be recalled, explicitly or by subtle association, at any time. At times, one cannot be certain who is speaking—the narrator, Biberkopf, or some interpolated, seemingly unrelated source. It becomes clear, however, that all of these voices, the author's included, are speaking to Biberkopf, that most of the novel is a multiple voice speaking to him.

At the beginning of the book, Franz Biberkopf emerges into Berlin from the gate of Tegel Prison, where he has served his term for a violent crime. He is determined to "go straight" and "keep his nose clean." The narrator says: "The punishment begins." Biberkopf's subsequent fortunes show what is meant by this curious remark. All that he has to learn still lies ahead of him. He is mistaken to believe that serving a prison sentence has made a new man of him; in fact, he has learned nothing. With good intentions and unwarranted self-confidence he believes he can do it alone. He is struck down three times by fate, each time more brutally than the last, but the assaults are ones which he himself has defiantly provoked in his moments of greatest satisfaction with his own progress. In fact, as the author has hinted in his preface, the unexpected force which strikes Biberkopf down only "looks like a fate." Not until the final blow is struck and Biberkopf finds himself implicated in a murder trial and committed to a mental hospital does he recognize the "fate" as Death, which has spoken to and in him throughout the novel. When finally Death speaks plainly to him, it says that it is life, since only death can lead the submissive individual back into the eternal anonymity that the self-confident Biberkopf has sought to deny. True to its rhythmic-repetitive pattern, the world of the Alexanderplatz in Berlin goes on—and so does Biberkopf, but broken outwardly and inwardly, no longer self-reliant, now a willing part of the anonymous world in which he understands his place.

Whether and how much Döblin may have borrowed from the techniques of James Joyce's *Ulysses* (1922) or John Dos Passos' *Manhattan Transfer* (1925) is subject to dispute. Both of these novels had appeared in German translations in 1927, but Döblin denied that either had had any significant influence on *Alexanderplatz, Berlin*. As the models for his montage technique, he cited instead the Expressionists and Dadaists and the techniques of filmmaking. The more important point here is that the montage furnished Döblin with the means for overcoming, insofar as that is possible, the sequential nature of narrative art and lending it an illusion of simultaneity that relates the seemingly unrelated in a single image of countless parts. *Alexanderplatz, Berlin* is thus an intimation of the infinitesimal and the infinite combined, an extraordinary example of "narrated world."

During his exile in France, and with little time lost following the completion of his South American novel, Döblin began work on *November 1918*, now republished as the four-volume edition it might have been much earlier but for the complications of exile and its aftermath. This expansive work is a pairing of two concurrent narratives: the story of the World War I veteran, Friedrich Becker, and his return to defeated Germany; and the fictionalized historical account of the events most Germans would associate with its title: the failed Communist Revolution of November and December, 1918, immediately following the collapse of the German Empire. As one form of Döblin's coming to terms with his own and Germany's fate, the work mixes individual and political-historical probings, psychological and epic processes.

The psychological component is the great innovation of *November 1918* for Döblin's literary development. The collective anonymity of human masses, familiar already from his early novels, finds expression in the depiction of the 1918 revolutionary turmoil; the probings into individual consciousness are undertaken most fully, but not exclusively, with the character of Becker, a man physically and psychologically crippled by the war. His sense of sharing in Germany's guilt and his powerlessness to effect change in the German mind by precept or by force torment him to the point where he becomes a fanatical seeker of God. Döblin's extension of interest from the collective to the individual psychological level is surely a reflection of his personal questioning and searching, marked clearly by his conversion to Christianity in 1941. It would be unfair, however, to say that he accepted the validity of the psychological novel he had eschewed earlier in his career, since his analysis of Becker's condition is not a "studio exercise" in the abstract, but an expression of urgent personal doubts.

Doubts and reservations affect the tone of the novel. Both Becker and the Spartacist revolutionary leaders have their doubts about the rightness of their cause, and both the revolutionary and the religious quests in *November 1918* come to unhappy ends. The Berlin revolts are frustrated until they can be crushed by the reactionary forces, and Becker falls the victim of a familiar error: the fatal hubris of believing he can stand alone. Döblin's ambivalent attitude toward the leftist cause, although he was generally in sympathy with it, is evident in farcical, satiric, and ironic passages. The style tends toward objective sobriety and understatement, placing Döblin in the company of other post-World War II German realists with their sense of minimal intact resources for artistic expression. The narrative control, once so sure in *Alexanderplatz, Berlin*, gives evidence of weakening in *November 1918*. Sharply drawn individual scenes contrast with an absence of clear overall structure. In fact, the attitude—or pretense—of narrative helplessness may be the more honest gesture for one writing in the early 1940's. Friedrich Becker surely reflects Döblin's thoughts on Germany when, near the end of the novel, he talks about Richard Wagner's *Tristan und Isolde*: "The opera is a terrifying document of the times. Love-death, alcohol-death, opium-death, war-death; what death will people flee to next?"

Hamlet, written in 1945 and 1946 and bridging Döblin's exile and repatriation, is again the story of a war veteran who returns home with severe physical and emotional wounds. This "Hamlet" is an Englishman, however, not a German, and the war from which he returns is World War II. Thus, Döblin chose characters and a setting in which he could analyze the human conflicts and relationships much more intensely than he had done in *November 1918*. The probings of *Hamlet* are Döblin's most direct confrontation with his own childhood experience of the tensions in his parents' marriage and the emotional complex brought on by the nature of their separation.

Like Friedrich Becker of *November 1918*, the principal figure in *Hamlet*, Edward Allison, returns home in confusion, questioning the sense of the war. Like his Shakespearean namesake, he finds there a tangle of lies and deceit which he must cut apart in the search for his own identity. For his parents, whose marriage is a bond of love and hate, the result is disastrous. For Allison himself, once "the long night of lies is past," the revelation is poor comfort, since it has shown him that dark instincts indeed seem to dominate human fate. Döblin originally had Allison enter a monastery at the novel's close. The publisher preferred—and received—a more optimistic ending in which "a new life began" for Edward Allison. Perhaps characteristically, Döblin left the literary world without a clear statement of his own wishes regarding the revised ending. His last major work thus remains as ambiguous in its philosophical conclusions as many of its predecessors; for a writer who saw the epic as a never-ending form, the lack of a final answer seems fully in character.

Major publications other than long fiction

SHORT FICTION: *Die Ermordung einer Butterblume*, 1913; *Die Lobensteiner reisen nach Böhmen*, 1917; *Der Oberst und der Dichter: Oder, Das menschliche Herz*, 1946; *Die Ermordung einer Butterblume: Ausgewählte Erzählungen 1910-1950*, 1962; *Die Pilgerin Aetheria*, 1978; *Erzählungen aus fünf Jahrzehnten*, 1979.

PLAYS: *Lydia und Mäxachen: Tiefe Verbeugung in einem Akt*, 1906; *Lusitania*, 1920; *Die Nonnen von Kemnade*, 1923; *Die Ehe*, 1931.

POETRY: *Manas: Epische Dichtung*, 1927.

NONFICTION: *Das Ich über der Nature*, 1927; *Alfred Döblin: Im Buch; Zu Haus; Auf der Shasse*, 1928; *Jüdische Erneuerung*, 1933 (*Jews Renew Yourselves!*, 1935); *Schicksalsreise*, 1946 (*Germany Is No More*, 1946); *Unsere Sorge der Mensch*, 1948; *Aufsätze zur Literatur*, 1963; *Unser Dasein*, 1964; *Reise in Polen*, 1968; *Briefe*, 1970; *Der deutsche Maskenball von Linke Poot: Wissen und Verandern!*, 1972; *Schriften zur Politik und Gesellschaft*, 1972; *Autobiographische Schriften und letzte Aufzeichnungen*, 1980; *Gespräche mit Kalypso: Über die Musik*, 1980; *Der unsterbliche Mensch: Ein Religionsgesprach, Der Kampf mit dem Engel, Ein Gang durch die Bibel*, 1980.

Bibliography

Kort, Wolfgang. *Alfred Döblin*, 1974.

Kreutzer, Leo. *Alfred Döblin: Sein Werk bis 1933*, 1970.

Müller-Salget, Klaus. *Alfred Döblin: Werk und Entwicklung*, 1972.

Prangel, Matthias. *Alfred Döblin*, 1973.

Schröter, Klaus. *Alfred Döblin in Selbstzeugnissen und Bilddokumenten*, 1978.

Michael Ritterson

HEIMITO VON DODERER

Born: Weidlingau, Austria; September 5, 1896
Died: Vienna, Austria; December 23, 1966

Principal long fiction

Die Bresche, 1924; *Das Geheimnis des Reichs*, 1930; *Ein Mord den jeder begeht*, 1938 (*Every Man a Murderer*, 1964); *Ein Umweg*, 1940; *Die erleuchteten Fenster*, 1950; *Die Strudlhofstiege*, 1951; *Das letzte Abenteuer*, 1953 (novella); *Die Dämonen*, 1956 (*The Demons*, 1961); *Die Merowinger*, 1962; *Die Wasserfälle von Slunj*, 1963 (*The Waterfall of Slunj*, 1966); *Der Grenzwald*, 1967 (fragment).

Other literary forms

In addition to the novels mentioned above, Heimito von Doderer published several volumes of short stories, poems, aphorisms, and essays, as well as his diary for the period from 1940 to 1950.

Achievements

The mention of Doderer's name among people familiar with German literature invariably evokes the image of Austria, particularly of the last few decades of the Austro-Hungarian Empire, which ceased to exist in 1918, and of the first Austrian Republic, which came to an end when Hitler annexed it to Germany in 1938. Doderer's major novels not only contain detailed and loving depictions of the Austrian landscapes and of the cityscape of Vienna, but also fascinating social panoramas of these singularly troubled periods in the country's history. Perhaps most important, these social panoramas are made up of characters whose personalities reflect the author's deeply felt concerns about the essence of modern man.

Biography

Heimito von Doderer was born on September 5, 1896, in Weidlingau, near Vienna. His father was Wilhelm Ritter von Doderer, a government architect and the builder of the Karawankenbahn and other Alpine railways. Doderer spent his youth in Vienna where he attended the *gymnasium*. During World War I, he served as an officer of the Dragoons in the Imperial Austrian Army. In 1916, he was captured on the Russian front and spent the next four years in various prisoner-of-war camps in Siberia.

In 1920, Doderer escaped from Siberia by walking across the Kirghiz Steppe. He returned to Vienna and studied history and psychology at the university there. In 1921, he wrote his first novel, *Die Bresche*, and in 1925, he received his Ph.D. in history. Beginning in 1927, he wrote for several newspapers, an activity which he gave up in 1931 to devote himself exclusively to his own literary production. In 1930, Doderer married Gusti Hasterlik; they were divorced in 1934. In 1933, he joined the outlawed Austrian National Socialist Party. When he moved to Munich in 1936, however, he came into direct contact with the political reality of Nazi Germany, particularly since he could find lodgings only in Dachau, a Munich suburb that was the site of a concentration camp. When he returned to Vienna shortly before the Anschluss, Doderer left the National Socialist Party and warned his Jewish friends of the impending danger. During World War II, he served as a captain in the German Air Force and in that capacity spent varying periods of time in France, Russia, Germany, Austria, Czechoslovakia, and Norway, where he was captured by the British in 1945.

During the period from 1946 to 1948—the worst postwar hunger years—Doderer completed the manuscript of his most humane and lighthearted novel, *Die Strudlhofstiege*. When this work and *Die erleuchteten Fenster* were published, Doderer was firmly established as a major literary figure. In 1952, he married Maria Emma Thoma. From 1950 to 1956, Doderer worked on his *magnum opus*, *The Demons*. It was published on his sixtieth birthday. Shortly afterward, in 1957, the *Times Literary Supplement* called him "the most formidable German-speaking novelist now living." In 1958, he received the Austrian State Prize for Literature, the first of several awards from various parts of the German-speaking world.

During the last years of his life, Doderer worked on a series of four novels which were to stand in the same thematic arrangement to one another as the four movements of a symphony. In their totality, these four parts were to constitute a panorama of the modern age, as seen from an Austrian vantage point. Unfortunately, Doderer was able to write only one complete novel of this series, *The Waterfall of Slunj*, and a fragment of a second one, *Der Grenzwald*. He died of cancer in Vienna on December 23, 1966.

Analysis

One of the most striking impressions one receives from a reading of Heimito von Doderer's novels is that most of his characters are somehow incomplete. At the outset of the novels, the physical, intellectual, and emotional circumstances of his personages are usually presented in great detail, and they often appear to be quite commonplace and normal to the reader, yet, by various means, Doderer always manages to convey the notion that they are deficient in some way. Their deficiency often consists of the preponderance of one character trait at the expense of others or of the domination of one part of man's nature (such as his intellect) over another one (such as his emotions). Such one-sidedness results in disharmony between the character concerned and the world around him and, in Doderer's terms, constitutes a deficiency in that character's humanity. In the course of the novels, some of his characters achieve a complete integration of the various aspects of their personalities and hence what he considers their true humanity. The successful integration of the characters' personalities establishes harmony between them and the world, or to use Doderer's terms, their universality. In Doderer's view, *homo universalis* must be able to come to grips with the rational and irrational forces within and outside himself, with beauty and ugliness, with richness and poverty—in short, he must accept life in all of its manifestations, and he must reconcile all of its extremes. The general theme of Doderer's novels is man's achievement of his own humanity.

According to Doderer, the universal man must be free in the Schillerian sense; he should do by inclination that which it is his duty to do. He must, of his own accord, accept life as it is, and he must participate in it to the best of his ability. Having understood Doderer's standard, one can proceed to the deviations from it which constitute the points of departure for his plots. Anyone who has a fixed notion as to what his life or his environment ought to be or why it does not correspond to his notion, and who consequently attempts to change his life or his environment, is caught in a situation which Doderer calls "the second reality." He is caught within the confines of ideology, idiosyncrasy, milieu, or whatever the case may be; he sees everything through glasses of a certain tint, his actions are conditioned in a certain manner, and he moves in a reality different from the generally accepted normalcy as postulated by Doderer. One such character is Frau Schubert, a middle-aged servant who wants to get married, even though there is not a chance in a million that she will find a husband. Nevertheless, she makes preparations, quits her job, rents a flat, buys furniture, and finally commits suicide out of desperation about her deceived hopes.

The plots of Doderer's novels are invariably concerned with the liberation of the protagonist from his or her "second reality." The treatment of the subject may at times be comical (as in Schlaggenberg's *chronique scandaleuse* in *The Demons*), but the basic problem is Doderer's most serious concern and directly related to some of the larger issues of the twentieth century. In his epilogue to the novella *Das letzte Abenteuer*, he differentiates between a pragmatic way of life ("thinking commensurate with life") and an ideological way of life ("living commensurate with thought") and he considers the latter doomed to end in doctrinairism, in reformism, and finally in the totalitarian state. Elaborating on this point, Doderer says in the same epilogue that during World War II, he discovered "how much more important it is to see what is, than to ascertain what ought to be, for the latter leads to the refusal of apperception, i.e. to that devastating form of modern stupidity which, by means of so-called convictions . . . makes impossible any communication about the simplest things."

The theme of man's achievement of humanity is presented throughout Doderer's novels with increasing emphasis. Some of his early works could conceivably be read as "stories" (to use E. M. Forster's term), without an awareness of the theme. This is particularly true of the second half of *Every Man a Murderer*, which has all the suspense of a whodunit. Conrad Castiletz, the protagonist of this novel, becomes obsessed with the idea of discovering the murderer of his wife's sister, whose death occurred eight years earlier. Conrad neglects his wife and starts on a wild-goose chase, searching for the jewelry which the woman in question had carried with her and for the one suspect in the case, whom the police had been compelled to release for want of evidence. In the end, Conrad finds out that he himself, together with a group of students in a train, unintentionally killed the woman. After this discovery, Conrad makes another one—namely, of his wife's infidelity. The next morning he dies in an explosion. Conrad's obsession with his wife's sister constitutes his "second reality," which he is unable to leave in spite of several warnings by friends and associates, who admonish him to lead and enjoy his life in the normal "first reality." When he is finally forced to accept the irrefutable evidence of his own unwitting complicity in his sister-in-law's death, he cannot live with this knowledge.

Conrad is the only character in *Every Man a Murderer* that is caught in the "second reality." This is typical of Doderer's early novels, where there are usually only a few characters directly concerned with his central theme. As Doderer develops, the number of characters in his novels increases, as does the complexity of their plots, but his central theme—man's attainment of true humanity—remains paramount. In *Die Strudlhofstiege*, Doderer presents this theme by means of a vast and complex array of characters. It is true that the protagonist (Lieutenant Melzer) is the only character that is involved in all the essential events of the novel, but the events do not take place solely because of him or for the sake of his development. The process of Melzer's complete humanization serves as a basis for comparison and contrast to various other characters whose humanization is achieved only partially or not at all.

Die Strudlhofstiege is in many ways a precursor of *The Demons*: Many of the characters of the earlier novel reappear in the later one. The German title of Doderer's novel, *Die Dämonen*, was adopted from the identical German title of the work by Fyodor Dostoevski, which is known in English as *The Possessed* or *Devils*. There are several thematic and structural similarities between Dostoevski's and Doderer's works. The main difference on the thematic level lies in the nature of the characters who are caught in the "second reality," of those who are possessed. In Dostoevski's work, the primary concern is with a group of fanatical ideologists whose ill-defined political pursuits bring harm to the lives of others. In Doderer's novel, all the major characters are possessed or, to use his terminology, have entered a "second reality." Only those characters whose illusions and activities are on a political plane, however, bring permanent misfortune and doom upon themselves and others.

In *The Demons*, the theme of man's attainment of true humanity is presented by means of a multitude of interrelated actions involving a total of 142 characters. While most of the principal characters are members of the upper-middle class and professionals, the scope of the novel also includes members of the highest ranks of the aristocracy as well as criminals and prostitutes. The main events of the novel take place between the fall of 1926 and July 15, 1927, the day of the general strike and the burning of the Palace of Justice in Vienna. Most of the many strands of the action, both private and political, are parts of the tissue of a conventional, almost classical, plot centered on the unveiling of the origin of a natural daughter and the bringing to light of a previously suppressed last will.

A synopsis of the plot of so long a novel (1,345 pages) must necessarily be incomplete and selective. For the sake of the present discussion, the fates, actions, and developments of seven key characters have been chosen for a detailed examination: Georg von Geyrenhoff, René von Stangeler and his fiancée Grete Siebenschein, Kajetan von Schlaggenberg and his supposed sister Charlotte, and Leonhard Kakabsa and his beloved, Mary K.

Georg von Geyrenhoff, a bachelor and a high-ranking civil servant, has recently regained a considerable sum of money which had been deposited in England and was thus inaccessible during World War I and for some time thereafter. Because of his financial independence and because of his dissatisfaction with his work, he retires prematurely from the civil service and devotes himself to the writing of a chronicle about the activities of a group of friends who are usually referred to as "Our Crowd." At first, he stands aloof from the lives of his friends and simply observes and records them, but soon he becomes intellectually and emotionally involved in their affairs; it is he who is responsible for bringing to light the suppressed last will, and in the end he marries Friederike Ruthmayr, the rich widow of Charlotte's father.

Dr. René von Stangeler, a recently graduated historian, at first is seen as struggling for intellectual, personal, and financial independence. He does not want a regular appointment (such as a professorship) and he does not want to be tied to the woman he loves, Grete Siebenschein. Grete, on the other hand, has to contend with her solidly middle-class family, as well as with her own often ruffled pride and self-respect. Their relationship and their lives change for the better when René is offered a job as a consultant by Jan Herzka, a businessman who inherits a castle in Carinthia. This job leads to a permanent position as librarian and book buyer for Herzka; it also helps to establish René's scholarly reputation because of his excellent critical edition of an original medieval manuscript which he discovers in the castle. Now that he feels financially and professionally independent and secure, René has much more self-assurance in his dealings with Grete and her family, and at the end of the book he refers to her as his fiancée.

Kajetan and Camy von Schlaggenberg's marriage has been a failure because of a fundamental emotional incompatibility. At the beginning of the novel, their definite separation has just taken place, and Kajetan suffers great emotional pain which impairs his creativity as a novelist. In addition, he has pecuniary problems and is forced to waste much time on journalistic hackwork. After he receives some financially important commissions from a large newspaper concern, he is in a position to pursue his theory of sexuality—that of the "Fat Females." According to this theory, only experienced, rather abundantly endowed middle-aged women who have no ambitions regarding marriage and family life are suitable mates for men of the postwar generation. He unfolds a great flurry of activity and wastes much money on this project until he eventually realizes how foolish and ridiculous it is.

Meanwhile, his supposed sister Charlotte is in dire financial straits as she practices her violin, preparing for a career as a soloist. During her first important audition, the insurmountable tremor of her hands (of which she had been aware all along) becomes evident once more, and the conductor for whom she auditions persuades her to abandon her goal. Upon returning to her home, she finds a letter informing her of a legacy of 250,000 schillings, which, however, is only a fraction of the fortune which she will eventually inherit. Even though she learns shortly afterward that she is not Kajetan's sister, she gives him a considerable sum of money. Kajetan is thus able to take a trip to London, where he has one last brief encounter with his wife. After this painful experience, he begins to devote himself to his real literary work. Charlotte marries Géza von Orkay, a Hungarian diplomat who is Geyrenhoff's cousin.

Leonhard Kakabsa, a simple worker, one day follows an impulse to buy a Latin grammar. He begins to study Latin and in the course of his studies develops a very keen understanding of grammar, which leads him in turn to master standard German diction. At first, he applies this diction only in his thoughts, nourished by the Greek classics, which he reads in German translations. He cultivates an acquaintance with several young persons, some of whom attend the *gymnasium*. One of them introduces him to her mother, Mary K. This strikingly beautiful widow has managed to overcome the effects of an accident in which one of her legs was cut off above the knee. She does not hobble about with her artificial leg but has learned to control it completely, and thus continues not only to appear, but also to be, graceful and poised. Her physical victory and Leonhard's intellectual victory at once point to an affinity in spirit. They are attracted to each other, fall in love, and accept this love with all of its implications.

In *The Demons*, the theme of man's humanization is presented by means of one main motif which pervades the entire novel and which involves all the major characters. This motif is man's passage from his self-constructed "second reality" into the factual, everyday reality. Motifs from Doderer's earlier novels, such as confinement and freedom, or imperceptiveness and perceptiveness, are all present in *The Demons*, but they are integrated or submerged in the main motif. While the various characters are in their "second reality," they are represented as being confined, as being unable to lead their own lives, and as being imperceptive in the sense that they have no understanding of their own afflictions or of their unsatisfactory relationships with others. At the end of their development—that is, once they have attained humanity in Doderer's sense—they understand and accept their own personalities and their positions in the world. Once they have attained this understanding and acceptance, they become sovereign masters of their own lives.

The main characters of the novel could well be categorized with respect to the amount of imagination which they possess and the measure in which they are involved in a "second reality": The spectrum would range from Camy von Schlaggenberg, who is represented as completely matter-of-fact and self-contained, to Alois Gach, an instinctively integrated personality, to Leonhard Kakabsa, whose initial mania for independence and noninvolvement is already somewhat akin to a "second reality," to René, Geyrenhoff, Charlotte, Kajetan, and Jan Herzka, not to speak of the political agitators or of Achaz von Neudegg, the medieval witch hunter and sex pervert. One cannot but agree with H. M. Waidson when he says that "the really interesting people in the novel are those whom the second reality has invaded, but who are capable, even if only with great effort, of focusing the double vision into one, subduing the imagination within its limits.

The question arises how the author conveys the idea that a given character has reached the turning point, that he or she has managed to "focus the double vision into one." There are several instances in the novel where choral characters make general philosophical statements on behalf of the author. These abstract statements, however, are outweighed by the all-pervading patterns of imagery which Doderer uses in applying his theory to particular characters and situations. The existence of a given character within a "second reality," his realization of being in this state, and his eventual attainment of true humanity—that is, his acceptance of factual reality—these phases of his development are indicated by means of telltale images, thoughts, and occurrences. In this manner, a certain rhythm is established which is very helpful for purposes of orientation within the many different strands of action in this long and complex novel.

At the end of the novel, all the major characters, with the sole exception of the political fanatics, have entered or reentered factual reality. They have learned to accept life as it is; they have attained true humanity. This affirmation of life is expressed in an almost ritualistic manner through the many marriages which conclude the novel.

No consideration of Doderer's novels would be complete without at least mentioning *The Waterfall of Slunj*, his last complete novel, a work that is masterfully constructed according to the sonata form. It includes all of his usual motifs and images, but they are subordinated to the overall musical structure. It is certainly a masterpiece and makes one regret that the author was unable to complete the remaining three parts of his projected tetralogy.

Major publications other than long fiction

SHORT FICTION: *Die Peinigung der Lederbeutelchen*, 1959; *Meine neunzehn Lebensläufe und neun andere Geschichten*, 1966; *Unter schwarzen Sternen*, 1966; *Frühe Prosa*, 1968 (includes the novella *Jutta Bamberger* and the novels *Die Bresche* and *Das Geheimnis des Reichs*).

POETRY: *Ein Weg im Dunklen*, 1957.

NONFICTION: *Der Fall Gütersloh*, 1930; *Julius Winkler*, 1937; *Grundlagen und Funktion des Romans*, 1959; *Tangenten*, 1964 (diaries); *Repertorium*, 1969.

Bibliography

Bachem, Michael. *Heimito von Doderer*, 1981.
Books Abroad. XLII, no. 3 (1968). Special Doderer issue.
Haberl, F. P. *Theme and Structure in the Novels of Heimito von Doderer*, 1965 (dissertation).
Hamburger, Michael. *From Prophecy to Exorcism*, 1965.
Weber, D. *Heimito von Doderer: Studien zu seinem Romanwerk*, 1964.

Franz P. Haberl